The Blue Guides

D1284325

Albania

Austria   Austria
Vienna

Belgium and Luxembourg
China
Cyprus
Czech and Slovak Republics
Denmark
Egypt

France   France
Paris and Versailles
Burgundy
Loire Valley
Midi-Pyrénées
Normandy
South West France
Corsica

Germany   Berlin and eastern Germany
Western Germany

Greece   Greece
Athens and environs
Crete
Rhodes and the Dodecanese

Holland   Holland
Amsterdam

Hungary   Hungary
Budapest

Ireland

Italy   Northern Italy
Southern Italy
Florence
Rome and environs
Venice
Tuscany
Umbria
Sicily

Morocco
Moscow and St Petersburg
Poland
Portugal

Spain   Spain
Barcelona
Madrid

Sweden
Switzerland
Thailand
Tunisia

Turkey   Turkey
Istanbul

UK   England
Scotland
Wales
Channel Islands
London
Museums and Galleries of
London
Oxford and Cambridge
Country Houses of England
Literary Britain and Ireland
Victorian Architecture in Britain
Churches and Chapels of
Northern England
Churches and Chapels of
Southern England

USA   New York
Museums and Galleries of
New York
Boston and Cambridge

Equestrian statue of Frederik V, Amalienborg Palace Square, Copenhagen

Blue Guide

DENMARK

W. Glyn Jones & Kirsten Gade

Maps and plans by John Flower

A & C Black · London

W W Norton · New York

Second edition 1997

Published by A & C Black (Publishers) Limited
35 Bedford Row, London WC1R 4JH

A CIP catalogue record of this book is available from the British Library.

ISBN 0–7136–4274–2

Published in the United States of America by
WW Norton and Company, Inc
500 Fifth Avenue, New York, NY 10110

Published simultaneously in Canada by
Penguin Books Canada Limited
10 Alcorn Avenue, Toronto
Ontario M4V 3B2

ISBN 0–393–31639–4 USA

The authors and the publishers have done their best to ensure the accuracy of all the information in Blue Guide Denmark; however, they can accept no responsibility for any loss, injury or inconvenience sustained by any traveller as a result of information or advice contained in the guide.

Kirsten Gade was educated at Copenhagen and worked for many years for the Greenland Education Service. She has taught Danish language at the universities of Newcastle upon Tyne and East Anglia. Her publications include Danish textbooks, children's books and, with Glyn Jones, *Danish. A Grammar* and *Colloquial Danish.*

W. Glyn Jones was educated at Cambridge and Århus and has taught at universities in England, Iceland and the Faroe Islands. He is now Professor Emeritus of Scandinavian Studies in the University of East Anglia. His publications include, in addition to numerous translations, critical studies: *Johannes Jørgensens modne år, Johannes Jørgensen, William Heinesen, Færø og Kosmos, Tove Jansson, Denmark. A Modern History, Georg Brandes. Selected Letters,* a history of Faroese literature and, with Kirsten Gade, *Danish. A Grammar* and *Colloquial Danish.*

Cover picture: red and black timbered house in Ærøskøbing by Adam Woolfitt/Corbis

Printed in Great Britain by Butler & Tanner Ltd, Frome and London

Introduction

In this revised edition we have provided a new range of practical information, including some guidance on accommodation. In the larger towns we list the names, addresses and telephone numbers of two hotels and the nearest youth hostel. These are not strictly speaking recommendations, but are intended to give visitors a little initial help in finding somewhere to stay. As far as possible, we have chosen hotels placed centrally in the town, and the first mentioned hotel is usually more expensive than the second. It can be assumed that all will be of good quality. The Danish youth hostels, too, all have a very high standard, as have Danish camping sites. This new edition also refers to a small number of restaurants, but apart from mentioning a few which we have found to be particularly attractive, we leave the choice to our readers. Denmark offers restaurants and cafés of all kinds, and you can be sure of a perfectly satisfactory standard in all of them. This includes the Danish *kro*, the inn, which often has a long tradition of catering behind it.

Denmark is also provided with a fine system of tourist offices, and these are listed in the text, with addresses and the telephone numbers of the main ones. You will find the staff in these offices both helpful and well-informed. Tourist offices sporting a green I are open all year round, sometimes even on Sundays. Their staff speak a variety of languages, are willing to answer written enquiries, and can provide information on the whole of Denmark. Many tourist offices with a red I are only open in the main tourist season and can only give information on their own areas.

We have, as far as possible, tried to detail new attractions which have opened since the first edition of the guide. New museums have appeared—for instance the very popular Experimentarium in Copenhagen and the new museum of modern art, Arken, at Ishøj—and they are included. Likewise, the National Museum has been completely re-designed since the first edition appeared, and we have taken note of this.

At the time of writing, the fixed link across Store Bælt has not been finished, but it will be open in 1998. This will change your travel arrangements when you cross from Sjælland to Fyn. And remember the fixed link to Sweden is also coming, though that is further ahead. By 1998, however, you should find that the rail link from Copenhagen to Kastrup Airport is open, making for much more rapid transport to and from the city. An exhibition showing plans for this fixed link has opened in Kastrup Strandpark 9.

Acknowledgements

The authors would like to express their thanks to the many people who have helped in the writing of this book. In particular, we thank the Danish Tourist organisations: the Danish Tourist Board's London office, the members of its headquarters in Copenhagen, and the many representatives of individual tourist offices and museums throughout Denmark, whose help in some cases has been quite outstanding. For photographs we are again indebted to the

Danish Tourist Board, individual Tourist Association offices and museums. Likewise we are grateful to representatives of many Danish churches and historical buildings for their courteous assistance. Last, but by no means least, we thank Gemma Davies and Judy Tither of A&C Black for a repeat of the help they gave us in preparing the first edition of this Guide.

KGJ, WGJ.

Using this Guide

Like many Blue Guides, detailed practical information is given at the beginning of the book. The guide to Denmark is split into 24 routes or chapters. Route summaries appear at the start of each chapter, giving information on distances and road numbers. Excursions off the main routes are indicated by paragraphs beginning ▶ and ending ◀. Information on tourist information offices, hotels, restaurants, etc., is given within the routes. A brief history of Denmark and a chronology of events is given at the back of the book, along with a short description of Danish churches and artists.

Contents

Maps and plans

Practical Information

Before you go

General information can be obtained from the **Danish Tourist Board**, 55 Sloane Street, London SW1X 9SY, tel. (0171) 259 5959; or, in the USA, 655 Third Avenue, New York, NY 10017, tel. (212) 949-233. A range of useful brochures is available including guides to hotels, inns, youth and family hostels, camping, cycling, ferries, events lists and maps.

Getting to Denmark

By air

Copenhagen's Kastrup Airport is one of the major European airports, with regular services to all parts of the world, and with frequent connections to Danish provincial airports. Most air traffic to Denmark will take you to Kastrup, though there are a few international services to the provinces, e.g. to Esbjerg, Århus and Billund (for Legoland).

Kastrup Airport is some 12km from Copenhagen centre, and there are frequent SAS buses to the central station, Hovedbanegården. The journey takes about 20 minutes. There are also rather slower—and cheaper—services by ordinary bus (Service 32) to Copenhagen Town Hall Square (Rådhuspladsen).

The following airlines run regular scheduled flights to Denmark from the **UK**: **Scandinavian Airlines**, tel. (0171) 734 4020; **British Airways**, tel. 0345 222 111; Air UK, tel. 0345 666 777; Maersk Air, tel. (0171) 333 0066; **British Midland**, tel. 0345 554 554; **Aer Lingus**, tel. (0645) 737 747; **Business Air**, tel. 0500 340 146; **New Air**, tel. 0161 489 2830; **Debonair**, tel. 0500 146200. For scheduled flights from the **USA** contact: **Scandinavian Airlines**, tel. (800) 221-2350; **Finnair**, tel. (800) 223-5500; **Icelandair**, tel. (800) 223-5500. **Canada**: contact **Air Canada**, tel. (416) 925 2311.

By rail

There are good rail services connecting with cities throughout Europe, with daily connections both to and from London, Victoria via Ostende. The journey takes approximately 24 hours. For information and bookings contact British Rail International Rail Centre, tel. (0171) 834 2345/828 0892; Eurotrain, tel. (0171) 730 3402. Thomas Cook's European timetable gives details of all rail and ferry services in Europe.

By coach

Several coach services are available to Denmark. London Coaches, tel. (0171) 227 3456, travel to Copenhagen, Fyn and Jutland three times a week (journey time approximately 26 hours). Roundabout Enterprises, tel. (01923) 835696, run a weekly service to Copenhagen, Odense and Fredericia via France (journey time approximately 25 hours). National Express Eurolines, tel. 0345 626452, also run a regular service, via Amsterdam (journey time approximately 26 hours).

By sea

There are connections most days between London, Liverpool Street and Copenhagen via Harwich and Esbjerg (London–Harwich an hour and a half, sailing time 18 hours, Copenhagen–Esbjerg 5 hours). The ships on this route are operated to a high standard by Scandinavian Seaways, tel. (01255) 240240, which also operates an equally convenient route between Harwich and Hamburg. If you are taking your car, these are the obvious ways to go, unless you want to drive up through Germany.

By car

The Harwich–Esbjerg route is the easiest. However, you can drive from any of the Channel or North Sea ports by good motorways, usually using the E45, entering Denmark, via Jutland or the E47 via Lübeck and taking the ferry from Puttgarden to Rødbyhavn (sailings every half hour, although it is advisable to book beforehand to avoid delays), from where there is a motorway to Copenhagen. There are also three-hourly departures from Rostock to Gedser and departures four times a day from Warnemünde to Gedser. From Gelting there are up to three sailings daily to Fåborg, and from Kiel up to three to Bagenkop in Langeland and one to Halsskov on Sjælland. If you are going to Bornholm, you might consider travelling via the the north German island of Rügen (reached by bridge and causeway), where you can take a ferry from Sassnitz or Neu Mukran to Rønne. Only a little further along the Baltic coast, there is a ferry from Swinoujscie in Poland to Rønne and from the same town there are five sailings a week to Copenhagen.

It is also possible to take the W coast route N of Hamburg via Husum to Tønder. There are minor frontier crossings from Germany as well, though they are little used except for local traffic.

From Sweden there are very frequent ferries from Hälsingborg to Helsingør and also from Malmö to Copenhagen. Other services: from Limhamn to Dragør, Göteborg to Frederikshavn, Halmstad to Grenå, Hälsingborg to Grenå, Varberg to Grenå, Landskrona to Copenhagen (Tuborg Havn). From Norway there are ferries from Larvik, Oslo, Moss and Frederiksstad to Frederikshavn and from Oslo, Egernsund and Kristiansand to Hirtshals. Larger ferries sail between Bergen and Stavanger and Hirtshals and between Oslo and Copenhagen.

Customs

For travellers arriving from another EU country checks are minimal, and in general informality is characteristic of customs inspections. If you take the main frontier crossing from Germany via Padborg you may encounter delays in the summer.

Travelling around Denmark

Domestic ferry routes

Denmark consists of the peninsula of Jutland (Jylland) and a large number of islands, many of which are connected by bridge. However, ferry connections are common between many of the islands, and at weekends and in the summer holiday months you are advised to book beforehand to avoid waiting for free space. The State Railways, DSB, run many of the ferries, and you can book on these at any railway station or by telephoning 33 15 15 15. Other ferry services are private, but the following telephone numbers can be useful: Copenhagen-Rønne (Bornholm): 56 95 18 66 or 33 13 18 66; Århus-Kalundborg by catamaran: 89 41 20 00; Grenå-Hundested: 86 30 96 88; Ebeltoft-Sjællands Odde: 89 52 52 52 or 89 32 32 32; Korsør-Nyborg by 'Vognmandsruten': 53 57 12 33. For others you should seek advice in a travel agency or Tourist Information Office.

By car

Main roads in Denmark are systematically numbered. Those connected with international routes have a number prefixed by E: E20, E55, and indicated by **green signs**. Next in the hierarchy come other main roads, designated on **yellow signs** by a 2-digit number: 11, 13. In this book we have prefixed these routes with an A: A11, A13. Good secondary roads have 3-digit numbers on **white signs**: 160, 283. In addition there are many unclassified roads, all of high quality. You need never be afraid to use them—and there is often remarkably little traffic on them.

Motorways are provided with **blue signs** indicating places served by the next exit and **green signs** indicating places reached by driving straight on. Exits are all numbered.

Speed limits. The general speed limits are 50kph in built-up areas, 80kph outside urban areas, 110kph on motorways—though individual speed limits are frequently imposed. Built-up areas are indicated by the name of the town/village, together with a sketch of houses and a church. The speed limit is then cancelled by the same sign with a line drawn through it.

Warning triangles. Motorists are expected to carry warning triangles with them in Denmark.

Headlights. You **must** by law drive with dipped headlights throughout the day in Denmark. Remember to have them masked for driving on the right.

Parking. Parking meters will be encountered in Copenhagen and other major cities. Many car parks in the provinces are free, but you are limited to time. You need to obtain a parking disc (available in banks, tourist information offices, garages and a host of other places) to attach to your windscreen, indicating your time of arrival. If you fail to use it, you risk a fine.

Road maps. These are available from petrol stations and tourist information offices. If you want a detailed map of the whole country, we recommend *Danmark. 1:100 000. Topografisk Atlas* published by Kort-og Matrikelstyrelsen. It is excellent—but expensive.

By rail

The Railway network (DSB) covers most of the country and is very efficient, clean and reliable. Inter-City trains run between Copenhagen and Jutland every hour, with connections to towns not served directly. Tickets should be bought in advance. Fares are calculated on a zonal system, the cost per km reducing on longer journeys. Nationwide information available by telephone: 33 14 17 01.

There are several fare reductions available, the main ones being: **Cheap Day tickets**, which offer a reduction on 2nd class travel when a journey covers at least 13 zones (approximately 100km) on Tue, Wed, Thur, Sat. Senior citizens can buy a '65 Billet', which allows price reductions on any day, but a higher reduction on days when 'Cheap Day' tickets are generally available. There are certain restrictions in connection with public holidays. **Group reductions** are available when three or more adults travel together 2nd class. **Child reductions**: children under four travel free, and children under twelve at half fare. A child under twelve travelling with an adult will go free if the adult asks for a 'børnerabat' on purchasing his or her own ticket. There are family compartments on Inter-City trains, in which children under four can have their own seats: they travel free, but the seat must be paid for.

Trains are taken on the ferry across Store Bælt, sailing time c 1 hour, and there are cafeterias and restaurants on board. **Seat tickets** on the train are required if you are crossing Store Bælt by rail, and it is in any case advisable to get one if you travel by Inter-City trains, even if you are not crossing Store Bælt.

By bicycle

Cycling is very common in Denmark, and cycle paths are very widespread, both in towns and on the busier country roads. Cycling is, however, prohibited on motorways and on certain major roads called 'motortrafikveje'. You can easily hire a bicycle in Denmark: information from Dansk Cyklist Forbund, Rømersgade 7, DK-1362 Copenhagen K (tel. 33 32 31 21).

By coach

Long-distance coach travel is not very common in Denmark, and prices tend to be the same as for rail travel. Some routes, however, might be useful, e.g. Billund-Odense (tel. 64 71 29 10); Esjerg-Frederikshavn via Ålborg (tel. 98 16 09 99).

General information

Accommodation

Inns and **hotels** vary in price and quality. However, the Royal Privilege Inns (*Kongeligt priviligerede Kroer*), an almost 800-year-old institution, are scattered throughout the country (there are about 800 altogether) and offer you comfortable accommodation—and good food—at reasonable cost. There are other good inns (*Kroer*), too: *kro* means inn. The Danish Tourist Board produces a list of hotels, and a booklet that gives details on how to book accommodation in hotels, manor houses, inns, holiday homes and farms. In many instances you will find guidance on finding accommodation in the text of this book.

A particular kind of accommodation is offered under the name of Dansk Kroferie. This allows you price reductions in 88 different Danish inns, but you must obtain beforehand a 'Krocheck' as part payment. Information of obtaining these can be had from tourist information offices, while information on the scheme as a whole, and the addresses of inns taking part, can be obtained from: Dansk Kroferie, Vejlevej 16, DK-8700 Horsens; tel. 75 64 87 00.

Some of Denmark's many manor houses have now been turned into hotels of a rather special kind. Information is obtainable from: Danish Castle and Manor House Hotels, Annasvej 9, DK-2900 Hellerup; tel. 39 40 02 77.

Another useful, illustrated and priced, hotel guide is available from Larsen

Hotel og Kroferie, Kongevejen 155, DK-2830 Virum; tel. 45 83 12 14. It is in Danish, but you will quickly get the idea.

There is a good supply of **bed and breakfast** accommodation. Information can be obtained from local Tourish Information Offices or from: Dansk Bed & Breakfast, tel. 31 61 04 05.

There are over 500 **camp sites** in Denmark. Information on them can be obtained from *Camping Denmark*, price including postage DKK 100, available from Campingrådet, Hesselgade 16, DK-2100 Copenhagen or from camping sites, bookshops, kiosks and tourist offices, price DKK 70.

Farm holidays

Staying on a farm is a popular way of spending a holiday in Denmark at a modest price. Information from: Dansk Bondegårdsferie, Søndergade 26, DK-8700 Horsens (tel. 75 62 38 22).

Self-catering

There is a myth that food in Denmark is very expensive. It is only a myth, though it would be wrong to assert that food is cheap. However, if you eat as the Danes eat—e.g. rye bread, liver paste, vegetables, dairy produce—you will find prices quite tolerable. If, however, you insist on eating the food you like at home but which is not common in Denmark—then you will help perpetuate the myth.

Banks

Banks are usually open from 09.30 to 16.00. They do not open on Saturdays. There are, however, plenty of cash dispensers.

Beaches

Denmark has a vast coastline, over 7000km, and most of the beaches are suitable for bathing or sunbathing. Notable are Rømø and Fanø, the west coast of Jutland, the north coast of Sjælland, Lolland and parts of Bornholm. Some of the best are referred to specifically in this book, but we have not been able to cover them all. The tourist information offices have free maps showing beaches for bathing.

Churches

Many churches are open during daylight hours, but thefts and vandalism over recent years have led to more and more being kept locked. However, when a church is locked it is usually possible to obtain the key from an address displayed at the entrance either to the churchyard or the church.

Country walks

The Danish countryside is less private than, say, that in Britain. There are certainly private estates, but you will have access to much more than you might imagine. You are, of course, expected to respect the countryside.

Currency

The main unit is the *krone*, which is divided into 100 *øre*. Foreign currency is freely exchangeable, and the major credit cards are widely accepted, as are Eurocheques. Denominations are—coins: 25 øre, 50 øre, 1 krone, 2 kroner, 5 kroner, 10 kroner, 20 kroner; notes: 50 kroner, 100 kroner, 500 kroner, 1000 kroner.

Disabled travellers
Denmark is well aware of the need for facilities for the disabled, and great care has been taken to provide them in all areas.

House numbers
In Denmark house numbers follow the name of the street, and we have adopted the same system in this book. So the address is Jyllandsgade 5, not 5 Jyllandsgade.

Museums
Museum opening times vary greatly, and it has not been possible to give exact opening times for all the museums to which we refer, although we have on the other hand, tried to give some indication. In general, you must be prepared for museums to be closed on Mondays—though this is by no means always the case. When no opening times are given this indicates that the museum is open all year round, but not on Mondays.

Personal names and place names
Without resorting to affectation or artificiality, it has proved impossible to be completely consistent in our treatment of personal names and place names. On the whole, unless there is a totally accepted English equivalent, we have followed the principle of using the Danish form. Hence Fyn and Sjælland, but Jutland, not Jylland. That we use Copenhagen, and not København, goes without saying, but there was a problem with Helsingør/Elsinore. We chose the Danish form—but have given the English form in parenthesis in the chapter heading. Slesvig/Schleswig and Holsten/Holstein gave even greater problems due to the historical meeting of languages and cultures in this area; we decided on Schleswig and Holstein purely because these are the forms normally found in English references to the area.

One personal name proved difficult: Knud or Canute. The king who tried to stop the waves is inevitably Canute to the English reader—but what when we come to his namesakes St Knud and Knud Lavard? Canute hardly seemed fitting here. The problem is compounded by the fact that the modern Danish, Knud, is in any case not the form they used! However, we decided that, as the Cathedral in Odense is definitely Sankt Knuds Kirke, and as street names including the name Knud cannot be juggled with, we would keep to the Danish form—though again we have on occasion put the English Canute in brackets, just to keep you on track.

Pleasure parks
We have referred to a number of pleasure parks, but as they are now mush-rooming, it is simply not possible to mention all of them. All over the country you will see 'Sommerland' or 'Ferieland', both of which indicate pleasure parks of one sort or another. Hygiene and safety standards are high, and in many there is an entrance fee, after which all entertainments are free.

Postal services

There is a post office in each town and village, but there is no system of sub-post offices such as in the UK. However, you can buy stamps in the many 'kiosks' and in most bookshops. Danish letter boxes are red.

Public holidays

The following are public holidays in Denmark: New Year's Day, Palm Sunday, Maundy Thursday, Good Friday, Easter Sunday, Easter Monday, *Store Bededag* (Common Prayer Day: 4th Friday after Easter), Ascension Day, Whit Sunday, Whit Monday, Constitution Day (5 June: shops shut at noon), Christmas Day (most shops will shut at midday on Christmas Eve), Boxing Day.

School holidays

The main school summer holidays are from mid-June to about 8 August. Autumn holidays are the week including the 3rd Tuesday in October. Easter holidays last from Palm Sunday to the Wednesday after Easter, and Christmas holidays about a fortnight, beginning around 22 December.

Shopping

Shops are normally open from 09.30 to 17.00, but many bakers are open much earlier—from 07.00 in many cases. Bakers may well remain open on Saturday afternoons, but **all** other shops will close by 14.00. Many bakers open at 07.00 too on Sundays—not least because of the Danish love of fresh bread and rolls for Sunday breakfast. Bakers usually also sell a limited amount of dairy produce, including cheese and ice cream, and often have newspapers on a Sunday.

Sightseeing

Information on the wide selection of sightseeing tours can be obtained from tourist information offices.

Several cities, not least Copenhagen, offer tourist cards providing free public transport and free access to an array of museums. In Copenhagen, you can buy a **Copenhagen Card**, valid for 1, 2 or 3 days, in larger railway stations, travel bureaux, tourist information offices, etc., in the major towns.

Sporting facilities

Tourist information offices will have pamphlets giving you full information on the various sporting facilities available, although we list information here on a few sports.

Canoeing

If you want to explore the Danish rivers by canoe, it is possible to hire canoes by the hour, day or week. Typical costs are kr. 100 a day or kr. 1000 a week.

Fishing

Anglers require a licence to fish anywhere in Denmark, costing kr. 25 for a single day or kr. 75 for a week, kr. 100 for a full year. In addition, most streams and lakes are private and you will therefore require a further permit. The general fishing licence can also be bought in post offices.

Sailing

There are some 350 marinas, large and small, in Denmark with charges varying from nothing to about kr. 100 per day.

Telephones

There is a good provision of telephone booths in Denmark. For local calls you insert 1 krone, for long-distance calls 5 or 10 kroner and then simply dial the number. Telephone cards are also available, and an innovation is that in the main railway station, and a few central places in Copenhagen, there are telephones that will accept British 10p coins.

If calling Denmark from abroad, you should prefix the telephone numbers given in this book by (+45) e.g. from the UK: 0045.

Tipping

Tips are not expected in Denmark, as all indicated prices are inclusive, whether they be for taxis, meals or hotels. If, on the other hand, you have found the service outstandingly good, no one is going to be insulted if you offer a tip.

Traffic lights

Traffic lights in Denmark apply to pedestrians as well as wheeled traffic. When the lights are at red, you are expected to wait. On the other hand, when they are at green, traffic turning in at a junction will wait for you as you cross—but you may find it less willing to stop at zebra crossings! When driving a car, remember to keep a look-out for cyclists when turning right.

VAT

In Danish: MOMS—can be reclaimed for large purchases by non-EU citizens by arranging first with the shop concerned and then reclaiming the amount paid at the border crossing on leaving the country.

Some useful words

Most Danes will speak English, but you might find the following of use as you look around:

afgang: departure	godnat: good night
ankomst: arrival	havn: port/ harbour
apotek: chemist's shop	herregård: mansion/manor house
banegård: railway station	højre: right
benzin: petrol	ja: yes
bil: car	kirke: church
by: town/ village	kloster: convent/monastery
Bælt: Belt	landsby: village
fare: danger	lufthavn: airport
farvel: goodbye	lukket: closed
færge: ferry	læge: doctor
gade: street	nej: no
goddag: hello	olie: oil
godmorgen: good morning	politi: police

rutebilstation: coach station
skov: forest
slot: castle/ palace
strand: beach
stræde: street
sund: sound
sø: lake
tak: thank you
tandlæge: dentist
til togene: to the trains
tog: train
torv: square/ market square
vej: road
venstre: left
øl: beer
å: river
åben: open

Numbers

0 nul
1 en
2 to
3 tre
4 fire
5 fem
6 seks
7 syv
8 otte
9 ni
10 ti
11 elleve
12 tolv
13 tretten
14 fjorten
15 femten
16 seksten
17 sytten
18 atten
19 nitten
20 tyve
21 enogtyve
30 tredive
40 fyrre
50 halvtreds
60 tres
70 halvfjerds
80 firs
90 halvfems
100 hundrede
200 to hundrede
1000 tusind

Months

January: januar
February: februar
March: marts
April: april
May: maj
June: juni
July: juli
August: august
September: september
October: oktober
November: november
December: december

Days of the week

Monday: mandag
Tuesday: tirsdag
Wednesday: onsdag
Thursday: torsdag
Friday: fredag
Saturday: lørdag
Sunday: søndag

And a useful sign. You will find this sign very often: ⌘
It indicates a museum or place of historical or cultural interest.

Danish cuisine

The Danes know how to enjoy their food, and they have a characteristic, though not exotic, list of typical dishes. A one-time British ambassador to Denmark, Robert Molesworth, writing at the end of the 17C, bewailed the lot of the Danes who, as he saw it, failed to cultivate decent wheat and were forced to grow rye instead. Little did he know! Few Danes would do without their rye bread (rugbrød), which they eat mainly at breakfast and lunch. If anything is typical of the Danish taste in food, this must be it. Always cut in much thinner slices than the white bread (which you also find), it is dark brown, firm, but not heavy, and can be made from finely or coarsely ground rye flour. It forms the basis of most of the open sandwiches (smørrebrød) for which Denmark is renowned.

Breakfast (Morgenmad) is likely to consist of ryebread and white bread (franskbrød) with sliced cheese, jam and possibly salami or some other sliced meat. If you want a rather better selection of bread, you can try one or more of the many kinds of rolls on sale. Traditionally, *rundstykker* (crusty rolls) and *kryddere* (the dictionary translation of rusks gives no idea of these crisp, extra-baked tea-cake-sized rolls) are the most common, but there are many others, and the traditional ones are nowadays supplemented with 'healthy' rolls made of various kinds of flour. All these rolls are given the generic name of *morgenbrød* ('morning bread'), and many Danes will go out of their way to have them for breakfast on a Sunday. They will also be on offer for your breakfast in hotels. Breakfast cereals such as cornflakes are also eaten, but you will just as often find oatflakes eaten raw with sugar and milk. You may be offered one or other of the soured milk products in the same family as yoghurt or fromage frais; yoghurt itself is among the many on offer, but perhaps the finest is *ymer*. The unimaginatively named A38 is a lighter type. Many of these products are eaten with a mixture of brown sugar and grated rye bread. If they want something sweet, Danes are just as likely to eat jam or honey as orange marmalade.

You can drink either tea or coffee to taste. In hotels you will also be offered juice, and it is not at all uncommon to have a glass of milk. You may occasionally see a Dane drinking a bitter snaps (Gammel Dansk) with breakfast, and this is certainly available in hotels and restaurants, but the habit is not all that common, even if it is very much to be recommended. In hotels you will find Danish pastries (Wienerbrød) on offer. This is an old custom, and many people will still buy it as part of their Sunday morning breakfast.

Lunch (Frokost) is usually eaten between 12.00 and 13.00. A typical family lunch will often be a basic meal consisting of a couple of rye bread open sandwiches, with liver paste, sliced meat, salami, egg, cheese and possibly a little green vegetable (often raw) or fruit. This will be accompanied by milk, beer, tea or coffee. A slightly more elaborate lunch will include more expensive meat slices and some kind of fish, in particular marinated or smoked herring (Bornholm smoked herring is particularly good). The herring will often be washed down with an ice-cold snaps. Some lunches will also include some kind of warm dish, possibly *frikadeller* (rissoles, or meat balls—but much better than these names imply) or some other light meat dish, perhaps a fried breaded fish such as a plaice fillet. At still more expensive lunches there may well be smoked eel or *gravad laks* (salmon treated with herbs), or perhaps shellfish. And there will almost certainly be one of the countless varieties of salads available in Denmark.

Dinner (Middag) is usually eaten between 18.00 and 19.00. An ordinary family meal will often consist simply of a meat or fish dish with potatoes and some kind of salad, supplemented with a little fruit as a second course. Danes do not eat anywhere near as many sweet dishes as are common in England, though there is no lack of splendid desserts for those who want them.

If you eat out, or if you are entertained to dinner, a two- or three-course meal is the norm. The choices are legion, and the following are just a few of the dishes likely to be on offer.

Soups. Many Danes still tend to make their own soups rather than rely on cans; consequently, their soups are good. In general Danish soups do not differ from those eaten in most other European countries, such as chicken soup, oxtail soup and vegetable soups. However, some differences can be found. You will often find small meat balls, dumplings and vegetables in the soups. You will also often find the meat or chicken on which the soup is based, served together with it, but on a separate plate, often accompanied by (mild) mustard or horseradish sauce. One typical Danish winter soup deserves special mention. This is *gule ærter* (split pea soup). It is made of split peas boiled with pieces of pork, cured gammon, or possibly *medisterpølse* (similar to Cumberland sausage), and containing various vegetables such as carrots, celeriac, leeks, onions and potatoes. At a time when traditional dishes are tending to be replaced by more exotic offerings, this is still very much in vogue and one of the few hot dishes with which a snaps and a beer are considered in good taste.

Main Courses. Danish cuisine is these days pretty untraditional, but various specifically Danish dishes are still quite common:

Hakkebøf: a superior kind of burger made from the finest minced beef unmixed with other ingredients. Fried in a frying pan and usually served with fried onions.

Frikadeller: fried minced pork mixed with egg, flour, milk and onion. They are often served with *rødkål*, boiled red cabbage with a sweet-sour taste.

Karbonader are 'burgers' made of minced pork.

Cuts of meat are often different from the English custom, and so you are likely to find other names on your menu. Thus, a *flæskesteg* may well be a leg of pork, but it can equally well be the joint which in England is used for chops—which you will, of course, also find in Denmark. *Mørbradbøffer* are delicious small steaks of tenderloin. You will find the traditional roast of beef, *oksesteg*, but you will just as often find smaller joints known as *culottesteg* or *cuvettesteg*, cut from a leg of beef and—providing they have been well hung—extremely well tasting.

You should also try Danish sausages, which normally are of a very high quality. *Medisterpølse* with red cabbage (*rødkål*) is another traditional dish, while frankfurters are yet another which you may get in a private home, but which you really ought to try from a *pølsevogn*, one of the stalls selling them everywhere you turn—the Danish equivalent of fish and chips.

Potatoes are not mere filling in Denmark, and they are normally very tasty and much firmer than the usual English varieties. They will be served boiled or, often, baked.

Desserts. The huge variety of cakes in Denmark is usually of a very high quality. You will often find *lagkage* (layer cake) as a dessert, though you should not expect to find it served with extra cream. You are unlikely to need it.

Fromage, made with raw egg and gelatine, is rather similar to the English 'fool', tasting of one of a variety of fruits or spirits.

Budding is not like English 'pudding', but is rather like blancmange or real custard. *Rombudding* (rum pudding) is the traditional flavour, but there are many other varieties.

Ris à l'amande is a special Danish dessert consisting of boiled rice, whipped cream and almonds. It is quite a light dish and is eaten with stewed fruit—or fruit preserved in spirits. It is the traditional Danish Christmas Eve pudding.

Is (ice cream) is a very common dessert—and Danish ice cream is very good indeed, though not so sweet as is common in England.

After a restaurant dinner it is worth asking whether you can have *kransekage* with your coffee. These are small individual cakes based on almonds and eggs. And if you want a short drink with your coffee, this is **not** the time to ask for snaps, which is drunk purely and simply with lunch, and then mainly if accompanying marinated herring! It was, on the other hand, an old Danish custom to have a snaps poured into your (black) coffee, but you will not often find this today.

It is worth noting that alcoholic drinks are rather expensive in Danish restaurants. In shops, however, wines tend to be a little cheaper than in the UK, and spirits rather more expensive.

The times indicated above are the traditional Danish meal times—though guests may well find that dinner is served rather later, as in other European countries. One result of the earlier times is that between-meal coffee etc. is also drunk rather earlier: *formiddagskaffe* (morning coffee) between 10.00 and 11.00, and *eftermiddagskaffe* (afternoon coffee) at about 15.00. If you have anything to eat with your morning coffee, it will be a *småkage* (cookie) rather than the English biscuit, which is not common in Denmark (though they are available in shops). In the afternoon you are more likely to have a *konditorkage* (fancy cake, cream cake) or a piece of *wienerbrød* (Danish pastry) of one kind or another. The northern English 'high tea' is unknown in Denmark.

Bibliography

Gorm Benzon: *Vore gamle kirker og klostre*, Lademann, Copenhagen 1973.

Jens Fleischer: *Ture i København*, Politikens Forlag, Copenhagen, 1986.

J. Broby Johansen: *Kunstvejviser over Danmark*, 1–15, Hamlet, Copenhagen, 1978–1986. *Den danske Billedbibel i Kalkmalerier*. Gyldendal, Copenhagen, 1948.

Svend Cedergreen Bech: *Københavns historie gennem 800 år*, P. Haase & Søns Forlag, Copenhagen, 1967.

Svend Cedergreen Bech and Jan Danielsen (eds.): *Danmark*, 1–10, Gyldendal, Copenhagen, 1986–89.

Odd Brochmann: *Seværdige København*, Arkitektens Forlag, Copenhagen, 1968. *Danmark 1:100 000. Topografisk Atlas*, 3rd ed., Kort- og Matrikelstyrelsen, Copenhagen, 1989.

Dræbel, Eilstrup, Meyer, Rasmussen: *Danmarks Kongeslotte*, Lademann, Copenhagen.

Fakta. Gyldendals Etbindsleksikon, Gyldendal, Copenhagen 1988.

Fakta Danmark '95, Systime, Herning, 1994.

Lise Gotfredsen & Hans Jørgen Frederiksen: *Troens Billeder. Romansk kunst i Danmark*, Systime, Copenhagen 1988.

Harry Hjortaa: *Naturen Danmark rundt*. Politikens Forlag, Copenhagen, 1979.

Ulla Kjær & Poul Grinder-Hansen: *Kirkerne i Danmark III*, Boghandlerforlaget, Copenhagen 1988–89.

Hans Edvard Nørregård-Nielsen: *Dansk Kunst 1–2*, 1983.

Jytte Ortmann: *Guide over Danske Herregårde og Slotte*, Herluf Stokholms Forlag, Copenhagen, 1985.

Niels M. Saxtorph: *Danmarks kalkmalerier*, Politikens Forlag, Copenhagen, 1986.

Poul Svendsen: *Museer og seværdigheder i Danmark* I–II, Branner og Korch, Copenhagen, 1989–1990.

Tourist in Copenhagen and North Zealand, Dansk Bladforlag, Copenhagen, 1990.

J.P. Trap: *Danmark*, 5th edn. 1–31, G.E.C. Gad, Copenhagen, 1953–72.

Further reading

Annie Christensen: 'The History of the Main Axis Through Fredensborg Palace' in *Garden History*, Vol. 16, No. 2, Autumn 1988, pp. 144–60.

Bent Rying: *Denmark*. History, Royal Danish Ministry for Foreign Affairs, Copenhagen, 1988.

P.V. Glob: *The Bog People*, Faber & Faber, London, 1971. *Danish Prehistoric Monuments*, Faber & Faber, London, 1971.

W. Glyn Jones: *Denmark. A Modern History*, Croom Helm, London, 1986.

Elisabeth Munksgaard: *Denmark: An Archaeological Guide*, Faber & Faber, London, 1970.

Otto Norn & Søren Skovgaard Jensen: *The House of Wisdom*, Christian Ejlers Publishers, Copenhagen, 1990

Stewart Oakley: *The Story of Denmark*, Faber & Faber, London, 1972.

Bente Scavenius (ed.): *The Golden Aged Revisited. Art And Culture in Denmark 1800–1850*, Gyldendal, Copenhagen, 1996.

Claus M. Smidt & Mette Winge: *Strolls in the Golden Age City of Copenhagen*, Gyldendal, Copenhagen, 1996.

The Royal Danish Ministry of Foreign Affairs: *Denmark*. Compiled by the editors of the Danish National Encyclopedia, 1996.

Danish literature in translation

Works by many of the Danish writers mentioned are available in translation. We refer you to the following:

Hans Christian Andersen: The *Fairy Tales* are available in a host of translations of very varying quality. We suggest those by Reginald Spink or R.P. Keigwin as being the best British versions. A good American version is Patricia Conroy and Sven Rossel, *Tales and Stories* by Hans Christian Andersen, University of Washington Press, Seattle and London, 1980.

Andersen's autobiography, *The Fairy Tale of My Life*, tr. W. Glyn Jones. Copenhagen 1954; London, New York 1955.

Herman Bang: *Tina*, tr. Paul Christophersen. London, Dover, NH, 1984.

St. Blicher: *The Diary of a Parish Clerk and Other Stories*, tr. Paula Hostrup-Jessen, London and Atlantic Highlands, NJ, 1996.

Karen Blixen (Isak Dinesen) is generally available in English, as much of her work was originally published in English.

Steen Steensen Blicher: *Diary of a Parish Clerk*, tr. Alexander Fenton, Herning, 1976.

Martin A. Hansen: *The Liar*, tr. John Jepson Egglishaw. London, Melbourne, New York, 1986.

William Heinesen: *The Black Cauldron*, tr. W. Glyn Jones, Dedalus, 1992

Peter Høeg: *Miss Smilla's Feeling for Snow*, tr. F. David, Harvill, 1995. *Borderliners*, tr. Barbara Haveland, Harvill, 1995. *The History of Danish Dreams*, tr. Barbara Haveland, Harvill, 1995.

Jens Peter Jacobsen: *Marie Grubbe*, New York, 1952. *Niels Lyhne*, New York, 1967.

Jørgen-Frantz Jacobsen: *Barbara*, tr. George Johnston, Norvik, 1993.

Johannes V. Jensen: *The Fall of the King*, tr. Alan G. Bower, Seattle, 1992.

Johannes Jørgensen: *St Bridget of Sweden*, tr. Ingeborg Lund, London, 1954.

Søren Kierkegaard: all his works are now available in English.

Svend Åge Madsen: *Days with Diam*, tr. W. Glyn Jones, Norvik, 1994.

Henrik Pontoppidan: *The Royal Guest and Other Classical Danish Narrative*, tr. P.M. Mitchell and Kenneth H. Ober, Chicago, London, 1977.

There are two comprehensive bibliographies of Danish literature in English translation: Elias Bredsdorff: *Danish Literature* in English Translation, Copenhagen, 1950.

Carol L. Schroeder: *A Bibliography of Danish Literature in English Translation 1950–1980*, Copenhagen, 1982.

The Guide

1 • Esbjerg to Odense

Total distance 137km. E20 to (91km) **Lillebælt**. *E20, 161 to (46km)* ***Odense***.

Esbjerg

- **Tourist information**: Skolegade 33; tel. 75 12 55 99.

- **Railway station**: Jernbanegade.

- **Ferries**: DFDS, Englandsterminalen, tel. 75 12 48 00.

- **Hotels**: Britannia, Torvet; tel; tel. 75 13 01 11; Ansgar, Skolegade 36; tel. 75 12 82 44.

- **Youth hostel**: Gammel Vardevej 80; tel. 75 12 42 58.

Esbjerg (pop. 83,500), the main port of entry into Denmark from England, can almost be described as a city without a history. The town was founded in 1868 (when there were said to be 20 people living in the area on a couple of windswept farms) with the express intention of its becoming an export centre, and it was given its charter as a market town in 1899. Until then, Hamburg had been an important centre for Danish overseas trade, but with the 1864 war and the subsequent loss of Denmark's other small west coast ports in South Jutland, a new outlet became necessary, not least because of the rapidly growing British market. The establishment of Esbjerg had long been discussed, but the final initiative was taken despite a great deal of scepticism by the much-maligned autocratic prime minister J.B.S. Estrup. Esbjerg is now Denmark's biggest port, not only for overseas trade, but as the home of some 150 fishing boats, and encompasses a large container terminal. It is Denmark's fifth largest town.

In a sense, Esbjerg has represented the modernisation of Denmark, the growing awareness at the end of the 19C that Denmark was what would nowadays be called an under-developed country, living in a grandiose dream of the past. After the 1864 war, which reduced Denmark to the smallest area it had ever known since becoming a united kingdom in the early Middle Ages, the decision was taken that 'what was lost abroad shall be won at home'. There is, then, little point in searching in Esbjerg for the 17C and 18C half-timbered houses for which Denmark is famous. Even the small houses here are brick-built, with an exterior reflecting modest affluence.

Esbjerg is a city representing the new dynamism of an age of internal and external trade, a symbol of expansion. Its energy and ambition are perhaps already demonstrated by the watertower, looking like the remains of a medieval castle, built on the highest point, **Baunehøj**, dominating the town and visible from far out to sea. And the general architecture in the town centre reflects this: the impressive railway station, with its twin towers looking for all the world like the gateway to another castle, and the Den danske Bank building on the Market

Square (TORVET), with its splendidly extravagant corbie-stepped façade. Indeed, the Market Square is in general a fine piece of architecture, one of the more expansive creations in a town otherwise bustling with business activity. The shopping centre is excellent, and the dead-straight pedestrian precinct, GÅGADEN, belies its straightness, and has a charm of its own with a spaciousness leaving room for rows of small trees on either side of the main thoroughfare.

Yet there is also, as in most Danish centres, an interest beyond the merely commercial, and Esbjerg is well equipped with museums. Combined tickets giving admission to most of the following can be bought in the tourist information office—and you get a trip round the harbour into the bargain. At HAVNEGADE 20 an art gallery, the **Esbjerg Kunstmuseum**, was opened in 1962—with a 3m-high piece of metal sculpture by Robert Jacobsen entitled *Esbjerg*, representing the brash energy which has gone into the town, adorning the gardens. This museum contains c 600 paintings and sculptures and over 1000 graphic works from 1920 to the present day by important 20C Danish artists as well as a large collection of lithographs.

The **Esbjerg Museum** at TORVEGADE 45 specialises in local history and archaeology, and contains a fascinating series of reconstructions of façades, shops and dwellings from the early part of the century. Here you will also find the West Jutland Amber Museum and a reconstruction of an Iron Age house, together with a series of Viking exhibits. The Esbjerg Historical Archives are also in this complex.

Another museum, the Museum of Printing (**Bogtrykmuseum**) at BORGERGADE 6–8, close to the railway station, is unique in Scandinavia. Dedicated to the history of printing and containing a range of old presses, all in working order, it provides a very special experience.

In Tarphagevej, reached along the HERTINGVEJ, there is a splendid museum dedicated to fishery and seamanship: **Fiskeri- og Søfarts museum**. It is particularly well arranged, with extensive collections of old equipment as well as models of old fishing boats. It also houses a saltwater aquarium containing most species of fish found in the North Sea, and a sealarium. An outdoor area offers reconstructions of a harbour, a stretch of sand dunes, a World War II shelter, a ropewalk and a lifeboat station, in all of which you are free to move about and explore the exhibits. Children will love it.

Many of Denmark's towns and villages can boast of their old churches, and Esbjerg is no exception. The village of Jerne was incorporated into Esbjerg in 1945, and its 12C church, on STRANDBY KIRKEVEJ is a fine example of Danish Romanesque architecture with, like many of its kind, Gothic additions. It contains a late Renaissance pulpit and a carved Baroque altarpiece from 1653. Otherwise, Esbjerg takes pride in its modern churches, three of which are of special interest. On FYRVEJ, to the north of the city, there is **Sædden Church**, designed by the architects Inger and Johannes Exner, and incorporated into a large shopping mall. A little further north, in Hjerting, there is now a new church designed by Alan Havsteen-Mikkelsen and containing sculptures by Robert Jacobsen. Closer to the centre of Esbjerg, in KIRKEGADE, there is the Roman Catholic **Sankt Nicolaj Kirke**, designed by Otto von Spreckelsen, who achieved world-wide renown by his design for the monumental Arc de la Défense in Paris.

If you do not intend to return to this part of Denmark, it is worth making a trip 30km to the south of Esbjerg to the ancient city of *Ribe (p 203).

►Excursion from Esbjerg to Fanø

Before leaving Esbjerg, you should take a trip by ferry (20 mins) to Nordby on **Fanø** *(pop. 3200), the low-lying island with 18km of spreading white sandy beaches and the North Sea Swimming Baths (**Vesterhavsbad**) opposite the harbour—you have a good view of it to starboard (on the right side) on arrival at Esbjerg and can scarcely fail to note the wind farm on the coast.*

This small island, which is now a tourist paradise with excellent sports and camping facilities, has had a mixed history. Originally the King's hunting ground, it was sold to the inhabitants themselves in 1741. These must have been lively people, for in 1685 they had managed to ensure the right to sell their own fish without paying dues on them. After buying the island they made considerable profits from coastal traffic—and smuggling—and they subsequently established no fewer than four shipyards on the island. The income from these, together with the existing seafaring tradition, led to a period of prolonged prosperity, which is reflected in the well-to-do aspect of the neat thatched houses in **Nordby** and the other small town on Fanø, **Sønderho**, 12km to the south, with its 100–200-year-old seamen's houses, one of which, **Hannes Hus**, is a museum seeking to recreate the typical Fanø house of former times (open school summer holidays).

Fanø has maintained much of the island tradition, and both Nordby and Sønderho have kept much of their old character; they still seek to show their traditions during weekends in July, when you are likely to find people in national costume, dancing traditional dances and even celebrating traditional weddings. Nordby has its Fanø Fair during the first weekend and Sønderho its Sønderho Fair in the third weekend.

Both Nordby and Sønderho have simple small churches with seafaring associations, that in Nordby dating from 1786, that in Sønderho from 1782. The **Fanø Museum** in Nordby has a fine collection of seafaring relics and many examples of the national costume which was long worn on Fanø (open Jun–Aug). At HERLUF TROLLESVEJ 1 there is a **toy museum** with an array of toys, dolls and models from the past two centuries (open May–Oct).

Sønderho is the home of Denmark's oldest licensed inn, with a licence going back to 1722. The old lifeboat station from 1887, **Sønderho Gamle Redningsstation**, and the windmill from 1895 are now both museums (both open summer school holidays).◄

There are two very different routes across Jutland from Esbjerg to the **Lillebælt** strait. The direct route (total distance 91km) has very little to offer apart from the lower mileage, while the alternative route (109km) takes you to sights both ancient and modern.

Direct route to Lillebælt

Total distance 91km

The road east of Esbjerg is low-lying, much of it reclaimed from the marsh and moorland which were once the hallmarks of Jutland. On reaching (33km) Holsted, you should drive a further 2km and then turn off right to **Tirslund** (4km), where, in the woods, you will find a huge erratic boulder, 3.5m high and 5.6m in diameter, standing on its own in a clearing, transported there by the ice in a distant past. Legend has it that Harald Bluetooth wanted to use the stone as a memorial to his parents at Jelling (p 292), but that when he had got it as far as this he heard that his son was organising a rebellion, and so he took it no further. But this is only legend. Judging by the name (Tirslunde = Tir's Grove), this must once have been a shrine of the god Tyr.

Back on the E20 you pass through the grounds of **Estrup manor** (built 1721) before you arrive at (15km) **Vejen** (**Tourist Information**: Nørregade 42), where there is a gallery of works by South Jutlandic artists. Standing in front of it there is a striking statue by Niels Hansen Jacobsen, *Troll Scenting Christian Blood*, from 1896. It clearly shows the influence of Rodin, with whose work Hansen Jacobsen had become acquainted during a stay in Paris.

Near the southwest outskirts of Vejen lies **Askov**, the site of one of Denmark's great folk high schools.

Askov Folk High School

Askov is inevitably associated with N.F.S. Grundtvig, whose idea of a high school movement to give a non-academic education to the rural population, and to fill them with Christian and patriotic ideals, was first put into practice by C. Flor at Rødding just south of Askov. This first folk high school was, however, situated on territory that was lost in the 1864 war, and consequently a new start had to be made in 1865. The main building of a disused farm in Askov was then chosen, just north of the Kongeå river (the Danish–German border between 1864 and 1920), and with its views across the lost Danish lands it soon became a place of great emotional significance. Askov Folk High School has since attracted all the great popular Grundtvigian orators of its time, and although the ethos of the folk high schools today is different, Askov has retained a central position in the Danish consciousness. An offshoot of 19C National Romanticism, the folk high school movement has for more than a century fostered a cultural awareness and a sense of a Danish Scandinavian cultural identity which it is perhaps difficult for non-Scandinavians to appreciate.

As a result of the growing importance of this non-academic education, Askov Folk High School has been subjected to various extensions over the years, and few of the original buildings are now left. Visits are possible on application.

A minor road south from Askov will take you to **Skibelund Krat** (3km), a wooded area just north of the old border. This, too, has memories of Grundtvigian patriotism, and was a spot where large popular gatherings were organised in the period up to 1920. There is a large amphitheatre with seating for 4000, and there are monuments to many Danish patriots.

The 12C Romanesque church in **Malt** just west of Askov is known for having one of the best-preserved Romanesque fonts in Denmark. The motifs on it are in themselves curious: in addition to complex ornamentation, four men are portrayed engaged in combat, while a woman is seen fleeing and carrying a child. At the west end there is a handsome modern stained glass window, a late work by Sven Havsteen-Mikkelsen.

From Vejen you follow the E20 east through increasingly undulating country. At 20km you meet the E45 motorway from Germany. From here the E20 (your route) follows the E45 north for 7km, at which point the two roads divide again and you follow the E20 to (14km) Lillebælt. If you want to visit Kolding (p 180)—and you really ought to—you drive straight ahead where the E20 meets the E45. (For Lillebælt see below.)

At the time of writing, a motorway is being built between Esbjerg and Kolding. When completed, during the lifetime of this guide, it will considerably reduce the journey time to Lillebælt and will inevitably entail the renumbering of the old road forming the basis of the direct route as described above.

Alternative route from Esbjerg to Lillebælt—via Legoland
Total distance 109km

You leave Esbjerg on the E20, after 11km turning left on to the A30 to (35km) the industrial town of **Grindsted** (pop. 1700; Tourist Information: Østergade 25). The very large church here is sometimes referred to as the Heath Cathedral. In 1921–23 an impressive new nave and tower were added to the original Romanesque church. The old altarpiece and much of the old furniture is now on view in the tower, to which access may be had on application.

You now turn right on to the A28, which takes you direct to (12km) **Billund** (pop. 8300).

- ■ **Tourist information**: at Legoland; tel 75 33 19 26; and in the airport; 75 35 41 00.

- ■ **Hotels**: Legoland, Aastvej 10; tel. 75 33 12 44; Svanen, Nordmarksvej 8; tel. 75 33 28 33.

Billund is now mainly known as the home of **Legoland**. Over 33 million Lego bricks are said to have been used in building this pleasure park, with among other things its miniature reconstructions of buildings from all over the world. You can see eminently recognisable reconstructions of Copenhagen, Amsterdam, London, Stockholm and many other famous cities. Legoland also has a huge collection of antique dolls, the oldest being from c 1580, as well as a comprehensive collection of antique toys of all kinds. Then there are dolls' houses, including, as the jewel, **Titania's Palace**, said to be the most elaborate miniature palace in the world. There are 18 rooms in it, and over 3000 pieces of furniture and equipment. It took the maker, Sir Neville Wilkinson, 15 years to complete his building, which was bought by Legoland in 1978. Another special feature of Legoland is a collection of 19C toys recently recovered from a ship which sank in 1870. Surmounting the whole site with its Legotrain, Indian Legoredo town, miniboats and Traffic School is a rotating restaurant at the top of the Legotop observation tower. Very much for the children, but acceptable for all ages, being kept in good Danish taste and beautifully laid out.

Here too you will find the Center Mobilium, containing a motor car museum, **Danmarks Bilmuseum**; an aircraft museum, **Danmarks Flyvemuseum**; the museum illustrating the history of the Falck Emergency Service, the **Falckmuseum**.

Leave Billund on the 176 south, a good and not-too-busy road. In 17km you will pass through **Egtved**.

Egtved parish is known to contain some 260 burial mounds, though only a small number have been preserved. However, on excavation in 1921, one of these revealed one of Denmark's major Early Bronze Age finds, the **Egtved Find**. The mound contained the body of a 20–25-year-old woman, the **Egtved girl**, in a remarkable state of preservation and surrounded by a large collection of grave goods. She was in an oak coffin, lying on cowhide, fully dressed, and wearing two bracelets and an earring of bronze. The charred remains of a child, possibly a sacrifice, lay close to her. The mound, to the northwest of Egtved, is still visible, but the find itself is now on show in the National Museum in Copenhagen. However, a wooden hut on the spot contains photographs demonstrating the excavation and the opening of the coffin, and there is a reproduction of the clothing worn by the Egtved girl.

The Romanesque church in Egtved has an octagonal tower resulting from a fit of zealous restoration in the 1860s. The purist will regret this zeal, but will look with interest at the fresco frieze of the Dance of Death which was uncovered in 1969. There are two other friezes of this kind in Denmark, one in Nørre Alslev in Falster and one in Jungshoved on Stevns (both see p 155). This one is nevertheless different in that the heads are missing from all the figures! All three friezes seem to be related to the famous one in Lübeck.

In the nearby **Tørskind gamle grusgrav** (Tørskind Old Gravel Pit) there is a sculpture park containing an integrated collection of nine open-air sculptures by Robert Jacobsen and Jean Clareboudt, in which the two artists seek to fuse nature and culture.

14km further on you reach the 441. Here you turn right, and in another 5km you meet the E20, which by now has become a motorway, but also acts as a sort of glorified ring road to the splendid old town of Kolding (p 180) which, time permitting, should be visited. If, however, you decide against a visit, you just join the E20 east to (17km) Lillebælt.

Lillebælt, the sound that separates Jutland from Fyn, is the narrowest of the three stretches of water separating the Kattegat from the Baltic. Whereas Storebælt (The Great Belt) and Øresund (The Sound) are considered international shipping routes, Lillebælt has much more of a local Danish character. It is about 130km long and at the narrowest point no more than 700m wide. It is

Little Belt Bridge (new)

only 13m deep at the entrance, and so it is impossible for large ships to sail through.

The stretch along Lillebælt is very beautiful, and both to the north and to the south there are often large numbers of sailing ships to be seen. This is particularly so in July during the annual sailing race around Fyn known as 'Fyn Rundt'. However, Lillebælt has other things to offer—magnificent beaches for bathing, ideal conditions for windsurfing and sailing, and excellent fishing.

There are two bridges across Lillebælt. The old Lillebælt Bridge, opened in 1935, is a combined road and rail bridge: there are two railway tracks, a roadway and a footpath. Its total length is 1178m, 825m of which is over the water.

Building commenced on the new motorway bridge in 1965, and it was opened in 1970. It is 1080m long and has two 120m-high towers.

From Lillebælt you have the choice of two routes across Fyn to Odense. The fast direct route (total distance 46km) is described first; see below for the slower, winding one (64km). However, Middelfart (p 176), 2km south of the motorway, is an optional digression on both, but the decision for or against a visit there has to be made within 1km after leaving the bridge!

Direct route from Lillebælt
Total distance 46km

Leave the E20 motorway at (10km) Junction 57 and continue your route on the 161, the old main road across Fyn.

21km ahead you reach Vissenbjerg, where you will find at Roldvej 53 Fyns Akvarium, with some 300 species of fish including piranha, surgeon fish and sharks, and at Kirkehelle 5 a large Terrarium (reptile zoo).

It is now only 17km to Odense (see below).

Alternative route from Lillebælt to Odense—via Mid-Fyn
Total distance 64km

This secondary route from Lillebælt to Odense is slower but more idyllic and will take you past two mansions. At 22km (Junction 55 on the motorway) you turn south on the 329 towards Årup. After c 2km, you will find an estate, **Erholm**, on the left. The 'English' park is open to the public, and you will have a view of the neo-Gothic mansion dating from 1850, which is open to parties of 25 or more by arrangement beforehand.

4km further south lies the village of **Skydebjerg**, with a curiously stumpy Gothic church tower which was never quite finished. Another 6km of this lovely, hilly, wooded countryside will bring you to a minor road on your left leading to (5km) **Krengerup**, a glorious, harmonious, neo-classical mansion from 1772, flanked by a half-timbered home farm and outbuildings from 1771. The farm-yard opens straight on to the road, giving a fine view of the mansion. There is public access to the park during daylight hours and there are marked walks. During the summer public concerts are held in the house.

Drive on now to (2km) Nårup where you turn right, joining the 168 east after 3km to (11km) **Bellinge**. Here there is a Gothic *church containing some of the best of Danish church frescoes, uncovered in 1883 and restored the following year, portraying scenes from the Old and New Testaments. There is also a painting of St George and the Dragon, and in between the principal motifs there are all kinds of small figures—jugglers, men carrying guns, etc. Most unusually, these frescoes are signed and dated: Ebbe Olesen and Simon Pedersen, 1496. The brick-built altar is from 1595 and is surmounted by an altarpiece from c 1525. From Bellinge the road leads you straight into (9km) Odense.

Odense

■ **Tourist information**: Rådhuset; tel. 66 12 75 20.

■ **Hotels**: Grand, Jernbanegade 18; tel. 66 11 71 71; Ansgar, Østre Stationsvej 32; tel. 66 11 96 93.

■ **Youth hostel**: Kragsbjergvej 121; tel. 66 13 04 25.

Odense (pop. 182,000) is the principal town and administrative centre of Fyn. It has been the seat of a bishop since the 10C and, since being overtaken by Århus (p 232 ff) in the 1880s, is now the third largest city in Denmark.

It is the centre of Odense which is particularly interesting, the quite small area immediately south of the railway station and down to the river. Here the streets are busy where traffic is permitted, but there are many pedestrianised streets which allow the visitor to savour that mix of old and new in architecture and manner of life which is one of the hallmarks of modern Denmark: old shops and houses stand cheek by jowl with modern counterparts. The area is architec-turally dominated by St Knud's (St Canute's) Cathedral, and it is here, too, that the birthplace and the later home of Hans Christian Andersen are to be found. The area has been renovated rather than modernised on the outside, and has something of the fairytale air of the past which it is intended to invoke. Whether the clean, tidy exteriors of these old houses today bear much resemblance to what they were at the time of Andersen, must stand open to question. But a certain charm cannot be denied.

History

The earliest known reference to Odense is found in a document from 988 and, consequently, the town celebrated its millennium in 1988. It is likely, however, that, with its central situation, a crossing point of the river, and with river access to the sea, it is much older, as is suggested by the name itself, almost certainly meaning 'Odin's shrine'. Attempts have been made to find relics of the heathen cult, and there are signs of earthen ramparts like those in Trelleborg (see p 45) on present-day Nonnebakken, south of the river.

In 988 Emperor Otto III issued a letter to the Archbishop of Bremen in which he exempted the town from taxes and declared his support for the creation of a bishopric there. The 11C historian Adam of Bremen talks of Odense as the 'magna civitas' of Fyn, and large numbers of coins were struck there in the reign of Knud I the Great (1000–35) and for successive centuries. Although Knud the Great (King Canute of England 1014–35) was associated with Odense, it was Knud II, St Knud> (1040–86), who came to occupy a central position in the town's history. In his efforts to establish a firm royal and ecclesiastical power, he caused a rebellion in Jutland. He fled to Odense, where he sought refuge in the then wooden church of St Alban (relics of whom had been brought from England, probably in 1075). There, kneeling before the altar, he was murdered together with his guard. By the end of the century the mood had changed, and in 1101 he was canonised, his body having already been moved in 1095 to a stone-built church for which he himself was responsible. The canonisation of St Knud led to Odense's becoming a place of pilgrimage, the home of six convents and monasteries, including two of the biggest in the country.

It is uncertain when Odense received its charter, though it may have been under King Valdemar III (1326–30), and from the beginning of the 15C it became the residence of many members of the Pomeranian, and later Danish, aristocracy. This, together with the large number of clerics attached to the See and the monasteries, gave the city its special character. Odense maintained its position as a centre of ecclesiastical affairs around and after the Reformation, when meetings of the aristocracy and of clerics were held to further the cause of the reformers.

In 1529 Odense was devastated by fire, and this was followed by further difficult years of suffering during the Count's War, when it was occupied first by one and then by the other side. By the mid-16C, however, it was on its way up again, and in the following hundred years it benefited greatly from the upsurge in foreign trade. Its position as a centre for great assemblies was re-established by the kings, and it was here the assemblies took the decision to open war on Sweden in 1654 and 1657. In 1658 Odense was occupied by the Swedish army, which stayed for a full two years and imposed crippling taxes on the citizens.

With the establishment of the absolute monarchy in 1661, the city lost its influential position as a meeting place, and a period of poverty ensued, lasting until the 18C. It was King Frederik IV who was largely responsible for improving the position. He and his Queen were fond of Odense, and in 1720–21 he had the old Sankt Hans Monastery transformed into Odense Castle (where he in fact died in 1730). The King's frequent visits to Odense brought back some of the aristocracy, and trade flourished once more. A sugar factory was established in 1751, followed by a soap works two years later and other industries throughout the rest of the century. In 1795 a theatre was opened.

War again put an end to this flourishing time. From 1807 to 1814 Denmark was involved on the French side in the Napoleonic Wars, which led to a period of impoverishment here as elsewhere in the country. Nevertheless, by the mid-19C the gradual move towards present prosperity began, partly as a result of the canal opened in 1804. Linking Odense direct to the Odense Fjord this led to the establishment of a harbour in the city. Moreover, Odense came to enjoy an advantageous position as a meeting point for virtually all the railways in Fyn.

One native of Odense associated with the wealth created in Denmark in the late 19C was Carl Frederik Tietgen, the financier and banker who was Director of Privatbanken in 1857 and who was one of the driving forces behind the establishment of the shipping company DFDS, the Great Northern Telegraph Company, the Danish Sugar Refineries, and the Tuborg Breweries. There is a statue in memory of him in the park, Kongens Have, immediately opposite the railway station. There, too, is a statue to Christmas Møller, the Conservative politician who during World War II was forced to flee to London, where he became the spokesman for Danes in exile.

To the southeast of Kongens Have stands **Odense Castle**, partially rebuilt on the site of the old St John's (Sankt Hans) Monastery by Frederik IV, and now, partly as the residence of the Chief Administrative Officer of Fyn, in the possession of the City of Odense. Immediately adjoining, in NØRREGADE, is **Sankt Hans Kirke**, once the monastery church. It is the only church in Denmark to have an outdoor pulpit. It fell into disrepair after the Reformation, and has been the subject of a good deal of rebuilding and restoration.

Odense is a busy city and was renowned for its traffic problems until the ring road was completed. Now, however, it is possible in parts to forget traffic and to stroll quietly along streets which have stood here for many years, streets with charming names such as Filosofgangen (Philosopher's Walk), Vintapperstræde (Tapster Street) and Pogestræde (Infant Street).

A walk from the railway station down the busy Jernbanegade will take you past the impressive **Fyn Art Gallery**, built in 1883–84 and extended in 1897–98. Here there are extensive collections of Danish art, from the great early figures such as Jens Juel and Christoffer Wilhelm Eckersberg to major modern figures like Asger Jorn, Richard Mortensen and Robert Jacobsen. Beyond the heavily restored former **Greyfriars' Monastery**, Jernbanegade brings you to the pedestrian precincts and the older part of the town.

A left turn into VESTERGADE will soon see you in FLAKHAVEN, with the *Town Hall** (1883) on one side. The 57m-long façade facing the square with its statue of Frederik VII by H.W. Bissen and the large abstract metal sculpture presented by Robert Jacobsen on the occasion of Odense's millennium, is a mixture of neo-Gothic and Italian, surmounted by figures representing the legislative and judicial powers. The internal decorations of the Town Hall are partly by the Fyn painter Johannes Larsen and can be seen on conducted tours in the afternoons in summer. The lateral wings of the original three-winged building were demolished in the 1940s. In 1955 they were replaced, and a fourth wing added to a design by Helweg Møller. One wing overlooks **Albani Torv** with its Roman Catholic Sankt Albani church (built 1906–08) in North German style and the old Odense **Adelig Jomfrukloster** (residence for ladies of the aristocracy). Beyond lie two parks, **H.C. Andersen Haven** and the **Klosterhave**.

The *****cathedral** is one of Denmark's major cathedrals, with the shrine of St Knud in the crypt, and with several royal tombs. St Knud was himself responsible for the original travertine church, in which he was subsequently buried. After fires in 1157 and 1247 a virtually new building was commenced under the guidance of Bishop Gisico, resulting after almost two centuries in the wholly brick-built Gothic cathedral now standing. The strikingly lofty nave with its elegant arches was finished by 1300, the chancel being added towards the end of the century. This chancel is approached by a broad flight of steps—its height derives from the fact that the crypt from the original church was left in place, if not entirely intact.

The immediate impression of this cathedral is one of lofty harmony and space, though the whitewashed walls give it a slightly severe appearance. This is offset, however, by the *altar, a magnificent triptych by Claus Berg, almost 5m high, which was originally made in 1521 for the old Greyfriars' Church and installed in its present position in 1885. Based on a painting from 1515 by Lucas Cranach, it is Claus Berg's masterpiece, containing almost 300 carved figures and representing the work of redemption. It consists of a huge central panel with eight smaller panels in the triptych wings and a further panel at the bottom. In addition to Christ crucified and the Apostles and the Virgin, there are recognisable portraits of the Church Fathers, of St Francis of Assisi and members of the Danish Royal Family. An inordinate amount of gold has been used on the altarpiece, which stands as one of the most impressive, perhaps *the* most impressive in Denmark, both for the splendour of the figures and for the intricacy of the decoration.

The cathedral's other principal treasures are in the *crypt, where there are two Romanesque reliquaries, one containing the relics of St Knud, the other now generally thought to contain the relics of his brother, but by some thought to be those of St Alban. These reliquaries have had a complicated history: probably hidden at the Reformation and found again walled up in 1582, they were finally removed and put in place in the cathedral in 1833. In 1806 the remains of King Hans, Queen Christine, and their sons Frants and Christian (the later Christian II) were moved to the cathedral on the closing of the old Greyfriars' Church; they are now in a vault in the east end of the north nave, surmounted by a splendid epitaphium to King Hans by Claus Berg, dated 1513 and thought to be a true likeness of the king. A memorial tablet to Prince Hans, also attributed to Claus Berg's workshop, can be seen near the entrance to the crypt. At the east end of the north aisle is the Valkendorf Chapel, containing a monument by Thomas Quellinus and enclosed in a wrought-iron gate by Christian IV's metal-

KØTTESGADE

Railway Mus.

Railway Station

ØSTRE   STATIONSVEJ

Kongens Have

Odense Slot

Skt. Hans

JERNBANEGADE

NØRREGADE

STATIONSVEJ

Falck Mus.

HANS TAUSENS GADE

KLOSTERVEJ

VESTRE

VINDEGADE

Fyn Art Gallery

GRAVENE

HANS

JENSENS STR.

DRONNINGENSGADE

KONGENSGADE

VINEGADE

SLOTSGADE

Greyfriars Monast.

VINTAPERSTR.

JERNBANEGADE

VESTERGADE

FLAKHAVEN

Rådhus

ℹ

ODINSGADE

VINEGADE

GRØNNEGADE

PANTHEONSGADE

BRANDT'S PASS.

Brandts Klaedetabrik

KONGENSGADE

SS. Knud & Alban

Kloster have

VESTERGADE

SANKT KNUDS KIRKESTR.

H.C. Andersen House

MUNKEMØLLESTRÆDE

KLAREGADE

KLOSTERBAKKEN

VESTERBRO

SØNDERGADE

FILOSOFGANGEN

Munke Mose

HUNDERUPVEJ

NONNEBAKKEN

ALLÉGADE

MIDDELFART & KOLDING

BOULEVARD

SØNDER

Odense A

JAGTVEJ

LÆSSØEGADE

E66

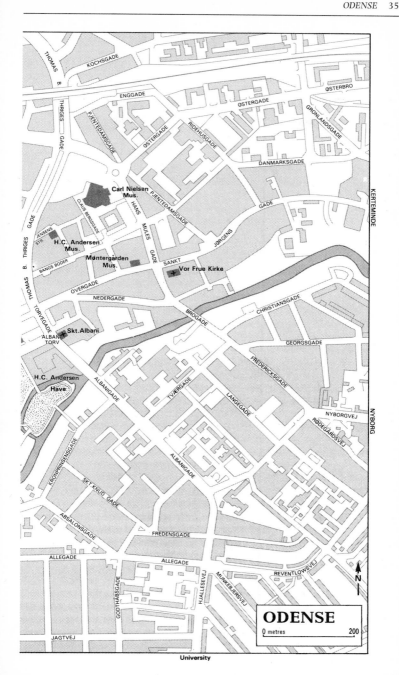

ODENSE

0 metres 200

University

work artist, Caspar Fincke. Opposite is the Ahlefeldt Chapel, also with a memorial monument by Quellinus.

Adjoining the cathedral on the south are the former domestic buildings of the Benedictine St Canute's Monastery, now the **Diocesan Library**. In the courtyard there is a bust of Thomas Kingo, Bishop of Odense (1634–1703) and one of Denmark's great hymn-writers. A Baroque poet of great note, Kingo was given the task of compiling a new hymn book, but the job was taken away from him again when it was discovered that he was filling it with his own hymns. Ultimately, however, the undertaking was returned to him, and he produced what became known as Kingo's Hymn Book, containing some of the finest hymns ever written in Danish, and used in some parishes into the present century.

On leaving the cathedral, if you proceed down SANKT KNUDS KIRKESTRÆDE, you will come to MUNKEMØLLESTRÆDE, where at Nos 3–5 there is a relic of a different kind in the house in which **Hans Christian Andersen** lived from the age of two until, at 14, he went to Copenhagen. Serving as an annex to the Hans Christian Andersen Museum proper, this tiny house contains an exhibition seeking to illustrate the author's childhood. There is not room for more:

> The home where I spent my childhood was one single little room where almost all the space was taken up by the workshop, the bed and the settle on which I slept. The walls, however, were covered with pictures; on the chest of drawers there were some pretty cups, glasses and ornaments, and over my father's bench there was a shelf containing books and songs ...
> By means of a ladder it was possible to go from the kitchen on to the roof, and there, in the gutters between it and the neighbour's house, stood a box of soil with chives and parsley growing in it;—it was all the garden my mother had, and in my story of *The Snow Queen* that garden still blooms.

The main ***Hans Christian Andersen Museum**, however, is the house in which Andersen was born, in HANS JENSENSTRÆDE 37–45. This is most easily reached by retracing your steps to the Town Hall, crossing Vestergade and going up Dansestræde to GRAVENE, which will lead you under the ring road into Hans Jensenstræde. Here, several houses have been converted into a museum,

containing spoken commentaries on the writer's life, rooms containing his furniture, letters, photographs and manuscripts, together with a large collection of Andersen's work in many languages. Andersen was a great traveller, and the museum contains his trunks, his hat case (and hat) and, not least, the length of rope which he always took with him in case of fire. Certainly a museum for the

Hans Christian Andersen's House

tourist, but the serious Andersen scholar will also find plenty of interest. The central hall is decorated with paintings by Niels Larsen Stevns illustrating episodes in Andersen's life.

Close by, in CLAUS BERGSGADE at the further end of Hans Jensenstræde, is the **Carl Nielsen Museum**, giving a visual and aural presentation of the life and work of the great composer and of his wife, the sculptress Anne Marie Carl Nielsen. This museum makes no concessions to the olde worlde atmosphere of this part of town, and is a modern, purpose-built edifice.

If you walk down to the other end of Claus Bergsgade, you come to OVERGADE, and a left turn will bring you to the **Møntergården Museum** based on 16C and 17C buildings from Odense, and intended to illustrate the history of the city. There is also a numismatic collection (open Mar–Dec).

A few metres further along Overgade will bring you to **Vor Frue Kirke** (Our Lady's Church), the oldest surviving church in Odense, part Romanesque, part Gothic, though heavily restored in the 19C. Built in brick, it contains remnants of an older, stone-built church on the same spot. It was in this church that Claus Berg's altarpiece was placed before being removed to the Cathedral in 1885; that replacing it is more modest, a painting of the Crucifixion by A. Dorph, 1885. There is a carved wooden font from c 1650 and an impressive Baroque pulpit by Anders Mortensen, dated 1639.

Odense is well furnished with museums, most of which are within easy reach of each other. Retrace your steps again and walk down the busy Vestergade until, on your right, you come to Brandts Passage. There at No. 37 you will find the old cloth mill, **Brandts Klædefabrik**, which houses an art gallery (**Kunsthallen**) with travelling exhibitions, a **Museum of Photographic Art**, unique in Denmark, and **Denmark's Museum of Printing** and **Danish Press Museum**. **Tidens Samling**, in the same complex, provides an impression of Danish living in the 20th century.

Two more museums in the city itself must be mentioned. The **Falck Museum** in Klostervej contains a historical collection of old fire engines and ambulances such as those which have been used by the Falck ambulance and fire service (open May–Oct). And, returning to the station and going beyond it, there is the **Danish Railway Museum**, a large collection of old rolling stock and other relics from the past 140 years (open summer; limited opening winter).

North of Odense, beyond the airport, there is yet another museum in the **Jernalderlandsbyen** (Iron Age Village), where archaeologists have sought to recreate an Iron Age atmosphere.

Odense is the home of one of Denmark's modern universities. It is situated about 3km southeast of the centre, and can best be approached via ALBANIGADE and HJALLESEVEJ, turning left into NIELS BOHRS ALLÉ; the *University then stands a few hundred metres on the right on Campusvej, a large, monumental building from the 1960s, in rust and black.

At Hestehaven 201, south of the University, lies the 16C mansion of **Hollufgård**, now owned by Odense City Council. It is used as a prehistoric museum, incorporating historical workshops and a Bronze Age milieu.

2km east of the University you will find **Den fynske Landsby** (The Fyn Village), one of the largest of Denmark's open air museums. It contains farms, houses, mills and other buildings such as a toll booth and a prison house, all taken there from different parts of Fyn (open Apr–Oct; limited opening winter).

The river, Odense Å, runs nearby, and for those with a will to walk, there is a path all the way along this charming river to the environs of Fyn village. (In the opposite direction the path follows the river through and well beyond the city of Odense, broken only briefly at Filosofgangen and Klosterbakken, and re-starting at Albanitorv.) For those wanting a more leisurely approach to Den fynske Landsby, there are sailings from the central Munke Mose and Filosofgangen to **Fruens Bøge**, from where Erik Bøghs Sti leads to the village. These boats call on the way at the **Fyns Tivoli** (fairground) and **Odense Zoo**, both of which also can be reached by car of course, leaving Odense along Søndre Boulevard.

Close to Den fynske Landsby, on Dalumvej, lies **Dalum Kloster** (Dalum Convent). The convent and its church were founded around 1200 by Benedictine nuns, many of whom belonged to the nobility, and it developed into one of the richest convents in Fyn, owning a great deal of land. At the Reformation it became Crown property, though the nuns were allowed to remain there until the last died sometime before 1580. Christian IV invested Ellen Marsvin, the mother of his morganatic wife Kirstine Munk, with the freehold of the estate, and his children from that marriage were brought up there. The King himself often visited Dalum Kloster. In 1682 the estate was sold to Didrik Schult and was given the name of Christiansdal, a name which it retained until 1906 when it was bought by the Order of St Hedvig, who turned it into a rest home. The original convent buildings have all disappeared, apart from the church, **Dalum Kirke**, originally the north wing of the convent, and modified in the 17C. In 1930 the St Hedvig's Sisters had a new church built for their own use.

▶Excursion from Odense to North Fyn and Bogense
Total distance c 70km.

Take the 303 west from Odense via Korup to (15km) Morud, stopping at (14km) **Langesø Skov**. These woods, containing the elegant 18C neo-classical Langesø mansion, are a favourite spot for the people of Odense.

From Morud follow the 335 north to (7km) **Søndersø**, where there is a splendid and largely Romanesque church. The horizontally striped exterior of granite ashlars alternating with whitewashed brick is unusual, while the interior exhibits some outstanding frescoes from c 1500, depicting the Immaculate Conception, the Annunciation, the Birth of Christ and the Adoration of the Magi. There is a Romanesque font, and the north door, from 1483, has an inscription in letters of iron.

Now take the 311 to (15km) **Bogense** (pop. 6000; **tourist information**: Adelgade 40; tel. 64 81 20 44), passing just south of the town Harritslevgård, a mansion from 1606, now used as a residential college. Bogense is the smallest market town in Fyn, with a charter from 1288. It has a fishing harbour, and a modern marina dating from 1976. There are splendid views of Jutland and the tiny island of **Æbelø** from the harbour and from other vantage points.

At the end of the remarkably long market place, Torvet, on the northwest side, stands the church, originally dedicated to St Nicholas, the patron saint of seafarers. Other old houses are **Den gamle Købmandsgård** in Annagade, and in Østergade **Erik Menveds Kro**, the oldest building in Bogense. In Adelgade there is, surprisingly, a copy of the famous Manneken Pis from Brussels, presented to Bogense in 1943 by Consul Willem Fønns. The old railway station in Jernbanegade is now the **North Fyn Museum** (open June–Aug; limited opening winter).

The 327 will take you all the way back to Odense. At 3km east you will catch a glimpse to the right of the impressive **Gyldensten mansion**, dating from 1640, standing in the largest estate in North Fyn. 13km further on you reach Uggerslev, from where it is a short drive west to **Skamby** (3km). The church here is one of the oldest in Fyn and has a fine crucifix by Claus Berg. Close to Skamby, between Torup and Glavendrup, you will find the **Glavendrupsten** (The Glavendrup Stone), bearing Denmark's longest runic inscription.

From Uggerslev it is 17km to Odense. ◄

►Excursion from Odense to the Hindsholm Peninsula, Kerteminde and Ladby
Total distance c 78km

This tour takes you to the northeast corner of Fyn and back. Leave Odense on the 165 and drive to (15km) **Munkebo**, once a small fishing village, but now dominated by the modern Lindø shipyard. From Munkebo you drive uphill along the Munkebo Bakke hill, providing spectacular views towards Hindsholm, across the Odense Fjord and the Kerteminde Fjord. Fork left towards (8km) **Mesinge**, where there is an unusual church with a pre-Reformation copper spire surmounting a corbie-stepped gable, next, passing the village of **Dalby** and the mansion of **Scheelenborg**, with a history going back to the 13C (not open to the public). At (5km) **Stubberup** you will find a village church—known locally as 'the white virgin'—standing high, with splendid views across the sea.

> Legend has it that this is the burial place of the regicide turned national hero, Marsk Stig, who died in 1293. As he was outlawed, his funeral had to take place in secret, and the story goes that the local priest was awakened one night and ordered to say a requiem mass for an unnamed dead person. He went to the church, found a grave already open in front of the altar and a coffin lying before it. He was sworn to secrecy after the funeral had taken place, but the maid in the presbytery had seen what had happened, and took the splendid drapings off the coffin in order to make her wedding dress of them. Unwittingly, she told her lover, who declared that she thus knew where his master was buried, and so must die. She was then buried in the cloth she had intended for her wedding dress. Despite the trappings, there is some chance that the main story is founded on fact, though Stubberup is not the only church in Denmark to claim to be the burial place of Marsk Stig.

Finally, driving through Martofte you will reach the very tip of **Hindsholm**, at (8km) **Fyns Hoved**, remembering that this peninsula was an island until the early 19C, when a land reclamation programme joined it to mainland Fyn. Fyns Hoved is a cliff 25m above the sea, and there are striking views from it of the North Fyn coast, north up the Belt to the island of Samsø, and even across to Sjælland.

This is also an area with a large number of neolithic and Viking burial sites, and the landscape is dotted with burial mounds. On your way south you should try to visit **Mårhøj**, just north of Martofte and a couple of hundred metres from the road. It is the biggest passage grave in Fyn, dating from c 200 BC. The main chamber, reached through a narrow passage 7m long, is over 10m long and almost high enough to stand up in. It is made of 18 large upright megaliths surmounted by seven cover stones. Two other passage graves are Tornehøj and Hestehøj.

Now drive as far south as Mesinge, there turning left and following the minor road to (2km) the village of **Viby**, where there is a restored windmill (limited opening), and an early Gothic church with a half-timbered tower which was added in 1718. Continue south to (6km) Kerteminde, noting the late 18C mansion of **Hverringe** on the way. The present rococo house was built in 1790, but the estate goes back to the days of King Valdemar IV.

KERTEMINDE (pop. 10,500) is another of the idyllic small market towns of Fyn, with a charter dating from 1413. There is a market, an old harbour, a large and well-equipped marina and many old buildings, mainly in a simple style, for instance those in Fiskergade. A harbour festival is held the first weekend in August, and every year on Midsummer's Eve, when bonfires are lit all over Denmark, there is a large bonfire on the north beach.

■ **Tourist information**: Strandgade 1B; tel. 65 32 11 21.

■ **Hotels**: Tornø, Strandgade2; tel. 65 32 16 05; Feriehotel Pax, Klintvej 45; tel. 65 32 30 26.

■ **Youth hostel**: Skovvej 46; tel. 65 32 39 29.

One of the fine old houses, **Farvergården** (The Dyers' House), in LANGEGADE, is now the town museum, with exhibitions covering local history and art, and including a reconstructed interior from the 19C (open Mar–Oct). Also in Langegade there is an alderman's house from 1630, while an old half-timbered house has been adapted as a bank. Close by, in Trollegade, is the **Høker** (Grocer), a 17C house renovated and turned into an olde worlde village store or 'museum shop' (open June–Aug, and Dec).

The old customs house in Strandgade now exhibits the work of local artists, but the local artist par excellence is, of course, Johannes Larsen, whose home on MØLLEBAKKEN is now the **Johannes Larsen Museum** dedicated to his work and that of other local painters (open Apr–Oct).

Close to the museum is **Svanemøllen** (The Swan Mill), from 1853, which actually belonged to Johannes Larsen, and is the only surviving mill of three which once stood on this hill. It has been carefully restored, and is open Apr–Oct.

Kerteminde was also the birthplace of the late Romantic poet Frederik Paludan Müller, whose verse novel *Adam Homo* (1842–49) was a precursor of Danish realism.

Copenhagen has its little mermaid, and Kerteminde has its Amanda, a granite

Johannes Larsen

Johannes Larsen, one of the Fyn School, is famous for his bird paintings, combining both accuracy and great artistry, and for his impres-
sionistic recreations of Danish provincial scenes. One of his most
famous paintings, *View across roofs in Kerteminde, early morning in May*
from 1896 or 1897 is for many the epitome of Danish provincialism,
and Kerteminde seeks to preserve this as its ideal. Others of Johannes
Larsen's pictures can be seen in the restaurant Pavillon Pax.

statue, on **Langebro**, of a fisherman's daughter. Amanda's real name was Sofie
Krag, and her life as a review actress in Copenhagen was somewhat less idyllic
than the statue seems to indicate.

A visit to **Højskolernes Håndarbejde** in TYREBAKKEN 11 is well worth
while. A folk high school with exhibition and shop, this represents the efforts to
preserve Danish traditional handicrafts, sewing, embroidery and design, and it
is possible to buy a host of tasteful designs and materials to carry on the good
work yourself.

On the south outskirts of Kerteminde lies **Lundsgård**, a mansion dating from
1765; and a little further south another one, **Risinge**, from c 1750.

To return to Odense from Kerteminde, you should follow an unclassified road
southwest, in the first instance as far as to (3km) **Ladby**, from where a minor
road northwest will take you to one of the major Scandinavian ship burials,
found in 1935. The Viking ship used in this 10C burial was 22m long and 3m
wide, and the Viking warrior was buried in it together with 11 horses and five
hunting dogs. It has been possible to reconstruct the outline of the ship, thanks
to nails which were still in place, and the remains of the horses and dogs and
some harnesses are still clearly visible. The whole is now a sophisticated *museum
housed in what looks like a burial mound. Tickets are available near the parking
area in a small house, where you can also buy yourself a cup of coffee.

Now continue southwest to (4km) Hundslev, where you can take a detour left
as well as right. To the right lies **Ulriksholm** (3km), a 17C mansion now an
hotel, and to the left the village of **Rynkeby** (2km), the special feature here
being the frescoes in the *church. These frescoes were not discovered until the
1960s, and when uncovered they turned out to be quite sensational. Thought to
be from between 1562 and 1565, they are unusual both in being post-
Reformation, and also because of their subject: they represent a company of 31
angels playing medieval musical instruments, many of which were not otherwise known. A visit to this 'angelic orchestra' is therefore a must for anyone
interested in old musical instruments. There are other interesting features in the
church, including three Romanesque gravestones.

3km south of Hundslev there is another possible detour to the left, this time to
the village of **Birkende** (3km), which is noted as the birthplace of Hans Tavsen
(pp 41–42).

Back on your route again you will, at 2km, meet the 160 in Vejruplund, from
where it is only 9km back to Odense. On your way you will pass Fraugde Kærby,
where you will find the **European Automobile Museum** containing some 80
cars from the 1950s, the largest of its kind in the world. Open June and July. ◄

2 • Odense to Copenhagen

Total distance 149km (39km on Fyn and 110km on Sjælland) if you follow the E20 motorway. However, we take you along two parallel routes on Fyn, one north and one south of the E20.

On Sjælland there is easy access from the E20 to the main towns, i.e. to (17km) **Slagelse**, *to (15km)* **Sorø**, *to (15km)* **Ringsted** *and to (30km)* **Roskilde**.

Our suggested route, however, follows the E20 only part of the way. We take alternative routes between Slagelse and Sorø and again between Ringsted, Roskilde and **Copenhagen**.

At the time of writing, it is necessary to take the ferry from Fyn to Sjælland, but by 1998 the connection will be by a combination of bridge and tunnel, one of the longest such in the world, providing for both road and rail traffic across Storebælt. A museum illustrating the history of the Great Belt has now opened at Knudshoved Ferry Terminal. Open 10.00–20.00 summer, 10.00–17.00 winter. Closed Mon.

The motorway is by far the quickest way of driving to (37km) the Knudshoved ferry near Nyborg. It can best be reached either by taking the A9 in the direction of Svendborg, joining the motorway after 7km at junction 49, or by taking the 160 in the direction of Nyborg and after 13km following the spur on the right to join the motorway at Langeskov—junction 47. You will, of course, join either of the roads leading east of Odense via the ring road.

There are, however, two alternative, more interesting routes from Odense to Knudshoved. The direct route mainly follows the 160 (the old main road), and offers several interesting detours (see below for the alternative route).

Direct route from Odense to Knudshoved (and ferry)
Total distance 39km.

12km from Odense you can visit **Birkende** (1km), noted as the birthplace of the 16C Reformer Hans Tavsen, in memory of whom there is a statue by Aksel Hansen in the village.

Hans Tavsen

Hans Tavsen is remembered in Denmark as the dominant figure in the Reformation movement and the translator of the Bible. Originally a monk, he went to study in Wittemberg, where he was strongly influenced by Luther. On his return to Denmark he began to introduce Luther's ideas and, in these pre-Reformation years, he was protected by the King. His translation of the Bible was later of profound significance for the newly established Lutheran Church, and its language played much the same role for Danish as that of Luther's Bible did for German. In 1541 Hans Tavsen was made Bishop of Ribe, where he remained until his death.

After a further 7km you reach Ullerslev, where the 315 south will take you to **Hindemae** (2km), a splendid neo-classical mansion from 1787 which now houses a permanent exhibition of antiques from the 17C, 18C and 19C. Twelve rooms in the main building are open to the public every day in the main holiday season and on Saturdays and Sundays in the spring and autumn. There is a large selection of antiques for sale, and there are café and restaurant facilities.

Back on the 160 you fork right after 5km in order to join the E20 to (10km) the **Knudshoved ferry harbour**. However, yet another splendid mansion is within easy reach from here. Instead of forking right, you can first proceed a further 500m and turn left to have a look at **Juelsberg** (1km), from 1771. The adjoining park is open to the public, and paths are marked for walking.

Now there is only one more temptation before the ferry, but that is a real one, a visit to the old town of **Nyborg**, which is described on p 195.

Alternative route from Odense to Knudshoved (and ferry)—via Fraugde
Total distance 39km

Take the 301 southeast to (8km) **Fraugde**, where there is an important church. First mentioned in 1239, it was extended in the early 15C. Some fine murals were discovered and restored in 1974. In the north chapel there are the tombs of Admiral Frederik Christian Kaas and his wife Birgitte Kaas, together with memorials to members of the Marsvin family.

However, the name of Fraugde is primarily associated with Denmark's great hymn-writer, Bishop Thomas Kingo. He is buried in the south chapel, together with his third, much-loved wife Birgitte Balslev. His first wife had died within a year of marrying. His second marriage, with a woman 16 years his senior, had presumably been a marriage of convenience, though perhaps it was inconvenient for Kingo that she lived to be 76. Within seven months, at Christmas 1694, the now 60-year-old Kingo married the 30-year-old Birgitte Balslev, who had grown up at nearby Fraugdegård. On the death of Birgitte Balslev's father, the mansion had passed into the hands of her brother, from whom Kingo now bought it. He and his wife spent much of their time there, and Kingo regularly preached in the chapel there. As early as five years prior to their marriage, he had been inspired by Birgitte Balslev to write one of his most beautiful secular poems, *To Candida*, an amazingly fresh and youthful expression of devotion for a man of his age in the 17C. The marriage lasted until Kingo's death in 1703. The coffins stand in front of an epitaphium by Thomas Quellinus, containing a poem written by Kingo in memory of Birgitte Balslev's parents, and surmounted by a medallion of Kingo and Birgitte Balslev. The work was done in 1702, and one must assume that Kingo himself saw it.

Continue now on the 301, turning left after 5km to visit the unspoilt village of **Davinde** (1km), where there is another interesting, but very different, church. Although there are inevitably Gothic extensions, thanks to its low vaulting the Romanesque nave has retained much of its original character. The village also boasts one of the best preserved of Danish thingsteads, the place where village meetings were once held. It dates from the 18C and consists of a circular area surrounded by 13 large stones with, in the middle, a lime tree growing up through the central hole of a millstone standing on three stone pillars.

Another 4km brings you to Ferritslev, where you turn left towards Nyborg, driving through (3km) **Ellinge**, where the young Carl Nielsen worked as a grocer's assistant. When 7km later you meet the A8, you turn left again and drive as far as (2km) the E20, which will take you direct east to (9km) **Knudshoved ferry harbour**. However, being as close to **Nyborg** as you are now, a visit to this historical town is worth contemplating (p 195).

The ferry crossing from Knudshoved on Fyn to Halsskov on Sjælland takes about 1 hour, and there are regular sailings. You can book beforehand from any railway station or at DSB, tel. 33 15 15 15, though this is not normally necessary except at busy holiday weekends. In **Halsskov** there is another museum, similar to that at Knudshoved, illustrating the history of the Great Belt.

There are two routes covering the initial stretch on Sjælland, that between Halsskov and Sorø is the direct route (total distance 32km), mainly following the E20 and calling at Slagelse. Korsør, just south of Halsskov is incorporated in the alternative route (71km; see below).

Direct route from Halsskov to Sorø
Total distance 32km.

From Halsskov you follow the E20 as far as (11km) Exit 40, where you turn off to (6km) **Slagelse** (pop. 35,000). There are relatively few old buildings left (though you can see the restored executioner's house in Fruegade), and Slagelse stands mainly as a thriving modern town.

■ **Tourist information**: Løvegade 7; tel, 53 52 22 06.

■ **Hotels**: Frederik II, Idagårdsvej 3; tel 53 53 03 22; Regina, Sct. Mikkelsgade 22; tel. 53 52 41 29.

■ **Youth hostel**: Bjergbygade 78; tel. 53 52 25 28).

History
Now one of the more important industrial towns in West Sjælland, Slagelse has a history going back to pagan times, when it is thought to have been a religious centre, with a temple standing on the site of the present Sankt Mikkels Kirke. By the 11C coins were being minted here, and a century later there were two churches, one of them, Sankt Peders, where the later local saint, Anders, was a priest.

King Erik Menved granted Slagelse a charter in 1288, and this was renewed and extended in the following centuries. Largely because of the fertile countryside around, the town flourished and grew until the beginning of the 16C, when it suffered both fire (there were 16 major fires between 1515 and 1804!) and Swedish occupation. At the beginning of the 18C it became a garrison town, but otherwise suffered seriously from a nationwide fall in agricultural prices. A new period of growth began at the end of the century, not least thanks to the opening of the main road from Copenhagen to Korsør. The railway came in 1856, ensuring sustained growth.

Sankt Mikkels Kirke, high above the town, was founded in the 11C, and traces of the original structure were found during repair work in 1970. The present church, a pseudobasilica, dates back in part to 1333, and the interior still bears many traces of the original workmanship. Nearby stands the old Gothic tithe barn, which at various times has served as a hospital, a grammar school and a police station. A marble plaque in the south wall lists famous pupils who attended the school. Hans Christian Andersen's name is among them—though in fact the school was not on this spot when he attended it.

Sankt Peders Kirke, in HERRESTRÆDE, dates from c 1150 and contains traces of its original Romanesque form; the old north door and some Romanesque windows can still be distinguished, though they are bricked up. The church was considerably extended in later centuries. St. Anders is believed to be buried in the north transept. Nearby, in BREDEGADE, stand the remains of the old monastery, **Helligåndshuset**, from the late 15C. It was restored in 1935 and contains frescoes by Niels Larsen Stevns. Also on Bredegade you will find Slagelse **Museum of Trade, Handicrafts and Industry**, demonstrating workshops of various kinds (open mid-June–end Aug).

One of Denmark's most famous old monasteries, **Antvorskov**, lies on the outskirts of Slagelse. It is reached by going south from the town centre, along Slotsgade and then Slotsallé (past the memorial stone to Hans Tavsen). At the end of Slotsallé you turn right along Hunsballevej, where, on the left, you will find the monastery ruins—at least those which are not covered by the motorway.

Founded in 1165 by Valdemar I, this was the home of the Knights of St. John of Jerusalem, and one of the largest and most influential of Danish monasteries. It was here Hans Tavsen became incensed at what he considered the luxurious manner of life in the monastery. Consequently, on Maundy Thursday 1525, he preached the sermon which is generally considered to have initiated the Danish Reformation movement. Most of the buildings were demolished in the 19C, and only a few ruins now remain. A little of it can, however, still be *heard*: the bell, from 1490, rings every day before morning service in the Cathedral in Copenhagen.

From Slagesle you can, if you wish, take the E20 to (15km) Sorø.

►Excursion from Slagelse to Trelleborg

The huge Viking encampment of Trelleborg, dating from c 980, lies about 8km from Slagelse. To reach it, first drive southwest along the 150 for 5km, turning right on a minor road to (3km) **Trelleborg**. It is a circular structure, surrounded by 5m-high ramparts, and with gates at the four points of the compass. The wooden streets linking these gates intersect in the middle of the complex. In each quarter of the circle there are four halls each 29.4m long, forming a square, and 15 similar, but smaller, buildings are placed side by side outside the main ramparts in such a way that their axes all point to the centre of the complex. Close to these is a burial ground. The original ramparts have been restored, and there are now cement piles to show the original position of the halls; a reconstruction of a hall has been built outside the complex.

This was the first of the Viking fortresses to be found; three others are known: Fyrkat, near Hobro (p 287), Aggersborg (p 315) on the Limfjord and Nonnebakken in Odense. (Nonnebakken is covered over and cannot be seen.)◄

Indirect route from Slagelse to Sorø

Total distance 27km.

The trip will take you through a typical Sjælland landscape and past a series of churches.

You leave Slagelse south on the 259 turning left after 3km to **Slots Bjergby**. Here, on a rise just south of the old Gallows Hill, stands a large whitewashed church, partly dating back to the Romanesque period. In the east wall in the porch there is a stone known as the *Krummerygsten* (Bent Back Stone) which, according to local tradition, was once used in the punishment of miscreants. The Gallows Hill (Galgebakken) and Hashøj, just north of the church, are ancient burial mounds. The Gallows Hill was excavated in 1946 and revealed plenty of evidence that this prehistoric burial mound had indeed been used for executions right up to the 19C.

Driving south on the 259, it is only 2km to **Gerlev**, the site of one of west Sjælland's finest village churches. The nave and chancel are Romanesque, and both the original doors have survived as have many other individual features. However, it is the wealth of Gothic frescoes in the chancel and nave that is most striking, signed by Martin Maler, Martin the Painter ('Martinus Malera bene fecit') and now splendidly restored. In the chancel there is a painting of Judgement Day and one of a Last Supper consisting of Danish medieval dishes, while in the nave there are representations of the Passion and Christ in Glory. The antemensale of the altar is from 1589, and there is a noble carved altarpiece by Lorentz Jørgensen, from 1667. The font is Romanesque.

While in Gerlev you should drive the short distance northeast to the small mansion of **Falkensten** (2km), from 1774, said to be built of material from Antvorskov Monastery. The most striking building is the enormous half-timbered *barn from 1862, with a sweeping thatched roof.

From Gerlev a minor road takes you south east to (3km) Skørpinge, where you turn right and drive a further 3km south to **Flakkebjerg**. Here, there is a fully preserved Romanesque church of unusual asymmetrical shape. Here, too, there are some fine frescoes dating from c 1300 (women at the tomb of Christ) and c 1450 (Christ as Judge of the World).

Yet another 3km—this time to the northeast—and you come to a third church worth visiting, that in **Gimlinge**, also Romanesque. Once more it is the frescoes which are the great attraction, some painted by Martin the Painter and dated 1409. Others are from between 1375 and 1400. Martin has again painted the Day of Judgement and scenes from the Passion. The antemensale is from c 1600, as is the ornate Renaissance altarpiece. The pulpit dates from 1594.

From Gimlinge a minor road east takes you to (3km) the A22, where you turn left, past the mansion of **Gyldenholm**, back to (10km) Slagelse.

Returning to the main route, from the centre of Slagelse the 150 leads on to (9km) **Kindertofte**, where the altarpiece in the church is a painting by Lucie Ingemann, the wife of the Romantic poet and novelist B.S. Ingemann.

The main road now takes you through lovely wooded terrain to (6km) Sorø (see below).

Alternative route from Halsskov to Sorø—via Korsør and Skælskør

Total distance 71km.

Leave the motorway at Exit 42 only 2km after joining it in Halsskov and drive across the bascule bridge into **KORSØR** (pop. 20,000), immediately to the south.

- **Tourist information**: Nygade 7; tel. 53 57 08 03.

- **Hotels**: Jens Baggesen, Batterivej 3-5; tel. 58 35 10 00; Skovhuset, Skovvej 120; tel. 53 57 52 52.

- **Youth hostel**: Tovesvej 30 F; tel. 53 57 10 22).

- **Sporting facilities**: Korsør has a good golf course and a first-rate marina, and it also has a busy fishing harbour. For those wanting to fish in the sea, there are plenty of possibilities along the coast, and fishing excursions by boat can also be arranged.

History

There are references to Korsør as early as 1241, but there are signs of much earlier settlements in **Korsør Nor** (Korsør Cove) and the islands in it. The Cove is immediately east of the town, and the entrance to it divides Korsør from Halsskov. The now ruined castle of Tårnborg to the north of the present town was established here as a defence against the Wends, and after a chequered period it saw a small settlement, Korsør, develop over the following centuries.

Korsør received its first charter in 1425. It was a natural port for communications with Fyn, and in the 17C it was decided that Korsør should become a main port for foreign trade. It was, however, the opening of the railway across Sjælland in 1856 that gave the impetus for the major expansion. Industry, not least the shipyard, made its home there, and connections by sea were established with Kiel and Århus. With increasing traffic, Korsør has maintained its position as one of the major ferry ports in Denmark, and all railway traffic between Sjælland and Fyn/Jutland still uses it, while until the opening of the fixed link most cars use the nearby Halsskov ferry terminal.

The old Korsør castle keep still stands, one of the only two medieval fortress towers remaining in Denmark, the other being in Vordingborg (p 139). Standing 25m high, it can clearly be seen from the harbour as the ferry approaches. It now houses a ***museum** illustrating the history of the town and the ferry connections to Nyborg. Nearby there is a powder store built by Christian IV (not open to the public) and the coastal battery once built to defend Korsør from attack from the sea.

As Korsør developed relatively late—and like so many other towns suffered from fires—there are few very old buildings. On the other hand there are many interesting 18C houses. They are centred on the charming main streets Algade, Slottensgade and Havnegade. Among them is Rasmus Langeland's house from 1761, also known as *Kongsgården* (The King's House), so called because this is where royal parties waited for suitable sailing conditions for crossing the Great

Belt. It is a long single-storeyed house with a mansard roof. The façade is decorated with inscriptions and reliefs and four statues, while Rasmus Langeland's
gravestone is fixed in the east end. A collection of sculptures by Harald Isenstein
(1898–1980) is now housed here. Note, too, the small but ornate toll booth
from 1785, now used for small exhibitions. On HAVNEPLADS you will find the
statue of the poet Jens Baggesen, who was born in Korsør in 1764. Baggesen is
one of the major poets of the late 18C and early 19C, and the only one really to
bridge the pre-Romantic and Romantic periods.

Korsør has another museum, the **Sparekassemuseum** (Savings Bank
Museum) c 4km south of the town, close to the house of **Klarskovgård**. This
museum illustrates the development of the Danish savings banks since 1810,
and shows the vast changes that have taken place over that time in furniture,
office equipment—and atmosphere.

You leave Korsør to the south on the 265, making your first stop at (9km)
Boeslunde. Here, overlooked by a 54m-high mound in which six golden bowls
were found at the end of the 19C, and on top of which archaeologists have found
the remains of another medieval castle, stands Boeslunde *church, dating back
to the 14C, once a place of pilgrimage thanks to a sacred spring, the Holy Cross
Spring—which still exists. The altarpiece is by Niels Skovgaard, replacing a very
special and ornate medieval folding altarpiece which could be changed
according to the calendar—and which is now in the National Museum in
Copenhagen.
    Continue along the 265 and you will come to (6km) **Skælskør** (pop. 11,300)
a small, out-of-the-way market town which in the distant past was the main
ferry link between Sjælland and Fyn, and which received a charter as a market
town in 1414. Having lost its former status, it has on the other hand retained a
good deal of charm.

■ **Tourist information**: Algade 1; tel 53 59 53 74.

■ **Hotels**: Kobæk Strand, Kobæksvej 85; tel. 53 59 45 15; Postgården,
    Strandgade 4–6; tel. 53 59 40 01.

■ **Youth hostel**: Kildehusvej 1; tel. 53 59 4384.

The church, formerly dedicated to St. Nicholas and going back in part to the
early 13C, is mainly Gothic, with a fine Gothic altarpiece from c 1475. The
carved pulpit is from 1630. Built into the churchyard wall in Gammelgade is a
medieval stone-built house which at various times has been a tithe barn,
grammar school and almshouse. Most of the other old houses are of modest
dimensions, though there is a picturesque half-timbered house in Vestergade
and a more imposing example in the same style from c 1600 in Algade.
    2km south of Skælskør, reached by a minor road running close to the fjord,
stands the striking manor house of **Borreby**, the scene of Hans Christian
Andersen's story *The Wind Tells of Valdemar Daae and His Daughters*, and one of
the oldest and best preserved of Danish Renaissance castles. It was erected in
1556 by the great chancellor Johan Friis, and stands almost unchanged,
surrounded by a moat, part castle, part mansion. In the 17C it came into the
hands of Valdemar Daae, the central character in Andersen's story. It is an ironic

twist that the steps in the spiral staircase in the tower are made of gravestones taken from the old Carmelite convent in Skælskør. The park and parts of the building (now including an exhibition of Sjælland handicraft) are open to the public. Borreby Marsh is a bird sanctuary.

Leave Skælskør on the 265 east, turning right at (9km) Bøgelunde to (3km) **Ørslev**, the site of one of the most famous of Denmark's church murals. This is the mid-14C 'dance frieze', a lively presentation of the medieval chain dance which now only survives in the Faroe Islands. The dancing figures are lifelike in their dress and movement, and provide a striking insight into medieval life. There are other quite unusual frescoes, too, with both religious and secular motifs.—Just south of Ørslev, approached via an embankment, lies the tiny island of **Glænø**, a delightful holiday area.

After your visit to Ørslev you should drive east again, past the mill to (4km) **Holsteinborg**, another magnificent mansion, built between 1598 and 1651, this time with four wings and corner towers. Another of Hans Christian Andersen's favourite places, it was once surrounded by a moat, only part of which remains. The park is open to the public.

From Holsteinborg a minor road takes you north across the 265 to (4km) **Venslev**, the centre of some of the popular religious movements in the early 19C, one of which ultimately became the evangelical wing of the Danish church, Indre Mission (Home Mission). From here you take the road north through the village of Hyllested to (5km) Dalmose, where you turn right into the 157. At (3km) **Ting Jellinge** can boast of one of the country's smallest churches, built in the North German style in the 14C, and complete with tower and porch.

Continue now along the 157 to (10km) **Lynge Eskilstrup**, where you will find **Kongskilde Friluftsgård**, an estate of 400 hectares in the midst of the Tystrup-Bavelse Nature Park. The entire park, which contains many prehistoric monuments, is open to the public, and there are facilities for eating and for overnight accommodation. And while you are here you should follow the lakeside road opposite to **Tystrup** village (3km), delightfully situated beside the beautiful **Tystrup Sø** lake. The church here, standing high above the lake, is from c 1370, with extensions from 1450. There are some interesting frescoes of Judgement Day and Christ in Majesty, with inscriptions in Danish, as opposed to the customary Latin, and with a clear connection with frescoes in the Chapel of the Magi in Roskilde Cathedral.

From Lynge Eskildstrup it is only a further 8 beautiful kilometres to Sorø.

Now we are back on the main route. **SORØ** (pop. 14,400), once stood on an island, and in practice is still three-quarters surrounded by two lakes—**Sorø Sø** to the west and south and **Tuelsø** to the northeast—and these in turn are surrounded by forest. There is a certain amount of light industry, but Sorø owes its renown less to that than to its historical significance.

■ **Tourist information**: Rolighed 5C; tel. 57 82 10 12.

■ **Hotels**: Postgården, Storgade 25; tel. 53 63 22 22; Sorø Storkro, Abildvej 100; tel. 53 63 56 00.

History

A monastery was founded here in the 12C by Asser Rig, the father of Bishop Absalon, the founder of Copenhagen. The island, as it then was, was an out-of-the-way place, ideal for a monastic foundation. After a period of decline the monastery developed into a wealthy institution until it was abolished at the Reformation in 1536. There had already been a school there, laying the foundations for an academic tradition, and this was allowed to continue. In 1623 Christian IV decided to develop the school as an academy for the sons of the aristocracy, thereby founding one of the most distinguished of Danish boarding schools, to this day known as Sorø Academy. Some of Denmark's leading scholars were associated with the school, Ludvig Holberg, the 18C dramatist, essayist, historian and novelist, being perhaps the most famous. In the 19C there were the poets B.S. Ingemann and Carsten Hauch. By their time the original structures had been replaced by Peder Malling's present building.

Sorø Academy, now a State-run co-educational boarding school, is private, but the area around the buildings and the surrounding park bordering the lake—corresponding more or less to the former monastery grounds—are open to the public. Lying in the south of the town close to the market place (**torvet**), it is approached through the original monastery gate, the only one left in Denmark, and now, as the home of one of the teachers, the oldest inhabited house in the country. This leads into an open square where, as well as the Academy buildings, 100m in front of you to the left is the longest monastery church in Denmark, dating back to 1201 and, together with Ringsted Church, one of the two oldest brick-built buildings in the country. Absalon is buried here behind the high altar, while several members of the Royal Family, including Valdemar II and Christoffer II, and other ancient and distinguished figures, are buried elsewhere in the church. Ludvig Holberg lies here, too. Queen Margrethe I was originally buried here, but her body was subsequently removed to Roskilde Cathedral on the orders of her Chancellor, Peder Lodehat, who was also Bishop of Roskilde.

This elegant Romanesque church, built in the 1160s to the pattern of the mother monastery at Fontenay, with its long nave flanked by aisles on either side, has vaulting from the following century but has otherwise retained much of its original character, despite some 15C alterations. The monks' misericords are still in place, as is the original night staircase leading up to the dormitory, though most of the furniture is of later date. The oldest piece is a large wooden crucifix from c 1247, with the cross and the figure of Christ all carved from a single piece of timber. Also medieval is the carved reliquary. From a later period there is the huge 1527 *crucifix by Claus Berg, at 8m in height the biggest in Denmark. The tall 1654 altarpiece has carved figures by Lorentz Jørgensen. Below the windows in the nave there are frescoes of the coats of arms of many of those buried in the church, especially the ancient Hvide family, to which Asser and Absalon belonged. The oldest date back to the late 13C, but they were repainted c 1515. The churchyard dates from the time when the church was built, and is still in use. The east wall is from the old monastery.

Apart from the Academy and church, Sorø has other areas of interest. Immediately west of the market square, in SØGADE is a row of old houses mainly from the 18C and 19C, although one of them, once used as residences for the pupils, is from 1650. The Library, in STORGADE, was established by Christian IV. Next to it stands the art gallery, **Vestsjællands Kunstmuseum**, containing an excellent collection of Danish paintings from the 18C to the present day, supplemented by another of fine medieval wooden sculptures gathered from the churches around Sorø. Also in Storgade there is **Sorø Amtsmuseum**, housed in a beautiful half-timbered building and offering a comprehensive collection of local historical exhibits, including a memorial room for the poet B.S. Ingemann (open summer; limited opening winter).

The entire region around Sorø is one of historical interest, whether you look to the Middle Ages or to more recent times. Of these latter **Tersløsegård** is of particular interest. Situated near the village of **Tersløse**, 11km northwest of Sorø, this three-winged thatched house was the home of Ludvig Holberg, and is now a museum (open Apr–Nov) containing many memories of one of the truly great figures of Scandinavian literature (p 119).

Leave Sorø on the 150 east. At (4km) **Slaglille**, where there is an unusually ornate stone-built Romanesque church, you should leave the main route, turning off left, to **Bjernede** (2km) to visit yet another church, this time a round one standing by the village pond.

*Bjernede church is the only round church on Sjælland, and the most elaborate of the seven still left in Denmark. A Latin inscription over the entrance says that it was the work of Sune Ebbesen, a cousin of Absalon, which dates it to before 1186. Over the years, the church has undergone a good deal of rebuilding, and the present strictly Romanesque exterior is in fact the result of a restoration from 1892. The interior is notable for four massive pillars supporting the vaulting, surmounted by a further four columns supporting the octagonal tower. A spiral staircase gives access to the upper church, which was probably a place of refuge in earlier times. Much of the furniture is either Gothic or Renaissance. Of particular interest is a late medieval tabernacle on the south wall of the choir.

Now follow the 150 to Ringsted. After c 2km you will come to Fjenneslev, and immediately after that you will see, on your right, **Kirke Fjenneslev**, with its unusual twin-towered church. The church itself dates from c 1130 and the towers from c 1200 (though they were reconstructed in the 20C). It was built by Asser Rig, and legend has it that he had to go to war and leave his pregnant wife behind. He told her that if the child was a girl she should add a spire to the church, and if it was a boy, she should build a tower. When he returned, he saw—two towers. However, this is *only* a legend, as Asser Rig's two sons Absalon and Esbern were not twins. Besides, Asser Rig and his wife were both dead by the time the towers were erected. At all events, this is an impressive Romanesque church with walls that are notably high in relation to their length.

There are some fine frescoes from 1150–1200, mainly on the chancel arch, with two figures which might possibly represent Asser Rig and his wife. The altar is thought to be original, and above it there is a crucifix by Claus Berg. The font is Romanesque. There is a 1.7m-long runestone in the churchyard, with the inscription 'Sasser raised the stone and made the bridge'. (There is in fact a bridge known as Sasser's Bridge crossing the river south of Fjenneslev!)

Now continue to (7km) **RINGSTED** (pop. 29,000), another of the historic towns in this part of Sjælland.

■ **Tourist information**: Sankt Bendtsgade 10.

■ **Hotel**: Scandic, Nørretorv; tel. 53 61 93 00.

■ **Youth hostel**: Amtsstuegården, Sankt Bendtsgade 18; tel. 53 61 15 26.

History

Now a modern city, Ringsted is closely associated with the history of Denmark in the Middle Ages. However, its history goes much further back, to the times when it was a major centre of the pagan religion, corresponding in its cultic significance for the people of Sjælland to Odense for Fyn and Viborg for Jutland. It has been surmised that the oldest church here was built on the site of the pagan shrine, as has happened elsewhere. It is here that the present Sankt Bendts Kirke stands.

Thanks to its central geographical position, Ringsted maintained its importance throughout the Middle Ages; coins were minted here in the 11C, and its significance is underlined by the fact that when King Knud Lavard was murdered in 1131, his body was brought to Ringsted for burial. He was proclaimed a saint and officially canonised in 1161, and at his shrine a monastery was built in the mid-12C. Valdemar I was closely associated with Ringsted, and lived here for a time. He designated the church the site for royal burials, and c 20 members of the medieval royal family are buried here.

Ringsted, too, was the scene of many important political meetings in the Middle Ages. It was given a royal charter in 1441. It was not, however, of great significance as a trade centre, and it was not until the advent of the railway in 1856 that Ringsted emerged as a geographically well-positioned trade and business centre, a position it has maintained ever since.

The central feature of medieval Ringsted is without doubt *Sankt Bendts Kirke, the old monastic church originally known as Sankt Knuds Kirke, one of the oldest and most impressive brick-built churches in Denmark. It dates back to c 1160, when it replaced the earlier and more modest church in which Knud Lavard was originally buried, and was completed at the beginning of the 13C. It suffered from a fire in 1241 and was rebuilt with a splendid vaulted ceiling, the new building being consecrated in 1268 by the Bishop of Winchester, in whose own cathedral both Hardeknud and Knud (Canute) the Great were buried. It is in the shape of a cross, with five apses in the east end and four chapels on the east side of the transept. The tower is from the 16C.

Over the centuries the church suffered from neglect, and the present elegant building is the result of a restoration from 1900–08. It contains many frescoes, including some particularly impressive ones in the central vaulting, with portraits of St. Knud and King Erik Plovpenning, King Knud IV, the Virgin and St. Catherine, and memorial friezes to Danish kings and queens as well as the coats of arms of some 100 members of the nobility. The auricular altar is from 1699, the altar crucifix from 1650 and the font from c 1150. The splendid pulpit, similar to the royal pew in Roskilde Cathedral, is from c 1600. Of the 20 royal tombs, mention should be made especially of those of Knud Lavard, Valdemar I and Valdemar II.

Valdemar II's much-loved Queen Dagmar was also buried here in 1212, as was her less loved successor Queen Bengerd (1221). Here, too, lie Erik Plovpenning and Erik Menved. The graves of Queen Dagmar and Queen Bengerd have been despoiled, but in that of Queen Dagmar was found a small Byzantine reliquary in the form of a crucifix, now on display in the National Museum and known as the Dagmar Cross. All these tombs, and many more from the Middle Ages, are to be seen in what is one of the main royal churches in Denmark.

Ringsted has few other remains from bygone ages. However, there is a further relic of the Middle Ages on the Market Square (**torvet**) in the form of three flat stones, traditionally thought to have been the site of the medieval *thing*—the public assembly. These are the only ones extant in Denmark. One of them is adorned with a 19C graffito—a games board inscribed by English soldiers garrisoned there during the occupation of Sjælland in 1807. The statue of Valdemar I on the Market Square is from 1937, the work of Johannes Bjerg. Of other older buildings there is the old posting house, Postgården, from 1795, an imposing building which is now a bank, and the Mahler houses, close to Sankt Bendts Kirke and dating from the late 18C. Nearby is the **Agricultural Museum**, illustrating 200 years of Danish agriculture. On the corner of Kongensgade and Køgevej you will find the restored **Ringsted Mill**.

►Excursion from Ringsted to Haraldsted

Take the 215 northwest from Ringsted and turn right after 7km to **Haraldsted**, from where there is a minor road leading east to the chapel on the edge of the forest. Haraldsted is where St. Knud Lavard was murdered in 1131 by his cousin Magnus in an effort to remove a rival contender for the throne. A sacred spring is said to have appeared on the spot where the deed was done. A chapel was erected close by, and the foundations are still visible. A 4m-high wooden cross was erected here in 1902.

In Haraldsted itself there is a stone standing on the site of the house in which Knud Lavard had spent the previous night, and close by there is the church in which he was originally buried, containing a great deal of medieval furniture in addition to frescoes in the chancel. On 26 June each year Roman Catholics walk in procession from Ringsted to commemorate the burial of Knud Lavard.◄

After returning to Ringsted, you continue your route north on the A14 north. At Ørtved (6km) you should turn right to **Vigersted** (1km), where you will find Knud Lavard commemorated in one of the 15C frescoes in the church. You now return to the A14 and continue for a further 4km, turning left to drive through Jystrup to the mansion of **Skjoldenæsholm** (4km). Built in 1766, this is now a conference centre and also an hotel. It stands near the site of Valdemar IV's Skjoldenæs castle; nothing remains of the original castle, though the mound on which it was built can still be seen. Close by is the large-scale tramcar museum, **Sporvejsmuseet Skjoldenæsholm**, with some 30 tramcars from Copenhagen, Århus and Basel, all in working condition and running on two tracks. In addition there are exhibitions and models (limited opening May–Oct). Back on the A14 it is now only 20km northeast to Roskilde.

Roskilde

Roskilde (pop. 50,700) received its charter in 1268. Of all the historical towns in this part of Denmark, it must surely be the most important. Indeed, it could be argued that it is the most famous of Danish cities outside Copenhagen, its present-day fame doubtless based on the magnificent cathedral with its many royal associations—but its importance goes far back in history.

■ **Tourist information**: Fondens Bro 3; 42 35 27 00.

■ **Hotels**: Prindsen, Algade 13, tel. 42 35 80 10; Maglegården, Maglegårdsvej 10; tel. 42 35 66 88.

■ **Youth hotel**: Hørhusene 51, tel. 42 35 21 84.

History

Roskilde was admirably sited to play an important part, being on the major land route across Sjælland, and with a deep fjord giving easy access to open waters. Certainly the name is known from the time of Harald Bluetooth, but it was Knud the Great who first saw its potential, and he created a bishopric there in 1020, making generous gifts to it to establish its churches and other ecclesiastical buildings. In 1370 the diocese owned 2600 farms in Sjælland, and by the Reformation a quarter of all the farms on the island as well as 30 large estates belonged to it.

The Reformation was catastrophic for Roskilde, which owed its status almost entirely to its ecclesiastical significance. Most of the churches were demolished, and the stones and bricks were used elsewhere—in Copenhagen, at Kronborg, on estates throughout Sjælland. Many of the art treasures in the cathedral were destroyed, and the chancel containing Queen Margrethe's sarcophagus was closed off for a century and a half. Things began to change though towards the end of the 16C when James VI of Scotland visited Roskilde to discuss questions of dogma with the famous theologian Niels Hemmingsen, who had been dismissed from Copenhagen and exiled to Roskilde as a crypto-Calvinist. Roskilde now became the home of several Renaissance artists and craftsmen, whose work is still well known in Danish churches.

The 17C Swedish wars brought great suffering to the city, and there was a terrible visitation of the plague in 1711, followed by serious fires between 1731 and 1735, some the work of an arsonist (who was caught and executed). Consequently, there are no 17C houses left and few from the first half of the 18C, though the main outline of the old city was retained in the rebuilding.

As elsewhere, the advent of the railways brought renewed growth, and Roskilde benefited by becoming an important rail junction. Nowadays, the ease of communication with Copenhagen has added to this; only 30 minutes away by rail, Roskilde has acquired many of the characteristics of a commuter town.

Duke Knud Lavard was born here in 1096, and the 16C hymn-writer Hans Christensen Steen in 1544. Roskilde has also been the birthplace of many other important figures in the history of Danish culture.

It is the glorious ****CATHEDRAL**, the fourth to be built on this site, that gives Roskilde its special significance for Denmark. The east section was completed by the mid-13C, and the entire structure was in place by 1282. The north tower is from the late 15C.

The overall plan of this magnificent brick-built cathedral was new for its time and remains impressive to this day. It consists of a lofty nave with a broad aisle on either side and ending in a great apse, though the original plan for a transept with three aisles was never carried out. The north and south aisles are lined with a series of chapels which are mainly the burial places of Danish royalty. More than 20 kings are buried here and 15 of their queens, as well as many of their immediate families.

Pride of place goes to Queen Margrethe I, who lies behind the high altar in a magnificent marble *sarcophagus surmounted by a figure of her as a young woman. Immediately north of the great west door—the main entrance—you will pass St. Sigfred's chapel, from 1405, and beyond that—on the north side—*Christian IX's chapel, built between 1917 and 1924 and the burial place of 20C Danish royalty.

Moving towards the east, you pass St. Bridget's and St. Andrew's chapels before reaching the bombastic *Christian IV's chapel, built between 1614 and 1640 partly under the supervision of Christian IV himself, and protected by ornate wrought-iron gates, the work of Casper Fincke. It is the most Gothic of all the chapels, which are otherwise predominantly Renaissance in style. At the centre is the surprisingly modest black sarcophagus surmounted by the king's sword, and surrounded by other royal sarcophagi. Notable, too, are the 19C frescoes, depicting scenes from the life of Christian IV and the bronze statue of the king by Thorvaldsen.

Continue east past Oluf Mortensen's porch at the start of the apse (perhaps better appreciated from the outside); then behind the altar around the apse, where you come to the Absalon Arch. This once linked the cathedral with the Bishop's Palace and, subsequently, with the royal palace designed by Laurids de Thurah in 1736.

On the opposite side of the nave from Oluf Mortensen's porch stands the chapter house, now the sacristy, dating back to the early 13C. Then, now moving west, you will come to *Frederik V's chapel, directly opposite that of Christian IV, and in striking contrast to it. Built in 1774 and completed by the neo-classical architect C.F. Hansen in 1820, it is dazzlingly light, a total contrast to the sombre splendour of Christian IV's chapel. Although the chapel contains numerous royal sarcophagi, the centre piece is the neo-classical sarcophagus of Frederik V by Wiedewelt, surmounted by an ornate pillar on which there is a profile of the King.

Further west again comes *Christian I's chapel, otherwise called the Chapel of the Magi, from 1459, containing the sarcophagi of Christian I and Queen Dorothea; here, too, is the monumental tomb of Frederik II, and the chapel is richly decorated with frescoes. Another feature of this chapel is the *Royal Column on which many crowned heads have had their heights measured and marked. Adjoining this chapel is the southwest porch, the present main entrance.

The last of the chapels is *outside* near the northwest corner of the cathedral, where an open octagonal *chapel contains the tomb of Frederik IX (d. 1972),

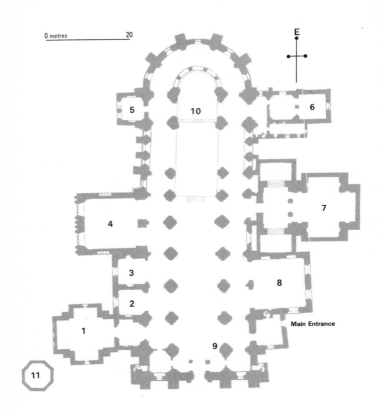

1   Christian IX's chapel
2   St Bridget's chapel
3   St Andrew's chapel
4   Christian IV's chapel
5   Oluf Mortensen's porch
6   The Chapter House
7   Frederik V's chapel
8   Christian I's chapel
9   The Clock
10 Queen Margrethe's sarcophagus
11 The open octagonal chapel

ROSKILDE CATHEDRAL

who expressed the wish not to be buried within the cathedral itself. This chapel was designed by Inger and Johannes Exner.

The central feature of the cathedral nave is, naturally, the high *altar, an ornate triptych from c 1560, made in Antwerp and considered one of the most splendid of its kind. Although in Renaissance style, it is composed in the manner of the older Gothic triptychs, with four main panels and four smaller ones, depicting scenes from the Bible in reliefs which are almost freestanding figures. There are known to have been at least 70 altars in the cathedral at one time, but little remains of them, no more than two figures from the 16C. The crucifix on the high altar is from c 1250. The choir stalls and lectern are richly carved Gothic work from the early 16C. In the nave, too, is Christian IV's pew, a richly carved and arcaded Renaissance work on two levels. The organ loft is from 1554, as is, in part, the organ itself. In the west end there is a famous *clock, from c 1500, including mechanical figures of St. George and the Dragon. Every hour on the hour, St. George's horse rears and tramples the dragon underfoot, at which the dragon issues a pitiful howl. Do time your visit so that you can watch this intriguing clock in action.

There are countless memorial plaques in the cathedral, and 176 gravestones. Allow more than the odd half hour for your visit. There is now a permanent exhibition showing the history of the cathedral in the new **Cathedral Museum**, opened in the Great Hall above Christian I's chapel. Guided tours of the cathedral are arranged by the Tourist Information Office.

Immediately to the east of the cathedral, and linked to it by the Absalon Arch from c 1200, is Laurids de Thurah's Palace, (Palæet), now partly a **museum** containing paintings and watercolours portraying Roskilde, together with a collection of 18C and 19C relics (open summer; limited opening winter). Also in the Palace is the **Museum of Contemporary Art**, which mounts exhibitions of modern art. Among the uses to which the Palace has been put was that of housing one of the elected Regional Advisory Assemblies (*Stænderforsamlinger*) set up in the 1830s as a move towards parliamentary government in Denmark. The town square, STÆNDERTORVET, is so named in commemoration of this. Further east, in a house from 1804 at SANKT OLSSTRÆDE 15, is **Roskilde Museum**. This contains a comprehensive collection illustrating the history of the Roskilde area from prehistoric times to the present century.

The statue of Roar and Helge on Stændertorvet illustrates the legend that the name of Roskilde stems from them and really means Roar's Spring. The square was the medieval market square, and here once stood the great Sankt Laurentius Church. Only its magnificent tower now remains, incorporated into the 19C town hall.

Going west from Stændertorvet, via SKOMAGERGADE to RINGSTEDGADE, you will find at No. 6 another section of Roskilde Museum, housed in **Brødrene Luetzhøfts Købmandsgård**, a proper old grocer's shop preserved in the style of the early 20C. It actually functions as a shop, and you can buy your goods there as they did in great-grandmother's time. Also in Ringstedgade, at No. 68, lies the **Håndværksmuseum**, a museum of old tools.

Retrace your steps as far as Jernbanegade, turn right, and take the third road on the left, FRUEGADE, where you come to the other old church in Roskilde, **Vor Frue Kirke**. If Saxo is correct in dating it to 1073–88, this is the oldest church

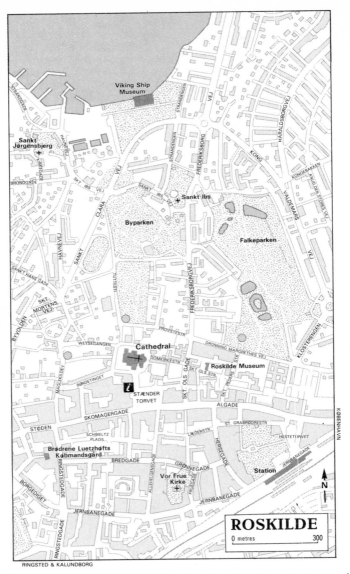

RINGSTED & KALUNDBORG

in Roskilde, and a find from 1060 in the churchyard nearby makes it seem that this might indeed be the case. However, in its present shape, the church stems rather from the mid-13C. (Open June-Aug, 12.00–14.00.)

Older than this is the now unused **Sankt Ibs Kirke** north of the town centre, on FREDERIKSBORGVEJ; only the nave remains standing, but it is from the beginning of the 12C. (Open Apr-Oct.)

If you leave Sankt Ibs Kirke along Sankt Ibsvej and continue into Havnevej you will soon come to what in medieval days was the separate village of **Sankt Jørgensbjerg** which grew up around a lepers' hospital. The area still has a village atmosphere, with many old fishermen's cottages and narrow streets, and here, in Kirkegade, stands the church of **Sankt Jørgensbjerg**. This singular church is very old, again one of the oldest in the country, dating back to c 1100, with a Romanesque nave and chancel to which have been added a Gothic tower and porch. Although built of stone, some of the architecture is reminiscent of 11C wooden stave churches. A drawing of a medieval ship has been carved into the east jamb of the door, together with a runic inscription. Other runic lettering is to be found in the chancel arch. None of the inscriptions has been interpreted. The north portal is believed to be the oldest extant piece of stone architecture in Denmark, with an unusual rounded relieving arch. As a church providing for a leper hospital, Sankt Jørgensbjerg church had special access and accommodation for the lepers, who were kept away from the rest of the congregation. Traces of this accommodation are still to be seen beneath the tower. The entire church was carefully restored between 1953 and 1955.

You are now quite close to one of the modern sights of Roskilde, the **Viking Ship Museum** down by the water. There is a path leading straight down to it from St Jørgensbjerg, but there are also ample parking facilities on the site if you prefer to take the car. The five ships of different types, once sunk in the fjord some 20km north of Roskilde in order to protect the approaches to the town, were salvaged in 1962, preserved and restored as necessary, and are now exhibited in this first-rate museum, which is well equipped with illustrations and regularly shows films in different languages. These ships are merchant ships, not those that carried Viking warriors; the largest, a sea-going vessel is 16.5m long and 4.6m wide. Replicas of them have been made, and it is now possible to go for a sail in one of them during the summer months.

▶**Excursion from Roskilde to Ledreborg mansion and the historical village of Lejre**

Leave Roskilde along the A14 south and turn right into the 155 c 3km from the town centre. Immediately after this you must turn left, and now you will find yourself in a very special 7km-long straight avenue of lime trees, some of which have recently been replanted, leading up to the mansion of **Ledreborg*. Dating back to the 17C, Ledreborg was redesigned and extended by Laurids de Thurah and J.C. Krieger in the 1740s, resulting in one of the most outstanding pieces of Baroque architecture and landscaped gardening in Denmark. It is open to the public throughout July and on Sundays from mid-June and until the end of August. The park is open throughout the year.

Driving back along the avenue you will come to a road pointing left to **Gammel Lejre** (1km), believed once to have been the seat of the ancient and more or less legendary kings of the area, the Skjoldungs, who are mentioned in the Anglo-Saxon 'Beowulf'. Much of the material on these kings is doubtless pure legend, and the 'King's House' (Kongsgården) can scarcely have belonged to them, dating only from the 18C. Nevertheless the museum in it is well worth a visit, consisting of furniture and implements used by the farming family which lived in this house for 200 years. There is, too, in **Lejre**, a very large Viking ship setting, at 80m the largest known, as well as the remains of others. Excavations have revealed a Viking Age burial site. The large burial mound outside the village is from the Late Iron Age, the time of the legendary Skjoldungs. Lejre today is a charming village, with many half-timbered cottages. It also has a *Historical Archaeological Experimental Centre with a reconstruction of an Iron Age village where, in the summer, it is possible to spend a time living in much the same way as did the people of the Iron Age. ◄

Just east of Roskilde there is access to the motorway 21/23 which will quickly take you through a mainly residential area to (28km) Copenhagen.

3 • Copenhagen

COPENHAGEN (København) (pop. 1,343,000) today, broadly speaking, consists of Copenhagen proper, Frederiksberg and a good deal of the island of Amager, which is linked to the mainland by a series of bridges.

■ **Tourist information**: Bernstorffsgade 1; tel. 33 11 13 25.

■ **Hotels**: The many hotels in Copenhagen make it impossible to list just two representative ones. Information can be obtained from the tourist information office; in addition, hotel reservations can be made by telephone on (+45) 33 12 28 80. Hotel reservations can also be made in Kastrup Airport on arrival.

■ **Parking**. In the centre of Copenhagen you will find parking meters (Look for P or Billetautomat). The area is divided into four zones, each with its own colour and its own rates, ranging from kr. 15 an hour in the red zone to kr. 4 in the blue. You pay your fee and take a ticket. At the top of the ticket there is a narrow strip, in the colour of the zone, telling you where you have parked and how long you have. You should take this narrow strip with you and stick the rest visibly on your windscreen.

You are not allowed to stay overnight in mobile homes in Copenhagen, but there is now a centrally situated site for mobile homes at Kalvebod Brygge.

Public transport

The public transport system within the Copenhagen area (as far out as Roskilde and Køge and covering much of northern Sjælland) is highly co-ordinated. This means not only good connections, but also that tickets purchased are available for use on all buses (though not private buses) or trains within a certain period. You can buy discount tickets valid for varying distances and times, but you must insert them in the yellow machines on the railway stations or on entering buses to have them clipped and time-stamped, and then remember how long they are valid. The Copenhagen area is divided into zones, for which you must have the appropriate number of clips. Bus drivers and station offices will advise you on what is needed. Children under 12 pay approximately half fare. There are also discount tickets valid for anywhere in the Greater Copenhagen area for either 48 or 72 hours. They are available from stations and tourist offices in the Greater Copenhagen area, or at DSB travel centres anywhere in Denmark. You need to have the card clipped as you start out, but there are no further restrictions.

Copenhagen canal trips

There are canal tours throughout the summer, with or without guides, leaving at half-hourly intervals from Gammel Strand and Kongens Nytorv.

Copenhagen Card

Visitors to Copenhagen will be interested in the Copenhagen Card, which gives free admission to over 40 museums and sights in and around Copenhagen, and also free travel on buses and trains in the Copenhagen area. You can buy cards valid for 1, 2 or 3 days in all main railway stations and travel bureaux, in many hotels and in Danvisit, H.C. Andersens Boulevard 22.

Bicycles

In Copenhagen bicycles can be borrowed from any one of about 120 unmanned points in the city. You insert a deposit of 20 kroner and the money is then refunded when you return the bicycle to any one of the points. These bicycles can only be used in the central area, and you should not try to go further afield on them: they are easily recognised, and the police will stop you.

Copenhagen sightseeing buses

Sightseeing buses without a guide leave Town Hall Square every half hour from 10.00 to 16.30 in the summer months. Tickets are valid for 24 hours, and you can get on and off as you like at any of nine designated stops. Half price for holders of Copenhagen Cards.

Copenhagen tours and excursions

Longer tours of Copenhagen and North Sjælland are on offer throughout the summer. Details from Tourist Information Offices.

A further tour from Copenhagen is **Øresund Rundt**, which takes you from Copenhagen to Malmö, Lund, Landskrona, Helsingborg and Ven (also spelt Hven) in Sweden, and back to Copenhagen on a choice of routes via Helsingør. You can go the opposite way round if you wish and you can break your journey as often as you like. Information from DSB Travel Centres or from Flyvebådene at the end of Nyhavn, tel. 33 12 80 88. **Youth Information Copenhagen**, Rådhusstræde 13, tel. 33 15 65 18 provides suggestions for touring Copenhagen by ordinary bus, by bicycle or on foot.

Copenhagen This Week, a weekly publication available from the central station, the airport and Tourist Information Offices, gives a comprehensive review of all that is available. Along with a vast amount of practical information, including hotels and restaurants, tours and excursions, it also lists the addresses and telephone numbers of foreign embassies, and kiosks, etc. selling foreign newspapers. A must.

History

There was a village called Havn on the island now known as Slotsholmen as early as 1025, and archaeological evidence even points to there having been a Stone Age settlement here. In the 1160s King Valdemar I gave this village to Bishop Absalon of Roskilde as a gesture of gratitude for his political help. In 1167, in order to secure the population against attack from the sea, Absalon set about building a castle here, and it is from this event that Copenhagen's history dates. Not only did the castle afford security, but it also ensured that trade flourished. The name of Copenhagen still echoes this process, meaning in fact 'merchants' harbour'.

The earliest town grew up in the area between the shore and Vestergade/Gammeltorv. Copenhagen changed hands several times during the early Middle Ages, sometimes belonging to the king, sometimes to the Bishop of Roskilde, and for a time it was even in the hands of the Lübeckers, who saw its prosperity as a threat to themselves, and consequently razed it to the ground in 1368–69. By 1417, however, it was firmly in the hands of the Crown in the person of King Erik of Pomerania.

Throughout the early Middle Ages Danish kings moved from one part of the country to another, but by the 15C Copenhagen had become established as the capital of a united kingdom. It might seem surprising that this city far out on the east of the country should have achieved this, but it must be remembered that the southern part of present-day Sweden was then part of Denmark, and that Copenhagen thus occupied a fairly central position.

With its establishment as the administrative centre, Copenhagen grew in importance, and by 1479 the University was founded. In the 16C the city suffered from the political upheavals. It was twice besieged, the second time in connection with the Reformation movement. The Reformers won, to a large extent with the backing of the ordinary populace. Then, in 1588, King Christian IV came to the throne, and although his foreign policy was disastrous and almost led to national bankruptcy, his urge to create a splendid capital was never-ending. Copenhagen owes many of its finest buildings to him.

In the 17C Copenhagen was again besieged, this time by the Swedes, and the very existence of Denmark was at stake. The Copenhagen citizens defended the city bravely and brilliantly when the Swedes tried to storm it, for which King Frederik III rewarded them with a great deal of municipal freedom. He then received *his* reward in 1660 when the citizens of Copenhagen supported him in his struggle with the aristocracy. He won, and established the absolute monarchy.

By now Copenhagen was a sizeable city, with narrow streets and houses crowded close together. Hygiene was non-existent, and fire precautions were poor. In 1711 the plague broke out and about a third of the citizens died from it. In 1728 there was a disastrous fire that laid waste to the centre. Now, with the ambitions of the absolute monarch and a growing awareness of international architecture, Copenhagen was largely rebuilt, and some of the most elegant of its mansions and palaces made their appearance. In 1795 there was another great fire, and in 1807 the British fleet bombarded Copenhagen in an effort to bring Denmark into the Napoleonic Wars on the side of Britain. They failed. The centre was again rebuilt, this time largely on neo-classical lines, as is clearly seen in the area around the University, the Cathedral and Gammeltorv/Nytorv squares.

The ramparts were demolished in the 1850s, allowing concentrated building outside them. Great blocks of flats now appeared in the Vesterbro, Nørrebro and Østerbro areas, some of good quality, some little more than slums. The 20C has had the task of clearing the poorer ones up, and a good job has been made of it.

Frederiksberg, immediately to the west of central Copenhagen, has a history going back to the time of Absalon, when there was a village here called Solbjerg. By 1417 it was in the ownership of Erik of Pomerania, and it has since then traditionally been associated with the Crown—and always independent of Copenhagen. In the 17C Christian IV settled a number of Dutch smallholders from Amager (see below) along what is now Allégade in an attempt to improve local agriculture and horticulture. The experiment was a failure, but one result of it can still be seen in the Dutch character of Frederiksberg Church. When Frederik IV built a castle here in 1699, the area was given the name of Frederiksberg. By the end of the 18C it was becoming a place where the citizens of Copenhagen had their summer residences, and in 1857 Frederiksberg was given the status of an independent 'kommune', which it still retains.

Amager is the small island southeast of Copenhagen, joined to the capital by a series of bridges, and in effect largely a Copenhagen suburb. It is the site of the new University campus, in Njalsgade, and, at Kastrup, of Copenhagen airport. The fixed link to Sweden, which is being constructed at the time of writing, goes via Amager, passing close to the airport. There is evidence of settlement on the island from as far back as the early Stone Age, and the fertility of the soil quickly established Amager as a source of agricultural produce for Copenhagen. In 1521 Christian II—who had close links with Holland and considered Dutch market gardeners to be better than the Danes—brought a number of Dutch families to live and work here, settling them in Søndre Magleby. The colony grew and spread to other parts of the island, leaving clear influences on customs and dress.

In 1617 Christian IV decided to found a new town at the north tip of Amager; this became known as Christianshavn, and is to some extent inspired by Dutch town planning of that time, not least in the canals for which it is noted.

Amager is, of course, now totally assimilated into the rest of the country, but its curious history has resulted not only in the very special area called Christianshavn, but also some villages rather different in character from those otherwise found.

Like other old cities, Copenhagen had a central area which could not cope with modern traffic. However, the 19C demolition of the ramparts had left wide streets on what were then the outskirts. It has thus proved possible to keep much of the traffic away from the central area, which consequently is unusually well provided with pedestrian streets.

The other modern feature of Copenhagen is its notably well-organised integrated public transport system. Both the city itself and a very wide area around it are divided into zones, and within this zonal structure tickets are transferable at will between train and S-train to bus within given periods of time.

A brief tour of Copenhagen by car

There is much to see in Copenhagen, but like most cities, it presents problems for drivers partly because of the many one-way streets and partly because of parking problems. So, as a quick introduction to Denmark's capital city, we have designed a fairly quick and easy run around for you in your car, noting briefly the main places of interest and giving as much information as can reasonably be coped with on such a trip.

You start your tour in front of the pseudo-Byzantine main railway station, **Hovedbanegården** from 1904–11, where there is a small car park.

   With the station on your right, turn right into BERNSTORFFSGADE. You will then have the other entrance to the station on your right and on your left the side entrance to the famous **Tivoli Gardens** from 1853.

   In about 250m you reach traffic lights, where you turn left into TIETGENS-GADE. Here you continue with Tivoli on your left, and on your right, in c 200m, the side of the art gallery the **Ny Carlsberg Glyptotek**, usually simply known as **Glyptoteket**. You will catch a glimpse of the front façade of Glyptoteket at the crossing with H.C. ANDERSENS BOULEVARD 100m further on. On DANTES PLADS, just in front of the main entrance, stands the Dante Column, erected here in 1921 to commemorate the 600th anniversary of Dante's death.

   Take a quick glance right further down H.C. Andersens Boulevard and notice the **Langebro** lifting bridge, leading to the island of Amager. The present bridge dates from 1954, but there has been a bridge on this spot since 1686.

   Go straight on into STORMGADE, and continue over the next crossroads at Vester Voldgade. On your right you now have the **National Museum**.

   A further 200m brings you, after the traffic lights, to a stretch of Copenhagen's canals. First there is FREDERIKSHOLMS KANAL on your right, with a small bridge, **Marmorbroen** (The Marble Bridge), designed in 1739–45 by Eigtved on the orders of Christian VI. It gives access to a complex (in fact a tiny island) called **Slotsholmen**, which is the islet on which Bishop Absalon, the founder of Copenhagen, built his original castle. The imposing parliament building, ***Christiansborg** is part of this complex, and dominates the scene. To your right, though partly out of sight behind Christiansborg, lie the Royal Arsenal Museum **Tøjhusmuseet**, housed in a building by Christian IV, the National Archives, **Rigsarkivet**, and the Royal Library, **Det kongelige Bibliotek**.

   Meanwhile, you should drive straight on, now with another canal, GAMMEL STRAND on your left. Gammel Strand was the major Copenhagen quayside in the Middle Ages, and until recently an important fish quay. There was a fish market here until the 1950s, and there are still some excellent fish restaurants. (Note the statue of the fishwife at the far end.) After c 150m you will have on your right **Thorvaldsens Museum**, looking for all the world like an Egyptian temple. Part of the building was once the royal coach-house.

   The street you are driving in is now called VINDEBROGADE; continue along it, following the traffic right at the traffic lights, perhaps casting a quick glance left where you will see the **Højbro** bridge and beyond it the square, HØJBRO PLADS leading to AMAGERTORV and the main shopping street, STRØGET (the overall name for several streets).

As you round the bend you will have the façade of Christiansborg on your right. You are now going to turn left, so keep in the left-hand lane in order to cross the canal on the next bridge on your left. While the driver is concentrating on this, the passengers can look to the right and see the Stock Exchange, **Børsen**, built 1619–41 on the command of Christian IV, with its spire of inter-twined dragons' tails. Beyond it is the **Knippelsbro** (1937), another lifting bridge leading to Amager, where the remarkable spire of Our Saviour's Church **Vor Frelsers Kirke** in Dutch Baroque from 1682–96 can also be seen. The spire, with steps running around the outside and topped by a 3m figure of Christ, was designed by Laurids de Thurah in 1750.

The bridge you are now crossing is **Holmens Bro**, and you are in a street called HOLMENS KANAL. On your right you have the naval church, **Holmens Kirke**. Bear left with the main stream of traffic, passing the statue of **Niels Juel** unveiled in 1881 to commemorate the bicentenary of the Battle of Køge Bay. The National Bank, **Nationalbanken**, from 1970, is now on your right.

After about 200m Holmens Kanal brings you to one of Copenhagen's most magnificent squares, **Kongens Nytorv**. It was designed on the orders of Christian V, whose equestrian statue stands in the middle of the square, and it was intended to link the old town to the splendid new buildings being erected to the east of this area in what was to be known as Frederiksstad. On your left as you enter the square you will see one of Copenhagen's oldest and biggest depart-ment stores, **Magasin du Nord**, and on your right the Royal Theatre, **Det kongelige Teater**. The present building was built 1872–74 and modernised in the 1980s. As the traffic bears right at this point you will pass the front of the theatre; note the statues of Denmark's two great dramatists by the entrance, one of Adam Oehlenschläger, the other of Ludvig Holberg.

Having passed the Royal Theatre you will on your right—just before another canal— catch a glimpse of **Charlottenborg**, which houses the Academy of Fine Arts. This building in Dutch Baroque was built 1672–83 as the residence for the Viceroy of Norway, Ulrik Frederik Gyldenløve, son of Christian IV.

Here you leave the Square, driving straight on into BREDGADE. But do note the area on your right, where you have another canal, NYHAVN. It was dug 1671–73 and is lined with an array of 17C and 18C houses, and now consti-tutes an attractive street known for its cafés and restaurants. Note the anchor close to the road. Made in 1857 and taken from the 19C frigate *Fyen*, it lies there as a memorial to Danish seaman who died in World War II.

BREDGADE is a very dignified road lined with neo-classical mansions. After 150m you pass SANKT ANNÆ PLADS (St Anne's Square) on your right, with a bronze equestrian statue of Christian X, and after that (No. 28) the rococo **Odd Fellow Palæ** built 1751–55 to a design by Nicolai Eigtved, and now a concert hall for chamber recitals. It was seriously damaged by fire in 1992, but has now largely been restored.

About 450m down Bredgade you will come to traffic lights. On your left you will see the Marble Church, **Marmorkirken** or, to give it its proper name, **Frederikskirken**, again to a design by Nicolai Eigtved, continued after his death by Laurids de Thurah and Nicolas-Henri Jardin and finally completed in 1894 by Ferdinand Meldahl.

Here you should turn right, into FREDERIKSGADE, which will lead you to the royal palaces of *Amalienborg, built around a square with the equestrian statue of Frederik V at the centre. Considered one of the finest pieces of European Baroque architecture, these palaces are again to a design by Eigtved and were built between 1749 and 1760. The palace on the right nearest the harbour is the Queen's residence. You can drive straight on, right down to the water's edge, to see the **Amaliehaven** park or just drive around the AMALIENBORG SQUARE. But whichever you choose: return to the one-way-road Bredgade, and continue your trip, soon passing, on your left, the Russian Orthodox church, the **Alexander Newski Kirke** from 1883.

The next traffic lights along Bredgade are at Fredericiagade, beyond which, on your left, you have the Eastern Regional Court and, on your right, at Bredgade 62 the Museum of Medical History, **Medicinsk Historisk Museum** in a building from 1785–87, originally the Academy of Surgery. On your right, too, you pass Denmark's principal Catholic church, **Sankt Ansgars Kirke**, designed by Gustav Friedrich Hetsch in 1842. A little further on the right lies the museum of decorative and applied arts, the **Kunstindustrimuseum**, in a building by Eigtved and Thurah from 1752–57, restored 1921–26 by Ivar Bentsen and Kaare Klint.

Where Bredgade ends at ESPLANADEN you bear right. The park on your left now is the **Churchill Park**. Then, also on your left, comes the Resistance Museum, **Frihedsmuseet**, with exhibits from the Danish Resistance Movement of World War II. As you come to the end of Esplanaden and cross Amaliegade, you will on your left see the huge **Gefion Fountain**, designed by Anders Bundgaard in 1909. Also in the Churchill Park stands the English church, **St Alban's Church**, built in typical English neo-Gothic in 1885–87.

It is no longer possible to drive through the park, so you will have to go back to the traffic lights at the end of Esplanaden, turn right and follow Grønningen to the next traffic lights, turn right again, and go down Folke Bernadottes Allé, to reach the green area again from the north. You can park here along with all the other cars if you want to pay a visit to the nearby Little Mermaid, *Den lille Havfrue*, sculptured in 1913 by Edvard Ericsen. On your way over to her, you will, on your right, see the Citadel, **Kastellet**, the fortress built by Christian IV in 1629.

From the Little Mermaid you return along Folke Bernadottes Allé to the traffic lights at the busy Grønningen. You should cross it, noting on your left a statue in memory of Carl Nielsen, *Pan Playing the Flute*, the work of the composer's wife, Anne Marie Carl Nielsen.

Once you have crossed this main road you are in ØSTER VOLDGADE, i.e. East Rampart Street, so called because it follows the old ramparts surrounding the city. On your right you can see the **Øster Anlæg** park, and on your left is the 'housing estate' which Christian IV had built for his sailors between 1631 and 1639, **Nyboder**.

700m further on you cross SØLVGADE, on the corner of which you have Copenhagen's main art gallery, **Statens Museum for Kunst**. Behind it, in the same park, but not visible from this road is the smaller, but impressive **Hirschsprungs Samling** gallery.

Immediately after Sølvgade you pass, on your right, the museum of geology, **Geologisk Museum**, standing in the botanical gardens, **Botanisk Have**. On your left is the **Kongens Have** park with Christian IV's sumptuous *****Rosenborg Palace** from 1634.

A further 400m brings you to traffic lights, at the crossing with GOTHERS-GADE. Turn right here and drive along Gothersgade, with the **Botanical Museum** on your right. Cross FARIMAGSGADE and continue until you reach the Copenhagen Lakes (Søerne), about 500m in all, where you turn right into ØSTER SØGADE, catching a glimpse of the Queen Louise Bridge, **Dronning Louises Bro**, leading over the Lakes on your left as you turn. There has been a bridge across the Lakes here since 1562, and the present one dates from 1885–87.

Stretching from GAMMEL KONGEVEJ in the west to ØSTERBROGADE in the east, and crossed by several bridges, Copenhagen's three Lakes were originally reservoirs, as the westerly Sankt Jørgens Sø still is. They lie outside the old city, and are now a much-loved open space. The banks are lined with greensward and paths with benches, and where Gyldenløvesgade crosses them there is the idyllic **Søpavillon** restaurant, with lawns and gardens.

You are driving with part of the **Sortedams Sø** on your left, and, on your right, the Copenhagen Municipal Hospital, **Københavns Kommunehospital**, designed by Christian Hansen and built between 1859 and 1863 in neo-Byzantine style.

When you come to the next major crossing, easily recognisable by the **Fredensbro** bridge from 1904, you turn right into SØLVGADE and across SØLVTORVET. You will now find you have the *Botanical Gardens* on your right and *Statens Museum for Kunst* on your left. On reaching the traffic lights, you turn right, into ØSTER VOLDGADE. You have been here before, and we have simply taken you along four sides of a square in order to show you the Lakes.

This time you drive across GOTHERSGADE, coming to a very busy part of Copenhagen, NØRREPORT. This is the site of the medieval North Gate, and now the location of one of the busiest suburban S-train stations. As you approach the station you will find on your left the pedestrian street FRED-ERIKSBORGGADE leading to KULTORVET square, beyond which stands the Round Tower, **Rundetårn**, the 34.8m-high observatory tower built for Christian IV in 1642.

On passing **Nørreport Station** you should move into the left-hand lane, ready to turn (at the next traffic lights) into the rather narrow NØRREGADE. The church which can soon be seen on your right is **Sankt Petri Kirke**, one of Copenhagen's four medieval parish churches.

About 250m down Nørregade you pass the old buildings of the **University** on your left. The main building, built 1831–36 to the design of Peder Malling, faces the cathedral **Vor Frue Kirke** on your left. This is a neo-classical building from 1811–29, designed by Christian Frederik Hansen, replacing the older building destroyed by the British bombardment of Copenhagen in 1807.

Nørregade now continues to **Gammeltorv** (Old Square), where you will see the magnificent Renaissance **Caritas** fountain, a gift to the citizens of Copenhagen from Christian IV in 1608, intended to provide them with fresh water. Immediately on reaching Gammeltorv you turn right, down VESTER-GADE, but you should try to gain a quick impression of the lively scene on Gammeltorv, crossed by the pedestrian street, **Strøget**, with the square, NYTORV beyond it, flanked by Christian Frederik Hansen's neo-classical law courts, **Domhuset**.

After 200m Vestergade brings you to VESTER VOLDGADE (West Rampart

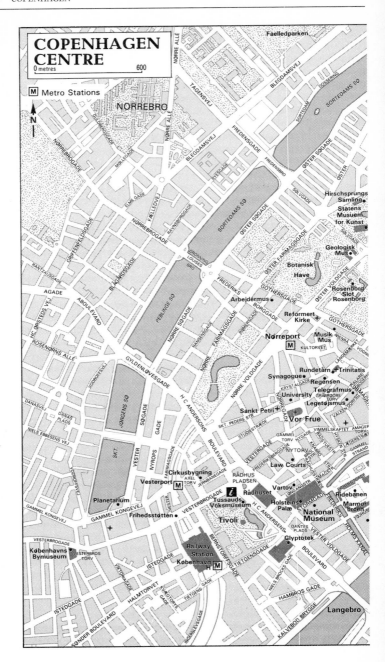

COPENHAGEN CENTRE

0 metres — 600

Ⓜ Metro Stations

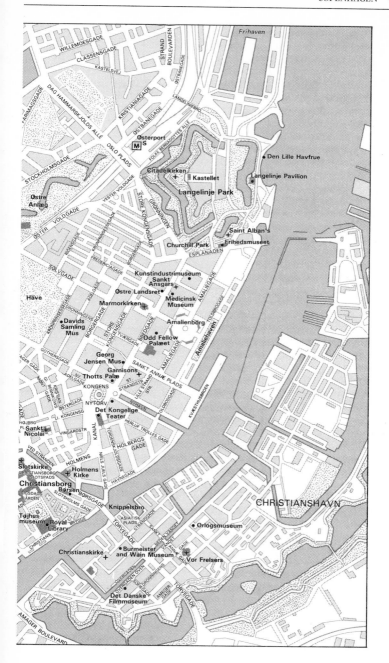

Street), where you turn left into **Rådhuspladsen**, Town Hall Square. The vast Town Hall, **Rådhuset**, itself was built between 1892 and 1905, designed by Martin Nyrop. As you approach the Town Hall, you will see just in front of you the statue of the horn-blowing Vikings, **Lurblæserne**. They stand close to where the Strøget pedestrian shopping street meets the Town Hall Square.

The Town Hall Square is now pedestrianised, so you should continue along Vester Voldgade, turning right at the traffic lights into Stormgade. Turn right at the next traffic lights again into H.C. Andersens Boulevard and then left at the next set of traffic lights into VESTERBROGADE. In 150m you will, on your left, pass the main entrance to **Tivoli**, built in 1889. In front of the entrance a quick glance in the opposite direction will give you a glimpse of the elegant roof of the old **Circus Building** from 1886 on Axeltorv square.

Drive straight on past the next traffic lights, where you have the **SAS head-quarters** on your right. The road soon leads you over the main railway line and passes **Frihedsstøtten** (The Liberty Column), a sandstone obelisk from 1792–97 commemorating the emancipation of the peasantry. Immediately after this column you turn left and find yourself where you started, at the main railway station.

Copenhagen on foot

In the following, **Copenhagen**, including Frederiksberg and Christianshavn, is divided up into seven areas, for each of which we have planned a walk taking you past the most important features. Naturally, in a city the size of Copenhagen, not all attractions are so close to the centre that they can be reached on foot. For those not included in the walks, but easily reached by public transport, the bus numbers or S-train routes are indicated.

See pp 68–69 for Copenhagen centre plan.

Bus timetables, and S-trains maps, can be obtained from stations and tourist informations offices.

Walk One ~

c 3km. The walk starts and ends in front of the main railway station, **Hovedbanegården**.

Main sights: *Tivoli, Rådhuset, Ny Carlsberg Glyptotek, National Museum.*

The main railway station was built of brick in 1904–11 to a design by Heinrich Wenck in pseudo-Byzantine style and is topped by a pyramid-like roof. The main entrance facing the railway cutting north is a Copenhagen landmark. The huge main hall is spacious and impressive, especially after being redesigned in the 1980s, and contains, in addition to kiosks, snack bars and a cafeteria, banks, a post office, a small supermarket, an office giving information on accommodation, a baker and outstanding facilities for inter-railers.

Immediately in front of the main entrance you will find access roads running alongside the railway track. These will lead you to (100m) VESTERBROGADE, one of Copenhagen's main thoroughfares, a busy shopping street with little of architectural interest. Here, you turn right, in 100m crossing Bernstorffsgade and 100m further on coming to the main entrance to **Tivoli** on your right. The gardens open before lunch, but in the afternoon they are rather quiet, an excellent pleasure park for children, and the adult entertainment does not really come into its own until the evening (open May–Sept). Tivoli has of late also been open around Christmas.

Tivoli, bounded by Vesterbrogade, Bernstorffsgade, Tietgensgade and H.C. Andersens Boulevard, was founded in 1843 by Georg Carstensen and inspired by the London Vauxhall Gardens and the Vauxhall–Tivoli in Paris. The Government made the land available, left over from the old fortifications, and the Tivoli Lake is in fact part of the old moat. The 'Renaissance' main entrance, with its Corinthian columns and dome, is from 1889. The site, which is not far short of 80,000 sq m, is part park, part pleasure gardens. And there are entertainments of all kinds, from the modern fairground to the Pantomime Theatre where classical pantomime, which can be traced back to the Italian *commedia dell'arte*, is still performed in the original manner. Built in 1874 in the style of a Chinese pavilion, the Pantomime Theatre is the oldest building in Tivoli. There is another 'Chinese' building, the Chinese Tower, while the Nimb restaurant is in 'Turkish' style. There is an open air stage for performances by acrobats and jugglers, the 'Tivoli Guard' marches around with its band, and there are musical performances of all kinds. A modern concert hall was opened in 1956, replacing the earlier one which was blown up in 1944.

Continue now for a further 200m to H.C. Andersens Boulevard, on the other side of which are Copenhagen's Rådhuspladen (Town Hall Square) and the Town Hall.

Rådhuspladsen (Town Hall Square), cleared with the removal of the city ramparts in the 1850s, is, after Kongens Nytorv, the largest square in Copenhagen and was pedestrianised in 1994. There are several sculptures to be seen, of which the statue by Anton Rosen of the Viking Lur Blowers is perhaps the most famous. Joakim Skovgaard's and Thorvald Bindesbøll's Dragon Fountain is also splendid. Standing in front of the Town Hall, note, on the top of the building on the far-side corner of Vesterbrogade and H.C. Andersens Boulevard, an enormous neon barometer topped by figures reflecting the weather—a girl carrying an umbrella when it is going to rain, and riding a bicycle when the sun is shining. On the far side of the square, at Rådhuspladsen 57, in practice the continuation of Vester Voldgade, you will find the **Believe It Or Not Museum**, with an fascinating collection of unusual artifacts from all over the world.

Rådhuset (The Town Hall), Copenhagen's sixth, stands some distance from the site of the earlier ones in Gammeltorv. When the city ramparts were removed in the 1850s an open space was cleared and used as an exhibition park. It was then decided to build the new Town Hall here. The competition for the design was won by Martin Nyrop, and building commenced in 1892. The official opening was in 1905. The huge rectangular building with four wings enclosing a lofty covered courtyard (24m × 44m), is inspired partly by northern Italian architecture (very obvious in the courtyard), but to a very large extent must be seen as a piece of 19C National Romanticism, reflecting Danish medieval brick buildings. The tower is open to the public, and offers a magnificent view of Copenhagen.

In the Town Hall you will also find Jens Olsen's unique astronomical **World Clock** (access all year). Guided tours in English.

Turn right down H.C. ANDERSENS BOULEVARD to (50m) **Louis Tussauds Voksmuseum** (Louis Tussaud's Wax Museum), at No. 22, containing wax models of famous personalities in the Tussaud tradition. Here, too, is the **Holografisk Museum**, a permanent exhibition of international holography. Both are open all year. And here, too, is the **Tivoli Museum** with 6000 sq. m of displays showing the history of Tivoli.

■ Open daily 10.00–22.00 during the Tivoli season; daily except Mon 10.00–16.00 in the winter season.

The walk now continues along H.C. Andersens Boulevard, with the Town Hall on your left, across TIETGENSGADE to (300m) the **Ny Carlsberg Glyptotek**, Dantes Plads 7.

The ornate buildings date from between 1892 and 1906. Vilhelm Dahlerup's façade is inspired by Venetian architecture, and the interior is richly stuccoed. On entering, you will find the ground floor of this impressive museum mainly dedicated to sculpture, including works by Thorvaldsen, Herman Wilhelm Bissen and Jens Adolf Jerichau, but also a great deal of French sculpture, not least Rodin. The two upper floors are occupied by painting. The French Impressionists are particularly well represented, but there is also an outstanding collection of Danish art.

The second phase of building was by Hack Kampmann, in a more severe neo-classical style. This extension houses the largest collection of Etruscan art outside Italy, and in addition there is the famous collection of Egyptian, Mesopotamian and Greek art, much of it presented to the museum by the brewer Carl Jacobsen, son of the founder of the Carlsberg Breweries. A third phase of building has taken place in the 1990s, resulting in greatly improved facilities, including a specially built glass wall to exhibit the Egyptian mummies in a pollution-free environment. There are is also a new gallery for the 30 Gaugins, and one for the large Degas collection. Finally, a roof terrace provides the opportunity for splendid views of Copenhagen. (Open all year.)

Just in front of Glyptoteket stands the Dante Column, erected in 1921 in commemoration of the 600th anniversary of Dante's death. It was presented to Copenhagen by the City of Rome, and is now surmounted by a bronze statue of Beatrice, executed by Einar Utzon-Frank. To the east of it there is a bronze plaque with a relief of Dante by the Italian sculptor S.L. Andreotti.

Some 400m beyond the Glyptotek you can glimpse the **Langebro** the lifting bridge leading to the island of Amager. There has been a bridge here since 1690, and the present one is from 1954.

After visiting the Glyptotek you should walk the few metres back to Tietgensgade, cross H.C. Andersens Boulevard at the traffic lights and continue past the next set of traffic lights at (100m) Vester Voldgade. Continue in a straight line into STORMGADE, where on the left, at No. 10, you will find the dignified **Holsteins Palæ**, a luxurious mansion built 1683–87, the third storey being added in 1756. Once the Natural History Museum, it is now the head office of an insurance company.

Opposite, flanked by a colonnade, is the **NATIONAL MUSEUM**. The main entrance in NY VESTERGADE is reached by walking first down FREDERIKSHOLMS KANAL and then taking the first turning on your right again. (On your way you will see on your left Christiansborg Palace and the Thorvaldsen Museum, which are described in Walk 3.)

The core of Denmark's National Museum is Eigtved's **Prinsens Palæ** from 1743–44, extended by further wings in Stormgade, Ny Vestergade and Vester Voldgade. Until 1807 such collections as there were, were housed in various parts of Copenhagen. Then in 1807 the Prinsens Palæ was designated the Royal Museum for Nordic Antiquity, being renamed the National Museum in 1892. The ethnographic collection was moved here in 1845, the collection of antiquities in 1851, the Scandinavian antiquities in 1855.

The Sun Chariot

The Museum was radically extended in the 1930s and has been the subject of a massive redevelopment in the 1990s, making this splendid collection, covering almost 10,000 sq m, into one of the most modern and architecturally pleasing museums in Europe.

The entire museum is divided into eight departments, of which six are housed in this complex and open to the public: 1: Danish Prehistory including the Viking Age; 2: Middle Ages and Renaissance; 3: 1660 to the 1830; 4: Ethnographical Collections (filling 22 rooms); 5: Egyptian, Classical and Middle East Collections; 6: Numismatics; (7: Open Air Museum—is in Lyngby, see below); 8: Research Department (not open to the public). Smaller exhibitions are regularly arranged in the foyer.

This is a National Museum in the grand style, with a wealth of exhibits from all areas. The Viking Age is particularly well represented, with most of the major finds from Denmark exhibited according to the most modern principles. There are reconstructions of milieux and dress throughout, together with explanatory photographs and texts, many in English.

You must allow plenty of time to see this outstanding museum, which now has a special exhibition for children. Plans and descriptions in English are available in the entrance hall and there are guided tours in English July–Aug. An excellent brief guide in English is available called *10,000 Years in 60 Minutes*.

■ Open daily 10.00–17.00 except Mon.

On leaving the National Museum you retrace you steps and then cross

Stormgade into RÅDHUSSTRÆDE. As you walk along here you should notice on your right the old houses in MAGSTRÆDE, a road from 1520 (the name really means something like Loo Lane). The oldest extant houses in this now quite idyllic street, Nos 17 and 19, are from the mid-17C. On your left you will find the small square, Vandkunsten, where in the 15C there was a watermill, driven by water from the neighbouring streams. Christian III constructed a pump here to supply water to Slotsholmen, the small island on which Christiansborg Palace stands, and in 1910 the fountain was erected, with water pouring from four lions' heads into a basin. The street sign 'Wand Konsten' on the corner is one of the oldest in Copenhagen, dating from c 1770.

The walk now continues along Rådhusstræde, but you may first like to walk left through Vandkunsten and along LØNGANGSSTRÆDE to take a look at (150m) **Vartov**.

Ultimately deriving from the old Holy Ghost Hospice, Vartov Hospital on the corner of Vester Voldgade and Løngangsstræde was built 1724–44. In the 19C it became a home for the elderly, with at one time provision for 450 people. The old buildings were restored in 1950 and now comprise various offices, private flats and a restaurant. Vartov is mainly known by the public for its church, as it was here that the great theologian and hymn-writer N.F.S. Grundtvig was pastor from 1839 to 1872. Built in 1754–55, it has balconies on three sides. The pulpit is above the altar, framed in the Corinthian columns of the altarpiece from c 1725. There is a statue of Grundtvig, kneeling, in the courtyard, the work of Niels Skovgaard.

The walk continues now 150m along Rådhusstræde when you will come to BROLÆGGERSTRÆDE, which in the 17C was the centre of the brewing industry in Copenhagen. It was here that J.C. Jacobsen, the founder of the Carlsberg Breweries, was born in 1811, as a memorial plaque indicates. (The actual name Carlsberg derives from the name of J.C. Jacobsen's son, Carl.) The house is today the offices of the Carlsberg Foundation.

Rådhusstræde now opens into a large open space which in fact consists of two squares, first **Nytorv** (New Square) and then **Gammeltorv** (Old Square or Old Market Place).

Since the 14C Copenhagen's Town Hall had stood on the south side of Gammeltorv, and in the 17C Christian IV ordered the space south of it to be cleared in order to give the Town Hall a more dignified aspect. Thus Nytorv came into being. After the fire of 1795, when the Town Hall was destroyed, Gammeltorv and Nytorv were joined to form a single open square.

To the left as you enter NYTORV you will see the **Law Courts and Lock-up**. Built in 1805–15, they are among the neo-classical buildings by C.F. Hansen designed to restore the centre of Copenhagen after the fire of 1795 and the British bombardment of 1807. Some of the materials used came from the first Christiansborg and others from Hørsholm Castle (p 105).

Linked to the lock-up by a bridge and facing Nytorv is the temple-like **Copenhagen City Court**, with a portal consisting of six Ionic columns. Note the inscription above the porch, the first words of the 1241 Jutlandic Law: 'With law the land shall be built'.

Gammeltorv to the north is indeed the old market place, dating back to the 12C, when Absalon founded Copenhagen. None of the really old buildings around it still survives, as Gammeltorv was razed during the great fire of 1728.

On the other hand the only monument from Christian IV's time standing in a public square is to be found here. Erected 1609–10, the copper and gilt **Caritas Fountain** was the King's gift to the citizens of Copenhagen, intended both to embellish the city and to improve the supply of fresh water. Caritas is represented as a pregnant young woman holding one child in her arms and with a boy at her side, the whole surrounded by dolphins.

Nytorv and Gammeltorv are crossed by Copenhagen's most famous shopping street, best known as **Strøget** (see below). You should turn left into it. Lined like the rest of Strøget with a host of shops, this western end is correctly called FRED-ERIKSBERGGADE, and will bring you in c 250m back to Rådhuspladsen.

Now cross the square diagonally to your right, and go over H.C. Andersens Boulevard into Jernbanegade, which will lead you to another square, **Axeltorv**, a small open space with seating and several sculptures. Here on one of the corners you will find the **Cirkusbygning**. Purpose-built in 1885 and claiming to be the oldest circus building in the world, this has now served for circus entertainment of various kinds, plus other grandiose shows, for over 100 years. Opposite, with its colourful, not to say gaudy, decorations, is the striking **Palads** theatre which houses altogether 19 cinemas.

Go across Axeltorv, past the Vesterport S-train station, across Vester Farimagsgade and into GAMMEL KONGEVEJ. Here, just at the end of the Lakes, at No. 10 and c 400m in all from Axeltorv, you will find the **Tycho Brahe Planetarium**. Dating from 1989, it includes a space theatre and sophisticated equipment to give you the feeling of space travel (open all year).

The walk now goes across GAMMEL KONGEVEJ and then left through the 100m-long STENOSGADE, passing the neo-Gothic Jesu Hjerte Kirke on your left. On reaching Vesterbrogade you turn right and proceed for c 200m to a small square, VESTERBROTORV. Immediately after this, at Vesterbrogade 59, you will find **Københavns Bymuseum & Søren Kierkegaard Samling**, housed in a neo-classical mansion from 1782–86. It became the Copenhagen City Museum in 1956, and offers a collection of relics from old buildings, tradesmen's signs, bicycles and street furniture to give an impression of what Copenhagen once looked like. These are supplemented with a collection of paintings and prints vividly illustrating the development of Copenhagen and the manner of life there over the centuries. There are models of Copenhagen in the late Middle Ages and at the time of Christian IV. The first of these large-scale models stands in front of the building in the summer. The Søren Kierkegaard collection was opened in 1960 (open all year).

ABSALONSGADE, running alongside the museum, has been maintained to give the appearance of an old street, with cobbles, gas lamps, benches and an old telephone kiosk, such as would have stood there between 1860 and 1940.

You now return along Vesterbrogade, where you will soon see **Frihedsstøtten** (The Freedom Column), standing in the middle of the road above the railway track. This sandstone obelisk, standing on a plinth of Norwegian marble and surrounded by four marble statues by different artists, commemorates the emancipation of the peasantry in 1788. It was designed by Nicolai Abildgaard and erected in 1797. Abildgaard was also responsible for the reliefs on the plinth.

The main railway station is now on your right.

Walk Two ~

c 2km. The walk starts and ends on the Rådhuspladsen.

Main sights: *Strøget, Rundetårn, the University, the Cathedral.*

The walk starts at the east end of RÅDHUSPLADSEN close to the column with the figures of two Vikings blowing *lurs*, the ancient curved horns which have now become the symbol for Danish butter. With the column on your right you start to walk up FREDERIKSBERGGADE, the west end of the main shopping street, Strøget.

A good deal of what is known as *Den indre by*, 'the inner city' is now pedestrianised. **Strøget** is not the name of a single street, but means 'principal shopping street' and is the popular name for what is claimed to be the longest pedestrian street in the world. It links the two principal squares, Kongens Nytorv and Rådhuspladsen, and incorporates from the Rådhuspladsen end: FREDERIKSBERGGADE, NYGADE, VIMMELSKAFTET, AMAGERTORV and ØSTERGADE. It became pedestrianised in 1962 and crosses the other main pedestrian street, Købmagergade. Some of the side streets off Strøget have benefited from its exhilarating atmosphere and have been turned into fashionable shopping and café streets, for instance the area around Pistolstræde, behind Hotel d'Angleterre at Kongens Nytorv. Not everything, however, is shops and cafés: at Østergade 16 you will find the **Guinness World of Records Museum**, exhibiting records of all kinds.

After 250m you will come to and cross Gammeltorv/Nytorv (see p 74). Walk down Strøget as far as Vimmelskaftet 38, where you will find **Haandarbejdets Fremme**, the best-known shop for Danish embroidery, knitting, etc. A source of inspiration for the craftswoman.

The area you are in here is the oldest part of Copenhagen. On your right, after passing Gammeltorv/Nytorv you will find KNABROSTRÆDE and BADSTUESTRÆDE, where the butchers had their booths in 1377 before moving to Købmagergade around 1400. A public bath house was then erected here, from which it derived its name in the 17C. The next road on your right is HYSKEN-STRÆDE, also one of the very oldest streets, referred to even in the 15C as being 'old'. The name means 'little house', and almost certainly refers to a public lavatory that is known to have been nearby in the 14C. The street's reputation improved with time, and in the 18C and 19C it had people of repute living here. It was badly damaged in the 1728 fire and widened in the subsequent rebuilding.

Moving into the funnel-shaped part of Strøget, called **Amagertorv** you will, on the left, find **Helligåndskirken**, the Church of the Holy Ghost. A hospice existed on this site as early as 1296, and in 1474 was incorporated into an Augustinian monastery, which after the Reformation became a hospital. The present church was the south wing of this monastery. It was extended in 1582, when the tower was added; the spire is from 1594. The porch on the south side was the commission of Christian IV, incorporating a doorway originally intended for the Stock Exchange. In 1672 the King's Chancellor, Griffenfeld, built the round sepulchral chapel on the north side. The church was badly damaged in the 1728 fire, but by 1732 had been repaired and reconstructed, thereby losing most of its medieval character.

At the wider end of Amagertorv—the part that really is the square—you will pass some of the most distinguished of Copenhagen's shops, including Illums Bolighus (furniture and furnishings), and the main **Danish Royal Porcelain** shop in the magnificent Dutch Renaissance twin-gabled merchant's house (1616) at No. 6. For those interested in visiting the Royal Porcelain factory in Smallegade, Frederiksberg, free transport can be arranged from this shop by telephoning 31 86 48 48.

Opposite, at Amagertorv 9, is an old tobacconist's shop founded in 1864, which now houses the small **Larsen's Pipe Museum**.

There was a market square here on Amagertorv in the 15C, and in 1684 it was designated the market place where peasants from the island of Amager were to sell their wares. In 1795 it was joined to HØJBRO PLADS—the area leading down to the canal and through which you can see right down to Christiansborg Castle and Slotsholmen (Walk 3)—when this was established after the 1795 fire, replacing a number of narrow streets. Højbro Plads itself contains some excellent examples of the neo-classical architecture of its time. Note especially the corner building, No. 21, with a façade of Corinthian pilasters above the present shop windows. The fine but somewhat romanticised equestrian statue opposite this building is of Bishop Absalon by Vilhelm Bissen. The fountain, **Storkespringvandet**, is from 1894.

Diagonally across Højbro Plads you will see the entrance to Sankt Nicolai Plads on which stands **Sankt Nicolai Kirke**, St. Nicholas' Church. The present church is from 1915–17, though there was one on this spot certainly as early as 1261, and probably rather earlier.

This is where the first Lutheran sermon was held in Denmark, and when the leading Reformer Hans Tavsen became parish priest here in 1529, it became the focal point of the Copenhagen Reformation movement. By the end of the 17C an imposing tower had been added, and St. Nicholas' Church was the most splendid in Copenhagen after the cathedral. It was almost totally destroyed in the 1795 fire, the tower being the only part of it left standing. After the Napoleonic Wars the ruined tower was actually used as a fire station, and St. Nicholas' Square became a market place.

In 1908–10 the tower was repaired and the spire, paid for by Carl Jacobsen, was added. The new church was then built between 1915 and 1917 to a design by H.C. Amberg. The intention was as far as possible to reconstruct the old church, of which there were detailed drawings. It was, however, not to be used as a church, and acted as a library until it was taken over in 1957 by the Church Army. The church is now used for travelling exhibitions, and there is a restaurant here, too.

At Amagertorv you leave Strøget and turn left into KØBMAGERGADE, another busy shopping street and, like Strøget, a pedestrian precinct. Købmagergade is thought to have been a main approach to the original Copenhagen as early as 1200. By the 15C it was the street in which the butchers had their booths, and the present name is in fact a distortion of the old 'Kiødmangergade', meaning, precisely, Butchers' Street. It is a rather winding street with many ancient associations, in particular the Round Tower and Regensen. Many of the present buildings are from the 18C, and you will gain a better impression of what this street really represents in terms of architecture if you keep your eyes, not on the shop windows, but on the first floors and beyond.

However, among the signs of past times, there are also signs of the present, where, close to the mundane Illum department store, you will find the **Museum Erotica**. Open all year, varying times.

On the right, 200m up Købmagergade, you will find KLAREBODERNE, which used to give access to a convent of nuns of the Order of St. Clare that had been established in this part of Copenhagen in the 15C. After the Reformation a royal mint was established on the site, giving rise to the nearby streetname of Møntergade. Of the present-day buildings it is Klareboderne 3, from 1731–34, that is of particular interest. Since 1787 it has been the home of Denmark's oldest publishing house, Gyldendal, and a plaque in the court-yard recalls that Søren Kierkegaard used to pass through daily on his way to school 1821–30.

Directly opposite the spot where Klareboderne enters Købmagergade stands the **Main Post Office**, behind which, entered from Valkendorfsgade is the **Post-og Telegrafmuseum**, a museum illustrating the history of the Danish postal service. In addition to photographs and models, as well as old equipment, it contains a complete collection of Danish postage stamps (open all year).

In a 19C warehouse at VALKENDORFSGADE 13 you will find the toy museum, **Legetøjsmuseum**, the ideal museum for children, with a splendid collection of over 25,000 items, including toys and dolls from former times and many countries. On the first floor there is a model town and a model railway layout thought to comprise one of the biggest gauge 0 model railway collections in Europe. There is a also tiny children's cinema. (Open all year, Mon-Thurs 09.00–16.00, Fri closed, Sat and Sun 10.00–16.00.)

The next road to the left along Købmagergade is LØVSTRÆDE, a street with an idyllic name (Leaf Street, Foliage Street). In the 19C the street had many literary associations. The author Meir Aron Goldschmidt lived in No. 8 in the 1840s. A short walk down Løvstræde and back again should really not be missed, as it will take you to the very intimate little square called **Gråbrødretorv** at the other end with its delightful cafés and restaurants. Try the cellar restaurant called Bøf og Ost! Or its big brother just above it: Peder Oxe.

This area was occupied by a Franciscan monastery in 1238, with its main wing in the present KLOSTERSTRÆDE. The monastery was demolished after the Reformation, though remains of the foundations are still to be seen in some of the buildings. Most of these are from the period of rebuilding after the fire of 1728, though those to the west are from a later rebuilding, after the English bombardment of 1807. In No. 3, Wessels Gård, there are two rooms to commemorate the 18C Dano-Norwegian poet Johan Herman Wessel, whose charming and amusing play *Love without Stockings* is one of the classics of Scandinavian drama.

Walk back to Købmagergade and turn left. In c 200m you will reach **Rundetårn** (The Round Tower), with **Trinitatis Kirke** on your right and **Regensen** on your left. Built by Christian IV in 1642 as an observatory, the Round Tower now acts as the church tower to Trinitatis Kirke. A rather stubby cylinder decorated on the outside with pilasters, it is 34.8m high, with an external diameter of 15m. A broad spiral ramp inside leads to the top, and it is documented that Tsar Peter II rode to the top in 1716, followed by the Tsarina in a carriage drawn by six horses. Remember Hans Christian Andersen's *The Tinderbox?* When the third dog has eyes as big as 'round towers', that is not what

Andersen said. He said the Round Tower—and he meant this one. There is a splendid view of Copenhagen from the top. (Open all year).

Trinitatis Kirke (Trinity Church; 1637–57) was started by Christian IV and finished by Frederik III, and was intended as something approaching a University church. At the same time the upper floor was to be the University Library. The Round Tower was then added as an observatory. The roof and upper floor, including the library, were badly damaged in the 1728 fire, and countless irreplaceable books and manuscripts were thus lost. On the other hand neither the church nor the tower was damaged in the 1795 fire or the 1807 bombardment. The present church is essentially 18C, with carved altarpiece and pulpit in rich ornamental Baroque by Fridrich Ehbisch. A huge rococo clock from 1757 stands against the wall opposite the pulpit. The pews are from 1731, each with a carved shell on the bench end.

Of the many distinguished men buried here, mention must be made of the great Icelandic historian Arne Magnusson, while the most magnificent of the memorial tablets is that from 1698 on the north wall of the chancel to Field Marshal Hans Schack by Artur and Thomas Quellinus.

Regensen just opposite is the most famous of Copenhagen's old student residences. It was built 1618–28, also by Christian IV, and consists of four wings around an open square in the centre of which stands a lime tree. Regensen is still used for its original purpose, and the courtyard, entered from STORE KANNIKESTRÆDE, is open to the public.

A further 200m along Købmagergade brings you to **Kultorvet**, which was established after the 1728 fire. Charcoal burners from North Sjælland used to come here to sell their products—hence the name Kultorvet, 'Coal Market'. Now, however, it is a pedestrian area, with pavement cafés and fruit and flower stalls.

Beyond Kultorvet you can now see **Nørreport**, the site of one of Copenhagen's medieval gates, Nørreport (North Gate). Today Nørreport is one of the city's busiest S-train stations.

From Kultorvet, we suggest you retrace your steps the short way towards Regensen, turning right immediately before reaching it, down KRYSTALGADE, a street known to date back to 1492. The main city library is in this street, but the main historical interest is the **Synagogue**, standing just over half-way down on your right. It was built 1830–33 after the loss in the 1795 fire of the old Synagogue, to a design by Gustav Friedrich Hetsch. A basilica, it has its side to the street with windows and doors in what has been described as 'orientalised neo-classicism'. It was extended in 1885 and restored in 1958 by Henning Meyer.

Just beyond the Synagogue you reach NØRREGADE, where you turn left. You are now in the university area, with the side of the old University buildings on your left.

Copenhagen University was founded in 1479 and was originally housed in the Cathedral School. After occupying various buildings in the area, in 1731 it was installed in the purpose-built premises here on Nørregade now called Kommunitetsbygningen. The neo-classical 69m-long main building, facing south on to Frue Plads, was then erected to a design of Peder Malling in 1831–36 as part of the grandiose scheme for rebuilding the centre of Copenhagen. The entrance hall was decorated with frescoes (1844–53) of scenes from Greek mythology, the work of Constantin Hansen.

Adjoining the main University complex in FIOLSTRÆDE—a pedestrian precinct with many second-hand bookshops—is the University Library, built 1857–71 to a design by Johan Daniel Herholdt. At right angles to the main building, immediately behind the Cathedral, is the University Annex, formerly the Metropolitan School, by C.F. Hansen. However, this annex is no longer big enough, and the University is now largely housed on an entirely new campus on Amager.

Just before you reach the Cathedral Square, Vor Frue Plads, you will see **Sankt Petri Kirke** on your right. There has been a St. Peter's Church here on the corner of Nørregade and Sankt Pedersstræde at least since 1304. It burned down and was replaced on several occasions, but although it was badly damaged in the 1728 fire, the walls remained standing. Further damage was done in the 1807 bombardment, but the early 16C tower survived. Rebuilding was completed by 1816. More restoration work was carried out in the 1960s and 1970s, and in view of the many catastrophes and resultant rebuilding, it is remarkable that part of the 15C building can still be seen, facing Nørregade. The church has belonged to the German-speaking community in Copenhagen since 1586.

The interior is vaulted throughout and most of the furniture is 19C. There are, however, some older memorial tablets, one by Thomas Quellinus removed from the crypt in 1865, another by Johannes Wiedewelt in memory of his father, the sculptor Just Wiedewelt, also placed in the church in 1865. The vaulted sepulchral chapel contains many ornate tombs and memorials. There are other memorials, including one by Wiedewelt, in the churchyard to the north of the sepulchral chapel.

The University building faces on to **Vor Frue Plads**, where the main building is clearly Copenhagen Cathedral, **Vor Frue Kirke**. The cathedral, formerly known as St. Mary's Church, is already mentioned at the end of the 12C, and was even then the most important in the city. There is evidence to indicate that it was founded somewhere between 1190 and 1200 by Peder Suneson, Absalon's successor as Bishop of Roskilde. The 1728 fire destroyed most of the Gothic structure which had grown up on the spot, but the chancel survived until the 1807 English bombardment, when it was severely damaged.

C.F. Hansen was given the task of rebuilding it. He demolished the remains of the Gothic chancel, retaining only the walls of the side aisles and the tower, and produced a dignified neo-classical building fronted with an impressive main entrance behind Doric columns. The nave is flanked by arcading, rounded arches on square columns supporting balustrades. These in turn bear columns supporting the barrel vaulting of the roof. The light enters from between these columns. The figures of the Apostles standing in the nave are by Thorvaldsen, as is the famous figure of Christ constituting the altarpiece. The font, a kneeling angel bearing a shell, is also the work of Thorvaldsen and was presented to the cathedral by him. The cathedral underwent a complete restoration 1975–79.

Opposite the front façade, on the corner of Nørregade and STUDIESTRÆDE, you will find the Bishop's Palace, **Bispegården**. This dates from 1732, replacing a medieval palace destroyed by fire. It was restored by Martin Nyrop in 1896, and while it has brick walls facing the road, the courtyard is half-timbered and has an external gallery along one of the walls (not open to the public, though it can be seen from the gateway during office hours).

If you now continue along Nørregade, you will shortly come back to

Gammeltorv. Here you turn right, along Vestergade, which you follow for 300m, reaching Rådhuspladsen, on the corner of which you will find the offices of one of Denmark's leading newspapers, 'Politiken'.

Walk Three ~

c 1.5km. The walk starts and ends in front of **Christiansborg Palace** *and is limited to* **Slotsholmen**—*the island in the middle of Copenhagen, which besides Christiansborg is occupied by a host of historical buildings.*

Main sights: *Christiansborg Palace, Thorvaldsens Museum, the Parliament building.*

According to the medieval historian Saxo, Bishop Absalon, the founder of Copenhagen, established a **castle** on what is now called **Slotsholmen** (Castle Island) in 1167 as a defence against marauding pirates. Early 20C excavations have indeed uncovered the remains of this castle, which is portrayed on the oldest known Copenhagen Seal from 1296. As it was built for defence, so it courted attack, and both the Wends and the Lübeckers partly destroyed it in the 13C and 14C. Although it was originally in the ownership of the bishops, first Absalon and then the Bishops of Roskilde, King Erik of Pomerania took it into the Crown's possession and turned it in practice into the royal castle, which it remained until after the Reformation.

In the early 18C Frederik IV had the then antiquated castle modernised and extended. Later that same century Christian VI had it demolished and replaced with the first Christiansborg, a modern Baroque palace partly designed by Eigtved and Thurah. The main wing looked on to a square ending at the Marble Bridge. This was the Royal Mews, looking much as it does today. The palace burned down in 1794. A second Christiansborg was then designed in neo-classical style by C.F. Hansen, whose aim was to reconstruct the entire centre of Copenhagen on neo-classical lines. That, too, burned down—in 1884. The third Christiansborg, the work of Thorvald Jørgensen, incorporates the only surviving parts of the earlier palaces, principally the Royal Mews of the first and the Chapel of the second. The foundation stone was laid in 1907, and the royal chambers were not finished until 1928. Unlike its predecessor, this palace has never been used as a royal residence, and it is now the home of the Danish Parliament.

This new **Christiansborg Palace** observes the general plan of its predecessor, facing northeast and overlooking Christiansborg Slotsplads (Christiansborg Palace Square) and, beyond that, the Holmens Bro bridge and Holmens Kanal leading to Kongens Nytorv. The style is neo-Baroque, the 25m-high main façade clad in granite ashlars collected from 750 different Danish municipalities. The remaining façades are in Bornholm granite, except Prins Jørgens Gård between the main palace and the chapel. This ensures a certain material continuity between the new and the old parts of the complex. The main palace complex is in the form of a square, with the rear wing opening on to the Mews, which in turn give on to the Marble Bridge and Frederiksholms Kanal. The copper-roofed main wing is surmounted by a massive tower, ending in a grandiose crown. The weather vane is 104m above ground level.

Christiansborg is not generally open to the public, though there is access both to the Mews and to Prins Jørgens Gård. There are conducted tours with English-speaking guides through the royal reception rooms at 11.00, 13.00 and 15.00 during the summer months and otherwise at 11.00 and 15.00. The Parliament is also open for conducted tours at limited times throughout the summer. More easily accessible are the palace ruins, which are open to the public from 9.30–15.30 daily May-Sept and 09.30–15.30 except Mon and Sat from Oct to April. Access is from Slotsplads. These fascinating and very extensive ruins take you right back to Absolon's original castle and show the process of extension and rebuilding that has taken place since.

The equestrian statue of Frederik VII standing in front of Christiansborg is by Herman Wilhelm Bissen and his son Vilhelm Bissen. Unveiled in 1873, it commemorates the signing under Frederik VII of the first Danish Constitution in 1849.

You should start your walk by going northwest from the main entrance on Christiansborg Slotsplads, i.e. to your right as you face the palace. You will soon come to the entrance of Prins Jørgens Gård. You should, for the moment, go past this to visit, immediately beyond the gateway, the Palace Chapel, **Christiansborg Slotskirke**, from 1826, the work of C.F. Hansen. It is in the neo-classical tradition, with the main entrance, to the northeast, through a porch flanked by four Ionic columns. The rectangular building has a flat roof, with a shallow dome in the centre. The ceiling is vaulted, with the dome as its central feature. The altar, to the southwest, is in a niche flanked by Corinthian pillars beyond which are figures of two Evangelists, the other two being in the west end. The royal balcony is above the entrance, and the organ is above this again. The chapel was badly damaged by fire in 1992, but at the time of writing is well on the way to being restored.

On leaving the chapel you should go back the 10m to the entrance to **Prins Jørgens Gård**, the great courtyard between the main palace of Christiansborg and the chapel. The right wing is, of course, formed by the chapel and, behind it, Thorvaldsens Museum. To the left there is access to the Royal Reception Rooms in the Palace proper.

They are reached by an imposing staircase, with statues by Jerichau and reliefs by Svend Rathsack. The impressive suite of rooms and halls includes the Fredensborg room, decorated with a painting of Christian IX and Queen Louise with their family in the garden of Fredensborg Palace, while the dignified Throne Room, with tapestry-covered walls, is dominated by two thrones designed by C.F. Hansen. The Christian X room contains the famous painting of Christian X crossing the border on a white horse to reclaim the lost lands of southern Jutland in 1920. The Danish Gallery, 40m long, is decorated with six huge allegorical paintings, while the Great Hall, **Riddersalen**, also 40m long, is resplendent with an intricate stuccoed ceiling, glorious candelabras and tapestries with motifs from the Scanian War. The patterned floor is made of black and white marble slabs.

On leaving the Royal Reception Rooms you continue through Prins Jørgens Gård, passing, at the end, the Supreme Court. On your right you will now find the entrance to the **Thorvaldsens Museum** on PORTHUSGADE. Open all year 10.00–17.00; closed Mon.

When Denmark's great 19C sculptor Bertel Thorvaldsen presented his works to his native city in 1838, it was on condition that a suitable museum should be found. Frederik VI provided the site of the old royal coach house, and the architect Gottlieb Bindesbøll designed the present museum, incorporating some of the original walls. It is considered to be one of the finest of Copenhagen's neoclassical buildings, carefully matched with the Castle Chapel adjoining. The ochre exterior is partly decorated with murals by Jørgen Sonne, one being a portrayal of Thorvaldsen's return to Copenhagen. The five imposing portals are surmounted by a triumphal chariot designed by Herman Wilhelm Bissen, and the copper roof behind is crowned by a low dome. The major part of the collection is made up of completed works, models and sketches by Thorvaldsen himself, including many of the models for his major European monuments. In addition there is his collection of prints and sketches, his extensive library and his private collection of Classical sculptures, vases and bronzes.

On leaving the museum, you continue along Porthusgade as far as **Frederiksholms Kanal**, where you turn left. On your right you will now see the National Museum. Some 50m on your left, you will find the entrance to the Royal Mews, via the Marble Bridge, **Marmorbroen**, an elegant rococo bridge and one of Eigtved's finest works, completed in 1745. The name the Marble Bridge stems from its marble pavements. Note the elaborate symbolical decoration, which was carefully restored in the 1970s and early 1980s.

Ridebanen, the Royal Mews, remains from the first Christiansborg and was designed by the architect Elias David Häusser. The whole forms one of the finest pieces of Danish Baroque architecture. Two magnificent pavilions by Eigtved from 1741 flank the entrance, which opens on to a wide courtyard. The north (left) wing houses the manège, while the low buildings behind colonnades on the right, contain, in addition to stabling, the **Karetmuseum**, a collection of royal coaches, and the Court Theatre. The oldest extant court theatre in the world, this is now the **Theatre Museum**, with a collection of paintings, drawings and photographs, posters, costumes and tickets, illustrating the history of the Danish theatre from the 18C to the present (open Wed, Fri, Sun, 14.00–16.00). The equestrian statue of Christian IX by Anne Marie Carl Nielsen is from 1927.

From the Royal Mews you enter **Rigsdagsgården**, the large courtyard in front of the main entrance to the Parliament, the Folketing, housed in the south wing of Christiansborg Palace. This is the entrance used by visitors to the Folketing.

The archway at the north end of this courtyard connects the Parliament building to the much older administration buildings on the other side. Closest to the archway is the three-storeyed **Gehejmearkivbygning** (State Archives Building) from 1715–20. It was taken into use in 1721, and in the course of the 18C the archives from Gottorp were removed here. After the loss of Norway in 1814 many of the Norwegian archives were added, and the collection was greatly increased as a result of political developments during the 19C. In 1889 the building was given the name of Rigsarkivet, and in 1908 it was necessary to take over the adjoining building, the former Royal Library, erected 1665–73 on the orders of Frederik III.

The present **Royal Library** is reached through a gateway diagonally opposite the Parliament steps, leading first to some delightful gardens containing a pond and a statue of Søren Kierkegaard by L. Hasselriis.

The Royal Library can be said to have been founded by Frederik III, who began the serious purchase of learned books in the 17C. It was, however, Christian V who moved the collection to the building commissioned by Frederik III. The present somewhat ponderous building in red brick is from 1898–1906 to the design of Hans J. Holm. The Entrance Hall, where there are extensive exhibits, is open all year round. The Reading Room is open to all for serious research but not for viewing.

Go back now to the Rigsdagsgård, and turn left. Through the archway 50m ahead you will come to TØJHUSGADE, where, on your left, you will find the Royal Arsenal Museum, **Tøjhusmuseum**, which is part of a complex established by Christian IV around a dock from which the Navy's ships took on supplies. The present museum is housed in the former Royal Arsenal from 1604. On two floors, it contains a vast collection of arms from pistols to heavy guns as well as uniforms and armour, many of great age. (Open all year.) The **Isted Lion**, a statue by Herman Wilhelm Bissen commemorating the Danish victory of Isted Heath in 1850, is in the courtyard.

If you now continue along Tøjhusgade you pass the Ministry of Education on your left. You should turn left at the end of the main wing, keeping the canal on your right, and walk to the end of the complex, where you will see the vast sweep of the roof of Christian IV's Brewery (1599–1605), one of the most impressive Copenhagen buildings of its time.

You are now on CHRISTIANS BRYGGE. Turn left again, and you will have the remaining old government buildings on your left, and the harbour on your right. You will pass the back of the Royal Library, and 50m beyond you will come to SLOTSHOLMS-GADE. Turn into this. Here on your right you will see the Stock Exchange, **Børsen**, one of Copenhagen's finest Renaissance buildings, 127m long and 21m wide, built 1619–23 on the initiative of Christian IV and designed by Lorenz and Hans van Steenwinckel. In his eagerness for a grandiose building Christian IV had its original

Christiansborg (right), the Stock Exchange (left)

unadorned façade, facing BØRSGADE, decorated and the spire consisting of four intertwined dragons' tails erected in 1624–25. The east end was decorated in 1640, and the entire building was restored by Eigtved in 1745. (Not open to the public.)

At the end of Slotsholmsgade, on your left, adjoining the archway, you come to **Den Røde Kancellibygning**, the Chancellery Building, which was constructed by Frederik IV to house the 'Colleges', the forerunners of ministries. (Not open to the public.)

Christiansborg Slotsplads is now immediately in front of you.

Walk Four ~

c 2.5km The walk starts and finishes on **Christiansborg Slotsplads**.

Main sights: *the Christianshavn area, Vor Frelsers Kirke, Holmens Kirke.*

With Christiansborg behind you, you go right, along the main road, BØRSGADE, which runs past the Stock Exchange, Børsen (see Walk 3).

Beyond the Stock Exchange you come to one of Copenhagen's lifting bridges, the **Knippelsbro**. With the establishment of Christianshavn in 1617, Christian IV found it necessary to build a bridge here to connect his new town with Slotsholmen and Copenhagen. Knippelsbro was then built 1618–20 and owes its name to a counsellor from Christianshavn called Hans Knip, who had the right to demand tolls from the passing ships. The present lifting bridge, from 1937, is the fourth to bear the name.

On the other side of the bridge, on the island of AMAGER, lies **CHRISTIANS-HAVN**, which was established by Christian IV as a fortress-like town separate from Copenhagen. With one small exception, all its streets are straight and meet at a right angles and, unlike Copenhagen proper, Christianshavn has never been devastated by fire and has therefore retained much of its old character.

The main road here is TORVEGADE, and on your left, immediately after the bridge and on the corner of Torvegade and STRANDGADE, you will see the splendid modern **Foreign Ministry** building standing on an area known as Asiatisk Plads. However, you should not cross Torvegade to take a closer look, as you are going to turn right into the other half of Strandgade, noting—and perhaps visiting—the 17C café on the corner. Strandgade 6, **Tordenskjolds Gård**, a fine stone façade with a splendid half-timbered courtyard behind, houses the Danish Society of Authors, while No. 4 is the **Burmeister and Wain Museum** illustrating the history of the great shipbuilding firm. At the very end of this part of Strandgade you will find the rococo **Christianskirke**.

This very unusual church was designed by Eigtved only a year before his death and built between 1755 and 1759. It was originally intended for the German congregation in Christianshavn. In many ways it resembles a theatre, with a series of 'boxes' on three levels surrounding the altar. Directly opposite the altar is the royal 'box'. In keeping with the style of the Reformed Church, the altar is surmounted by the pulpit, which again is surmounted by the organ. N.F.S. Grundtvig was allowed to preach to his congregation here between 1832 and 1839.

You now return to the main road, Torvegade, and turn right, when you will come to a curious road consisting of a row of houses on either side of a canal, with the equally curious names of Overgaden neden Vandet and Overgaden oven Vandet (Upper Street Below the Water and Upper Street Above the Water). It is a street of particular charm, with old houses in various colours lining the canal where barges and all kinds of sailing ships are moored. Overgaden oven Vandet 10 is a small museum, **Brøstes Samling**, illustrating the history of Christianshavn. At its south end this road is crossed by STORE SØNDERVOLDSTRÆDE, where, at No. 4, you will find **Det danske Filmmuseum**, the Danish Film Museum, containing in all some 13,000 films and huge numbers of photographs and posters, mainly connected with the Danish film industry.

Store Søndervoldstræde leads you to Dronningensgade. Turn left here and take the first street on your right, Sofiegade. The second street you come to is AMAGERGADE, where, at No. 11, you will find one of the most picturesque of all the half-timbered courtyards in Christianshavn, complete with outside gallery. Note, however, that this is a house in which people live and not a museum. Now continue along Amagergade to Torvegade and turn left, walking as far as the Dronningensgade crossing (the second street). Cross Torvegade here and continue straight ahead along Dronningensgade, and you will very quickly come to **Vor Frelsers Kirke**, the Church of Our Saviour. It is distinguished by its unusual tower, surmounted by a copper steeple, designed by Thurah, with a stairway of 150 steps encircling it on the outside. The height of this steeple, including the globe and surmounting figure, is 86.6m. Built 1682–96, to a design by Lambert van Haven, the church itself is in the style of Dutch Baroque and shaped like a Greek cross. The main entrance, flanked by Corinthian columns, leads into a space of impressive proportions. Separated by pilasters adorned with cherubs, there are slender windows of clear glass beneath lofty vaulting embellished with golden stars. The altarpiece, ordered by Christian V from Nicodemus Tessin in 1694, is an impressive example of Baroque bombast, and six large-scale Baroque angels are incorporated into the altar rail. The organ loft, too, is a huge piece of ornate Baroque carving. (Open all year, with admittance to the tower, which is the highest vantage point with public access in Copenhagen.)

On leaving the church, we suggest you follow SANKT ANNÆ GADE down to the canal, where you again come to Overgaden oven Vandet. Turn right here and walk the 200m along the canal to reach Overgaden oven Vandet 58, where the naval museum **Orlogsmuseum**, is housed in the dignified old naval hospital, **Søkvæsthuset** (1755). Here you will find 300 ships' models (the oldest from 1687) as well as a graphic history of Danish seafaring. (Open Tues-Sun, 12.00–16.00.) The author Johan Ludvig Heiberg and his wife Johanne Luise Heiberg, one of Denmark's greatest actresses, lived here in the 19C, and the trees in the garden are said to have been planted by Mrs Heiberg.

To get across the canal you will have to walk back to Sankt Annæ Gade and then turn right. At the top of the road you reach Strandgade once more, where, overlooking the harbour, a row of old warehouses, now serving various purposes, has been modernised, while facing them there is a row of 17C merchants' houses. Turn left here and when you reach Torvegade you have completed your Christianshavn circle.

Now cross the Knippelsbro bridge, but this time you should stay on the right-hand side of the road and turn right again just opposite the Stock Exchange. In the midst of a small patch of green on your left here you will find the naval church, **Holmens Kirke**, to which the entrance is reached 100m further on, from HOLMENS KANAL.

The tall gable of Holmens Kirke overlooking the canal is from an earlier 16C church and is Italian inspired, but the present building is otherwise from 1641, the time of Christian IV, and stands virtually as it then was, having avoided damage from fire and bombardment. The low vaulted ceiling in the nave has stucco decorations from the 1640s, while the brass rail dividing the nave from the chancel is from 1668. The auricular oak altarpiece is from 1661, with carved figures of the four Evangelists and reliefs of the Last Supper, Crucifixion, Burial of

Christ and Ascension. The pulpit is also an outstanding piece of auricular work, supported on a figure of Moses and topped by a canopy in the form of a lantern.

Attached to the church, along the canal, there is a large sepulchral chapel from 1705–08, containing many sarcophagi. Pride of place goes to the naval heroes Niels Juel and Tordenskjold. The composer Niels Wilhelm Gade is also buried here, as are the architects C.F. Hansen and Gustav Friedrich Hetsch.

In the courtyard of the church there is a statue of Tordenskjold, the work of Herman Wilhelm Bissen, while a bronze statue of Niels Juel by T. Stein to commemorate the Battle of Køge Bay can be found in Holmens Kanal, 100m to the right of the main entrance.

However, on leaving the church you should now cross Holmens Kanal and follow it to the left till you reach VED STRANDEN, the road running alongside the canal, but on the opposite side of Christiansborg Palace. Keeping the canal on your left, walk as far as the bridge and you will now have the **Højbro Plads** square (Walk 2) on your right, and just in front of you the quay area called GAMMEL STRAND. As the name implies, this was part of the shoreline in the Middle Ages, and is thought to be the place where fishermen landed their catch. Until new laws prevented it in the 1950s, the Copenhagen fish market was here and consequently a long row of fish stalls, and those good old days are commemorated by the statue of the fishwife in her traditional dress now standing here. Many of the buildings facing Gammel Strand are 18C. Note particularly the sandstone porch of the old **Isenberghs Gård**, No. 48 (by Andreas Gercken). The fish restaurants here are also to be recommended.

You can now cross the Højbro bridge over the canal and then the main road— and you are back at Christiansborg.

Walk Five ~

c 3.5km. The walk starts and ends in front of the Royal Theatre on Kongens Nytorv.

Main sights: *Kongens Nytorv area, Amalienborg, Gefion Fountain, the Little Mermaid, the Marble Church.*

Kongens Nytorv was intended to link medieval Copenhagen with the new districts being developed, first by Christian IV and then by Frederik III. It was, however, Christian V who set about converting what had been the site of the gallows into a square of great elegance, the virtual centre of modern Copenhagen. The exquisite buildings, many of which still survive, began to appear in the late 17C. At the centre of the square there is a park area, the main feature of which is the proud Baroque equestrian statue of Christian V, from 1688, the work of the French sculptors Abraham César and Claude l'Amoureux. It commemorates Christian V as the real creator of Kongens Nytorv and is the oldest equestrian statue in Scandinavia. It must be admitted, however, that the present statue is a bronze copy by Einar Utzon-Frank of the original which was done in lead and was in a state of decay by 1946.

Kongens Nytorv still has an air of distinction, partly the result of the open space, with its statue and trees in the centre, partly because of the associations of some of the buildings on it. At the side of the Royal Theatre there is one of Copenhagen's most famous department stores, Magasin du Nord. To the left of

Magasin, at Holmens Kanal 2, is **Erichsens Palæ** which, built 1797–99 for one Erich Erichsen, was once the most magnificent neo-classical private building in Copenhagen, and the only one to have a façade facing Kongens Nytorv that included six Ionic columns. The architect was Caspar Frederik Harsdorff and the reliefs over the columns were the work of G.D. Gianelli>. The building now houses one of Denmark's largest banks. This building is on the corner of VINGÅRDSSTRÆDE, where, at No. 6, now the Kong Hans Restaurant, there is a huge medieval vault.

Beyond Magasin du Nord comes ØSTERGADE, the eastern end of Strøget, notable at this end for its fine shops, and beyond this again stands perhaps the most dignified of Copenhagen's old hotels, **Hotel d'Angleterre**. Then comes NY ADELGADE, which, for those interested in the history of the theatre, used to be called Lille Grønnegade and was the home of the first real theatre in Copenhagen, for which Ludvig Holberg wrote his first plays. There is nothing left of the theatre now, but the building has been splendidly restored to house the **Galerie Asbæk**, where some of Denmark's best contemporary artists exhibit their work on five floors. The gallery also contains a restaurant (closed in July). On the corner of the nearby HOVEDVAGTSGADE you will find one of Copenhagen's historical wine bars, Hvids Vinstue, with echoes of the Royal Theatre opposite, and on the other side of Hovedvagtsgade, facing the Royal Theatre is the A'Porta restaurant and bar, also with its historical and cultural links.

Det Kongelige Teater, the Royal Theatre, has stood on the same spot in Kongens Nytorv since 1749. The original building, by Eigtved, was rebuilt 1773–74 by Caspar Frederik Harsdorff. This was in its turn replaced 1872–74 by the present building in Italian Renaissance style, designed by Vilhelm Dahlerup and Ove Petersen. In front of the entrance are statues of Ludvig Holberg (by Theobald Stein, on the right) and Adam Oehlenschläger (by Herman Wilhelm Bissen, on the left). To the left of the main theatre, in Tordenskjoldsgade, is the entrance to the smaller stage, **Nye Scene**, from 1929. A bridge connects the two.

You start this walk by going from the Royal Theatre in an anti-clockwise direction, and following the traffic. You will first come to (100m) **Harsdorffs Hus**, an elegant neo-classical town house which was the work of Caspar Frederik Harsdorff, a former Professor of Perspective at the Academy of Fine Arts. The relief in the gable is by Wiedewelt. Built 1779–80, the house influenced subsequent architectural taste in Copenhagen. (Not open to the public.)

Immediately beyond Harsdorffs Hus comes the mansion of **Charlottenborg**, built 1672–83 by Ulrik Frederik Gyldenløve, the son of Frederik III. This is the first major example of Danish Baroque architecture, and was partly built with material taken from Kalø Castle (p 125). There is a bust of Frederik V over the balcony above the entrance. The façade is of small dark brick with sandstone decorations while the central section of the roof and the lantern above are of copper. Since 1734 it has been the home of the Royal Academy of Fine Arts, the first Principal of which was Eigtved. Now it also houses frequent art exhibitions. In the courtyard behind the main building there is a statue of Thorvaldsen by Einar Utzon-Frank.

Just beyond Charlottenborg you come to the end of NYHAVN.

Frederik III planned this canal, allowing ships to sail from the harbour right

Nyhavn

up to Kongens Nytorv and enabling merchants to build their houses directly along the wharves. It was completed in 1673. Hans Christian Andersen lived here at various times, in Nos 18, 20 and 67. Throughout the whole of the first half of the 20C the north side was a place of ill repute, but in the 1970s and 1980s a total transformation took place, and it is now a fashionable restaurant area, much frequented by locals as well as visitors to Copenhagen during summer months. Small ships are moored the length of the canal, adding to its atmosphere. The anchor standing at the Kongens Nytorv end is a memorial to Danish seaman lost during World War II; it bears the date of 1857 and once belonged to the 19C frigate *Fyen*. Nyhavn is one of the places from where you can take a boat trip round the Copenhagen canals and harbour.

From the Kongens Nytorv end of Nyhavn you take either STORE STRANDSTRÆDE or LILLE STRANDSTRÆDE to (150m) SANKT ANNÆ PLADS. You should cross the wide boulevard diagonally to the right into AMALIEGADE, which will take you to (300m) **Amalienborg Slotsplads**, Amalienborg Palace Square.

On the occasion of the 300th anniversary of the royal house of Oldenborg in 1748, Frederik V decided to found a new district for Copenhagen's most distinguished citizens, to be called Frederiksstad. The central feature was to be an octagonal piazza designed by Eigtved and containing four identical Baroque mansions. These were to be financed privately by four wealthy owners, to whom the king gave the necessary land. Consequently the four mansions became known as the Brockdorff, Levetzau, Moltke and Schack mansions. Apart from the period 1848–63, one or other of them has been the royal residence since the royal palace of Christiansborg burned down in 1794.

Queen Margrethe II lives in the Schack mansion, now known as **Christian IX's Palace**. Part of **Christian VIII's Palace**, now Crown Prince Frederik's residence, is open to the public daily during the summer from 11.00–16.00, and daily except Mondays in the winter, allowing access to three generations of royal private apartments. This collection should be seen as a continuation of the collection in Rosenborg and shows the rooms as used by monarchs in the period 1863-1947. Under the personal guidance of Queen Margrethe, the first floor has been carefully restored over the past twenty years and from May 1996 is open for 20-minute-long guided tours every other Sat and Sun and every other Wed, with tours commencing at 11.00, 12.30 and 14.00. As this palace is still in use as a royal residence, there may be changes to this, and if you want to make sure, you should ring to 33 12 21 86 for further information.

Christian VIII House, Amalienborg Palace

The square, with Italian mosaic cobbling from 1886, has at its centre one of Europe's finest neo-classical equestrian statues. The work of Jacques-François-Joseph Saly, it commemorates Frederik V, and was unveiled on Amalienborg Palace Square in 1771.

When the Queen is in residence the ceremony of **Changing the Guard** takes place on the square at 12.00 each day. The Guard leaves Rosenborg Palace at 11.30 and marches along Gothersgade, Nørrevold, Frederiksborggade, Købmagergade, Østergade, Kongens Nytorv, Bredgade, Sankt Annæ Plads and Amaliegade, returning via Frederiksgade, Store Kongensgade and Gothersgade.

While on Amalienborg Palace Square you should take the exit to the right, towards the harbour, to see the small **Amaliehaven** park, established in 1983 and sponsored by the huge shipping line A.P. Møller (Mærsk Line) to the design of the Belgian garden architect Jean Delogne and the Italian sculptor A. Pomadoro.

Then return to the square and turn right, continuing along AMALIEGADE. As you walk along here, with tall 19C façades on either side, take the time to peer into some of the courtyards, especially on the left-hand side, where you will suddenly find yourself in 17C and 18C surroundings, showing clearly how the 19C built on to what was already there.

About 500m further on you cross ESPLANADEN and here, just to your left, is **Frihedsmuseet**, the museum of the Danish Resistance, containing a large collection of exhibits from the World War II Occupation. (Open all year.)

Right in front of you, you will find the biggest public monument in Copenhagen, the **Gefion Fountain**. This most impressive fountain is from 1908 and the work of Anders Bundgaard. It illustrates the legend of the goddess Gefion, who could take as much of Sweden as she could plough in a single night. She transformed her sons into oxen and ploughed out the whole of Sjælland. (Much of Bundgaard's other work is to be seen in the Tingbæk Limestone Mines, p 243.)

If you now continue north along the sea front, you will, in c 200m, come to **Den Lille Havfrue**, the famous Little Mermaid, sitting on a rock by the water's edge. This bronze statue, from 1913, is the work of Edvard Eriksen and the idea of erecting a statue inspired by Hans Christian Andersen's story came from Carl Jacobsen of the Carlsberg Breweries. The figure is modelled on the sculptor's own wife.

The area north of Esplanaden is normally known as the **Langelinje Park**. Covering some 20 hectares in all, it includes besides the Gefion Fountain and the Little Mermaid, the Citadel, the Liberation Museum and the English church. There are also other sculptures. Captain Ivar Huitfeldt and his crew, heroes of the Battle of Køge Bay, are commemorated here, as are the polar explorers Ludvig Mylius-Erichsen, N.P. Høeg and Jørgen Brønlund, and King Frederik IX.

Langelinje was always a favourite spot for outings for Copenhageners, not least the old romantic Langelinje Pavilion which, however, was sabotaged during World War II. The new Langelinje Pavilion, on the same site close to the Little Mermaid, from 1957, is in a totally different style, built to the design of Eva and Nils Koppel. From the restaurant behind the glass façade you have a splendid view of the sea front and the many passing ships, and parking is seldom impossible.

Behind the Langelinje Pavilion lies **Kastellet** (The Citadel), the popular name for Frederik III's fortress, Citadellet Frederikshavn. There were fortifications here under Christian IV, but the Citadel proper was built 1662–63 under Frederik III. From the south it is approached through a gateway called **Sjællandsporten** (The Sjælland Gate) bearing the date 1663, and directly opposite, to the north, there is **Norgesporten** (The Norway Gate). In typical Baroque fashion, the blocks of old buildings, residences and storehouses are grouped symmetrically around the main street linking the two. The Dutch windmill is from 1847. The Citadel is no longer used as a barracks, but houses military offices and the Army Library.

The church, **Citadelkirken**, is from 1703–04. It is a small building with a saddle roof surmounted by a ridge turret. The original entrance, now bricked up, was through a porch flanked by four Doric columns in the long east façade. In 1728 the church was linked to the then prison behind the west wall. The original large windows to the west were bricked up and replaced by 'peep-holes' through which prisoners could take part in services without being seen. Little remains of the original church furniture, except the carved altarpiece and two brass candlesticks. The organ loft is from 1756. (The Citadel is open all year round.)

When you are finished with the park, go back towards Esplanaden. Here, in the south part of Langelinje, which has since World War II been known as the **Churchill Park**, you will pass the English **St. Alban's Church**, built in typical English neo-Gothic of brick covered with flint between 1885 and 1887 to a design by A.W. Blomfield.

On reaching Esplanaden you should cross it and walk the few metres to the right, until you come to BREDGADE, a dignified thoroughfare running parallel with Amaliegade, and leading back to Kongens Nytorv. Some 100m down Bredgade you will find, on the left at No. 68, a Rococo building from 1752 by Eigtved, flanked by two Baroque pavilions by Thurah from 1757. This is the **Kunstindustrimuseum**, the Danish Museum of Decorative and Applied Arts. The complex originally constituted the Frederik's Hospital, which is the scene of part of the action in Hans Christian Andersen's *Galoches of Fortune* and also the place where Søren Kierkegaard died, but the hospital was closed in 1919, and the buildings were then turned into the present museum housing a collection of European and Oriental decorative art. The main emphasis is on furniture, but there are special collections of porcelain, silver, textiles and book bindings. There are also collections of Chinese and Japanese work. (Open all year, daily except Monday 13.00–16.00.)

Just beyond the Kunstindustrimuseum is the principal Roman Catholic church in Denmark, **Sankt Ansgars Kirke**.

There was a chapel here as early as 1764, for the use of foreign embassy staff, but the present building dates from 1841–42. Although taken into use in 1842, it was not actually consecrated until 1865, on the thousandth anniversary of the death of St. Ansgar, who converted Denmark. The design is by Gustav Friedrich Hetsch and aims at maintaining the simplicity of early church architecture. The church itself stands a little back from the street, but with two pavilions—one a chapel, the other the side entrance—reaching the building line. When this was built, Catholic churches were not allowed to ring bells, and so the belfry, standing behind the actual church and invisible from the road, was not erected until 1943.

Immediately beyond the church, at Bredgade 82, is the **Medicinsk-historisk Museum**, the Museum of Medical History. This neo-classical building was designed by Peter Meyn for the Academy of Surgery in 1785–87. The museum illustrates the history of medicine and dentistry, and the original auditorium with dissecting table, lit from above, is as when built. (Open for conducted tours Wed 11.00–15.00.)

On the opposite side of Bredgade here, on the corner of FREDERICIAGADE, you will see the imposing buildings of **Østre Landsret**, the Eastern Regional Law Court. The elegant building in a mixture of Dutch and Italian styles facing Bredgade was built in 1701–02 by Frederik IV as a new opera house, and was used as a theatre between 1705 and 1708. The main building, in Fredericiagade 24, was the seat of the Danish Parliament from 1884 to 1918.

A little further down Bredgade you cannot fail to notice the golden onion domes of the Russian Orthodox Church, the **Alexander Newski Kirke**. It was built at the suggestion of the Russian Government 1881–83, to a design by the Russian architect David Grimm, in the style of 17C Moscow church buildings. The granite and brick façade, with a relief statue of Alexander Nevsky, is surmounted by three gilt onion domes, and the church itself, on the first floor, is reached by a marble staircase and decorated with Russian and Byzantine motifs.

On the opposite side of Bredgade, a little closer to Kongens Nytorv, at No. 54, you will see **Dehns Palæ**, a Baroque mansion from 1755, designed by Johann Gottfried Rosenberg. It is now owned by Danmarks Apotekerforening (The Danish Pharmaceutical Association). (Not open to the public.)

You are now almost at FREDERIKSGADE, leading on the left to Amalienborg Palace, and on the right to **Marmorkirken**, the Marble Church.

Officially called Frederiks Kirke (Frederik's Church), this was originally intended as one of the centrepieces of the planned, but never completed, Frederiksstad district. The original drawings were by Eigtved, but after his death the work was continued by Nicolas-Henri Jardin. Because of the cost, the project was then shelved in 1770 and not taken up again until the financier Carl Frederik Tietgen undertook to complete it in 1874, this time with Ferdinand Meldahl as his architect. The finished church was then consecrated in 1894. The copper-covered dome (one of the largest in Europe) with an internal diameter of 30m is clearly inspired by St. Peter's in Rome and St. Paul's in London. The cylinder bearing the dome is encircled with arcading, and on the balustrade there are figures from the Bible and Danish church history. The interior consists of an enormous circular nave surrounded by arcading.

On leaving the Marble Church, continue along Bredgade, where after c 300m you will see on your left, at No. 28, **Odd Fellow Palæet**, another beautiful house from 1755, designed by Eigtved. Originally called Berckentins Palæ, in the 1880s it was turned into a concert hall with 1500 seats, and in 1900 it was acquired by the Order of Oddfellows. It has been used as a concert hall until severely damaged by fire in 1992, and at the time of writing is undergoing restoration.

A little further, and you cross Sankt Annæ Plads to the left, where, under the trees, you will see a statue of Christian X on horseback. The image of Christian X seems to be that of the equestrian king, as it was on horseback he crossed the German border in 1920 and it was on horseback, in his seventies, that he rode through all parts of Copenhagen during the Occupation to keep up Danish spirits, until a fall from the horse finally put a stop to it and confined him to a wheelchair until his death in 1947.

The church on the right-hand side of Sankt Annæ Plads is the Baroque **Garnisons Kirke** built 1703–06, with a tower from 1886. Despite its name it is no longer a garrison church. Built of brick, the west front is divided by Tuscan pilasters supporting a gable. There is a small spire above. The seating inside is on two levels. The marble altar, from 1724, is by Just Wiedewelt and Didrik Gercken. The composer J.P.E. Hartmann is buried here.

Opposite Sankt Annæ Plads, at Bredgade 11, you will find the **Georg Jensen Museum** with a splendid collection of silverware from 1904–40 by this famous company (open all year). In the same building, antique and second-hand silver by Georg Jensen and A. Michelsen, and porcelain by Royal Porcelain and Bing & Grøndahl, are on sale. Bredgade is now famous for its antique and art dealers.

You are almost back in Kongens Nytorv now. On the corner of the square and Bredgade there is one more very imposing building to note: **Thotts Palæ**, which is now the French Embassy. It was built 1683–86 for Admiral Niels Juel, who died here in 1697. The original architect of the house is unknown, but we know that the modernisation of the façade was done by Nicolas-Henri Jardin in 1763–64, when the pilasters on the façade were crowned with Corinthian capitals, and the balustrade was added above the first floor.

You have now reached Kongens Nytorv, and the Royal Theatre is straight ahead.

Walk Six ~

*c 2.5km. The walk starts and ends outside **Østerport S-station** in **Oslo Plads**. The suggested detours will add a further km to the walk. Østerport Station can easily be reached by S-train and is about 5 mins from the Central Station.*

Main sights: *Statens Museum for Kunst (The Royal Museum of Fine Arts), Rosenborg Palace.*

Coming out of the S-train you would be wise to cross the busy OSLO PLADS road in front of the station by the subway so as to emerge on the western side of the road. On emerging, turn right and right again into ØSTER VOLDGADE (East Rampart Street) at the lights, and you should now be walking parallel with the railway track on your right. Note, in the triangular space ahead of you just before leaving Oslo Plads, the statue of the flautist by Anne Marie Carl Nielsen, made in memory of her husband Carl Nielsen.

A few metres down Øster Voldgade you cannot fail to notice, on your left, the group of striking old houses, all painted ochre. These are known as **Nyboder**,

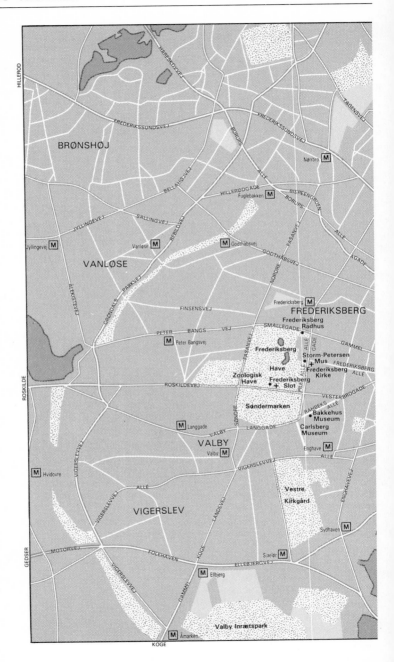

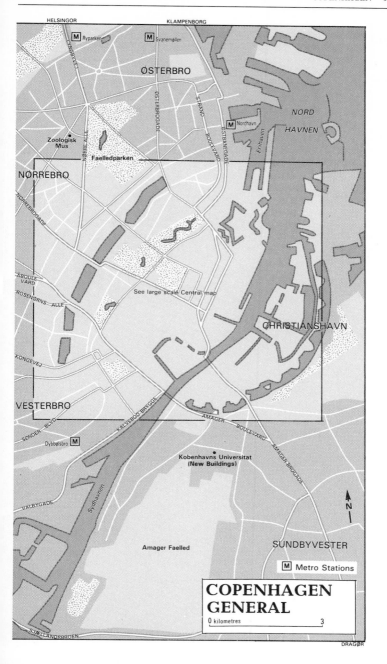

HELSINGOR   KLAMPENBORG

M Ryparken   M Svanemøllen

ØSTERBRO

M Norchavn

NORD
HAVNEN

Zoologisk
Mus
Faelledparken

NØRREBRO

See large scale Central map

CHRISTIANSHAVN

VESTERBRO

Dybbølsbro M

Kobenhavns Universitat
(New Buildings)

N

Amager Faelled

SUNDBYVESTER

M Metro Stations

COPENHAGEN
GENERAL

0 kilometres   3

DRAGØR

and they were built when Christian IV decided to provide free housing for his sailors.

Originally there were 616 single-storeyed houses, but numbers were increased in the 18C, and then again reduced in the 19C. Of those still standing (and there are many) only the Museum, called **Nybodernes Mindestuer**, at Sankt Paulsgade 20, is left from the original buildings from c 1630, the remainder being from the later extensions. It is still a remarkable area, with clear, straight lines of houses and unadorned but pleasing architecture. The museum, which was founded in 1931, consists of rooms, furniture and objects showing a typical Nyboder house from the 19C. A bronze statue commemorating Christian IV as the founder, executed by Vilhelm Bissen in 1900, stands in the area, visible from Øster Voldgade.

On your right you will now have the remains of the ramparts and a park called **Østre Anlæg**, constructed on the ground cleared when the ramparts were removed. After about 800m you come to the crossing with SØLVGADE, where, on your right, you will find **Statens Museum for Kunst**, the Royal Museum of Fine Arts.

The building, by Vilhelm Dahlerup, is from 1895 and was originally intended as a home for the royal collection of paintings after the Christiansborg fire of 1884. The basic construction, on two floors, is two long wings connected by a short wing at either end. Apart from the removal of Dahlerup's grandiose entrance, the exterior is still unchanged, but the interior was partly redesigned in the 1960s. The very extensive collection covers West European art from Byzantine icons to contemporary work, with particularly extensive collections of Dutch and Flemish art (including Pieter Brueghel the Elder, Rubens, Jordaens, Frans Hals and Rembrandt) and a splendid collection of early Italian painting (Titian and Tintoretto) in addition to both French and German collections, and work by El Greco. From a later period the French Impressionists are well represented, and there are important collections of Matisse and early 20C French painting.

The Danish collection is of outstanding importance, covering the entire development from the late 18C to the present day. Abildgaard, Jens Juel, Eckersberg, Købke and Lundbye are all well represented, and there is an entire room devoted to Hammershøi. The 20C is mirrored in the work of artists such as Harald Giersing, Asger Jorn and Per Kirkeby. There is a very large collection of prints and drawings including work by Dürer and Rembrandt. (Open all year.)

The very extensive Collection of Plaster Casts belonging to the museum is now housed in Vestindisk Pakhus in Toldbodgade.

Opposite Statens Museum for Kunst, on the other side of Sølvgade, lies the Geological Museum, **Geologisk Museum**, at Øster Voldgade 5–7. This museum of geology contains comprehensive collections of minerals, fossils and meteorites, with outstanding exhibits illustrating the geology of Denmark and Greenland. (Open daily except Mon 13.00–16.00, all year.)

If geology does not tempt you, then go diagonally across the traffic intersection to see **Rosenborg Have** (Rosenborg Gardens), which is the park—also known as **Kongens Have** (The King's Gardens)—covering some 12 hectares around Rosenborg Palace. Originally designed for Christian IV in 1606 when he started building Rosenborg, it is the oldest park in Copenhagen and since the 19C has been one of the most popular in the capital. In the northeast is the

Hercules Pavilion from 1773, by Harsdorff, and there are numerous statues, including one of a horse and lion by Peter Husum from 1617. In the south end stand two columns once used in jousting tournaments, and here, too, you find 17 marble balls the size of cannon balls arranged on the lawn. As befits a park intended for a leisurely stroll, there is also a café for your refreshment.

Not only is a walk through Rosenborg Have a delight in itself, but it will also bring you to KRONPRINSESSEGADE, where, at No. 30, there is a small but very choice art gallery, **Davids Samling** (the David Collection). Housed in an unpretentious mansion from 1806–07 this is one of the finest collections of Oriental art in Scandinavia, founded in 1945 by C.L. David and presented by him to the State. The most important part of the collection consists of Persian art from the 8C to the 16C, and comprises both illuminated manuscripts and collections of glass, pottery, metal work and silks. There is also a collection of English furniture, Danish silver from the 17C and 18C and Danish porcelain. (Open all year.)

While in Kronprinsessegade you should also note the curious booths lining Rosenborg Have known as **Meyns Pavilloner**. Kronprinsessegade was a new street built after the 1795 fire and the 'Pavilions', linked by elaborate wrought-iron railings, were a series of 16 individual small booths (4m × 4m × 4m) in neo-classical style built 1803–04 by Peter Meyn between the road and Rosenborg Park. They were intended as shops, but the experiment failed.

When you have seen all this, you should visit **Rosenborg** itself. The entrance to the castle is from Øster Voldgade, about 200m from Sølvgade, but it can be approached through the park from the south. This most interesting museum is virtually packed with people in the tourist season, but it is well worth joining the crowd. Guidebooks in English can be bought with the tickets.

Christian IV's small palace of Rosenborg, built 1606–34, with its 45.5m-high square tower to the west and the two lower ones to the east, is one of the most famous buildings in Copenhagen. It is built of brick, with horizontal lines and other decorations of Gotland sandstone.
There are elaborate gables at either end. On the west façade there is a lead bust of Christian IV and 12 busts brought to Denmark from Italy by Frederik IV. The copper roof is from 1712. Rosenborg was at first surrounded by a moat, part of which still remains.

Christian IV and his second wife Kirstine Munk had their rooms at opposite ends of the ground floor; these rooms still exist, and those of Christian IV are largely in their original state, particularly the oak-panelled **Winter Room**, with over 90 paintings in the panelling, and Christian IV's study with its oaken ceiling and

Rosenborg Palace

Chinese lacquered panelling. Kirsten Munk's bedchamber was changed in the 1660s into a Baroque chamber with stuccoed ceiling and marble decorations.

The rooms on the first floor are the result of rebuilding in the 18C, and the second floor contains the Great Hall, transformed by Christian V and decorated with tapestries. Frederik IV then had an opulent, barrel-vaulted stuccoed ceiling constructed, turning this into one of the most impressive of all Baroque rooms in Denmark. However, in 1917 the tapestries were removed for restoration and, as they were never returned, some of the former splendour has been lost. A special feature now is the three silver lions standing in front of the throne.

In the course of time Rosenborg was used less and less as a residence, and the royal family began to house many of their treasures, including the crown jewels, here. Even in the 17C there are signs that outsiders were allowed access to some extent.

In 1849 Rosenborg was transferred to State ownership, and is now open to the public. The exhibits are arranged chronologically to give an impression of changing tastes and fashions from the time of its creator, Christian IV. It also contains exhibits from earlier times collected by successive monarchs, for instance Christian I's horn of silver gilt. Since 1922 the Crown Jewels have been on show in Christian V's Room. Clothes worn by kings and queens can also be seen, including the bloodstained tunic worn by Christian IV at the Battle of Kolberger Heide (1644).

On leaving Rosenborg you continue along Øster Voldgade to the crossing with GOTHERSGADE (c 250m), where, on your left you have the Guards' Drill Ground and, at No. 100, **Livgardens historiske Samlinger**. Housed in a 200-year-old barracks, this Royal Life Guards Museum exhibits an array of uniforms, weapons and documents pertaining to the Royal Life Guards over the past three centuries. (Open all year.)

Opposite is the Reformed Church, **Reformert Kirke**. Despite the monopoly of the Lutheran church, immigrant Calvinists living in Copenhagen were given permission to hold services in 1685. In 1688–89 they built this church in Dutch Baroque style, rectangular, with saddle roof and ridge turret, and with a façade decorated with pilasters.

Beside the church you will find ROSENBORGGADE, leading to ÅBENRÅ, where at No. 30 there is the **Musikhistorisk Museum**. Founded in 1898 and since 1977 incorporating **Carl Claudius' Samling**, the Carl Claudius Collection of musical instruments from 1905, this museum is housed in a building from 1730. It contains a very large collection of instruments as well as a library and archives. Visitors are able to hear many of the musical instruments as they go through the collections. An extensive guide is available on entry. (Open daily except Thur 13.00–16.00 during the summer, but only on Tues, Thur and Fri in the winter season.)

Now go back to the intersection of Gothersgade and Øster Voldgade. Here, on the northern corner, there is an entrance to **Botanisk Have**, the Botanical Gardens. Before going in, however, you might like to go just a little further along Gothersgade and turn into Rømersgade, on the left, where you will find, at No. 22, the **Arbejdermuseum** (The Workers' Museum), founded in 1983 to illustrate the history of the working classes in Denmark. It contains a room in which you can eat and drink as people did in 1892!

Return to the entrance to the extensive **Botanisk Have**, Botanical Gardens, where the collections of palms and cacti are of particular note. The present gardens were established between 1871 and 1874 on undulating land available on the demolition of the Copenhagen ramparts. The greenhouses (4000 sq m) were inspired by those in Kew Gardens in England and the Brussels Botanical Gardens. There are over 15,500 plant species in the gardens. The museum building, on Gothersgade, is from 1875–76, and contains a large library and extensive collections, including 200,000 specimens of plants from Denmark and 160,000 from Greenland and the Faroe Islands. The general herbarium contains over a million specimens of flowering plants. The entire area is under the control of Copenhagen University, and as a guide to your tour you can hire a personal stereo together with a tape in one of several languages.

You should leave the Botanical Gardens by the north exit, which will lead you, 200m to the right, to **Sølvtorvet**. Here, you cross Sølvgade and go into STOCK-HOLMSGADE, where, 100m on the right, you will find another of Copenhagen's principal art galleries, the **Hirschsprung Collection**. This gallery, founded by the cigar manufacturer Heinrich Hirschsprung, offers an exquisite, chronologically arranged collection of 19C Danish painting, including the early 19C Eckersberg, Købke, Bendz, Roed, P.C. Skovgaard and Constantin Hansen, and the late 19C Skagen painters Anna and Michael Ancher, Viggo Johansen and Krøyer. The late 19C Realists and Naturalists Zahrtmann, Hammershøi and Ring are among others represented, as are the Fyn painters Peter Hansen, Fritz Syberg and Johannes Larsen. The relief in the tympanum is by Kai Nielsen. This purpose-built museum from 1908–11, designed in classical style by H.B. Storck, is open afternoons all year.

On leaving the gallery you continue along Stockholmsgade which in c 250m will bring you back to Oslo Plads, where you will see Østerport Station diagonally to your right.

Walk Seven ~ Frederiksberg

*c 3.5km. This walk begins at **Frederiksberg Rådhus** (Frederiksberg Town Hall). You reach it by bus, taking either No. 1 (Frederiksberg. Ålstrupvej) or No. 14 (Vanløse. Jydeholmen), both of which can be boarded on **Rådhuspladsen**.*

Main sights: *Frederiksberg Have, Zoologisk Have.*

Frederiksberg Town Hall, opened in 1953, stands at the junction of GAMMEL KONGEVEJ, SMALLEGADE, FALKONER ALLÉ and ALLÉGADE. It is brick built, in five storeys, with its main entrance facing Allégade. Perhaps the most striking aspect is the 60m tower, with an observation platform and the curious pavilion above. It is a clock tower, with faces on each side, and contains a magnificent carillon of 48 bells which plays different tunes at certain hours during the day.

At Smallegade 45, 600m behind the Town Hall, is the Royal Porcelain factory, the **Kongelige Porcelænsfabrik** (1775), which can be visited Tue and Thur, except late July and early August.

Return to Allégade, turn right, and walk for 400m to the **Frederiksberg Runddel** roundabout, where FREDERIKSBERG ALLÉ, another main thoroughfare from central Copenhagen, emerges. Here you will find the main entrance into **Frederiksberg Have** park. But before this, there are two places worth a visit at the roundabout: Frederiksberg Kirke and the Storm Petersen Museum.

The modest **Frederiksberg Kirke**, octagonal in shape and with a steep pyramidal roof, is built in the Dutch Protestant tradition and reflects the influence of the Dutch community in this area in the 17C and early 18C. It is the work of a Dutch architect, Felix Dusart. The roof is supported inside on eight pillars, and there is a gallery all round. The monograms of Christian VI and Queen Sophie Magdalene can be seen in the vaulting. As is usual in Dutch Protestant churches, the pulpit is above the altar. The altarpiece is by Eckersberg. To the north of the altar there is a memorial plaque to the 19C poet and dramatist, Adam Oehlenschläger, who is buried in the churchyard.

Just opposite the church to the left of the entrance to Frederiksberg Have is the **Storm-Petersen Museum**, dedicated to the drawings, paintings and personalia of Denmark's most famous cartoonist and humorist. A particularly attractive feature is a collection of pipes which Storm Petersen—himself a dedicated pipe smoker—had collected throughout his life.

Now go through the gates to **Frederiksberg Have**, which, together with the adjoining **Søndermarken** south of ROSKILDEVEJ, forms one of Copenhagen's major parks, the two together making up 64 hectares.

Frederiksberg Have was originally established close to Frederiksberg Palace (see below) by Frederik III in 1651 and redesigned around 1700 by Frederik IV. A century later Frederik VI developed it further, providing for canals, bridges, islands, and in general giving it the informal, relaxed feel which it has today. There is a Chinese pavilion (1798–1800), and a Swiss cottage to a design by Nicolai Abildgaard from 1800–01. The main entrance, from 1755, is by Thurah. Nearby stands a statue of Frederik VI by Herman Wilhelm Bissen.

On your left (i.e. to the south) you will see **Frederiksberg Slot** (Frederiksberg Palace), standing impressively above open ground; the original wing, an 'Italian villa', was built 1699–1703, overlooking the park, and is still much as it was then. The two lateral wings were designed later, between 1733 and 1738, by Thurah and Elias David Häusser. The palace was long used as a royal residence, but since 1869 it has been Denmark's Military Academy.

You now leave the park through the palace grounds where, in the east wing of the palace, you will see **Frederiksberg Slotskirke**. This is a small Baroque chapel from 1710 by W.F. von Platen. A feature of the narrow nave is the Ionic columns on either side, while both the walls and the ceiling are elaborately stuccoed. On reaching ROSKILDEVEJ turn right and 100m further on your right you will find the entrance to Copenhagen Zoo, **Zoologisk Have**.

Copenhagen Zoo was established here in 1859, and has since been steadily developed to contain some 2500 animals and birds. It is run on the most modern principles, containing animals you can look at as well as animals you can play with. With its restaurants and its accessible tower it is said to be the most popular Copenhagen attraction after Tivoli. (Open all year.) (If you want to visit the zoo without seeing the other sights in Frederiksberg, you can take buses 18, 27, 28 or 39 from Rådhuspladsen.)

On leaving the zoo, you should turn left into Roskildevej and walk back as far as Frederiksberg Palace. Here you cross the road and go into the park called **Søndermarken**. Just inside the entrance you will find a long avenue going off obliquely in a southeasterly direction. Take it, and it will bring you out at the end of PILEALLÉ. Just to the left of this exit, on the other side of Pileallé you will find RAHBEKS ALLÉ. No. 23 is the **Bakkehus Museum**. Hidden well away in a garden full of old trees, Bakkehuset (c 1764) does not look like a museum. It seems to be just another private home as indeed it was under the ownership of the writer and critic Knud Lyne Rahbek, when it became a focal point for the writers and artists of the Danish Golden Age, many of whom actually lived there for a time. It is furnished as far as possible in the original style, often with the original furniture, in an attempt to preserve the atmosphere of the Rahbeks' home. There is even a coffee table with imitations of the cakes baked at that time! A room in Bakkehuset is dedicated to the leading 19C Romantic dramatist Adam Oehlenschläger and to the 18C poet and dramatist Johannes Ewald, in the opinion of many the greatest Danish poet ever. (Open all year.)

From Bakkehuset you really ought to go back to Pileallé and finish your walk with a little refreshment, for just to the left here, where Pileallé bends and becomes VALBY LANGGADE, you cannot—on looking down Ny Carlsbergvej—fail to see the entrance to the world-famous **Carlsberg Breweries**. Here is Vilhelm Dahlerup's huge **Elephant Entrance**, with four giant elephants of Bornholm granite supporting the upper building, and the motto *Laboremus pro Patria* inscribed above the archway. The Breweries behind are open for individual visits Mon–Fri at 09.00, 11.00 and 14.30, or, for groups by arrangement, and a visit will also include the **Carlsberg Museum** (Valby Langgade 1), which illustrates the history of the Breweries and the work of the Carlsberg Foundation. In the museum you will also find portraits of the Jacobsen family, antique statues and a staircase flanked by Thorvaldsen figures.

A walk back to the centre of Copenhagen is possible from here, taking a short cut through Rahbeks Allé to Vesterbrogade and then proceeding along this busy shopping street for the rest of the way, but the distance is close on 3km, and you may prefer to take the bus No 6.

Some more Copenhagen sights ~

Not all the sights in Copenhagen can conveniently be grouped in walks, and some are a little too far out to reach easily on foot. The following list comprises some of these attractions, together with the way of reaching them by using public transport.

Arken. Museum for Modern Art, Ishøj Strandpark, Skovvej 42, Ishøj, is an imposing new museum built to mark Copenhagen as European City of Culture 1996. In addition to the permanent collection, Arken puts on travelling exhibitions of Scandinavian and international art. The complex also contains a concert hall. Reached either by road or S-train to Ishøj. (Open daily 10.00–17.00, Wed 10.00–22.00, closed Mon.)

Brede Museum, I.C. Modewegsvej, Lyngby, is part of the National Museum, exhibiting Danish cultural history over the last 300 years. (Open all year, varying times.) Distance from Copenhagen 15km. S-train to Jægersborg, where you change to the Nærum Line to Brede.

Danmarks Akvarium, Strandvejen 1, Charlottenlund. Situated in an area of parkland this modern aquarium is one of the largest in Europe and presents a well-arranged collection of some 3000 fish from all over the world. (Open all year.) The nearby **Skovriderkroen** is a well-known restaurant. Distance from Rådhuspladsen c 7km. (Bus 6 or 176 from Rådhuspladsen.)

Dragør is one of the villages on **Amager** founded by Dutch immigrants, and it has a rather different character from ordinary Danish villages. It is characterised by carefully preserved narrow cobbled streets, their sometimes thatched and half-timbered houses built close together near the harbour. This harbour is surprisingly big, and reflects the fact that in the 19C Dragør was the third largest port in Denmark after Copenhagen and Helsingør. But with the advent of bigger ships, that all stopped. There are several large old buildings near the harbour, including the old **Pilot's House**, with a small tower above the roof. The old warehouse from 1682 is now the **Dragør Museum** with an excellent local history collection, in addition to which there are re-creations of the interiors of old seamen's and fisherfolk's houses. (Open 1 May–30 Sept.) There are regular ferry sailings from Dragør to Limhamn in Sweden. Distance from Rådhuspladsen c 15km. (Bus 30, 33, 34, 73E.)

The Eksperimentarium, Danmarks Science Center, is a so-called 'activity centre' with a range of exhibits concerned with the environment, technology, energy and health, and is now one of the most popular of all Danish museums, offering almost 300 experiments for you yourself to try. (Open Mon, Wed, Fri 09.00–18.00, Tues Thurs 09.00–21.00, Sat Sun 11.00–18.00.) Distance from Rådhuspladsen c 7km. (Bus 6 from city centre, e.g. main railway station, Kongens Nytorv, Østerport Station or S-train to Svanemøllen and then Bus 21 or 23.)

***Frilandsmuseum**, Kongevejen 100, Lyngby. This open air museum is the 7th Department of the Danish National Museum and contains nearly 100 old farms and houses of all sizes and in all styles from the whole of Denmark. The buildings have all been dismantled and reconstructed in a large park. Most are equipped with appropriate furniture and implements. (Open all year; varying times.) Distance from Rådhuspladsen c 15km. (S-train to Lyngby, then Bus 184 or 194 in direction of Holte. Or S-train to Sorgenfri and then 10-minute walk along Hummeltoftvej and Skovbrynet.)

Grundtvigskirken, På Bjerget. Designed by Peder Vilhelm Jensen-Klint, this huge church was built 1921–40 as a memorial to N.F.S. Grundtvig. It is based on the shape of a traditional Danish village church, but has the dimensions of a cathedral. There are variations on corbie steps both in the west façade and on the north and south walls, and there are flying buttresses around the apse. Much of the interior—the altar, font and pulpit—are designed by the architect's son, Kaare Klint. Distance from Rådhuspladsen c 7km. (Bus 10 from Hovedbanegården, 16 from Rådhuspladsen, 19 from Rådhuspladsen, 43 from Nørreport Station.)

Karen Blixen Museum, Rungstedlund, Rungsted Strandvej 111, Rungsted Kyst. Karen Blixen's home, containing exhibitions of books, paintings and manuscripts, surrounded by a park and bird sanctuary. Karen Blixen (Isak Dinesen) is buried in the grounds. (Open May-Sept daily 10.00–17.00; Oct-Apr Wed-Fri 13.00–16.00, Sat-Sun 11.00-16.00, closed Mon, Tues). Distance from Rådhuspladsen c. 20 km. (Train from Central Station, Nørreport or Østerport to Rungsted Kyst, and then bus 388, or S-train to Lyngby and then Bus 388.)

Mindelunden i Ryvangen, Tuborgvej. This is a Memorial Park to Danish Resistance Fighters from World War II. Situated close to where captured members of the Resistance were executed, it was once the burial place of 198 of them. About 100 are still buried here, in identical graves. A statue, representing a mother with a dead son, the work of Axel Poulsen, is at the centre. (Open all year.) Distance from Rådhuspladsen c 7km. (S-train to Hellerup Station.)

Ordrupgårdsamlingen, Vilvordevej 110, Charlottenlund. The Ordrupgård Gallery, developed from the private collection of Wilhelm Hansen and housed in a purpose-built gallery in landscaped gardens, offers a comprehensive collection of Danish 19C and 20C art (including Købke, Hammershøi and Ring). Housed in a separate gallery is a very extensive collection of French 19C and 20C paintings (Degas, Renoir, Pissaro, Cézanne, Gaugin and many others). Distance from

Rådhuspladsen c 13km. (S-train to Klampenborg or Lyngby and then Bus 388.)

Store Magleby was the village in which the Dutch peasants were originally settled on Amager in 1521, and for two centuries it was predominantly Dutch. Church services were held only in Dutch or Low German. The church itself dates from 1611, with alterations from 1731. The pulpit is Renaissance (1614), and the pews and altarpiece are 19C neo-Gothic. The 18C half-timbered **Amagermuseum**, at Hovedgaden 4, has collections of local dress (showing the influence of Dutch national costumes), paintings and interiors of cultural interest. (Open all year; varying times.) Distance from Rådhuspladsen c 13km. (Bus 30, 33 from Rådhuspladsen.)

Tuborg Bryggerier, Strandvejen 54, Hellerup. The Tuborg Breweries, which have stood on this site since 1873, are open all year for individual visits Mon–Fri at 10.00, 12.30 and 14.30, and, by arrangement, for groups. Distance from Rådhuspladsen c 7km. (S-train to Svanemøllen and then Bus 1 or 21.)

Zoologisk Museum, Universitetsparken 15. This is a modern zoological museum, with a large number of models and exhibits of animal life. Children will love it. (Open all year.) Distance from Rådhuspladsen c 3km. (Bus 18, 42, 43, 184.)

4 • Copenhagen to Helsingør (Elsinore)

Total distance 47km. The route follows the 152 throughout.

From Central Copenhagen you should first make your way to Klampenborg, either by driving via Østerport and there following the ring road 02 and the 152 through Hellerup, or by joining the E47/E55 motorway and turning off at Junction 16 towards Klampenborg from where you follow the 152, STRANDVEJEN north.

Now you are travelling into North Sjælland, the traditionally idyllic countryside north of Copenhagen, discovered and much loved by the Romantics in the 19C and still the favourite area for day trips by Copenhageners on summer Sundays. It is nowadays increasingly a popular commuter belt, well served by first-class roads and the excellent integrated public transport system. As far as Rungsted you will find many large houses, built by affluent families seeking beautiful surroundings, but further out the smaller fishing villages have retained much of their character, though they, too, are now being taken over by families moving out of the city. Visitors delight in the beaches, the light effects, the wide expanses of the Sound (Øresund) and the views of the Swedish coast to the right on driving north.

You will go through **Klampenborg**, 11km north of Copenhagen, passing the **Bellevue** beach, one of Copenhagen's favourites, where summer days see sun worshippers in their thousands sunbathing or swimming in the waters of the Sound. To your left you will find **Jægersborg Dyrehave**, the great deer park, once the domain of royalty, now a vast open space where people can roam at will, still catching frequent glimpses of the many deer on the hilly terrain. It is almost 3km across and, if you include the more northerly **Jægersborg Hegn**, stretches north for some 7km of unbroken open green land.

Jægersborg Dyrehave

Jægersborg Dyrehave has been parkland of differing kinds since the Middle Ages, and is referred to in the 13C 'Valdemars Jordebog'. You enter the park through red-painted gates bearing the monograms of different kings. If you turn left off Strandvejen on to PETER LIEPS VEJ and continue along **Fortunvej**, you will come to the former home of one of Frederik VIII's gamekeepers, **Peter Lieps Hus**, now a popular café. Continue along FORTUNVEJ, and you come to the site of what was once a sacred spring, **Kirsten Piils Kilde**. It was a place of pilgrimage in the 16C, and subsequently a fairground developed there. This gradually grew into the nearby *Dyrehavsbakken, Copenhagen's first great amusement park, still said to be the biggest in North Europe. It has an older tradition than the 19C Tivoli, representing a more 'popular' form of entertainment, and today, alongside modern fairground entertainment, it has succeeded in preserving much of its original character. Perhaps a little noisier than Tivoli, it has a dynamism of its own, and is, in fact, very different. Dyrehavsbakken is signposted from Klampenborg and can be approached either from Fortunvej or from DYREHAVEVEj. Dyrehavevej will also bring you to **Galopbanen**, the Copenhagen Trotting Course.

On one of the highest points of Jægersborg Dyrehave stands the elegant rococo hunting lodge, **EREMITAGEN**, built in 1736 by Laurids de Thurah for Christian VI, and still in the possession of the Royal Family. The name, 'the hermitage', suggests the private nature of the original building, when it even contained a lift on which an entire dining table could be sent up to the royal apartments so the family could eat without the attentions of servants. The level ground outside was, incidentally, the site of Denmark's first football match, in 1879.

Following the 152 north you will clearly see Eremitagen on your left, and beyond it the continuation of the park, Jægersborg Hegn. After 5km you pass through **Skodsborg**, and then (3km) **Vedbæk**, a small fishing village now equipped with an excellent marina. Continue for a further 4km and, on your left, just opposite the busy Rungsted yachting harbour, you will see **Rungstedlund**, the home and burial place of Karen Blixen (Isak Dinesen). It is a house with a long history, and was originally an inn, part of which still survives. In 1773 another great Danish writer, Johannes Ewald (1743–81), lived there and wrote some of his finest poetry. A mound in the park close to the road is known as **Ewald's Mound**. Rungstedlund now houses the Karen Blixen Museum. Open daily from May to Sept and from Wed to Sun otherwise.

Just after Rungstedlund the 207 leads to **Hørsholm** (3km), once the site of a royal castle which was allowed to fall into disrepair in the 19C, and nothing now remains. In its former stables and barn, however, there is a museum, **Jagt-og Skovbrugsmuseum**, illustrating the history of hunting and forestry. In 1822 the architect C.F. Hansen, who was responsible for redesigning much of central Copenhagen, built a church in his typical neo-classical style in the castle courtyard. This is now **Hørsholm Church**, containing an altarpiece by Thorvaldsen and a Rococo font from the chapel of the now vanished castle. On SØNDRE JAGTVEJ you will find **Hørsholm Egnsmuseum**, with exhibits of local interest, particularly from the 18C and 19C.

Back on the 152 you continue north to (6km) **Nivå**, where, in the mansion of **Nivågård**, there is a very fine collection of 16th and 17th century European paintings (including Ruisdael and Rembrandt) and a small, but exquisite collection of paintings from the 19C Danish Golden Age. (Open Tue-Fri 12.00–16.00; Sat-Sun 11.00–17.00.) 3km further north you reach **Sletten**, from where you can take a trip to the island of **Ven**. This is now Swedish, but it has a Danish history, being the site of the great 17C astronomer Tycho Brahe's famous observatory.

Yet another 2km, and you are in **Humlebæk**, where, on GAMMEL STRANDVEJ (clearly signposted on the right of the 152) one of modern Denmark's most famous art galleries and artistic centres, *****Louisiana**, is situated. Lying in delightful surroundings sloping down to the Sound, and surrounded by lawns dotted with sculptures by Jean Arp, Max Ernst, Calder and Henry Moore, it is an internationally renowned gallery of Danish and international modern art, with a permanent collection and regular major exhibitions. There is a concert hall, and concerts and recitals are regular features. Open daily 10.00–17.00.

Immediately south of Humlebæk is the **Niels W. Gade Museum**, commemorating the famous Romantic composer (Sat, Sun). Humlebæk is itself an old fishing village, and many of the old fishermen's houses still stand, giving their own charm to the beautiful surroundings. The church here is not old, but it does contain some fine modern stained glass by one of today's most important church artists, Sven Havsteen-Mikkelsen. Humlebæk is, too, the site of the mansion of **Krogerup** (1779), now Krogerup Folk High School, situated on the road towards **Kvistgård** to the left of the 152.

Helsingør
Continue to (9km) Helsingør (Elsinore) (pop. 56,800) which is far more than Hamlet's Castle.

■ **Tourist information**: Havnepladsen 3; tel. 49 21 13 33.

■ **Hotels**: Marienlyst, Nordre Strandvej 2; tel. 49 21 40 00; Skandia, Bramstræde 1; tel. 49 21 09 02.

■ **Youth hostel**: Nordre Strandvej 24; tel. 49 21 16 40.

History
Helsingør has a history going back to the beginning of the 13C, possibly earlier, and owes its growth and importance to its position on the narrowest part of the Sound, now with ferry and hydrofoil connections with Sweden. It also had a strategic position, and when King Erik of Pomerania introduced Sound dues in the 15C, he built a castle to enforce them. At the same time he established Helsingør as an important ecclesiastical centre, helping

to found no fewer than three monasteries in the town: Franciscan, Dominican and Carmelite. The present mansion of **Marienlyst** occupies the ground on which the Franciscan monastery stood. The Dominican monastery became a hospital after the Reformation, but no longer exists, though remains were found in Fiolgade in 1936. The Carmelite monastery did better, and some of the buildings still stand, in particular the church, **Klosterkirken**.

In the 16C the town was destroyed by the Lübeckers, and it was twice visited by the plague. That same century Frederik II had the old castle dismantled and replaced by the present Kronborg (1574–83). This move, which was supplemented by the stationing of a barracks in the town, revived Helsingør. The 17C and 18C were a period of growth, lasting until the Napoleonic Wars, when Helsingør suffered badly. With the abolition of the Sound dues in 1857 it was hit yet again, as this meant that ships no longer all put in and brought trade. On the other hand, the opening of the railway in 1864, followed by the introduction of steam ferries to Sweden, brought new life to the town.

*Kronborg Castle (open all year 10.30–17.00. Closed Mon, Oct–May) must remain the special attraction of Helsingør. It is situated on a promontory to the north, overlooking the harbour and the Sound. By the end of the rebuilding, the resplendent Renaissance edifice stood, as it does today, as four wings roofed with copper (hence the present green colour) around a magnificent central court-yard. It was badly damaged by fire in 1629, but rebuilt by Christian IV. After the rather sombre approach to the castle, the first sight of the interior is an experi-ence, a glimpse of the inner courtyard through a rounded archway flanked on either side by two Ionic columns with statues of Neptune and Mercury in the niches between them. The archway is surmounted by a bay window beneath which is a series of coats of arms.

The courtyard is enormous and light, and it is from here that you follow the set route through the rooms and halls. They vary from the intimate to the splendid. In the north wing there is the king's chamber, with its stuccoed window recesses, the painted panels in the ceilings by Gerrit van Honthorst, and the alabaster and marble fireplace. In the **Lesser Hall** (Lille Sal) there are seven of the tapestries ordered by Frederik II, huge portraits of Danish kings. These, and the 104 others (!), were intended for the 63m-long **Great Hall** (Riddersalen) with its floor of Gotland marble, but here, in a space made even more vast by the total lack of furnishings, there are painted portraits instead. Most sumptuous of all, perhaps, is the ***Chapel** (Slotskirken), entirely furnished as it was at the time of Frederik II, with gloriously painted and carved bench ends and royal balcony, not to mention the organ from the time of Christian IV.

The castle now includes a museum of commerce and shipping—the **Handels- og Søfartsmuseum**—which illustrates Danish maritime history and Denmark's colonial past, and beneath the castle the *casemates are partly open for inspection. Here sits brooding the stone statue of Holger Danske, the legendary hero who will come back to save Denmark in its hour of need.

The remainder of Helsingør needs to be seen on foot. Start from the square in front of the station, and cross over to STRANDGADE with its old houses:

Stephan Hansens Gård from 1760, **Claessens Palæ** from 1790 and **Mester Peiters Bod**, the old apothecary's shop. Now turn down any of the streets on your right to the carefully preserved STENGADE, where you will find more excellent examples of old buildings: **Odernes Gård** (No. 66) from 1459, the late Gothic houses at Nos 70, 72 and 74 from the 16C. No. 76 is a Renaissance house from 1579, while No. 64 is Baroque, from 1739. There is a wealth of fine old houses in Helsingør—the whole of this quite compact district is distinguished by them, many of high architectural quality.

Now walk north along Stengade until you reach SANKT ANNA GADE on your left. Here, on the corner of Sankt Anna Gade and SANKT OLAI GADE you will find the Cathedral Church, **Sankt Olai Kirke**, easily recognised by its tall tower. Its history goes back to c 1200, but the present Gothic structure dates mainly from 1450; it has a broad lofty nave and chancel, both whitewashed, with massive Gothic arches on either side. The furniture is outstanding, mainly Renaissance and Baroque. The auricular high altar from 1664 is by Lorentz Jørgensen and stands over 11m, with reliefs representing scenes and characters from the New Testament.

The exuberant rood screen from 1652–53, supported by 76 brass balusters, is by Claus Brahmeier of Hamburg and Jens Mortensen of Helsingør. The crucifix above it is Gothic, late 15C. The pulpit, from 1568, is one of the earliest Danish Renaissance works. Some of the bench ends are inscribed with coats of arms of the nobility or with that of Helsingør City, dated 1560. Of particular interest is the baptismal chapel, while an amusing detail (seen with 20C eyes!) is the black tablet on which parishioners were named if they had committed an ecclesiastical peccadillo.

It is now only a few steps further along Sankt Anna Gade to **Sankt Marie Kirke**. This is the south wing of the Carmelite monastery, which is the best preserved monastery in Denmark. St Mary's Church, brick built, consists of a tall nave with side aisles, ending in both east and west with Gothic gables and windows; the light from these windows is the only direct light to the nave. The pointed arcades separating the side aisles stand on heavy square columns. On the north side of the nave the royal gallery bears the initials of Frederik III and Queen Sophie Amalie. There are late Gothic frescoes in the vaulting in the nave and on the wall of the south aisle. The Baroque altarpiece is from 1637, the organ loft from 1630–40, the bench ends from 1700. The organ itself is from 1635 and was played by the composer Didrik Buxtehude when he was organist here from 1660–68. The church is notable for a large number of gravestones and memorial plaques. Christian II's mistress, Dyveke, is said to be buried here.

The adjoining **Vor Frue Kloster** consists of the remainder of the Carmelite monastery, the whole of it surrounding the monastery cloisters. Immediately to the west stands the corbie-gabled **Carmelite House** (Karmeliterhuset), most of it dating from the early 16C and now, together with Marienlyst (see below), forming the Helsingør City Museum, illustrating the history of Helsingør and the Sound dues.

Continue your walk now along Sankt Anna Gade and its curiously named continuation, Lappen (The Patch), to the beautiful park surrounding the elegant neo-classical mansion of **Marienlyst**. Originally called Lundegård, it was designed by Nicolas-Henri Jardin in 1759 to the order of Adam Gottlob Moltke and bought by King Frederik V in 1760. On the death of the King it was taken over by Queen Juliane Marie, from whom it derives its name. The park was designed according to Romantic ideas and furnished with an artificial burial mound which was given the name of Hamlet's Grave, and it is still to be seen. It is, however, not one of the various places claiming to be the authentic burial place of the elusive prince.

The science museum, **Danmarks Tekniske Museum** is 1km further west on NORDRE STRANDVEJ, the continuation of Lappen. Its exhibits illustrate scientific developments over the centuries, and include a room dedicated to H.C. Ørsted, the discoverer of electro-magneticism, a typewriter from 1867 and the first aeroplane to fly in Europe.

If you now return along Nordre Strandvej and turn left down STRANDALLÉ (at the junction with Lappen) and follow this round into STRANDPROMENADEN, you will come, on your right, to the **Øresunds Akvarium**, where you can see living specimens of the fish and marine animals from the Sound. Just opposite you will find **Grønnehave Station**, from where in the summer months you can travel by vintage railway to Gilleleje and back.

▶Excursion to the west of Helsingør
Total distance c 56km.

The north coast of Sjælland is famous for its sandy beaches and clear water and is much loved by holidaymakers.

Take the 237 from Helsingør to (5km) **Hellebæk**, where the old **Hammer Mølle**, founded by Christian IV in 1597 and in its time copper mill, gun foundry and clothing mill, is now a working museum (open summer). Hellebæk is also notable for its workmen's cottages, the oldest dating from 1735.

Continue now to (7km) **Hornbæk**, with its popular beaches and sand dunes. 5km further finds you in another beautifully situated bathing resort, **Dronningmølle**. If you take the minor road south here towards **Villingerød** and turn left at Villingerød Church (2km), you will come to an area called **Rusland** (see Brother Rus, below), where the **Rudolf Tegner Museum and Sculpture Park** exhibits the work of the Symbolist sculptor and painter who himself founded the museum in 1937 (open summer).

From Dronningmølle it is otherwise no more than 3km to **Nakkehoved**, with its 18C lighthouse (and inn), and a further 3km to **Gilleleje**, the northernmost fishing village on Sjælland, and now a much-visited tourist resort. Again, there is a magnificent beach, and daily fish auctions. This is the terminus of the vintage railway from Helsingør. The **Gilleleje Museum**, housed in the old school house, a fisherman's cottage and Nakkehoved lighthouse, boasts an excellent collection of exhibits illustrating local life over the centuries (open summer).

If you take the 227 south from Gilleleje and turn right after 4km, you will come to **Søborg** (2km) with the remarkably well-preserved ruins of the 12C castle which was the first brick-built castle in Scandinavia. The large—also brick built—Romanesque church here is contemporary with it; the tower is mid-13C. The original south door is still in use, while the north door has been bricked up, but is still visible. There are a few frescoes on the walls and columns in the nave. The altar is medieval, with an altarpiece from 1593 (originally in St Mary's Church in Helsingør), the work of Hans de Brügge. The land around Søborg was once a lake—still called Søborg Sø. Draining began in the late 18C by means of the canal to Gilleleje, which still exists.

Just west of Gilleleje the 251 south will take you to (8km) **Græsted**, where you will find **Nordsjællands sommerpark**, which is said to be one of the best tourist attractions in northern Sjælland. (Open 25 May-25 Aug.) Now take the road to (4km) Kirke Esbønderup, where you will find a minor road leading to (2.5km) **Esrum Kloster**, a Cistercian monastery founded by Archbishop Eskild around 1150. King Erik Menved's twin sons were buried here, as was Valdemar IV's Queen, Helvig. Only the south wing now remains, of which the west part, the administration block, is late 14C and is said to be the oldest secular building in Denmark. Until recently it was a private residence, but steps have now been taken to restore as much as possible of this building, to use it as a museum dedicated to the Catholic period in Denmark and as a concert hall. Perhaps this will act as a counter-balance to the Reformation polemic telling the story of how the Devil, under the name of Brother Rus ('rus' means intoxication) set about seducing the monks and did very well until he was finally unmasked and driven out. Perhaps it is not too much to assume that it is his name that is attached to the nearby Rusland—see above.

From Esrum Kloster drive south 1km to join the 205 east. On your right now is **Esrum Sø**, the second biggest lake in Denmark—9km long—and one of the deepest—21m. Drive along the 205 through Horserød Hegn wood and past **Horserød Prison** (a camp for Russian prisoners of war in World War I, an internment and later concentration camp during the Nazi occupation in World War II, and now an ordinary prison) back to (15km) Helsingør. ◀

5 • Helsingør to Copenhagen via Hillerød

Total distance 64km. E47/E55, 213 to (8km) Gurre. Unclassified road to (4km) Tikøb. 235, A6 to (18km) **Hillerød**. *201, A19 to (34km)* **Copenhagen**.

Leave Helsingør (p 106) south on the E47/E55, turning off at (6km) Junction 3 on to the 213 turning north to (2km) **Gurre**. Just beyond the village, idyllically situated on the south bank of **Gurre Sø** (lake) are the ruins of one of the most famous of Danish medieval castles.

Gurre Castle was the favourite castle of Valdemar IV, whose mistress Tove, according to legend, was murdered in a particularly nasty way by his Queen. She invited Tove into the sauna, pushed her in first, locked the door and roasted her. Valdemar was distraught and cursed God, for which he was condemned to hunt the forests of Sjælland until Judgement Day. He is said to have uttered the words: 'Let God keep His Heaven, if only I can keep my Gurre.' This is the legend taken over by the 19C poet Jens Peter Jacobsen, which, in German translation, forms the text of Schönberg's *Gurrelieder*. (Historically, Tove was actually the mistress of Valdemar I, but that is another matter.)

The ruins now stand in places to a height of 5m, and indicate that the castle originally consisted of a late 12C rectangular central tower surrounded by a more or less square ring wall with a tower at each corner. It is thought to have been demolished about the time of the Reformation, and the materials in part used in the building of Frederiksborg Castle (see below). Other material from it was used in the 19C to build artisans' houses. Just east of the castle the foundations of a 14C chapel are visible.

An unclassified road west takes you to (4km) **Tikøb**. The imposing late 12C Romanesque church here was given by King Hans to Esrum Monastery (p 110) in 1489. Some of the original windows are visible, and both the original doors, though the elegant south door is now walled up. The round-arched windows in the east are from c 1200, as is the porch, though this was later altered. The vaulting in the nave is 15C. The splendid Renaissance pulpit is from the late 16C, and the Baroque altarpiece from 1723. A single bench end is dated 1597, but most are modern.

From Tikøb you continue south on the 235 to the A6, where you turn right and follow this road to (9km) *****Fredensborg Palace**. This magnificent Baroque palace, started by Frederik IV in 1720 and given the name Fredensborg ('Peace Palace') to celebrate the end of the Great Northern War, stands in a large park sloping down to Esrum Lake. The complex consists of 28 buildings in all.

The central section of the palace, designed by Johan Cornelius Krieger, was built between 1720 and 1724, other parts following in succeeding years. The four side wings by Nicolai Eigtved are from 1753, and Laurids de Thurah was responsible for the palace steward's residence and the notably tall chimneys at the corners of the central cupola—necessarily built to this height in order to create sufficient draught. The white palace, with green copper roofs, is approached via an avenue leading to a circus surrounded to the left and right by two-storey buildings each forming three sides of an octagon. To the right of the palace are two lower wings, the knight marshall's residence and the domestic wing, known as 'Damehuset', and between them the chapel, all overlooking a green flanked by long, low buildings on two sides.

The interior of the palace is of a splendour befitting its surroundings. On entering you will come to the hall beneath the central cupola, the **Kuppelsal**, with its ornate stucco ceiling and its marble floor in black and white. The **Garden Room**, too, deserves special attention, having a magnificent stucco ceiling forming a framework around a painting by Henrik Krock representing Denmark and Norway asking the Olympic gods for peace. The Rococo walls are decorated to match, with large-scale paintings of ancient Rome. Hendrik Krock is responsible for other splendid painted ceiling panels surrounded by intricate stucco work by the brothers Sturmberg. A total contrast is the strictly neo-classical 'Damegemakket' (**Ladies' Chamber**) from 1776.

The Baroque **Chapel**, surmounted by a steep saddle roof topped by a ridge turret, is in the form of a cross with a gallery supported by Doric columns below and supporting Corinthian columns above. The pulpit, font and altarpiece are by Friedrich Ehbisch, and the painting in the central panel of the altarpiece is by Hendrik Krock.

Fredensborg was the setting for large gatherings of European royalty during the 19C, when Christian IX could claim to be the father-in-law of Europe. It is still the spring and autumn summer residence of the royal family, but in July the palace and the private garden, **Marmorhaven**, with statues by Johannes Wiedewelt, are open to the public, with **conducted tours** every half hour in the afternoons.

The wooded **park**, which is open to the public all year round, was designed by Nicolas-Henri Jardin in the 1760s. The sophisticated layout with vistas across Esrum lake provides for lime tree walks fanning out from the palace, and in particular a splendid avenue immediately behind it. A walk known as **Nordmandsdalen** presents a remarkable series of figures of Norwegian and Faroese peasants in national dress, commissioned by Frederik V.

From Fredensborg you continue south on the A6 towards (9km) Hillerød. As you approach the town you will, on your right, find a road (RENDELÆG-GERBAKKEN) leading straight to ***Frederiksborg Castle**.

Built on three islets in the Slotssø lake, this is surely the most famous historical castle in Denmark after Kronborg (see p 107). In 1577 the future Christian IV was born here, and as he grew up he decided to create

Frederiksborg Castle

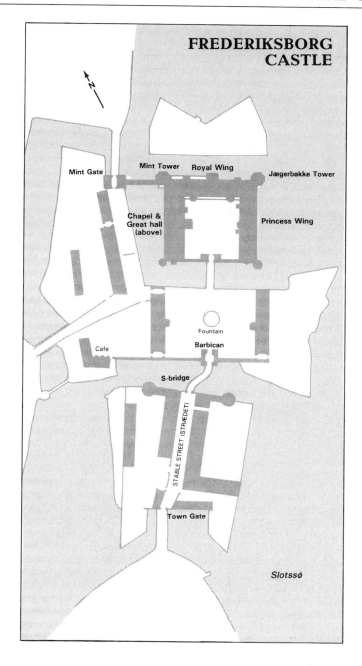

FREDERIKSBORG CASTLE

N

Mint Gate

Mint Tower

Royal Wing

Jægerbakke Tower

Chapel &
Great hall
(above)

Princess Wing

Fountain

Cafe

Barbican

S-bridge

STABLE STREET (STRÆDET)

Town Gate

Slotssø

of it a castle in the grand style. He succeeded in his ambition. In 1599 he started a lodge called 'Sparepenge' (Savings), in which he lived while the old castle was demolished, and the new one built. The Royal Wing was finished by 1605, followed by the Chapel Wing in 1606. The exterior, symmetrically built in Dutch Renaisssance style, was more or less finished by 1611, with the exception of the Princess Wing, which was not completed until 1615. Work on the interior continued for many years, and a good deal of redesigning took place in the 18C. In 1859 the entire castle then went up in flames. Funded by J.C. Jacobsen, the wealthy brewer who founded the Carlsberg Breweries, it was then restored to something like its original state in order that it should become the **Museum of National History**, which it now is. The Chapel Wing (beneath which are the King's treasury and wine cellar) was the least damaged by the fire.

The resplendent **Chapel**, the setting for the coronations of the Danish absolute kings from 1671 to 1840, is one of the most magnificent parts of the present castle. Entered through a sumptuous Renaissance doorway, it is surmounted by intricate vaulting, while the richly decorated arcading on either side supports a gallery running right round. The ebony and silver pulpit and the flamboyant altarpiece, with a silver-gilt relief of the Crucifixion in the main panel, are the work of the Mores workshop in Hamburg, c 1606. The famous **Compenius organ** from 1610 is still in use, and there are recitals on Thursdays from 13.30 to 14.00. The carillon above the chapel plays a hymn melody every hour throughout the summer months.

The **Great Hall** is immediately above the Chapel, but the original was badly damaged during the fire, and this is a reconstruction which, good as it is, lacks the splendour of the original carved panelling. That and the vaulted ground-floor dining room known as **Rosen**, were the first to be completely restored, as they were the ones about which most was known. **Christian IV's Chamber** is another room successfully restored, now containing large-scale paintings by Carl Bloch and Otto Bache portraying events from the life of Christian IV, while the **Audience Chamber** with its lofty stucco ceiling is much as it was in 1688.

As the Museum of National History, Frederiksborg now contains countless relics from the nation's past, including both memorabilia, portraits, coats of arms and paintings depicting scenes of national importance. Added to this there is the outstanding collection of historical furniture which has been gathered from many sources over the past century. Some of the earlier exhibits reflect a 19C Romantic view of Danish history, while later additions to the collection reflect a more scholarly approach.

*Hillerød (pop. 34,700) originated as a village near Hillerødsholm, gaining in importance when Frederik II came into possession of the estate in 1560. It thrived on the numerous visitors to the royal estate, and Frederik II made a vain attempt to establish it as a market town. It grew further under Christian IV, providing for the large numbers of workers and visitors. However, after suffering from a great fire in 1692 it was further reduced in status when the Court moved to Fredensborg in 1720. A certain amount of trade was now developed, until, in 1834, there was another catastrophic fire, followed by yet another a year later.

The result is that few of the old buildings in Hillerød have survived. The establishment of the Museum of National History in Frederiksborg Castle, linked with

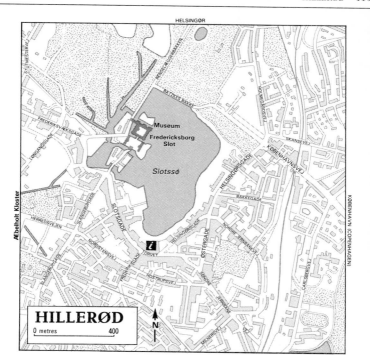

the opening of the railway, has brought new growth, and Hillerød is now a busy, thriving town, an excellent shopping centre, catering for the large numbers of tourists attracted by Frederiksborg.

■ **Tourist information**: Torvet 1; tel. 42 26 28 52.

■ **Hotels**: Hillerød, Milnersvej 41; tel. 48 24 08 00; Missionshotel, Slotsgade 5 A; tel 42 26 01 89.

There are nevertheless a few older buildings still standing, for instance the old parsonage in KANNIKESTRÆDE, the **Lowzowske Gård** from 1758 on the corner of SLOTSGADE and MØLLESTRÆDE, and the **Batzke house** from 1720 on the edge of the Castle Park. The ethnographical museum, **Nordsjællands Folkemuseum**, is situated in HELSINGØRGADE, containing both local historical collections and exhibits reflecting the history of North Sjælland's rural culture.

▶**Excursion from Hillerød to nearby Gribskov forest and Nødebo**
Gribskov forest lies just north of Hillerød and is reached by taking the A6 north and then either the 267 or the 227. (The latter will bring you direct to (6km) Nødebo on the west shore of Esrum lake, a spot of interest in itself, see below.) Gribskov covers 56 sq km and encompasses several lakes. You can wander at

will—but watch it: you can easily get lost! It was a place much loved by the philosopher Søren Kierkegaard, to whom there is a memorial stone at **Stjernen**, about 1.5km west of Nødebo, where he was fond of meditating. His wonderful lyrical description of Gribskov can be found in *Stages on Life's Way*.

Nødebo is the village on the shore of Esrum Lake, just opposite Fredensborg. Its tiny stone-built Romanesque church (with a later and inappropriate ridge turret and belfry) was built by the monks of Esrum Monastery (p 110) and despite later additions has many original features left. There are frescoes from c 1425 and c 1460. Those in the chancel and nave are by the 'Big Nose Master', a series of anatomically impossible figures, many adorned with very large noses. Those beneath the tower are the work of the artistically far superior Union Master. The Baroque pulpit from 1668 is by Esben Børresen. Nødebo also has a **Dolls' Museum** of an unusual kind: dolls in historical costumes, including figures representing Christian IV's daughter Leonora Christine and Queen Victoria. (Open Easter and July.) ◄

▶**Excursion to Æbelholt Monastery**

Take the road west via Tjæreby to (6km) the junction with the A19, where the remains of the Augustinian **Æbelholt Monastery** from c 1230 can be found just opposite the junction. It became a place of pilgrimage for the old and infirm after the early Abbot Vilhelm was declared a Saint and after one of his teeth was reputed to work miraculous cures. Together with a garden of medicinal herbs, there is now a museum on the spot, exhibiting bones and skeletons illustrating illnesses prevalent in the Middle Ages. Little is left of the monastery except the buttresses and foundations of the chapel, although an extensive programme of restoration has been carried out over the past few years. (Open daily in summer; Sat, Sun at other times.) ◄

As you drive south from Hillerød on the 201, on the outskirts of the town you will see, on your left, a modern church, **Præstevang Kirke**, designed by Holger Jensen and built in 1962 to the pattern of the old Viking houses in Trelleborg (p 45).

After 13km the 201 will bring you to **Birkerød**.

■ **Tourist information**: Rådhuset.

Once a village, but now, no more then 20km away from Copenhagen, largely a dormitory town, Birkerød stands in lovely wooded countryside, and there are still a few older buildings to be seen, harking back to former times. Among them the Romanesque church deserves special attention. Dating back to the 12C, this brick-built church contains a good collection of 16C frescoes, including one of the oldest portrayals of Judgement Day; you will also find there the chains worn by the local pastor when imprisoned by the Swedes in 1659. The late Gothic altarpiece from c 1475, with a central panel representing the Crucifixion, was probably made in Lübeck, and the auricular oak font is from c 1650. The Renaissance pulpit dates from c 1600. The important late 19C novelist Jakob Knudsen is buried here.

Just outside Birkerød, to the north, lies **Sjælsø** lake. In the woods nearby there is a restaurant called **Jægerhytten** (The Hunter's Lodge), said to be the spot where the English-born Queen Caroline Mathilde used to meet her court doctor and lover, Count Struensee, in 1770. As a consequence, she ended in exile, he on the scaffold.

4km south on the 201 lies **Holte**, another old village that is now an affluent Copenhagen dormitory. It is magnificently situated, surrounded by woods and on the shore of the idyllic lake **Furesø**.

Holte is mainly residential; there are few really old buildings among the rather fine turn-of-the-century villas, but **Gammel Holtegård**, a mansion built in 1757 by Laurids de Thurah for himself, stands on Attemosevej. To find this, you turn left at the traffic lights in the centre of the town and drive along ØVERØDVEJ towards Vedbæk. ATTEMOSEVEJ is then c 3km on the right. In addition to mounting travelling exhibitions, Gammel Holtegård contains the local archives and a collection of prehistoric finds made in nearby Vedbæk. The central feature is 22 Stone Age skeletons unearthed in 1975; many of them are well-preserved and they are exhibited together with the ornaments and weapons found with them, producing a vivid picture of the life of coastal hunters some 7000 years ago. Follow Attemosevej south now and turn right after 2km into SØLLERØDVEJ, where after a further kilometre you will find the 300-year-old **Mothsgården**, which is a local history museum. Close by is **Søllerød Kro**, one of the finest inns in the area. Continuing along this road, you come back to Holte.

From Holte the main road takes you to (17km) Copenhagen (p 60 ff).

6 • Copenhagen to Århus

Total distance 98km plus ferry (3hrs). 156 to (30km) **Roskilde**. *155, A23 to (68km)* **Kalundborg**. *Ferry to* **Århus**.

The 156 from Copenhagen to Roskilde (p 54) offers only a few minor items of interest; however, from Roskilde to Kalundborg there are two suggested routes. The direct route (total distance 68km) is given first; see below for the alternative route via Dianalund.

Direct route east from Roskilde east to Kalundborg
Total distance 68km.

Leave Roskilde on the A14 south and turn right after 3km into the 155 west, which will take you to (5km) **Kornerup**. Here is one of the smallest churches in the country, with a Romanesque chancel and nave, Gothic porch, 18C porch and 19C belfry. The altarpiece, a triptych, is from c 1500, and the pulpit from 1590.

Continue another 15km and turn left into the A23. After 10km you come to the village of **Nørre Jernløse**. Here there is an interesting 12C Romanesque church with a wealth of decoration on the apse and chancel, and containing some exquisite frescoes from c 1500 representing Christ in mandorla, with Mary and John. There is a late Gothic antemensale, a Baroque pulpit and Renaissance pews for the local aristocracy.

3km north of Nørre Jernløse lies the impressive three-winged Renaissance mansion of **Løvenborg**, built 1630, not open to the public, but clearly visible from the road. It ranks among the finest mansions in Sjælland.

Back on the A23, you now drive 8km and turn right into **Mørkøv**, where there is one of the most richly decorated of Danish *churches. Virtually all the walls and vaulting are covered in a wealth of well-preserved frescoes from c 1450, the work of the Isefjord Master; their unusually light colours result from the techniques used when restoring them in the 1940s.

From Mørkøv you might like to drive southeast on the 231 to the mansion of **Torbenfeld** (2km), the east wing of which was built in the 1570s. The impressive house, standing on a small island, is furnished with towers and spires; the south wing is a much altered medieval building, with cellars from c 1400, while the east wing was built in the 1570s. Two corner towers are from 1906. (Not open to the public.) If you continue along this delightful road, in 3km you will pass another splendid mansion, **Kongsdal**, and, after yet another 2km, arrive at the beautifully restored church at **Undløse**, containing the Union Master's finest work in Denmark (most of this painter's work in fact being in Sweden).

Another brief excursion from Mørkøv is to drive along a small road SW to **Skamstrup** (3km). Here is another church containing a wealth of frescoes, some from c 1350, some by the Isefjord Master from c 1450; among the earlier ones is the oldest authentic—and quite detailed—painting of a ship in Denmark. It is seen in the legendary contest between St Olav and King Harald III of Norway (who was killed by the English King Harold at Stamford Bridge).

From Mørkøv you follow the A23 to (6km) the idyllic village of **Jyderup**, where the small Romanesque church still stands in its entirety, though with later additions. Facing it is the fine half-timbered parsonage. Soon after Jyderup you will drive through the **Grevindeskov** forest, just to the south of which is **Skarresø** lake.

8km beyond Jyderup you reach the 155, where you might like to turn right to **Bregninge** (3km), where again there is a church with a large number of fine frescoes from three different periods. They include a frieze with pictures of the Creation from c 1300, a Wheel of Fortune (1400) and scenes from the life of St Catherine from 1425. The altarpiece, too, from 1654, is a fine piece of Baroque work originally sited in Dragsholm (p 131).

Return now to the A23, where after 2km you could visit the church in Viskinge before driving the last 10km to Kalundborg (see below). The frescoes (1425) in **Viskinge Church**, beautifully restored in 1965, are thought to be based on an altar painting in Wildungen in Westphalia. Of particular interest is the scene showing a serene face on a Christ weighed down under the burden of the cross He is bearing.

Alternative route from Roskilde to Kalundborg—via Dianalund
Total distance 83km.

To take this more roundabout route, you leave Roskilde on the A14 south, turning right after 3km into the 155 west for another 18km. Here you turn left to (3km) Tølløse. The road turns to the right in the village; follow it to 1km Gammel Tølløse, where you will find **Tølløsegård**. This has a history going back to 1370, the present main building being a 1944 recreation of it as it looked at the time of the Renaissance. Continue now via (2km) Nørre Vallenderød to (4km) Ugerløse, then to (7km) Stenlille, turning right there into the 255 towards (5km) Dianalund.

Immediately before reaching Dianalund you might turn left to Tersløse (2.5km), where you will find **Tersløsegård**, once owned by the daughter of Esbern Snare (see below), but most famous as the home of the 18C dramatist, essayist and historian Ludvig Holberg. This is not a museum proper, but it contains three rooms devoted to Holberg, restored to what is thought to have been their appearance when the great writer lived there during the summers of 1745–53. The collection comprises portraits of Holberg, illustrations, early editions and other memorabilia (open Apr–Oct).

From Dianalund you now follow the 255 to (4km) Skellebjerg and from there the 219 west to (4km) Ruds Vedby, with the mansion of **Vedbygård**, dating back to the 14C. The present south wing is from c 1500 and the imposing north wing from c 1540, while the west wing is partly 18C and partly 19C. The great Baroque poet Thomas Kingo was tutor to the family here in 1659. (Not open to the public.)

The 219 now continues to (5km) **Sæby**, where the church contains frescoes from three periods; those in the apse, in an Italianate style, are from c 1150–75 and thus the oldest on Sjælland. Immediately north of the village lies the large **Tissø** lake. To see the lake you should drive north along the 219, which runs along its east side, passing on your right the mansion of **Sæbygård**, where Thomas Kingo also taught the children in his day, and which is the scene of one of his less devotional poems, 'Sæbygaards Koeklage' (The Lament of Sæbygård's Cows)—the object of their lament being the bull which has drowned in the local pond.

From Sæby it is only 5km further along the 255 to **Gørlev**. As a small town, Gørlev has little intrinsic interest, but it is nevertheless the home of the **Gørlev Stone**, one of the most interesting of the Danish runestones. It now stands in the porch of the Romanesque church, the inscription telling us that a certain Thjodvi had the stone raised, after which it lists the entire runic alphabet.

■ **Tourist information**: Algade 47.

■ **Hotels**: Reersø Kro, Strandvejen 46, Reersø; tel. 53 55 90 22; Postgården, Strandvejen 45, Reersø; tel. 53 55 91 18.

Leave Gørlev north on the A22 and drive 9km to Svallerup, where you should turn right to (3km) **Ubby**. The church here is an exceptionally fine late medieval building.

Built in brick by Esbern Snare in 1179, it has an impressive nave lined with four pillars on either side, all with trapezium capitals typical of the buildings attributed to the Hvide family, supporting a series of Romanesque arches. The chancel is also vaulted. The magnificent auricular altarpiece carved in unpainted oak by Lorentz Jørgensen is from 1677. The carved Renaissance bench ends are from c 1600 and the pulpit from c 1620. There is a late Gothic crucifix, the work of the Store-Fuglede Master.

This is an area rich in prehistoric monuments, but those in Ubby are worthy of special attention. There is a dolmen chamber and six passage graves, two of which are double.

From Ubby you can follow the 219 back to (3km) the A22 and go on to (2km) **Rørby**, where, in a church standing on a steep slope and overlooking Kalundborg Fjord, there are 15C frescoes from the Union Master's workshop (only discovered in 1981 and carefully conserved by 1983) and a large Gothic triptych altarpiece from c 1500.

From Rørby it is only 5km along the main road to **Kalundborg** (pop. 19,200).

- **Tourist information**: Volden 12; tel. 53 51 09 15.

- **Hotel**: Ole Lunds Gaard, Kordilgade 1–3; tel. 53 51 01 65.

- **Youth hostel**: Stadion Allé 5; tel. 59 56 13 66.

History

Kalundborg grew up around a castle and church founded c 1170 by Esbern Snare, the brother of Bishop Absalon. The oldest known charter is from 1485. Esbern Snare's castle, built as a defence against marauding pirates, was replaced with a much larger one further to the east by Valdemar IV, but his structure was virtually destroyed during the Swedish occupation of Sjælland 1658–60. All that is now left is the ruins of Esbern Snare's castle in the **Ruinpark** on Lindevej at the west end of the harbour, and those of Valdemar IV's on **Volden** closer to the centre of the town. The original church, on the other hand, still stands as one of the most unusual churches in Scandinavia.

The importance of Kalundborg at the time of Valdemar IV is signified by its role as a place of assembly for the nobility, and it was here that Valdemar signed his coronation charter in 1360. A Benedictine monastery was founded here in the 13C, but became a home farm for the castle after the Reformation, the buildings themselves being razed during the 18C. Kalundborg was an important centre during the Middle Ages, but its role was diminished in succeeding centuries. It regained its importance as a transit port for Århus in the 19C, more particularly with the building of the railway in 1874. Two big fires, one in 1901 and one in 1920, destroyed much of the old town, the former, which burning down about a quarter of the buildings.

Despite these fires, however, Kalundborg has retained much of its old character. Particularly in the west part of the town there is a host of old streets and alleyways, and Kalundborg is the only Danish market town to possess four stone-built medieval buildings.

Esbern Snare's ***Vor Frue Kirke** (Our Lady's Church), built between 1170 and 1190, and now world famous, is the natural point of departure for a tour of the town. Its shape is unlike anything else in Denmark, reminiscent rather of Byzantine or Russian churches. Instead of the long nave and shorter transept, it is in the form of a Greek cross, with more or less equidistant arms. Each of the arms ends in a hefty octagonal tower surmounted with a spire, and an even higher spire towers over the crossing. This major tower, **St Mary's Tower**, collapsed in

Vor Frue Kirke, Kalundborg

1827 due to insufficient foundations, and it has taken two major operations to restore it and the church interior to their original state.

The nave is square, and at the corners there are four granite pillars supporting the central tower. The four outer towers, named after SS Anna, Gertrude, Maria Magdalene and Catherine, rest partly directly on the barrel vaulting of the four arms. In view of the grandeur of the exterior, the vaulted interior seems remarkably small. The altarpiece is an ornate, richly carved Baroque piece by Lorentz Jørgensen, similar to those found in the churches at Køge (p 146) and Helsingør (p 106), with relief carvings of the Birth of Christ, the Last Supper, the Crucifixion, Resurrection and Ascension. The altar crucifix is from the 12C.

Just east of the church, in KIRKESTRÆDE, there is a row of old houses. Walk past these to **Torvet** (The Square), on the east side of which you will find the remains of Valdemar's castle, the tower known as **Folen** (The Foal). Immediately west of the Square is the neo-classical **Gyths Gård** (Gyth's House), where the Norwegian Nobel prize-winner, the novelist Sigrid Undset, was born; there is a memorial plaque on the front. From the Square issue the two main streets of the medieval city, ADELGADE and MUNKESØGADE. Adelgade 6 is the old **Bishop's Palace**, and presumably forms half of a four-winged residence; the west wing, with its imposing gable facing Adelgade, was used as a town hall from 1539 to 1854; after restoration in 1970 it has again been used for meetings of the town council. On the south side of Adelgade there is a row of half-timbered houses, one of which is early 17C.

Now walk past the churchyard, with its medieval mortuary chapel, probably originally the house of one of the priests, to the complex of half-timbered houses known as ***Lindegården** to the west of the church. The oldest of these buildings, forming the north wing on Adelgade, is from c 1650, the rest from c 1755 to 1786. Lindegården is now the ***Kalundborg and District Museum**. This is a delightful museum, one room of which, the Rococo Room, is thought to be by the same team as was responsible for the Lerchenborg mansion (see below). In an area so rich in archaeological finds as this, there are obviously going to be excellent prehistoric exhibits. The Viking Age, too, is well represented, as are the Middle Ages, when Kalundborg was at its zenith. Other exhibits illustrate life in the 18C and 19C, and there are also reconstructions of rooms and a collection of peasant dress from the 19C (open daily in summer; limited opening in winter).

There is a **Local History Archive** at VOLDEN 12, close to the tourist information office; and to the west of Lindegården you will find the ruins of Esbern Snare's original castle.

Returning via PRÆSTEGADE, you will pass the medieval tithe barn in the wall of the churchyard. Continue to Torvet now, cross it diagonally to your left and go down Volden to LINDEGADE and KORDILGADE. In Lindegade you will find more half-timbered houses on the corner of SKIBBROGADE and also, at No. 4, a charming Baroque house from 1763. In Kordilgade, now a pedestrian precinct, there is a fine half-timbered merchant house, **Ole Lunds Gård** (now an hotel and restaurant), as well as the Baroque **Bryggergård** (The Brewer's House). The important 19C painter Johan Thomas Lundbye was born at SKIBBROGADE 8 (south of Kordilgade), and a plaque commemorates this.

3km south of Kalundborg stands the great mansion of *****Lerchenborg**. This is one of the most perfect Baroque mansions in Denmark, built 1743–53 by General Christian Lerche. The design is the general's own, but as he was a close friend of Laurids de Thurah and Nicolai Eigtved, the principal architects of his day, their influence can be guaranteed. Built on symmetrical principles, with a pointed gable over the main entrance and rounded gables at the end, the main wing, in white, comprises 17 windows on two floors overlooking a symmetrically laid-out French garden by Jean-Baptiste Descarrières de Longueville. The south wing and certain other rooms are open to the public, and a visit is a must. The rooms, mainly Rococo, are furnished in the appropriate styles with family portraits on the walls. The vaulted ceiling in the great hall is decorated with white stucco reliefs, setting off motifs from Ovid on the walls. On the top floor there is a collection of prehistoric relics found on the estate. The ubiquitous Hans Christian Andersen was a guest here in 1862, and there are Andersen memorabilia in some of the rooms.

A series of musical events is arranged here in August every year, and concerts are given in the great hall. There is a cafeteria at the entrance to the park, which is also open to the public (open pm late June-mid-Aug; closed Fri).

Close to Lerchenborg you will find the **Asnæs Power Station** (Asnæsværket), the largest in Denmark. Conducted tours are arranged on Tue and Thur in Aug, starting at 10.00 and taking c 2 hours. (Tickets obtainable from the tourist information office in Kalundborg.)

Large DSB ferries sail between Kalundborg and Århus (p 232), telephone reservations 33 15 15 15, and these have now been joined by a hydrofoil, the Cat-Link, that halves the journey to an hour and a half; telephone reservations 89 41 20 00. From Kalundborg, too, you can take a ferry to **Samsø**, telephone reservations 33 15 15 15, a delightful little island filled with summer cottages, and producing the first eagerly awaited new Danish potatoes in the springtime.

7 • Århus to Roskilde via Ebeltoft

Total distance 134km plus ferry. A15 to (29km) Rønde. A21 to (22km) **Ebeltoft**. *A21 to (4km) Ebeltoft Ferry Terminal. Ferry to Sjællands Odde (1hr 40 mins). A21 to (80km)* **Roskilde**.

The direct route from Århus to Rønde takes you on the A15, allowing you occasional glimpses of the sea. At 16km you by-pass **Løgten**, where there is a six-sailed windmill, and a further 13km will see you in Rønde. The more interesting route (36km) takes you inland, via the manor of Rosenholm.

Follow the A15 N, but only for 18km, to a point just beyond Løgten, where you turn left on the 587 to (1km) the 563, which then takes you to (3km) **Hornslet**.

■ **Tourist information**: Tingvej 16.

■ **Hotels**: Den gamle kro, Rosenholmvej 3; tel. 86 9940 07; Gammel Løgten Strandkro, Strandvej 51; tel. 86 99 44 99).

For centuries this area has been deeply influenced by the Rosenkrantz family of Rosenholm (see below), and they have left their mark on the imposing *church, approached through a decorative Renaissance gateway. The earliest known reference to a church here is from 1355, but there is believed to have been one on the spot since the 9C. The central part of the nave is still part of the Romanesque building. Extensions took place in the following century, when the porch was added. In 1560 the Romanesque chancel was demolished and the nave was extended east. Later additions were the elegant tower and the Rosenkrantz family's sepulchral chapel to the south.

There are some very old, but very fine, frescoes from c 1250 on the north wall; their motifs include a castle under attack and also, unique in Denmark, a scene from the legend of Parsifal. The altarpiece is from c 1525, and Claus Berg's centre panel from c 1530 is a splendid and imaginative depiction of Golgotha. It is flanked by English alabaster reliefs from c 1450. Many members of the Rosenkrantz family are buried in the church, which consequently is provided with many ornate gravestones and memorials. A major restoration took place in 1963.

2km north of Hornslet stands the manor of ***Rosenholm**, the Rosenkrantz family seat and one of the most splendid and best-preserved of Danish Renaissance mansions. It was begun in 1559 by Jørgen Rosenkrantz, and has retained its outer appearance almost unaltered since 1600. There are four wings surrounded by a moat.

It is still the home of the Rosenkrantz family, but it is open from mid-Jun to 31st Aug, also Sat/Sun in May, the remainder of Jun and throughout Sep. The furnishings belong to all the different periods during which it has been the family home and include large-scale French and Flemish tapestries and Spanish and Moorish furniture. The large gardens, with their avenues and walks, were designed in the 18C. The Renaissance pavilion from the end of the 16C, known as **Pirkentavl**, is said in fun to be known locally as the first Jutland university, owing to the private academy for the nobility once run there by the rather unorthodox 17C theologian Holger Rosenkrantz. There is a small museum in the cellar, filled with pottery and various objects retrieved from the moat.

Leave Rosenholm by the minor road just opposite the manor and drive to (2km) **Mørke**, where there is one of the largest medieval churches in Djursland (i.e. the peninsula northeast of Århus), dating back to the 12C. The chancel and nave are both Romanesque, as is the very old granite font, and some particularly interesting features are the granite carvings on the south side; above the entrance there is a stone decorated with interlacing patterns like those found in Jelling (p 282), and there are two figures of dragons, one of them apparently eating a man lying beneath it.

A road east will now take you to (5km) **Thorsager**, where, occupying a commanding position at the top of a steep hill, you will find the only round church in Jutland, thought to have been built by Valdemar II —though like that in Horne on Fyn it has suffered from 19C extensions and improvements.

From Thorsager another minor road leads south to (5km) **Rønde**.

■ **Tourist information**: Ceresvej 2; tel. 86 37 23 66.

■ **Hotels**: Møllerens Hus, Århusvej 32, Ugelbølle; tel. 86 37 12 38; Hubertus Kroen, Møllerup Gods, Feldballe; tel. 86 37 10 03.

■ **Youth hostel**: Kaløvej 2; tel. 86 37 11 08.

From Rønde, there is a choice of routes to Ebeltoft—the direct route (19km) via the A21, or the alternative, coastal route (38km; see below).

Direct route from Rønde to Ebeltoft
Total distance 19km.

Follow the A21 east from Rønde as far as (4km) Bjødstrup, where you should turn right down a minor road to (1km) **Møllerup**, a manor house with outbuildings dating back to 1681. The main wing was rebuilt in 1868 and the outbuildings are now partly used as a riding school, partly as a restaurant. The park is open to the public.

The original house is believed to have been built by Stig Andersen Hvide, the 13C folk hero Marsk Stig, who took part in the murder of King Erik Glipping in 1286. Marsk Stig's house was demolished when the new buildings were erected in 1681. Excavations in 1920 uncovered the foundations of the original house, which like the present one had three wings.

Marsk Stig
According to the medieval ballad, Marsk Stig was sent to fight for the king, whom he asked to take care of his wife while he was away. The king did so only too thoroughly, and when he returned, Marsk Stig was greeted by a sorrowful wife, Ingeborg, who told him what had happened and demanded revenge. Marsk Stig then murdered the king, announced the murder according to the custom of the day, and was outlawed for his pains. (The tiny island of Hjelm, where he spent the rest of his life, is some 4km off the mainland coast, and can be seen as you sail from Ebeltoft.)

Møllerup is specifically mentioned in the ballad as the place where Marsk Stig returned to tell his wife of their fate.

Leaving Møllerup, following the same road east, after 1.5km you will meet the A21 again. Here you turn right and drive to (13km) Ebeltoft (see below).

Alternative route from Rønde to Ebeltoft—the coastal route
Total distance 38km

This route takes you on a good unclassified road south from Rønde through wooded, hilly countryside to (2km) **Kalø**. On your right you will find the archetypal romantic ruined castle, King Erik Menved's **Kalø Slot** from 1314, outlined against the sea, standing isolated and inaccessible except on foot (open).

The castle stands on a tiny islet approached by a 500m-long medieval cobbled causeway with a drawbridge giving access to the square courtyard. The tower, 10m high and 12m square and with walls 3m thick, is now the best-preserved part of the original complex, though there are remains of walls and some cellars. The original castle was dismantled on the orders of King Christoffer II, the brother of Erik Menved, but it was presumably rebuilt by Valdemar IV. In 1519 the future King of Sweden, Gustav Vasa, was held prisoner there by Christian II, but he escaped to lead Sweden in its breakaway from the union between the two countries. In 1672 Christian V gave the castle to his half-brother Ulrik Frederik Gyldenløve, the first husband of Marie Grubbe, who dismantled much of it and transported it to Copenhagen in order to build the mansion of Charlottenborg (pp 65, 88).

On the other side of the main road lies **Kalø Hovedgård**, the home farm originally belonging to the castle. The present half-timbered buildings are from the first half of the 18C. It is now used as a training school for hunters and as a biological research station.

From Kalø you drive south along the coastal road with magnificent views across Kalø Bay to (9km) **Knebel**, where there is a Romanesque/Gothic church restored by Axel Skov in 1956. The altarpiece was plundered from the Swedes some 300 years ago.

In Knebel, too, there is a memorial to the people of the Mols peninsula, the 'Molboer', the Danish equivalent of the English Wise Men of Gotham, about whose proverbial lack of intelligence many amusing stories have been told since the 18C. The water in the inlet here, Knebel Vig, is very deep, and afforded a safe harbour for medieval warships.

Just outside Knebel, on a road northeast towards Agri, you will find the 4000-year-old **Poskær Stenhus**, one of the largest of Danish stone circles, consisting of 23 standing stones (some as high as 2m) enclosing a pentagonal chamber.

Leave Knebel on a minor road running south and then west along the coast to (4km) **Tved**, where there is a mainly Romanesque church built largely of undressed boulders, which have been described as being 'of a strange barbaric beauty'. The walls in the west are extremely thick, suggesting that they were once meant as the foundations for a never-completed tower. It contains some

Poskær Stone Circle

well-preserved frescoes from the mid-16C, restored in 1942. The nearby parsonage is a beautiful half-timbered house and outbuildings.

If you drive a further 4km south from Knebel you will come to the imposing mansion of **Iisgård**, built in 1890, close to the mound upon which the original medieval mansion stood. You are in fact now at the tip of one of the forelands of the **Mols peninsula**, with views west towards Århus and southeast to another of the forelands, Helgenæs.

Back in **Tved** the route takes you east to (4km) **Vistoft**, where the Romanesque/Gothic church was restored in 1942 by Axel Skov.

From Vistoft you can, if you wish, turn south and drive across the isthmus to the **Helgenæs** peninsula, again offering extensive views in virtually all directions. At the narrowest point of the isthmus there is a medieval wall, which a doubtful tradition maintains was built by Marsk Stig. Beyond it again there are some 19C entrenchments dating from the Dano-Prussian war of 1848.

Again, the terrain is very uneven, rising to 53m at **Høghøj** in the south. It is here that Saxo maintains that King Harald Bluetooth and his son Svend Forkbeard fought a bitter but inconclusive duel, and where King Harald was then murdered by his archer warrior Palnatoke in revenge for having been forced by the king to shoot an apple off his own son's head. It was in the waters off Helgenæs, too, that Magnus the Good defeated Svend Estridsen in 1044.

If you decide not to take a look at Helgenæs, you should drive east from Vistoft through Fuglsø and follow the glorious road right round **Ebeltoft Vig** (Bay) to (15km) Ebeltoft itself.

Driving along you will have views across the bay, and on your left are the **Mols Bjerge**, one of the more idiosyncratic areas of Denmark formed during the last Ice Age. Like other places called mountains in Denmark, they scarcely merit the name, but admittedly the terrain does rise to 120m just north of Fuglsø and, at **Agri Bavnehøj**, even to 137m—though this is too far from your present route to be seen. There are, meanwhile, several roads leading off the coastal road, and they will take you further into this moorland and woodland area, with its varied animal and plant life. There are excellent parking facilities.

*EBELTOFT (pop. 13,400), lies on a natural, sheltered harbour, and this is presumably the reason for its having been established here in the Middle Ages. In the present century, of course, it is also conveniently situated close to Tirstrup (Århus) airport.

■ **Tourist information**: Torvet 9; tel. 86 34 14 00.

■ **Hotels**: Hvide Hus, Strandgårdshøj, tel. 86 34 14 66; Ebeltoft, Adelgade, tel. 86 34 10 90.

■ **Youth hostel**: Søndergade, tel. 86 34 20 53.

History

Ebeltoft was granted a charter in 1301 by King Erik Menved, possibly as a sign of gratitude for its help against the outlaws living on the island of Hjelm nearby. Little is known of its medieval history, though there is a reference to the church there in 1458.

It suffered severely during the 17C wars with Sweden, and after some recovery of its shipping it lost most of its gains during the Great Northern War (1700–21) and went into a period of stagnation from which it was long in recovering. Attempts to build a new harbour were successful for a time, but it was not until the 19C that better times really came. The local mayor then borrowed church funds (without permission) to build a new harbour. The project was successful, though the mayor nevertheless lost his job over it.

Even in the 20C, however, growth in Ebeltoft has been modest in comparison with that in nearby Grenå, probably largely because the main railway system never reached Ebeltoft. Ironically, however, this lack of modern developments has led to Ebeltoft's special position as a tourist attraction offering a modern version of much that is traditional in a small Danish town, with cobbled narrow streets and a wealth of unspoilt old houses. And despite its apparent outlying position, it offers a car ferry terminal to Sjællands Odde and is thus a very convenient transit point for motorists wanting to travel between Jutland and Sjælland. Allow yourself plenty of time to savour the charm of this now thriving Lilliput town.

Ebeltoft boasts the smallest town hall in the world, a single-storey half-timbered building topped by a small spire. It was built in 1576 and restored twice in the 18C and finally in 1909, when it was opened as the **Ebeltoft Folkemuseum**, mainly exhibiting furnishings and equipment from the locality, as well as archaeological and Siamese collections. The old lock-up lies beneath and is also open to the public. It now forms part of the Ebeltoft Museum, the other two parts being the **Dyer's House**, the oldest dyeworks in northern Europe, unchanged since the 19C, and **Helgenæs Vicarage**, with its collection of items of local interest.

If you walk down either NEDERGADE or OVERGADE, you will come to KIRKEGADE and **Ebeltoft church**. It was referred to as a 'chapel' in 1458, but has since been extended. There are frescoes from 1521, discovered in 1919 and since restored. The nearby old parsonage is now a doll museum, **Missers Dukkemuseum**, with a comprehensive collection of dolls and other old toys of many kinds (open summer).

In Overgade there is a large, well-preserved merchant's house, and there are others in ADELGADE, one of them having an outside gallery in the courtyard. However, it is the general atmosphere of an old provincial town, with its many small houses, many now scheduled, which constitute the main attraction of Ebeltoft. You will perhaps not find many imposing houses, but you will move into a past age. And that is emphasised, if you happen to spend the night there, by the presence of town 'watchmen', who patrol the streets and at intervals sing

Ebeltoft

out the old watchmen's rhymes telling the inhabitants what time it is and assuring them that all is well.

You will inevitably go down to the harbour, where you will find the frigate *Jylland*, launched in 1860. After many years of being left to rot, this fine old man-of-war is now restored to its former glory (open).

At STRANDVEJEN 8 there is a **glass museum**, where over 500 artists from 40 countries have 4000 works on show. A glassworks has been established at the side of it, and visitors can watch glass blowers demonstrate their skills (open summer).

Round trip to the area northeast of Ebeltoft
Total distance c 26km.

This short trip starts on a minor road northeast to (3km) **Dråby**. This delightful, idyllic village with its charming thatched cottages has an unexpectedly large 13C church with buttresses to the north and south, popularly known as **Mols Cathedral**.

One assumes that Dråby was once a harbour, and that the church originally belonged to the nearby Skærsø estate. This, at least, would account for the size of the church. To the east there is an apse, and to the west a slender and graceful stilted tower. There are frescoes from the 15C and 16C, some by the Isefjord Master. The rather bombastic Baroque altarpiece, with life-size figures of SS Luke and John, is from c 1700. The church was restored in 1967–70 by Inger and Johannes Exner.

In Dråby, too, you will find the manor farm of **Lyngsbækgård**. The main house, in what is known as Jutland Baroque, was built in 1784, and the principal half-timbered outbuildings, now protected, are two years younger.

You leave on a minor road north which will take you through (3km) Stubbe, along the south side of Stubbe Sø lake, through Gravlev to (5km) **Hyllested**, again an unspoiled village with narrow streets and thatched cottages.

Hyllested Church has a wealth of frescoes from c 1500, those in the nave by the Brarup Master. They were not discovered until 1967, and they have been conserved as near as possible to their original state. They represent both biblical scenes and grotesque fantasy figures. Outstanding is the Brarup Master's painting of the Creation.

East of Hyllested stands the late 16C manor house of **Rugård** (1km). With its two towers and its fortress-like appearance, Rugård is slightly forbidding. It must certainly have been forbidding to local people in the days of one of its owners, Jørgen Arnfeldt (d. 1717). He was a fanatical witch-hunter, who on the slightest excuse rounded up women he suspected of witchcraft, and had them 'tried' in the lake outside the house. If they floated, they were rejected by the waters and thus guilty—and so burned or tortured to death in the cellars as soon as they were dragged out. If they sank, they were innocent—but much good did that do them!

From Hyllested you drive west to (3km) Fuglslev, where you bear left after the church to (2km) Øksenmølle. Now turn left again into a road which takes you the west side of Stubbe Sø and back to (10km) Ebeltoft.

Direct route to Roskilde

Ebeltoft **ferry terminal** (Færgehavn) is c 4km south of Ebeltoft. This is one of the shortest ferry routes between Jutland and Sjælland with a sailing time of 1 hour 40 minutes, and a planned reduction to 45 minutes with the introduction of a catamaran service, telephone reservations 89 52 52 52. Jutting out into the sea here you will find a large windmill park which provides Ebeltoft with its electricity. And nearby is the holiday village, **Øer Maritime Ferieby**, with some 300 holiday cottages offering first-class accommodation and splendid facilities for 2400 visitors. The village has been built on an artificial saltwater lake which is entered via a lock. As might be expected, Ebeltoft is equipped with a first-rate marina at Ebeltoft Skudehavn, nearby.

Odden Ferry Terminal is right at the tip of the narrow spit of land on the northwest corner of Sjælland, known as Sjællands Odde (Sjælland Point). It is a low-lying area covered with weekend cottages, but otherwise with few salient features. On the other hand it has its historical significance.

7km along the A21 from the harbour, you will come to **Overby**, where you might want to make a short stop.

The waters around Odden were the site of a naval battle between the pride of the Danish navy, the 'Prins Christian Frederik', and a British naval squadron in 1808, when Denmark and Britain were on opposing sides during the Napoleonic Wars. It was a one-sided battle, which the Danish ship lost; it blew up and sank with the loss of 64 sailors and 129 wounded. The hero of the battle was a 25-year-old lieutenant, Peter Willemoes, who has become famous in Danish history.

In Overby the dead from the battle are buried in a common grave, and there are other memorials to the Battle of Sjællands Odde. A model of the *Prins Christian Frederik* hangs in the church, and the names of those killed are inscribed on oak panels. A memorial column by Thorvaldsen's pupil Vilhelm Bissen stands in the churchyard, inscribed with a poem by N.F.S. Grundtvig, whose father was pastor here from 1766–76.

The church itself has an early Gothic nave, with late Gothic extensions. Ironically, perhaps, three British airmen from World War II are also buried in the churchyard.

Now continue east along the A21 to (7km) **Lumsås**, from where you might make a detour by turning off left to visit (10km) Nykøbing Sjælland and its surroundings.

▶**Nykøbing** (pop. 7000) is full of tourists in summer, attracted by the wonderful beaches in the area, but it also has other things to offer. In

Kirkestræde there is the **museum**, with excellent collections of local historical interest; its gardens are themselves a museum, full of medicinal herbs (open summer).

■ **Tourist information**: Algade 52; tel. 53 41 08 88.

■ **Hotels**: Klintekroen, Klintvej 158, Klint; tel. 59 32 11 91; Klintebjerg, Havnevej 13, Klint; tel. 59 32 00 95.

■ **Youth hotel**: Egebjergvej 162; tel. 59 93 00 62.

2km south, near the coast road, you will find **Anneberg**, where there is a museum exhibiting, among other things, antique glass and Chinese porcelain (open summer). A further 3km will bring you to **Sommerland Sjælland**, a large-scale pleasure park with all kinds of family entertainment.

Instead of driving back through Nykøbing, from Anneberg you can head west, cross the 225 and drive to (5km) **Højby** to experience the impressive and high-lying church there for the sake of its magnificent Gothic frescoes. They are from c 1380 and of very high quality indeed, portraying Judgement Day, the voyage of St Olaf, St George and the Dragon, and the martyrdom of St Stephen. The bench ends in the church are from 1555 and are splendidly carved, and the altarpiece is a triptych from c 1630. The pulpit is from 1656.

Now drive another 4km west and you are back on your main route again. ◀

▶ If you decide not to visit Nykøbing, you follow the A21 south from Lumsås, perhaps taking a look at the double passage grave known as the **Troldstuer** after 1km, on your left. 2km further south, also on your left, you will find a road leading off to **Stenstrup** (1km), where you might visit the excellent ethnological museum containing many of the archaeological finds from the area here which is unusually rich in prehistoric monuments (open summer).

Still following the A21 south you will soon find yourself in **Trundholm Mose** (Trundholm Marsh), an area full of burial mounds. It is here the famous Early Bronze Age Sun Chariot ('Solvognen') was discovered in 1902. Now one of the great treasures of the National Museum, this represents a horse (the earliest model of a horse found in Denmark) pulling a six-wheeled chariot on which stands a gold-plated bronze disc representing the Sun. The wheels are themselves of particular interest in being the earliest known example of spoked wheels in Denmark. The Sun Chariot is thought to be a model of a full-sized chariot of similar nature, and is a clear indication of sun worship in Bronze Age Denmark. It was presumably deliberately broken and sunk in the marsh as a sacrifice. The marsh had been drained by 1902, and the chariot was turned up by a plough.

10km south of Lumsås you will reach the 225, and here there is an opportunity for an interesting detour, 17km out and 17km back again. ◀

▶ Leave the A21 and follow the 225 west which takes you along the coast through hilly countryside to **Høve** (8km), where there is a lively modern museum illustrating the development of this area over the ages. Continue now to **Fårevejle** (4km). Here there is a museum (open summer) showing the history of the stretch known as the Lammefjord, which was drained at the end of the

19C by the construction of an embankment across the narrowest point of the fjord. Much of the fertile land thus uncovered is below sea level. The museum also contains exhibits associated with the Earl of Bothwell, the third husband of Mary Queen of Scots, who was imprisoned in the nearby Dragsholm Castle (see below), and who is buried in Fårevejle Church. A mummified body in the church is said to be his, though this is by no means certain.

To see **Dragsholm Castle**, you follow the 225 another 4km south, turning left 1km after you have passed the 231. Standing 1km away from the main road on what was once a narrow spit of land, the only link between Odsherred to the north and the remainder of Sjælland, it dates from 1250, and once belonged to the Bishop of Roskilde. After the Reformation the bishop was forcibly turned out, and the king put his own lieutenant in. Later, Dragsholm became a prison for State prisoners, of whom the most famous was the Earl of Bothwell. He died here. During the Swedish wars Dragsholm was badly damaged, but it was rebuilt at the end of the 17C and given more the character of a Baroque palace, the appearance it now has. Today the castle is an hotel—said to have no fewer than three ghosts—and restaurant, and some of the historic rooms, the cellars and the park are open to visitors on application. Hotel bookings by phone 39 40 02 77.◀

11km after crossing the 225 the A21 brings you to the embankment across the **Lammefjord**. Old maps show that the Lammefjord used to stretch almost across to the west coast, virtually dividing Odsherred off as a separate island.

As part of the campaign to make up for the territory lost to Germany after the 1864 war the work of building the 2km-long embankment across the narrow part of the fjord was begun in 1873. This, together with a system of drainage canals, led by 1907 to the water level having dropped by 4.8m, and by 1943 by 7.5m, providing a huge cultivable area (5764 hectares), most of it of high quality soil. If you stop on the embankment and go to the top of the sea wall, you will gain some impression of what has been achieved.

8km later, you are on the outskirts of the village of **Tuse**, where there is a whitewashed church dating back to Romanesque times, though with many Gothic features. This church is particularly interesting for its very fine frescoes from the Isefjord Master's workshop, extending from the childhood of Christ to the Day of Judgement. The Three Kings are seen confronting three skeletons, while a girl churning butter is mocked by two devils. There is, too, a particularly graphic representation of other devils chasing people into Hell.

From Tuse you continue east, and in only 6km reach **HOLBÆK** (pop. 32,200).

■ **Tourist information**: Jernbaneplads 3; tel. 53 43 11 31.

■ **Hotels**: Strandparken, Kalundborgvej 58; tel. 53 43 06 16;
Jernbanehotellet, Jernbanevej 1; tel 53 43 41 06.

■ **Youth hostel**: Algade 1; tel. 59 44 29 19.

This is one of the oldest towns in Sjælland, with charters going back at least until the end of the 13C, by which time it was the seat of a Dominican monastery. It probably grew up around a castle built by Valdemar II (the mound on which it stood is still visible to the west of the town, near the shore), and owed its original success to the fact that the small medieval ships could sail into its harbour without difficulty.

It maintained its position until the late 17C, but then suffered from the Swedish wars, and only began to make progress again with the increase in the corn trade in the late 18C. The 19C brought industry, and Holbæk's geographical position on the railway between Copenhagen and Kalundborg has maintained its economic strength.

One of the striking aspects of Holbæk is the width of its main street, ALGADE, quite unusual in Danish provincial towns and giving it a rather special atmosphere. There are still a few old houses to be seen in Holbæk, the best preserved of which, at KLOSTERSTRÆDE 14–16, is now the Holbæk Museum (see below), standing next to the elegant old town hall from 1844. In the museum courtyard an old house from 1660 has been rebuilt after being removed there from its original position close to the harbour. In the courtyard of Algade 28 there is another two-storeyed half-timbered house dating partly from the Renaissance and partly from 1719. Other more modest half-timbered houses, mainly from the 18C and early 19C, are still extant. Nothing remains of the Dominican monastery except the remains of the old south wing, which now form the parish hall of the 19C **Sankt Nicolai Kirke** which, unusually, stands north–south. The hall was partially rebuilt and used as a mortuary chapel, but it was restored in 1972–74 and put to its present use.

The *Holbæk Museum in Klosterstræde, which is part of a complex of old buildings dating from 1660 to 1667 was founded in 1910, and contains no fewer than 51 exhibition rooms. As one of the best of Danish provincial museums, it is well worth a visit, both for the very special atmosphere created by these old buildings, and for its excellent collections. There are re-creations of old rooms and shops and exhibits reflecting the development of the area from prehistoric times to the German Occupation. Of particular interest is the collection of pottery and silver.

A museum of a different kind is the **Zonen Museum** in SKYTTENSVEJ 2, just to the west of the town centre. Zonen was the name of an ambulance, fire and rescue service which finally joined its former rival, Falck, to form the present Falck-Zonen, which operates all Danish emergency services, including ambulances. This museum is in the form of an emergency station from the 1930s and includes both vehicles and equipment (open school holidays).

While you are in Holbæk, the church at *Tveje Merløse 3km south on the A57 should really not be missed. It is one of the more unusual Danish village churches, dating from c 1125, probably built by the same Asser Rig who built the church at Kirke Fjenneslev (p 51), and thought by some to be a reduced-size copy of Roskilde Cathedral (p 55). It is larger than Fjenneslev, and its Romanesque character has been preserved, with windows with rounded arches, but the most notable feature is the twin towers, again reminiscent of Fjenneslev. Unlike Fjenneslev, however, this church is more or less in its original form, and is thus unique in Sjælland. There are some important frescoes from c 1200 in the apse, and the altarpiece is by Joakim Skovgaard.

We suggest that instead of taking the direct road from Holbæk to Roskilde, you make the following detour.

▶Follow an unclassified road east through Tjebberup until, at 8km, you cross Bramsnæs Bay on the **Munkholm Bridge**, opened in 1952.

On the far side, on the left, you will see the 18C **Langtved Færgekro** (Langtved Ferry Inn), echoing the time when it was necessary to be ferried across the straits here. It is a place with literary associations, both the mid-19C poet Christian Winther and the later 19C novelist Henrik Pontoppidan having been associated with it, while the surrounding area is scattered with burial mounds and kitchen middens.

It is worth stopping here, to admire the fine view and to walk through the forests with their prehistoric remains, while short drives in various directions will bring you to idyllic and unspoilt villages. Take, for instance, the 53 road north to (2km) **Ejby** and another 3km to **Kirke Hyllinge**, where the chancel arch in the church is decorated by the oldest known fresco on Sjælland. Drive 4km further north on the 53, turning right on a minor road past the mansion of Krabbesholm to (2.5km) **Gershøj**, with its healing spring. Here the road goes south through **Sæby** (with its idyllic parsonage) and then right along the coast through Lyndby, finally joining the A21/23 to (23km) Roskilde. ◀

If you choose not to take this detour, but to continue along the road east after Bramsnæs Bay, you proceed past Ryegård Deer Park. At the far edge of the wood, some 3km beyond the bridge the road passes the late 19C mansion of **Ryegård**, with a history going back to 1350.

After another 4km you join the motorway to (13km) Roskilde (p 54).

8 • Rødbyhavn to Ringsted

Total distance 112km. 153 to (18km) **Maribo**. *To (9km) Sakskøbing. (28km)* **Vordingborg**. *A22, unclassified roads, 265 to (32km)* **Næstved**. *A14 to (25km)* **Ringsted**.

Rødbyhavn, established when the old ferry port of Rødby found itself 5km from the coast with the draining of Rødby Fjord in the 1930s, is the port of entry to Denmark on arriving from the German port of Puttgarden.

■ **Tourist information**: Færgestationsvej 6; tel. 54 60 45 46.

■ **Hotels**: Lalandia; tel. 54 60 42 00; Danhotel, Havnegade 2; tel. 54 60 53 66.

You are on the island of **Lolland**, one of the flattest parts of Denmark (the highest point in South Lolland is only 22m). Some of the island is below sea level, and there are 60km of dykes to keep out the sea. It is an agricultural region famous for its beet crops. At the time of the Valdemars the region was the target of raids by the Slavic Wends, and some placenames (e.g. Kramnitze) still record their presence. In a later age, in the 19C and 20C, there was an influx of Polish workers eager to take part in the beet harvests. They, too, have left their mark.

You leave Rødbyhavn on the 153 and drive to (5km) **Rødby** (pop. 7000).

■ **Tourist information**: Vestergade 1; tel. 54 60 41 10.

■ **Hotels**: Euro Hotel E4, Maribo Landevej 4, Rødby; tel.54 60 14 85; Eggerts Hotel, Østergade 61, Rødby; tel. 54 60 12 01.

There is now little to show that Rødby was a thriving ferry harbour for centuries. Indeed, there is little to indicate its age, as it suffered from a series of fires in the 18C, that of 1774 leaving only five houses standing. A century later, in 1872, Rødby suffered further devastation from catastrophic flooding. Apart from a warehouse on the corner of Østergade and Sædingevej, there is hardly anything from before the 19C, except the carefully restored half-timbered **Willers Gård** in VESTERGADE, from 1729. In Vestergade, too, there is the old excise booth from 1690. The elegant town hall is from 1853.

Rødby experienced a period of growth in connection with the opening of the direct route to Germany in 1963, and in 1981 it was able to celebrate its 750th anniversary by erecting a fountain in the market place symbolically representing wild geese resting on their way.

From Rødby there are two routes to Sakskøbing: the direct route (23km) via Maribo, or the alternative route via Nysted (47km), which takes you through charming countryside (see below).

Direct route east to Sakskøbing via Maribo
Total distance 23km.

Just 2km north of Rødby, on the 153, you drive through **Sædinge**, a village in which the Brarup Master has been responsible for the frescoes in the church. Then drive 2km north, to follow the 297 east to visit **Holeby** (3km), where the area's first sugar beet factory was built. It still stands, though it is now a paper mill. On HØJBYGÅRDVEJ you will find, too, a museum, **Polakkasernen**, illustrating the work of the Polish girls who used to come annually to take part in the beet harvest (limited opening, summer). Beet harvesting may not sound particularly romantic, but it must be appreciated that beet and the sugar produced from it have had an inestimable significance for this part of Denmark.

Højbygård manor, which was the site of some of the earliest attempts to produce beet sugar at the end of the 19C, stands 2km south of Holeby. It dates back to c 1400, though the present buildings are from 1761. Note the huge granary.

Back on the 153 you drive direct north to (9km) the beautiful and historical town of **MARIBO** (pop. 11,350) situated on the narrow neck of land linking two lakes, Nørresø and Søndersø, around which there are now footpaths for those wanting a delightful walk.

■ **Tourist information**: Torvet 1A; tel. 53 88 04 96.

■ **Hotels**: Hvide Hus, Vestergade 27-29; tel. 53 88 10 11. Ebsens, Vestergade 32; tel. 53 88 10 44.

■ **Youth hostel**: Søndre Boulevard 82B; tel. 53 88 33 14.

History

Maribo has grown up around a Bridgettine convent founded in 1416 by King Erik of Pomerania at the wish of his mother, Queen Margrethe I. Queen Margrethe had herself been brought up by the daughter of St Bridget of Sweden, and it had been her wish to create a Danish equivalent to Vadstena, the home of the Bridgettine Order. The religious centre was constructed according to a vision of St Bridget, and was to provide a monastery to the south and a convent to the north. The monks and nuns were to be strictly segregated. The galleries used by the nuns to separate them from the monks and the congregation still exist in the church, which has had the status of Maribo Cathedral since 1809.

The convent was not closed at the Reformation, and the last Catholic nun did not die until the 1570s, after which the convent became a Lutheran 'adelig jomfrukloster', i.e. a religious house providing accommodation for the unmarried daughters of the nobility. These particular daughters frequently caused scandals, and the king had the establishment closed in 1624. The church belonging to it became the parish church of Maribo. The convent buildings continued in existence for some time, and Leonora Christine, the imprisoned daughter of Christian IV, after her release from Copenhagen Castle in 1685, was allowed to live in it until her death in 1698. She is now buried in the cathedral, and her minute coffin is visible through a window in the crypt (lit by a clearly indicated switch nearby).

The *cathedral, with a lofty main nave 60m long and two almost equally lofty aisles, was built 1410–70, and is unusual in that the choir is to the west, according to the wishes of St Bridget. The vaulted roof is supported by a series of octagonal columns. The original tower was demolished in 1736, but the remainder of the cathedral has retained much of its original character, not least thanks to a careful restoration carried out in the 1860s. A particular treasure is a late 14C painting representing St Bridget herself. It is thought to be the oldest extant painting on canvas in Scandinavia, but has suffered greatly from the ravages of time and is kept in the dark. Permission to view can, however, be obtained. A few remains of the convent and monastery are to be seen to the south of the cathedral. A further relic from Bridgettine days is the fact that the Cathedral bells are rung six times daily.

Outside the area associated with the cathedral there are some well-preserved tiny old houses which are still in use, some dating back to the end of the 18C. On the town square, TORVET, there is the splendid **Quades Gård** from 1825, a town house with a dignified neo-classical façade. There, too, is the old town hall from the 1850s. Close by, in JERNBANEGADE 22, is **Lolland-Falsters Stiftsmuseum** (Diocesan Museum), with extensive historical and archaeological collections, not least a room dedicated to the story of the Polish beet pickers, who once were an annual feature of Lolland. It also contains a collection of 13C crucifixes. Jernbanegade 24 houses the **Lolland-Falster Art Gallery** with an extensive collection of Danish art, including many major works, from 1750 to the present day. At MEINCKESVEJ 4, beautifully situated behind **Bangshave**, the park behind the cathedral, there is an open air museum, **Frilandsmuseet i Maribo**, exhibiting farm buildings from Lolland-Falster (open summer).

The poet and dramatist Kaj Munk was born in a house on the market square.

The actual house has given way to a supermarket, but there is a plaque in the wall commemorating him. A statue to Kaj Munk stands to the right of the town hall.

▶ A novel excursion can be made from Maribo on the **Museumsbane**, a private railway, the oldest in Denmark, through 8km of idyllic scenery close to the Knuthenborg Safari Park (p 162) and nearby Bandholm (p 162) with its excellent yachting facilities. ◀

3km east of Maribo in **Engestofte**, a Gothic church and a mansion are well worth a visit. The small church is surmounted by a ridge turret from 1660 and there is a north chapel from 1786, designed as a mortuary chapel and now used as a porch. The nave is in the shape of five sides of an octagon. The original lancet windows have been preserved on the northwest wall, and the interior is covered by cross vaulting. There is an ornate triptych from c 1510, originally from Maribo Cathedral. The centre panel is dominated by the Virgin, crowned and carrying the child Jesus. She is surrounded by five angels, and flanked by two saints on either side. The main figures on the very beautiful side panels are those of St Bridget and St Clare.

Engestofte mansion has a history going back to 1393, but the present harmonious building in yellow and white is from 1805–07. Until 1967 the manor was in the ownership of the Wichfeld family, and in the church there is a memorial plaque to the Scottish-Irish wife of one of the last members of the family, Monica Wichfeld, (b. Massy-Beresford) who was active in the Danish Resistance movement and ended her days in a German prison in 1945. In the woods nearby stands the half-timbered **Engestofte Hospital** from 1770; this was not a hospital in the modern sense, but rather a hospice, a home for the poor of the Engestofte estate.

From Maribo you follow the 153 and drive north to (9km) Sakskøbing (see below).

Alternative east route east from Rødby to Sakskøbing—via Nysted
Total distance 47km.

You drive east from Rødby on an unclassified road to (4km) **Tågerup**, where the Romanesque/Gothic church on your left, in which the Romanesque window in the chancel has been reopened in modern times, has frescoes from three different periods—1425, 1450 and 1500. It is those by the Brarup Master in the vaulting of the nave that are of particular interest. In their portrayal of biblical scenes they show a striking realism: Adam is seen both in Paradise and, later, hard at work in the fields, while Eve is working with a distaff, surrounded by her children, one of them with a whip and top. A runestone bearing the inscription 'Åsten's sons raised this stone after their brother Spærle, Esbern Næb's skipper', lies outside the porch.

1km further brings you to **Lungholm manor**. Its history goes back to 1450, but the present imposing main wing is from 1857, standing between, unusually, two oblique side wings from 1639. It is now a large riding stable. It also offers a wolf park and museum, the only chance in Denmark to see wolves in (well-fenced-in) natural surroundings (open summer). The house itself is open for conducted tours.

Continue now through (2km) **Errindlev**, turning left after 1km to drive north past (2km) **Bremersvold manor** from 1802. 1km further north you will see on your left **Kærstrup**, a manor house standing behind a moat and with a history going back to the 12C. The present elegant building is from 1765, though it was considerably altered and spires added in 1836. The 297 is now a kilometre further on, and here you turn right for 9km later to follow the 283 to (14km) Nysted.

Surrounded by wooded countryside, **NYSTED** (pop. 5600) is a delightful small coastal town, one of the smallest market towns in Denmark, with charters going back to 1409.

■ **Tourist information**: Adelgade 65; tel. 53 87 19 85.

■ **Hotels**: Hapimag, Stubberupvej 17; tel. 53 87 15 50; The Cottage, Skansevej 19; tel. 53 87 11 25.

As might be expected in a town of this kind, there are many old houses, often half-timbered, in streets which have kept much of their original character. In ADELGADE, where many of the half-timbered houses are to be found, you will also discover a large, two-storeyed half-timbered warehouse. Where Adelgade enters TORVET, the large early Gothic church (c 1300) stands, surmounted by an elegant lantern spire from 1649–50. At the north end of NY ØSTERGADE the **old watertower** has now been transformed into an observation tower, offering magnificent views, and with exhibits on four floors as you go up (open June–Aug).

Close to Nysted is **Aalholm Castle**, first mentioned in 1329, though its origins probably go much further back. Valdemar IV is known to have stayed here, as did several later monarchs. The present imposing though rather forbidding building, said to be one of the oldest inhabited castles in Europe, certainly contains sections surviving from the 14C, though other parts reflect 19C alterations.

Countess Amalie Raben of Aalholm was one of the great inspirations for the 19C poet Emil Aarestrup, who lived in Adelgade from 1827 to 1838 as the local doctor. It was to her he wrote some of his finest love poems. Others he wrote to his wife, with whom he had 12 children.

From Nysted an unclassified road leads north through (3km) **Kettinge**, where there is an old Dutch mill and a bird park (both open summer). From there the 297 takes you to (2km) Frejlev, from where you might like just to drive 4km further east to visit the delightful **Frejlev Skov**, the most southerly beech forest in Denmark, with many prehistoric monuments.

3km northeast of Frejlev you will pass the mansion of **Fuglsang**, built in 1869, but with a history dating back to the 15C.

2km later take a minor road left to (2km) **Toreby**. The enormous church here, the biggest village church on the islands of Lolland and Falster, has a history which can be traced back to the early 11C, when there was a wooden church here. Then a stone apse was fixed, and extension after extension was built in the 13C, 14C and 15C, resulting in the present impressive building.

Now take the A9 west, arriving in 7km at the village of **Radsted**, where the large Romanesque/Gothic church has for centuries been associated with the owners of the early 16C mansion of **Krenkerup**, which you will find 1.5km off the main road just opposite the church. Krenkerup is not open to the public, but can clearly be seen from the west.

From Radsted it is only 3km to Sakskøbing.

SAKSKØBING (pop. 9400) is an old town surrounded by wooded countryside and standing by an ancient ford. Its position made it an important traffic centre in the Middle Ages; now an important centre for the sugar beet industry and the site of a large modern sugar refinery.

■ **Tourist information**: Torvegade 4. tel. 54 70 56 30.

■ **Hotel**: Saxkøbing, Torvet; tel. 53 89 40 39.

■ **Youth hostel**: Saxes Allé 10; tel. 53 89 60 45.

There is a pleasing market square with a bronze statue (1940) by Gottfred Eickhoff representing two Polish beet pickers, while in the park in front of the church there is a bronze statue by Lise Ring: *Girl with Umbrella*. The heavily rebuilt **church** dates back to the 13C and contains a pre-Reformation altarpiece and a finely carved pulpit from 1620.

Of the old buildings in Sakskøbing, one of the finest is the 18C **Wichmanns Gård** in TORVEGADE. Also in Torvegade, in what is now a bank, there is a memorial to one of Sakskøbing's most famous residents, the mid-19C poet Emil Aarestrup. He is remembered today for his elegant love poems, often humorous, and sometimes daringly erotic for the time.

On the southern outskirts of the town, you will find an amusing **watertower**, in which the head-like shape of the upper portion has been exploited to provide a smiling face surmounted by a hat (open).

A road northwest leads 4km to the mansion of **Orebygård**, its towers rising majestically above the fjord and clearly reminiscent of Frederiksborg Castle (p 112). The park is open to the public.

From Sakskøbing you drive northeast along the 153, turning left after 2km to **Berritsgård** (1km), a dignified and well-preserved brick-built mansion from 1586, once the home of Arild Huitfeldt (1546–1609), Chancellor and the author of an important early history of Denmark. Adjoining the main house there is a huge barn from 1789. Note the avenue stretching in a straight line due north from the house to the Guldborg Sound, 7km away. Now drive back to the main road, turn left and proceed to the (10km) **Guldborg Sound**, which you cross by the 170m-long bascule bridge built in 1933–34. You are now on the island of **Falster**. 2km after the bridge you might turn right to **Brarup** (2km), where the Romanesque/Gothic church displays a wealth of frescoes. Those in the apse and chancel are from c 1300; those in the nave, covering all the wall space, date from the end of the 14C and are by the Brarup Master, who has been given his name from this church. The altarpiece is late Gothic. c 1450.

1km west of the 153, in **Kippinge**, is likewise an impressive historical church, crowned with a lofty lantern spire from 1701. This was one of the most important Danish places of pilgrimage in the Middle Ages, said to possess a relic of the Holy Blood. Consequently, it has been richly endowed, and still has some splendid furniture which was restored to its original colouring in 1928. In the chancel there are frescoes from 1300–50. The exquisite auricular altarpiece was richly carved in 1633 by Jørgen Ringnis, who was also responsible for the auricular pulpit two years earlier. There are two Gothic crucifixes, one from 1350, the other from 1400.

After the Reformation the relic remained an object of veneration for some time, but it is thought then to have been destroyed, and a triptych from the late 15C representing the crowning of the Virgin took its place. This in its turn gave way to a holy spring nearby, St Søren's Well, to which people travelled from afar, and which still exists. The significance of this shrine is confirmed by the fact that Christian IV's wife, Kirstine Munk, visited it in 1642—and was scolded by the king for kneeling before the altar, praying, he said, for his early death.

Continue now north on the 153, after 8km crossing the old **Storstrømsbro** (Storstrøm Bridge—Storstrøm being the name of the waterway crossed at this point). When it was opened in 1937 this 3.2km-long bridge was the longest in Europe—and the second longest in the world. It still carries both road and railway, but the carriageway is no longer sufficient for all the motor traffic across the water here, and so in 1985 the new Farø Bridges (p 150) were opened 5km to the east, carrying the E47 motorway. The bridge will bring you to (3km) **VORDINGBORG** (pop. 20,100), on the island of Sjælland.

■ **Tourist information**: Algade 96; tel. 55 34 11 11.

■ **Hotel**: Kong Valdemar, Algade 101; tel. 53 77 00 95.

■ **Youth hostel**: Præstegårdsvej 8; tel. 53 77 50 84.

History

Thanks to the castle which used to stand here, Vordingborg is one of Denmark's major historical towns, with charters going back to 1415 and possibly beyond. It is to be supposed that the town of Vordingborg grew up around the royal castle which was founded at the time of Valdemar I. The site was strategically important, ideally suited to expeditions against the Wends, and a natural spot for the ferry between Sjælland and Falster. It was not, however, a geographical position favouring rapid development, and Vordingborg's role during the Middle Ages seems to have been limited.

It was the castle that was important. Exactly when it was founded is uncertain, but it certainly existed under Valdemar I and, judging by piles driven into the fjord to prevent enemy ships sailing in, it was fortified long before this. Valdemar II extended it, as did Valdemar IV. Both Valdemar I and Valdemar II died here, and Valdemar IV was buried in the castle chapel until Queen Margrethe I had his body taken to Sorø monastery chapel. It was Valdemar IV who built the Goose Tower, which is the only part of the castle now standing intact.

The castle was the scene of meetings of the Danehof State Council, and it was here that the greatest of the Danish medieval laws, the Jutlandic Law, was signed by Valdemar II in 1241. The first phrase of this Law, 'With law the land shall be built', is known to every Dane and adorns the façade of the old Law Courts in Copenhagen.

Vordingborg remained a small town throughout the Middle Ages, still deriving its main importance from the castle, where both Frederik II and Christian IV were in residence for a time. In the 17C it was enfeoffed to

Prince Jørgen, the younger brother of Christian V. Prince Jørgen then married Princess Anne, the future Queen Anne of England. In this connection it is interesting to note that the music known in England as Purcell's (or Jeremiah Clarke's) Trumpet Voluntary is in Denmark known as Prince Jørgen's March! In 1655 the town was struck by the plague, and in 1658–60 it was totally plundered by occupying Swedish troops. In the 18C it became a garrison town (as it still is), but it was seriously damaged by a series of fires. It was not until the mid-19C that real growth occurred, thanks to the advent of the railway with the resultant easier access and the potential for industrial development. This trend was further helped by the building of the Storstrøm Bridge.

Very little remains of older buildings in Vordingborg. The old chemist's shop in ALGADE is from 1826, and there are old houses in RIDDERGADE, opposite. The important 19C novelist Meir Aron Goldschmidt was born at Algade 133 in 1816 and is commemorated by a plaque on his home. (His novel *A Jew* is partly set in Vordingborg.) The former **town hall**, from 1845, standing in Algade, is also a dignified neo-classical building, now used as a courthouse and lock-up.

It must, however, be the extensive ruins of the **castle** which are the main attraction. It was once an enormous complex, and the outer walls, of which several stretches are still to be seen, extended over a total of 650m; there were eight towers, of which the **Goose Tower** still stands (open summer).

In the castle complex you will find the **Sydsjællands Museum**, part of which is in what was once Prince Jørgen's Castle. The museum's exhibits cover the prehistory and history of this area, the oldest being a 12,000-year-old spear and arrow heads. There are naturally many exhibits connected with the history of the castle and with the town's military history, together with others of ethnographical interest—a reconstruction of a peasant's living room, a collection of costumes, a display of craft implements. There is also a room dedicated to Goldschmidt. Within the castle complex is a botanical garden with over 300 medicinal and culinary herbs.

The large **Vor Frue Kirke** church is Gothic, mid-15C, though the chancel may be from c 1400. There is a fresco of the Crucifixion on the chancel arch; both this and others discovered in the vaulting over the chancel are the work of the Helligtrekonger ('Three Kings') Master responsible for the Christian I Chapel in Roskilde Cathedral. The magnificent rood screen is from the same workshop. The ornate altarpiece, depicting the Crucifixion, is by Abel Schrøder from 1641, and the rather unusual Renaissance pulpit is from 1601. In the south aisle there is a late Gothic altar with a relief of St Anne. Most of the bench ends are from the 1930s, but there are six from the 1590s.

There are some fine mansions in the Vordingborg area. If you take the A22 north, after 1km you will find, on your left, a road leading towards **Rosenfeldt** (1km). Much of the complex was built 1776–78, of bricks taken from the ruins of Vordingborg Castle, but the main Renaissance-style building, giving on to a grass-covered octagon surrounded by lime trees, is from 1868–69. Having seen this, you should go further east along the curious **Knudshoved Odde** (Knudshoved Point). It juts 15km out into the sea. You can only drive half-way along it, to a car park, but then you can walk to the end if you wish, with the sea lapping the land to either side. There are numerous prehistoric remains on the Point.

1km northeast of Vordingborg, just south of the A59, you will find **Iselingen**, built in the style of an Italian villa by a Swiss businessman in 1802, a spire being added in 1920.

You leave Vordingborg by the A22, making a short detour into the village of **Kastrup**, only 3km north of the town, to see the Romanesque church there. It is built of unhewn boulders, unusually asymmetrical in shape, and with walls varying enormously in thickness. Standing on high ground and dedicated to St Clement, the patron saint of seafarers, it has retained two of its original windows in the north wall and one in the south wall. The altarpiece is late Gothic, c 1500, and there is an early Gothic (c 1300) crucifix as well as a great deal of other early church furniture.

Now drive north another 4km to a minor road east pointing towards (3km) Sværdborg. We suggest you leave the main road here and go across country.

In **Sværdborg** there is yet another church with some unique and fascinating frescoes. There is a host of them in the vaulting, including a primitive baptism, taking place in a barrel, and with God's hand raised in blessing and the Holy Spirit in the form of a dove swooping down to the spot where the font once stood. However, the really special ones are a series of apocalyptic pictures depicting the end of the world, showing the seas rising, the trees covered in red dew, towns and houses destroyed and fire devouring the entire Earth.

Follow this minor road through (2km) Lundby, turning right on the main road and then at the Romanesque church left to drive to (2km) **Lundbygård**, a manor given by the king in 1660 to one Svend Poulsen, better known as 'Gøngehøvdingen', in recognition of his determined (and bloody) opposition to the Swedes during the 1657–60 occupation. The present neo-classical main building of Lundbygård is from 1815, restored 1910 and 1943. The east wing is now a **museum** containing prehistoric exhibits found in the area.

After a left turn the road will bring you north to (2km) the main 265, where you turn left again and proceed to (5km) **Mogenstrup**. Here a sacred spring, St Magnus' (i.e. Mogens') Well was once the scene of midsummer fairs; the Romanesque church contains good frescoes from c 1425, signed *Martinus bene fecit*. Originally, as is common in this area, there was only one window in each wall of the nave; these original windows are bricked up now and have been replaced by others, but their outlines are still visible.

The road now continues to (10km) *Næstved, (pop. 45,350).

Næstved

■ **Tourist information**: Købmagergade 20A; tel. 53 72 11 22.

■ **Hotels**: Vinhuset, Sct. Peders Kirkeplads; tel. 53 72 08 07; Kirstine, Købmagergade 20; tel. 55 77 47 00.

■ **Youth hostel**: Frejasvej 8; tel. 53 72 20 91.

Næstved is a garrison town, and the Royal Guard Hussars parade through the streets every Wednesday morning. Wednesday and Saturday are market days, and on Saturdays in June and July there is musical entertainment in the pedestrian precincts.

History

Næstved certainly goes back to the 12C. At the mouth of the Suså river (the longest in Sjælland) and on the intersection of important roads from Ringsted and Slagelse, it was ideally placed for the development of a market town. Its earliest surviving charter is from 1426, but there were earlier ones. A monastery was founded here in c 1200 (on the site just outside the present town now occupied by Herlufsholm School), and Næstved was of sufficient consequence for medieval kings to visit it regularly and for important negotiations to take place here. The loss of the monastery at the Reformation was a blow to the town, as was the Swedish occupation between 1657 and 1659. A Danish garrison was subsequently established here, bringing some financial benefits, but the real improvement only came in the 19C with the growth in agriculture and the development of industry thanks to the advent of the railway running from Køge to Vordingborg. Further growth came after 1930 when the present harbour was established, and now Næstved is the biggest town on Sjælland after Copenhagen.

Næstved has grown up around the main square, **Axeltorv**, and it is in this area that the largest concentration of old buildings is to be found. There are two churches, Sankt Peders and Sankt Mortens. **Sankt Peders Kirke**, standing on the square by the same name, is a large, imposing Gothic building 56m long and 20m high. The tower is 35m. In the east wall of this tower and in the north arcade of the nave there are traces of an earlier Romanesque church, of which nothing else remains. Unlike any other church in Denmark, the chancel is in the form of seven sides of a decagon, with lofty pointed windows and buttresses. Among the frescoes there is one of Valdemar IV and his Queen, Helveg, kneeling before the Trinity, presumably done soon after the king's death in 1375. A late Romanesque crucifix hangs beneath this. The choir stalls are from c 1500, while the carved pulpit from 1671 is one of the major works of Lorentz Jørgensen, with reliefs of Adam and Eve. The bench ends in the closed pews are from 1580, the work of a local master.

Sankt Mortens Kirke is also Gothic and brick-built, but much smaller. This, too, is built on the site of an earlier Romanesque church, of which remains can be seen. There are frescoes showing St Martin of Tours, the patron saint of the church, but the main glory of this building is the exuberant 6m-high auricular altarpiece from 1664, the work of Abel Schrøder, the organist in this church for 42 years, showing reliefs of the Passion, the Last Supper, the Crucifixion and the Resurrection. The panels are divided by twisted columns. The pulpit, from 1602, is thought to be the work of Abel Schrøder's father. There are pews for the local nobility, dated 1598, and there are other bench ends from 1577.

On the north side of **Sankt Peders Kirkeplads** square you will find the medieval **town hall**, the only one of that time extant in Denmark, the oldest part being from the first half of the 15C. The ornate gable overlooks the road. Next to it on the left there is a beautiful half-timbered house from 1606, and on the right is **Gøyernes Gård** (The Gøye House), in which are incorporated the remains of a stone-built house from the 16C.

On the south side of Sankt Peders Kirkeplads there is a row of medieval brick-built houses. The oldest of them, **Gottschalk's House** (No. 8) dates from c 1400, and its western extension is from 1500. To the east of it are seven houses

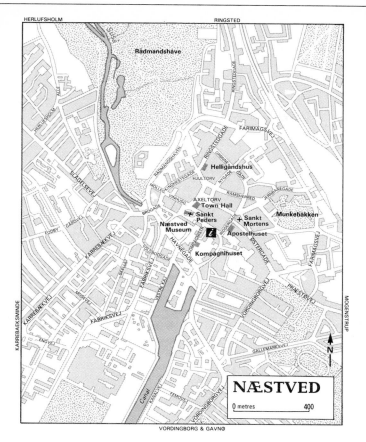

from 1482, probably shopkeepers' and artisans' houses, now known as
*Mogens Thuesens Stenboder (Mogens Thuesen's Stone Houses); two of
them now form part of **Næstved Museum** (limited opening). The row ends in
the east with the old grammar school, in which the early philologist and folk-
lorist Peder Syv lived from 1659–64 as headmaster. In KOMPAGNISTRÆDE, just
to the east, there is the 15C guildhall, **Kompagnihuset**, the only extant
medieval guildhall in the country. It has recently been restored, but is not open
to the public.

  None of these, however, is the oldest building in Næstved. That honour goes to
the old hospital, the **Helligåndshus** (The Holy Ghost House) on
RINGSTEDGADE, which is mentioned for the first time in 1398. It is now also
part of Næstved Museum and houses excellent exhibitions of local history and
handicrafts as well as a splendid collection of old carvings.

  A further house to be viewed is the half-timbered **Apostelhuset** (The Apostle
House) in RIDDERGADE, so called because there are reliefs from 1520 of Christ
and the twelve Apostles in the mullions between the windows of the façade. The

house was originally a guildhall. There are other half-timbered houses here and in Møllegade, Vinhusgade, Østergade and Ringstedgade.

In HJULTORV square you will find a tiny equestrian statue, reputedly the smallest in Denmark, standing opposite the courthouse. Conversely, there is an enormous statue of a troll near the **Munkebakken** hill, representing the legend that a great troll once set out to bury Næstved in sand, and dropped it all outside the town.

On the outskirts of the town, to the northwest, on HERLUFSHOLM ALLÉ, you will find **Herlufsholm School**. When the Benedictine monastery was closed after the Reformation, the buildings came into the ownership of Admiral Herluf Trolle who, together with his wife Birgitte Gøye, left the buildings to a trust as a school. It has since become one of the most distinguished of Denmark's ancient boarding schools, the school chapel is open to the public from May to Sept and contains a *crucifix from 1230, on which the body is carved from a single ivory tusk, the largest such in Europe.

Herluf Trolle and Birgitte Gøye lie in sarcophagi behind the altar, and the historian Arild Huitfeldt is also buried here.

Herlufsholm School overlooks a wooded park, Rådmandshaven, to the north of which there is the **Herlufsholm Pinetum**, a plantation of conifers established in 1890 and containing an array of coniferous trees, many of which are alien to Denmark. The pinetum is open to the public, and there are good parking facilities.

One of Denmark's great houses, **Gavnø**, is just outside Næstved. It is reached by driving south on the A22 to the southern outskirts and then turning right through Appenæs to Gavnø (3km).

As the name suggests, Gavnø was originally an island, but it is now connected to the mainland by an embankment. In 1398 Queen Margrethe I acquired it and founded a Dominican convent. Part of this still exists in the present chapel. After the Reformation the nuns were allowed to live here as before, but on their deaths the convent was secularised and adapted for use as a private mansion. It was further modified in the late 17C and finally in 1755–58 transformed into the magnificent rococo house of today—which nevertheless still bears traces of its medieval origins.

The house contains what is said to be the largest private art collection in Scandinavia—over 2000 paintings. Among them are the oldest extant portraits in Scandinavia, dating from the 15C and painted on wood. Of particular interest, too, is the sumptuous panelled **chapel** from 1401, which has been developed from the medieval convent chapel. The carved altarpiece is by Abel Schrøder, 1670, and the main panel is framed by 44 coats of arms; a further 16 coats of arms form the framework to the top panel. The pulpit, standing on a headless troll with his face on his stomach, is also from the Schrøder workshop. It was partially restored in 1913, when repairs were carried out to the bench ends, many of which are from 1576 and 1651–53. One rarity is a bridal pew from the late 16C.

A major tourist attraction in the spring is also the *Park with a host of tulips and other bulbs. An attraction of a different kind is the **fire engine museum**, also in the Park. Both the Park and the house are open to the public from 1 May to 31 Aug.

▶A trip out from Næstved along the 265 west will, after 7km, bring you to a fork. Take the left fork and drive to the delightful **Karrebæksminde**, or across the tiny bridge to **Enø**, both places providing you with marvellous bathing beaches.◀

▶The area east of Næstved also has its attractions. Leave on the A54 and drive as far as (7km) Holme-Olstrup; following the road left you pass **Holmegård** (2km), a mansion from 1635. This house, which is privately owned, has given its name to the parish and to the world-famous **Holmegård Glassworks**, 2km further on (open daily). Here you can see glass-blowing as well as the techniques of modern glass production. There is also a glass museum here and a shop where you can find good bargains.◀

You can now return to Næstved via (1km) **Fensmark**, where there is church from the time of Valdemar I. The 19C poet Christian Winther (1796–1876) was born in the idyllic parsonage here, as is recorded on a stone.

Leave Næstved on the A14, driving north through (14km) **Herlufmagle** and on to (9km) **Vetterslev**, where another splendid altarpiece from 1671 by Abel Schrøder is to be seen, as well as an auricular pulpit from 1628. While here, you should drive 3km northwest to the village of **Vrangstrup**, where you will find one of the smallest and most unusual *churches in Denmark, dating from c 1200. This asymmetrical but charming building bears many traces of its Romanesque origins. On the north side it has changed little since it was built, while on the south side a late medieval porch surmounted by a thatched ridge turret has been added. This church, too, possesses an altarpiece and pulpit by Abel Schrøder, as well as bench ends from 1550. And there is a host of late Gothic frescoes in the vaulting. For obvious reasons, the church is kept locked, but the key can be fetched from the house just opposite—and some key it is, too!

Now return to the A14 and continue to (6km) Ringsted (p 52).

9 • Copenhagen to Gedser

Total distance 155km. 151 to (39km) **Køge**. *(54km)* **Udby**. *E47/E55 to (31km) Ønslev. E55 to (31km) Gedser.*

It is possible to cover all this route on the E47 and E55, but we suggest other and more interesting routes. The trip to Køge is not exciting, though the coast road does have its compensations these days when you reach Ishøj. You can either take the motorway E20/E47/E55 and drive south to Junction 31, turning off there at **Jersie Strand** and joining the 151 south. Or you can take the 151 all the way from Copenhagen and drive through the suburbs and ribbon development all the way to (38km) Køge. If you take the 151, however, you will drive close to the grandiose project from 1980: **Køge Bugt Strandpark** (Køge Bay Beach Park), 7km of beaches, with artificial lakes and facilities for bathing and boating. There is a splendid marina, constructed around two islets, and now the imposing **Arken, Museum of Modern Art**, sleek and low in profile like the hull of a white ship. Built for Copenhagen as the European City of Culture 1996, and with over 9000 square metres, it houses galleries, a concert hall, theatre, cinema and restaurant and promises to be a highly individual cultural centre of real quality. It can be also reached by S-train to Ishøj Station, from where there are buses. Open daily 10.00–17.00, Wed 10.00–22.00, closed Mon.

Ishøj has in recent years made great efforts to provide a range of facilities: near the station there is a huge shopping centre also including a concert hall and swimming pool, and only a couple of kilometres to the north, in fact between two motorways, is a small wild-life park.

From Ishøj the road continues close to the coast to Køge, (pop. 31,000).

Køge

■ **Tourist information**: Vestergade 1; tel. 53 65 58 00.

■ **Hotels**: Hvide Hus, Strandvejen 11; tel. 53 65 36 90; Centralhotellet, Vestergade 3; tel. 53 65 06 96.

■ **Youth hostel**: Vamdrupvej 1; tel. 53 65 14 74.

History

Køge originated as a village at the mouth of the river and near a suitable ford, close to the present-day Gammel Køgegård. It was established in its present position during the 13C, where it thrived on herring fishing and trade with Germany. King Erik Menved gave Køge a charter in 1288, and throughout the Middle Ages Køge was an important trading centre. A large church, Sankt Nicolai Kirke, was built in the 14C. In 1484 King Hans established a Franciscan monastery which existed until 1531, when the buildings became a hospital. In 1633 there was a great fire, and the town suffered further from Swedish occupation during the 17C Swedish wars. It was also the scene of one of the great Danish naval battles, the Battle of Køge Bay (1677).

Unlike many other Danish towns, Køge was spared further major fires, and thus still has many of its older buildings—there are said to be more half-timbered houses here than in any other Danish town except Ribe (p 203). It experienced a new period of growth in the 19C with the advent of the railways, and it now has a direct S-train connection to the capital.

The broad market square, **Torvet**, with its statue of Frederik VII, is the biggest provincial market place in Denmark and the obvious place to start a tour of the town. The medieval whipping post, where the local prostitutes—referred to as 'Køge Hens'—were punished, is no longer there, but many of the older buildings are. The **town hall** has a neo-classical façade from 1803, but behind it there are buildings going back to 1552, making this the oldest town hall in the country still in use as such. To the left of it stands the old lock-up, which has now been incorporated into the complex. In the courtyard behind there is a fountain from 1979.

The building next to it is made up of two merchant houses with courtyards, from 1610 and 1619. It now houses the *****Køge Museum**, a splendid collection of local antiquities, distributed through 30 rooms. There are furnished rooms illustrating the style and manner of living of the area, costumes, furniture both ornate and simple, implements, coaches, and old coins—including selections of two very large hoards of silver coins discovered in 1978 and 1987, one weighing 35kg and thus the largest find of silver ever made in Denmark. Both hoards were presumably hidden from the occupying Swedes in the 17C. Another important archaeological feature is the **Strøby Egede Grave**, a find made on the coast just southeast of Køge. The grave from 4000 BC contained the skeletons of three adults and five children, the greatest number yet found in a grave of that age.

Køge

A literary curiosity is a windowpane taken from the nearby inn, *Norske Løve*, on which Hans Christian Andersen scratched the words: 'O God, O God, in Køge'. Out in the courtyard there is a butcher's booth from c 1500, moved there from the Square, where it was in use until 1914. (Open all year.)

In the wall of a corner shop opposite the the museum there is a plaque commemorating the 'Køge House Cross'—a supposed visitation by the Devil which resulted in the burning of several witches in 1612.

NØRREGADE is the pedestrian shopping area, and the original character of many of the buildings is hidden behind modern shop windows. It illustrates the good general principle that one should keep one's eye on the upper storeys, where there are still plenty of signs of the original half-timber construction. No. 29, a former school building, is a well-established art gallery of an unusual kind, **Køge Skitsesamling**, with sketches and models by 20th-century Danish artists. It also puts on regular visiting exhibitions. Open Tues–Sun 11.00–17.00, closed Mon.

The east end of the great **Sankt Nicolai Kirke*, Køge's main church, overlooks Nørregade. The church stands on the site of an earlier brick-built church from the first quarter of the 14C, some of which is incorporated in the tower to the west. This tower was long an important landmark, and it was used by Christian V as a vantage point from which to watch the Battle of Køge Bay. The main nave, vaulted and flanked by Gothic arcading and vaulted aisles on either side, is from 1375–1400. In the 15C there were some 15 side altars, none of which has survived. The choir loft is unusual in being decorated with a mixture of Evangelists, Muses and symbols of the Arts and Senses.

Køge church is one of the most richly furnished in the country, and the pulpit and canopy by Hans Holst from 1634 are probably the finest example of 17C Danish carving. The carved Baroque altarpiece from 1652 by Lorentz Jørgensen is also among this master's most outstanding works. The black marble and porphyry font is from 1613, holding a dish of Nuremberg silver from 1635. There are both Gothic and Renaissance bench ends, but the main impression is made by the 104 magnificent Baroque pews from 1624. Over 150 tombstones are found in the church, more than in any other Danish church except Roskilde Cathedral (p 55).

If you leave the church by the main entrance you will come into KIRKESTRÆDE, where just to your left in front of the library you will find the oldest datable half-timbered house in Denmark, with the year 1527 over the doorway. It now houses the children's library. Walking back through Kirkestræde towards Torvet you will find a whole row of old houses, including No. 13, **SMEDEGÅRDEN**, with two 16C benches outside.

Now cross Torvet diagonally to BROGADE, where there are yet more old half-timbered buildings, most of them again carefully restored. No. 7 is **Jensens Gård**, with storehouses in the yard; it has been carefully restored to give an idea of a complex of merchants' warehouses. The art gallery **Køge Galleri** is now housed here. No. 17 is **Langkildes Gård**, where the large silver hoard was found, and No. 19 is **Hugos Gård**, a 17C half-timbered house with a cellar from c 1300, now a wine bar.

The last road leading from Torvet, VESTERGADE, also contains some impressive buildings, of which the two-storeyed **Richters Gård** from 1644, now a restaurant, is outstanding.

There are many more old merchants' houses in Køge, and most of the courtyards are open to the public. The tourist information office here organises guided tours of them in summer.

Now continue along Vestergade and cross the ring road. Some 200m beyond, on the left, you will find an old avenue leading to the mansion of **Gammel Køgegård**. Here you can park your car and walk the 500m right up to the house, which is private, but has a park open Wednesday, Saturday and Sunday afternoons. Turn right in the courtyard, walk another five minutes west and you will reach the beautiful wooded, as well as geologically interesting area, **Køge Ås** (Køge Ridge) containing the enclosed graveyard, **Claras Kirkegård**, with the tomb of Nicolai Frederik Severin Grundtvig. He lies there with his second wife, Anna Marie, who was the sister of the then owner of Gammel Køgegård.

From Køge you have the choice of two major routes as far as **Nykøbing Falster**. The direct route (93km) is detailed first. For the alternative route (134km), via the island of Møn, see below.

Direct route from Køge to Nykøbing Falster
Total distance 93km.

Leave Køge on the 151 south, until, in 15km, you reach a road to your right to (7km) **Haslev** (pop. 13,900; **Tourist information**: Torvet 5A; tel. 56 31 52 00) a smallish town known as an educational centre, having both a folk high school and a teacher training college, each connected with the evangelical wing of the Danish Church, 'Indre Mission'. This is decidedly 19C provincial Denmark, with only a couple of small half-timbered cottages to remind one of the time when Haslev was a village. The **museum** on FREDERIKSGADE does, of course, contain exhibits from earlier days, the horse-drawn fire-engine and other exhibits reflecting its beginnings as a station town.

Haslev is an excellent centre from which to visit some of Denmark's more famous great houses. A minor road southeast leads to **Bregentved* (3km), the largest estate in Sjælland. There was a castle here in the days of Erik Menved, but the present white Rococo buildings are relatively modern. The north wing is from 1650 and the south and east wings from 1886–91; the chapel is from 1735. The park is open to the public, but the house is private.

Note the long **Holte Avenue** of 551 lime trees, planted in 1751, established in honour of Frederik V by the then owner Adam Gottlob Moltke. Hans Christian Andersen was a frequent 19C visitor here, and it was here that he wrote the beginning of *The Ugly Duckling*, the introductory scene being inspired by Bregentved park. The final scene, however, in which the swan comes into its own, is the park of the other great house in the area, Gisselfeld.

*Gisselfeld, with its red brick walls and corbie gables, stands 4km south of Haslev on the road to Vester Egede. Isolated on a tiny islet in the middle of a lake and approached by bridges on either side, it has a history going back to 1370. The present Renaissance castle was built between 1547 and 1575 by Christian III's seneschal Peder Oxe, who for a time was the virtual ruler of Denmark. The house is private, but the park with its beautiful lake and some 400 different tree and bush species is open to the public from Palm Sunday to October. The greenhouses, which are also open, contain many rare species. In the old watchman's house there is a museum illustrating the history of Gisselfeld.

Just southwest of Gisselfeld you will find **Hesede Skov** (Hesede Woods), an idyllic and charming forest area with a famous 19C restaurant, the Villa Galina.

Leave Haslev on the road southeast to (8km) Olstrup, where you rejoin the 151, passing the lakes. Torup Sø and Ulse Sø, on the way. You are now 3km from the crossroads at **Rønnede**, a town which itself is of no particular interest, but lies close to several places worth a visit.

In **Kongsted**, 2km southeast of the crossroads, there is a large late Gothic church with a splendid array of frescoes from c 1450 on the walls, and vaulting in the nave. Those in the vaulting illustrate the childhood and Passion of Christ, those on the walls consist of figures of saints together with a number of coats of arms. It is from this church the fresco painter called the 'Kongsted Master' is given his name. The altarpiece is from 1600 and the Renaissance pulpit from 1619.

With the church on your left you can now drive on a minor road to the 154, turn right and immediately left to **Lystrup** (3km altogether), a mansion from 1579 in Dutch Renaissance style by the same architect as was responsible for Vallø Castle (p 151).

Return now to Rønnede, cross the 151 and the motorway as far as **Vester Egede** (4km), where you turn left to go to **Sparresholm** (3km), a Renaissance mansion from 1609 consisting of a main wing and two short saddle-roofed side wings from about 1700. The **Sparresholm Vognsamling** (Sparresholm Carriage Museum) exhibits over a hundred horse-drawn carriages of many kinds dating back to the 17C, and is the only museum of its kind in Denmark (open summer for groups by arrangement only).

Now follow the 151 20km south. Here, just before the road dives under the motorway, on your left, lies the charming early 19C **Udby Kro**, one of the Royal Privilege Inns. These inns have a history going back to the 12C, when Erik

Glipping decreed that a system of inns should be built every 40km on important roads. Until 1912 they were only for bona fide travellers, and local people were not allowed to use them. There are now 113 such inns left, of which Udby is an excellent example.

You will find **Udby** itself just west of the 151 after you have passed the motorway. This is a very special village, both because it is largely unspoiled and possesses a great deal of intrinsic charm, and also for its historical association with the great hymn-writer and educationalist Nicolai Frederik Severin Grundtvig, who was born in Udby parsonage in 1783. He spent his childhood here and returned in 1811 to be his father's curate until 1813. On a 38m mound to the west of the church there is a 2.5m-high memorial stone to him. The parsonage, from c 1650, is still in use, but one of the four wings is the **Grundtvig Museum** (open pm Apr–Oct). The parsonage garden, a miniature park—and the subject of one of Grundtvig's best poems—is always accessible, but visitors are asked only to use the paths clearly indicated.

The Romanesque **church** consists of an apse, chancel and nave with Gothic vaulting. There are frescoes from five different periods: ranging from the late 13C to c 1578. The altarpiece from 1585 is by the prolific Sjælland master, Bertel Snedker of Vordingborg. The granite font is Romanesque and the pulpit early Renaissance from 1584.

From Udby we suggest you take the E47/E55 motorway south to (14km) the ***Farø Bridges**, Farø being the name of a small island in the straits between the islands of Sjælland and Falster. The new bridges carrying the motorway were opened in 1985, and consist of a low-level bridge from Sjælland to Farø, immediately followed by a high-level bridge from Farø to Falster, a total of 3322m in length. The central section of the high-level bridge is supported by two enormous concrete pylons which can be seen from far away. If you leave the motorway and make a brief stop on Farø, you will find there Denmark's sole **Traffic Museum**.

At 5km (Junction 43) you leave the motorway again, taking the 293 west to (5km) **Nørre Alslev**. Here in the church there is a most unusual and very famous late 14C fresco depicting a medieval chain dance, with a king and a bishop as well as lesser mortals holding hands and joining the dance. But the dance is led by—Death.

There are two other friezes like it in Denmark, one at Jungshoved near Præstø (see below), the other at Egtved (p 28). The theme is particularly associated with a frieze with the same motif in Lübeck in North Germany. Hence the Danish way of speaking of someone looking seriously ill: he looks like Death from Lübeck. The Nørre Alslev frescoes are the work of the 'Elmelunde Master' (see below) and is one of a large number of frescoes from four different periods in this church.

Now follow an unclassified road south for 5km and turn left into **Eskilstrup** (2km), the home of **Lolland-Falster's Tractor and Motor Museum** (open summer; limited opening winter). For those with literary interests it must be mentioned that, 5km further east, lies the village of **Torkilstrup** where, in the idyllic parsonage, Bernhard Severin Ingemann was born.

From Eskilstrup you can join the E55 and head south to (5km) Nykøbing Falster (see p 159) or—alternatively take a minor road south as far as to (5km)

Stubberup, from where you drive another 2km east to **Tingsted** (2km). In the Romanesque church here are again frescoes from 1475–1500 by the great 'Elmelunde Master', an artist of rare imagination and humour who here paints scenes from the life of Christ, but supplements them with the Wheel of Fortune and a little episode in which a Devil is spoiling the milk as it is being churned, the whole interspersed with intricate floral decorations. From Tingsted another minor road will take you to Nykøbing Falster and the E55.

Return to Stubberup, and drive south on the E47 to (5km) Nykøbing Falster (p159).

Alternative route from Køge to Nykøbing Falster—via Stevns peninsula and the island of Møn
Total distance 134km.

You leave Køge on the 209 southwest. After 4km you turn right and then 1km further left into a beautiful avenue of trees leading you to (3km) ***Vallø Castle**. The history of the castle goes back to the time of Christoffer II, but the present dignified Renaissance building is from 1580–86, with later additions in 1651 and (by Laurids de Thurah) 1735–38. Since the 18C it has been an 'Adelig Jomfrukloster'—a home for the daughters of the aristocracy—but wider access has been possible since 1976. The house is not open to the public, but the courtyard is, and the magnificent park is open throughout the year, as is the adjoining deer park, where suitable paths are clearly marked. The old Vallø inn just opposite the castle entrance comes in very handy and is very good.

From Vallø Castle, we suggest you do not return via the long avenue, but take the road east to (1.5km) **Valløby** village. There is a church here dating back to Romanesque times, but it is mainly Gothic with elaborate Renaissance additions, of which the magnificent east gable is the most striking. It completes the new Renaissance chancel from 1590, one of the few in the country.

On leaving Valløby you have the problem of getting across the **Tryggevælde river**, which virtually cuts off the **Stevns peninsula**. You will have to turn north on the 209, as though going back to Køge, turning right after 2km on the 261, initially a coastal road which will take you through **Strøby Egede** to (6km) **Strøby**, where the church has a Romanesque chancel and nave with a Gothic extension from c 1500. It is built mainly of limestone ashlars taken from the huge limestone deposits at Stevns Klint (p 153), and contains a series of 14C frescoes depicting the Passion. In the churchyard there is a memorial to the novelist Martin A. Hansen who spent his childhood here, and doubtless here acquired much of the sense of tradition and cultural history which marks his work.

1km southeast of Strøby you turn left on the road to (3km) **Magleby**, where there is again a church of interest. The earliest part, the nave, is 13C, with a late Gothic chancel from c 1500. At the east end of the nave there is a 17C sepulchral chapel. The Renaissance altarpiece is from 1606, with paintings from 1610; the pulpit dates from 1614; the pews are late Renaissance. A medieval tithe barn is incorporated into the churchyard wall to the east.

From Magleby the minor road continues to (3km) the impressive **Gjorslev Castle**. The first castle here was owned by Rane Jonsen, by tradition responsible for the murder of Erik Glipping, and executed in 1294. The present main wing was built c 1400 by Peder Lodehat, Queen Margrethe I's Chancellor, and Bishop of Roskilde.

It is one of the oldest inhabited buildings in Denmark today. The looming cruciform principal wing, dominated by a 30m-high tower, is unique among European castles. A Gothic hall in this wing is sometimes used for concerts. The north wing is from 1638, the south from 1843. The whole complex is encircled by a moat. Gjorslev remained in Church hands until the Reformation, since when it has been either in Crown or private ownership.

The approach from the east, along Bredgade, is a special sight. This wide road, cobbled apart from the central carriageway, is lined with half-timbered artisans' houses from the time of Frederik IV, and this scene must thus have remained almost unchanged since the early 18C. The 20 hectare park, containing many rare trees, is open to the public, but it can only be entered from the south. The castle itself is private.

Northeast of Gjorslev lies the delightful **Gjorslev Bøgeskov** (Gjorslev Beech Forest), a beautiful wooded area, with lakes and some 55 burial mounds, one of them 51m long, and with a magnificent view across Køge Bay. There is a restaurant here, too—right at the beach.

From Gjorslev you continue along a minor road through **Holtug** with its high-lying Romanesque/Gothic church (complete with runic inscription on the south side), long used as a landmark, to (7km) **Store Heddinge**, where the church is one of the most unusual in Denmark—though one wishes the restorers had left it alone.

Built of limestone ashlars, it consists of a rectangular Romanesque chancel (probably inspired by Byzantine models) and a unique octagonal Romanesque nave (apparently inspired by Aachen Cathedral), with a Gothic west tower and porch. The chancel is well preserved, but the nave has been drastically altered. As a drawing by a 17C historian clearly shows, it was once much higher than at present, with eight columns supporting a central section, and a vaulted aisle around it, more in the style of the round churches of Bornholm. The chancel is equipped with a confusion of more or less hidden passages and rooms, probably reflecting the original intention that it should be suited for defence. The construction of the very substantial west tower seems to indicate the same purpose.

In spite of its modest size Store Heddinge is actually a market town, with a charter from 1441 (and probably earlier). Like other towns, it suffered fires and a Swedish occupation, but there are still enough older houses to have preserved something of its atmosphere. Fitting for such a small 'town', it can boast Denmark's shortest street, no more than 1.85m—but with a street name: TRIANGLEN (The Triangle). It has also boasted five distilleries (at a time when the total population was 576!), of which one, at ALGADE 22, still stands, though it is no longer in use.

Round trip from Store Heddinge to Stevns Klint and Rødvig
Total distance c 17km.

Take an unclassified road southeast through **Højerup** to (5km) the limestone cliffs of this area known as **Stevns Klint**. In places the cliffs offer a sheer drop of 40m to the sea. They stretch over some 15km, are full of fossils, and are completely different from anything else in Denmark. For centuries limestone has been quarried here, and many of the local buildings are made of it. However, only the soft chalk from the lower layers is now used—for blackboard chalk. The **Stevns Museum** at HØJERUP BYGADE 38 illustrates the history of the area, with a geological section, exhibitions of implements used in the quarrying, local costumes and furniture—and relics from the Battle of Køge Bay. There are art exhibitions in the museum during the summer (open pm May–Oct).

Højerup Cw, or what is left of it, is one of the products of the local limestone quarries. Now standing starkly outlined right on the brink of the cliffs, it dates back to c 1250, and according to legend moves 'a cock-stride' inland every Christmas Eve to avoid falling into the sea. The sea got it in the end, when the chancel fell over the cliff in 1928. The altarpiece was severely damaged by the collapse, but parts of it were saved and are on view in the remains of the building today. The pulpit from 1605 is still intact. The cliffs are now reinforced at this spot, and the church is safe—but not in use (open summer).

Now follow a small coastal road southwest to (5km) **Rødvig**, a favoured tourist resort in the summer, with weekend cottages, good beaches and excellent facilities.

■ **Tourist information**: Østersøvej 6; tel. 53 70 64 64.

■ **Hotel**: Rødvig Kro, Østersøvej 8; tel. 53 70 60 98.

There is a small marine engine museum here, **Rødvig Skibsmotormuseum** (open June–Aug), with 80 fishing boat engines from between 1917 and 1970, all in working order. The **Rødvig Flint Kiln** (reconstructed, originally from 1870), once used to fire powdered flint for glazing porcelain, stands on HAVNEPLADS and is now a museum and viewing platform.

From Rødvig you take the 261 back to (7km) Store Heddinge again, possibly stopping after the first 2km in **Lille Heddinge**, where a ticket bought to the Stevns Museum (above) will—on application—grant you free entrance to both an old smithy here (at BROVESHØJVEJ 19) as well as to a village school, **Den gamle Rytterskole** at STORMARKSVEJ 1, one of 240 so-called 'cavalry schools' established by Frederik IV in 1721. It is now a small museum and includes a collection of works and memorabilia of the painter Niels Larsen Stevns (1864–1941) (responsible for the murals in Viborg Cathedral, p 282). Close by, there is a smithy and adjoining malt kiln from the 1790s. The limestone ashlar church in the village is part Romanesque, part Gothic, with an unusually lofty nave (8.5m). There were once three floors to the nave, the upper one being for storage and for keeping watch. It is assumed that this church formed part of the defences against the Wends. There is also a recently restored windmill.

From Store Heddinge you now continue west on the 154 for 12km to a crossroads where you have Karise on your right and Vemmetofte on your left.

Take a look first at **Karise** (3km), where there is yet another of the fortified churches of the region. Traces of embrasures and parapets are still to be seen. The building dates back to 1261. The brick-built chancel is again unusually high, 10m, suggesting that there were once two floors, while the nave is 6.9m. Despite the different heights of the chancel, nave, tower and north porch (built of alternating layers of brick and limestone), when seen from the north this church has a harmonious effect, with its five corbie gables. To the south, however, the effect is cancelled, thanks to the addition of the bombastic mausoleum chapel built by the influential Moltke family and designed in neo-classical style by Jardin and Harsdorff. It is dominated by the sarcophagus of Adam Gottlob Moltke, the one-time owner of **Bregentved** castle and close friend of Frederik V. This is surmounted by a medallion by Wiedewelt, who also designed the sarcophagus containing Moltke's first wife. It is not the design of the chapel as such that jars, but the fact that it is in such close proximity to a medieval church to which it is totally out of proportion.

Return now to the 154, cross it and drive to **Vemmetofte Kloster** (3km), not a convent in the ordinary sense, but another 'Adelig Jomfrukloster', a home for the unmarried daughters of the aristocracy. Like Vallø Castle, it had its rules altered in 1976, and is now a retirement home. Its history goes back to the Middle Ages, but the present Baroque house dates from 1715–24. It is not open to the public, but there is access to the park.

Just beyond the estate lies the lovely wooded **Vemmetofte Strand**, ideal for bathing. There is also a restaurant.

If you decided against both Karise and Vemmetofte you just follow the 154 for another 4km and then take the 209 to (5km) **Fakse**. The town has a distinguished son: it is the birthplace of the great Viking warrior Rollo who raided England and defeated King Athelstan, then proceeded to conquer and found what is now known as Normandy. He was given the title of Robert of Normandy before he died in 927. William the Conqueror was one of his descendants. There is a memorial stone to Rollo by the town hall.

To most Danes today, however, Fakse does not mean Rollo—it means beer. **Faxe Brewery** is among the biggest in the country, and it is open for visits (and tastes). The tiny thatched half-timbered house by the entrance in TORVEGADE is the place where it all started. Also in Torvegade you will find **Fakse Geologiske/Kulturhistoriske Museum** with a collection from this geologically exciting area, in addition to a local historical collection (open summer; limited opening winter).

2km south east of the town centre lies **Fakse Kalkbrud**, the limestone quarries, an impressive sight, 1km long by 500m wide—and up to 50m deep. Limestone has been quarried here since the 13C and has provided materials for many buildings. Some of the chalk is so hard that it has become known as Fakse marble, and has been used for facing buildings. The quarry welcomes visitors.

Having seen the quarry you really ought to drive just 3km further south east to the old village of **Fakse Ladeplads**, the harbour from which the local limestone is loaded for export, as it has been since the Middle Ages. There are huge silos at the water's edge, but there is also a modern marina, for outsiders have learned to appreciate this seaside resort just as much as the locals used to do.

On the road back to Fakse, you will in 4km come to **Blåbæk Møller**, a picturesquely situated watermill and windmill, the former certainly continuously functioning since 1664 (open on application).

2km northwest of Fakse stands the mansion of **Jomfruens Egede**, made up of two individual wings placed on either side of a small chapel. The south wing has 16C remains, while the north is from 1636; both were restored (i.e. redesigned) in 1797.

From Fakse it is easy, if you wish, to drive 6km west and join the faster direct route at Rønnede, but we suggest you stick to this route, having got this far, and with the splendid island of Møn so close at hand.

So follow the 209 south. In 11km you will find a road on your right leading to the **rag oak** (Kludeegen) in **Leestrup Forest**. You will have to park your car in the small car park and walk into the forest to find this curious phenomenon. In old superstition this oak tree had healing powers. A sick person had, on the Thursday night after the new moon, to pass nine times through the divided trunk to be cured. In addition to that, anyone seeking a cure had to hang an article of clothing in the tree as a sacrifice. There are still rags hanging here, and there are signs that the ancient practice is still continued.

Another 9km sees you in **Præstø** (pop. 7300), a quiet market town with a charter from 1403, snuggling splendidly at the south of the **Præstø Fjord**, with views of virtually the whole of the fjord coastline.

■ **Tourist information**: Jernbanevej 22; tel. 55 99 11 90.

■ **Hotels**: Frederiksminde, Klostermakken 8; tel. 55 9910 42; Kirsebærkroen, Kirsebærvej 1; tel. 55 99 39 55.

Præstø has retained a great deal of natural charm, with a tiny fishing harbour, winding streets with mainly 19C houses, a cobbled market square with its neoclassical **town hall** from 1823, designed by C.F. Hansen.

There was a monastery here before the Reformation. The **church**, from 1470, is all that is left. It is large and impressive, with three corbie gables on the buttressed south wall. From the outside these look like three chapels, but inside they turn out to be part of a wide extension to the original nave. At RØDELEDVEJ 1, the old pottery from 1898 is now a working **museum**.

On the coast immediate north of Præstø stands the mansion of *Nysø. The elegant Baroque building from 1671–73 was something of a cultural centre in the 19C. The then owner, Holger Stampe, put a studio at the disposal of Bertel Thorvaldsen, who executed some of his most important works here. The great sculptor was, however, not the only visitor, and many of the most prominent figures of the Golden Age of Danish Romanticism were frequent guests, including, of course, Hans Christian Andersen. There is a **museum** in Nysø now, dedicated to Thorvaldsen (limited opening). There is also access to the park when the museum is open.

To the east of Præstø there is the **Jungshoved** peninsula. This is the area once more or less ruled by the famous hero Svend Poulsen, better known as Svend Gønge or 'Gøngehøvdingen', during the Swedish occupation of 1658–60. He was what today would be known as a successful guerilla leader.

At the south of this small peninsula stands **Jungshoved Church**, one of the three Danish churches with a fresco portraying the Dance of Death (cf. Nørre

Church on the island of Møn

Alslev, p 150). The church, from c 1225 and unusual in itself in having the tower on the north side, stands beside the mound on which there was once a medieval castle which by tradition played a part in Svend Poulsen's operations.

You leave Præstø on the 265 south to (15km) Kalvehave, where you cross the 1943 11-arched **Dronning Alexandrines Bro** (Queen Alexandrine's Bridge) to the island of ***Møn**.

10km along the A59 brings you to **STEGE**, a small, idyllic, provincial market town dating back to the 13C, and with a charter from 1268. At the time of Valdemar I it was the site of a castle. Stege grew rich between the 13C and 16C, thanks to the herring fishing in the area, but it has since, apart from a period at the beginning of the 19C, stagnated—and thus kept its charm.

■ **Tourist information**: Storegade 2; tel. 55 81 44 11.

■ **Hotels**: Stege Bugt Langelinie 48; tel. 55 81 54 54; Pension Elmehøj, Kirkebakken 39; tel. 55 81 35 35.

You will find here delightful cobbled streets and half-timbered artisans' houses as well as early 19C merchants' houses recalling this later period of affluence; one of these, **Empiregården** in STOREGADE, is now the **local museum** with exhibits from 7000 BC to the present day. The adjoining **Mølleport**, the last of the town's three gate towers, still stands as the best-preserved town gateway in Denmark. Correspondingly, the medieval ramparts have also survived in good condition.

On the market square, TORVET, you will find a grand late 18C merchant's house, the **Kammerrådsgård**. There is a **doll museum** in GRØNNEGADE 14, and at HAVNEVEJ 14 you will find **Dansk Brandværns museum**, illustrating the history of the Danish fire brigades.

For so small a town, the Gothic **church** with a lofty and dignified nave from c 1525 is remarkably large, 60m long, and thus one of the biggest provincial churches in Denmark. The tower is characteristically built in alternating layers of red and limestone bricks.

►Excursion to east Møn
Total distance c 35km.

This excursion is really a must! Follow the 287 east, the first stop being at (4km) **Keldby** (or **Kelbymagle**). The *church here is from the early 13C, and entering it is like going into a medieval art gallery. It is a large church, and the vaulting is simply covered in frescoes from four different periods, from 1275 to 1600. Some are the work of the Elmelunde Master. The altarpiece and pulpit are of a splendour to suit the murals; the late Gothic altarpiece from 1500, ornate and richly carved, with Christ in the central panel surrounded by four panels depicting His life, and with the twelve Apostles in the outer panels. The equally ornate Renaissance pulpit is from 1586.

Only 1.4km to the south there is in **Keldbylille** a late 18C four-winged thatched farm which was left to the National Museum in 1864 and has been preserved in its original state as a museum (open summer; limited opening winter).

4km east of Keldby in **Elmelunde**, is the *church that has given its name to the great medieval Master. Like Keldby, this church too is filled with the most glorious frescoes, many illustrating Bible stories like the slaughter of the Holy Innocents, others exhorting the priest to speak loud and clear! The Elmelunde Master has painted Christ in Majesty over the altar. As you admire these sublime frescoes, you might reflect on the fact that they were whitewashed over after the Reformation! Elmelunde Church, partly dating from c 1075 and thus one of the oldest stone-built churches in Denmark, received a new altarpiece and pulpit as a gift from Christian IV's daughter, Leonora Christine, in 1636. Both are still in place, proudly showing Christian IV's monogram.

Immediately east of the church there is a large Bronze Age burial mound, and it is assumed that the church was built on a heathen shrine, as so many of the older churches were.

You continue east, through (3km) **Borre** with a church from 1250 remarkable for its decorative brickwork, to (3km) **Magleby**. ◄

From here there are three excursions. They are all quite short, and it would really be a pity to miss out any of them.

►If you drive 3km northeast you will find two mansions called **Liselund**, both close to the sea—the old one a delightful thatched house from 1772-95, now a museum in a romantic park reflecting the late 18C fondness for the idyllic (guided tours)—the new one, from 1887, now a splendid hotel and restaurant (tel. 55 81 20 81).◄

Liselund

►A   short   drive   east through the woods, brings you to the majestic ***Møns Klint*** (Møn's Cliff), a 'wild and weatherbeaten shore', towering limestone cliffs rising at their highest point to 128m, and constantly changing their profile thanks to winter storms. Those who have been here before will now look in vain for the impressive rock formation known as **Sommerspiret** (The Summer Spire)—it collapsed in January 1988, and there was a further major fall in 1994. The restaurant/hotel 'Store Klint' which is 25m from the Baltic—and 75m above it—has a splendid sea view (tel. 55 81 90 08). ◀

▶Driving south from Magleby you will pass the **Klintholm manor**, approached by an imposing avenue, but not open to the public. In **Klintholm Havn**, 3km further, you have a busy little fishing harbour dating back to 1878. It has well-known fish restaurants and a smokehouse where you can buy products on the spot. ◀

Leave Stege on the 287 south and stop for a while at (7km) **Damsholte**, where the tiny Rococo church from 1743 is unlike any other in Denmark. The nave is rectangular, with a five-sided extension at either end. It was the work of the age of pietism, and according to pietist custom the altar and pulpit are in one.

After another 5km you will come to a crossroads leading north to **Tostenæs** and south to **Kokseby**.

If you are interested in archaeological remains—and there are a great number around here—you should turn north to visit **Klekkende Høj** (2km), a large burial mound with two entrances and, after a further 3km along the same road, **Kong Asgers Høj** (2km), a huge passage grave with an 8m passage leading to a 10m-long burial chamber. Take a torch with you.

Archaeologists will also be interested in a third important monument, this time 3km south of the crossroads, through Kokseby and **Fanefjord**. **Grønjægers Høj** is the biggest long barrow in Denmark, surrounded by a stone circle made up of 134 enormous boulders.

Nearby **Fanefjord Church* is the third of the Elmelunde Master's churches, his finest work in the view of many. Fanefjord was once an important medieval harbour; the now isolated church, originally dedicated to St Nicholas, dates from the late 13C, when there was a busy market town on the spot. It is filled with frescoes, those on the chancel arch from c 1350, the remaining exuberant array from c 1500 by the Elmelunde Master—colourful, imaginative, drastic: scenes from the Old and New Testaments, Christ as Judge of the world, figures of saints, grotesque figures of demons, and a wealth of floral decoration.

Return to the 287 from Fanefjord.

Your route now continues south and west to the small island of **Bogø**. Just south of Bogø town you take the ferry (half-hourly sailings) to Stubbekøbing on the island of Falster. (You can also, if you so wish, drive right across the island to (6km) the Farø Bridges, and from there follow the direct route above.)

Stubbekøbing (pop. 6870) is another small fishing port that was of strategic significance in the Middle Ages. It then grew with the herring fishing, but has since sunk into provincial idyll, with old half-timbered houses in quiet streets.

■ **Tourist information**: Vestergade 43; tel. 53 84 13 04.

■ **Hotel**: Elverkroen, Vestergade 39; tel. 53 84 12 50.

The main street, VESTERGADE, contains several old buildings, for instance **Trojels Gård**, from 1708, once part of a merchant's house with courtyard.

It has been claimed that the dignified **church** is one of the most interesting buildings on Falster. The Romanesque nave is late 12C, the chancel from c 1250, the St Anna chapel on the north wall late Gothic. The main structure is lime-stone, though brick has been used in some of the arcading. There are frescoes from five different periods, ranging from 1250 to 1520. The altarpiece is High Renaissance, from 1616, and the rood screen four years younger. The auricular pulpit and canopy date from 1634. On Nykøbingvej you will find a museum, **Motorcykel og Radiomuseum** (limited opening).

▶A short excursion from Stubbekøbing takes you along the 293 east to **Næsgård** (5km), Denmark's first agricultural college from 1849. From this spot a road north leads down to **Borrehuset**, where Marie Grubbe of Tjele (see p 286) lived in her final years as a ferrywoman, rowing travellers across the Grønsund Straits to Møn. It was here Ludvig Holberg met her. There is nothing left of her house, of course, but it is moving to stand here and think of the fate that was worked out on this spot.

Continue south on minor roads through **Korselitse Østerskov**, the longest stretch of coastal forest east of Storebælt to (6km) **Hesnæs**, a tiny fishing village with beautiful thatched cottages. They were architect designed in the late 19C and have all their walls insulated with straw on the outside.

Return to Stubbekøbing via (3km) **Moseby** with its idyllic parsonage from the 1770s and (2km) **Åstrup**, where the Elmelunde Master is again responsible for a wealth of frescoes, supplementing others from the 13C on the chancel arch. ◀

From Stubbekøbing take the 271 south through Horreby to (19km) **NYKØBING FALSTER** (pop. 25,200).

■ **Tourist information**: Østergade 7; tel. 54 85 13 03.

■ **Hotels**: Falster, Skovalléen; tel. 54 85 93 93; Teaterhotellet, Torvet 3; tel. 54 85 32 77.

■ **Youth hostel**: Østre Allé 110; tel. 54 85 66 99.

History

Nykøbing Falster, one of the three Danish towns by the name of Nykøbing, was given a charter by Valdemar II. It originated as a defence against the Wends, and a large castle was established here. In the 13C the king was often in residence, and here Valdemar IV signed a peace treaty (one of many) with the Hanseatic League in 1365. In 1419 a Franciscan monastery was founded, and since 1532 its chapel has been the parish church. The castle brought affluence and trade to the town, and this continued until the mid-17C, when Nykøbing went into decline. The castle was sold for demolition in 1767. Agricultural improvements in the 19C brought renewed prosperity, and this was accelerated after the establish-ment of the first bridge to Lolland in 1867, followed by the arrival of the railways, and finally the opening of direct connections with Germany via Gedser to Warnemünde in 1903.

The buttressed late Gothic **church**, standing at the junction of STORE KIRKESTRÆDE and KLOSTERSTRÆDE is the old Franciscan monastery church and at one time formed the south wing of the monastery, the west wing of which is also partially extant, now used as a parsonage. The tower, with its onion spire, is from 1766. The vaulted nave is whitewashed, emphasising the ornate carving of the Renaissance altarpiece presented by Frederik II's queen, Sophie of Mecklenburg, in 1618. There is an auricular pulpit, supported by a figure of Moses; it and its canopy are from 1640, the octagonal metal font from 1648.

The most curious feature is Queen Sophie's genealogical table on the north wall of the chancel, with portraits of each ancestor painted in 1626 and surmounted by a carved top section from 1627. One of the numerous sepulchral tablets contains a well-preserved painting by Lucas Cranach the Elder, from c 1540. In the gardens near the church there is a medicinal herb garden, laid out in 1969.

A few old buildings are scattered around the central part of the town, but do not give an overall impression. Best known of the old houses is **Czarens hus** (The Tsar's House) on the corner of LANGGADE and FÆRGESTRÆDE—perhaps symbolically now facing a small square with Mogens Bøggild's delightful granite fountain representing a bear, from 1939. The carefully restored and maintained house from c 1700 was indeed used briefly by Peter the Great on his way to Copenhagen in 1716. A wooden plaque, written in German, commemorates this.

Czarens hus is now part restaurant, part the **Falsters Minde** museum (entrance in Langgade) with exhibits from a unique Viking shipyard south of Stubbekøbing and a model of Nykøbing Castle. Of this once splendid castle there are now only a few ruins left at the north end of SLOTSGADE. The **Halskov Vænge Museum** in PARKVEJ provides an experience of life—and death—in the Bronze Age.

The two routes merge in Nykøbing, and from here you follow the E55 south, soon passing on your right, **Hasselø Nor**, where there was a settlement of Dutch market gardeners in the early 17C. 7km south of Nykøbing you reach **Væggerløse**, where the newly restored **Stouby Mølle** from 1790 is the only post mill of this particular type in Denmark (limited opening).

Immediately south of Væggerløse you will see a road east to (3km) **Marielyst**, a seaside resort par excellence. It is in the centre of a 10km stretch of magnificent beaches, one of the best in Denmark, with all conceivable facilities for holiday-makers.

Following the E55 south from Væggerløse you pass through the **Bøtø Nor**, another area once cultivated by Dutch farmers. A small area of this low-lying land has not been entirely drained, and in it there is a 100 hectare bird sanctuary, the home or resting place of many rare birds, including cranes. 12km south you reach the gentle village of **Gedesby**, with its half-timbered thatched cottages and the ramparts of Valdemar II's castle of Gedesgård.

In 4km you reach **Gedser**, which owes its existence to the ferry connections to Germany. There are today ferries to Rostock every two or three hours, and the journey takes about two hours. (Reservations tel. 33 15 15 15.) Places of interest in Gedser are the **Gedser Remise** railway museum in Stationsvej, with locomotives and passenger coaches from c 1900 onwards (open weekends Apr–Sept), and the **Geological Museum** in SKOLEGADE (open all year). **Gedser Lighthouse** is also open for visitors in the summer.

10 • Maribo to Odense via Svendborg

Total distance 105km—plus ferry. A9 to (34km) Tårs ferry harbour. (Ferry Tårs–Spodsbjerg 45mins). A9 to (9km) **Rudkøbing**. *(17km)* **Svendborg**. *A9, A43 to (45km)* **Odense**.

From Maribo to Tårs ferry harbour you have a choice of three routes: the direct route (34km, listed first), via Knuthenborg (45km), or via Nakskov (49km).

Direct route from Maribo to Tårs ferry harbour
Total distance 34km.

Take the A9 west to (6km) Nørreballe, turning left here to **Østofte** (1km), where there is an interesting large church, partly dating back to the Romanesque period. Its brightly coloured and well-preserved frescoes contain some amusing motifs, one of them unique in Denmark: Eve being produced out of Adam's back. Elsewhere God is creating the animals, while at the Gate of Heaven the Archangel Michael is giving Adam the acorn from which will grow the tree providing the wood for the Cross. Not far from the church you will find an old post mill.

A further 6km on the A9 you come to **Stokkemarke** where there is an impressive church with a late Romanesque nave and subsequent Gothic additions. The church tower is a particularly solid structure, with corbie gables on each side. The stained glass windows in the apse are by J.Th. Skovgaard.

Your next stop is in (9km) **Halsted**. The 12C church here once formed the north wing of a Benedictine convent founded by Jutta, the daughter of Erik Plovpenning. There are still some remains of the original building, e.g. a carved tympanum above the south door, while later features of note are some fine carvings on the 1636 pulpit and the entrance to a sepulchral chapel, from 1643.

Instead of now driving direct to (13km) Tårs, you might make the short detour to visit the biggest town on Lolland, **Nakskov**. To do this you take an unclassified road west from Halsted leading direct to Nakskov (6km) (p 163).

Alternative route from Maribo to Tårs—via Knuthenborg
Total distance 45km.

Follow the A9 north out of Maribo to (3km) the 289. Here you should turn right and drive north to (5km) **Knuthenborg**, the site of an elegant mansion standing in a very large privately owned park, part of which is now the most comprehensive **safari park** in Denmark, crisscrossed by a full 16km of roads. It is approached through elaborate wrought-iron gates and offers not only a large stock of wild animals, but also a children's zoo, pony-riding and a model of the islands of Lolland/Falster (open summer).

From Knuthenborg it is only 1km to **Bandholm**, a small fishing village with picturesque old warehouses, and the terminus of the Maribo-Bandholm vintage railway.

Remain on the 289 northwest for 12km towards **Birket**. Immediately before the village you will find a minor road going off left to **Lindet** (1km), where you will find Birket church. It is less the church that is of interest than the free-standing wooden bell-tower near the entrance to the churchyard. It dates from 1350 and is thought to be the oldest extant wooden building in the country.

Continue on the 289 for a further 3km, to a road leading south to **Pederstrup** (2km), a neo-classical mansion designed by C.F. Hansen. It has been restored and contains a museum commemorating the 18C land reformer Christian D.F. Reventlow. It moreover contains a collection of good sculptures. Open all year.

You should now return to the 289, turning off left again almost immediately to see **Kong Svends Høj** (King Svend's Tumulus), a huge passage grave, with a central chamber 12.3m long. Another 10km on the 289 sees you in **Lille Løjtofte**.

Here there is a very small but almost totally unspoiled Romanesque church, the only later addition being the porch. Not only has this church retained its original appearance and atmosphere, but it also possesses a very special font, the work of the Majestas Master from the Swedish Baltic island of Gotland. It rests on a foot carved in the shape of four lions, and the outer facing is richly carved with reliefs of Christ in Majesty, the Annunciation, Mary's meeting with Elizabeth, the Birth of Christ, the Shepherds in the fields and the Three Kings.

1km beyond Lille Løjtofte you turn right and drive through Sandby to (10km) Tårs and your ferry.

Alternative route from Maribo to Tårs—via Nakskov
Total distance 49km.

Leave Maribo on the 153 southwest, driving through (4km) Hillested and turning right after a further 1km on to a road to (3km) Øster Skørringe. Here you turn right on to the 275 and drive west past the mansion of Kristianssæde to (9km) Bjergeskov, where you should take the road south through Dannemare to (9km) **Tillitse**.

There is a small Romanesque church here, but the interesting feature is the runestone near the porch, with two inscriptions, one of them Christian: 'Eskil Sulkeson had this stone raised to himself. As long as the stone lives this memorial inscription, done by Eskil, shall stand. May Christ and St Michael help his soul.'

Back on your route again you pass (3km) **Rudbjerggård**, a large half-timbered 17C mansion with an octagonal tower. In the course of its history it has belonged to two morganatic royal wives, Kirsten Munk and Countess Danner. 2km further on your left will give you a glimpse (if you want it), of **Sølvbjerg**, the site of the last public execution in Denmark in 1882. After another km you should follow a road leading right to (8km) Nakskov.

NAKSKOV (pop. 15,650) is the largest town on Lolland, with a charter dating back to 1200.

■ **Tourist information**: Søndergade 17; tel. 53 92 21 72.

■ **Hotels**: Skovriddergården, Svingelen 4; tel. 53 92 03 55; Harmonien, Nybrogade 2; tel. 53 92 21 00.

■ **Youth hostel**: Branderslevvej 11, Branderslev; tel. 53 92 24 34.

Formerly a shipbuilding town and ferry port, Nakskov has gone into decline since the shipyard was closed and the Langeland ferry transferred to Tårs. Like other parts of Lolland, Nakskov suffered at the hands of Lübeck in the 15C and 16C and was occupied by Swedish forces in 1659. However, the picturesque roads leading from the centre of the town to the harbour with its half-timbered warehouses (some dating back to 1600) point to a high level of trade and affluence in the past.

Standing on the corner of the market place, AXELTORV, is the elegant Rococo Theisens gård from 1786. If you go into the courtyard you will find a series of renovated warehouses from the 18C, now used for meetings and other local activities. At the furthermost end of the complex, standing on the corner of BADSTUESTRÆDE and HAVNEGADE is a splendid half-timbered warehouse dating back to at least 1702. The long wing in Badstuestræde has been described as one of the most picturesque half-timbered buildings in the country. Axeltorv itself is unusual in being triangular, a shape going back to the Middle Ages.

To the north of it lies Nakskov Church, **Sankt Nikolai Kirke**. Mainly from the 16C, it still contains parts of the original Romanesque structure from the 13C. The elegant altarpiece is the work of Anders Mortensen, 1656, and the pulpit, from 1630, is by Jørgen Ringnis, as is the panelling beneath the tower. The great chest, with its five locks, is from 1573, while the tall spire dates from 1906.

In TILEGADE nearby, east of Axeltorv, a working museum has been installed in **Den gamle Smedie** (The Old Smithy), where a blacksmith works, using tools some of which are 200 years old. There is a statue in Axeltorv of King Christian X, placed there in 1952 in commemoration of the Liberation.

The Catholic church of Saint Francis is from 1921, built largely for Polish sugar workers in the sugar refinery which has long been one of the main sources of industry in the town. The harbour area in Nakskov is characterised by a collection of charming old warehouses, outstanding among which is **Dronningens Pakhus** from 1590, the oldest building in the town.

On leaving Nakskov, you drive north through Branderslev to (5km) the A9. Here a left turn will quickly bring you to (6km) **Tårs**, where the ferry from **Tårs** sails (45 mins) to **Spodsbjerg**, a small village on the island of Langeland, from where the A9 takes you to (9km) Rudkøbing. The old main road is still in existence, and provides a more leisured and picturesque route.

RUDKØBING (pop. 7000) is the principal town on the island and was once an important trade centre, which received its charter in 1287.

■ **Tourist information:** Torvet 5; tel. 62 51 35 05.

■ **Hotels**: Rudkøbing Skudehavn, Havnegade 21, tel. 62 51 46 00; Skandinavien, Brogade 13, tel. 62 51 14 95.

■ **Youth hostel**: Engdraget, tel. 62 51 18 30.

■ Rudkøbing is well equipped for the tourist trade, and has much to offer in the way of cafés, restaurants and street entertainment. Sightseeing **walks** are arranged on Thurø in the summer. Apart from its road connections to Fyn, Rudkøbing also provides a **ferry** connection to Marstal on the island of Ærø (p 170) and to the tiny island of Strynø, no more than 3km × 2km, with its small population of close-knit islanders.

The town centre has maintained much of its old aspect, with decorative old-fashioned cobbled streets, an impressive church—possibly partly dating back to 1105, but mainly from the 16C and 17C—a windmill placed high above the town, and numerous old fishermen's houses which have been thoroughly restored. One, in Brogade, was converted into a tiny Catholic church in 1925, to serve the many Poles who used to come to work in the sugar beet fields.

Other characteristic features are the numerous old merchants' houses, half-timbered, with impressive steps leading to sometimes quite ornate main entrances. Outstanding among them are **Den bayske Gård** in ØSTERGADE, now a private house, and the **Old Chemist's Shop** (open summer) in BROGADE, dating from 1856. This was the birthplace of the Ørsted brothers—Hans Christian (1777–1851), the discoverer of electromagnetism, the founder of modern science in Denmark, and a leading influence on the Danish literary Romantic movement, and Anders Sandøe (1778–1860), an influential jurist and statesman in his day. The shop, which houses a collection of old furniture and equipment, and the garden behind it, containing a chestnut tree said to date from the beginning of the 18C, is now part of the Langeland Museum.

Hans Christian Ørsted is commemorated by a statue by Bissen on the picturesque **Gåsetorv** square, while Anders Sandøe Ørsted has his statue by J.C. Berg in the **Ørstedpark**.

The **Langeland Museum** in JENS WINTHERSVEJ offers a large collection of relics from the island. Langeland is rich in archaeological sites, and it is thus natural that over half of the museum collection should be of archaeological interest, with many exhibits reflecting the discovery of rich Viking graves in the area.

▶**Excursion from Rudkøbing to north Langeland**

As its name suggests, **Langeland** is long and narrow, and it would be a pity to leave it without exploring some of the charming villages.

The 305 road runs north-south through the whole island. Drive first towards the north, to (10km) the village of **Tranekær**, dominated by its splendid castle, which can be traced back to the 13C. Since 1672 it has been the residence of the Ahlefeldt family. Resulting from several alterations and restorations, the present building consists of two wings linked by an octagonal tower surmounted by a spire. There is a public pathway through the park, giving clear views of the castle which is otherwise not open to the public. A recent innovation in the park is the establishment of **Tranekær International Centre of Art and Nature** (TICKON), a 'land art' centre with works of art created from natural materials.

Perhaps the most famous member of the Ahlefeldt family was Count Frederik, still known as the General. He attempted to create in Tranekær something approaching a South German duchy, and the relationship between the castle and the surrounding village—a relationship unique in Denmark—reflects clearly the feudal nature of this attempt. The old stables are now a restaurant (**Café Herskabsstalden**), and are situated opposite the private theatre which the General had constructed near the entrance to the castle. Even the poultry did well, and the old henhouse, topped by a tower used as a dovecot, is now a small **art gallery**.

Other buildings of note in this idyllic village are the inn (**Tranekær Gæstgivergård**), dating from the 18C and, immediately south of it, the musicians' houses, two long, half-timbered houses intended to house the General's musicians and players.

Opposite the castle there is a sculpture park, **Galaksen** (The Galaxy), the work of the modern sculptor Jan Axel Starup. It consists of 27 boulders, the largest weighing ten tonnes, arranged in a spiral and bearing inscriptions and symbols. 1km north of the Castle lies **Slotsmøllen** (The Castle Mill), a well-preserved windmill, completely restored in 1985 (open summer).

Of the many mansions on Langeland, one of the most famous is **Egeløkke**, situated 1km west of the main road to Lohals 5km north of Tranekær (park occasionally open; house private). This is the mansion where the young Grundtvig was appointed tutor, only to fall in love with the mistress of the house, Constance Leth, one result of which was his first religious awakening. A visit to the churchyard in **Bøstrup** (immediately west of the main road just before you turn off to Egeløkke) will give a sight of Constance Leth's grave.

2km north a minor road leads west to **Dageløkke** (1.5km), a holiday centre,and 6km further north you pass the 400-year-old mansion of Steensgaard before reaching (3km) **Lohals**, the northernmost village on Langeland, which has a small harbour with yachting facilities and a ferry connection to Korsør on Sjælland. It is also a fishing port. A popular site for weekend cottages, this area has first-rate bathing facilities; you can hire boats and bicycles, and fishing trips can be arranged in the Langeland Belt which is famous for its cod fishing. ◄

►Excursion from Rudkøbing to south Langeland

Take the 305 south from Rudkøbing as far as (9km) **Lindelse**. Here you turn left and bear left again at the village of **Hennetved** (1.5km) to reach the mansion of **Skovsgaard** (1.5km), now owned by Danmarks Naturfond (the equivalent to the National Trust). The mansion itself is not open to the public, but the park and shore are, and **Langelands Museum** has an exhibition of horse-drawn carriages from the late 19C and early 20C here (open summer).

4km south of Lindelse you will come to the village of **Humble** with its long dolmen known as **King Humble's Grave**, probably the best known of all the prehistoric monuments on Langeland. There are parking facilities outside the impressive, partly Romanesque Humble church; follow the road for about 100m before turning into a path leading through a farmyard to the dolmen itself, well preserved and positioned high above the surrounding countryside. It measures 55m × 9m and is surrounded by 77 large stones. It is to be assumed that 'King Humble' was mythological.

Returning to the main road, you should drive through the village and then fork right to **Ristinge** (5km) to see the long dolmen at **Ristinge Nor** (clearly marked to the right of the road) and the dolmen chamber at **Ristinge Klint**. This latter is reached by following the beach at Ristinge along the cliff face from where there is a path leading up to the dolmen. The beach at Ristinge is one of the finest of the many in Langeland, with sand stretching for several kilometres and ideal bathing waters.

The 305 south from Rudkøbing leads ultimately to the lively port of **Bagenkop** (28km), from where there are regular ferry connections to Kiel (two and a half hours). There is also a well-equipped yachting harbour. ◀

Returning to the main route, the A9 from Rudkøbing runs across a bridge to the flat island of Siø and then by causeway to the wooded and hilly island of Tåsinge. It skirts Tvede Skov forest on the right, and keeps close to the coast. In Lundby, 10km from Rudkøbing, you will find a road to your left leading to **Landet** (1km) where the famous romantic couple, the Swedish Count Sixten Sparre and his beloved tightrope dancer Elvira Madigan, lie buried. When she left him in 1889, the Count followed her to Denmark and shot her before committing suicide himself. Of older date are the many fine Romanesque granite sculptures in the church.

In (3km) **Bregninge** there is one of the churches most frequently visited by tourists, a heavily restored Romanesque church from the tower of which there are wonderful views over the whole of the archipelago to the south of Fyn. It was once said to be possible to see 65 church towers, 20 mansions and 30 windmills from here. Bregninge also houses a small museum illustrating life on the island in a bygone age. Just outside the village an old windmill has been adapted and turned into an excellent café/restaurant, also with splendid views.

On the southern outskirts of Bregninge there is a road to the right leading to **Valdemars Slot** (Valdemar's Castle) (3km). The wooded road first passes the remnants of an old fortification, **Kærstrup Voldsted** (Kærstrup Ramparts) and then one of the most famous trees in Denmark, the **Ambrosiuseg** (Ambrosius Oak), so named because the 18C poet Ambrosius Stub, who was a tutor in Valdemars Slot, is said to have been fond of sitting under its branches to write his poetry. The tree is thought to be between 400 and 500 years old, and the 20m-high trunk has a girth of 7m.

*Valdemars Slot itself was built by Christian IV between 1639 and 1644, and was intended for his son, Count Valdemar Christian, who, however, was killed in battle in 1656. It was a mansion truly worthy of a king's son, designed by Hans van Steenwinckel, the architect responsible for Rosenborg Palace in Copenhagen, and bigger than Rosenborg. The original building, badly damaged in the wars against Sweden (1657–60), was later presented to the naval hero Niels Juel for his part in the wars. In 1678 he began a reconstruction in the Baroque style of the day, and it is this magnificent building which now stands on the original site.

One of the largest privately owned mansions in Denmark, it is open to the public, and great efforts have been made in the 21 rooms to which access is given to preserve the appearance of a house in use, even to the extent of lighted candles on some of the tables. The style of the rooms varies from the royal apartments through the great hall and the chapel to the servants' quarters. There are also many important historical relics, not least among which is Niels Juel's own sea chest. The house itself looks out on to a park and an artificial lake surrounded by 18C outbuildings and a pavilion overlooking the sea. In summer, light refreshments are served in this, while there is a bistro in the north wing. The crypt under the chapel houses a restaurant. Part of the house is now an hotel, and the whole mansion can in fact be hired for special occasions.

Instead of returning straight to the main road, you could continue north and drive through (1km) **Troense**, an old shipping village characterised by its old half-timbered cottages. There is a small maritime museum (**Søfartsmuseum**) here with relics of the China trade for which Tåsinge was once a centre. From the harbour there is a clear view of the island of Thurø, now linked to Fyn by a bridge. The road leads via Eskær back to the A9.

North of Bregninge the A9 crosses a bridge opened in 1962 linking Tåsinge and Fyn and leads you straight into (4km) Svendborg.

SVENDBORG (pop. 42,400) is the second largest city on the island of Fyn.

■ **Tourist information**: Centrumpladsen 4; tel. 62 21 09 80.

■ **Hotels**: Ærø, Brogade 1; tel. 62 21 07 60; Royal, Toldbodvej 5; tel. 62 21 21 13.

■ **Youth hostel**: Vestergade 45; tel. 62 21 66 99.

It was founded in the 13C, the earliest record of the name dating from 1229. It was granted a charter in 1253. Built on high ground overlooking the islands of Tåsinge and Thurø, it commands splendid views of the South Fyn coast and archipelago. It has a good, sheltered natural harbour, and this contributed to its growth in the Middle Ages, when trade with the Baltic and the Hanseatic League flourished, to become one of the most important market towns in Denmark. It suffered from the many wars in the Middle Ages, and was burned down on more than one occasion. After a period of peace, Svendborg again suffered under the 17C wars against Sweden, being occupied by the Swedes for 18 months and partly destroyed. The Napoleonic Wars also saw foreign troops here, this time French and Spanish, but since then Svendborg has grown steadily, to become a centre for trade and communication with the islands off the south coast of Fyn.

The old part of the town has maintained its character, with steep streets and many impressive old houses. Of particular interest are HULGADE and BAGERGADE. The area is dominated by one of Svendborg's principal churches, **Vor Frue Kirke** (Our Lady's Church). It was originally built between 1253 and 1279, and still bears traces of its early Romanesque character, though alterations in the late Middle Ages have resulted in a predominantly Gothic structure. The spire dates from 1768. The interior is well-proportioned and spacious, giving a sense of light and harmony. The pulpit bears the dates 1597 and 1599, though the carved figures were added in the course of a radical restoration in 1884. The simple altar is from around 1600, but the altarpiece is the work of the important 19C painter Eckersberg. The 27 bell carillon in the tower plays hymns four times daily.

Vor Frue Kirke stands on the highest point in Svendborg (originally the site of the castle), and overlooks the market square with its town hall, theatre and the elegant **Wiggers Gård**, a half-timbered building of 1939. Although now principally a car park, the square is, for several days in August every year, the site of a re-creation of a typical 19C market.

Vor Frue Kirke is not, however, the oldest church in Svendborg. That honour goes to **Sankt Nicolaj Kirke** in GERRITSGADE nearby. It dates back in part to the mid 13C, and thanks to a sensitive restoration in the 1890s is now largely returned to its original form. The granite font is late Romanesque, and the Renaissance pulpit is from 1585. The altarpiece from 1894 is the work of Joachim Skovgaard.

North of Vor Frue Kirke runs FRUESTRÆDE, an unspoilt old street in which the poet and hagiographer Johannes Jørgensen lived as a child, and to which he returned in his old age after spending many years in Assisi. Part of the house (No. 15) has been turned into a memorial museum (**Johannes Jørgensens Mindestuer**) and is open to the public on Tue. No. 3 is **Anne Hvides Gård**, the oldest dwelling house in Svendborg, built in the 1560s, and now part of the **Svendborg and District Museum**. However, the main part of this museum is in the old workhouse, Viebæltegård, at GRUBBEMØLLEVEJ 13, where in addition to static exhibits there is a goldsmith's workshop. The most recent addition to Svendborg's museums is the **Toy Museum** at SANCT NICOLAIGADE 1B (open Wed–Sat) with an extensive display of toys both Danish and foreign from the past hundred years.

The elevated part of the town is ringed by a road called DRONNINGEMAEN, on which (No. 30) is situated **Svendborg Zoologiske Museum**, with zoological collections tracing the development of animal life over the last 13,000 years (open summer; limited opening winter).

Beyond Dronningemaen is a hill called **Ovinehøj**, in fact the old site of execution. From here there are views over the town and the surrounding countryside and sound. To the east of the town, on another hill, is **Svendborg Navigation School**. It stands close to the site of the medieval **Ørkild Castle**, long in the possession of the bishops of Odense, and burned down during the Count's War at the time of the Reformation. There is little to see of the castle now, though there are a few traces in the **Caroline Amalielund** park, where a further attraction is an open air theatre.

A walk east from Svendborg, along the coast, brings you to the wooded area encompassing the old Christiansminde Hotel, recalling an elegant past age, with views across the harbour and sound, and of the bridge linking Tåsinge and Fyn. A great bonfire is lit here every year on Midsummer's Eve. The sculptor Kai Nielsen was born in Svendborg, and several of his bronzes are to be found in the town.

From Svendborg the A9 continues towards Odense through a wooded and at first fairly flat landscape. After 16km you will come to the village of **Kværndrup**, where, situated on a hill there is an originally Romanesque church unusually with the tower in the east. Among the many tombstones in this church is that of Frands Brockenhuus, who had the nearby castle of

*Egeskov (open summer, p 192) built in the 1550s. Egeskov Mill can be seen in Kværndrup, at GRØNNEBJERGVEJ 1, open daily 11.00–17.00.

A further 5km towards Odense will bring you to the village of **Ringe**. Here, too, there is an interesting church, originally Romanesque, but with Renaissance additions, and this time with its tower on the south side. The south chapel, designed by Harsdorff and Wiedewelt, contains the tombs of General H.H. Eickstedt (d. 1801, one of the conspirators who betrayed Struensee) and his family. Ringe Museum contains a good collection illustrating village life in mid-Fyn from prehistoric times, but with the emphasis on the 18C and 19C (open summer).

A short journey east on the 323 here will take you to **Ryslinge** (3km), the site of the first Grundtvigian folk high school, founded in 1850. Apart from its early medieval church in which a feature is the Romanesque granite sculptures, the village also contains the Nazareth Church, a *valgmenighedskirke* (free church) built in 1866 for the Grundtvigian pastor Vilhelm Birkedal, who had been dismissed from his post as a pastor in the Lutheran state church, and whom his parishioners were reluctant to lose. It is the first such church to be built in Denmark. To the south of it stands a memorial statue of Birkedal.

5km north of Ringe you will find a road off to the right to **Sønder Højrup** (1km), where there is an art gallery: **Lindeskov Hansens Kunstsamlinger** (open weekends).

At (3km) Årslev we suggest that you leave the A9 and turn left to (4km) **Nørre Lyndelse**, where you can visit the childhood home of the composer Carl Nielsen (1865–1931). The house (described by the composer in his autobiography *My Childhood in Funen*) is now a museum illustrating Nielsen's life, and with particular emphasis on his childhood. His wife, Anne Marie Carl Nielsen, was a sculptress, and a beautiful statue by her in memory of her husband and portraying him as a boy playing the flute, stands to the west of the village.

From Nørre Lyndelse you can follow the A43 to (12km) Odense (see pp 30–38), passing on your way **Bramstrup**, the manor dating back to 1689 where the boy Carl Nielsen worked as a cowherd and goose herd.

11 • Rudkøbing to Middelfart via Ærø

*Total distance 102km. Ferry crossing to **Marstal** (1hr). Unclassified roads to (12km) **Ærøskøbing**. (16km) Sæby. Ferry to **Fåborg** (1hr). 329 to (36km) **Assens**. 313, unclassified road to (38km) **Middelfart**.*

From Rudkøbing (p 164) you take the ferry to Marstal on the unspoilt island of *Ærø, which for centuries belonged first to the Margrave of Brandenburg and then the dukes of Holstein and Schleswig, being left as an integral part of Denmark after the 1864 war which otherwise detached the duchies from the kingdom.

Small as it now seems, **MARSTAL** (pop. 3500) is a town rich in seafaring history. It has been said that there is not a sailor anywhere who has not heard of Marstal, and in terms of tonnage it was once the largest port in Denmark.

■ **Tourist information**: Havnegade 5; tel. 62 53 19 60.

■ **Hotels**: Ærøstrand, Egehovedvej 4; tel. 62 53 33 20; Mejerigården, Vestergade 30 B; tel. 62 53 32 38.

■ **Youth hostel**: Færgestræde 29; tel. 62 53 10 64.

The harbour in Marstal is not entirely natural, and the mole is supposed to have been constructed in a somewhat unusual manner: the sea used to freeze over during the winter, and when the ice was thick enough, huge boulders were dragged out on to it and carefully arranged so that, when the thaw came, the boulders fell into position on the sea bed.

Marstal reached its peak of affluence in the 18C, the age of mercantilism, and the seafarers who formed its inhabitants have put their stamp on the town's appearance. With the advent of the steamship, the town lost its importance, but it has in recent years made a comeback with coaster traffic. There are also plenty of square-rigged sailing ships to be seen there in addition to countless small yachts, and there is a small modern shipyard. Most of the narrow streets, many named after Danish heroes, slope down to the harbour. The houses in them, mostly from around 1800, are tiny and stand on minute plots, an arrangement stemming from the system of taxation in operation at the time. Some are built of brick, others are half-timbered.

There is a splendid ***church** in Marstal, built in 1738 on high ground so as to be seen from the sea, and full of hints of the seafaring nature of the town, not least in the shape of six ships' models hanging from the roof, while the organ loft is called the bridge. The altar candlesticks had their first home in a temple in Peking. The altarpiece (1881) by Carl Rasmussen shows Christ calming the waters, and the figures portrayed are those of sailors well known in Marstal at the time.

One interesting, perhaps unique, feature is the existence of two fonts; one dating from c 1150 and made of granite, used to be reserved for children born in wedlock, the other, in black stone, being for the less fortunate. The present clock is the work of Jens Olsen, famous for his world clock in Copenhagen City Hall. The churchyard, too, reveals a seafaring tradition and contains a famous gravestone with the inscription: 'Here lies Christen Hansen at anchor with his wife; he will not weigh until summoned to God's throne.' **Marstal Søfartsmuseum** is rich in seafaring exhibits.

From Marstal follow an unclassified road west for 8km and branch right there to (4km) ***ÆRØSKØBING** (pop. 4136).

■ **Tourist information**: Torvet; tel. 62 52 13 00.

■ **Hotels**: Ærøhus, Vestergade, tel. 62 52 10 03; Det lille hotel, Smedegade 33; tel.62 52 23 00.

■ **Youth hostel**: Smedevejen 15; tel. 62 52 10 44.

■ There is also a **camping and holiday ground** in the town, and *bicycles* can be hired for a modest charge—an ideal way of experiencing the relatively traffic-free roads and the none-too-hilly terrain.

■ **Free guided walks**, with an English-speaking guide, are arranged on Wed mornings by the Tourist Information Office.

Even at first sight Ærøskøbing is quite remarkable. It received its charter in 1398, and is the only town in Denmark to be scheduled a conservation area in its entirety, much of it being virtually as it was in the 17C: altogether 36 houses are Class A listed. In place of the minute sailors' houses in Marstal, here there are splendid dwellings, often half-timbered, with bow windows, gables and impressive steps and doorways, redolent of the wealth of the town in the 17C before Marstal began to usurp its place in the 18C.

The two oldest houses are in SØNDERGADE: **Kjøbinghus** (now a café) from 1645, and **Priors Hus** from 1690. The general 17C charm can be experienced by a walk along the narrow, cobbled streets from the GAASETORV square along Søndergade, passing through the main square, TORVET, with its two wooden pumps and the old grammar school, then right into Vestergade and right again down GYDEN, left into BROGADE, right into NØRREGADE and back to Gaasetorv. The street lamps are now electric, but they have retained their original shapes.

There are three museums, the main ethnographical collection being in **Ærø Museum** in Brogade (open summer). In the **Museumsgård** in SMEDEGADE there is a collection of bottle ships and carvings. Then there is the beautiful half-timbered **Hammerichs Hus** containing a valuable collection of china and porcelain. This was the gift of the sculptor Gunnar Hammerich, who also gave Ærøskøbing the 150 plaster casts of his works which are now housed in the **G. Hammerichs Skulptursamling** in the cellar of the Town Hall. The present, whitewashed copper-spired **church**, the second or third on this site, is quite modest in size, and was built 1756–58 (restored 1950); it contains a medieval font (13C) and 17C pulpit.

Ærøskøbing was the birthplace of Anders Arrebo (1587–1637), the father of Danish prosody and the author of a large-scale epic poem entitled *Hexaemeron*; there is a bust of him in the park near the harbour.

From Ærøskøbing there is a ferry connection (an hour and a quarter) to Svendborg (pp 167–168), a delightful sail through the archipelago, passing between the islands of Drejø on the left and Hjortø on the right.

You leave on the unclassified road leading towards Søby. Turn right on reaching the main road from Marstal to Søby, and you will almost immediately come to the village of (5km) **Tranderup**. Here there is an unusual, rather intimate **church**, with a tower surmounted by a wooden superstructure in French Empire style built in 1832 and designed by C.F. Hansen, the architect responsible for the Copenhagen Cathedral. The Romanesque church houses a pre-Reformation altar, and above the chancel arch there are early 16C frescoes, one portraying the Virgin and Child, the other a bishop. The chancel is built at an angle from the nave.

Without noticeably leaving Tranderup you suddenly find yourself in (1km) **Vindeballe**, and from here you could just take a quick trip west to some chalk cliffs, **Vodrup Klint** (2km), which give views across the Als peninsula.

A walk south (4km) along the coast will bring you to one of the largest windmill farms in Denmark. **Ærø** is well placed to make use of wind power; some 10 per cent of the electricity here is already so produced, and there are plans to make the island totally independent of electricity produced by traditional methods.

A further 3km on the main road brings you to the delightful village of **Bregninge**, where there are views across the sea on both sides of the island. Here, too, is a very fine church, lying in a secluded position in a large churchyard to the left of the road and of particular interest in that it houses an unexpectedly ornate altarpiece, carved c 1530 by Claus Berg. It is a triptych, the centre panel portraying the Crucifixion, and the two side panels representing the Apostles and a group of saints. There are early 16C frescoes including, behind the altar, a representation of Christ the Judge of the World, while opposite the pulpit there is the head of a jester. A bell rope once came out of his mouth, and the hole, worn askew, is still there.

Another 1km north will bring you to **Søbygård Voldsted** on the right. These 12C earthen ramparts built by Valdemar I as a defence against the Wends lie beside a large farm (privately owned) partly dating from the 16C. **Vester Mølle** windmill at the top of the hill beyond the ramparts was in use until 1980 and is well preserved—but can only be seen from the outside. The view from it is magnificent.

Søby is only 500m away now, a small but lively town which is the home of a sizeable fishing fleet, a shipyard and a dry dock. The streets were once quite broad and winding, and in places (e.g. in NØRREGADE and SØBAKKEVEJ) small houses have been built 'in the ditch', on tiny roadside plots of land made available to the less well-off workers. Beyond the town it is possible to walk to the tip of the narrow strip of land leading to **Næbbet** (The Beak), an area with good bathing, fine views and teeming bird life.

There are ferry connections from Søby to Mommark on the island of Als (pp 187–188), and to Fåborg on Fyn, each journey taking about an hour. On the latter route there is a view of the tiny islands of Avernakø on the right and Lyø on the left. If, on your trip across Ærø, you have fallen for its unspoilt charm, **FÅBORG** (pop. 17,300) will provide a gentle transition to mainland life.

■ **Tourist information**: Havnegade 2; tel. 62 61 07 07.

■ **Hotels**: Færgegaarden, Christian IXs Vej 31; tel. 62 61 11 15; Faaborg, Torvet 15; tel. 62 61 02 45.

■ **Youth hostel**: Grønnegade 70-71; tel.62 61 12 03.

Fåborg is one of the coastal towns established in southern Denmark after the final defeat of the Wends in the 12C. It is first mentioned in 1229 in a document written by Valdemar II, and it received its charter in 1251. The castle built here was destroyed during the Count's War, and it was really only in the 19C, with increased trade, that Fåborg flourished in earnest, becoming a centre for the corn and meat trade with Norway, England and the Duchies. It was badly hit with the loss of the Duchies in 1864, but by then its character as the home of well-to-do merchants was established, and much of that character still exists today.

There are, however, still signs of earlier times. The 15C **Vesterport**, at the end of VESTERGADE, is the old gateway to the town, carefully restored in 1917. It has a rounded archway and is surmounted by corbie steps to a height of some 10m. In LILLE TÅRNGADE, close to the market square, there is a 19m-high bell-tower with carillon from the second half of the 15C. Close by there are a number of late 18C half-timbered houses.

The main square, TORVET (where the old lock-up is now a museum), is the highest point in the town—7m above sea level—and there you will find the town hall (1840) and a fountain in bronze by the Svendborg sculptor Kai Nielsen, the impressive **Ymerbrønd**, portraying the giant Ymir drinking milk from the cow Audhumla as it licks the boulder from which was to emerge a man, Burir, whose grandsons were to be the first three gods of Norse mythology, Odin, Vili and Ve.

The square is at the centre of the oldest part of the town, which stretches from HOLKEGADE in the west to JOMFRULÅGEN in the east. Together with many small half-timbered houses there are two fine 18C merchants' houses in Holkegade, one of which, ***Den gamle gård**, Holkegade 1, is now a museum housing furniture and other exhibits relating to Fyn. Holkegade 2 is a **Model Ship Museum**. In Vestergade there is the well-preserved **Voigtske gård**, now partly a furniture and clothing shop, the home of the Voigt family with whose daughter, Riborg, the young Hans Christian Andersen fell in love.

The present parish church is **Helligåndskirken** (The Church of the Holy Ghost), a large late 15C Gothic structure once forming part of the Holy Ghost Monastery, traces of which can still be seen on the north wall. The nave is divided into three, giving on to a narrower and lower chancel. The altarpiece, portraying Christ in Emmaus, is the work of Vilhelm Marstrand (1858), and was given to the church by L.P. Voigt on the occasion of his golden wedding.

The ***Fåborg Museum for Fynsk Malerkunst** (Fåborg Gallery of Fyn Painting), GRØNNEGADE 75, was founded in 1910 and now ranks among the leading art collections in Denmark, far more comprehensive than Carl Petersen's tiny neo-classical entrance might suggest. The building is small, consisting of two main rooms and a number of side rooms in which there is a collection of paintings and sculptures by artists associated with Fyn. The original granite sculpture for the Ymerbrønd is here, as are other works by Kai Nielsen, and there are paintings by Johannes Larsen, Poul Christiansen, Anna Syberg, Fritz Syberg, Peter Hansen, Jens Birkholm and others less well known. These are not minor works of art, but paintings of international stature, occasionally on classical themes, but mainly representing the Fyn landscape and rural life.

In addition to the Ærø ferry, there are others from Fåborg to the small islands of Bjørnø, Avernakø and Lyø, as well as a car ferry to Gelting in Germany. For those interested in **vintage railways**, there is also the Syd Fyenske Veteranjernbane, running between Fåborg and Ringe and using rolling stock from the 1930s and 1950s.

►An interesting brief excursion from Fåborg is to the **Kaleko Water Mill Museum** on PRICES HAVEVEJ about 2km from the town. You drive east on the A44 and on the outskirts of Fåborg turn left towards **Diernæs**. The Mill is then c 1km ahead on your right. There is thought to have been a mill here since the mid-15C, and the present one is from the 17C. The idea is to give visitors a glimpse of a miller's life in past centuries.◄

Leave Fåborg on the 329 northwest and drive to (5km) **Millinge**, where, in an old half-timbered grocer's shop at ASSENSVEJ 279, there is a **museum** of toys ranging from an 18C Italian doll to 20C model cars. 1km further you will find **Stensgaard**, a splendid half-timbered mansion mainly from the 16C, but partly going right back to the 14C. It is now an hotel.

Continue to (3km) **Faldsled**, where there is a good inn, and 4km later you pass on your left the mansion of **Damsbo**. It dates from 1656, and consists of two parallel single-storeyed wings with ornate gables at either end, and joined by a high wall. In (2km) **Jordløse** there is a church dating back to Romanesque times, but mainly built in the late Middle Ages. The principal item of interest is a carved late Gothic altarpiece from c 1515, the work of Claus Berg's Odense workshop, representing the crowning of the Virgin. The nearby parsonage is a delightful half-timbered house with outbuildings around a courtyard. Originally built in 1734, it was badly damaged by fire in 1981, but has since been restored.

The road now continues to (5km) **Hårby**, from where you have a choice of routes to Assens, the direct route (16km), or the alternative route via Gummerup (25km, see below).

Direct route from Hårby to Assens
Total distance 16km.

From Hårby you take the 323 west. After 5km you will find a minor road on your left to **Dreslette** (2km). The church here dates back to Romanesque times, and there are a few Romanesque traces left. At the end of the 18C it was 'modernised', and the huge three-storeyed tower was added. There are 111 steps to the top, but there are breathtaking views when you reach it. Return to the main road and continue to (5km) Ebberup, which itself has nothing of interest to offer, but you should turn south here to **Hagenskov** (2km), otherwise known as **Frederiksgave**, a magnificent neo-classical mansion from 1774–76, designed by Georg Erdmann Rosenberg, a pupil of Nicolas-Henri Jardin. 600m southeast of the present house you can see the mound on which the medieval Hagenskov stood.

1km further south you will find in **Å** the very beautiful botanical gardens, **De 7 Haver**, displaying trees, shrubs and plants from seven European countries and boasting specialised collections, for instance of old-fashioned roses and rhododendrons.

Return now to Ebberup and follow the 323 for c 3km. Here you will find the **Kærum Church** on your right. It is to be assumed that the entire church was once decorated with frescoes in an elaborate—and unique—pattern of branches, leaves and flowers, many of which have survived.

From Kærum the 323 takes you straight into (3km) Assens (see below).

Alternative route from Hårby to Assens—via Gummerup
Total distance 25km.

Leave Hårby on the 329 north to (4km) Gummerup, where you will find the large **Vestfyns Hjemstavnsgård**, one of the finest half-timbered farms in an area full of them. It was bought in 1930 by the Vestfyn Hjemstavnsforening

(West Fyn Regional Association) and is now open as a museum illustrating rural life in former times in this part of Fyn (open summer).

From Gummerup you drive further on the 329 to (2km) Glamsbjerg, where you take the 168 west past (6km) **Øksnebjerg**, easily recognisable by the Dutch windmill from 1859. This was the scene of a bloody battle during the Count's War in 1535, when Christian III's ruthless commander, Johan Rantzau, confronted the Lübeck army seeking to restore the hapless Christian II to the throne. Rantzau won, and slaughtered 3000 peasants supporting the other side. There is a memorial here to the peasants killed on this occasion.

Continue now past (1km) Øksnebjerg Mill to (13km) Assens.

ASSENS (pop. 10,720) is known as far back as 1231, though the date of its first charter is uncertain. After the Battle of Øksnebjerg Rantzau's troops sacked Assens, before proceeding to mete out the same treatment to other towns on Fyn. In 1658 Assens suffered Swedish occupation. It is now a quiet, small port, used mainly for fishing and yachting (there is a marina with room for 600 yachts), and with a ferry to the small island of Bågø. The main source of income is a sugar factory.

- **Tourist information**: Ladegårdsgade 1; tel. 64 71 20 31 and Næsvej 29; tel. 64 71 35 80.

- **Hotels**: Marcussens, Strandgade 22; tel. 64 71 10 89; Stubberup Kro, Middelfartsvej 113; tel. 64 79 10 49.

- **Youth hostel**: Adelgade 26; tel. 64 71 13 57.

- There are good **bathing beaches** close to the town, and further excellent opportunities for bathing on the coast both north and south. The tourist information office can arrange for **fishing** excursions in Lillebælt.

The town centre and the harbour have retained much of their old-fashioned character. Near the harbour there is a statue of one of Denmark's great naval heroes, Peter Willemoes (1783–1808), who was born here. He stands on a plinth, and is surrounded by a cobbled area in the shape of the *Prins Christian Frederik*, the ship on which he was killed in battle off Sjællands Odde (p 129). Just in front of the statue is a small hut, a **cooking house**, built in the days of sailing ships to provide sailors with hot food, for they were forbidden to have fires on their wooden ships while in harbour.

The birthplace of Peter Willemoes is one of the most spendid houses in the town, situated on the main street, ØSTERGADE 36. Built in 1675, it is now a museum with a special emphasis on maritime exhibits. Adjoining is a new **museum of art** in the artist Dankvart Dreyer's birthplace, containing works by 11 artists associated with Assens. Also in Østergade stands the striking **town hall** dating back to 1781, though the façade in Renaissance style is the result of radical rebuilding in 1891 and 1917.

In the same street there is a statue of Klaus Berntsen, who was Prime Minister from 1910–13, representing Assens in the Danish parliament for 40 years. Still in Østergade, there is a plaque on No. 23 commemorating the sculptor Jens Adolf Jerichau who was born here.

Close to the Peter Willemoes house stands the church, **Vor Frue Kirke**, after St

Knud's Church in Odense the longest in Fyn, and characterised by the lofty, light impression it imparts. The oldest parts, the Holevad Chapel and the base of the steeple, date back to 1295, though the building was not completed until 1488 and is thus mainly Gothic in character. The steeple stands 48m high, and is the only octagonal steeple in Denmark apart from Kalundborg (p 120). There is a gravestone from c 1200 by the wall between the chapels. Close to the font, dating from 1910, stands a marble angel by Jerichau, and a large painting by Dankvart Dreyer, *Christ appearing to the Apostles and the Three Mary's*, adorns the south wall.

There is a Catholic church in Nørregade, **Vor Frelsers Kirke** (Our Saviour's Church), run by Redemptorists. Built in 1927, it is in a pleasing, simple style. Signs of earlier affluence are found in several merchant houses. There is an ethnographical museum in **Mands Samling**, DAMGADE 26, and the biggest private collection of silver, glass and antiques in Denmark in **Fabrikant Ernsts Samlinger**, Østergade 57.

For the direct route from Assens to Middelfart, the 313 north, winding through wooded countryside, brings you to (5km) **Holevad**, where the old schoolhouse is now a café containing old furniture and antiques. From here the 313 continues north and after 22km you will come to an unclassified road leading west to (11km) Middelfart (see below). For the more interesting, coastal alternative route follow the 313 north to (7km) Salbrovad, turning left here to (9km) **Wedellsborg**, the largest estate in Fyn. The large whitewashed mansion dates in part from the 14C, though it is mostly from the 15C and 16C. It can be seen from the large park, to which there is public access.

Now take a minor road from Wedellsborg north through Eskør to (7km) **Tybrind**. This is the area of a major Bronze Age find, and two of the best-preserved *lur* (Bronze Age horns) ever discovered were unearthed nearby. The road forks in Tybrind and you take the left fork, proceeding through Rud and Føns to (6km) **Rönæs**, where there is a museum of Asiatic antiquities and Chinese and Tibetan costumes. 1km further you turn left again and remain on coastal roads to (5km) Gamborg, from where there is only another km to a main road taking you (left) direct to (7km) Middelfart.

MIDDELFART (pop. 18,900) was historically the site of a ferry between Fyn and Jutland—and it retained that function until the first bridge was built across Lillebælt in 1935.

■ **Tourist information**: Havnegade 10; tel. 64 41 17 88.

■ **Hotels**: Kongebrogaarden, Kongebrovej 63; tel. 64 41 11 22; Hindsgavl Slot (Mansion), Hindsgavl Allé 7; tel. 64 41 88 00.

Middelfart is mentioned in the early 13C King Valdemar's Landbook and in the Knytlingesaga, and received its charter in 1496. As a ferry site, it has had its share of famous historical personages on their travels, not least Christian II, who spent a month here in 1523 after the Jutlandic nobility had renounced their allegiance to him, and it suffered both under the Count's War and the 1658 war against Sweden.

Middelfart has never been one of the richer towns on Fyn, and this is seen in the modest nature of many of the older buildings, though the charm of the half-timbered houses is ever present. There are some larger ones, however, one of which, BROGADE 8, dates from c 1600 and is now a folk museum. **St Nicolas' Church**, over 40m long, with corbie gables, mainly late Gothic, though with a Romanesque chancel, stands on ALGADE, on a hill overlooking the harbour. The richly adorned auricular altarpiece is from c 1650, and the predella contains a painting by Eckersberg from 1842. The bench ends are mid-17C, and two of them bear the insignia of Christian IV. The marble font in the form of an angel dates from 1845 and is the work of Thorvaldsen's pupil H.W. Bissen. There is a large collection of gravestones in the church, several dating from the mid 16C.

If you are interested in construction, you might visit the **Bridge Exhibition**, Broudstillingen, in ALGADE 4, illustrating the building of the old bridge across Lillebælt, 1924–35.

Middelfart is exactly half-way between the two bridges spanning **Lillebælt**. Immediately west of the old bridge stands the mansion of **Hindsgavl**, dating back to c 1200 (remains of the original ramparts can be seen), but now a neo-classical building from 1784. It is used as an hotel and a conference centre. The delightful park, with views across the sound and to the tiny island of Fænø, is open to the public.

12 • Tønder to Kolding

*Total distance 81km. A11/A25, A25 to (15km) **Løgumkloster**. (18km) Toftlund. (48km) *Kolding.*

You leave *Tønder (p 198) on the A11/A25, driving north for c 6km. Turn right on the A25, and follow it for c 9km until you meet the 401. Here you should divert by turning right and going to (2km) **Løgumkloster**, (pop. 7000).

■ **Tourist information**: Østergade 13; tel. 74 74 41 65.

■ **Hotels**: Central, Markedsgade 15; tel. 74 74 30 50; Løgumkloster Refugium, Refugievej 1; tel. 74 74 33 01.

■ **Youth hostel**: Vænget 28; tel. 74 74 36 18.

■ The annual fair in August, **Kloster Mærken**, is the largest in Scandinavia. Originally called **St Bartholomew's Fair** (Bettemøs Mærken), it starts on the third Saturday in August, close to St Bartholomew's Day, the 25th.

Løgumkloster is a large village with wide streets and greenswards and many 18C houses. It contains the remains of a Cistercian monastery founded in 1173. Building on the *church began in 1190 and was completed more or less in its present form by 1325. The oldest extant part is the present north door, while the chancel and impressive corbie gable are high Gothic. Note in particular the splendid east end, with its intricate windows and gabling. The monastery was suppressed after the Reformation, in 1548, though the buildings were left standing for some time. A section of the west wall can still be seen, and on the east wing the chapter house and dormitory have been restored.

The chancel is large in relation to the nave, reflecting the fact that the clergy sat there, while the nave was reserved for the lay brothers. One notable architectural feature is the lack of vaulting at the intersection of the nave and transept, giving it the appearance of a cupola. There are, as is customary in a Cistercian monastery, few decorations in the spacious and beautiful church, but in the chancel there are some interesting misericords from c 1500. There is also a 14C reliquary in the wall, with space for 16 relics. An elaborate antependium from 1325 is now in the National Museum in Copenhagen. In the crypt there is an exhibition illustrating the history of the monastery and of the Cistercian order in general.

Immediately adjoining the west wall of the church is a building known as **Slottet** (The Castle), now used as a training centre for the clergy. It was built as a hunting lodge in 1614 by Duke Johann Adolph of Gottorp, and has subsequently been used for various purposes. The bishop and poet Hans Adolf Brorson lived here for a time, and it is said that it was here he was converted to his pietist views.

An attempt has been made in the present century to re-create something of the spiritual calm with which Løgumkloster was formerly associated, and in 1959–61 a **Refugium** or Retreat Centre was built and opened. It is connected to the church by a covered walkway and is open to people of all religious persuasions seeking a respite from everyday life. On the opposite side of the river there is now a folk high school, and close by a modern bell-tower, **Frederik IX Klokkespil**, with a carillon of 49 bells on which aspiring carilloneurs are trained. It can be heard six times a day.

A museum called **Holmen** contains exhibits reflecting medieval church life and modern church art (open Easter–Oct). In front of it there is a statue by Alice Buchhave of a Cistercian monk. On the town square there is a statue of three jugglers commemorating St Bartholomew's Fair.

A more sombre commemoration is found in the cemetery immediately south of the town, where there is a **memorial** to 70 Russian, Belgian and French prisoners of war who were held here during World War I (when this was German territory), and who died during a typhoid epidemic. The memorial was placed there by their fellow prisoners.

From Løgumkloster you drive northwest to (2km) **Løgumgårde**, where the old parish church of **Nørre Løgum Kirke** is situated. This consists of a Romanesque chancel and nave, with Gothic extensions, including a late 14C tower. The auricular pulpit is from c 1630 and the (much adapted) altarpiece from 1400. The entire church is decorated with frescoes by the Lily Master.

You then drive north, through (4km) **Nørre Løgum** village, turning off left after a further 5km to (3km) **Arrild**. Here you will find an impressive church with a Romanesque nave and Gothic tower. The beamed roof is richly decorated with acanthus leaves. The altar has a painted Gothic antependium and is surmounted by an elaborate triptych from c 1475. Much of the remaining furniture is also of early date, not least the carved bench ends from c 1550.

In Arrild, too, there is a modern holiday village, consisting of some 400 holiday homes, many of them available for letting. Information on these can be had in Toftlund tourist information centre (tel. 74 83 11 19).

7km further north on the A25 you arrive at **Toftlund**, a small town, centrally placed, with excellent road connections to Tønder, Ribe, Haderslev, Åbenrå and Flensborg, and giving easy access to the beautiful countryside—woodland and moorland—in this part of South Jutland.

Toftlund *****church** is an unusual shape, the nave on the south side being lined with three gables which for all the world look like the gables of houses facing the road, such as are seen in Tønder and other towns in South Jutland. The pitched roofs on these gables are intended to harmonise with that surmounting the much older tower. They represent extensions from 1912 to 1913 to this otherwise Romanesque/Gothic church.

The nearby **Tislund Church** is the oldest in South Jutland. To reach this you take a road east from the northern outskirts of Toftlund towards Bevtoft, turning left after c 3km. The small church is entirely Romanesque with the exception of a porch from 1852. There are four original Romanesque windows, of which one, in the north side, has not been bricked up. Note the small, rounded chancel arch, unchanged since it was built. There is a reliquary in the medieval altar. The altarpiece is an early 16C triptych with simple but skilfully carved figures, and the granite font is Romanesque. The pulpit is from c 1575, unfortunately 'modernised' c 1700, when the original carving was planed off to make way for some second-rate paintings of the four Evangelists.

9km north of Toftlund the A25 runs through Gabøl, from where you should drive the extra 8km west along the A47 to **Gram** to visit the splendid mansion of **Gram Slot**.

■ **Tourist information**: Østergade 10; tel. 74 82 01 11.

■ **Hotels**: Den Gamle Kro, Slotsvej 47; tel. 74 82 16 20; Gram Slotskro, Slotsvej 52; tel. 74 82 16 14)

Standing on a bend by the main road, Gram Slot was built c 1500 to replace a castle dating back to 1231 which stood some 3km further northwest. Surrounded by woodland, and fronted by the castle pond, it now houses the **Central Southern Jutland Museum**, with archaeological and geological collections connected with the area. Perhaps most surprising is the six-million-year-old skeleton of a whale discovered in a claypit nearby. On the opposite side of the main road, you will find the **South Jutland Fire Service Museum** (open summer).

From Gabøl you drive further north on the A25 through delightful varied countryside to (13km) **Jels** (**Tourist Information**: Jes Møllegade 5; tel. 74 55 21 10). Here there is a thoroughly restored windmill (open summer), and here, too, in the woodland down by one of the three local lakes, there are ramparts dating from Viking times, **Jels Voldsted**. There is also an open air stage where there is so-called Viking entertainment in July.

The road now runs northeast to (11km) **Vamdrup**. This small town, now virtually unknown, was once the Danish border station for the main European railway lines to Scandinavia. It was built by the English when the Danish railways were expanding rapidly, and the English presence is still to be seen in some of the architecture. The old railway station is now a **museum** illustrating the history of the railways.

From Vamdrup the road continues northeast to (5km) **Hjarup**, where there is a 17C half-timbered former parsonage. 5km further on the road meets the E45, which you can join if you wish to go north or east without going in to Kolding. Otherwise you drive a further 5km to Kolding, (pop. 59,000), Denmark's seventh largest city.

Kolding

■ **Tourist information**: Akseltorv 8; tel. 75 53 21 00.

■ **Hotels**: Scanticon, Skovbrynet; tel. 75 50 15 55; Saxildhus, Banegårdspladsen; tel. 75 52 12 00;

■ **Youth hostel**: Ørnsborgvej 10; tel. 75 50 91 40).

■ Kolding has one of Denmark's largest **marinas**, situated at the mouth of the harbour. It is possible to **hire boats**, and there are **sailing trips** on the fjord on Wednesdays and Sundays in the summer.

History
Kolding is first mentioned in the 13C King Valdemar II's *Jordebog* (a kind of Domesday Book) and has a charter from 1321 (though this was probably not its first); it was an important commercial centre in the Middle Ages because of its position as a junction north–south and east–west and its proximity to the German-speaking lands to the south, and it still has a busy harbour, the most important in the country for the export of cattle.

In the Middle Ages the castle, Koldinghus, which King Erik Glipping saw as 'a gateway and key to the realm' was a place where the Court met, and many members of the nobility subsequently built mansions there or in the immediate neighbourhood. As a consequence, Kolding was the scene of more than one dramatic event. It was there in 1365 that Valdemar Atterdag was reconciled with the sons of the hated Count Gert of Holstein, who at one time ruled all Jutland and in 1340 held Kolding in pawn. In 1411 Erik of Pomerania concluded a peace treaty here with Duchess Elizabeth of Schleswig. Later, the ubiquitous Christian II met his uncle Duke Frederik (later King Frederik I) here in 1522, and Kolding was the site of an abortive attempt in 1534 to put an end to the Count's War. Skipper Klement, the peasants' leader during the Count's War, was imprisoned for a time in the fortress of Koldinghus.

A period of decline ensued in the 17C continuing until the mid-19C when the harbour facilities were greatly improved; later the advent of the railways brought new significance and new trade. In the 1848–50 war against Holstein, Kolding was at first the site of the Danish military headquarters, but was a time occupied by enemy troops.

***Koldinghus**, standing on high ground overlooking the surrounding country-side and fjord, is the only royal fortress now surviving in Jutland, and several kings have been closely associated with it.

It was the birthplace in 1545 of Duke Hans the Younger, the first ancestor of the present Danish Royal House, and the following year of his younger sister, Dorothea, an ancestor of the British House of Hannover. Christian II included it in a list of three castles (the others being Ribe and Skanderborg) which were to

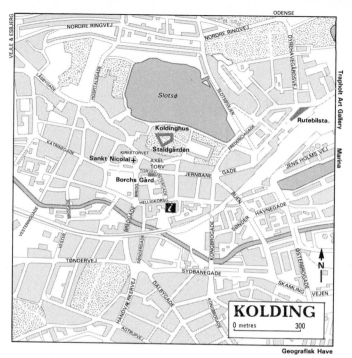

Geografisk Have

be maintained. Frederik II lived here as a boy, Christian IV is said to have written his first Latin essay here, and Frederik IV met his future mistress and subsequently queen here when he sought refuge against the plague in 1711. It was the favourite residence of Christian III, and he died there on New Year's Day 1559.

It is not known exactly when the first Koldinghus was built, but historical sources claim that it was founded in 1284 by Duke Abel as 'a defence or border fortress' after his brother, Erik Plovpenning, had burned down parts of Kolding. It is, however, certain that Erik Glipping helped rebuild the castle in 1268. Christoffer of Bavaria built the north wing in 1447, and Christian I added the west wing in 1470. Christian II was responsible for the south wing, with its royal apartments, and for the East Wing. Christian IV, the king who provided Denmark with many fine buildings and an enormous national debt, built the Chapel and the great tower on which he placed four 2.25m-high sandstone figures: Hannibal, Hector, Scipio and Hercules. High above the surrounding countryside, and each facing his own point of the compass, these figures, with the three Scandinavian crowns on their shields, symbolised Christian's dream of a united Scandinavia—under himself. Only Hercules survives, and he faces south.

Koldinghus has suffered from fire and damage on many occasions. The north and west wings burned down in 1533; there was another fire in 1597; and yet others in 1627 and 1644. In 1658 Polish troops stormed the castle, which at the time was in the possession of the Swedes. The greatest catastrophe, however, came in 1808 during the Napoleonic Wars. Spanish troops stationed in the castle accidentally set fire to it and it was almost completely razed to the ground. Christian IV's great tower collapsed and took much of the vaulting of the chapel with it. The decision to rebuild Koldinghus after the 1808 fire was not taken until 1867, the National Museum being given responsibility in 1890. The task has now been completed, and the castle is open to the public. Rather than attempt to return it to its original appearance, this highly original restoration complements the ruins and, by a series of galleries, allows free movement within. The castle also contains numerous exhibitions, both permanent and itinerant. Adjoining the castle is the well-preserved and charming old part of the town, largely reserved for pedestrians. Here, at AXELTORV 2, is **Borchs Gård**, a large, three-storeyed house said to have the most elaborately decorated gabled façade in Denmark. It was built in 1595 by an apothecary, Herman Reiminck, whose initials are worked into the decorations in the lintel over the front door. There are acanthus leaves and angels' heads, and at the top of the gable there is a huge rosette.

The oldest surviving house in Kolding, HELLIGKORSGADE 18, bears the date 1589 and was the home of a shoemaker; it is again three-storeyed, a typical Renaissance half-timbered house, restored in 1915. Together with the house next door, **Morten Eriksens Gård**, with an inscription stating that it was rebuilt in 1632, it gives some impression of what Kolding must have looked like when houses of this kind and size were commonplace.

The principal church in Kolding, **Sankt Nicolai Kirke**, standing on KIRKETORVET, was founded in the mid-13C, though after a thorough restoration in the 1880s there is now little left of the original building. Nevertheless, it still contains a splendidly carved and imposing Renaissance altarpiece and pulpit dating from 1589 and 1591. Claus Lauritzen's sandstone font, in the same style, is from 1619.

The 19C National Romantic poet Carl Ploug (1813–94) was born in Kolding. He is commemorated with a statue, and there is a plaque on the spot where his house used to stand. There is a certain irony in the fact that Carl Ploug's doggedly nationalistic ideas were those largely responsible for the Danish defeat at the hands of the Prussians in 1864. On JERNBANEPLADSEN there is also a statue to the Liberal politician Chresten Berg (1829–91).

The **Trapholt Art Gallery** opened in 1988 as one of the largest galleries in Denmark. Situated in a beautiful position overlooking the Kolding Fjord, it specialises in Danish art and handicrafts from the present century and incorporates all the most modern museum principles. **Geografisk Have** is a botanical garden, with a fine collection of trees and plants from all over the world, including a rose garden with 125 different varieties, a scent garden and the largest bamboo grove in Europe.

13 • Tønder to Nyborg via Sønderborg

Total distance 137km, plus ferry. A8 throughout. (37km) Kruså. (28km) **Sønderborg**. *(16km) Fynshav. Ferry to Bøjden on Fyn (50 mins). (11km)* **Fåborg**. *(45km)* **Nyborg**.

This route at first runs close to the 63km-long border between Denmark and Germany. The border has not always lain here; after the 1864 war it was much further to the north, but a plebiscite was held in the area in 1920 to decide on a final border between the two countries; voting took place parish by parish, and the present line follows the local wishes then expressed. Even after World War II, no changes were made to the 1920 border, which over the years has become less and less formal. For much of its length it follows the courses of rivers, but elsewhere you will find villages where it runs straight down the middle of a street, or farms with fields on either side of it.

There *is* a border, then, and it is both political and cultural, but there are equally areas of cultural affinity. One of these is the work of the great Expressionist painter Emil Nolde (1867–1956), who was born in the now Danish village of Nolde; but he was a German-speaker and by the art world has always been considered as belonging to German Expressionism. There are plenty of signs of his presence on the Danish side of the border, but the magnificent **Nolde Museum** is in Seebüll, just south of the border in Germany.

From *Tønder (p 198) you take the A8 east to (14km) **Burkal**, where there is a Romanesque church from the first half of the 13C, one of the most richly decorated in South Jutland.

The outstanding feature is the ornate 17C painted ceiling over the nave, which was revealed during restoration work in 1943. Against a blue and blue-grey background there are 13 medallions representing Christ and the Apostles, accompanied by 26 others representing the arts, virtues and seasons. The altarpiece is a rare piece of Renaissance work from 1622, the centrepiece containing reliefs instead of the more usual paintings; the pulpit and canopy, typical of this area, are from the same period. The crucifixion group fixed in the chancel arch is much earlier, from 1500–25.

In Burkal you will also find the large Grøndal farm with a barn built in the Holstein style—brick walls, whitewashed, surmounted by a sweeping thatched hipped roof, rounded over the doorways.

Before continuing you might also like to drive 2km south to **Rens**, where there is a large old watermill.

From Burkal you take the A8 to (11km) **Tinglev**. There is little of architectural interest here, but Tinglev is the focus of German cultural life in the region. Between 1920 and the period after World War II, great efforts were made by the minorities of both countries to maintain and support their cultures, and Tinglev provides plenty of evidence of this, with German schools and nursery schools, German-language newspapers and German-language political organisations. For many years nationalist feelings on both sides ran very high indeed, but now things are different, and tolerance reigns—though no one in this area can be unaware that two cultures meet here.

The A8 continues southeast through (10km) Fårhus where you turn right towards **Frøslev**, a place which has played a role in modern history. It was the site of a concentration and internment camp during World War II, and many of the 13,000 or so Danes held here were further despatched to concentration camps in Germany itself. After the war the name was changed to Fårhus Camp, and Danish collaborators were housed here to await trial. Now it has been thoroughly restored and is the home of several *museums: the National Museum has exhibits here, as have the Danish Civil Defence and Red Cross Organisation. Some of the accommodation has been left as it was when Frøslev was used as an internment camp, and there are also exhibits to show what life was like in South Jutland during the Occupation (closed Dec–Jan). There is also a UN museum illustrating the work of the Danish soldiers who have served under the UN flag since 1948.

From Frøslev it is only 2km east to **Bov**, north of Padborg. Again there are memories of wars here. On 9 April 1848 Danish troops fought and won a battle at Bov against Schleswig-Holstein troops, and there are graves in the churchyard to remind visitors of this event and of the 1848 war in general. Both north and south of the present border there are countless places with memories of border conflicts over the ages (often in the form of war memorials and soldiers' graves), ranging from the Dannevirke fortifications (now south of the border) to a memorial in Padborg to the three border guards shot on duty at the time of the invasion in 1940. **Bov Museum**, housed in a building from 1528, contains excellent local collections covering the history of the **Military Road** (p 293) and displaying uniforms from the various wars affecting the region.

A further Danish relic now south of the border is Christian IV's Copper Mill (Danish Kobbermølle, German: Kupfermülle), just south of Kruså, where much of the finest 17C and 18C Danish copper was produced. The mill itself has gone, but the houses which Christian IV built for his workers still stand, in much the same style as Nyboder in Copenhagen.

From Bov you should drive northeast 2km to the Danish frontier town of Kruså, and from there you can stay on the A8 right to (11km) Rinkenæs. However, we suggest you leave the A8 1km after Kruså towards Kollund, and cover this short distance along the slightly longer coastal road instead.

This *road, which provides outstanding views of the Flensborg Fjord and the German coast and town of Glücksburg opposite, has been called the most beautiful coastal road in Denmark. Certainly Hans Christian Andersen subscribed to the view: 'The countryside around the Flensborg Fjord is without doubt one of the most picturesque parts of Schleswig; there are great forests, hills almost as big as mountains, and the ever-varying scenery of the winding fjord and the many quiet freshwater lakes.'

On the way you will pass through (4km) **Kollund** with its church from 1971, built in traditional Danish village style. A further 3km brings you to **Sønderhav**, with a view of the tiny **Okseøer** islands where tradition has it that Queen Margrethe I died of the plague in 1412. From Sønderhav it is a further beautiful 5km to Rinkenæs.

In **Rinkenæs** there are two churches, of which the older, standing on high ground, but without a tower, is Romanesque, with a 16C porch. It still contains some, but not all, of its original furniture—two statues of saints from the original altarpiece, the Virgin and Child, and 12 figures of the Apostles. The pulpit is from 1606. There are many old gravestones, including that of the first soldier to fall in the war of 1848. Some of the remaining furniture—a crucifix from the chancel arch and some late Gothic candlesticks—have been transferred to the new church, built in 1928–32 in traditional village church style. The carvings on the pulpit were begun by the sculptor Otto Bülow, but he was murdered by Occupation forces in 1943, and the work was completed by others.

From the outskirts of Rinkenæs it is well worth taking a walk along the fjord on the old **Gendarmsti**, the path once used by patrolling frontier guards.

Now continue to (2km) **Alnor**, where you should leave your main route, turn left and drive to **Gråsten** (2km) for a short detour.

▶ As you approach Gråsten there is a view across the Nybøl Nor (Nybøl Cove) on your right, and then on your left the Slotssø, Palace Lake.

Gråsten

■ **Tourist information**: Kongevej 71; tel. 74 65 09 55.

■ **Hotels**: Axelhus, Borggade 16; tel. 74 65 06 15; Alnor Kro, Gammel Færgevej 38, Alnor; tel. 74 65 12 68.

After passing the lake you turn left on to the 481, and immediately on your left again you will arrive at what you have really come to see, **Gråsten Palace**. This three-winged structure dates from 1759 when it was built to replace the earlier palace, much of which was destroyed by fire in 1757. It was redesigned in 1842 and given in 1935 to the then Crown Prince and his wife, and it is still the summer residence of the Queen Mother, Queen Ingrid. When Queen Ingrid is not in residence there is public access to the courtyard, castle and exuberant Baroque *chapel, which, with an altarpiece stretching from floor to ceiling and much as when originally consecrated in 1700, is now used as a parish church. When the Queen is in residence, there is a ceremony of changing the guard on Fridays at 12.00. The deer park is normally open to the public.

Hans Christian Andersen visited the castle in 1845 as the guest of Duke Christian August of Augustenborg, and it was here he wrote his story *The Little Match Girl*. Here, too, the memories of a frontier area are preserved, in that there is a memorial outside the castle grounds to the colonel who, single-handed, offered resistance to the Gestapo in 1944 when they came to arrest him—and after a three-hour-long battle paid with his life.

During the third weekend in July each year, Gråsten has a festival of tilting in the ring, and during the last week of August there is a large-scale fair and market in the town. Throughout the summer pleasure boats sail on the fjord and you can enjoy the beautiful landscape from the water. West of Gråsten lies one of Denmark's finest beech forests. It is open to the public, and there are count-less paths for a walk in idyllic surroundings. ◀

Continuing your route from Alnor you should take the A8 east across the Egernsund narrows to (5km) **Broager** (**Tourist information**: Storegade 23; tel. 74 44 11 00), the main town on the undulating **Broagerland** peninsula dotted with small woodlands, criss-crossed with hedges, with steep cliffs overlooking the fjord to the east, and with long stretches of excellent beaches from which to bathe.

From far afield you can see **Broager Church**, with its twin towers, an unusual sight in Denmark. Legend has it that these towers, surmounted by decorated tiled spires, were built in memory of Siamese twin sisters who were joined at the hip. (And 19C excavations did in fact unearth the skeletons of such twins.) So tall are the towers that during the 1864 war the Prussians used one of them as a look-out post to direct gun fire at the Dybbøl fortifications further east. In 1923 restorations uncovered frescoes from both the 13C and 16C, including Christ in Majesty in the apse and, in the north transept, a series depicting in graphic detail the martyrdom of St George. Clearly connected with these is the splendid (though restored) life-size figure of St George on horseback slaying the dragon, standing in the tower.

To the east of the church is a free-standing wooden belfry of a type commonly found in this area. Topped with an octagonal spire, it dates from 1650, and is the largest in the country. Nearby there is a memorial mound surrounded by stones bearing the names of the 190 members of the parish, then German citizens, who were killed in World War I. Of older date are both Danish and German graves from the two Dano-Prussian wars.

If you take the A8 east from Broager and then turn right into the 481, you will come to (4km) **Dybbøl**. If any place in this part of Denmark signifies national feeling *vis-à-vis* German culture, it must surely be this.

Battles were fought here during the first Dano-Prussian war of 1848, and then the area was fortified in 1857 with extensive *earthworks to serve as a second line of defence in the event of the Dannevirke fortifications falling in a future war. On the night of 5 February 1864, during the second Dano-Prussian war, Dannevirke did indeed fall, but the Dybbøl fortifications were not yet complete, and after a violent bombardment lasting 34 days, they, too, were taken, an event which in practice brought the war to an end and put the entire area under German rule until 1920. After the war the Prussians completed the fortifications, and most of those now on view were in fact built by them, not the Danes.

Dybbøl has come to symbolise Danish defeat and Danish national aspirations, and the particular symbol of these is the **Dybbøl Mill**, standing on high ground, and offering panoramic views of the entire fortified area. Originally built on this spot in 1744 or 1745, the windmill has been burned down three times, twice as a result of the wars, and once by accident in 1935. The entire area is full of war graves, of both Danes and Prussians, one of the most touching being of two Danish soldiers buried in a private front garden beside the road at nearby **Bøffelkobbel**.

The area around Dybbøl has figured in patriotic poetry and in fiction, nowhere more poignantly than in the novel *Tina* by Herman Bang, where the mood of the Danes during the battle near Dannevirke is vividly portrayed. In addition to the small museum that has been there for some time, there is now the **Dybbøl Banke Battlefield Centre** (open summer), containing exhibits and memorials of the wars, including war graves and fortifications, and the area immediately surrounding Dybbøl Mill is a national memorial park. From an earlier period there is the Romanesque church from c 1250, with a crucifix above the chancel arch from c 1200. On the hill at Dybbøl you will also find the huge red granite erratic boulder, the **Dybbøl Stone**, 8.8m long, 6.7m wide and 2.7m high.

From Dybbøl it is only 3km along the 481, crossing the elegant high bridge built in 1980 to span the narrow Als Sound, to Sønderborg, the principal town on Als, the seventh largest of the Danish islands.

The island of **Als** is c 34km long from northwest to southeast, with a curved east coast lined with dunes and fine beaches, while the west coast is indented and irregular, approaching to within 120m of Jutland at **Als Sound** with its deep and sometimes fast-flowing water. The countryside is wooded and varied—and very beautiful. The roads are good and allow you to experience this rather special island at your leisure. And while you do so, you should remember that the present idyll covers over a past which has been marked by violence extending back to the Wends and the Vikings.

SØNDERBORG (pop. 29,000) meaning 'Southern Castle', has grown up around a royal castle dating back to the 12C, probably founded by Valdemar I (Valdemar the Great) as a defence against the Wends, and later becoming a residence both voluntary and involuntary for Danish kings when in the south of the country. It was here that Christian II spent 17 years of his life, from 1532 to 1549, after the safe conduct promised him had been broken by the nobility. As imprisonments go, his was probably rather comfortable.

■ **Tourist information**: Rådhustorvet 7; tel. 74 42 35 55.

■ **Hotels**: Scandic, Rosengade 2; tel. 74 42 19 00; City, Kongevej 64; tel. 74 42 16 26.

■ **Youth hostel**: Kærvej 70; tel. 74 42 31 12.

■ The medieval tradition of tilting has been maintained in South Jutland, and a four-day-long **festival of tilting** is held each summer, beginning on the second Saturday in July, preceded by a solemn procession of those taking part.

If there is a scarcity of old buildings in Sønderborg, with the exception of the area around HAVBOGADE, it is for once not because of fires, but because it was severely damaged by Prussian artillery during the 1864 war. However, the **Castle**, now a museum, stands, massive and impressive, on a tiny headland jutting out into the south entrance to the Als Sound. It forms an irregular rectangle, with a 10m-high tower built into the northwest corner, and shows traces of rebuilding in the 14C. The character of the castle changed in the period 1550–70, when it was transformed into a Renaissance palace with no military potential. During the 17C Swedish wars, however, it fell into disrepair, and it was then rebuilt in the 18C in Baroque style. In the 19C it was again severely damaged, serving for a time as a military hospital and then as a Prussian barracks. The 20C has seen a gradual restoration, first in the 1930s, then in the 1950s and 1960s. The chapel, often called the Queen Dorothea Chapel after the Queen who was responsible for much of the 16C rebuilding, was restored in 1954–55 and reflects the new church style deriving from the Reformation, with the pulpit occupying a central position.

As the largest provincial *****museum** in Denmark, the castle now has extensive collections illustrating the history of the castle and the surrounding area; it also contains a fine art collection including works by C.A. Lorentsen, C.A. Jensen and C.W. Eckersberg, who had his roots in this area and is sometimes called the father of Danish painting. Naturally, the Dano-Prussian wars of the 19C are well represented, as are the two world wars and the reunification of this area with Denmark in 1920. Of curiosity interest are the decrees issued by the self-styled President of Als when, in 1918, as part of a naval mutiny in North Germany, a disgruntled sailor by the name of Bruno Topff proclaimed Als a republic. His 'presidency' lasted for three days.

There are the remains of one other very old building in Sønderborg, though in the course of the 17C, 19C and 20C it has been extensively rebuilt. Even the name was changed in 1957 from St George's Church to St Mary's Church, **Mariekirken**. Nevertheless, there is some old furniture left, the altarpiece being from 1618, the font from 1600, and the carved pulpit (the work of Master Hinrich Ringerinck of Flensborg) from 1599. On the north wall there is a cupboard from the 15C. The other church in Sønderborg, built in 1957 and designed by Kåre and Esben Klint, the architects responsible for the Grundtvig Church in Copenhagen, is modern Gothic, an adaptation of the traditional corbie-gable village style.

From Sønderborg the main road goes northeast to (3km) Ulkebøl, where it rejoins the A8. **Ulkebøl** itself is now virtually a suburb of Sønderborg, containing a good deal of industry and the airport. Here, too, however, in what was once a separate village, stands the Romanesque *church which was formerly the principal church for Sønderborg, extended and rebuilt in 1787 to exhibit some of the architectural features of the Augustenborg Palace Chapel (see below). There is an ornate triptych from c 1525, carved in Antwerp, and, above the altar, a late Romanesque crucifixion group from c 1250. The tower is remarkable in being as broad as the nave.

From Ulkebøl the A8 continues to (5km) **Augustenborg** on the island of Als.

■ **Tourist information**: Storegade 28; tel. 74 47 17 20.

■ **Hotel**: Frydendal Kro, Helved 1; tel. 74 47 41 09.

Strictly speaking **Als**, does not form part of southern Jutland but is a separate entity, once the domain of the Dukes of Augustenborg.

It was a Duke of Augustenborg who built the first **Augustenborg Palace** in 1660, while a successor replaced it between 1770 and 1776 with the present three-winged mansion, the biggest and most imposing in this part of Denmark, dignified, totally symmetrical, slightly severe in its splendour. It has had a mixed fate, having been a military hospital and a barracks—and is now a mental hospital. The park is open to the public: note the memorial plaque near the tree under which Hans Christian Andersen used to sit. The splendid Baroque chapel is used as a parish church, with rich, ornate decorations in white and gold.

►Excursion to north Als from Augustenborg

From Augustenborg you take a minor road north to (3km) **Ketting**, where, standing on high ground overlooking the delightful village, there is yet another church with an unusually broad tower, dating back to the early 13C. The original chancel and nave, which were slightly older, were pulled down and replaced in 1773. The altarpiece is from 1743, but parts of two earlier altarpieces from c 1450 and 1500 can also be seen in the chancel and on the north wall, while there is a crucifix from c 1300 above the chancel arch. The large parsonage from 1802 is a little east of the village, approached by an avenue of elms and chestnuts. There is a bishop's palace (Bispegård) in Ketting, for this was the seat of a bishop from 1819, when Als and Ærø formed a diocese, until 1864, when Als became part of the diocese of Schleswig.

An unclassified road now leads north to (2.5km) **Egen**, another charming and idyllic village. Here you will find the largest (75m long) thatched church stable in Denmark, with stabling for 34 horses to rest while their owners are in church. The church itself, originally dedicated to St Martin, goes back to the 13C. The chancel and nave are Romanesque, the remainder later. There is a free-standing medieval bell-tower in the churchyard, erected on top of an ancient burial mound.

Continue north through (9km) Oksbøl to (2km) **Nordborg**, where the old village has been extended to the southeast and now adjoins the modern **Langesø**, built for the workers in the Danfoss factory only 4km away (see below).

■ **Tourist information**: Stationsvej 8; tel. 74 45 05 92.

■ **Hotels**: Havnbjerg Stationskro, Skolevej 30, Havnbjerg; tel. 74 45 10 19; Nørherredhus, Mads Clausensvej; tel. 74 45 05 35.

Nevertheless, Nordborg has its charm, and to the north lies **Nordborg Castle**, dating back to the 11C, and in its way forming a North Als parallel to Sønderborg Castle. And like Sønderborg, Nordborg has been used as a prison, for Bishop Valdemar of Schleswig, and for Erik Glipping (when he was 12 years old!). The original castle has been destroyed, and the present building dates from 1909. It is now a college, and the grounds are open to the public in summer.

From Nordborg the 405 goes southeast to (3km) **Havnbjerg**, where there is a Romanesque church containing remains of Romanesque and Gothic frescoes. The altar painting is by Eckersberg. Here, too, there is a splendidly restored thatched Dutch windmill from 1835 (open), together with a dwelling house and outbuildings of an unusual type. The 405 now continues to (1km) **Danfoss**, the home of the Danfoss factory—refrigerators, thermostats, central heating—which was the brainchild of a local inhabitant in the 1930s and since the 1950s has grown to employ over 6000 people.

Hjortspring, 2km further along the road, is where in 1920 a 4C ship, surrounded by weapons, was found in a bog where it is assumed to have been put as a sacrifice. It is now in the National Museum in Copenhagen.

From Hjortspring you return to (12km) Augustenborg.◄

▶Excursion to south Als from Augustenborg

This in effect a rather longer alternative to the main route (below) from Augustenborg to the ferry harbour at Fynshav, but it also gives you an impression of the beautiful scenery of South Als.

Leave Augustenborg on a minor road south to (3km) **Kirke Hørup**, where there is a Romanesque/Gothic church with a free-standing medieval bell-tower, partly rebuilt in 1689. Part of the altarpiece is from 1425. In Kirke Hørup, turning left on to the 427, you now travel via Skovby and across the Drejet embankment to **Sønderby** (17km), where there are panoramic views across the Flensborg Fjord. Here, too, is **Kegnæs church**, built 1615–16 by Duke Hans, with a porch from 1695, on the outside of which there is an original sundial. The altarpiece is from 1450, possibly transferred from Sønderborg, which received a new altarpiece in 1618; the chancel arch crucifixion group is from c 1500.

You will now have to return to Skovby by the same route, and from here you then take a minor road north to (2km) **Lysabild**, where there is a medieval pilgrims' church containing a chapel dedicated to the Holy Blood. There are also frescoes from 1425 depicting the Crucifixion. As part of the foundations to the north wall a Bronze Age cresset stone has been used and is still visible. West of the churchyard lies the parsonage, from 1826, with an impressive magnificent example of a Holstein type barn, from 1783.

From Lysabild you drive north to (2.5km) a crossroads. A right turn here will bring you to (2km) **Mommark**, where you can take the ferry to Søby on the delightful island of Ærø (p 172). Otherwise, you continue north through **Blommeskobbel**, with its prehistoric remains, to (8km) Fynshav ferry harbour.◀

Returning to the main route, on leaving Augustenborg you continue along the A8 for c 5km until you come to a road on your left pointing north to Hundslev. Take this and drive as far as **Notmark** (1km), where, standing in a beautiful churchyard, there is a fine church, with a Romanesque chancel and nave, and a late Romanesque tower of impressive proportions, finished with gables to the north and south. The nave has a beamed roof, while above the chancel there is vaulting bearing frescoes of coats of arms. A processional crucifix above the altar is from c 1525. Nearby there is a thatched stable in which parishioners could keep their horses while at church. The parsonage, clearly visible from the road, is from 1688, a delightful thatched half-timbered house with patterned brickwork, thoroughly restored in 1952. It is the only Danish parsonage originally having dwelling house, stables and barn all under one roof. And huge this hipped roof is, with its two broad gables.

Return now by the same road, and cross the A8 to go only as far as **Asserballe** (1km) where the Romanesque church stands on high ground. However, despite several pieces of old furniture, it is particularly for its literary associations you should see this church and the nearby parsonage. It was in the idyllic *parsonage here that the novelist Herman Bang was born in 1857, and it is this house in which much of the action in his autobiographical novel *The White House* is set. Asserballe is similarly the setting of Bang's novel *Tina*, with its moving portrayal of the Danish defeat at the hands of the Prussians in the 1864 war—though it has to be admitted that Bang was no longer in Asserballe when these events took place.

Go back again to the A8 and drive east to (4km) **Fynshav**, where you take the ferry to Bøjden on the island of Fyn (50 mins). Here you follow the A8 east to (6km) Horne.

Horne boasts one of the seven round churches in Denmark, and the only one on Fyn. Sadly, the original round church has been extended to comprise the usual chancel, nave and tower, though its original form is still clearly distinguishable, 17m in diameter and much like the round churches of Bornholm (pp 33 ff). There were been two floors in the original structure, and there are arrow slits placed high in the 2m-thick walls, indicating that the upper floor was at one time used for defence. The original Romanesque chancel has been replaced by a long Gothic nave of the same height as the rotunda. The vaulting is late Gothic throughout.

The grey, blue and gold furniture is early 19C, and the painting above the altar is by Eckersberg. The marble font used at present is by Bertel Thorvaldsen, while there is another Romanesque granite font near the northwest pillar in the round church. The crucifix above the chancel arch is from 1525. One of the impressive features in the church is the *balcony directly facing the pulpit. It was built for use by the Bille-Brahe family, the owners of the nearby mansion of Hvedholm; their imposing neo-classical chapel can be seen in the churchyard outside. Hvedholm itself, rebuilt in the late 19C, lies to the right of the road c 1km further east, and is now a rest home.

4km further on, the A8 brings you to the northern outskirts of Fåborg (p 172). Do not just pass through this old town. It is well worth a visit.

From Fåborg there are two suggested routes to Nyborg and the nearby ferry harbour of Knudshoved. The direct route to Nyborg (total distance 51km), listed first, goes straight across Fyn, the alternative follows its southern coastline.

Direct route from Fåborg to Nyborg
Total distance 51km.

Leave Fåborg by the A8 northeast, skirting the delightful wooded hills of **Svanninge Bakker** to (8km) Korinth.

In the village of **Gerup**, 1km west of Korinth, the old school from 1784 has been turned into a **school museum** (open Saturday afternoons). North of Korinth on the east side of the beautiful **Arreskovsø lake**, the biggest lake on Fyn, you will find the 16C Renaissance **Arreskov mansion**, where visits to the park and the house can be arranged.

2km further along the A8 you will reach the great mansion of **Brahetrolleborg**. This was originally a Cistercian monastery from 1172, called Holmekloster, and the 13C church constituting the present north wing is the only remaining part of the early buildings. Other parts date from the 15C, and alterations and extensions were also carried out in the 16C, 17C and 19C. A thorough restoration in 1985 uncovered remains of the original monastery. After the Reformation the complex was taken over by the Crown and the name was changed, first to Rantzausholm and then, in 1667, to Brahetrolleborg. In the 18C the estate was turned into a model of social and agricultural progress. The park is open to the public.

Egeskov Castle

From Brahetrolleborg you continue along the A8 for 9km, where, on your left, you reach ***Egeskov**. This is an absolute must. Dating from 1554, it is one of the best preserved and most romantic of all Denmark's Renaissance castles, standing in the middle of a lake on a foundation of oak piles and huge boulders. With its twin pointed towers and ornate gabled walls it is the archetypal fairy-tale castle. The surrounding park, also among the best kept in the country, dates from the 18C and is divided into sections representing gardens in different traditions. It is famous for its hedges, and it contains one of the few mazes in Denmark. The house itself has undergone several restorations, most recently in the 1970s and 1980s; one of its most impressive features is the great *hall, now regularly used for concerts. The grounds also house a **museum** of veteran cars, aeroplanes, motorcycles and horse-drawn carriages. Egeskov is open to the public from May to end of September.

2km beyond Egeskov you reach Kværndrup (p 168), from where you might take an unclassified road east in the direction of Gudbjerg as far as **Mullerup** (7km), an estate with a history going back to 1474, situated in idyllic surroundings in the midst of a series of lakes and canals. The present building is from 1887 and now serves as a centre for the sale of antiques.

Otherwise leave Kværndrup to the northeast and follow the A8 to (7km) **Gislev**, where there are some fascinating early 16C frescoes in the church. Done in an unsophisticated style, they represent scenes from the life of Christ, and it has been suggested that the way in which Mary is shown worshipping the Child may indicate the influence of Brigittine visions. These frescoes are all in the vaulting, and there are remains of others, portraying Gethsemane, on the north wall.

From Gislev you can drive straight on to (6km) Ørbæk. However, we suggest you take a slightly less direct route.

Turn left in the middle of Gislev on to a minor road leading north to the mansion of **Lykkesholm** (2km), dating from the 1780s, and, like so many of the mansions in this area, associated with visits by Hans Christian Andersen. It is not open to the public, but visible from the road to the north. Continue to (1km) Ellested and turn right into the 323. Ørbæk is now only 4km away, but just before reaching the village you will find a track to your left leading to the huge Lindeskov Dolmen, **Lindeskovdyssen**, surrounded by 126 large stones. Drive on now to Ørbæk.

In the Romanesque church in **Ørbæk** there is again a wealth of colourful frescoes from c 1500, the work of a local artist known as the Clog Master. The Baroque altarpiece is late 17C, incorporating figures from a late Gothic triptych; the pulpit dates from c 1592.

Just 1km south of Ørbæk stands the mansion of **Ørbæklunde**. It is visible from the road, and you can get closer to it on foot, but not in your car. It is unusual in being one of the last fortified houses to be built in Denmark (1560–93). The spire is from 1593, and the side wing was added in 1660 (no public admission).

From Ørbæk the A8 continues to (7km) **Vindinge**, where the church possesses a large and famous crucifix by Claus Berg from the 1520s.

Now you can drive into (4km) **Nyborg** (see p 195).

Alternative route from Fåborg to Nyborg—via Svendborg
Total distance 60km.

Leave Fåborg on the A44 driving east. In (16km) **Vester Skerninge** there is a Romanesque church with an altarpiece by Eckersberg (1817). 2km further on you come to **Ollerup** where you will pass its famous High School for Gymnastics, which is clearly visible from the road, an impressive set of buildings dating from between 1920 and 1939.

►You really ought to allow yourself a short detour here. Turn north near Ollerup church on to a small road leading towards Egebjerg, simply to experience the most impressive scenery in South Fyn, the **Egebjerg Bakker** hills some 3km away.◄

Immediately after the Ollerup High School you pass **Hvidkilde Lake**. Here you will find a car park from which there are marked walks through the beautiful park of **Hvidkilde House**. 1.5km further, on your left, you pass Sørup Lake before arriving in Svendborg (p 167).

From Svendborg you continue northeast on the 163 to (7km) **Skårup**. The church here dates back to 1319, and some of the original Romanesque features are still visible amidst the Gothic extensions. In the churchyard there is a Gothic tithe barn which was once used to house the poor of the parish. The altarpiece, which was restored in 1929, is an elaborate Gothic carving from c 1470. The pulpit is mid 17C. The nave and chancel have vaulted ceilings, but that in the late Gothic tower is flat; it is said that the pastor used to keep his beer on the floor above it. The east frame of the south door of the church reveals a primitive Romanesque carving of a ship.

2km further north, in Vejstrup, you will find **Vejstrupgård**, a small mansion from 1754, in the grounds of which there is **Vejstrup Watermill**, the biggest two-wheeled watermill in Denmark, built in the 1830s. From Vejstrup it is only 7km to Hesselager, our next stop on the main route. However, if you do not mind a little meandering, we can take you past a few more mansions and another church before then.

3km north of Vejstrup on the left you come to a road leading to Gudme. Take this, and immediately after leaving the main road, on your left, there is the mansion of **Broholm**, with a history dating back to 1326, though the present buildings are from 1642, the square tower having been added in 1895. The principal wing is on a small islet in the middle of a lake. The courtyard is open to the public.

Continue to (2km) **Gudme**, where there is a church of particular note. You will immediately notice the enormously wide late Gothic tower, much bigger than is to be expected on a church of this size, and somehow out of keeping with the corbie steps at the west end and over the south door from 1603. All the vaults inside are decorated with fresco ornamentation, and there is another large fresco on one of the walls illustrating the legend of St George. A date above the chancel arch indicates that they are from 1488. The altarpiece is a simple carving from the end of the 15C, and there are two late Gothic choir stalls, thought to be from Claus Berg's workshop.

Return now to the 163 via Broholm, turn right, and almost immediately left again on to a minor road leading to (4km) **Lundeborg**, a tiny fishing village with views across the water to the island of Langeland. There used to be ferries from here to Langeland, but the Svendborgsund Bridge has put an end to that. However, the village is well worth visiting. There are paths along the coast in each direction, and the bathing is good. If you need a nice inn at this stage, you will find one here too. Recent archaeological excavations have demonstrated that the Gudme-Lundeborg area was once an important trading centre, and a royal residence has also been discovered here.

On returning from Lundeborg, in 1.5km you come to a crossroads. Turn right here. This road will take you in the direction of Hesselager, and in particular past (2km) **Hesselagergård**, one of the oldest and most impressive mansions in Denmark. Hesselagergård is first mentioned in 1446, and the present building, dating from 1538, was erected on the orders of the great Chancellor Johan Friis (1494–1570). It is visible from the road, with an unusual rounded Venetian *gable thought to have been built to the orders of Johan Friis himself after he had seen similar structures in Germany. It is a splendid piece of Renaissance architecture. Not open to the public.

2km further on lies Hesselager village.

The rather atypical **Hesselager** *church repeats the rounded gables of Hesselagergård mansion (see above). On the orders of Johan Friis they were added to the original Romanesque church in 1550. There are some frescoes in the church, including an illustration of the fable of the fox and the stork (which, here, is a crane), and the coats of arms of members of the Friis family. Among the numerous gravestones and memorials in the chapel, there is one ordered in 1557 by Johan Friis in memory of himself and his family. It portrays a very realistic figure of Death holding the coat of arms of the Friis family. To the north there is a well-preserved tithe barn, half of which served as a school around 1600, later to be used as a poor law institution.

If you follow a minor road east of Hesselager church for 2km you will find the **Hesselager Stone**, otherwise known as **Dammestenen** (The Damme Stone), a granite boulder thought to weigh about 1000 tonnes. It is 12m high and 46m in circumference. Legend has it that a witch threw the stone at the church in Hesselager, but missed. In practice it was brought here by ice from Norway during the Ice Age and is the largest erratic boulder in Denmark.

From Hesselager, take the 163 and continue north for about 2km to Langå, where you can turn left past the church to **Rygård mansion** (2km). There is access to an area close to the house, but not to the house itself, which can only be glimpsed through trees. Rygård was built just before Hesselagergård (c 1530), but looks much more the sombre medieval castle as, with water on two sides, it stands on piles driven into the marshy ground of a tiny island.

After the medieval aspect of Rygård and the early Renaissance air about Hesselagergård, the time has now come to see the neo-classical façade of **Glorup**. To find this you return to Langå, drive 1km north and turn left towards Svindinge immediately on leaving the village. Glorup is about 1km down this road.

There has been a mansion here since 1599, but the present neo-classical building dates from 1765. It is not open to the public, but there is access to the park on Thursday afternoons and all day Sunday. This *park is itself well worth a visit, the work of the French garden architect Nicolas-Henri Jardin, containing areas in the French and the English styles. There is a 'temple' from the 1870s, containing a statue of Andromeda by Johannes Wiedewelt—possibly originally intended for the Moltke Mansion, part of the royal Amalienborg palace in Copenhagen (p 89).

Glorup was one of the many mansions on Fyn which Hans Christian Andersen was particularly fond of visiting. He went there for the first time in 1839 and returned no fewer than 24 times over the next 30 years.

Back on the 163, drive north for a further 4km and turn off to (2km) Frørup, where you will find **Østfyns Landbrugsmuseum**, the East Fyn Agricultural Museum, an extensive collection of old agricultural implements. There is a garden attached, where you can eat sandwiches or buy a cup of coffee. From Frørup you can continue north along a quiet road to (5km) Kogsbølle, turning right there to **Stevnshøj**, a vantage point 65m above sea level, with a splendid view across Nyborg and Knudshoved. From here, too, you can see Holckenhavn, the last call before Nyborg, reached by continuing to the 163 and turning left.

Holckenhavn, the largest private mansion in Denmark, was originally called Kogsbølle; it came into the possession of the Ulfeldt family and was then called Ulfeldtsholm until Christian IV's mother-in-law Ellen Marsvin acquired it and changed its name to Ellenborg. It was given the name Holckenhavn by its new owner, Eiler Holck, in 1672. Two wings of the present house were built in the 1580s, the principal and secondary towers in 1596 and the remainder in the 1630s. It was thoroughly restored between 1904 and 1910 with the intention of giving it back the appearance it had when Ellen Marsvin was in charge. She it was who was responsible for the unusually ornate chapel in which the carvings are said to have taken the artist seven years to complete. The house is not open to the public, but there is access to the park for limited periods on Tuesday and Saturday afternoons.

From Holckenhavn you drive across the narrow Holckenhavn Fjord to (2km) Nyborg, continuing past the harbour and on to (5km) Knudshoved if you so wish.

NYBORG (pop. 18,400) with a charter from 1292 is a major provincial port, of particular importance for its ferry connections with Sjælland. These used to go from the centre of the town, but most are now centred on **Knudshoved**, the ferry terminal on the spit of land stretching 3km to the east. The ferry crossing takes about one hour. With the opening of the fixed link to Sjælland, all this is about to change.

■ **Tourist information**: Torvet 9; tel. 65 31 02 80.

■ **Hotels**: Nyborg Strand, Østerøvej 2; tel. 65 31 31 31; Missionshotellet, Østervoldgade 44; tel. 65 30 11 88.

The town grew up around ***Nyborg Castle**, which was founded in 1170 by Knud Prislavsen, a nephew of Valdemar I.

History
This was one of a system of castles built along Storebælt as defences against the Wends. However, with its central position Nyborg soon became the meeting place for the Danehof and the Rigsråd assemblies and thus the capital of Denmark, until Copenhagen took over this function in 1413. Prior to this many official and royal documents were issued in Nyborg. Here, too, many events of national significance occurred: Erik Glipping signed his stern charter here in 1282; five years later, his murderers, Marsk Stig and Rane Jonsen, were outlawed here; in 1326 South Jutland was here enfeoffed to Count Gert of Holstein.

The original castle was surrounded by water and a brick ring wall. The keep was built into the east wing, while opposite, built into the west wing, was the dwelling house, the Palatium, where various kings and their retinues lived. Christian II was born here.

A period of decline began in the 17C. A great storm in 1620 wrought havoc, and during the war against Sweden 1658–60 such damage was done to the castle that it was no longer suitable as a royal residence. All attempts to maintain the building ceased, and in 1670 one of the towers was taken down. In 1702 a visiting French diplomat described it as 'an old castle falling in ruins, without tiles, and with several cracks in the walls'. In 1722 most of the castle was demolished, and some of the materials were used in building Odense Castle. Only the royal apartments and the keep were left standing, and the keep was reduced in size in 1822.

In 1849 the State took over the castle, and by the beginning of the present century its historical significance was becoming appreciated. In 1914 the National Museum was voted funds to begin the work of reconstruction, at the same time as carrying out archaeological excavations on the site. The old west wing was very largely restored to the appearance it had at the time of Christian III. This wing is now open to the public from March to October, sparsely furnished as it would have been then, though the furniture itself is mainly somewhat later. It is even possible to hire the old Great Hall and the old Danehof Hall for private formal receptions and dinners, and thus—against suitable payment—to entertain one's guests in the oldest royal castle in Scandinavia.

The main church in Nyborg, **Vor Frue Kirke** on Gammel Torv, was radically rebuilt in the 19C, but the west end of the nave is thought to have been built in 1389 on the orders of Queen Margrethe I, and the east end to be from 1428. The nave is separated from the aisles by arcading, and the pillars here clearly indicate the different period in which the two sections were built. The sturdy tower is from 1581, and the spire from 1588–89. Much of the furniture, including the altarpiece, is 19C, but there is a 1649 wrought-iron grating in the south side by

Christian IV's artist craftsman, Caspar Fincke. In the south chapel there are two fonts, one, Romanesque, of granite, the other, Renaissance, of wood. The pulpit is a richly carved work by Anders Mortensen from Odense, dated 1653.

Of other old buildings in Nyborg, mention must be made of a medieval stone-built house, the **Korsbrødregård** just south of the church, on the corner of ADELGADE and KORSBRØDREGADE. The oldest part is from the early 15C, the remainder early 17C. Likewise in Korsbrødregade, the old **parsonage** also dates back to the 15C, but it was also extended and rebuilt in the 17C. It has been restored in the 20C.

There are various half-timbered houses, of which **Mads Lerckes Gård**, SLOTSGADE 11, is undoubtedly the most impressive today. Built in 1601 by Mads Lercke, with side wings added in 1637 and 1643, this house of 30 rooms is now a local history museum, particularly interesting for its reconstruction of an affluent burgher's home from the mid-18C (open Mar–Oct). It stands next to another of Nyborg's grand houses, **Dronningegården**, from 1760.

Nyborg suffered from a serious fire in 1797, and much of the subsequent rebuilding was in neo-classical style. Many of the dignified new buildings still stand in TORVET, KONGEGADE and NØRREGADE. A particularly fine, but slightly later, example is found at KORSGADE 4.

A good stretch of the old ramparts to the north and west of the castle still exist, and they now form a public park. In particular there are good views from the section called Dronningens Bastion. The town gateway from 1666 has also survived.

14 • Tønder to Ringkøbing

*Total distance 160km. A11 to (46km) **Ribe**. (46km) Varde. (43km) Skjern. A28, A15 to (25km) **Ringkøbing**.*

If you approach Denmark by car from Germany, one of the likely points of entry is the crossing north of the German town of Süderlügum on the German highway 199, which in Denmark then becomes the A11 and takes you to Tønder. Other border crossings on the west coast will also almost inevitably take you there.

You are now in the area of Denmark known as **Sønderjylland**, Southern Jutland, which as a border region has in times past seen more than its share of wars, from the 13C to the 19C. The excruciatingly complicated problems of the region stem from the fact that the two former duchies of Schleswig (Danish: Slesvig) and Holstein (Danish: Holsten) each had a different relationship to the Kingdom of Denmark, to which they were both nevertheless linked, and whereas Schleswig was predominantly Danish speaking, Holstein was predominantly German. When national sentiments emerged, in the 19C, it turned out to be impossible to satisfy all parties, and war was the result. After the 1864 defeat of Denmark by Prussia, Southern Jutland became part of Germany, which it remained until 1920, when a parish-by-parish plebiscite determined the present border.

*Tønder is only some 3km north of the border, and stands at the south edge of the area known as **Marsken** (The Marshland). This is the almost totally flat region bordering the North Sea, much of it below or just at sea level, protected by dykes like those in Holland. So not only has the region known wars, but it has in the course of time been subjected to natural catastrophes in the form of flooding. On one occasion in the 14C, some 30 churches are said to have been washed away, while thousands of the local inhabitants perished. Little wonder that laws were introduced compelling those owning land to help build dykes. These and the system of drainage canals saved the land, but in the course of the resultant transformation, Tønder, which had once been a harbour and of great importance for the export of cattle, found itself surrounded by dry land in the 16C. It still has a ship in its coat of arms.

TØNDER (pop. 12,650) is first mentioned in 1130, and it was granted a charter as a market town in 1243. When it lost its harbour facilities it turned to other means of making a livelihood, and by the 18C lacemaking was the region's principal occupation. By the end of the century it provided work for some 12,000 people, many of them working in their own homes. Fortunes were made by the lace merchants, as is apparent from the opulence of some of the early houses still standing in Tønder. Gold and silver smiths added to the wealth.

- **Tourist information**: Torvet 1; tel. 74 72 12 20.

- **Hotels**: Tønderhus, Jomfrustien 1; tel. 74 72 22 22; Hostrup, Søndergade 30; tel. 74 72 21 29.

- **Youth hostel**: Sønderport 4; tel. 74 72 35 00.

A walk through some of the old streets with their characteristic end-facing gables will quickly reveal the affluence of a former age. Look, for instance, at the entrances to the 17C and 18C houses in ØSTERGADE or VESTERGADE, with their intricate carved portals in sandstone, impressive flights of steps, and sandstone lions guarding the entrance. And the doors themselves, with their exquisite Rococo decorations. To top it all there is the **Amtmandspalæ** (The Sheriff's Palace) from 1768 in JOMFRUSTIGEN. Even the more modest houses, often with bow windows, speak of more than modest means. Standing on the town square is the oldest house in Tønder, the **Old Town Hall** from 1520, restored in 1987.

There was once a castle in Tønder, but it has now disappeared without trace. However, the old gatehouse is still there, and together with an adjoining further building from the 1920s it now forms the **Tønder Museum** with, among much else, a collection of old Dutch tiles reflecting the life of the area in the days when the export of cattle established a close link with Holland. Reciprocal trade brought the tiles to Tønder, and it was common practice to tile the interior walls of houses. The museum also contains a truly impressive collection of local lace and silver-work.The old lock-up has been incorporated into the museum, as has the old whipping post in the shape of a man, the 'Kagmand', the only one left in Denmark.

Sønderjyllands Kunstmuseum is housed in the same building. Originally founded on Danish art presented by Danish artists to celebrate the return of southern Jutland in 1920, this gallery has grown over the years to include the work of mainly modern Danish artists. There are plans for a major expansion of these museums, to which will be added the nearby Water Tower offering impressive views of the low-lying countryside. A further **museum** containing the most comprehensive collection of old pharmaceutical apparatus in Denmark is to be found in **Det gamle Apotek** in SØNDERGADE.

Like the dwelling houses, the principal church in Tønder, **Kristkirken** with its 47.5m octagonal spire and its Renaissance and Baroque furniture, reflects the wealth of a past age. It was built 1591–92 to replace the earlier St Nicholas' church which was now too small. Nevertheless, this earlier church must also have had considerable character, and remains of it are still to be seen in the marble font (1350) and some of the carved bench ends, while the Renaissance pulpit from 1586 also stems from it. The Baroque altarpiece is from 1695, and the splendid choir loft with its 18 scenes from the Bible dates from 1623. A further striking feature of the church is the 14—often bombastic—memorial tablets dating from between the 15C and 17C, lining the nave.

Near the south wall there is a bust of Hans Adolf Brorson, who was pastor in Tønder from 1729–37 before becoming Bishop of Ribe. However, this pietist pastor and bishop was also a poet, one of the greatest of Denmark's hymn-writers, and it is for this he is remembered. The Danish hymn book has on more than one occasion been referred to as 'the best anthology of Danish poetry'. Even prior to the Reformation there were hymns of note in Danish, but the post-Reformation Lutheran church has fostered a large number, many of the highest literary value.

Danish poetry would be able to enjoy considerable distinction even if it had not produced more than the poetry of Brorson, Kingo and Grundtvig, all of whom are most noted as writers of hymns and all of whom became bishops. Thomas Kingo, who was the earliest of them, was the great Baroque poet. Brorson, a few years his junior, was the Rococo poet, the man who saw God's greatness even in the smallest things in creation. He endured much suffering in his life, with the early loss of his wife and the mental illness of his son, and some of his hymns betray a longing for death, though others are more optimistic. In particular his later work showed an impressive command of verse form and linguistic inventiveness.

▶Excursion from Tønder to Møgeltønder and Højer Dyke

Total distance c 26km. It is not only Tønder itself and its famous son that give this area a special interest. There is also Højer, 12km away on the west coast, and on the way there Møgeltønder and Gallehus.

You start your excursion by taking the 419 west, turning right after 3km to reach the tiny village of **Gallehus** (1km). There is not immediately very much to see here, only a few houses around a green on which there are two standing stones. Yet it was the place of two of the most important archaeological finds in Danish history, and because of them and their subsequent fate, the ultimate inspiration for one of the finest poems of the Romantic Age, *The Golden Horns*.

Return to the 419, cross it and drive to (3km) **Møgeltønder**. There is little else here than a castle, a church and a very beautiful main street. But all this makes it worth visiting. The main street, SLOTSGADE, is lined on both sides by carefully

The Golden Horns

The story must be told: in 1639 a young lacemaker, Kirsten Svensdatter, was walking through a field in Gallehus, when she stumbled on something lying just under the surface of the ground. She picked it up and found it to be a golden horn 75.8cm long and weighing just over 3kg. In 1734 a young farm labourer, Erik Lassen, walking nearby, stumbled over another one, rather shorter. The runic inscription and the ornamentation on the two horns suggest that they were made some time in the 5C. Christian IV actually used the first as a drinking horn, but in time both were put on display in the Royal Museum in Copenhagen. There, an enterprising goldsmith, Niels Heidenreich, decided he could put them to better use. He stole them and melted them down. Unfortunately for him, he was caught and spent the next 38 years in prison. Fortunately for us, drawings were made by Ole Worm, and on the basis of these it has been possible to reconstruct the horns, reproductions of which are now on view in the National Museum in Copenhagen.

A few doors from Niels Heidenreich in Copenhagen lived the budding young poet Adam Oehlenschläger, who just at this time became fired with the ideas of German Romanticism. He wrote his first major poem, *The Golden Horns*, in a verse form much like that of the old Eddic poetry and in expression a programme piece of Romanticism: the horns were the gifts of the gods to the innocent whom they had chosen—but they were put on display by unimaginative scholars with no sense of the real significance of the divine gift—and so the gods took them back. If there is any poem known by all Danes, it will be this. To return to Gallehus: the two inscribed standing stones mark the spots where the horns were unearthed.

tended old thatched houses once used by the castle staff. Many have the bow windows common in the Schleswig area. Both the footpaths and the road are cobbled, and between them is a row of lime trees on either side of the road.

As its name suggests, Slotsgade leads to the castle, **Schackenborg**. Built in 1664–67, this was extended and 'modernised' in the 18C, though the two side wings have retained much of their original character. It was the last fortified castle to be built in Denmark, and it still bears traces of its fortifications. It replaced the older Møgeltønderhus, which was given to Hans Schack in recognition of his victory over the Swedes at Copenhagen and Nyborg in the 17C Swedish wars, and remained in the possession of the same family until quite recently. It is now the home of Prince Joachim and Princess Alexandra. There is public access to the park.

The *church, which has been closely associated with the castle, is large and impressive, with special pews (from 1691–92) reserved for the owners of Schackenborg. The nave and chancel are Romanesque, and to them have been added a Gothic transept and west tower. Parts of the east end are from c 1200. You will find this church particularly striking for the great number of frescoes it contains. Those in the chancel date from c 1550, while others over the chancel arch are from c 1275. Others again are considerably later—some even from the 19C when the older frescoes were subjected to a thorough and somewhat heavy-handed restoration. There is a splendid late Gothic altarpiece from c 1500, a late

Romanesque granite font and a Baroque pulpit (1694). The organ, from 1679, is one of the oldest in Denmark, and a special wooden vault has been constructed above it to make room for the pipes. A reminder that this area was once part of Germany is found in the churchyard, where there is a memorial to soldiers killed in World War I while fighting on the German side.

Kniplehusets Museum, at SØNDERBYVEJ 1, is a museum of lace and lace-making from the 18C to the end of the 19C, demonstrating not only the products, but the methods used in lace-making (open summer; limited opening winter).

From Møgeltønder you will automatically continue on the 419 to (7km) **Højer**, an unspoiled village of narrow streets and thatched houses and farms, many of them scheduled, the centre of the system of sluices used to control the water level in the Marshland. Like many of the churches in this region, that in Højer seems to be huddled up to withstand the elements, sombre and tough. The old windmill is now a ***museum** demonstrating the battle against the threat from the North Sea (open Apr–Oct).

The system of ***sluices**, some from 1861, now supplemented by a new system from 1981, is most impressive, as is the double system of dykes, the new, outer one, running from Emmerslev, north of Højer, to the embankment connecting the German mainland to the island of Sylt. Take a look at the sluices and the museum (open Apr–Oct) in SLUSEVEJ, Margrethe-Kog just south of Højer. Nearby you will find the unusual farm called **Hohenwarte**, built in the 1860s as a replica of the University of Kiel and now a plant research station. Back in Højer you join the 419 again and drive back to Tønder. ◀

Returning to the main route, drive north from Tønder on the A11 to (11km) **Bredebro**, which, as the name implies, is the bridge over the river at Brede. Here there is an impressive and carefully restored church, originally from the 13C, but extended in 1772. The tower is from 1400 and the spire from 1694. A reminder of more modern times is the fact that the tower was struck by a shell in 1940, and that the shell is still there!

There is a poignant memorial here to a sailor, Jørgen Martensen, who was taken prisoner by Turkish pirates in 1678. The local population collected money for a ransom, but the poor chap died before it was handed over—and so the money went to a memorial instead.

From Bredebro the A11 continues north to (12km) Skærbæk. However, if you are not short of time, we suggest you take this alternative and much more interesting route.

▶Leave the A11 at Bredebro and drive west on an unclassified road through (9km) Randerup, the birthplace of Brorson, there turning left to (6km) **Ballum**, a coastal village with many old houses. It is quite a modest place, but to those who have read their Karen Blixen it will be of interest, for it is from here that the story *Sorrow Acre* (from *Winter Tales*) emanates. There is even a gravestone in the churchyard said to be that of the unfortunate mother, and locals might show you the field in which she harvested the rye. Believe it all if you like.

Drive north on the 419, after 5km passing on your right all that remains of **Misthusum**, a village that was washed almost completely away in a great storm in 1634. There is little left except a single house built from the ruins, and now a tiny museum of local history. 2km further brings you to the 10km-long causeway leading to Rømø.

Rømø

Rømø is a kind of tourist paradise, and the numbers of visitors in the summer reflect this. There is a broad shoreline, with excellent nude bathing facilities if you want them. The beach facing the North Sea is unbelievably wide: even where it is narrowest there is over 1km to the water at high tide. There is a wealth of animal life here, including many seals, and every conceivable sports facility.

■ **Tourist information**: Havnebyvej 30, Tvismark; tel. 74 75 51 30.

■ **Hotels**: Kommandørgården, Havnebyvej 201, Mølby; te. 74 75 51 22; Færgegården, Vestergade 1–5, Havneby; tel. 74 75 54 32.

■ **Youth hostel**: Lyngevejen 7; 74 75 51 88.

Traditionally, Rømø has been an old-fashioned seafaring island with scarcely any roads, and it was only in the 1960s, with the building of the causeway, that this came to an end. The inhabitants try to maintain some of their old customs, not least that of wearing national dress on festive occasions. Yet untouched by modern life as it was until a late stage, there are signs of plenty in the old houses on the island, outstanding among which is what is now the museum, **Kommandørgården**, an impressive, solid house on suitably high ground, built in 1744 and restored by the National Museum in 1951. (A ticket to this museum also gives you access to **Toftum gamle Skole** (Toftum Old School), the oldest and smallest school in Denmark, in use from 1784 to 1874.) Like many houses in the area, the inside walls of Kommandørgården are clad in Dutch tiles, and there are richly carved beams and decorations.

The island's wealth came from its seafaring tradition, particularly in the 18C, and its whaler captains ('kommandører') have left their mark on it both in the fine houses they built and, not least, in the splendid gravestones which they ordered for themselves and their families—and for which they tended to write their own inscriptions. Take a look at the churchyard; it is unusual. The church is medieval in origin, but was extended during the affluent 18C. It is a relatively large building, though it is not without a certain intimate charm. Model ships hang from the ceiling, and carved plants decorate the pews.

On returning to the mainland you stay on the 175 until, at 4km it crosses the A11 just north of Skærbæk. ◀

In **Skærbæk**, a former merchant's residence now houses a museum with a comprehensive collection illustrating everyday life in southern Jutland (limited opening all year).

On leaving the village you take the A11 north to (5km) **Brøns**, where there is a church with a magnificent painted ceiling and beams decorated with floral patterns; the pews are painted bright blue and equipped with carved bench ends, all overlooked by pale but beautifully preserved frescoes from the time of the Reformation. They are a graphic presentation of the debate of the day, with the Pope, prelates and high-ranking laymen gathered around what looks like a letter of indulgence, while a group of (smaller) ordinary people are clearly arguing with a monk. Meanwhile, this is a church of some size, the early parts dating from c 1250. In addition to a large Romanesque font, there is a tabernacle from c 1300 in the chancel and a late 15C crucifix over the chancel arch.

The road to Ribe will now lead you through (5km) **Rejsby**, where the late Romanesque church has an unusual octagonal spire and a painted wooden ceiling. A further 5km brings you to **Hviding**, which was once on the coast and furnished with a harbour. There are those who subscribe to the theory that this was the original site of Ribe, and certainly Hviding was a rival to Ribe in the 12C. The large church in the nearby **Gammel Hviding** reflects this early status and has an unusual late Gothic altarpiece portraying a host of figures surrounded by a rosary.

Just north of Hviding you will see a road to the left leading to Vester Vedsted (3km), from where you can see, and possibly reach, the tiny island of Mandø (7km). The Wadden Sea here is so shallow that there is a special bus service to Mandø at low tide—but do not try to walk or drive across yourself, as you are likely to stray from the road—which disappears at high tide in any case.

Because of its isolation, **Mandø** has maintained much of its old character as a fishing and seafaring community with a great deal of bird life, and Mandø village is no more than a cluster of houses, a church, a school and inn (with accommodation). There are some small museums, though. **Mandøhuset** (The Mandø House), a skipper's house from c 1830, offers exhibits illustrating early 19C life on the island (open May–Oct). At Midtvej 3 there is an ornithological museum (open Apr–Nov), while the windmill, Mandø Mølle, on Søndre Strandvej, has been restored and opened to the public. The tiny church, once described as '17 paces from the altar to the door', dates from 1727, with a porch added in 1792. The painter Joakim Skovgaard did an altarpiece which stood in the church from 1890 to 1895, when it was removed because the wet salt air was ruining it, and the present altarpiece is a copy of it. The reindeer antlers serving as coat racks were found in the sea west of Mandø and are thought to be 10,000 years old.

Ribe

Returning to the main route, on the A11, you only have another 5km to drive before you arrive in **Ribe** (pop. 18,250), one of the finest medieval cities in Denmark.

■ **Tourist information**: Torvet 3–5; tel. 75 42 15 00.

■ **Hotels**: Dagmar, Torvet; tel. 75 42 00 33; Den Gamle Arrest, Torvet 11; tel. 75 42 37 00—yes, it really is the old lock-up, and you sleep in the cells!

■ **Youth hostel**: Sanct Pedersgade 16, tel. 75 42 06 20.

■ Also Ribe Byferie, Damvej 34; tel. 79 88 79 88 offers a large array of **private flats and houses**.

■ A **Viking Fair** is held at the Ribe Viking Centre at the end of May each year.

History

Ribe has a long history. It is first mentioned c 860 when St Ansgar, who started the conversion of Denmark, was given permission to build his second church here (the first was in the now vanished Hedeby further south). From this it must be assumed that even at that time Ribe was a town of some importance, probably as a trade route to England and southern Europe. Certainly, archaeologists have uncovered over 60,000 artefacts from the Viking Age and before just outside the town. In 948 Ribe was given its first bishop, thus gaining yet more in importance, both as an ecclesiastical centre and as an increasingly busy trade centre. Its significance is further underlined by the fact that coins were minted here as early as the reign of King Knud the Great.

Valdemar II gave the town considerable privileges and tax dispensations, and these were renewed by succeeding monarchs, the earliest of them dated 1242, the latest 1766. In 1127 King Erik held his son's wedding here, and accounts talk of an inordinately busy harbour and thriving trade at that time. By 1200, Ribe was the most important trade and transit centre in Denmark, with close links with many of the major trading cities in Europe. Towards the end of the Middle Ages, with the advent of better sailing ships capable of rounding Skagen, Ribe's international importance as a transit harbour began to diminish. Nevertheless, it was one of the first towns in Denmark to own a printing press, and the first printed edition of the Jutlandic Law of 1241 was done in Ribe in 1504. At the time of the Reformation there were some 20 guilds in the town.

With the completion of the cathedral, a cathedral chapter was established in 1145, and Ribe possessed, in the course of time, a large convent and three monasteries as well as some smaller religious houses and hospitals. There were six churches in addition to the cathedral and the chapels in the convents and monasteries.

At the beginning of the 12C, Riberhus Castle was built to the west of the town, and this became the setting for many royal occasions. In particular there is a tradition that the Valdemars were particularly fond of Ribe, and the much-loved Queen Dagmar, the wife of Valdemar II, died here in 1212 (though she was buried in Ringsted). The cathedral chimes play the melody of the ballad of Queen Dagmar at 12.00 and 15.00. Riberhus is named in Christian II's charter as one of the three Jutlandic castles which should be maintained. Nevertheless, by the time of Christian IV it was in disrepair; it was demolished by the end of the 17C, and now the only trace of it is the mound on which it was built and the remains of the moat surrounding it.

Ribe as a whole was not enthusiastic about the Reformation, and indeed the Reformation with the resultant suppression of the religious establishments helped reduce its wealth and influence. Its trade also suffered through the emergence of other trading centres, not least Copenhagen. Another negative factor was the fact that Ribe's harbour was on a river, not on the coast, which limited the size of the ships able to use it. Most of the goods taken to and from Ribe by sea were carried by lighter between the city and the harbour, some 7km downstream. The position deteriorated yet more when the river silted up in the 18C. Whereas many other towns in Denmark experienced a new period of growth in the 19C, this did not happen in Ribe. The loss to Germany of southern Jutland robbed it of a natural hinterland, and the emergence of Esbjerg as a major export port towards the end of the 19C affected it yet more.

In the Middle Ages Ribe had a reputation for being strict in the application of its laws, and it is certain that at least 12 women were burned as witches between 1572 and 1652. In SØNDERPORTSGADE there is a memorial to one Maren Splid, burnt for witchcraft on 9 November 1641 'between the gallows hills near Ribe'. The strictness of the regime in the town is reflected in the story of a woman whose son had been condemned to death by the Viborg Court, and who, on seeing him hanging in the gallows there, sighed: 'Aye, my son, but be thankful you were not tried by the Ribe court!'

Many famous names are associated with Ribe: the great post-Reformation bishop Peder Palladius was born here in 1503, and the poet Anders Bording in 1619. The Reformer Hans Tavsen spent the last ten years of his life here, and here, too, lived the 17C humanist Anders Sørensen Vedel from 1581 to his death in 1616. Hans Adolf Brorson ended his days as Bishop of Ribe, and close to where he lived, the poet Ambrosius Stub died in poverty in 1758. The two probably never met. Stub was overlooked in his old age, and he has his parallel in the 20C composer Rued Langgaard, who spent the last 12 years of his life as cathedral organist here. Langgaard was not really accepted as a composer in his day, and it is only now that his genius is being acknowledged.

The *cathedral, with a floor level about 1.5m below the present-day square on which it stands, must remain the most prominent building in Ribe. It dominates the town, and its lofty 13C tower can be seen from miles around, high above the outline of the medieval buildings. In fact, this 48.6m tower was probably once even taller, but it partly collapsed in 1594, and the present shape was adopted when it was rebuilt in 1610. The other tower, the St Mary's Tower, is from 1896, when it was erected to replace an earlier tower which had collapsed in the 18C.

Consecrated in 1125, this glorious Romanesque cathedral is in the form of a basilica with a nave flanked by two aisles on either side, the only such church in Denmark. Originally, it was built with a single aisle on either side of the nave, plus a transept and chancel. At the intersection between this original transept and nave there is a great dome 21.3m high, unique in Scandinavia. The two outer aisles, which largely hide the original ground plan, were added after a fire in 1402. Thanks to the combination of breadth and height brought about by the six arches and then the twin aisles and further colonnades on either side of the nave, this massive cathedral strikes the visitor as being peculiarly spacious and light.

There are three doors to the church, the most interesting being the one known as the Cat's Head Door on the south side, so called because the lion's head in the door handle was once thought to be that of a cat. This huge door is set in a splendid portal with two columns on either side and horseshoe-shaped arches above enclosing a carved tympanum representing Christ being taken down from the Cross, one of the most important pieces of Danish medieval sculpture. The whole is surmounted by a triangular gable with figures of Christ and the Virgin surrounded by angels.

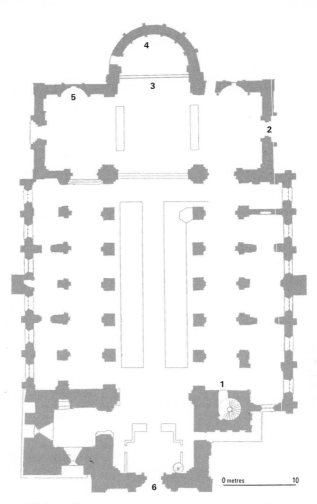

1 St Mary's Tower
2 The Cat's Head Door
3 Altar table from 1988
4 Frescoes: stained glass windows
  and mosaics from 1983-87
5 Tombstone of King Kristoffer I (1259)
  believed to be the oldest royal
  tombstone in Scandinavia
6 The West Portal from 1225, Bronze
  doors by Anne Marie Carl Nielsen (1904)

RIBE CATHEDRAL

There is a good deal of the medieval church furniture and decorations left in the cathedral, including some frescoes—though these have been damaged by the elements in the course of time. Now, in the midst of this magnificent Romanesque church, there is a modern altar, behind which some modern frescoes, mosaics and stained glass windows have been added, the work of Carl-Henning Pedersen between 1983 and 1987.

Quite apart from the cathedral, the *centre of Ribe has been scrupulously maintained to keep its medieval atmosphere as far as possible, with narrow winding cobbled streets and half-timbered houses, most of which are still inhabited. Close to the east end of the cathedral, on the Square itself, is **Weis' Stue**, a tiny inn from 1600 with a carefully preserved 18C interior with beamed wooden ceilings, and walls either panelled or covered with Dutch tiles, all filled with period furniture. At the other end of the Square is the town's old school, **Katedralskolen**, dating as a grammar school from the 16C, but with a history going much further back. Some of Denmark's most famous names went to school here. Nearby, also in SKOLEGADE, are the remains of the old 16C Bishop's Palace, where Hans Tavsen spent his last years. There is now an archaeological museum on this spot.

Many half-timbered buildings as there are in Ribe, they are not the only houses of interest; there are some very old brick-built dwellings, including the 16C Tårnborg in PUGGAARDSGADE (in which the 16C humanist Anders Sørensen Vedel lived). **Puggaard** itself, in GRAVSGADE, is a brick-built house from c 1400, at one time a residence for the canons of the cathedral. On the corner of STENBOGADE and SØNDERPORTSGADE with its entrance from VON STØCKENSPLADS square stands the oldest extant **town hall** in Denmark, dating from 1496. It was in this house that the poet Anders Bording was born in 1619, and it became the town hall in 1709. At von Støckensplads 2, there is now the **Ribe Toy Museum**, exhibiting toys from between 1860 and 1975 (open summer 10.00–17.00, winter Wed–Fri 12.00–16.00, Sat–Sun 12.00–16.00).

Further along DAGMARSGADE you come to Sankt Catherinæ Plads, the site of *St Catherine's Church and monastery, one of Denmark's best-preserved monastic churches. The Dominican monastery was founded in 1228, but the present church, the third to be built on this site, is from 1433 and apart from the cathedral is the only one of the old churches to survive. It is some 46m long, 21.5m wide, and consists of a nave and two aisles, but without a distinct chancel. The tower is from 1618, but it had to be reduced in height. The font is medieval, the richly carved pulpit from 1591, and the altarpiece from 1650. The old cloisters also survive, and can be reached through the church. If you go further along Dagmarsgade to the junction with SANCT NICOLAJGADE, you will find the **Ribes Vikinger Museum**, situated on the spot where Ribe is thought to have been founded in AD 700 and covering the history of Ribe from that date to 1700.

Go back now as far as SORTEBRØDREGADE, which will bring you to to *Quedens Gård on the corner of OVERDAMMEN. (A single ticket also gives you access to the **Town Hall Museum** on von Støckens Plads and **Hans Tavsens House** at Torvet 17.) This is a splendid merchant's residence originally from 1580, built around a courtyard; the dwelling house is from the end of the 18C. It is now a museum, and the interior seeks to re-create rooms from the 16C to the 19C. A walk further on, down the narrow cobbled and pavement-less FISKERGADE, will show you one of the lovely old streets, with alleyways leading off it.

The old harbour is no longer used for serious purposes, but there are facilities for private yachts and launches. There are some old Wadden Sea ships on display, and there is also a post showing the water levels during various floods—the greatest being the famous flood of 1634 which destroyed Misthusum (see p 201). In SKT NIKOLAJGADE there is an art gallery (**Kunstmuseum**) exhibiting a wide range of Danish art.

Slightly further out of the centre, on LUSTRUPVEJ, between the A24 HADERSLEVVEJ and the road from Tønder, the **Ribe Viking Centre** is being constructed, and when finished will contain life-size reconstructions of parts of Viking Age Ribe: the market place from c 720, a farm from c 980 and Ribe as it was c 1050.

Leaving Ribe, drive 7km north on the A11/A24 to just south of Gredstedbro, from where if you wish, you can follow the A11/A24 and later the A24 to (21km) Esbjerg (p 23). If you prefer to go straight to (31km) Varde, which is our next real stop, you also follow the A11/A24, but you must be sure to stay on the A11, when the A24 c 5km later forks left for Esbjerg. We suggest however, you leave the A11/A24 altogether, turning right into **Gredstedbro**, just before you reach the town. If you do this, you have the chance of seeing two interesting churches before you are back on track again 7km ahead.

The first of these, reached by a minor road, is 3km west of Gredstedbro, the rather fine Romanesque church at **Vilslev**. Here there are some well-preserved frescoes from c 1225, one of which, above the chancel arch, portrays a beautiful young Abel lifting his lamb up towards God. You will also find a stone showing the height reached by the 1634 floods.

From Gredstedbro you take the unclassified road north towards Bramming. At (4km) Sejstrup you should turn left to (1km) **Hunderup** to take a look at the church, in which there is a totally unexpected splendid marble sarcophagus, the work of the Flemish sculptor Cornelis Floris, who was responsible for the tomb of Christian III in Roskilde Cathedral (p 55). The tomb here is that of the owner of the nearby mansion of Kærgård, Niels Lange, and his wife.

Proceed now west through Hunderup and rejoin the A11 2km ahead, turning right for (25km) Varde.

VARDE (pop. 19,500) once enjoyed a strategic position in an otherwise marshy area as a firm crossing of the big Varde Å river, which in the early Middle Ages formed a trade route. There was a royal castle here, Vardehus, and this, too, contributed to Varde's significance. In 1439 the local peasants stormed and burned down the castle and then took refuge in Varde itself. In return, the king's troops burned down Varde. Varde's earliest known charter is from 1442, though one must assume there were earlier ones, not least because the town boasts the oldest civic coat of arms in Denmark.

■ **Tourist information**: Torvet 5; tel. 75 22 32 22.

■ **Hotels**: Arnbjergallé 2; tel. 75 21 11 00; Motel Varde, Tømrevej 18; tel. 75 22 15 00.

■ **Youth hostel**: Pramstedvej 10; tel. 75 22 10 91.

However, despite its long history, Varde has little in the way of old buildings, most of which have suffered in many disastrous fires. Even after the establishment of its great rival, Esbjerg, Varde continued to grow, partly because of the advent of the railway line. It is now a busy market town serving a thriving hinterland, and as a result of the demands placed on it, the old centre has been completely rebuilt, leaving little to remind one of the past except the general layout of the streets around the old square, TORVET.

Varde **church** on the west side of Torvet square was built around 1150, but suffered from the fires which ravaged the town. It was twice rebuilt in the 18C and then extended in 1812. The latest restoration was by Kaare Klint and Rolf Graae in 1965. The bombastic Renaissance altarpiece is from 1616, with 18C paintings in the panels.

There *are* some old buildings in Varde, first and foremost the elegant **Kampmannske gård** from 1781 on the corner of STOREGADE and KRÆMMERGADE. It was built after the great fire of 1777, as is recalled in the inscription over the doorway: *ex cinere redivivus anno 1781*.

Close to the Arnbjerg Park to the east of the town centre there is a delightful model of the Varde of 1860, **Minibyen**; the miniature town houses are built of brick and roofed with tiles, all one-tenth of normal size. In the Arnbjerg Park there is an open air theatre, a memorial to those killed during the World War II Occupation, and a 'geographical garden'. Here, too, is **Varde Museum**, with excellent archaeological and ethnographical collections, including textiles, silver and 'jydepotter', the curiously shaped black clay pots associated with this area. They have a very old history indeed, and were fashioned without the use of a potter's wheel. They were then fired over a low flame, which produced a black finish. Nowadays they are tourist wares, but here you will find the genuine thing.

Further to the east of the town there is the pleasure park of **Varde Sommerland**; pay the entrance fee, and everything is free inside.

From Varde to Ringkøbing you have the choice of two routes, the direct one (68km) taking you across country, and the longer and more scenic (87km) along the North Sea coast. The direct route is described first.

Direct route from Varde to Ringkøbing
Total distance 68km.

Although the A11 north leads straight from Varde to **Skjern**, our suggested direct route is via the A12 and is only slightly longer. Leave Varde on the A12/487 northeast to (10km) **Nørholm**. The mansion is not open to the public, but a narrow road just before the house leading right to **Nørholm Hede** skirts the gardens, and you can catch a glimpse of it from there. Nørholm Hede (Nørholm Heath) is a large expanse of moorland which, experimentally, has been left undisturbed so that studies of the flora and fauna of unspoiled moorland can be carried out, and a brief look at this area is well worth while. On returning to the A12/487 proceed north, after 1km taking the A12 fork to (11km) **Hjedding**.

One of the most important facets of Danish rural life for the past century or so has been the co-operative movement. Inspired by the co-operative movement in England, farmers joined forces at the end of the 19C to provide co-operative facilities instead of being dependent on their own efforts or on the private dairies, etc. which tended to be in the hands of the large landowners. First came co-operative dairies, but then came slaughterhouses and other large ventures. Hjedding is the site of Denmark's first co-operative dairy, and fittingly it is now a **Dairy Museum** containing all the original equipment from 1882.

A further 2km brings you to **Ølgod**, where, thanks to the discovery of 171 old coins under the floor during restoration work, the original Romanesque church can be traced back to the 12C. The font indicates that it was dedicated to St Laurentius. The tower and porch are Gothic additions.

Now follow the unclassified road past the church through **Tarm** (**Tourist information**: Stationsvej 4; tel. 97 37 18 28.) to (19km) Skjern.

You are now driving in an area that was once right off the beaten track, known as darkest Jutland, and it has thus developed its own local pride and its own local customs. It is an area where, perhaps because of the difficult conditions, Christianity flourished in a particularly demanding form, as is now borne out by the many churches in the area. As we shall see in a moment, it is a form of Christianity that has had far-reaching international reverberations.

Skjern (pop. 12,600; **Tourist information**: Østergade 8; tel. 97 35 18 55) was no more than a village until the railway came to it in 1875, and it now has the honour of being the most recent town in Denmark to be given a charter as a market town—in 1958. Not surprisingly, then, the oldest building, a water-tower, dates only from 1875. The impressive Skjern Church contains Romanesque remains, but has been extensively rebuilt and extended. The richly carved altarpiece is from 1610–20. Adjoining the watertower there is now a museum illustrating the development of the area. Another old building, the windmill, from 1882, is a scheduled monument (open summer). Both these are now incorporated into the **Vestjysk økomuseum** (West Jutland Ecological Museum), also called the Skjern-Egvad Museum. The other three departments are: **Bundsbæk Mill**, further north in the Dejbjerg Plantage, an old working mill, but also including a reconstructed Iron Age village; **Fahl Kro**, 10km south-west of Tarm on the 423, with an old inn, a museum and various activities for children and adults, including trips in Viking boats; and the **Hattemagerhus** (Hatter's House) in Tarm, giving an impression of the everyday life of west Jutland working families in the 19C. All five seek to combine the academic rigour of a museum with the friendlier approach sought by many tourists.

What you do have in this area, is excellent *fishing. **Skjern Å** is one of the biggest of Denmark's rather modest rivers, and near Skjern it is joined by several tributaries. These, together with associated lakes within a radius of some 15km, have been carefully developed for fishing—for trout, perch, pike and, near Borris (9km west), salmon. Licences for this area can be obtained at any of the tourist information offices in the area. Fishing on the fjords and along the coast is free.

▶**Excursion from Skjern to Sædding**
Total distance 20km, mainly on unclassified roads.

The A11 takes you north through a landscape dotted with burial mounds to (7km) **Hanning**, where the well-preserved Romanesque church has been newly restored. A partly decipherable runestone has been used as the lintel over a walled-up door in the south wall.

In Hanning you turn right, following a minor road to (3km) *Sædding, the place which Søren Kierkegaard in 1840 described as 'the poorest parish in the moorland region of Jutland'. Yet today it has been described as the nearest you can get in Denmark to a place of pilgrimage. This is clearly an exaggeration;

Sædding is generally quiet and deserted and makes no concessions to tourists, though it is certainly visited by many who are interested in Kierkegaard.

This is the village in which Søren Kierkegaard's father was born, and where, at the age of 12, he stood on a mound and cursed God—an event which he never forgot, which moulded him for the rest of his life, and which came to be of fundamental importance to Søren Kierkegaard, too. The modest and largely unaltered Romanesque church, with no tower, consists of chancel and nave, with a later porch. There is a commemorative tablet to Søren Kierkegaard on the walls inside, and the ship hanging from the roof, presented to the church in 1939, is called the **Regine**—clearly a reference to Søren Kierkegaard's unfortunate fiancée, Regine Olsen. Kierkegaard visited Sædding once only, though his brother, who became Bishop of Ålborg, actually preached in the church there. The father worshipped in it as a child, and the strict evangelical Christianity preached in it has reverberated to this day under the influence of his philosopher son. The family home no longer exists, but there is a stone to indicate the place where it once stood.

From Sædding you drive south to (4km) Sønder Årup, rejoining the A11 and returning to (6km) Skjern. ◄

The main route continues now along the A28, and you first pass through the **Dejbjerg Plantation**, which offers relief from the predominantly moorland landscape. In the middle of the plantation, 6km north of Skjern, you come to a crossroads.

If you turn left here, you will come to **Dejbjerg** (2km), where the church has some unusual features. Romanesque with Gothic extensions, it has a chancel arch decorated with carved intertwined serpents and vines. The splendidly ornamented pulpit is from c 1600, and there are elaborate benches for the pastor, the parish clerk and the nobility. In the tower you can see some rather less distinguished but very special benches. They were once provided for the use of the gypsies and social outcasts who frequented the area, and who were excluded from using the same pews as the rest of the local population.

Eight British airmen, shot down in World War II, are buried in the churchyard here.

In a field south of the church a stone commemorates the finding in 1881–83 of the Bronze Age Dejbjerg carriages, now reassembled in the National Museum in Copenhagen.

If, however, you are more attracted by mills than by churches, you follow the minor road right at the A28 crossroads, and after 1.5km you will come to the beautiful **Bundsbæk Mølle** (Bundsbæk Mill), a restored watermill now forming part of the museum complex of the area.

7km later on the A28 you can turn off again right at Højmark to visit **Sønder Lem** church (1km), where the ship hanging from the ceiling was made by English prisoners of war held in Ringkøbing in 1808 during the Napoleonic Wars. There is a striking number of prehistoric burial mounds around Sønder Lem, some 45 in all, many of which can be seen from the church tower.

Another 4km north will take you to the A15 which you then follow west to (8km) Ringkøbing (see p 216).

Alternative route from Varde to Ringkøbing—the coastal route
Total distance 87km.

This less direct, but much more varied and interesting route will take you through a completely different, and quite distinctive, part of Jutland, much of it on the narrow neck of land between Ringkøbing Fjord and the North Sea.

You leave Varde on the 181 west, turning off left after 4km into the 431 and driving to (4km) **Janderup**. Here, just south of the main road and overlooking Varde river, stands the magnificent **Janderup Church**, a Romanesque building from c 1200. The 16C vaulting is covered with frescoes, this time not of a figurative nature, but exclusively of fleur-de-lis designs. It is a style found in several churches in this area, and is ascribed to an artist known as Liljemesteren, the Lily Master. The altarpiece (1645) is the work of a local master. It is elaborately carved and richly coloured, and surmounted with a figure of Christ in glory. Also richly carved is the pulpit from c 1600. Above the chancel arch hangs a crucifix from c 1300, and nearby there are other medieval figures, the most splendid of which is a statue of the Virgin and Child from 1503, representing Mary as Queen of Heaven with the powers temporal and spiritual kneeling beside her.

A particularly interesting feature is the old oaken entrance door. It was removed when a new door was fixed in 1979–81. However, as it is believed to be the original door the decision was taken to save it. It now hangs just inside the new door, and can be swung open for inspection.

A further 3km along this road brings you to **Billum**, where there is another fine Romanesque church built of tufa. The lofty nave is less ornate than that in Janderup, but the apse is of special interest for its blind arcades. The apparently Romanesque windows are thought to be of later date. The altarpiece and pulpit are early 17C, the font Romanesque. The benches are old, probably 16C, and there are several medieval statues on the walls.

The road now continues towards (3km) Oksbøl—though you will have to leave the main road if you want to go into the village, which the 431 by-passes. **Oksbøl** (**Tourist information**: Vestergade 27; tel. 75 27 18 00) has a particular treasure in its church, **Ål Church**, situated in the north part of the village. The original Romanesque church, dedicated to St Nicholas, the patron saint of seafarers, was built in the first half of the 12C, though it was later extended. There are, nevertheless, still many original Romanesque features—windows, both doors, and the original chancel arch. The profusion of frescoes is contemporary with the oldest part of the building, and it is believed that there were once friezes along the walls of both the nave and the chancel. Best preserved now is a frieze portraying a battle between knights on horseback, which has been compared with the Bayeux Tapestry, with which it is of course roughly contemporary. Stylised indeed, but it gives a vivid impression of the dress, armour, coats of arms—and brutality—of armed combat at the time. There is nothing to indicate whether it refers to a specific battle. There are other frescoes depicting the life of St Nicholas, and there is a painted Romanesque lion over each door.

The wooden crucifix on the altar is an exact copy of the original crucifix from the early 12C. It is particularly interesting in that it demonstrates how crucifixes at that time portrayed Christ not as suffering, but as triumphant. The pulpit, with its carved figures of Christ and the four Evangelists, is Baroque, and there are modern stained glass windows.

Oksbøl *is* only a village, and by the end of World War II it counted fewer than 1000 inhabitants. However, by that time it had become host to the biggest refugee camp in Denmark. With its 38,000 German refugees, the **Oksbøl Camp**, adjoining the village, formed for a time the sixth largest town in Denmark, with an area of 4 sq km and a circumference of some 8km. It was run by its own 'local authority' of refugees headed by an elected German mayor. There was a courthouse here, and cinemas, theatre, churches and hospital, even a railway station. Little is now left of this enormous camp, from which the last refugees departed in 1948, though the present Oksbøl youth hostel is situated in what was the camp hospital.

There is, meanwhile, a museum here at KIRKEGADE 1, **Blåvandshuk Egnsmuseum**, with exhibits and a film illustrating life in the camp. The museum also contains exhibits illustrating the history of the area from prehistoric times to the mid-20C, including the Occupation (open summer; limited opening winter). There is a large army camp in Oksbøl, where the **Pansermuseum**, containing an assortment of tanks and armoured personnel carriers, is open to the public from 15 June to 15 August.

▶**Excursion from Oksbøl to Blåvandshuk Peninsula**

Before continuing north to Ringkøbing, you might make an excursion south to visit a very idiosyncratic area known as **Blåvandshuk**, the most westerly part of Denmark, and a peninsula giving access to 40km of unbroken sand and sand dunes. To do this you take the 431 from Oksbøl south to **Blåvand Kro** (Blåvand Inn) (17km). You are here in a village called **Oksby**, where you will also find the **Blåvand Museum** in the thatched and half-timbered former school, providing a graphic illustration of the difficult living conditions in this area in times past. Another indication of the same is in the other museum, **Blåvand Redningsbådsmuseum** (Blåvand Lifeboat Museum), at FYRVEJ 25. On the most westerly point you will find the lighthouse, from 1900, where there is limited access to the top.

South of here is the sandy area known as **Skallingen**, reached by driving along a narrow road east and south—and then walking. In driving there you will go through **Ho**, where there is a large sheep market on the last Saturday in August.

On returning along the 431 to Oksbøl you might wish, after 13km, to turn left to (7km) the very fine bathing beach at **Vejers Strand**.◀

From Oksbøl you should take the road diagonally opposite Ål Church, PRÆSTEGÅRDSVEJ, towards Børsmose, and drive through Ål Plantage. About 1km along this road, on the left, you will find a last, poignant, reminder of the great refugee camp in the form of the **German Refugee Cemetery**, where some 1400 refugees are buried. It is now tended by the German War Graves Commission, although the majority of those buried there are, in fact, civilians.

Now move on towards (5km) **Børsmose**.

This drive will take you first through a wooded area, and then out into a quite remarkable and desolate moorland which has been subjected to continuous sand drift. Even so, oak trees have managed to establish themselves and survive—in the most peculiar shapes. The road in fact passes through a military area, the presence of which has paradoxically allowed a rich animal and bird life to develop in the area, and kept the ubiquitous summer cottages away.

At Børsmose you turn north and continue for 8km along a minor road to join the 465. If you turn left here, you will come to (1.5km) another delightful beach **Henne Strand** (1.5km). If you turn right instead and just continue with your route, you will quickly find yourself in (1km) **Henne Kirkeby**.

Here, on high ground overlooking the Filsø lake (which used to be much larger), there is one of the Romanesque churches characteristic of the region, built in the second half of the 12C by the Bishop of Ribe, who also owned nearby Hennegård. The original church was extended in Gothic times, and contains a good deal of furniture from that period—an early 16C tabernacle fixed in a magnificently carved large altarpiece from c 1600, two side altars, one of them surmounted by a beautiful figure of the Virgin and Child. The pulpit, richly carved, is from 1573, the canopy from 1625. The church bell bears the date 1444.

Now turn left on to a minor road leading to (8km) Nørre Nebel, there joining the 181 northwest. You follow this road for c 6km to a road on your right pointing to Tipperne.

Tipperne, probably meaning 'the tufts', is a miniature peninsula jutting out into the Ringkøbing Fjord—which to all intents and purposes is an inland lake with access to the sea; Tipperne consists of marshland and sand deposits, and is now an outstanding bird sanctuary, the home or resting place of countless sea birds, both sedentary and migratory. There is a small museum here and also an observation tower. The area immediately before Tipperne, **Værnengene**, is meadowland, similarly with a rich bird life, which can be observed from the road. Tipperne is state owned, Værnengene in private ownership, but both are protected areas.

■ There is public access to Værnengene daily from 1 Apr–31 Dec, 09.00–18.00; Tipperne on Sun from 1 Apr–31 Aug, 05.00–10.00, and from 1 Sept–31 Mar, 10.00–12.00.

It should be noted that the whole of the Ringkøbing Fjord is a protected area, and that, although there are ample facilities for yachting and windsurfing on this very suitable stretch of water, they are not allowed anywhere near Tipperne. There are other parts, too, with restrictions. Tourist information centres will provide you with charts showing where, and where not, yachting and windsurfing are permitted.

Now follow the 181 and drive through **Nymindegab** to the area known as **Holmsland Klit**. This is a Nordic holiday paradise if ever there was one. Not only do you find here some of the most impressive of Danish sand dunes, but the beaches stretch the entire 35km of this neck of land which at its maximum is 2.5km wide; the sand is white, the sea is clean and, except where marked, safe. Or you can hire a pony and ride along the sea edge. There are plenty of carparking facilities. As you drive up, you cannot but be aware of the presence of the North Sea on your left, though you will only catch the occasional glimpse. On your right, however, you will have views across the Ringkøbing Fjord. There are, inevitably, cafés, cafeterias and camping grounds in the area, but there is room for them all. There are, too, some magnificent old farms, amazingly big for an area where life in the past has been hard indeed.

A drive of 15km will bring you to **(Nørre) Havrvig**, where there is an isolated church standing on high ground overlooking Ringkøbing Fjord. It is not old, and it is not architecturally splendid, but the churchyard is interesting, partly for the railings around the graves—a custom in this area—and partly because of the graves of several named Allied airmen shot down during World War II.

One more kilometre and you come to **Abelines Gård** (Abeline's Farm), one of the largest and best-preserved of the many thatched farms on Holmsland Klit.

This really impressive farm was built in 1871—significantly, by a receiver of wrecks—and is today owned by a trust aimed at preserving West Jutlandic historic buildings. It is open to visitors in the summer and, almost unchanged since it was a family home, provides an impression of the furniture and daily life of West Jutland in the past. Note that there is no real bedroom—the beds are all in alcoves, in the old Scandinavian tradition. Yet people lived in this house until 1954! (open mid-June to early Sept—with café facilities).

Continue now north along the 181 to (6km) **Hvide Sande**.

■ **Tourist information**: Nørregade 2 B; tel. 97 31 18 66.

■ **Hotels**: Holmsland Klit, Nørregade 2; tel. 97 31 16 00; Skodbjerge, Søndre Klitvej 172; tel. 97 31 50 24.

This busy town is new, having grown up with the establishment of access from Ringkøbing Fjord to the North Sea in 1931. Now all deep sea fishing from this area is based on Hvide Sande, which has become one of Denmark's major fishing ports. The machinery regulating the flow of water between the North Sea and the fjord is an impressive sight in itself.

About 5km north of Hvide Sande, on high ground, you will find **Nørre Lyngvig** lighthouse, originally built in 1906. It stands 36m high (53m above sea level in all), and there are 225 steps leading to the top from where you have panoramic views. At the bottom, while you are regaining your breath, there is a miniature museum illustrating local wild life (open Easter–Nov).

From Nørre Lyngvig it is 8km to **Søndervig**, another holiday home area and bathing resort. Here you will find what claims to be the only **Elvis Presley Museum** outside the USA. (Open daily 11.00–17.00.)

In Søndervig you turn right to join the A15, and after 7km you will be close to **Gammelsogn Kirke**. While the churches on Holmsland Klit are relatively new, this is an old one. It is a Romanesque building with a late Gothic tower and porch, standing behind a wall of huge boulders on the shore of the fjord. On the north side the Romanesque windows are still to be seen, but on the south side they were replaced by larger windows in 1880. The pyramidal spire is from the 18C. There is nothing opulent about this church, and it bears traces of having stood in a poor part of the country. It has, however, been the principal church in the area, to which the inhabitants of the Holmsland Klit used to sail or row on Sundays. There are paths along the shore of the fjord leading both to Søndervig and Ringkøbing.

Back on the road, **Ringkøbing** (pop. 17,175) is a mere 2km away, across the Vonå river linking Ringkøbing Fjord with Stadil Fjord to the north.

■ **Tourist information**: Torvet; tel. 97 32 00 31.

■ **Hotels**: Fjordgården, Vesterkær 28; tel. 97 32 14 00; Ringkøbing, Torvet 18; tel. 97 32 00 11.

■ **Youth hostel**: Kirkevej 28; tel. 97 32 24 55.

History

Ringkøbing is one of Denmark's older market towns, with a charter from 1443. Excavations indicate that it was founded as a port in the mid-13C, and the central area is still built around the old town—of which, however, the church is the only building remaining. Fishing and the cattle trade led to considerable affluence in the 16C and 17C. However, in the 18C the entrance to the Ringkøbing Fjord at Nymindegab was partly closed by sand, making access difficult, and Ringkøbing's residual importance as a port then ended with the opening of the railway line in the 19C.

The 19C had, meanwhile, been a time of prosperity, and the town's aspect is one of 19C brick houses with hipped roofs and white-painted cornices. It is a style typical of the architecture of the west coast of Jutland, and efforts have been made in recent years to ensure that these buildings are not superseded by 20C styles. Modern industry has come to Ringkøbing in the form of a shipyard and a factory for agricultural machinery.

One of Ringkøbing's oldest buildings, the former mayor's residence from 1807, stands on the main square, TORVET, close to the elegant old town hall, built in 1849. Nearby is the Hotel Ringkøbing, with parts dating back to the 16C. On Torvet, too, stands the rather modest, buttressed church, the oldest parts of which are from the early 15C, while the tower is some 200 years later, with gabling added in 1866. Notice that this tower is broader at the top than at thebase. The somewhat low nave is cross-vaulted; the pulpit is late 16C. There is a sundial from 1728 on the west buttress.

To gain an impression of the older part of town, you should take a walk through the streets near the square, between NØRREGADE and SØNDERGADE. Here you will find an array of mainly single-storey houses typical of West Jutland, and built at the turn of the 19C. The new town hall, near the harbour, is from 1969–70.

Ringkøbing Museum, KONGEVEJ 1, contains excellent archaeological and historical collections, including exhibits from the Mylius-Erichsen expedition to northeast Greenland in 1906–08 (open summer; limited opening winter). Mylius-Erichsen spent part of his childhood in Ringkøbing, and there is a statue of him in front of the museum.

►Excursion from Ringkøbing to Vedersø

Total distance c 51km. This trip will take you further along the North Sea coast, to several more of the best churches of the area, and to Vedersø with its reminiscences of the dramatist and priest, Kaj Munk.

You leave Ringkøbing on the A15, driving west for 5km and turning into a road on your right leading to (1km) **KLOSTER**, where you will find NYSOGN KIRKE. This name, meaning 'New Parish Church', indicates that it is the younger of the two churches in this area, the other being Gammelsogn (Old Parish). However,

Nysogn Church is not exactly modern, being late Romanesque/early Gothic in style, of considerable dimensions and beautifully proportioned. The large crucifix over the altar is from c 1500, though it has been extensively restored.

From Kloster you drive west along a minor road to join the 181 at (4km) Hovvig. This will take you north along the North Sea dunes (very close to the sea), with views across the **Vest Stadil Fjord** on your right. Here, as on Holmsland Klit, there are thatched farms, two of the best preserved being (5km) **Strandgården** and, 4km further on, **Bankgården**: both are now protected buildings. Strandgården, an elegant building from 1875, is now a museum illustrating life in this part of the country, with a good collection of old agricultural and fishing equipment. The rich bird life of the area is also illustrated, and the museum contains a collection of first editions of the author Kaj Munk, who lived in nearby Vedersø (open summer).

Vedersø itself is 4km east of the 181, the road leading to it being about 4km north of Bankgården. The relatively modest Romanesque/Gothic church here is built of granite ashlars, but has little architectural significance. The interest inevitably centres on the fact that it was here that Kaj Munk was pastor from 1924 to his murder in 1944. He is buried in the churchyard.

Kaj Munk

Kaj Munk was in some ways a curious anomaly, in that he was originally quite positive in his views on the Italian dictator Mussolini. He soon had doubts about Hitler, but his patriotic fervour was not fully revealed until Hitler occupied Denmark. He then fearlessly opposed the occupying forces in his writing as well as in his preaching, and in 1944 he was one night taken from his home by the Gestapo, shot, and dumped by the roadside near Silkeborg.

From Vedersø you should continue south to (5km) **Stadil Kirkeby**, where the *church is one of the most splendid in this part of Jutland. It is richly decorated, perhaps reflecting the fact that it once belonged to the canons of Ribe Cathedral. However, the church is dominated by the golden altar, the sister piece to that in Sahl Church (p 260).

There are indications that these so-called golden altars were quite common in the 12C and 13C; seven have survived, five of them being in the National Museum, those in Stadil and Sahl still being in the churches for which they were intended. Legend has it that the altars in Stadil and Sahl once formed the head and foot of the bed belonging to an English prince who gave them to the churches as a thanks offering for safe deliverance from a storm at sea. In practice, they are highly sophisticated expressions of medieval faith.

At all events, this altar is believed to date from the period when the church itself was built, i.e. c 1200. It is made from wood covered with copper and then gold leaf, and was once the antemensale, being later installed in an ornate Renaissance altarpiece. It represents Christ enthroned, surrounded by 14 panels illustrating His childhood together with figures of the Apostles, and studded with quartz crystals.

The pulpit and organ loft in the church are Renaissance work, as are the pews, including those reserved for the local lord of the manor. A Romanesque piscina from the chancel has been repositioned in the tower. The entrance door is thought to be original, which makes it one of the oldest church doors in Denmark.

4km northeast of Stadil lies **Tim Kirkeby**, where there is another interesting church, even if it cannot compare with Stadil. Situated in an isolated position, it has Romanesque, Gothic and Renaissance features, none of which has the sumptuous carving so often found. The elegant altarpiece, containing four Corinthian columns, is from c 1590. The side panels contain original paintings, the centre panel a later crucifixion scene. The altar itself is fronted with glazed tiling from 1957 depicting scenes from the life of Christ, the work of Jais Nielsen, who is also responsible for the stained glass windows in the tower.

You now drive 3km east to join the A28/A16, and you follow the A16 through Hee (p 227) back to (12km) Ringkøbing.

15 • Kruså to Århus

Total distance 178km. 170 throughout. (23km) **Åbenrå**. *(24km)* **Haderslev**. *(28km)* **Kolding**. *(30km)* **Vejle**. *(26km)* **Horsens**. *(26km)* **Skanderborg**. *(22km)* **Århus**.

If you approach Denmark on the motorway from Flensburg, you will enter via the crossing post at Kruså. From here it is possible very quickly to join the main E45 offering you a fast route to Århus. However, the route along the old main road, now designated the 170, is more interesting.

You immediately drive north along the 170 through Søgård village to (11km) **Søgård** house. Just before the house you will find yourself between two lakes, a large one on your left, a small one on your right.

The 170 here is actually built on the old ramparts of what was once the biggest castle in Schleswig—Søgård (Lake House). Its quite dramatic history goes back to 1357, and has been determined by the border conflicts over many centuries; in 1643–44 it was totally destroyed. It was not rebuilt until the mid-19C, and the present simple but elegant building—now a military barracks—dates from 1858–60. It was from here that a force of 32 men was sent on 9 April 1940 to confront the German army when it invaded Denmark. Seven of the Danes were killed before the entire force was overrun. There is a memorial to them, a sandstone obelisk, at the entrance to the barracks.

Just north of Søgård you might turn left on the 481 and drive to **Kliplev** (3.5km) to visit the former pilgrim church of St Salvator, one of several places of pilgrimage on the old Military Road (Hærvejen) (more about this road on p 293). Kliplev was also the site of a major horse and cattle market, and while the pilgrims no longer come, the market still exists. Nevertheless, the pilgrims' church is still there, built in stages between 1400 and the Reformation, but apparently never quite built to the planned size because the Reformation brought things to a halt.

The Chapel of St Salvator is on the north side of the large nave, and many members of the Ahlefeldt family, the former owners of Søgård, are buried here. There are frescoes from c 1600, and in the churchyard there stands an excellent example of the free-standing medieval bell-towers commonly found in this part of the country. Here, too, there is a wooden frame from a grave dated 1550, the oldest in Denmark. The porch is from 1775, and a sundial from that year is fixed in the wall. In an outbuilding near the church there is a hearse from c 1800.

Now follow the 170 and drive to (12km) **Åbenrå** (pop. 21,900), lying in wooded countryside and idyllically situated at the head of the Åbenrå Fjord.

■ **Tourist information**: H.P. Hanssensgade 5; tel. 74 62 35 00.

■ **Hotels**: Europa, H.P.Hanssens Gade 10; tel. 74 62 26 22; Missionshotellet, Klinkbjerg 20; tel. 76 63 00 91.

■ **Youth hostel**: Sønderskovvej 100; tel. 74 62 26 99.

■ The countryside immediately around Åbenrå is very beautiful indeed, as is the coastline. There is ample scope for **walking** and **cycling** in this ancient borderland, where relics of the past appear quite unexpectedly. Down by the fjord you will find the 4500-year-old burial chamber known as **Myrpold**. That there are good **yachting** and **swimming** facilities goes almost without saying. The annual **local festival** of tilting at the ring takes place here on the first weekend in July.

History

Åbenrå is the largest port in South Jutland, and it has grown around the excellent harbour facilities. It has a charter going back to 1335, but is much older, probably from the 12C. Like so many other towns in the area, Åbenrå has suffered badly from the border conflicts. After the 1864 Danish defeat, it became the centre of Danish national movements in the area. Then, with the return of the area to Denmark in 1920, it was soon a centre for the German minority in North Schleswig. There is still plenty to point to its position between the two cultures. On the one hand it has a modern German grammar school, built in 1964, while on the other it is the seat of the South Jutland Regional Library and the South Jutland Regional Archive. The *Folkehjem* to the north of the town betokens the efforts of the Danish population to maintain their own culture while under German rule.

Near the town centre stands **Brundlund Castle**, now the residence of the Sheriff of Åbenrå and Sønderborg. It was largely rebuilt 1805–07 by C.F. Hansen, whose design reflects the austere lines of his Copenhagen work, and seeks to maintain, as he put it: 'the Gothic shape, which is so well suited to the beautiful romantic surroundings'. The original castle, parts of which still survive, was built by Queen Margrethe I in 1411. It was here in 1945 that the Swedish Count Folke Bernadotte successfully negotiated the return of Danish and Norwegian prisoners from Nazi concentration camps. Some 75m north of the castle you will find the castle watermill, an almost square building with a steep-pitched roof, dating back to the mid-16C. It was restored in 1952.

Brundlund Castle is not C.F. Hansen's only work in Åbenrå. He also designed the neo-classical **town hall** on the main square, STORE TORV. The main hall is decorated with a large collection of portraits of Danish kings and queens.

Åbenrå's principal **church** stands just north of the old town centre and dates back in part to c 1250; the nave, transept and apses are largely original. The sacristy is late Gothic. However, the church was subjected to a major restoration in the 1880s, followed by another by Kåre Klint in the 1950s. The superb Renaissance pulpit is from 1565, and the grandiose Baroque altarpiece from 1642. The Romanesque font is decorated with sculptured animals and other ornamentation.

Åbenrå Museum, founded in 1887, is situated in H.P. HANSSENSGADE, and contains collections relating to the archaeology and history of South Jutland and to the history of navigation and shipbuilding. There is a large collection of bottle ships and another of Danish paintings. Among the more famous exhibits is the Bronze Age skeleton, the Nybøl Man.

A good deal of the old town has been preserved despite several fires in the 17C and 18C. As in Tønder (p 198) the old houses are built close together, with gables facing the road. Most of them are modest in size, and the main area concerned is close to the church. In particular VÆGTERPLADSEN can provide the atmosphere of a bygone age. There are a few larger houses, including the splendid *Postmaster's House** from 1755 at SØNDERGADE 20, without doubt the most imposing house in the town.

►Excursion to Varnæs church

While in the Åbenrå area you should take the opportunity of driving the 12km east on an unclassified road to **Varnæs** to see a rather fine, but heavily restored, Romanesque/Gothic church with a magnificent 15C late Gothic altarpiece displaying an array of carved figures and scenes. A 14C censer hangs in the chancel arch. Like other churches in the region, this has no tower, but there is a free-standing medieval bell-tower in the churchyard. Also in the churchyard there are two iron collars once used for punishing malefactors.◄

From Åbenrå you now drive north on the 170 for 4km, when you will come to a road east to **Løjt Kirkeby** (2km). In the sizeable *church here you will find the biggest and most ornate altarpiece in South Jutland, dating back to 1520, the work of Claus Berg. This altarpiece is richly gilded and in addition to the 12 Apostles has, as its centrepiece, a crucifixion scene with crowds of people, 45 in all, around the crosses. There are two representations of the martyrdom of St Erasmus, and one of the figures has been identified as that of St Ansgar, the monk who brought Christianity to Denmark.

The church is Romanesque, and contains frescoes from c 1520 which unusually have never been covered over, possibly because they are decorative rather than representational. There is a gilded crucifix from the early 15C, a pulpit from 1577, and a perspective painting from 1750: viewed from the right it shows the Crucifixion, from the left the Resurrection.

Now drive north 6km to **Knivsbjerg**, the highest point (97km) in South Jutland. Here a bombastic tower, the Bismarck Tower, was constructed in 1901 by the Germans to commemorate the incorporation of the area into Germany in 1864, but it was destroyed again by bombs planted in 1945. Knivsbjerg has, however, remained a focal point for the German minority, who hold rallies here, and there is a memorial to ethnic Germans who fell in World War II.

The road continues now to (14km) **HADERSLEV** (pop. 31.000) standing at the head of the narrow Haderslev Fjord and straddling the river connecting this to Haderslev Dam, the biggest lake in South Jutland.

- **Tourist information**: Honnørkajen 1; tel. 74 52 55 50.

- **Hotels**: Motel Haderslev, Damparken; tel. 74 52 60 10; Harmonien, Gåskærgade 19; tel. 74 52 37 20.

- **Youth hostel**: Erlevvej 34; tel. 74 52 13 47.

- The Haderslev area is well equipped for **sports and outdoor activities** of all kinds, including, rather unusually, the hiring out of 'water cycles' so that you can paddle out on to the lake at Haderslev Dam. There is also the **paddle steamer**, the *Helene*, that will take you on a leisurely trip around the Haderslev Fjord.

- **Concerts** are regularly given in the cathedral and other churches in the district.

History

Haderslev received its charter in 1292. It appears to have come into being in the 12C at the junction of roads from Kolding and Ribe, developing into a thriving trade centre in the Middle Ages. The large Benedictine church became a collegiate church under Schleswig Cathedral. The other major building was the castle of Haderslevhus, first mentioned in 1326, in which Christian I signed his Charter. It was here that Christian II proclaimed the first Lutheran church law.

Haderslev was once even a royal residence: Frederik II spent a time here, and Christian IV celebrated his wedding and had several of his children baptised here.

Much of the town was destroyed by fire in 1627, an event which heralded a period of decline lasting throughout the 17C and 18C, despite continuing trade with Norway. In 1864 the town was taken over by the Prussians, and remained in German hands until 1920, by which time trade in the area had improved, and with it Haderslev's prosperity. This prosperity continued after the return to Denmark in 1920.

Haderslevhus Castle is no more, and ***Haderslev Cathedral**, also known as St Mary's Cathedral, standing on the highest ground, is thus the dominant building, its mighty walls visible from far around as they tower over the surrounding buildings. The transept is from c 1250, the nave from c 1260, the soaring chancel, the most splendid Gothic chancel in Denmark, being added in c 1420; the remainder is of later date. There are signs in some of the ashlars used in the building that they must have formed part of an earlier granite church from c 1100. The final shape given to the church in the 13C was of a nave with an aisle on either side. The vaulting is some of the loftiest in Scandinavia.

The original cathedral was partly destroyed by fire in 1627, but later restorations have aimed at re-creating it in its original form. The windows in the chancel are strikingly tall. The crucifix behind the altar is late 13C, the figures of Joseph and Mary beside it are from 1425 and 1450, the pulpit and canopy from 1636. The unusual bronze font was cast in Flensburg in 1485; it stands on four legs fashioned as the four evangelists. The restored Sieseby *organ, which can be seen to the left of the nave, is of particular interest.

It is said that Lutheranism was preached for the first time in this cathedral, in 1525, and certainly Danish Lutheranism was partly fashioned in a synod held here.

However, the cathedral is not the oldest church in Haderslev. That honour goes to **St Severin's**, or Old Haderslev Church, in the west of the town, close to Haderslev Dam; unfortunately, its original Romanesque character has been altered over the centuries, not least through restorations in 1912. There are old frescoes as well as a striking modern one of the Apocalypse on the apse, painted in 1952 by Hjalte Skovgaard. The Romanesque font is decorated with carvings of animals and human heads.

In 1984 Haderslev was chosen as the 'town of the year' in recognition of the careful restoration of its **old houses**. These are particularly centred on the area near the cathedral. Immediately west of the cathedral, in APOTEKERGADE, there are remains of medieval vaulted cellars, but most of the half-timbered houses in the area are of rather later date. The former Duke Hans Hospital, in SØNDERBRO, dates back to 1569. SLOTSGADE 20 is a house dating back to 1580, though with 17C additions. This fascinating building now houses the comprehensive **Ehlers Collection** of pottery (open summer; limited opening winter).

In the monastery churchyard in PRÆSTEGADE you will find memorials to the dead from both sides in the Schleswig-Holstein wars and those who fought on the German side in World War I. Here, too, are buried many of those who were most politically active during the breakaway period in the 19C.

Haderslev Museum (open all year) is at DALGADE 7, a little east of the town centre. Archaeological exhibits account for a large proportion of the museum's collections, but there are sections devoted to local history and ethnography, and there is a re-creation of a 19C home. Among the exhibits is a copy of the clothes in which the early Bronze Age Skrydstrup Girl was dressed. (This remarkably well-preserved woman, now in the National Museum, was found in 1935 in an oak coffin in a burial mound at Skrydstrup to the west of Haderslev.)

The archaeological collections are all housed in a modern building opposite which there is a fine open air museum. Here you will find a large barn from 1620, once part of Øsby parsonage, now containing a collection of agricultural implements. There are also two 17C half-timbered houses, duly furnished, and a windmill.

Den slesviske Vognsamling (The Schleswig Carriage Museum) is just south of the museum, in SEJLSTENSGYDE, opposite the yachting harbour. It contains some 40 different horse-drawn carriages and carts. The building housing them is itself a splendid relic from the past, built in the 18C as a riding school for the Holstein Lancers (open mid-June to mid-Aug).

▶Excursion to the east of Haderslev
Total distance c 35km.

This trip takes you through the area immediately south of Haderslev Fjord. You leave Haderslev on an unclassified road east to (3km) **Starup**, where you will find a remarkable 11C church built of calcareous tufa and showing English influence in its architecture. The nave, chancel and apse are original and have undergone very little alteration, but the side aisles are inferior 20C reconstructions. On either side of the nave there is Romanesque arcading surmounted by Romanesque windows beneath a beamed roof. During work on the church in 1919 the remains of frescoes were discovered. These were used as a basis for the reproduction frescoes which are now a striking—and unfortunate—feature. The church contains a remarkable font from 1742 in which the bowl of the font is held by an angel surmounted by the Holy Ghost in the form of a dove.

From Starup you drive southeast through Hejsager to (7km) **Halk Church**, with corbie steps in the west and over the porch and north-facing chapel. Unusually, the tower is in the east, above the elongated chancel. However, it is not only the architecture which is of interest, but also the furniture. The large and impressive bronze font is from 1491, made in the same foundry as those in Haderslev and Århus Cathedrals. A Gothic Virgin and Child is, however, much older, from c 1275, and there is a crucifixion group from the same time. The centre section of the colourful altarpiece is likewise Gothic, though the side panels are Baroque. Also there is a number of Gothic altarpieces from former side altars, one of them portraying St George slaying the dragon. On the vaulting opposite the pulpit (from 1559) hang two pieces of armour and a sword, said by legend to have belonged to a cadet who murdered a local farmer one Good Friday—and who is now supposed to haunt the church at Easter.

Halk is very close to the coast, and here, at **Halk Hoved**, you will find an impressive 26m-high cliff. The stretch southeast of this is a favoured beach for bathing and sunbathing. And for countless holiday cottages.

Now drive back to Hejsager and on to (10km) **Årøsund**. Here, too, there are magnificent beaches, and you can take the hourly ferry to the tiny islet of **Årø**, only ten minutes away. There are only 200 inhabitants here, and this charming island has been left largely untouched by modern developments, though there is a camping ground here. There is plentiful bird life, too.

You will return to (15km) Haderslev through **Øsby**, where there is another large church dating back to Romanesque times, but mainly Gothic in its architecture. An interesting feature here is that it has no windows in its north wall. Another is that it contains one of the oldest Renaissance pulpits in Denmark, from 1559. On the west side there is a charnel house from c 1510, the only extant medieval charnel house in the country. The parsonage, standing nearby, is an imposing residence from 1765, brick-built and whitewashed. ◄

The 170 will take you from Haderslev direct north to (11km) the very unusual small town of Christiansfeld. However, we suggest a slightly longer indirect route to guide you past a couple of interesting churches and a mansion on your way there.

You leave Haderslev driving east on an unclassified road towards Fjelstrup, and c 3km from the town centre, at Neder Åstrup, you turn right on to a minor road leading to (2km) Over Åstrup. Almost immediately, on your left, you will see the elegant small mansion of **Åstrupgård**, built c 1780. A further 500m brings you to **Åstrup church**, also on the left. This has a unique, very elaborately carved panelled ceiling from 1675 above the unspoiled Romanesque nave. The grandiose altarpiece from 1638 is similarly ornate and contains a central picture of the Last Supper. The pulpit, also in Renaissance style, is from 1621. On the south wall there is a splendid crucifix from c 1525.

Continue along this relatively high ground overlooking the fjord, turn left in Over Åstrup, and then right when you reach the Fjelstrup road to (6km) **Fjelstrup**, where there is a late Romanesque church (c 1200) with Gothic additions. Over the walled-up south door there is a tympanum with relief carvings of the crucified Christ between Mary and St John. From Fjelstrup there is then a straight road to (6km) ***Christiansfeld** (pop. 9175), passing close to Tyrstrup, where the Moravian Brethren (see below) first established themselves.

■ **Tourist information**: Kongensgade 5.

■ **Hotels**: Brødremenighedens Hotel, Lindegade 25; tel. 74 56 17 10; Den gamle Grænsekro, Koldingvej 51; tel. 75 57 32 18.

History
Christiansfeld is the home of the Danish Moravian Brethren, the *Herrnhuter*, and their presence has marked the village since their arrival in 1773. Although reduced now to a couple of hundred members, they have managed to maintain the centre of the village as they originally planned it.

The village received its name after Christian VII, who invited the Brethren to settle in Denmark, knowing them for their skills and reliability both as craftsmen and tradesmen. In a Denmark which at the time was rigorously Lutheran, they were given virtually full control of their own affairs, including church and school, and they were exempted from military service. For ten years they were also exempt from taxes and duties—much to the annoyance of merchants in Haderslev.

Christiansfeld was thus designed according to quite specific principles, built in the shape of a cross with the church at the centre and with straight intersecting roads starting from it. These roads were—and still are—lined with lime trees. The individual houses were also built to a pattern established elsewhere by the Brethren. There were large communal houses for the unmarried men, for unmarried women, and for married couples.

The central section of the ***church**, known as the Hall, dates from 1776–77, the side wings from 1795–97 and, with the exception of the ridge turret constructed in 1897, it is virtually as it was originally designed. It is built of yellow Flensburg brick, without decoration except that every fifth row of bricks stands c 5cm further forward than the rest, thus breaking the otherwise gaunt façade. The interior is similarly without decoration of any kind, with long benches facing a podium behind which there is a reproduction of Thorvaldsen's statue of Christ. The floor is made of untreated deal. Men and women enter through different doors.

The ***cemetery**, to the east of the town, is quite different from normal cemeteries. It is known as **God's Acre**, and the graves, each marked by an identical gravestone, are carefully arranged in sectors divided by paths in the form of a cross. There are no family graves; men are buried to the west of the main path, women to the east. All the graves, some 2000 in all, are numbered. A notable feature is the lime trees marking the different sections; they are the originals, planted in 1773 and 1774.

The old ***communal houses** still stand, one for the men (the Brethren) on the corner of STOREGADE and KONGENSGADE, one for the women (the Sisters) on NØRREGADE, and one for the widows on BIRKEVEJ (now the **Brethren Museum**—open summer). They are all built of the same brick as the Hall. So, too, are the individual, mainly single-storeyed, houses. The Brethren own an hotel, built in 1773, and it was in this that the ceasefire between Denmark and Prussia was signed in 1864.

For all their strict manner of life, the Brethren put a great effort into their skills, not least in the manufacture of honey cakes, for which the town is still famous. Stop and have a taste!

Leaving Christiansfeld on the 170 north you will at (2.5km), near **Frederikshøj**, cross the pre-1920 border. There are still markers to be seen. If you are interested in experiencing some of the atmosphere of the old border region, you should make a detour here, instead of heading straight towards (11km) *Kolding (p 180).

►Leave the 170 a few kilometres ahead in Taps, turning right on a minor road through Åstorp to (4km) Sjølund. From here you follow an unclassified road north towards Sønder Bjert, but only as far as (3km) Skamling in order to visit the nearby **Skamlingsbanken** (Skamling Hill). Standing high above the surrounding countryside, and with a view across the straits to Fyn, this hill was the meeting place for mid-19C Danish nationalists. The first rally to be held here was in 1843, when some 6000 people met to show their patriotic sentiments. The following years they were addressed by some of the most famous of Danish national figures. In 1863 a 16m-high obelisk was raised at the top of the hill. In 1945 about 100,000 Danes gathered here to celebrate the Liberation. Today Skamlingsbanken is a national monument rather than a significant meeting place. From here the road takes you direct to (12km) Kolding. ◄

There is a ring road around Kolding, so you can by-pass it if you wish—though, if this is your only visit to the region, you are well advised to experience this most interesting town, described on p 180 ff.

North of Kolding the 170 continues. Follow it to c 15km from Kolding, when you will find a minor road west leading to (3km) **Øster Starup**.

The relatively unspoiled Romanesque church in Øster Starup is famous for the splendid relief carvings around the two doors. At the east side of the bricked-up north door there is an almost free-standing figure of a lion killing a man, a violent scene in which the symbolism is thought to be that of a man tied to his fate and entirely in the power of the lion. There is a similar figure on the south-west corner of the nave, and a beaked monster will be seen at the northeast corner. The triumph over this evil is represented to the right of the south door: here, too, there is a lion, but it is balanced by the figure of the Archangel Michael slaying the dragon. On the font there are reliefs of the Tree of Life and symbols representing Christ. These Romanesque carvings are quite unusual, well worth the short detour.

Now continue to (12km) Vejle (p 291), which is a beautiful little town in lovely countryside. If you are not coming this way again, do consider a short trip to the historic Jelling 11km northwest (described on p 292), before you continue north-east.

In addition to the motorway E45, there are two good routes from Vejle to Horsens: either direct (26km) or via the coast (63km).

For the direct route, take the 170 northeast to (8km) Bredal, where you turn right on to an unclassified road to (1.5km) **Engum**. The rather modest church here, thoroughly restored in 1977, is filled with impressive, bombastic rococo furniture—pulpit, altarpiece, organ loft, benches, all from c 1760. The chancel arch is flanked by two angels with flaming swords, and there are Romanesque frescoes in the arch and in the chancel.

Another 18km will see you in Horsens (see below).

Alternative route from Vejle to Horsens—the coastal route

Total distance 63km. This more leisurely route takes you along the beautiful Vejle Fjord to the ferry port of Juelsminde and from there to Horsens. On the way you will pass close to several mansions, none of which, however, is among the most outstanding in Denmark; nor are they open to the public, though in some cases there is access to the park. You will, however, also pass through Glud with its fine open air museum.

You take the 170 northeast for 6km, turning off right on the A23 to (6km) **Daugård**, where next to the Romanesque church you will find the small mansion of Williamsborg, from 1774. Continue towards Juelsminde. In 2km you will discover a minor road off right leading to (1km) **Rohden**, a mansion built in 1898; the road goes through the grounds.

A further 3km along the A23 comes Stouby, from where we suggest you follow minor roads south through the woods right down to the coast, eventually reaching (4km) **Rosenvold**. Built in 1586, Rosenvold is the most interesting of the mansions on this route, looking much as it originally did. For a time it was owned by Ellen Marsvin, the mother-in-law of Christian IV, and it was a favoured residence of her daughter, Kirstine Munk, Christian IV's morganatic wife, after Christian had rejected her.

Continue past Rosenvold and rejoin the A23 after some 5km at Smedskær.

Before driving further eastwards, however, you should cross the A23 and drive north to **Over Vrigsted** (2km). The church here is quite unusual, almost all of it dating from the beginning of the 12C, with remarkably few alterations. Some frescoes representing two heads were uncovered here in 1959; dating from between 1125 and 1150, they are thought to be the oldest surviving fresco paintings in Denmark. Now you return to the A23 and turn left.

Continue to (8km) **Juelsminde**, a ferry port with connections to Kalundborg (p 120). There is little of interest in Juelsminde, apart from the huge anchor from the frigate '*Jylland*'— which itself is in Ebeltoft (p 126)—though the wooded surroundings and coastline are beautiful.

In Juelsminde you turn north and follow the 459 for 5km to Hosby, where on the eastern outskirts of the town you will find the pleasing mansion of **Palsgård**, built c 1500 but radically rebuilt 1804–06. The park is open to the public.

Back on the 459 you continue north to (7km) **Glud**, where there is a small open air museum, **Den gamle Landsby** (The Old Village), containing one of the oldest dated houses in Denmark (1662) together with other houses, many from the 17C and 18C, which have been reassembled here. Most are complete with historical implements and tools (open summer).

From Glud you take the 459 northwest to (13km) Horsens (pop. 55,300) passing at (7km) **Boller Castle** on your right. This castle, built variously between 1550 and 1759, was also a much-loved residence of Kirstine Munk, who died here in 1648. It now serves as a rest home.

Horsens

■ **Tourist information**: Søndergade 26; tel. 75 62 38 22.

■ **Hotels**: Scandic, Schüttesvej 6, tel. 75 62 23 23; Jørgensens, Søndergade 17–19, tel. 75 62 16 00.

■ **Youth hostel**: Flintebakken 15, tel. 75 61 67 77.

■ **Horsens Fjord** is a yachtsman's paradise, with many hospitable small harbours, tiny islands, and a delightful coastline—which also invites **walking**.

History

Horsens has a history going back to the 12C and a charter from 1442. Lying in a fertile area, close to the fjord, it has had a less varied history of progress and poverty than many other Danish towns. Horsens has tended always to be relatively prosperous, though there was a lengthy period of stagnation in the 17C and 18C and, like so many other Danish towns, Horsens suffered badly during the 17C Swedish wars. It suffered, too, during the 1940–45 Occupation, when there was a good deal of Resistance activity in the town, followed by punitive action on the part of the occupying forces.

One curious feature of Horsens' history, however, is the presence there in the late 18C of exiles from the Russian royal family. They lived in the magnificent Baroque mansion called Lichtenbergs Palæ—now Jørgensens Hotel—in which a Russian Orthodox chapel was established.

SØNDERGADE, the main street, is unusually wide. It contains several 18C buildings, but was given its present appearance in the late 19C. It was at this period that the old town hall, now housing the town archive and the tourist information office, was built in Renaissance style. Helms Apotek (Pharmacy) dates from 1736, and Jørgensens Hotel from c 1744. Several of the rooms here have been maintained in their original shape. The only half-timbered house in the street is **Monbergs Gård**, from 1772.

Probably the most unusual of Horsens' houses is **Claus Cortsens Gård** from 1718, a magnificent three-storeyed half-timbered structure surmounted by an onion-shaped dome. It was originally situated in Søndergade, next to Helms Apotek, but has been moved to the east of the town, and now stands on SUNDVEJ, a little beyond **Horsens Museum**, which now is the home of many of the more interesting features from buildings demolished over the years. There are in addition archaeological collections and collections of silver, pottery and furniture associated with a now-vanished Horsens (open summer). A recent addition is an exhibition of memorabilia connected with Vitus Bering (1681–1741), the Horsens-born explorer who, working for the Russian Czar Peter the Great, discovered the Bering Strait between Alaska and Siberia. The exhibition includes a reconstruction of Bering's head made after his grave was discovered and exhumed in 1991. The museum is not only the place in Horsens with memorials to Vitus Bering. His name appears in one street name and in the Vitus Bering Park near the railway station. There is a memorial plaque in the park flanked by two guns from the ship on which Bering sailed for the last time in 1741. They were a gift to Horsens by Nikita Khrushchev when he visited Denmark in 1957.

Behind the museum, on CAROLINELUNDSVEJ, stands the art gallery, **Lunden**, with a large collection of paintings and graphics by Mogens Zieler as well as collections of classical and modern Danish art.

A museum of an entirely different kind is the **Arbejder-, Håndværker- og Industrimuseum** (Museum for Crafts and Industry), reached by going down NY HAVNEGADE, opposite Horsens Museum, and turning right into STJERNHOLMSGADE. This museum, the only one of its kind in Denmark, is housed in the former power station from 1906, and contains exhibits demonstrating the industrial development of Denmark, and its effect on the way of life (open Jun–Sept).

As might be expected in a town of this kind, there are some interesting old churches. First, on TORVET (the Square), there is **Vor Frelsers Kirke** (Our Saviour's Church), built in the 13C, possibly by Valdemar II, though the onion-shaped dome above the tower is 18C. It is a large basilica, high to the vaulted ceiling, with brick interior as well as exterior. The pulpit and canopy, from 1663–70, with carvings of scenes from the Passion, are ascribed to Peder Jensen Kolding, and are considered among the finest of their kind in Denmark. Note, too, the imposing west door.

At the other end of BORGERGADE, which leads from Torvet, you will find the other old church, **Klosterkirken** (The Monastery Church). This is the only remaining part of the former Franciscan monastery, and was the subject of rebuilding in the 18C. However, nine of the monks' carved choir stalls are still there, with figures of SS Erasmus and Gertrude on the gabling at the ends. Nor are these the only items of furnishing of interest: the altarpiece is late medieval, a crucifixion scene in the centre panel, with side panels containing the figures of the 12 Apostles and four saints, including St Francis. An ornate carved rood screen stands at the entrance to the chancel, surmounted by a late Gothic crucifix, and there is a carved and gilded font screen from 1716 in the north aisle. The Lichtenberg sepulchral chapel is situated in the south aisle.

On approaching Horsens from Vejle, you will have passed a church of an entirely different kind at the southern end of the town: **Sønderbro Church**, a strikingly modern structure designed by Paul Nieport—perhaps a little in the style of Le Corbusier.

To the left of the 453 west of Horsens you will find in a well laid-out park, **Bygholm**, a three-winged mansion from 1775, but with a history going back to the 14C. It is now an hotel.

There are again two routes to choose from between Horsens and Århus: the route via Skanderborg (48km), described first, or the alternative route (47km), via Odder.

Horsens to Århus via Skanderborg
Total distance 48km.

From Horsens you take the 170 north, passing on your right close to the mansion of Serridslevgaard, where accommodation is available by arrangement (tel. 75 66 73 75), and then proceed straight to (26km) **Skanderborg** (pop. 19,785). The later part of your journey will be through increasingly hilly and wooded countryside, and 5km from Skanderborg you will come to Skanderborg Lake. You are here on the fringe of the Silkeborg–Skanderborg lake district.

■ **Tourist information**: Adelgade 105; tel. 86 52 27 44.

■ **Hotels**: Skanderborghus, Dyrehaven 3; tel. 86 52 09 55; Slotskroen, Adelgade 23; tel. 86 52 00 12.

■ **Youth hostel**: Dyrehaven 9; tel. 86 51 19 66.

History
Skanderborg was the site of a royal castle in the early Middle Ages, and there are many references to it in the medieval ballads. According to these, Valdemar II was here when in 1212 he heard that Queen Dagmar lay ill in Ribe, and it was here Marsk Stig came to renounce allegiance to King Erik Glipping and subsequently to announce that he was responsible for his murder in 1286. It was during a siege of this castle that Niels Ebbesen, another of Denmark's great medieval heroes, was killed in 1340. Frederik II (1534–88) extended the castle and in 1583 decided to found a market town around the castle. It never became a centre for trade, but there is now a certain amount of industry here, and the town is one of the centres for the tourist industry in this particularly attractive part of Jutland. As Crown Prince, Christian IV spent a good deal of time in Skanderborg, and here his sister, later to marry James VI of Scotland and I of England, was born. By the 17C, however, there was little use for a great fortified castle and it gradually fell into disrepair. It was sold in 1767 and demolished soon afterwards. With the exception of the chapel, which was retained as Skanderborg parish church, there is now nothing left of it although we know what it was like from contemporary drawings and etchings.

This *chapel was built in 1570 by Frederik II as a chapel royal, and much of the resplendent carved panelling is still to be seen—the bench ends with the royal coat of arms and royal motto carved into them, and the pulpit. All was carefully restored in the original style 1944–48. The crypt beneath, originally the castle wine cellar, was restored for use as a chapel in 1969. It is not open, but admission can be gained on application to the verger.

A little to the north stands **Skanderup Church**, dating back to c 1050. Although there have been later additions (including a tower with an onion-shaped dome from 1741), most of the original Romanesque structure is intact. In particular the apse is unusual; it is shaped like a horseshoe and has seven sections of exterior arcading into which open three circular windows. Apart from roof renewals, it is thought to have stood unaltered since it was built and is the only example of this design in Denmark. However, this is not the only very old feature remaining in the church. There are frescoes from c 1170, again with motifs such as the crucifixion of St Peter and the death of Simon Magus which are unique in Scandinavian churches. There is a dramatic battle scene, too, which is earlier than others of a similar nature. The Baroque pulpit and altarpiece from 1650 with ornate auricular carvings are probably by Peder Jensen Kolding.

The old part of Skanderborg is largely made up of modest **half-timbered houses**, often with a courtyard behind. A number of these still stand, especially in BORGERGADE and ADELGADE, just north of the Castle Church. In Adelgade you will find **Skanderborg Museum**, in a building from 1888 overlooking the Lille Sø lake. It is particularly concerned with local history, but also has some interesting prehistoric exhibits.

To the west of the Castle Church lies the **Skanderborg Deer Park** on a headland jutting out into Skanderborg Lake, a delightful large wooded area with marked paths. There is an open air theatre, a kiosk for refreshments and a lakeside bathing area.

From Skanderborg you take the 170 north through (8km) **Hørning**, a delightful village with a pond in wooded surroundings and the charming **Bodilmølle**, a knife factory from 1740. The 170 then continues to (14km) Århus (see below).

Alternative route from Horsens to Århus—via Odder

Total distance 47km.

To drive by this route you leave Horsens east on the 451. After about 5km, however, at Stensballe, you should turn off left and visit **Vær Church** (1km).

This detour is less for the sake of the church itself than to see the grave of one of the great figures of 17C Denmark, Griffenfeld (1635–99). Born Peder Schumacher, this brilliant man rose to the highest post as Chancellor for the new absolute monarch Frederik III, and he was responsible for establishing Absolutism in law in 1665. He was ennobled for his work. By 1676, however, he was accused of treason and sentenced to death. After mounting the scaffold he was given a royal pardon and condemned to life imprisonment, first in Copenhagen, later in Trondheim, where he died. His remains were brought to Vær, and he now lies in a black coffin in a sepulchral chapel at the foot of the church tower.

About 1km on the other side of the 451 at Stensballe lies **Stensballegård**, a Baroque mansion built in the 1690s by Frederik Krag, the son-in-law of Griffenfeld. It is visible from outside the park, but is not open to the public.

Continue on the 451 to (17km) Ørting, perhaps turning off right c 1km before Ørting to visit the church in **Falling** (1km), which is large and contains an altarpiece from 1635 by Peder Jensen Kolding. Particularly striking is the very large gateway leading into the churchyard.

5km north of Ørting you arrive at **Odder** (pop. 19,000; **Tourist informa-tion**: Banegårdsplads 3; tel. 86 54 26 00), one of the largest towns in Denmark without a charter, though its history certainly goes as far back as the 14C. It is a small road and railway junction with a good deal of light industry. There are few old buildings, but a large church stands in the centre of the town. The apse, chancel and nave are Romanesque, the remainder Gothic. This was once the home of one of Denmark's golden altars, but it has been removed and is now in the National Museum. There is nevertheless a beautifully carved altarpiece by Peder Jensen Kolding from 1645. The impressive archway leading into the churchyard is similar to that in Falling.

Odder **museum**, in an old watermill, has a good local ethnographical collec-tion. Also one illustrating the history of the hunting rifle (open pm).

From Odder the 451 continues through (8km) Malling. 5km further on you turn right to **Moesgård** (1.5km) where the old half-timbered mill is now a restaurant. **Moesgård House** from 1780–84 has since 1970 been a prehistoric museum, **Forhistorisk Museum**, giving a graphic presentation of the develop-ment of Denmark from the Stone Age to the Viking Age. Among the most impor-tant exhibits is the Grauballe Man, the well-preserved body found in a bog near the village of Grauballe in 1952. There are also ethnographical collections from Greenland and Afghanistan. In the park outside there is what is called a 'prehis-toric path', leading to reconstructions of prehistoric houses and barrows of various kinds.

It is now only 7km to Århus.

Århus

■ **Tourist information**: Rådhuset; tel. 86 12 16 00.

■ **Hotels**: Atlantic, Europaplads 12–14; tel. 86 13 11 11; Ansgar, Banegårdsplads 14; tel. 86 12 41 22.

■ **Youth hostel**: Havnegade 20; tel. 86 19 20 55.

■ A large harbour provides a major **ferry terminal**, not only for domestic routes, but also for routes to Sweden. The terminal is about 1km from the railway station, well signposted. From here there are six daily ferries to Kalundborg (p 120) (sailing time 3hrs 10 mins; tel. 33 15 15 15), from where you will find excellent roads or fast railway connections to Copenhagen (pp 60 ff). There is also a fast **catamaran** connection to Kalundborg (the CAT-LINK, sailing time 1hr 20 mins; tel. 89 41 20 20) with five departures most days.

■ **Tirstrup airport**, 35km to the northeast serves the city, mainly with domestic flights, but with a growing number of international connections (e.g. to London).

History
Århus is Denmark's second city. It appears to have originated no later than the beginning of the 10C, and by 948 it had a bishop; its coat of arms is known from c 1250, and its earliest known charter is from 1441. In addi-tion to a great deal of industry and commerce, it has all the other marks of

a major city—a university (founded 1928), music conservatory, business high school, and virtually every kind of educational establishment one can think of. There is a fine theatre, orchestra and concert hall, as well as the biggest provincial library in the country. And a host of museums, including the Old Town, one of Denmark's two major open air museums.

There is a theory that the original town was centred on the area around Vor Frue Kirke (Our Lady's Church), and it is beneath this church that the remains of the original episcopal church from the 10C have been discovered. The present cathedral was started in the final years of the 12C, bringing with it the increased trade that automatically came with a major ecclesiastical centre, even if medieval Århus could not compete with Viborg (p 282). Nevertheless, Århus underwent a period of rapid development in the Middle Ages, not least because of its harbour facilities, though it declined when its role as an ecclesiastical centre came to an end with the 1536 Reformation. Its geographical position though allowed it to recover, and after a period of stagnation in the 17C it started to grow again from about 1750. It suffered severely from the blockades in the Napoleonic Wars, but later in the 19C, with the advent of the railways and the steamship, trade increased greatly, and Århus established itself as a major centre in Jutland, a development which continued throughout the 20C, until today it stands as a major city by any standard.

Århus (pop. 274,500) is a busy city, and can best be seen and appreciated on foot. The main railway station (built 1926–29) is as good a place as any to start a walk. You should bear diagonally right and go down RYESGADE and SØNDERGADE, the main shopping streets. Søndergade is now a rather brash pedestrian precinct, but as you walk down them you might give a thought to what these streets were like until the 1960s, when tramcars thundered down them, very close to the pavement on the right-hand side. You will soon come to the **Roman Catholic church** on your left in Ryesgade, built 1879–80 in neo-Gothic style. After crossing the bridge over ÅBOULEVARDEN you will find on CLEMENSTORV (Clement's Square) the large Unibank on your left. In the basement of this building there is the ***Vikingemuseum** illustrating the history of Århus in Viking times. Almost opposite you now come to BISPETORV (Bishop's Square) with its equestrian statue of Christian X, and you will be facing Århus Theatre from 1898–1900, with a scene from Holberg adorning its façade.

On the opposite side of Bispetorvet stands ****Århus Cathedral**, originally dedicated to St Clement. With a nave 93m long, this is the longest church in Denmark and certainly one of the most resplendent. The first church was built here in the 11C, and this, the third to stand on the spot, incorporates elements of the 13C Romanesque church. It dates from the 15C and apart from the Romanesque remains is predominently late Gothic.

The best-preserved Romanesque remains are the four chapels off the chancel, all of which have retained their original vaulting. The Gothic nave is the same width as the chancel, with lofty cross vaulting dating from 1477–87, and there is an aisle on either side. The pillars supporting the vaulting at the west end, which are based on the older church, are square, while the new ones at the east are octagonal. An impression of lightness and elegance is given by the tall, broad windows in the arcading on the north and south sides.

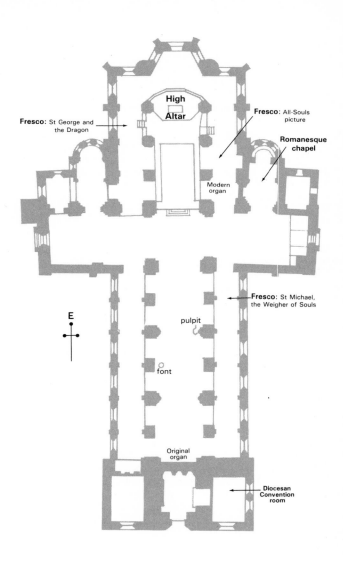

Fresco: St George and the Dragon

High Altar

Fresco: All-Souls picture

Romanesque chapel

Modern organ

Fresco: St Michael, the Weigher of Souls

E

pulpit

font

Original organ

Diocesan Convention room

ÅRHUS CATHEDRAL

The cathedral boasts a wealth of frescoes, by five different masters, from the end of the 15C. They vary in content from decorative designs, coats of arms and Danish fables to the martyrdom of St Christina, and, in the transept vaulting, a glorious representation of Christ as the Judge of the World, dated 1480. On the wall of the north aisle there are figures of St Anthony and St Barbara, and on one of the pillars on the south side Christ, crowned with thorns, is appearing to Pope Gregory. The Virgin enthroned is seen on one of the columns to the north. There is a St George, and a picture of the Day of Judgement, and many more. For anyone interested in Danish frescoes, this is a must, quite different in character from the frescoes in the village churches. Some of them have clearly surmounted side altars in times past, but the side altars have disappeared.

The *High Altar, however, is still there, one of the glories of Danish churches. The altarpiece is one of the biggest and most elaborate in the country. The main section is the work of the Lübeck master Bernt Notke, presented to the church in 1479 by Bishop Jens Iversen. The centre panel contains three large-scale figures, of St Anna with St John the Baptist on the right and St Clement on the left. The side panels contain figures of the 12 Apostles. The whole is surmounted by a baldachin put there in 1514 by Bishop Niels Clausen, representing the Assumption of the Virgin. The great silver candlesticks on the altar are from 1706.

The bronze font from 1481 rests on figures of the four Evangelists, and is richly decorated with figures and inscriptions. The large crucifix hanging on the north transept wall is from the same period. The pulpit is a magnificent Renaissance work from 1588 with carved reliefs of biblical motifs. There is moreover a large number of, often ornate, memorial tablets, as well as intricate wrought-iron gates to some of the chapels and to the chancel. These include works by Thomas Quellinus and Caspar Fincke. The tombstones here go as far back as 1100.

After leaving the cathedral, you should take a look at the old part of Århus to the north of the cathedral, walking through MEJLGADE, ROSENSGADE, GRAVEN, PUSTERVIG and KLOSTERGADE. These streets were allowed to fall into disrepair until the 1970s, since when they have been renovated and restored to something like their old state. Many of the ground floors are now small boutiques. At DOMKIRKEPLADS 5 there is an unusual museum, **Kvindemuseet**, dedicated to the history of women and their lives (open all year). The same building houses a museum presenting the Occupation as experienced in Århus (open Sat, Sun).

In this area you will also find Lille Torv square, beyond which is VESTERGADE, the site of the other very old Århus church, ***Vor Frue Kirke**. This was built by King Erik Ejegod at the end of the 11C, and is the oldest building in Århus. Originally the episcopal church, it later became the chapel of the Dominican monastery, the buildings of which, now called Århus Hospital, still stand to the north and west of Vor Frue Kirke. The church has five sections of arcading on either side of the nave, of which the two easternmost form the chancel and are the oldest part of the building; the nave is from c 1400, while the south aisle and the tower are late medieval. There are frescoes from 1300 to 1350 in the chancel, and from the 16C in the south aisle. The ornate altarpiece from 1520 is by Claus Berg. During excavations in the 1950s an old *crypt was discovered; this has now been completely restored for liturgical use and is open to the public.

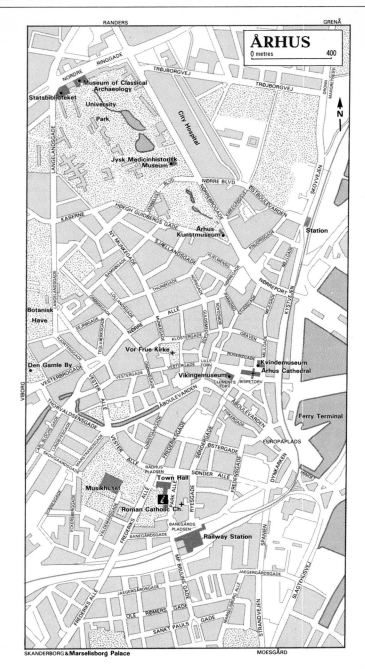

It dates from c 1060, is built of calcareous tufa, and is the oldest-known vaulted room in Scandinavia.

Now walk along Vestergade to THORVALDSENSGADE; turn right and go as far as VESTERBROGADE. Cross it, and you will find the entrance to the famous open air museum ***Den gamle By** (The Old Town). Despite its name, this is not an old part of Århus, but a reconstruction of an old town, incorporating almost 70 half-timbered houses transported here from different parts of Denmark, reassembled and arranged to form a very charming and authentic-looking village. There are houses and buildings of many varied kinds, including the mayor's residence standing on the market place. Many of the houses are themselves open for inspection, and are equipped with furniture and household implements suited to their age. The museum is open all year,

Den gamle By Museum

though times of opening vary according to season. You are, however, at any time able to walk through the streets, even if the individual houses are closed.

Beyond the Old Town are the botanical gardens, **Botanisk Have**, which have a large collection of plants and trees of interest to specialist and layman alike. There is an **open air theatre** in this park.

Retrace your steps now, and continue along Thorvaldsensgade and VESTER ALLÉ, passing the Business Archives on your left as you walk up the hill. At the top of this hill you should turn right into FREDERIKS ALLÉ; in a park on your right you will then see the concert hall, **Musikhuset**, the impressive complex built in 1982 as the home of the Århus Symphony Orchestra, The Danish National Opera and the Århus Festival.

Now make your way back along Frederiks Allé, to RÅDHUSPLADSEN, the Town Hall Square, with the famous **Grisebrønd**, the beautifully fashioned figure of a pig and its young, one of which relieves itself at regular intervals. Here, too, of course, is the main entrance to the **town hall**, from 1941, one of the best-known examples of Scandinavian architecture of its time, with its striking and unusual tower. Parts of the town hall are open for guided tours. You can go to the top of the tower at 12.00 and 14.00 on weekdays in the summer. But you can hear the splendid striking clock and its chimes at 12.00 all the year round. Now turn right into PARK ALLÉ, and you will soon be back at the railway station.

There is more to see in Århus. This time a car will be useful, but not absolutely necessary. You should make for NØRREPORT and drive/walk up NØRREBROGADE. You will then, on your left beyond SABROES PLADS, come to **Århus Kunstmuseum** (Århus Museum of Art) in the splendid modern building designed by C.F.Møller. Originally dating from 1859, this was the first art museum to be established in Jutland. The collection covers an outstanding range of Danish painting and sculpture from the past 300 years, from Eckersberg and Lundbye in the early 19C, through Michael Ancher and Vilhelm Hammershøi in the late 19C to modernists like Giersing, Lergaard and Peter Brandes. Foreign artists are naturally also well represented.

On leaving the museum, you should go further up HØEGH GULDBERGS GADE as far as C.F. MØLLERS ALLÉ. Turn in here into the beautiful University Park, and you will come to the **Steno Museum** (open 10.00–16.00 closed Mon). Named after the great 17th-century scientist, who ended his days as a Roman Catholic bishop—and who was canonised in 1988—this is a very comprehensive museum of the history of science and medicine. Among other things, it contains a reconstruction of a medieval herbal garden. Off C.F. Møllers Allé you will find MEYERS ALLÉ, containing another of Århus University's museums, this time the **Natural Historical Museum**. Meyers Allé will bring you back to Nørrebrogade, opposite one of Denmark's major hospitals, Århus Kommunehospital. Turn left and walk alongside the **University Park**, past the main university buildings, dating back to 1928. The campus has been carefully designed to give an impression of space and relaxed beauty, and the halls of residence are placed in pleasing groups.

Turn left at NORDRE RINGGADE, passing by the main University buildings (which house a **Museum of Classical Archaeology**), and at the next main crossing, with LANGELANDSGADE, you will find the main University Library, **Statsbiblioteket**. If you now turn down Langelandsgade, you will return to the centre of the city.

3km south of the town centre you will find, standing in a great park, the royal residence of **Marselisborg Palace** (built 1899–1902). The park is open to the public when the Royal Family are not in residence. Beyond it is the arboretum, **Forstbotanisk Have**.

In the same area, on CHRISTIAN FILTENBORGS PLADS square, there is a museum, **Det danske Brandværns Museum**, containing over 80 fire engines from many different times (open summer), and from here again it is not far to the pleasure park **Tivoli Friheden**.

16 • Århus to Ålborg

A. Via Hobro

Total distance 108km. E45 to (36km) **Randers**. *(27km)* **Hobro**. *(46km)* **Ålborg**.

The main E45 north from Århus (p 232 ff) is a good straight road, clearly marked.

After c 13km, you might turn off right to **Todbjerg** (3km), where there is a church in which the old and the new are tastefully and artistically combined. On the north wall there are some late 12C frescoes. The late Baroque altarpiece contains paintings done in 1979 by Sven Havsteen-Mikkelsen. The church also contains a Rococo pulpit and a large painting from 1725 over the chancel arch. In the medieval church chest a 14C parchment letter (one of very few found in Denmark) and some 13C and 14C coins were discovered in 1905.

Return to the E45 and drive to (23km) **RANDERS** (pop. 61,500) the sixth-largest town in Denmark.

■ **Tourist information**: Tørvebryggen 12; tel. 86 42 44 77.

■ **Hotels**: Randers, Torvegade 11, tel. 86 42 34 22; Kronjylland, Vestergade 53, tel. 86 41 43 33.

■ **Youth hostel**: Gethersvej 1; tel. 86 42 50 44.

■ There is ample provision in Randers for **sporting activities**, and **canoes** can be hired by Randers Bridge.

History

Its history goes back certainly to the 11C, when coins were minted here, while in 1086 it is mentioned as the place in which the rebels opposing St Knud were to meet. After the murder of the Holstein Count Gert by Niels Ebbesen, it was the bridge across the Gudenå river at Randers which was the escape route used by Niels Ebbesen and his men. Randers was then at the centre of a Jutlandic revolt against Valdemar Atterdag when he tried to raise taxes. The oldest charter known for Randers is from 1302, issued in Viborg by Erik Menved, but it is assumed there were earlier ones.

In the Middle Ages Randers was an important trade centre in the hands of the Lübeckers, thanks to its position at the mouth of the river. Three convents or monasteries were established here—first the Benedictine Vor Frue Kloster in the second half of the 12C, a Greyfriars monastery in 1236, and then, in 1417, a Holy Ghost Monastery, to which St Martin's Church was later attached. There were three other churches in the Middle Ages.

There was a rampart around Randers in the 15C, and after the Reformation the Greyfriars monastery was given a less spiritual mission and transformed into Randers Castle. In the 16C the town suffered two great fires and was largely destroyed. This catastrophe was followed by the plague in 1602 and the usual series of occupations and sackings in the 17C wars against Sweden. It fared little better in the 19C wars against Prussia and Holstein, during both of which it was occupied. Meanwhile, maritime trade increased, and Randers had a large fleet of freighters by the end of the century. Heavy industry came to the town, not least in the shape of the railway's rolling stock works.

The only one of the medieval churches to have survived in any form is **Sankt Mortens Kirke** (St Martin's Church) on Kirketorvet. Even this is not one of Randers' very early churches, the chancel apparently dating from c 1494 and replacing the original medieval structure. The nave and the St Hans chapel on the south wall seem to be slightly later. The transept arch collapsed in 1632 and was rebuilt in 1634, the new arch bearing the insignias of Christian IV and

Queen Anna Cathrine. The tower was added in 1795–96. The lofty nave with pointed vaulting borne on octagonal pillars, separating it from the aisles, is light and spacious.

Of particular interest is the ornate west door, from 1700. It was formerly only used to allow the passage of coffins into the church, and the carved panels reflect this. The richly carved altarpiece is from 1765. The 1686 pulpit, a magnificent piece of Baroque carving, is thought to be the work of Laurids Jensen from Essenbæk and harmonises with other outstanding Baroque carvings, not least the organ loft. The font is from 1695. The model ship in the nave is dated 1632 and is the oldest known church ship in Denmark.

Nearby is the imposing **Helligåndshuset** (The Holy Ghost House), once part of the monastery of that name. It is one of the remaining medieval buildings in the town, built c 1500 and standing in the middle of the town on Erik Menveds Plads. It is on two floors plus cellar, with corbie steps at either end. After the Reformation it was sold to a noble family, but has since served as a school (Steen Steensen Blicher was both pupil and teacher here) and offices. Yet Helligåndshuset is not the oldest brick-built house in Randers. That honour goes to the three-storeyed **Paaskesønnernes Gård**, from 1468, on the old Town Hall Square, RÅDHUSTORVET.

One end of Helligåndshuset, at which there is a statue by Ane Brügger of **The Woman with Eggs**, looks out on HOUMEDEN, a lively pedestrian shopping street containing some attractive **half-timbered houses** from a slightly later period in Randers' history. After Ribe, Randers is said to have more extant half-timbered houses than any other town in Jutland. Oldest of them is NYGADE 4, a house from 1550, restored in 1985. It is interesting to note that Nygade with the adjoining ROSENGADE formed the old Jewish quarter of Randers. There was a thriving Jewish community here in the 19C, a fact which is still echoed in the existence of a synagogue and a Jewish cemetery dating back to 1807.

Another splendid half-timbered house stands on the corner of NØRREGADE and LILLE VOLDGADE, and STOREGADE can also boast some fine specimens. Half-timbered houses, carefully tended, are the hallmark, too, of another principal shopping street, BRØDREGADE, which is known to have been there since 1468. One of the most elegant of them is now the **Toy Museum**, with a unique collection of toys and dolls from the turn of the present century.

Many of Randers' medieval buildings have been lost, but the town can claim three fine modern churches: **Sankt Clemenskirke** from 1963, by Inger Exner, Johannes Exner and Knud Erik Larsen, which was awarded an architecture prize, incorporating rooms suitable for use other than for church services, with textile decorations, an altar of Norwegian marble, and a pulpit of stainless steel; the square **Sankt Andreas Kirke** from 1971, designed by Holger Jensen, deriving its light through windows in the roof; **Johanneskirken** from 1978, with concave walls and a separate bell-tower, and decorations by Herluf Tarp.

There is a flourishing cultural life in Randers, which has its own symphony orchestra. It performs in a new concert hall and theatre complex constructed in the old power station now known as **Værket** (The Works). In addition there are two major museums in the town, the Art Museum **Randers Kunstmuseum** and the Museum of Cultural History **Kulturhistorisk Museum**. Both are now housed in a purpose-built gallery from 1969, known as **Kulturhuset** (The House of Culture), standing in STEMANSGADE.

The ground floor of this is taken up by the Library, while the Museum of Cultural History is on the first floor, offering artefacts old and new, and showing, too, a re-creation of rooms from the turn of the present century. There are also some etchings by Rembrandt and Adriaen van Ostade. The Art Museum is on the second floor, with an extensive collection of Danish painting from the late 18C to the present day, including paintings by Abildgaard, Eckersberg, Hammershøj and Købke. More modern works include paintings by, among many others, Weie and Giersing, a representative collection of works by the Cobra artists and both paintings and sculptures by Sven Dalsgaard in addition to many contemporary works by Danish artists.

▶Excursion along Randers Fjord
Total distance 58km.

If you want to experience the beautiful Randers Fjord landscape you should leave Randers on an unclassified road northeast towards **Harridslev**, very soon turning right and driving through the village of Albæk to (12km) **Støvringgård**, a mansion dating back to the 16C, with the existing buildings from the early 17C; they are now used as residences for unmarried ladies of a certain rank. The great hall and chapel (unchanged since the 17C) are usually open to the public in the afternoon.

Proceed now to (2km) **Mellerup**. The small church, which has retained many of its Romanesque characteristics including an original chancel arch, possesses a particularly interesting early Gothic crucifix, beautifully restored in 1944.

The route continues northwest to (4km) **Tvede**, which is also worth visiting for the sake of its Romanesque church. It stands on high ground, and has some richly carved furniture from the late 16C—including ordinary pews and more elaborate ones for the gentry, and an intricately carved pulpit and altarpiece, both from 1594. An hourglass is fixed to the pulpit to remind the pastor to keep his sermon within reasonable limits.

Continue north past Gjessinggård house on your right to (4km) **Øster Tørslev**. The church here is late 19C, but it was constructed of material from its Romanesque predecessor, of which it bears clear signs. A special feature is a crucifix from c 1250, in which the Cross is fitted into a carved arch.

A further 4km brings you to **Råby**, where there is a church with a most unusual collection of frescoes. These date from 1511 and represent on the one hand the more customary Apostles and Saints (e.g. St Gertrude), and on the other a collection of fantastic figures including centaurs and mermaids, and in one case verging on the pornographic. (There is a suggestion that it was the intention to render these fearful figures harmless by painting them in a holy place.)

The road continues northeast, and you should take a minor road to (5km) **Sødring**. Here you will find the small mansion of **Sødringholm**, built 1752, but with a history going back to the 13C. The small 15C church in Sødring is pure Gothic. Some elegant frescoes from 1491 were discovered in the vaulting in 1902, done by an artist who has become known as the Sødring Master, one of whose characteristics is the rather feminine character of the male faces he painted.

You have now reached the mouth of the fjord and return to (27km) Randers. ◄

Returning to the main route, drive north from Randers on the E45. In 8km you will reach **Råsted**. Again there is a church to see, and once more a church redolent with history, the main interest being the well-preserved 12C frescoes in the chancel and nave and over the transept arch, the most extensive well-preserved Romanesque frescoes in the country.

The south wall is decorated with a large-scale, detailed and realistic painting of the Crucifixion. Over the transept arch sits Christ enthroned, giving the Keys to St Peter and a book to St Paul, while the other Apostles look on. The arch also contains references to other scenes from the Bible and seems to symbolise the entire story of the Redemption. Then the chancel, which is elaborately decorated throughout, provides a much fuller and more tangible account of the Redemption, with the Holy Innocents being slaughtered by medieval knights, the whole being arranged with a beautiful sense of artistry and symmetry. Drive for another 10km through gently undulating country, and you will come to **Handest**, which is the terminus of the Mariager–Handest **vintage railway line** running 17km between Handest and Mariager. At the Mariager end there is a large collection of rolling stock as well as three steam engines (from 1909, 1928 and 1949), diesel engines and diesel railcars, all lovingly restored and maintained. In the summer some trains go as far as Randers instead of stopping at Handest.

The E45 now takes you to (9km) Hobro (p 287) and then to (15km) **Rold**, where there is a large **Circus Museum** (open summer).

A road off right in Rold will take you through Arden to the small mansion of **Villestrup** (10km), where the large Baroque park is open to the public in the summer months. It dates from 1750 and has recently been totally renovated. Villestrup House itself is a stately home built in 1538 and is not open to the public. If you go another 1km east you reach **Astrup**, where there is an imposing church. This was originally Romanesque, but the first owner of Villestrup, Axel Juul, had it rebuilt in 1542 and transformed into what in effect is the first Renaissance church in Denmark. The octagonal tower and copper spire are unusual.

Return to Rold, cross the E45 and drive to the mansion of **Nørlund** (5km). The original Nørlund, first mentioned in 1414, was a fortified tower owned by a robber (the forest of Rold Skov was a good place for robbery of one sort or another—even into the 19C!). This robber band became too active, and Queen Margrethe I brought cannon in and destroyed the tower—and hanged its inmates. The present Nørlund, the third, was built between 1581 and 1597 by Ludvig Munk, who married Ellen Marsvin in 1589; their daughter Kirstine Munk, subsequently Christian IV's morganatic wife, was born here in 1598.

You should now follow the E45 north into **Rold Skov**, the largest forest in Denmark, covering an area of some 80 sq km—certainly enough to get lost in if you start walking. The most convenient place to leave your car is 8km north of Rold village, where there are ample parking facilities near the road leading off to Skørping.

We suggest that you get a local map before venturing too far afield. This is a forest rich in wild life, with numerous lakes (some of them suitable for bathing) and many burial mounds. There are also lots of streams in Rold Skov as well as the three largest natural springs in Denmark. The water from them maintains a constant temperature, resulting in flora and fauna different from that found elsewhere in the country. There are both red deer and roe deer, foxes, badgers, martens, squirrels, and even the odd wild boar. Birds of prey are relatively common, but there is a vast array of other birds, from the nightjar to the thrush and from the heron to the kingfisher. And for those interested in insects, there is a host to choose from. As for flowers and plants, they are legion, and Rold Skov is the only place in Denmark where the Lady's Slipper orchid is found.

Within a short walking distance from where you are parked you will find **Rebild** and **Rebild Bakker** (Rebild Hills).

This area has always been associated with Danish-Americans. After the large-scale emigration from Denmark to the United States at the end of the 19C, many first and second generation Danish-Americans went to great lengths to maintain their links with the 'old country'. In 1912 a group of Danish-Americans collected sufficient funds to buy some 100 hectares of land in Rebild Bakker, making a present of this area to the Danish people, on condition that it should remain in its natural state and be open to everyone, and that Danish-Americans should be able to hold their own celebrations there. The area has since been extended to cover a further 100 hectares. Now, every year on American Independence Day, 4 July, Danish-Americans and their Danish relatives gather to celebrate.

The park contains a replica of the house in which Abraham Lincoln was born; this is a museum of pioneering times in the USA, and there is a prairie schooner to add to the atmosphere (open daily June–Aug, weekends May and Sept). There is also a museum dedicated to old folk instruments and their music. However, irrespective of all these overtones, Rebild Bakker is an area of outstanding beauty, a clearing in the great forest, a terrain covered with heather and scrub, a jewel in what many would refer to as one of the most beautiful areas of Denmark.

On the opposite side of the E45 from where you have parked are the **Tingbæk Limestone Mines** (open summer). Limestone is no longer quarried here, and the old workings have been turned into one of the most idiosyncratic art galleries in Denmark, with sculptures and plaster casts by Anders Bundgaard, Carl Johan Bonnesen and Anton Laier. Bundgaard's most famous work is of course the Gefion Fountain in Copenhagen (of which there is a smaller version here), but he was also responsible for sculptures outside Copenhagen Town Hall and Christiansborg Palace, and for the Cimbrian Bull in Ålborg.

Your next stop on the E45 could be in (2km) **Gravlev**. Apart from possibly visiting Anders Bundgaards grave here, there might be one more memorial for you to see before leaving this area: the **Airmen's Stone** near **Årestrup**. The easiest way to find Årestrup is to turn left off the E45 at Gravlev and drive 5km south. You will see the stone just to the east of the village. It was placed there and inscribed in memory of the crew of a Liberator bomber shot down on this spot during World War II. All eleven on board were killed. Part of the memorial consists of one of the propellors from the crashed aircraft. The airmen were buried in a common grave at the time, but they were then reburied in Årestrup churchyard, where their graves can now be seen.

Continue now on the E45 to (4km) Støvring, where you turn right to the rather unusual village of **Volsted** (5km).

Once more, a church is the attraction, and at first sight you might wonder why. It is a small Romanesque building, without a tower, indeed at a distance without any striking features, more the sort of church found in the poorer areas of West Jutland than in this affluent region. Even inside, there appears to be little of interest. Yet at the entrance to the porch there *is* something, the very thing you have come to see—the 'signature' of the man who built it. It is the work of a 12C sculptor/architect called Goti, who is known to have been responsible for various churches in Jutland, and whose style can be sensed in sculptures in yet other churches. The porch itself is of later date, certainly not his work, but the sculpted ashlars from an earlier door have been incorporated into this, representing a lion at the top, the Temptation on the left and a bishop on the right. There are furthermore an Agnus Dei and other figures, while the name of Goti is actually inscribed on a stone in the porch.

Driving north you again have a choice. The E45 will take you direct to (18km) Ålborg (see below), and Exit 27 or 26 will take you right to the centre. You could, however, leave the motorway 7km north of Støvring, turning at junction 29 on to the 180 towards Svenstrup for a short detour.

▶Follow the 180 for another 7km and turn left into the 187 west through Frejlev (4km). 4km further, on your right, you will find one of Denmark's major long barrows, now known as **Troldkirken** (The Troll Church). The central feature is a hexagonal burial chamber c 55m long, and it is surrounded by a circle of 47 large stones, some of those at the south end standing as much as 2.5m high. Placed high on a hillside, the Troll Church is an impressive monument, and there is an equally impressive view from it.

You now continue to the next village, **Sønderholm** (1km), where there is a Romanesque church with Gothic extensions and later additions. One of the notable features is the large number of Renaissance frescoes, including 32 coats of arms, perhaps reflecting the fact that a sign of true nobility was the claim to coats of arms stretching back over 16 generations. The altarpiece and pulpit are both 16C. Among the many graves is that of Christence Kruckow, who was beheaded in 1621 for witchcraft.

7km further on lies **Nibe** (pop. 7600) which has a charter dating back to 1727, though it is little more than a large village with a small amount of light industry. Its streets are narrow and winding, and most of the houses are modest single-storey structures—modest but by no means unattractive. Indeed, Nibe is one of those small fjord towns which have a very special idyllic charm of their own.

■ **Tourist information**: Torvet 2; tel. 98 35 35 00.

■ **Hotels**: Store Restrup Herregård, Restrupkærvej 10; tel. 98 34 18 88.

You should now return to the 180 which will take you straight into the centre of (20km) **ÅLBORG** (pop. 158,150), the fourth largest city in Denmark.

Ålborg

■ **Tourist information**: Østerågade 8; tel. 98 12 60 22.

■ **Hotels**: Heinan Phønix, Vesterbro 77; tel. 98 12 00 11; Chagall, Vesterbro 36-38; tel. 98 12 69 33.

■ **Youth hostel**: Skydebanen 50; tel. 98 11 60 44.

History

Ålborg was first mentioned during the reign of Hardeknud (Hardecanute) (1018–42) (the son of Knud the Great), who was King of Denmark from 1035–42 and King of England from 1040–42. Thanks to its position, it grew quickly as a trading centre for other towns on the Limfjord, and it grew rich on the herring fishing and trade links with Norway.

The earliest known charter is from 1340, but it is believed that there were earlier ones. The first municipal law was granted by Valdemar II in 1342. The Benedictine Convent of Our Lady was founded as early as 1116, while the Greyfriars' Monastery is mentioned in 1268, and the Holy Ghost monastery was founded in 1451. There are references to the city's having been fortified in the Middle Ages, but no remains of either moat or mound are now to be seen. By 1310 there was a castle in the south part of the town and King Hans died there in 1513. However, during the Count's War the castle was so badly damaged that it had to be abandoned. In 1915, during the building of the new police station in Rantzausgade, parts of the foundations of this early castle were found.

Ålborg suffered two disastrous fires, one in 1501 and one in 1530, but the major catastrophe was during the Count's War, when Skipper Klement took the town, only to be driven out by the merciless Johan Rantzau in 1534, after which the town was plundered by Rantzau's troops and all fortifications demolished. However, profits from the herring fishing quickly put Ålborg on its feet again, and the early 17C was a period of affluence, from which many of the splendid houses stem. Nevertheless, during the 17C wars, Ålborg changed hands on various occasions and was once more plundered and heavily taxed, and in 1663 it suffered another great fire. There followed a period of varying fortunes, and it was only in the latter part of the 19C that the city really began to flourish once more with the advent of the railways and the modernisation of the harbour. These developments brought the industries which are today associated with Ålborg: cement, shipbuilding, building materials, iron and steel, and—akvavit (i.e. snaps). 'Let's have an Ålborg' is at least one very common way of suggesting a glass of this Danish national drink.

In 1970 Ålborg was officially united with **Nørresundby**, which until then had been Ålborg's sister town on the north bank of the Limfjord, linked to Ålborg by bridge and tunnel. Together, the harbours of Ålborg and Nørresundby constitute the largest provincial port in Denmark. Just to the east of the city is the Greenland Dock, now the port for all sea-borne freight between Denmark and Greenland.

Present-day Ålborg has its own university and symphony orchestra as well as the second largest zoo in Scandinavia and several first-rate museums.

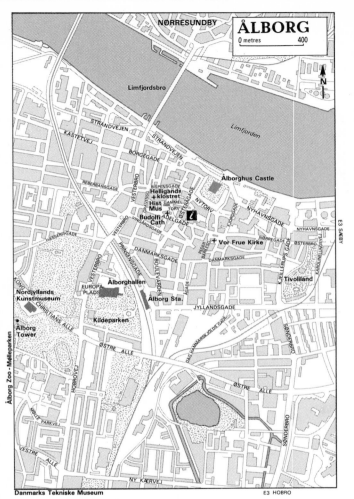

There is a good choice of car parks in the centre of Ålborg though you may have to look around for space. Perhaps that on STRANDVEJEN, down by the Limfjord, will be the easiest to find; it is close to the castle, and it is here you might start your exploration of this fascinating city.

The present **Ålborghus Castle** was built on the orders of Christian III between 1539 and 1555. Although this was a royal palace, it was little used by royalty. Only two wings remain today, of which the east wing is in more or less its original shape, a compact half-timbered building. The wall of the north wing facing the courtyard is likewise of half-timbered construction, though slightly higher and to a different design. It is now the official residence of the chief administrative officer of the county and houses the county administration. The courtyard is open to the public during daylight hours, and there is access to the old dungeons and underground passages.

West of the Castle, at ØSTERÅGADE 25, is **Jørgen Olufsens Gård**, one of the fine 17C merchants' houses. Elegant as it is, it is put in the shade by another house in Østerågade: **Jens Bang's House** at No. 9, from 1623–24, which is generally acknowledged to be the finest merchant's house in Denmark. It is five storeys high, and is equipped with three impressive gables overlooking Østerågade and one overlooking ADELGADE. At first-floor level on the front there is an octagonal bay, topped by a copper roof with a statue of Flora at the apex. There is a famous wine cellar, **Duus' Vinkælder**, beneath the house, open now as it has been for the past 300 years. The chemist's shop, Svaneapoteket, which is at ground-floor level in this building, has been there since 1651— owned by the same family throughout.

Nearby, in GAMMEL TORV, stands an elegant Baroque building, the former **city hall**, built between 1757 and 1762. On a gable above the front entrance there is the Danish coat of arms and Frederik V's motto 'Prudentia et Constantia'.

Round the corner, in ALGADE, there is the *****Budolfi Cathedral**, named after the English St Botolph. The oldest parts of this elegant building date from 1100, but most of it is from 1400. It consists of a nave with an aisle on either side, the nave continuing straight into the chancel. The west tower was rebuilt in 1663 after one of the great fires, and the Baroque spire was added in 1780. As befits a church of this size and dignity, there is a splendid Baroque *altarpiece from 1689 and a pulpit from 1692, both made in the workshop of Laurits Jensen from Randers. Both are massive and richly carved. The font is of marble. There are also frescoes from the beginning of the 16C, and among the paintings there is a portrait of the English-born Queen Caroline Mathilde (1751–75), the sister of George III. A special feature of the church is the carillon, which plays on the hour during the day.

The other principal church in Ålborg is **Vor Frue Kirke** (Our Lady's Church), which you reach by crossing Østerågade again, and walk down Algade. Vor Frue Kirke is then on your right. This was originally the church attached to the Convent of Our Lady, and was probably the main church in Ålborg in the 16C and 17C—even being referred to as the cathedral in several documents. In its original form it stems from the second half of the 12C, and the Norwegian King Sigurd Slembe was buried there in 1140. The present building, consisting of a nave and two aisles, is the result of very extensive rebuilding in 1878. Even this church suffered from a fire in 1902, which destroyed most of the 17C altarpiece, and the present one is a 20C product. The metal font, on the other hand, is from 1619, and the carved pulpit from 1581. One relic from the first church is found at the west door, which is set in sculpted 12C ashlars saved from the original north door.

Retrace your steps now, walk past Budolfi Cathedral, turn right at GRAVENSGADE and then right again at Adelgade; you will now find, on C.W. OBELSPLADS, the remains of the Holy Ghost monastery, **Helligåndsklostret** from 1431, claimed to be the best preserved monastery in Scandinavia. The present west wing is original, while the north and east wings are 16C. The chancel of the chapel is from 1681, and the whole was subjected to a 19C restoration in 1847–48. There are frescoes from c 1500. Also known as Ålborg

Hospital, this has been called Denmark's oldest charitable institution, and to this day it provides 26 homes for the elderly. Parties are conducted through it at 14.00 Mondays to Fridays in the summer season, and it is well worth a visit.

In general, you should wander through the old streets in this part of the city and savour the atmosphere of the remaining half-timbered buildings, or discover the narrow lanes like LATINERGYDEN beside the monastery. In HJELMERSTALD, SØNDERGADE, NØRREGADE and FJORDGADE some of the remaining old houses have been carefully restored.

Ålborg, however, is not only old buildings and statues, but it provides a host of entertainment possibilities. The famous JOMFRU ANE GADE (quite close to Helligåndsklostret) is almost entirely dedicated to restaurants, cafés and clubs, and is one of a number of pedestrian streets in the centre.

East of the central area there is entertainment of a different character in Ålborg's **Tivoliland**, Ålborg's very effective answer to Copenhagen's Tivoli.

VESTERBRO is the main artery in the city, and here you will find Anders Bundgaard's statue of the *Cimbrian Bull*, from 1937, the symbol of Himmerland drive and expansion, relating to the fact that the Cimbrians emanated from this area of Denmark known as Himmerland. There is a much gentler statue too: Gerhard Henning's *Goosegirl*, from 1937. Yet another contrast is Erik Heide's *The Animal* in the courtyard of the **Medborgerhus** (Civic Centre) on Nytorv.

Further south on Vesterbro, on your left you will come to **Ålborghallen**, the Ålborg Hall on EUROPA PLADS, a cultural centre opened in 1953 with theatre, concert hall, exhibition and conference facilities as well as a restaurant and bowling alley. The Ålborg Hall stands on the edge of the **Kildepark**, a beautiful small park containing a large number of classical statues, including Thorvaldsen's *Three Graces* and Anne Marie Carl Nielsen's *Child of Bacchus*. A little further on, on the opposite side of Vesterbro which here becomes HOBROVEJ, you cannot miss the **Ålborg Tower**, an observation tower rising to 105m above sea level and offering panoramic views of the city and the surrounding area.

In the same area as the tower, in **Mølleparken**, lies **Ålborg Zoo**, where there is a large collection of animals and birds, many in enclosures offering them a good deal of freedom.

Ålborg has an excellent selection of museums, chief of which must surely be ***Nordjyllands Kunstmuseum**, dating from 1966, also very close to the Ålborg Tower, but entered from KONG CHRISTIANS ALLÉ to the north. Designed by the Finnish architects Elissa and Alvar Aalto and their French colleague Jean-Jacques Baruel, this is one of the most successful of Danish museums. It caters exclusively for 20C Danish and international art, containing extensive collections of work by the Cobra and Fluxus groups and is the venue for many visiting exhibitions.

Further south, on RIIHIMÄKIVEJ just off Hobrovej, is **Danmarks Tekniske Museum**, the Science Museum. As the name suggests, it is a museum dedicated to the history of science, and there are both permanent and visiting exhibitions. There are various gadgets at which you can try your hand.

Another museum is **Ålborgs Historiske Museum** (The Ålborg Historical Museum), at Algade 48, with a large collection of exhibits ranging from the Stone Age to the 19C, and including Aalborg silverware and Danish glass. Of the reconstructions of old rooms, the Ålborg Room is of particular interest. The doors, panelled walls and magnificent ceilings were taken from one of the old merchant houses demolished in 1866, so there is a completely authentic appearance.

The local history archives are in PEDER BARKESGADE 5, close to Vor Frue Kirke, and in the same building there are the Emigration Archives, containing material on Danish emigrants (open summer, limited opening winter).

B. Via Hadsund

Total distance 126km. E45 (52km) **Randers**. *507 to (31km) Hadsund.* **Ålborg**.

Drive north from Århus on the E45 for 24km, then turn right to (5km) **Voldum**. There is a rather splendid 17C church here, with a Gothic porch. The furniture is ornate Baroque, the carved altarpiece being the work of one of Peder Jensen Kolding's pupils. The pulpit from c 1600 is supported on a figure of Moses. The pew for the local aristocracy on the north side is particularly elaborate.

The church stands at a crossroads. Turn left here and drive north for a further 2km, and you will come to the large, three-winged mansion of **Clausholm**, a fine example of Baroque art. Dating from the end of the 17C, it stands in an elegant park in the Italian style, with avenues of lime trees and some magnificent fountains. Concerts are given in the sumptuous chapel, where there is an organ thought to be from 1601. Clausholm is open to the public in the summer months, and there is a cafeteria in the cellar—where a collection of antique stoves is on display.

You now continue north to (2km) Årslev, there turning right to (4km) **Hørning**, where there is yet another and extremély interesting *church. It is quite small, consisting of a Romanesque chancel and nave built of granite ashlars. Vaulting was added in the Middle Ages, as was the transept; the tower, with an octagonal lantern standing 32m high, is early 18C. At the end of the 17C elaborate stucco decorations were added to the vaulting in the nave and chancel, giving the entire church an atmosphere at once intimate and opulent. The Baroque altarpiece is mid 17C, as are the wrought-iron font and the richly carved pulpit.

Although the present appearance of this church is fascinating in itself, however, it stands as a token of the continuity of religious practice. During restoration work in 1886–88, an oak beam from c 1050 was discovered; it bears carvings in much the same style as the Jelling Stone (p 292)—a leaf decoration on one side, and a carved serpent on the other, still showing the remains of the original yellow and red paint.

During further restoration work in 1964 excavations uncovered evidence that a wooden church had formerly stood on this same spot. At a lower level still the excavations uncovered a burial mound from c 1000, in which there was an undisturbed burial chamber containing the skeletal remains of a woman beside whom was positioned a table—the oldest known such in Denmark—and a decorated bronze dish. The chamber in which she was buried is similar in shape to that in the northernmost burial mound in Jelling. These old relics have been taken over by the National Museum, where they are now on display.

From Hørning you drive 1km northeast to the A21. Turn left and continue to (14km) Randers (see above).

The distance from Randers to Hadsund is served by two good routes: that via Hald (31km) is described first; for the alternative route via Mariager (35km) see below.

Randers to Hadsund via Hald
Total distance 31km.

Leave Randers on the 507 north, driving to (12km) **Hald**, where, in the Romanesque church, you will find an *altarpiece from 1500 that was once in St Martin's Church in Randers. It stretches across virtually the whole of the chancel and completely dominates the little church by dint of its size and its splendour. The central panel represents the Holy Trinity flanked by the Virgin and St Martin, while the two wings represent the twelve Apostles and the four Fathers of the Church. Some late Gothic frescoes were uncovered in 1899 on the chancel arch, and more were found in 1924 in the vaulted roof of the chancel.

Continue to (4km) **Gjerlev**, where the church has an altarpiece by Skovgård. Before reaching (15km) **Hadsund** (p 252) a detour can be made, turning off towards **Havndal** 7km north of Gjerlev.

▶Here you will first drive past the 17C mansion of Trudsholm before reaching one of the sights you have come to see, **Lyshøj Mølle** (4km). This mill, from 1894, has been thoroughly restored and is in working order (open summer). A minor road now continues to **Udbyneder** (1km), where in the Romanesque/Gothic church you will find a large number of fine frescoes from 1515–20 depicting the Day of Judgement and various saints and coats of arms, one of the best works by the Sødring Master.

A further 3km along this road will bring you to the mansion of **Overgård**, one of the most imposing in this part of Jutland, dating from the end of the 16C, and still retaining much of its original Renaissance character. Overgård is not open to the public, but there are sometimes concerts there in the summer.◀

Drive back now to the 507 and cross into (8km) Hadsund (p 252) by the new (1978) bridge across the Mariager Fjord.

Alternative route from Randers to Hadsund—via Mariager
Total distance 35km.

From Randers you drive north on a good but unclassified road towards Mariager. After 9km you should turn right to **Spentrup** (2km), where there is yet another church to visit, this time one with literary associations.

Spentrup Church is not one of the largest, but it still retains much of its original Romanesque character, not least an interesting fresco from c 1200. This represents two female figures, one blindfolded and holding a lance which has transfixed a lamb, while the other has a chalice into which the blood from the lamb is running. The blindfolded figure represents Jewry, unable to see the truth, and in its blindness doing to death the Lamb of God, while the other figure represents the Church, sighted and redeemed by the Blood of Christ.

The real interest in this church, however, is the fact that the important 19C poet and short story writer Steen Steensen Blicher was pastor here from 1825 and lies buried in the churchyard. A large boulder decorated with a lyre and a laurel wreath stands on the grave in memory of him. (There is more about this very important 19C figure in chapters 20 and 23, which are concerned with a number of places with which Blicher is especially associated.) In **Malvines Hus**, STATIONSVEJ 47, here in Spentrup, you will meanwhile find a museum containing Blicher's works and a large number of his personal effects (limited opening summer).

Steen Steensen Blicher

Blicher was born in Vium in Jutland and quickly grew aware of the beauty of the then Jutlandic heath and the fascination of the stories, legends and people associated with it. In 1824 he published a short novel entitled *The Diary of a Parish Clerk*, which has established itself as one of the classical works of Danish literature. One of his finest short stories, *Late Awakening*, is a fictitious account of the occasion in Spentrup when he discovered that his wife was unfaithful to him. He was severely criticised by his contemporaries for publishing a story which was too open and dealt with subjects best left alone.

Back on the main road you drive north through a beautifully hilly and wooded area to (14km) **MARIAGER** (pop. 8167), one of Denmark's smallest market towns, with a charter dating from 1592.

■ **Tourist information**: Torvet 1 B; tel. 98 54 13 77.

■ **Hotels**: Postgården, Torvet 6; tel. 98 54 10 12; Motel Landgangen, Oxendalen 1; tel. 98 54 11 22.

■ There are **bathing** facilities at the harbour.

■ The **vintage railway line** between Mariager and Handest has its terminus here. Trains run on Sundays in June, July and August, and additionally on Tuesdays and Thursdays in July.

History

Mariager grew up around the Bridgettine convent which was founded there in 1410, when it was no more than a tiny hamlet. The convent was given the right to establish a harbour, and this brought trade to the locality, even though only small boats could enter it. Neverthelesss, local bricks and lime were loaded in Mariager in considerable quantities, mainly for domestic use, though some were exported to Germany. The town's dependence on the convent and the trade created by visitors and pilgrims meant, however, that it went into decline after the Reformation, more particularly after 1588, when the former convent lost its new position as a residence for unmarried daughters of the aristocracy.

Mariager suffered serious fires in 1573 and 1583, and the importance of the limestone quarry diminished. A further blow was the re-routing of the main road between Randers and Ålborg over Hadsund rather than

Mariager, as it had traditionally been. Nor did Mariager benefit from the advent of the railways to the extent that many had hoped, and it has remained a small, idyllic town situated on a very beautiful fjord. In recent years a great deal has been done to maintain this image, and to make the most of Mariager's charm for the growing tourist industry of the region.

In view of its former dependence on the Bridgettine convent, it is not surprising that Mariager should be dominated by the **convent church** standing on a wooded hillside overlooking the yachting harbour. Nevertheless, what is now left is only a small part of the original building from 1460–80. The present cruciform church has a transept with wings roughly the same size as the nave and chancel. The north, south and west wings formed part of the original convent church, but the east wing is modern, dating from rebuilding in 1933. In its present shape it is some 43.5m long including the tower, though excavations have shown that it was at one time 75.7m. There was a danger of collapse in the 18C, and consequently the size of the original convent church was greatly reduced. The chancel was drastically lowered, but this was corrected in the rebuilding work carried out in 1931–33.

The present carved oak altarpiece is from the 17C, and the pulpit from 1724. More interesting is the pre-Reformation *Grave of Christ, a wooden coffin containing a life-size figure of Christ, formerly used in Holy Week rituals. You have to open the door to the room and switch on the light yourself—and the effect is quite startling. There is another life-size figure of Christ as the man of sorrow behind the main altar.

Among the many tombstones is that of Stygge Krumpen (c 1480–1581), the last Catholic Bishop of Børglum and of his brother Otte Krumpen (c 1485–1569), who led Christian II's campaign against Sweden in 1520. Stygge Krumpen's tombstone—bearing a portrait said to be a true likeness—stands in the church, but the bishop's body is now buried in the churchyard. The only other remaining building of the original convent is the north wing, which stands close to the church and is used as a court registry.

Of other buildings in Mariager, mention should be made of the 18C merchant house, **Den gamle Købmandsgård** at KIRKEGADE 2, a beautiful building which is now a most interesting museum and art gallery with a good local historical collection and a model of the old convent and church (open summer). Close by is the old **Post House**, a half-timbered building from the 18C, which for a time was used as a parsonage and is now an hotel and restaurant containing furnishing from the 17C.

The old **apothecary's house** is built on a 15C basement foundation and stands on the site of a former guest house belonging to the convent. The 1850 **fire engine house** is also still standing, and the old brewery from 1876 has recently been restored.

Near the central area is Munkholm Park, in which there is a sacred well, St Helen's Well.

From Mariager you drive on the 555 alongside the fjord straight to (12km) **Hadsund** (pop. 10,600; **Tourist information**: Storegade 20; tel. 98 57 20 66) which is little more than a village and owes its existence purely to its position as a suitable place at which to cross the Mariager Fjord. Historically, it was a ford, and as late as 1840 there were only seven inhabitants. In 1860 a small transit harbour was established here, and a steamship route was opened between Hadsund and Copenhagen. The advent of the railways brought more growth, and a bridge was built over the Mariager Fjord in 1904.

Hadsunds Egns Museum has a good collection illustrating life in the area over the past 300 years (open summer; limited opening winter). Hadsund was the birthplace of the 20C novelist Hans Kirk.

Between Hadsund and Ålborg there is again a choice of routes: the direct route (43km) comes first; the alternative route (62km) via the coast follows below.

Direct route from Hadsund to Ålborg
Total distance 43km.

The 507 is a straight road through undulating countryside. After 7km you arrive at a crossroads, indicating Korup on the right and Astrup on the left.

Take the left turning and drive to **Astrup** (6km), where there is a rather splendid church, one of the earliest Danish Renaissance churches, from 1542. It consists of a chancel and nave, separated by a very wide chancel arch, an elegant porch, and a tall octagonal tower in the west. The 1634 carved altar-piece, depicting the Last Supper, was made in Ålborg. The granite font is Romanesque, with reliefs of a man's head flanked by two lions, and a heavily armed man in battle with a dragon.

Continue west for a further 1km to see the imposing late Gothic mansion of **Villestrup** from 1538–42. The splendid 5-hectare Baroque park, for which loam was brought from the surrounding countryside, was established around 1750 in the style of French and Italian parks, and has been open to the public since 1988 (open at varying times during the summer).

Back on the 507 you drive 16km north, where you should turn off right to Komdrup (4km) and Sønder Kongerslev (a further 2km), both of which have churches of interest.

The small church in **Komdrup** is Romanesque, from c 1200. The original north door is still in use, while the south door has been bricked up. No original windows have survived, and the church was the subject of rebuilding in 1884. The altarpiece is late Gothic, probably the work of one of Claus Berg's pupils. A triptych, has, in the centre panel are figures of God the Father, Christ, Mary with the Child, and John the Baptist, and 12 Saints in the side panels.

Take the road south-east from the church to **Sønder Kongerslev**, where there is another interesting small Romanesque church. The octagonal Renaissance tower is one of only two of this shape in Denmark, the other being in Astrup, above. There is an altarpiece from 1597 and a beautifully carved pulpit from the same time.

The 16C mansion of **Kongstedlund**, which has been associated with this church, lies c 1.5km southeast. From high ground here, looking east, you have a view of the unreclaimed, and now protected, marshland **Lille Vildmose**.

Back on the 507 you drive past one of the biggest and most interesting mansions in North Jutland, **Lindenborg**. It has a history going back to the 14C, when it probably originated in connection with a ferry across the Lindenborg Å, on which it stands. There are three wings, of which the south wing from 1583 was possibly designed by the same architect as designed Kronborg Castle in Helsingør (p 106). Not open to the public.

4km further on, at **Gunderup**, there is a large church (34.8m long) of unusual design, sometimes referred to as 'Himmerland Cathedral'. The nave and chancel are Romanesque. The Romanesque north door still survives, as do two of the original north windows. The Romanesque font is of granite and in it are carved a human head and two animals with intertwined tails. There are two runestones in the porch; one of them was found by a burial mound and is of particular interest. The inscription on it reads: 'Toke raised this stone and made this memorial to his stepfather Abe, a stout yeoman farmer, and Tove his mother. Both lie in this mound. Abe left his possessions to Toke.' There is a very similar inscription on runestones found in the church in Sønder Vissing (p 305). As the Sønder Vissing stones show, Toke was the grandson of King Gorm the Old, who is remembered on the runestone in Jelling (p 292).

After a further 9km north on the 507 you take a road left leading to (6km) Ålborg (p 245 ff).

Alternative route from Hadsund to Ålborg—via the coast
Total distance 62km.

Leave Hadsund on the 541 east to (12km) Als, calling first at (3km) **Visborg**, where the 16C church has an unusually large array of Renaissance furniture: an altarpiece from 1600, still containing an original painting, a pulpit in the same style, carved benches in the chancel, other pews from the 16C and 17C, an elegant wrought-iron altar rail from 1600, and above the sacristy door a painting of the Seefeld family, mother, father and eleven children, who then owned the mansion of Visborggård nearby. A memorial stone to them stands at the side of the altar. It was in fact Jakob Seefeld—who died in 1599 and was buried in this church—who was responsible for the building. The Seefeld family grave is in the churchyard.

The mansion of **Visborggård** is a huge house surrounded by a broad moat and looking more like a castle, the south wing of which dates back to 1575–76. Of the original seven towers only two remain to flank the imposing façade with its magnificent sandstone gateway. It was Jakob Seefeld who had it built—or rebuilt—in the grand Renaissance style after an older castle had been burned down by Skipper Klement's followers.

Visborggård is now a home for the mentally ill and not open to the public. There is, however, public access to the park, where there is a memorial of special significance to the Danes. When, in 1920, southern Jutland was returned to Denmark, King Christian X marked the occasion by riding over the border on a white horse. That horse had come from Visborggård, and it is now buried there in a marked grave.

Soon after leaving Visborg, you will drive out of the undulating terrain and come to a flat expanse of land, which will extend most of the way along this coastal road. You will soon reach **Als**, where there is a regional museum in the form of a typical Himmerland farmhouse from the mid 19C, with contemporary furniture and farm implements from the area.

The 541 will now take you north along the coast through a flat landscape to (5km) **Øster Hurup**, a fishing village with excellent bathing facilities.

On your way north you will now pass **Lille Vildmose** on your left. This is an area of 55 sq km of drained marshland, largely now under cultivation, but much of the south part is kept in its natural state and is not open to the public. In the centre of Lille Vildmose lies Tofte Lake, a bird sanctuary, to which there is also no admittance, though you can drive up to an observation platform from which you can follow the bird life.

12km further north brings you to **Dokkedal**, another fishing village which has become a bathing resort. It has a very fine beach, safe for children, and is well equipped with car parks, toilets, etc.

Six more kilometres and you are in Egense, where you turn west on to the 595. Just after entering this road you will come to a large house called Egense Kloster (Convent), formerly belonging to Mariager Convent, though there has never really been a convent here (no public admittance).

Drive 9km west on the 595 to a road leading left to **Sejlflod** (2km). This is the only place in Denmark actually to boast a *pyramid (open). Standing 8m high, this is a copy of the Egyptian Cheops pyramid and was built by a psychologist who believed that special healing powers could be attributed to it.

Rather older are the extensive prehistoric remains centred on **Tofthøj**, a burial mound just to the west of the village. Artefacts and graves from as far back as 3500 BC have been found there, leading to the suggestion that Sejlflod is actually the oldest settlement in Denmark. It is moreover situated in extremely varied and interesting terrain, surrounded by hills, heathland and, over the drained marshes, in close proximity to the sea.

Back again on the 595 you come to (5km) **Klarup**, where there is a charming small Romanesque church with a Gothic tower. There are clear traces of the 18C, including several pietist-inspired rococo paintings.

Just beyond Klarup, on the right, lies **Klarupgård**, a splendid, low-built half-timbered house from the 18C, ultimately with a history going back to the time of Erik Menved. From Klarup you drive straight into (13km) Ålborg (see above) by crossing the E45 and continuing on over the railway line. You then take the second road right (Hobrovej), which will take you straight into the centre.

If you wish to go north without visiting Ålborg, you simply take the E45 on the outskirts of the city.

17 • Århus to Thisted

Total distance 165km. A26 to (67km) **Viborg**. *(37km)* **Skive**. *(30km) Nykøbing Mors. (31km)* **Thisted**.

From Århus (p 232) the A26 takes you through undulating countryside to (23km) **Voldby**, where the church boasts a splendid auricular altarpiece by Claus Berg portraying the martyrdom of 10,000 knights. The pulpit is contemporary with it.—A narrow road north just before the church will take past to

Frijsenborg (4km), the majestic 19C neo-Renaissance mansion at the centre of one of the largest estates in Denmark.

7km further on you come to a road leading south to **Gjern** (3km). Here there is a motorcar museum, **Jysk Automobil Museum**, displaying some 135 cars, lorries and motorcycles of 65 different makes, all painstakingly restored. The oldest car is a Belgian Vivinus from 1900, and the motorcycles come from countries as diverse as the US, Denmark, Sweden, England and Germany (open summer).

Gjern's other claim to fame is that the artist Erik Raadal was born here and used the village as the motif for most of his work, thus producing the most comprehensive picture in art of any village in Denmark. There is also a new Lake Uplands Holiday and Course Centre offering accommodation for 110 on seven farms. Nearby flows the Gudenå river, and the old towpath along its banks offers the opportunity of splendid walks.

Returning to the A26, you can now continue to (4.5km) Fårvang, where you might turn left and drive south to **Tvilum** (5km).

Standing alone here in idyllic surroundings, close to the Gudenå river, is a church which once formed the north wing of an Augustinian monastery from the early 13C, and where there is now a copy of the first complete Danish translation of the Bible, from 1550, known as Christian III's Bible. The church is small and unadorned, with a simple dignity of its own. There is a Romanesque font and a carved late medieval altarpiece.

A further 4.5km on the A26 will bring you to **Kongensbro**, where a famous old inn stands at the crossroads, a favourite haunt of anglers. Drive on through (6km) Ans, with the 13km-long **Tange Sø** on your right. This lake was created in 1920 when the biggest hydro-electric power station in Denmark was built in Tange, just to the north. If you turn right immediately after the lake you will come to **Tange** (4.5km), where part of the power station is a well equipped and very popular **electricity museum** (open summer).

Otherwise you drive straight on to (22km) Viborg (p 282). If you do not want to visit the fine old capital of Jutland, you can remain on the A26, which is clearly marked on the ring road, and drive straight to (30km) Skive (see below). This direct route has little of interest, however, so at (10km) Fiskbæk we suggest you leave the A26, driving north for a time along the west side of the **Hjarbæk Fjord**.

The unclassified road you should follow turns off right just after you have passed the high-lying church, and will first take you past the little inlet where Canute is said to have gathered his fleet to sail to England. A further 12km along this road, will bring you to **Ørslev Kloster**.

Like so many other monasteries and convents, Ørslev Kloster was turned into a private residence after the Reformation, though, as elsewhere in Denmark, the nuns were allowed to remain in the convent until their death—the last lived for 60 years after the Reformation was proclaimed. It remained in private hands until 1964, when it became a study centre for Kulturhistorisk Museumsforening (The Cultural History Museums Association); since 1969 it has been a place of retreat for writers and artists.

Standing surrounded by trees on raised ground, the whole complex has meanwhile retained much of its original ponderous dignity. The large church, the north wing of the complex, is part of the original building from c 1200, with Romanesque apse, chancel and nave in the general style of village churches of the time, though a good deal larger. The tower is Gothic, though it underwent considerable alteration in the 18C. Among the objects of interest in the church is a memorial to the Faroese patriot (and pirate) Magnus Heinesen, who was a friend of the then owner. He was beheaded in Copenhagen in 1589, and a year later, when the execution was declared to have been a mistake(!), permission was given for his body to be taken to Ørslev and buried.

From Ørslev Kloster you return to the 579, which you will just have crossed, turn right there and drive along this road and later the A26 to (14km) **SKIVE** (pop. 27,250), which lies at the neck of the Skive Fjord, where Karup Å (river) enters it.

■ **Tourist information**: Østerbro 7; 97 52 32 66.

■ **Hotels**: Gammel Skivehus, Søndre Boulevard 1; tel. 97 52 11 44; Hilltop, Søndre Boulevard; tel. 97 52 37 11.

Skive received its charter in 1231 and its history goes as far back as AD 1000, but it has suffered from fires on several occasions, and there are few really old buildings left.

However, just outside the town, on the shore of the fjord, stands the 16C mansion of **Krabbesholm**, a large dignified brick building which is now a folk high school. The other principal historical building in Skive is the old church, **Fruekirke**, which has a history going back to 1304, and stands in an almost Italianate churchyard.

The chancel and nave are Romanesque, but there are Gothic additions. By the 19C the church was becoming too small for Skive, and there were plans to demolish it. It was then discovered that beneath the whitewash there was an elaborate collection of frescoes, and it was decided to restore them and maintain the church. There are some 50 figures from the Bible and church history, surrounded by a flowered pattern, and there is an astounding wealth of colour and invention in a church which has retained much of its Romanesque character. The altarpiece is from 1600 and the altar candles from 1650. One of the candelabras is 17C, while the other two are copies.

In HAVNEVEJ, between ÅGADE and the railway line, stands **Skive Museum**, where in addition to antiquities and Denmark's largest collection of amber (11,000 pieces) there is a good art collection and a Greenland Room containing a large number of Greenlandic exhibits. Another building of particular interest is **Gammel Skivehus** on the corner of ØSTERTORV and SØNDRE BOULEVARD. Today an hotel, it is on the site of an 11C castle, and incorporates a splendid early 18C half-timbered wing which is open to the public and contains a collection of relics from the earlier Skivehus Castle.

Skive is a good centre for excursions.

▶ Excursion from Skive to Spøttrup Castle, Lihme Church and Lem Church
Total distance c 44km.

Leave Skive to the west on the 573 and drive straight to (20km) ***Spøttrup**, said to be the most perfectly preserved medieval castle in Scandinavia. It is unusual to begin with in that it stands empty, with public admission to all parts; unusual,

Spøttrup Castle

too, in its compact, forbidding aspect, as it stands on low unwooded ground, un-adorned, isolated and surrounded by a moat behind high ramparts, approached through an austere gateway across a narrow bridge—clearly intended to be a castle capable of being defended. And defended it was when Skipper Klement's followers attacked it during the Count's War in 1534. The original building of three wings is from c 1500, the fourth wing being late 16C (open May–Sept). In the adjoining park there is a reconstructed medieval herb garden with some 300 different herbs; there is also a rose garden—and, very conveniently close by, a restaurant.

Follow the road north turning left at the first crossroads. This minor road will take you along the coast to (8km) **Lihme** (or **Lime**), where there is a large and architecturally interesting church, one of the oldest in Denmark, built probably around 1100 and reconstructed c 100 years later. The tower in the west exhibits an arched frieze decorated with carved heads. The apse is enclosed on the outside by half columns, and at the east corners of the chancel, just below the roof, there are jutting figures of animals carved in the ashlars, reminiscent of the figures often found jutting out of the wooden stave churches of Norway. Inside, in the chancel, there are frescoes from 1507, in which the tracery is possibly Irish-inspired, but the most interesting feature is doubtless the stone font with its beautiful symbolical frieze depicting stags, knights and dragons, which has not so far been finally interpreted.

From Lihme a further 3km east on the 189 will bring you to **Lem**. Here, too, there is a church of note. The combination of Romanesque apse, chancel and nave, and a Gothic tower is not unusual, but the carvings on the Romanesque granite ashlars are, and they are remarkably well preserved. There are late 16C frescoes in the chapel.

From Lem it is 15km on the 189 back to Skive. ◄

►Excursion from Skive to the island of Fur
Total distance c 57km.

The tour starts on the 551 north from Skive, following the road along the fjord for 12km, when you turn right to **Jenle** (1km) near the coast. From 1907 this was the home, and is now the burial place, of the Jutlandic poet and novelist, Jeppe Aakjær. In poems of great lyrical intensity and showing a deep love for the ordinary Jutlandic peasant struggling for his existence, and in novels remarkable for their revelations of the brutality of 19C rural life, Aakjær established himself as a leading literary figure at the turn of the 20C. Jenle (the name means 'isolated' in Jutlandic dialect) is now in State ownership, and the house, very much as when Aakjær lived there, is open to the public in the summer, giving a lively impression of the poet's writing and work for cultural and political progress, not least in the form of great rallies held in the grounds.

Return to the 551 and drive north to (3km) **Grinderslevkloster** where the church once formed part of an Augustinian monastery founded c 1150. It is part Romanesque, part Gothic, with an apse surrounded by half columns surmounted by carved heads. The prior's door on the south side is flanked by carved ashlars in the form of a lion and a dragon, and surmounted by a tympanum with a cross carved inside a frieze. Mid-16C frescoes by the Torum Master include a Madonna and Child, in which the realistically portrayed child Jesus is reaching for a pear, the traditional symbol for the mother's breast.

The Torum Master takes his name from the village of **Torum**, 6km further north. Here he is thought to have been responsible for most of the extensive and well-preserved frescoes in the church. Discovered in 1952, they cover both walls and vaulting with motifs from the Bible as well as several figures, including SS Paul and Christopher. The Romanesque granite font is decorated with 16 carved figures.

Another 4km sees you at the narrow **Fur Sound** separating the mainland from the tiny island of **Fur**. There is normally a ferry connection every 30 minutes, and the crossing takes 5 minutes. Fur is one of the areas in Denmark (the others are on Mors) famous for deposits of mo-clay, also known as diatomaceous earth or kieselguhr, and made up of the skeletons of microscopic algae mixed with clay. The substance is both light (it will float) and tough, and it is used largely for insulation. These are the only known deposits of mo-clay in the world; they are 60m deep in places, and the countless fossilised plants, fish and insects in them provide a paradise for anyone interested in biology or geology. Some of the best fossils are found in the museum (open Apr–Oct) in **Nederby**, 2km north of the Sound.

You return to (29km) Skive on the 551. ◀

▶Excursion from Skive to Hjerl Hede and to the churches at Sahl and Ejsing
Total distance c 49km.

From Skive you take the A34 south to (6km) **Estvad** with its Romanesque church and tower from c 1470. The magnificent carved Gothic altarpiece, a triptych, is from 1502, and the church possesses a Romanesque chalice and censer. There are also some late Romanesque frescoes.

Now follow the A34 south for 7km. Here you come to a crossroads, and if you turn right you will in a further 6km arrive at Sevel. (To make a short cut driving across the **Hjelm Hede** heath as far as Søgård is an experience, but you need a good map to find the old track, and a good car to drive along it!)

Just before reaching Sevel you will see **Stubberkloster** convent signposted to the left. You can only cover some of the distance by car, but it is well worth the trouble to walk the rest, for the landscape around here has a grandiose rugged beauty of its own. There is not much left of the 13C Benedictine convent down by the side of Stubbergårdsø lake, but the ruins are scheduled, and there are well-preserved remains of cellar vaulting inside the present building. In more recent times, this area has provided the inspiration for one of Denmark's best-known women writers, Marie Bregendahl, who was married to Jeppe Aakjær from 1893 to 1900.

In **Sevel** itself there is again a delightful church, standing on high ground in a well-kept churchyard. The chancel and east part of the nave are Romanesque, the remainder Gothic. Traces of the former men's entrance are clearly seen on the south wall, and of the women's entrance on the north wall, but neither corresponds to the present entrance through a porch from 1765. The pulpit is from 1605, while the gallery is slightly older. The tower contains not only an impressive church bell, but also a carillon, which plays three different hymn tunes morning, noon and evening, and which was given to the church in 1938 by one Andreas Gade, the great-uncle of one of the present authors.

Another attractive feature in Sevel is the old inn, Sevel Kro.

From Sevel it is only 4km to ***Den gamle Landsby Museum** at **Hjerl Hede**. This is one of Denmark's most famous and extensive open air museums, a reconstructed village comprising more than 40 buildings brought from all over Jutland, and illustrating the development of Danish village life from 1500–1900—a grocer's shop, a smithy, a school, workshops of different kinds, a Romanesque church with murals, a windmill, and several farmsteads. The 'village' is open from April to November, but in July each year not only does it show off its buildings, but large numbers of people dress in the appropriate costumes, demonstrate their skills and trades, and bring everything to life. At the same time there is a reconstruction of a Stone Age settlement—also with volunteers suitably dressed.

When you have seen the village, you should not miss a walk out on to the broad heath. It is protected, and gives an excellent impression of what virtually the whole of Jutland was like 150 years ago. It is well worth walking as far as the long and curiously shaped **Flyndersø** lake, the largest moorland lake in Denmark. It originated at the end of the Ice Age, when the retreating ice left behind vast accumulations here. On melting, these formed so-called kettle-holes which then filled with water.

You should now drive to (3km) **Sahl**, again to see a church, but once more with something very special. Sahl Church contains the best preserved of Denmark's *golden altars. The church itself is quite large, Romanesque from c 1150. The pews are closed, with carved bench ends. It used to be the custom for men and women to sit on their own sides of the church, and it is interesting to note here that the benches for men on the south side are higher and sturdier than those for women on the north side.

Meanwhile, it is the altarpiece which is bound to attract your attention. It now stands as a single unit, but it once consisted of an antemensale, standing in front of the altar, and a predella, standing on the altar itself. It all consists of an oak base covered with chased copper which in its turn is gilded. The whole is covered with biblical figures, scenes from the life of Christ, and Christian symbols, and the effect is quite remarkable. There is a very similar altar in Stadil (p 218).

Now drive 3km west to the 189, where you turn right after 2km and then left to **Ejsing** (2km). Yet again, it is a church you should visit, and yet again it is a large one with special features. The chancel and nave are Romanesque, and there are sizeable late medieval extensions including an aisle with columns and vaulting. The blue-painted pews and bench ends from c 1760 are decorated with pietist symbols. The pew for the local squire is Rococo in style, the glorious oak pulpit and canopy Baroque (and said originally to have been intended for Viborg Cathedral), the sculpted font Romanesque (the oldest piece in the church). There are excellent frescoes (including a very obviously male Adam) from c 1500 in the chancel, behind the altar and in the south chapel—where there is a pompous memorial stone to Axel Rosenkrantz and his wife.

It is, however, in the sacristy that you find the most unusual features. Here, there is a Lutheran confessional from the 17C, and here, too, through a large trapdoor in the floor, you might (on request) see the mummified remains of a fully robed 18C pastor and his wife, lying on beds of hops in open coffins.

Leaving Ejsing, you rejoin the 189 north and drive back to (18km) Skive. ◀

Returning to the main route, from **Skive** you drive north along the A26 to (25km) Sallingsund. The region you have been crossing is called Salling, and on the other side of the sound lies the Limfjord island of **Mors** (pop. 23,300). This island is similar in shape to Jutland itself, and legend has it that when God was making Jutland He first made this as a model; however, as the model ended up being so beautiful God could not bring Himself to destroy it, and so He placed it in the middle of the Limfjord.

Mors is now connected to the mainland by bridges. There are 17 villages here and a sole town, Nykøbing.

■ For the tourist there are plentiful facilities for hiking, cycling, fishing, sailing, and there is a full range of overnight accommodation (for information, contact the Tourist information office in Nykøbing Mors, see below).

After crossing the elegant 1730m-long Sallingsund Bridge, you will very soon find signs pointing left to **Jesperhus Blomsterpark** (Jesperhus Flower Park) (1km), a favourite place for excursions. The park, in the wooded, undulating countryside of Legind Bjerge (mountains!), covers some six hectares and boasts half a million summer flowers in beautiful surroundings, with fountains, lakes, aquarium and aviary. It also claims to have the 'largest and longest waterfall' in Denmark—though this is surely an example of Danish humour. It does, however, have plenty of amusements for children (open mid-May to mid-Sept).

Back on the A26 you almost immediately turn off right to (3km) **Nykøbing Mors**. The town is locally only called Nykøbing, but as there are three major towns in Denmark called Nykøbing, their location is often added to the name. Though only small, the town has nevertheless had a charter since 1299, and today has a small amount of light industry, not least a plant processing the oysters for which the Limfjord is famous.

■ **Tourist information** (summer): Havnen 4; tel. 97 72 04 88.

■ **Hotels**: Pakhuset, Havnen; tel. 97 72 33 00; Sallingsund Færgekro, Sallingsundvej 104; tel. 97 72 00 88.

■ **Youth hostel**: Morsø Vandrehjem, Østerstrand; tel. 97 72 06 17.

The oldest building in Nykøbing is the former **Dueholm Monastery**, approached via VESTERGADE and DUEHOLMGADE. The monastery formerly belonged to the Order of St John of Jerusalem, and was established by the Bishop of Børglum in 1371. The present 16m-long west end of the main building is from 1450, while the remainder of the main building together with the side wing was added after the Reformation, when the monastery went into private ownership. The monastery now houses **Mors historiske Museum** (The Mors Historical Museum).

In addition to paintings of Mors, this contains local historical finds, while in the loft, with its original roofing construction, there is a collection of ploughs, a reconstruction of the interior of a peasant house and, in the east end, a reconstruction of a small church with old local church furniture. The side wing contains the archaeological collection, and the garden some reassembled Bronze Age graves from Mors.

On RÅDHUSTORVET (Town Hall Square) there is a foundry museum—the **Støberimuseum**—housing a collection of products from the old Mors Foundry and, in addition, some old Norwegian and German stoves (open Jun–Aug).

Nykøbing **church** is neo-Gothic, from 1891, and contains some misericords, presumably from Dueholm Monastery, and a fresco by J.T. Skovgaard.

The Dano-Norwegian novelist Aksel Sandemose (1899–1965) was born here, and there is a memorial plaque on his childhood home in FERKENSTRÆDE. It was good of Nykøbing to put it there, as Sandemose's portrayal of his home town, under the name of Jante, is anything but flattering.

►Excursion from Nykøbing to West Mors
Total distance c 24km.

Take the 545 road west for 17km to Hvidbjerg, turning left after the church on a minor road to **Glomstrup mansion** (3km). Glomstrup, from 1797, but with a history going back to 1376, is now a museum, supplemented by an open air museum of 14 various buildings on a 2500 sq m site (open July). They house collections of 18C and 19C furniture and tools in their contemporary settings. There is a children's museum, too.

Return to the 545 and drive on to (4km) **Karby** where there is an unusual, recently restored and splendidly appointed church, part Romanesque and part Gothic, with, in the sacristy, some 17C frescoes which still exhibit medieval qualities. There is a Romanesque granite font, a pulpit from 1600, an auricular altarpiece from 1690, and two richly decorated pews for the local nobility.

You now return on the 545 to (20km) Nykøbing. ◄

►Excursion from Nykøbing to North Mors
Total distance c 50km.

Leave Nykøbing on the 581, driving 24km north to **Feggesund** sound. The last 2km are driven on a very narrow spit of land, with views of Thy to your left and straight ahead, and of the small island of Livø and the mainland coast near the town of Løgstør (both p 314) on your right.

This is a wild, desolate area to which many legends are connected. It seems likely that this was one of the places where the Vikings gathered their ships before sailing out into the North Sea (as was then possible via Thisted). Legend also tells of one King Fegge who became jealous of his brother, Horvendil, murdered him and then married his wife. Following ancient Scandinavian tradition it then fell to Horvendil's son to avenge him. The son's name was—Hamlet! Fegge is said to be buried here, and a stone has been raised in memory of all this.

If you wish to go straight from here to Thy and Thisted, there is a ferry every half hour, the journey taking five minutes, and Thisted is then 20km away (p 301). However, there are other things to see in this northern area of Mors. On your way back to Nykøbing you could turn off right at 5km (in Hesselbjerg) to visit the mo-clay deposits and the **Mo-clay Museum** (1.5km) at SKARREHAGEVEJ 8.

Back on the 581 you drive a further 3km south and then turn right again on to a minor road leading to (2km) **Nørre Dråby**, passing a small archaeological and geological museum within the first kilometer. From Nørre Dråby you should follow a coastal road south along splendid beaches to (5km) Flade, where, at the nearby **Salgjerhøj** you will find the highest point on Mors, offering a magnificent panorama of the island, the fjord and the countryside all round. It is claimed that on a clear day you can see 34 church towers from here. 3km further west **Hanklit**, a mo-clay cliff, rises vertically 60m above the Limfjord, a sight of great majesty, and now a protected area.

From Flade you return to (13km) Nykøbing.

From **Nykøbing**, the last part of this route follows the A26 northwest. 21km ahead you come to the 381m-long **Vilsund Bridge**, built in 1939 as one of the several bridge projects introduced to counter the unemployment of the great Depression. On arriving on the mainland region of Thy across the sound, you drive north along the coast to (10km) Thisted (p 301).

18 • Thisted to Ålborg via Skagen

*Total distance 307km. A11 to (43km) Fjerritslev. (29km) Åbybro. A55 (25km) Løkken. (27km) **Hjørring**. (16km) Hirtshals. E39, 597, A40 north to (47km) **Skagen**. A40 S to (41km) **Frederikshavn**. E45 to (12km) **Sæby**. E45, unclassified roads, 559 to (33km) Dronninglund. 559, E39 to (34km) **Nørresundby** (for Ålborg).*

From Thisted, take the A11 as far as (25km) **Øsløs**, where you will find a small museum in the house where the novelist Johan Skjoldborg was born. Skjoldborg has no international reputation, but he was known in his day as one of a group of writers fighting for better conditions for the developing rural proletariat.

The direct route from here to (18km) Fjerritslev (see below) is via the A11, passing at 4km **Bygholm Vejle**, an area famous for its teeming bird life, especially in the migration season—6000 hectares are designated a bird sanctuary.

A more interesting alternative route however, is as follows.

In Øsløs leave the main road, turning left on to a minor road north to (3km) **Højstrup** where there is a Viking burial ground. This consists of about 25 small burial mounds, some partially preserved ship burials, and some 75 standing stones. Continue north along this road through Tømmerby to (4km) **Tømmerby Kirke**.

One of the largest churches in the region, this originally consisted of a Romanesque apse, chancel and nave built of granite ashlars. In the late Middle Ages a brick tower and porch were added. The ashlars forming the outer wall of the apse contain numerous sculpted human and animal figures, and above the north door there is the figure of a dragon carved in the tympanum. The altar consists of a massive stone slab containing a reliquary (now empty) and supported by four octagonal granite pillars. The altarpiece is from c 1600, while the pulpit, probably the work of the same local artist, seems to be inspired by that in Thisted. The church contains two Romanesque gravestones, one from c 1200.

From Tømmerby church you drive west to (1km) Frøstrup, where you reach a main road and turn right for Fjerritslev.

Art lovers will want to make a slight detour first. Instead of turning right on the main road, turn left, drive for 3km and then turn left again towards **Langvad** (1km) where there is a delightful art gallery, **Kirsten Kjærs Museum** exhibiting 200 paintings and 100 sketches by Kirsten Kjær, who was born nearby in 1893.

Driving north from Frøstrup, you should make a detour after 4km to see the special North Sea coastline around here. Turn left to **Bulbjerg** (3km), which is a 47m-high moraine-covered limestone formation ending in a sheer cliff over-looking the coast, reached by a winding path, and giving extensive views. There is a shelter, with illustrations explaining the countryside around. **Skarreklit**, or what is left of it, a few hundred metres further on, is on the actual coast. This limestone pillar used to stand about 100m from the shore, the last relic of the former coastline and a landmark famous for its jagged outline; in September 1978 it collapsed in a ferocious storm. Over recent years a 160km-long cycle path has been constructed from here along the shore to Skagen.

You should now return to the main road, turn left, and follow it to (16km) **Fjerritslev**.

■ **Tourist information**: Østergade 1; tel. 98 21 16 55.

■ **Hotels**: Klitrosen, Slettestrandvej 130, Slettestrand; tel 98 21 72 55; Svinkløv Badehotel, Svinkløvvej 593, Slettestrand; tel. 98 21 70 02.

■ **Youth hostel**: Brøndumvej 14-16; tel. 98 21 18 55).

As a town Fjerritslev has little to offer apart from its busy shops and a local brewery which is now a museum illustrating the history of brewing (limited opening mid-June to Aug). However, it is within reach of some of the most beau-tiful stretches of the North Sea coast, and that is why we give two routes covering the distance from Fjerritslev to Åbybro. The direct route largely follows the A11 throughout; see below for the alternative North Sea route.

Direct route from Fjerritslev to Åbybro

From Fjerritslev you drive east along the A11. At (13km) Svenstrup a minor road leads right to **Kokkedal** (3km), a 16C mansion standing on high ground and surrounded by a moat, one of the few medieval palaces fully open to the public. It is now an hotel and restaurant, with an art gallery and a splendid hall used for concerts and meetings.

2km further ahead on the A11 you reach **Brovst**, where **Landsbymuseet** (The Village Museum) in the 18C north wing of **Bratskov mansion** is a working museum, including a smithy and a school room from about the turn of the century. The 16C main wing is also open to the public.

5km south of Brovst lies another mansion, **Oksholm** from c 1470, which was once part of a Benedictine convent called **Øland Kloster**. The convent chapel now forms the north wing of the mansion and is used as a parish church. There is a balcony for the nuns, presumably formerly with access from the former east wing. The late Gothic altarpiece, representing the Virgin and eight figures of saints, is of particular interest, as is a 6m-high pre-Reformation tabernacle. The house itself is not open to the public. Nearby is the carefully restored **Oksholm Mill.**

From Brovst you drive another 8km east along the A11. Here you reach a minor road right signposted **Gjøl** (9km). Admittedly it is a fairly long detour, but the village has got something rather special to offer.

*Gjøl Church, with its unusually long Romanesque nave, is famous for its stone engravings, many by the 12C master Goti, who is responsible for stone carvings in other Jutland churches, too. Here, on the south door in Gjøl, he has even left a portrait of himself, sitting chipping away at the stone with his pick hammer. Nearby, he has carved his own name and those of his helpers. They have depicted the Fall, Mary with the Infant Jesus watched over by an angel, a bishop, a lamb carrying a cross, and two lions held apart by a cross. Master Goti has included himself in the scene depicting the Fall, sitting just behind Adam, and in almost exactly the same position as Adam.

This particular relief classes Gjøl Church as a 'Paradise Church', the only one in Scandinavia. Other churches with the same motif are known from Gorki in Russia and in France, and the symbolism signifies that in entering this church one is going back to the springs of life. The church also contains frescoes from the 1530s representing the Tree of Jesse, the sacrifice of Isaac and Jacob's ladder. The altarpiece is a richly carved late Gothic work from c 1520, possibly the work of Hans Brüggemann, with a centre panel representing the Adoration of the Magi.

Back on your main route again you follow the A11 through the village of Birkelse to (6km) Åbybro, passing the elegant 16C manor house of Birkelse on your right.

Alternative route from Fjerritslev to Åbybro—the North Sea route
Total distance 35km.

This route, which follows unclassified roads, will be particularly attractive to those who like walking. It first takes you from Fjerritslev northeast along a country road to (8km) **Hjortdal**, where there is a small, relatively unspoiled

12C church. Its tower is remarkably squat, and it is said that the taller one preceding it was demolished during the Napoleonic Wars, when Denmark was at war with England, so as not to act as a landmark for the enemy.

Immediately beyond the church the road goes left, right down to the shore at (2km) **Slettestrand**, where you may find fishing boats landing their catch on the sand and have the opportunity to buy the freshest plaice imaginable. You should park your car and walk west along a beautiful shore overlooked by **Svinkløv Plantage**, a plantation of pine and spruce, which like most plantations is open to the public. (For accommodation in the Slettestrand area see under Fjerritslev above).

Now drive east between the sea and the extensive wooded bank known as **Lien** (The Brae) until, 3km further on your right, you reach a farm called Fosdalgård. Here again, you should park your car and take a delightful walk, this time up the narrow, densely vegetated Fosdal valley to **Lerup** (2km), where there is a church and a sacred spring called Vor Frue Kilde (Our Lady's Spring), from which water still flows. This used to be a place of pilgrimage. The 12C church in Lerup contains some 16C decorative frescoes and a carved 17C altar-piece. The Romanesque font is interesting for the primitive outline figures engraved on it.

The Lien area is almost mountainous in character, and many artists have chosen to live here, often offering their products for sale to passers-by.

You now drive a further 6km north, turning right here at a T-junction to (16km) Åbybro.

Back on the main route, from Åbybro you take the A55 north turning briefly left off the main road at c 4km to follow a parallel road through Kås. Immediately north of this village you will find (3km) **Jetsmark Church**, dating back to c 1100 and containing some of Jutland's most famous frescoes.

The nave, chancel and apse are Romanesque, the tower late medieval. The frescoes, which cover all the vaulting, are from 1474. Against a background of stars in the chancel there are the symbols of the four Evangelists, prophets and Fathers of the Church, and in the nave there are New Testament scenes and portraits of saints. The figures represented are, of course, in medieval dress, and the liveliness of the proceedings is best indicated by a painting above the pulpit representing the murder of the Holy Innocents, in which one woman is robustly wielding a club in defence of her child. The porch contains a runic stone from the Viking Age. You now continue north and rejoin the A55.

3km later you should make a detour turning left on to the 559 to the favoured seaside resort of **Blokhus** (6km).

■ **Tourist information**: Støvesvej 2; tel. 98 24 85 11.

■ **Hotels**: Nordsøen, Høkervej 5; tel. 98 24 93 33; Karnappen, Strandvejen 14; tel. 98 24 90 20.

■ **Youth hostel**: Kirkevej 26; tel. 98 24 91 90.

With wide, firm sands stretching for many kilometers, the whole of the west coast of Jutland offers splendid beaches for bathing. This is one of the best, the ideal place for a family holiday by the sea, and without the over-commercialisation associated with many seaside resorts—though there is plenty of entertainment, from bridge drives to horse racing, and open air sports from football to surfing. It is an area rich in summer cottages, many of which can be rented.

From Blokhus you return to the A55 and drive 5km north and through the village of Saltum. Here, at a crossroads, stands the monumental **Saltum Church** dating from c 1150 with an impressive, broad tower, famous for its frescoes from 1525; these include the Tree of Jesse amidst an arabesque-like pattern of leaves, together with many directly amusing motifs. Unlike many medieval frescoes, these have never been completely whitewashed over. There is also much interesting furniture in the church, not least the richly carved hexagonal pulpit from the end of the 16C, while on the north wall there are several medieval carved figures.

2km west of Saltum lies **Fårup Sommerland**, an entertainment centre with amusements of many kinds including horse riding for the young, and a miniature railway. Everything is free once you have bought your admission ticket, which lasts all day.

Totally free is the **Saltum Beach** (4km west), another splendid bathing area. From Saltum you drive north to (10km) **Løkken**.

■ **Tourist information**: Mostingsvej 3; tel. 98 99 10 09.

■ **Hotels**: Kallehavegaard Badehotel; tel. 98 99 10 30; Klitbakken, Nørregade 5; tel. 98 99 11 66.

■ **Youth hostel**: Sankt Thøgersplads 2, Vrensted; tel. 98 88 90 33.

Løkken is, if anything, an even more popular resort than Blokhus, likewise with fine beaches and excellent holiday facilities, including sports hall, swimming baths and tennis courts. **Løkken Museum**, in an old skipper's house from 1850, has a local history collection (open May–Sept).

On leaving Løkken on the A55 you drive northeast for c 2km, turning right on an unclassified road to **Børglumkloster monastery** (4km), a place with a long and turbulent history. (There is admission to part of the castle, the courtyard and the church from Whitsun to the end of August.)

Børglumkloster Monastery

Børglum was originally a royal residence, and it was here that St Knud was staying when the Vendsyssel rebellion, which was to lead to his death in Odense, was instigated. By 1139 there was a Bishop of Børglum. It is not known exactly when the Premonstratensian monastery here was founded, but it was certainly in existence by 1205. The Bishop of Vendsyssel chose Børglum as his residence, and Børglum then became in effect the Cathedral of Vendsyssel, replacing Vestervig (p 299). With the passage of time the monastery gathered great wealth, and the bishops gradually became powerful men in the realm. Not all of them, however, were men of humility; one, Bishop Tyge, expelled the monks and fortified the monastery in defiance of the king; but most infamous were Niels Stygge Rosenkrantz and Stygge Krumpen, who stand as symbols of the corruption in the Church in Denmark before the Reformation.

After the Reformation the monastery was secularised and the buildings fell into disrepair. At the beginning of the 18C a local farmer, later ennobled under the name of Frederik Kjærskjold, began to restore the buildings. On his death the task was continued by his wife and finished c 1750 by his daughter and her second husband, the highly gifted architect Laurids de Thurah, who designed many of the most important 18C buildings in Copenhagen. It was doubtless he who was mainly responsible for the impressive mansion we know as Børglumkloster today.

The present buildings largely preserve the aspect of the medieval monastery, consisting of four unadorned wings around a courtyard. The magnificent *church, 39m × 20m, forms part of the north wing of Børglumkloster and is thought originally to date back to c 1220. It consists of a lofty vaulted nave with an aisle on either side, mainly late Gothic, but with remains of the original Romanesque building. In one of the pillars there is a man's head carved into the ashlar. Most of the furniture is Rococo—the pulpit, the enclosed pews, the altar rail. On the north wall stand two important tombstones, those of Bishop Jep Friis and Bishop Niels Stygge Rosenkrantz. One of Frederik Kjærskjold's achievements was to restore the church, which he did in the grand style, in 1734 providing it with a huge altarpiece 12m high and almost as wide, all backed by painted drapery creating the impression of black velvet.

Before returning to the A55, you might like to go a further 10 km to **Vrå**, where, centred on the Folk High School, there is a splendid art gallery devoted to the work of artists who have become known as the Vrå painters, dominated by Svend Engelund, but including many others. Art of a different kind is to be found in the early 16th-century frescoes and the carved 15th-century altar in the nearby Romanesque church.

Return now to the A55 and drive north for 5km, turning left towards (8km) Lønstrup. On your way there you will pass minor roads leading off left to Rubjerg Knude and, later, Mårup church.
    Rubjerg Knude is a 74m-high cliff. The former lighthouse there is now a museum (open May–Oct), demonstrating the effects of sand drift. The trip there is itself an experience, for this is an area profoundly marked by sand drift. The astounding effect of this process is clearly demonstrated in the museum—and, if more be needed, by the abandoned Rubjerg church, only part of which has survived.
    The tiny Romanesque **Mårup Church** stands only a few metres from the edge of the cliffs and is therefore threatened with closure. Many of the graves in the churchyard are surrounded by fences to prevent the flowers on them from blowing away, and at the west end of the church there is an anchor from an English man-of-war, The Crescent, that was stranded here during the Napoleonic Wars, in 1808: 226 members of a crew of 300 are buried in the churchyard.
    From Lønstrup you move east again, soon passing a very high-lying church on your left. This is **Vennebjerg Church**, situated higher than any other in this county of Vendsyssel, a clear landmark which can be seen from afar, and for this purpose the north side is always painted white.
    A further 12km brings you to **HJØRRING** (pop. 34,950), which received its charter in 1243, growing during the Middle Ages into a flourishing and rela-

tively large town with three churches standing quite close together, all of which, unusually, have survived. A period of decline followed the Reformation, but new life came at the end of the 18C, and Hjørring has continued to flourish.

■ **Tourist information**: Markedgade 9; tel. 98 92 02 32.

■ **Hotels**: Phønix, Jernbanegade 6; tel. 98 92 54 55; Hjørring Kro, Birthesvej 2; tel. 98 92 53 29.

■ **Youth hostel**: Thomas Morrildsvej 11; tel. 98 22 67 00.

A particular feature is Hjørring's keen interest in the arts; since the 1960s it has accumulated a unique collection of modern Danish sculpture which is distributed in key positions throughout the town with the intention of introducing art into everyday life. A pamphlet available from the tourist information office lists 52 localities with almost 100 sculptures, some of them of considerable size.

Most impressive perhaps is **Springvandspladsen** (Fountain Square) in the centre of the town, with its water organ amidst sculptural decorations by Bjørn Nørgaard. In SEIDELINSGADE you will find the art gallery, **Hjørring Kunstmuseum**, containing some impressive frescoes by Niels Larsen Stevns depicting the history of North Jutland; in addition there is a good collection of other North Jutland art. The local history museum, **Vendsyssel Historiske Museum** close to the old AXELTORV, was established in 1889 and contains old statues from pre-Reformation churches as well as prehistoric and medieval exhibits.

The three old churches in Hjørring, all from the 13C, are well worth a visit. The oldest is **Sankt Olai**, dedicated to the Norwegian King and Saint, Olaf, and standing on the site of an older wooden church, remains of which were found in the 1960s. It is built of granite ashlars, and has no tower. **St Catherine's Church** is the largest of the three, but it has been so thoroughly rebuilt that most of its early character has gone. The present transept is in fact based on the original nave, the present nave being a later addition. The large auricular altarpiece is from 1651. Architecturally rather better preserved is the brick-built Romanesque **Sankt Hans Kirke**, in which both the nave and chancel are nevertheless late Gothic. This church contains some fine frescoes.

Hjørring was the birthplace of the late 19C dramatist and novelist Henri Nathansen and the 20C novelist Knuth Becker, both of whom are commemorated by plaques.

From the outskirts of Hjørring the A55 takes you north to (9km) **Tornby**, where there is a Romanesque church containing a small but ornate late Gothic altarpiece from c 1525. There is a runic inscription on the north wall. When it was first interpreted in 1913 it was thought to say that the writer of the runes had one Whitsun morning enjoyed Joan in the church. Alas, nothing so exciting. Later scholarship has shown that it was not Joan, but **tone**, i.e. music, that gave Thorstein such pleasure. Unusually, the ship hanging in this church is a lightship. Around Tornby there is a large nature reserve.

After a further 3km you might turn right to visit **Horne** (2km), where a stone burial chamber from the Early Bronze Age can be seen to the west of the Romanesque church. An inscription on the pulpit from 1589 contains a quotation from Luther: 'A good priest must do these three things—enter the pulpit, say something, and descend again.'

Returning to the A55 you go on to (4km) **Hirtshals** (pop. 14,630), the third of the major ports on the west coast of Jutland.

■ **Tourist information**: Nørregade 40; tel. 98 94 22 20.

■ **Hotels**: Hirtshals, Havnegade 2; tel. 98 94 20 77; Skaga, Willemoesvej 1; tel. 98 94 55 00.

■ **Youth hostel**: Kystvejen 53; tel. 98 94 12 48.

With its harbour completed in 1930, Hirtshals is now an important centre for the fishing industry, with ferry connections to Norway. For the tourist, the main attraction must be the **Nordsømuseum** (North Sea Museum); indoors there is an aquarium showing some 70 species of North Sea fish, as well as seals and dolphins, and illustrating the fishing industry of the region.

Hirtshals Museum at SOPHUS THOMSENSGADE 6 is housed in a fisherman's house from 1880, and is furnished to show the living conditions of a fisherman and his family at the beginning of the 20C. It also contains a section illustrating the history of the local bitter *snaps.*

From Hirtshals take the E39 southeast, turning off left after 4km on the 597 towards (14km) Tversted. Instead of going straight there, we suggest a detour. On reaching (7km) Uggersby, you should turn right to (5km) Mygdal, where in the old mansion of **Odden** there is a collection of no fewer than 1200 sketches and studies by J.F. Willumsen, a valuable supplement to the Willumsen Museum in Frederiksund. (Open daily all year.)

From Mygdal you continue along the minor road towards **Bindslev** (4km). Just before reaching the village you will discover the church, which has a most unusual 13C fresco of the Madonna and Child; there is clearly Byzantine influence at work here, and it has been suggested that the fresco was inspired by an illuminated book. You then drive on to **Tversted** (**Tourist information**: Østervej 10; tel. 98 93 11 26).

Leaving Tversted on the 597 east you pass a large eagle reservation (**Tuen Ørnereservat**) (open mid-June to mid-Sept), before at 15km you reach the A40. Here you turn left and drive to (6km) Hulsig where you turn left again to visit Råbjerg Mile and Kandestederne (4km).

Go for a walk in **Råbjerg Mile**, a wild area of sand and sand dunes, so vast and so untouched that at times you could imagine yourself in the Sahara. You will find nothing like it anywhere else in Denmark. Nearby **Kandestederne** is again a well-known holiday area. You can in fact drive as far as this on the broad sandy beach all the way from Tversted!

Driving north again on the A40 you should turn off right after a further 9km. Here you will come to yet another example of the effects of sand drift in the church buried in the sand, **Den Tilsandede Kirke**. Built in the 14C, this church was originally Skagen Church, dedicated to St Laurence, the patron saint of seafarers, and was the longest church in Vendsyssel. Then, around 1600, sand drift began to affect the area, threatening the church itself by the end of the 18C. For 20 years people dug their way into it every Sunday, but by 1795 it was abandoned by royal decree. The furniture and church fittings were sold, and the nave was used as a quarry, only the tower remaining intact, used as a landmark for shipping. It still stands, and is now a favourite spot for tourists.

You now return to the A40, turn right, and are soon in (3km) ****SKAGEN** (pop. 13,300).

■ **Tourist information**: Sankt Laurentivej 22; tel. 98 44 13 77.

■ **Hotels**: Clausens Hotel, Sankt Laurentivej 35; tel. 98 45 01 66; Brøndums Hotel, Anchersvej 3; tel. 98 44 15 55.

■ **Youth hostel**: Rolighedsvej 2; tel. 98 44 22 00.

Skagen is the most northerly town in Denmark, situated on the narrow spit of land dividing the waters of the **Kattegat** from the **Skagerrak** and because of its situation a birdwatchers' paradise at certain times of the year. You can drive almost to the tip, **Grenen**, walking the last stretch to see where the waters of the two meet, and feeling almost surrounded by

Grenen

water. In so doing you cannot fail to notice the intensity of the light reflected from the sea on all sides. You can, if you wish, stand in the sea, with one foot in the Kattegat and one in the Skagerrak—but **you must not try to bathe at this spot**. The currents are extremely dangerous. If you want to bathe, choose some of the other excellent beaches nearby.

History

Skagen was granted a charter in 1413. It was an important shipping and fishing centre, and in the 16C it was actually bigger than Copenhagen. However, sand drift occurred, Skagen suffered under the various 17C wars and went into serious decline, and by the beginning of the 19C it was in a miserable state, with no doctor, no lighting, scarcely any roads. A road constructed in the 1850s was buried in sand. However, life returned in the second half of the 19C, and then came the event that really put Skagen on the map again—its discovery by a group of Danish artists, who saw the artistic possibilities of an old-fashioned community, and who appreciated the intensity of the light on the landscape.

Skagen now became a focal point of Danish art, and a school of 'Skagen painters' arose, ably supported by many writers, too. Names such as Michael and Anna Ancher, P.S. Krøyer, Viggo Johansen and Laurits Tuxen are inextricably associated with Skagen. Some settled there, others visited regularly. And they attracted painters from Norway and Sweden, too. The poet particularly associated with the group, and himself an able painter, is Holger Drachmann, whose poems inspired by the sea are in the same spirit as the paintings of his fellows.

Apart from the general charm and exhilaration of the place, it is the work of these artists which makes Skagen an absolute must. ***Skagens Museum** contains some 1500 paintings, sketches and sculptures, some of them on a very large scale, which together constitute the very essence of the Skagen painters' work. They are all housed in a splendidly planned gallery where it is possible to view even the largest paintings from the distance from which they have the best effect (open summer; limited opening winter).

Close by is **Brøndums Hotel**, a favourite haunt of the artists, and a place filled with reminders of them. Today we can be thankful that the artists had a tendency to pay their hotel bills in kind!

A different impression of these same artists in their daily lives, however, is to be found in ***Michael & Anna Ancher's House**, two minutes away from the Skagen Museum and not to be missed either. The Anchers lived there from 1884, and it was this delightful, low-ceilinged house that became one of the meeting places of the Skagen artists. After the death of her parents, their daughter Helga, also a painter, lived here until her death in 1964. The house has since been carefully restored, and great efforts have been made to re-create the atmosphere of the artists' home; their furniture is here, their piano, their china, their artists' equipment. There is even an unfinished sketch on an easel. The walls are covered with paintings and sketches. One almost feels that the artists themselves could appear at any moment. The adjoining **Saxilds Gaard** puts on exhibitions of sketches by Anna, Michael and Helga Ancher (open summer; limited opening winter).

A little further away, at HANS BAGHSVEJ 21, lies **Drachmann's House**, where the poet and painter lived from 1902 until his death in 1908. In 1911 it was opened to the public, and is filled with paintings by Holger Drachmann himself and his contemporaries (open June-mid-Sept). So closely bound was Drachmann to Skagen that he chose to be buried here, and his tomb, designed by Krøyer, stands in the dunes at the very north of the peninsula.

Although Skagen is particularly associated with the art of the turn of the century, modern artists, too, have flocked here, and their work is to be seen in **Grenen Museum** at the northernmost tip of the land (open May–Sept).

A museum of a slightly more usual kind is **Skagen Fortidsminder**, in P.K. NIELSENSVEJ. This open air museum consists of eight buildings which have been moved here from the vicinity—a poor fisherman's home from the mid-19C alongside that of a more affluent fisherman, both furnished in the appropriate style. There is a lifeboat station, a windmill, a memorial hall, and a fishery museum containing many exhibits of local interest (open Mar–Nov). At BANKVEJ 2, there is a **museum** filled with amber exhibits. (Limited opening winter), while at FLAGBAKKEVEJ 30 there is a **natural history museum** devoted to the Skagen area (open May-Oct).

When you have savoured the art and atmosphere of Skagen you should try one of the numerous small **fish restaurants** around the harbour. Modest on the outside, they are almost without exception very fashionable inside and justly deserve their reputation as some of Denmark's finest fish restaurants. **Gammel Skagen** on the western outskirts of Skagen has some very nice restaurants too.

It is scarcely surprising that Skagen should be about the most popular holiday resort in Denmark.

You leave Skagen again by the A40, passing Ålbæk and **Råbjerg Mose**, an area of marshland and heath. 34km south of Skagen you should turn left to visit **Strandby** (2km). Strandby itself is a fairly ordinary small coastal town, but it contains a most unusual modern church, from 1966, the work of the architect Jacob Blegvad. Apart from the bell-tower and the office building to the west of the church, there is not a straight wall in sight. Instead, the lines are those of a ship, with a great, sweeping tiled roof, and the comparison with Le Corbusier's chapel in Ronchamps is inevitable. From the shore near Strandby you can glimpse the tiny **Hirsholmene** islands, only the largest of which is inhabited— by some 20 people.

Return to the A40 and drive the remaining 7km south to **Frederikshavn** (pop. 35,200), which was not given a charter until 1818, but today is the largest city north of the Limfjord, the terminal of the main railway line from Copenhagen (there is a private railway taking you on to Skagen), and a ferry port serving several towns in both Norway and Sweden, in addition to the Kattegat island of Læsø.

■ **Tourist information**: Brotorvet 1; tel. 98 42 32 66.

■ **Hotels**: Hoffmanns, Tordenskjoldgade 3; tel. 98 42 21 66; Stena, Tordenskjoldgade 14; tel. 98 43 32 33.

■ **Youth hostel**: Buhlsvej 6; tel. 98 42 14 75.

There is a shipyard in Frederikshavn and a good deal of industry, in addition to the fishing industry. On the other hand, there are relatively few old buildings apart from the early 19C fishermen's houses at FISKERKLYNGEN, standing cheek by jowl in narrow lanes, and the old **Gunpowder Tower**, now a military museum (open Apr–Oct). The main church, a colossus from the late 19C, has an altarpiece by the Skagen painter Michael Ancher; the town hall is from 1977, pleasing but not outstanding. Close by is the **Kulturhus**, containing a museum offering a good collection of ex-libris, and travelling exhibitions of modern art.

There is, however, something special very close to Frederikshavn. In the western outskirts of the town, 1km south of the 585, lies the exquisite small mansion of **Bangsbo**. Although its history can be traced back to the 15C, the present buildings date from the 18C, thoroughly restored 100 years later by the then owner, Johan Knudsen. Knudsen, together with his brother, started a literary periodical in Copenhagen, and thus came into contact with many of the leading literary figures of his day, in particular becoming a close friend of the novelist Herman Bang. Bang spent much time in Bangsbo and even went so far as to express the vain wish that he might be buried here. When Johan Knudsen retired from Copenhagen, he turned Bangsbo into a cultural centre. Anne Marie Carl Nielsen designed the garden, and the architect Thorvald Bindesbøll the entrance porch, over which Johan Knudsen's initials are to be seen. His guests here included some of the most famous (and, in the eyes of some contemporaries, infamous) names in Scandinavian culture from the end of the 19C.

Bangsbo is now a *****museum** owned by Frederikshavn. Along with local and literary exhibits the main building contains Europe's largest collection of hair decorations (an amazing sight). The outbuildings have exhibits of an entirely different kind. One contains an excellent museum of the World War II Occupation of Denmark—uniforms, weapons, vehicles, proclamations, all chronologically arranged to give an impression of developments over the years. Another is dedicated to shipping and includes a fascinating collection of figure-heads. And by no means least among the attractions at Bangsbo is a remarkably well-preserved merchant vessel from the 12C—the **Ellingå ship**.

Adjoining Bangsbo there is an extensive deer park to which there is free admission.

Some 2km further west on the 585 will bring you to **Cloostårnet** (the Cloos Tower), an observation tower built in 1962, standing 160m above sea level. It affords panoramic views of the whole of Vendsyssel. On the opposite side of the road here you will find **Flade** church, dating back to the early 13C, but with modern frescoes from 1958.

You leave Frederikshavn on the E45 and drive south along the coast to (12km) **SÆBY** (pop. 18,200). If Frederikshavn bears the stamp of modern times, Sæby clearly reflects its long history, an enchanting small town idyllically situated.

■ **Tourist information**: Krystaltorvet 1; tel. 98 46 15 19.

■ **Hotels**: Viking, Europavej E3; tel. 98 46 17 00; Hillers, Vestergade 31; tel. 98 46 15 90.

■ **Youth hostel**: Sæbygårdvej 32; tel. 98 46 36 50.

History

In the Middle Ages Sæby (meaning the town by the sea) belonged to the Børglum Monastery (see p 267), as did the nearby Sæbygård mansion (see below). The river provided a natural though unreliable harbour, through which the monastery transported goods. In the late 15C a Carmelite monastery was established, dedicated to the Virgin, and the town became known for a time as Mariested. The church belonging to it still stands, but the remaining buildings have disappeared. To this day the Virgin and Child form the town's coat of arms. Sæby flourished even after the Reformation until Frederikshavn took over the lead, when for a time Sæby went into decline. By the 19C, however, it was on its way up again. Nevertheless, it has not grown into a large town, and although there is some light industry, Sæby has maintained its unspoiled character.

The artists and writers who frequented Skagen also found Sæby. Holger Drachmann stayed at Clasen's hotel in Algade, as did Herman Bang—and Bang based one of his most wicked novels on his observations there. The novelist Gustav Wied was there for a time, and Ibsen was a visitor in 1877; it was probably there that he wrote his *Lady from the Sea*.

ALGADE is the original main street, leading to the imposing church deriving from the Carmelite monastery. Most of the houses are of historical interest. They include the old courthouse (No. 7) and the former Clasen's Hotel (No. 3), now a home for the elderly. Here, too, is a former town hall as well as an old home for the poor, Rhuuses Hospital, established in 1723. The old Town Hall, now the police station, is from 1847, but it is predated by an even older one, from the early 18C, in STRANDGADE, at the east end of Algade. Opposite is one of the oldest buildings in the town; built as a hospital in 1565, it has stood in its present form since 1675 and has now been turned into accommodation for pensioners.

On the corner of Algade and SØNDERGADE stands the 17C **Konsul Ørums Gård**, now **Sæby Museum**, containing local history exhibits and reconstructions of an old shop and a schoolroom from c 1920.

At the east end of Algade is KLOSTERTORVET with the *church dedicated to the Virgin. It is a remarkably narrow building (8m) in relation to its length (54m), really consisting of an extension of the small church standing here before the establishment of the Carmelite monastery. The Carmelites lengthened it without widening it. One of the features is the murals uncovered during restorations in 1905–06. On the north wall of the original part of the nave there are biblical motifs and several coats of arms, from c 1465; in the three east severies (bays of vaults) there are later representations of the story of Joachim and Anna and of the Day of Judgement—these include a famous grotesque representation of a devil taking away the soul of a dead man, while his grieving wife is already giving in to the charms of a new lover; in the vaulting of the south chapel there is a later mural, a design from c 1520, consisting of leaves around the coats of arms of the last two bishops of Børglum.

The altarpiece, a triptych, is from c 1520 with a carved centre panel representing the Virgin and Child standing on the Tree of Jesse; the side panels are paintings of the shepherds and the Magi worshipping the Child. In the chancel there are 20 misericords from c 1500, two of them with elaborately carved bench ends, and there are many other pieces from both before and after the Reformation. Of particular interest is an unusual wooden font from 1645 in the south transept. The splendid Renaissance pulpit and canopy are dated 1577, and were restored in 1906.

West of the town centre lie Sæbygård woods and further on Sæbygård mansion. Both can be reached on foot by following the stream, or you can drive if you prefer. The woods—largely a conservation area—cover 120 hectares and consist mainly of beech. They are high-lying and have to be approached via a steep slope which denotes the coastline of 14,000 years ago.

The original **Sæbygård mansion** belonged to Børglum Monastery, but the present house, surrounded by a broad moat, dates from 1576. The octagonal spire over the main entrance is from 1861. There are four wings, of which the main one, to the north, is still in use as a private dwelling. Sæbygård houses extensive collections of paintings and porcelain, and the great hall with its beamed ceiling is particularly impressive. The mansion is open for conducted tours every day in the main season, and arrangements can be made for groups at other times through Sæby Museum.

On leaving Sæby you turn south following the E45 for 14km. Here a road leads left to (2km) *Voergård, an impressive and ornate Renaissance mansion surrounded by a broad moat.

Again, this is a building once owned by Børglum Monastery, and it was Bishop Stygge Krumpen who built the north wing. The remainder was built by 1591. The exact date of building is not known, though the first reference to the house is from 1481, and that part still stands, incorporated into the north wing within the courtyard. Voergård is private, but there are conducted tours of the main wing throughout the summer months. It is not strictly speaking a museum. Consequently, in the setting of a magnificent house you will find paintings by, among many others, Raphael, Frans Hals, Rubens, Corot and Goya; splendid furniture from the time of Louis XV and Louis XVI of France; a collection of Sèvres porcelain, along with the porcelain used by Louis XVI and Marie Antoinette during their imprisonment, counterbalanced by that used by Napoleon during his 100 days; there is Spanish furniture, Flemish tapestry, and a Chinese room. This is a home of great splendour, and one of the most comprehensive private collections open to public view in Denmark today (limited opening from Easter to beginning of Sept).

After the Reformation Voergård was owned by the Crown, but in 1578 it came into the hands of one Karen Krabbe, who gave it to her daughter Ingeborg Skeel. It was she who was responsible for building the east wing, and so impressed was King Frederik II that in 1588 he presented her with the ornamental portal, which according to tradition was originally intended for Frederiksborg Castle (p 112). After Ingeborg Skeel's death in 1604 Voergård fell into neglect and was severely damaged during the 17C wars. Despite restoration work in the 18C, it was not until the house came into the ownership of Peder Brønnum-Scavenius and subsequently of Erik Scavenius that it was restored to its present state. In 1955 it was bought by the Papal Count E. Oberbech-Clausen, who was responsible for adding to the collection of art treasures in the house, decreeing that the art and antique collection and the main wing should be opened to the public on his death. The north wing, on the other hand, is reserved for the Order of St John of Malta, for which a Chapel has been established.

1km further down the road lies **Voer Kirke**, the church built by the earlier owners of Voergård. On the south side, and fundamentally out of proportion to the structure as a whole, there is a huge square tower from 1585 forming a sepulchral chapel. It contains an elaborate monument from 1600 to Erik Banner and Ingeborg Skeel, the owners of Voergård. Erik Scavenius, the controversial Danish Prime Minister during part of the World War II Occupation, lies buried in the churchyard here.

Driving east again, you turn right in the village of Præstbro and continue through Dronninglund to (14km) the 559. Here you make another right turn and drive on to (2km) the mansion of **Dronninglund Hovedgård**. A Benedictine convent was established here c 1268, thriving and growing until the nuns complained of bad treatment by Bishop Stygge Krumpen of Børglum. After the Reformation the convent became a private house. The present Dronninglund Hovedgård, now an hotel (tel. 98 84 33 00), is partly based on the convent buildings, as is particularly obvious in the east wing.

The adjoining *church is considered one of the best examples of Romanesque architecture in Vendsyssel. During restoration work in 1943 a large number of 16C murals was discovered, representing biblical motifs and knights; one depicts Alexander the Great on an elephant doing battle with a King Arthur on horseback. There is a very large Renaissance altarpiece from c 1600, a carved pulpit from 1580 surmounted by an auricular canopy, and a gallery for the owners of the house, from 1600.

A further 7km west on the 559 brings you to **Hjallerup**, in June the scene of Europe's biggest horse fair. This is an event which is now of diminishing importance, but the fair has a history going back many centuries.

12km beyond Hjallerup, still on the 559, you come to the E39. Here at the crossing you will find **Tylstrup Kro**, one of the historical Royal Privilege Inns, where you can still find everything from a cup of coffee to a well equipped room for the night. If you want something more elaborate, you can proceed a further 1.5km and turn left here to **Gammel Vrå Slot** (1km), an old mansion now serving as a luxury hotel while maintaining the atmosphere of the great house (tel. 98 23 36 22).

However, the main object of coming to Tylstrup is to turn south on the E39 in order to visit (5km) **Sulsted Church**. Hidden away 1km east of the main road, and reached on the 559/585, this contains some of the most impressive and famous murals in the country. If it is closed the key can be obtained from a house adjoining, and it is worth going to the slight trouble of getting it. The vaulted ceiling is sumptuously decorated with frescoes from 1548 depicting the life of Christ, with accompanying text, unusually, in Jutlandic dialect. Not only are they impressive in their array and variety, but they clearly demonstrate the dress of the time at which they were painted, and thus provide a fascinating social document. A further interesting feature is that they include a portrait of the Virgin as Queen of Heaven—yet they were painted **after** the Reformation. Most of the remaining church furniture is from c 1600. Steen Steensen Blicher's favourite daughter, Malvine Steensdatter, is buried in the churchyard.

You now return to the E39 and drive the remaining 10km to Nørresundby. Here the main attraction, **Lindholm Høje**, a ridge to the west of the town, is one of Denmark's most important and extensive archaeological sites. It contains the remains of a large settlement dating back to between AD 600 and 1100; almost 700 Iron Age and Viking Age graves, including 150 ship settings, have been discovered here, all excavated 1952–58. Grave goods found during excavations are now housed in a purpose-built museum in VENDILAVEJ, just west of the site. The site itself has been preserved in its excellent state thanks to the activities of sand drift, which seems to have taken place in the 10C, covering the earliest part of the town to a depth of 3–4m. Also west of the site, on FR. RASCHS VEJ, there is a herb garden containing 250 medicinal herbs carefully arranged. Here, too, there is a half-timbered pipe-making house containing collections of pipes and textiles.

From Nørresundby you have a choice of routes south across the Limfjord to Ålborg (p 245 ff) and beyond. There is the bridge from 1933, 635m long and 12.5m above the surface at its highest point, which will bring you into the centre of the city. Alternatively, you can follow the E45 and take the more recent, but naturally less picturesque, 552m-long tunnel, 10m below the surface. If you do not intend to stop in Ålborg, this is clearly the route for you.

19 • Ringkøbing to Hobro

Total distance 130km. A16 to (43km) **Holstebro**. *(51km)* **Viborg**. *A16, 517, E45 to (36km)* **Hobro**.

From Ringkøbing (p 278) the A16 leads north to (8km) **Hee**, a small village where there is a remarkably large church built of granite ashlars, one of the most interesting Romanesque churches in Jutland. The chancel, nave, porch and tower are all Romanesque (though the subject of radical neo-Romanesque rebuilding in the 19C), while the two chapels on the south side are of later date. Despite the efforts of the 19C, the west end still has some splendid original features, and is at times reminiscent of Ribe Cathedral. The late Renaissance altarpiece is from 1635, its three sections being defined by white columns. Two heads jut out at the top of the tower; according to one legend the church was built by a troll, and the heads are those of him and his wife. J.C. Christensen, the Danish Prime Minister who presided over the introduction of democratic rule into Denmark in 1901, is buried in the churchyard. There is also a memorial to him in the garden of his house in the main street and a memorial room has been established in the house itself. Open during the summer and autumn holidays 13.00–17.00 except Fri and Sat.

Now follow the A16/28 to (18km) **Ulfborg Kirkeby** with an interesting Romanesque/Gothic church with some unusual features. Even the exterior is striking, consisting of a transept as high as the nave, with a gabled chapel beside it to the west, and to the east a gabled porch beneath a substantial tower— certainly not a poor church, but perhaps reflecting the austerity of the area in its small windows and the general sense of compact strength. Inside, the chapel and the transept are joined by a series of rounded arches. It is, however, the pulpit, from c 1587, which immediately attracts attention, projecting from a carved gallery stretching the width of the nave. It is one of only two such left today, though the signs are that this construction was once fairly common. The painted panels in the gallery represent the 12 tribes of Israel. In the chapel there is an ornate, large-scale sandstone and marble memorial to the State Councillor Preben Gyldenstierne and his two wives.

The A16 will now take you to (18km) Holstebro, through countryside which bears the traces of the harsh weather West Jutland has been subjected to. To the east of Ulfborg there is a wide undulating tract of heathland, now a conservation area. It is intersected by several streams, the vegetation is mainly heather and juniper, the soil sandy. Few people live there, the villages are small, their churches tiny and without towers. It is worth driving along some of the narrow roads to gain a feeling of this quite unusual area and to sense what West Jutland was once like.

HOLSTEBRO (pop. 39,050) is first mentioned in 1274 and has a charter from 1584, though it is thought that there were earlier charters which were burnt in a fire in 1552. As a market town Holstebro flourished in the 16C, with a large ox market and with trade via Hjerting (near Esbjerg) with Holland. After a period of decline in the 18C, it gradually recovered in the 19C, largely thanks to the advent of the railways, and attracted a good deal of industry. Since World War II it has been a garrison town.

■ **Tourist information**: Brotorvet 8; tel. 97 42 57 00.

■ **Hotels**: Schaumburg, Nørregade 26. tel. 97 42 31 11; Krabbes Hotel, Stationsvej 18; tel. 97 42 06 22.

At the centre of the inner ring road lies **Store Torv** (Grand Square), which has always been the focal point of the town. However, there are no really old buildings left, as Holstebro suffered no fewer than 13 fires in the space of 200 years, and what did not disappear on one occasion vanished on the next. Even the main church, **Holstebro Kirke**, is only from 1907, and is of little intrinsic architectural interest, though it does contain some splendid church furniture.

A total contrast is the **Nørrelands Kirke**, from 1969, designed by Inger and Johannes Exner and containing rooms and buildings intended to incorporate the church into the daily lives of the local inhabitants. It is in the shape of a cube, and receives its light mainly from slit windows in the roof. The pews are grouped in a fan-like pattern around the altar. The free-standing bell-tower consists of a belfry standing on narrow girders and reached by an open spiral staircase.

Like several other Jutland market towns, Holstebro shows a great interest in the arts. The **Holstebro Kunstmuseum** in SØNDERBROGADE contains collections of mainly post-1930 Danish art and graphic art by Picasso, Matisse and Giacometti among others. There is also an extensive collection of non-European art. Adjoining the Art Museum in new premises opened in 1991 is **Holstebro Museum**. It contains a very extensive collection of mainly Jutlandic artefacts from prehistoric, historical and modern times, including a collection of silver and a reconstructed silversmith's workshop. There is a working meteorological station and exhibitions of early local industry. Downstairs is the Hans Dissing collection of tin toys and the museum's collection of dolls. Here, too, is the Dragoon Museum and exhibits from the Second World War occupation of Denmark.

The **Jens Nielsen and Olivia Holm-Møller Gallery** in NØRREBROGADE exhibits work by these two artists and other contemporary Danish painters. In SØNDERLANDSGADE there is a museum for miniature works of art, the **Museum for Kleinkunst**, containing nothing larger than 10cm × 15cm.

Like other towns, too, Holstebro has made great efforts to embellish its streets, and there are many pleasing sculptures scattered around the town, outstanding among which must be a Giacometti in front of the old town hall in Nørregade. For philatelists the attraction must be the **Old Post Office** in ØSTERGADE (open Sat).

▶**Excursion from Holstebro to the North Sea coast and Lemvig**
Total distance c 138km.

Leave Holstebro on the ring road, taking the A16 southwest to (18km) the A28, where you turn north to (1km) Ulfborg Kirkeby (see above). Continue another 3km on the A28 and on your left you will find a striking archway, built in 1790, leading to the mansion of **Nørre Vosborg**, the oldest of the medieval fortified houses of West Jutland. It is thought that King Erik Menved once owned it. The original house was destroyed in a storm in 1532, and the present building from 1552 was a replacement for it (open summer). Hans Christian Andersen visited Nørre Vosborg in 1859 and there met Captain Marryat, the author of *The Children of the New Forest*—but without any obvious meeting of minds.

The A28 continues north through Vemb village, east of which there is a bird sanctuary, to (11km) Bækmarksbro. Here you turn left, driving past (9km) **Bøvling Church** with its 18C onion-shaped spire, and 1km further on **Rysensten house** on your right. With a history going back to 1414, and once known as Bøvling Castle, the present Rysensten has a main wing dating largely from 1638–39.

7km north of Rysensten you arrive at Dybe, where you take a minor road west to (4km) the coastal village of **Ferring**, once a favourite resort of authors and artists, the most important being the Expressionist painter **Jens Søndergaard**, whose former summer cottage here is now a **museum** (open summer; limited opening winter). Ferring old church contains some unusual 12C frescoes which were restored in 1987, and which seem to show English influence.

You can walk along the broad sands both north and south of Ferring and gain an impression of the grandeur of this West Jutland coastal scenery—though in the summer you will have to share the experience with a lot of others. You might also gain an impression of the violence of which the sea is capable here! All along the coast there are remains of World War II coastal defences, and 2km south of Ferring there is the 26m high **Bovbjerg lighthouse**, standing on a 46m-high moraine cliff.

Return to the 181, and turn north once more towards (c 18km) **Harboør** which is a sizeable fishing port, one of the centres of the west coast fishing industry to this day, and one where life in the past has been unusually demanding. According to one source, the parish of Harboør has been subject to more flooding and sand drift than any other except Agger immediately to the north. It is, however, the harsh life of the fishermen one thinks of first and foremost. In 1893 this was the scene of one of the most famous tragedies in 19C Denmark, when 26 fishermen were drowned during a storm. There is a memorial to them in the churchyard, which contains many other reminders of tragic events, not least a memorial wall inscribed with the names of all fishermen who have drowned here. Inside the church the Renaissance altarpiece is fittingly equipped with a central panel from 1910 showing Christ among the fishermen's families.

Before proceeding north, just take the minor road west from Harboør to **Langerhuse** (2km), where **Flyvholm Rescue Station**, from 1847, is now open as a museum illustrating the work of the coastal rescue service. Over 700 stranded seamen have been saved by crews from here (open summer).

The drive north from Harboør to (10km) **Thyborøn** is along a narrow spit of land, where you can see water on both sides.

■ **Tourist information**: Nordsøkaj 41.

■ There are excellent **bathing** facilities in the neighbourhood of Thyborøn and Harboør, not least along the shore of the Channel, and **angling** from the moles is permitted.

■ A tiny **ferry** crosses the Channel once an hour.

Thyborøn itself is a modern fishing port which has grown up this century on the south side of the narrow Thyborøn Channel. The harbour was constructed between 1914 and 1917. On the square, **Torvet**, you will find the anchor of a Russian frigate, the *Alexander Nevsky*, which sank off Thyborøn in 1868. The son of Tsar Alexander II was on board, and both he and virtually all the crew of 734 were brought ashore alive. Only eight members of the crew died, two of whom are buried in the churchyard in Harboør. On a totally different level, there is the attraction of the **Snail House**, a house covered with snail shells from all over the world (open summer).

The time has come to turn south again on the 181, this time making for

Lemvig, joining the 513 after 18km. 3km after this you pass the small Romanesque **Heldum Church** with some good frescoes and an altarpiece by the distinguished Jutlandic artist Niels Bjerre. The church bell, now in a belfry outside the church, is from the 14C. From here it is only 2km to **Lemvig** (pop. 19,000; **Tourist information**: Toldbodgade 4; tel. 97 82 00 77), a town with privileges dating back to 1545, lying on low ground by the Lem Bay, and surrounded by quite high terrain. It is mentioned as early as 1234, but it has never been of great significance. Nevertheless, the idyllic setting and the charm of the area give Lemvig and its surroundings an undeniable attraction.

Now you should turn south down the A28, after 8km turning left into the 521, which on your left will take you past **Kronhede Plantage** and **Klosterhede Plantage**, together forming the biggest tree plantation in the country, back to (25km) Holstebro. ◀

Returning to the main route, you leave **Holstebro** east on the A16, passing at (26km) the confluence of the Karup and Haderup rivers at **Hagebro**. This is an anglers' paradise, well provided with overnight accommodation. 5km further sees you in **Sjørup** and from here—weather being good—a short excursion south is well worth making.

Follow the 186 south for 5.5km and turn right here in the middle of nowhere into the area called **Kongenshus Mindepark**. Leave your car in the car park a little further on and have a brisk walk!

You are now in the midst of what used to be known as the **Alhede** (The Great Moorland), a desolate area which was populated in the late 18C by German settlers brought in from the Rhine and Main areas by the king in an attempt to cultivate the vast tracts of moorland covering Jutland. (Even as late as 1850 a third of all Jutland was moorland.) Each family was provided with primitive accommodation, two oxen, a cow, and implements to set about cultivating the infertile moorland. (Karup, nearby, is said to have the poorest soil in Denmark.) This they did, with great difficulty and at great expense, succeeding in cultivating first buckwheat, then rye and potatoes—for which they became known as 'Potato Germans'. They retained many of their German characteristics until the mid-19C, but have now become totally assimilated.

What is now called Kongenshus Mindepark (Kongenshus Memorial Park), covering 1200 hectares, is one of the first areas in which cultivation was attempted, in 1754. The king financed buildings here, but the original scheme was a failure—as was an attempt early in the 20C to introduce reindeer—and, ironically, the area is now a conservation area intended to preserve part of Jutland as the whole of the region once was, and to remember the many unknown men and women who spent their entire lives cultivating the moorland. The names of some 1200 others, high and low, are still known, and these have been engraved partly on the large boulders along the path in the Mindedal (Memorial Valley) and partly on the smaller stones forming a circle at the end of the valley.

Take a walk along the path here and perhaps beyond. The heather is a splendid sight when in full flower, and there are many kinds of berries and a rich and varied bird life—including the rare black grouse.

There is an hotel in the area and a small museum illustrating the flora and fauna and showing a collection of household implements associated with the cultivation of the moorland (open mid-May to end Aug).

Back on the A16 after 3km you will reach the village of Daugbjerg. To your right you will see **Daugbjerg Dås** (Daugbjerg Hill), rising 71m above the surrounding countryside, and affording a grand view of the area for those who climb it. But if that does not attract you, you should turn left to visit the abandoned lime workings, **Daugbjerg Kalkgruber**, in Dybdalsvej (open May–Aug); there are conducted tours by torchlight.

These workings, thought to date right back to the 10C, stretch underground for many kilometres, reaching a depth of 70m in places.

The mines have proved a source for legend and superstition in their time, and a gipsy woman caught here was burned as a witch on Daugbjerg Dås in 1602, accused of having eaten the hearts of six new-born children in order to become invisible: she only needed to eat a seventh in order to achieve her objective, but was, inevitably, caught in time. Blicher also set some of his most dramatic stories in the Daugbjerg mines. It is now only 18 km to Viborg (pop. 40,300), the old capital of Jutland.

Viborg

■ **Tourist information**: Nytorv 9; tel. 86 61 16 66.

■ **Hotels**: Palads, Sankt Mathiasgade 5; tel. 86 62 37 00; Golf, Randersvej 2; tel. 86 61 02 22.

■ **Youth hostel**: Vinkelvej 36; tel. 86 67 17 81.

History

Viborg is one of Denmark's really old cities, with a history going back to the 8C. The first element in its name, *vi*, suggests that it was once a sacred spot, and there is thought to have been a place of sacrifice close to where the present cathedral stands. Viborg's charter as a market town dates from 1150. For centuries this was where the nobility elected and did homage to their king—from 1027 with the election of Hardeknud (Hardecanute) until 1665 when homage was done to Prince Christian, subsequently Christian V. King Erik Glipping was crowned here in 1259 and, after being assassinated in 1286, buried before the high altar of the cathedral (though his tomb was almost entirely destroyed by fire in 1726).

Viborg was the site of one of Denmark's four regional assemblies, the seat of a bishop from 1065, the site of a stone-built cathedral from c 1130, the home of five monasteries and convents and ten other churches. It was in Viborg that Hans Tavsen launched the Reformation movement, and it was in Viborg that Skipper Klement, the leader of the peasantry during the Count's War, was hanged in 1536. The law courts were situated here, and when, in the 19C, Denmark made its first hesitant move towards popular government, one of the regional advisory assemblies was set up here.

Nevertheless, with the establishment of the Absolute Monarchy in 1661 and the gradual concentration of power and administration in Copenhagen, Viborg's importance declined, a process which was enhanced by the city's lack of easy access to the sea. As in the case with other towns in Jutland, it underwent a period of growth in the 19C with improved communications and especially the arrival of the railway, and in the 20C it has experienced

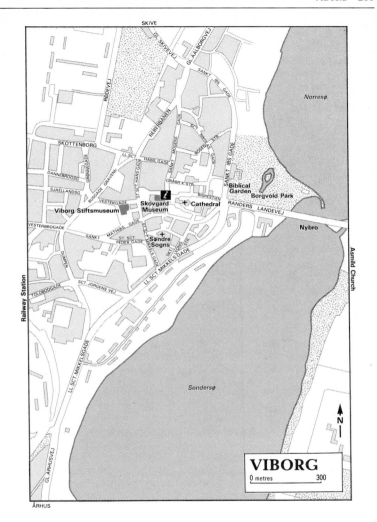

further expansion and seen the establishment of thriving industrial concerns. At the same time, much of the older part of the city remains, and it has retained the feel of an old cathedral city, combining this with the informal modernity which is a characteristic of so many Danish cities.

The old city was grouped around the ***cathedral**, but it is useless to seek in this monumental building the features which make, for instance, the cathedral in Ribe so outstanding, for little remains of the original structure from 1130 apart from the crypt. The present building dates from 1876. The original granite building, one of the largest such buildings in Europe, was demolished in 1863.

It had suffered a great deal of damage and decay—and reconstruction—over the years, and it was decided to replace it with a dignified neo-Romanesque building of grey granite, like the cathedral in Lund in Sweden inspired by Rhineland churches. It is severe in its design, but austerity is combined with a monumental grandeur, and all is now set off by the vast frescoes (1899–1906) by Joakim Skovgaard in the nave, chancel and transept, which add colour and warmth, and which are a major attraction for visitors.

The paintings on the walls of the nave depict scenes from the Old Testament, while the rather later oil paintings on the ceiling and dome represent scenes from the childhood of Christ and figures of the Prophets. The New Testament is represented in the transept, while the chancel and apse present Christ in glory. One of the qualities of these murals is Skovgaard's wish to paint in a Danish national spirit. Whether his great project is entirely successful is a moot point, and opinions are divided. Nevertheless, it should be experienced.

The nave, in which so many of these paintings are to be seen, is flanked by seven rounded arches on either side, surmounted by arcades, while the huge transept arches are similarly rounded. Most of the furniture in the cathedral is 19C, but there is a fine 14C seven-branched candlestick standing almost 3m high and a late Gothic crucifix as well as several ancient gravestones and memorial tablets.

The cathedral stands on high ground overlooking a pleasing square, and surrounded by streets with names betokening the ecclesiastical past of the city: GRÅBRØDRE KIRKESTRÆDE (Greyfriars Church Street), BISPESTIEN (Bishop's Walk), SORTEBRØDRESTRÆDE (Blackfriars Street)—and quite close by is the street with the curious forlorn designation of NAVNLØS (Nameless). These are the streets to wander about in if you want to have at least some feel of what old Viborg was like. Close by are the pedestrian streets of VESTERGADE and SANKT MATHIASGADE, busy as are all shopping precincts, but yet with a good deal of charm. In the middle of them, in HJULTORVET square, stands **Viborg Stiftsmuseum** (Viborg Diocesan Museum—formerly the town hall) with a collection of exhibits relating to the history of Viborg from prehistoric times to the present century. On DOMKIRKESTRÆDE, immediately south of the cathedral, there is the **Skovgaard Museum**, with a collection of paintings by Skovgaard and others associated with him.

Leaving the Cathedral Square at the west end, close to the Skovgaard Museum, you should go down SANKT MOGENSGADE, cross Sankt Mathiasgade and go down MAGELØS ('Matchless'), diagonally to your left. This will bring you to what is the oldest surviving church in Viborg, **Søndre Sogns Kirke**. It was once called Blackfriars Church and until 1529 was part of a 13C Dominican monastery. It is thought that the central part of the nave is actually from this original church. The remainder is later, the 23m-high tower being from 1702. The ornate gilt altarpiece, standing well forward in the nave and leaving room for a confessional behind, is an early 16C triptych carved in the Netherlands, and brought to Viborg in 1728 from the chapel in Copenhagen Castle; it has been called 'the finest of Denmark's carved Flemish altars'. The pulpit is from 1728, in its over-rich decoration reflecting the pietist domination of Danish church life at this time, culminating when the pietist Christian VI came to the throne in 1730. The closed pews, too, are decorated in the pietist spirit, with over 200 paintings by Mogens Christian Thrane. In SANKT LEONISSTRÆDE at the end of SORTEBRØDRE KIRKESTRÆDE you will find the 15C brick-built **Domprovstegård** (Dean's Residence) which in a varied career once served as a women's prison.

To the east of the cathedral, skirted by SANKT IBSGADE and RANDERS LANDEVEJ (the A16), lies the charming **Borgvold Park**, leading down to the lake which once denoted the boundary of the city. On Sankt Ibsgade, too, you will find a **Biblical Garden** containing a unique collection of plants and trees associated with the Bible. Viborg also houses comprehensive **Local History Archives** and the **Public Records Office** for North Jutland, both of which are open to the public.

On RANDERSVEJ, on the east side of the lakes the Heath Society (Hedeselskabet), which has been responsible for the cultivation—and now the preservation—of the Jutland heath, has its offices, with exhibits to which access is granted on application. Here, too, very close to the lakes stands **Asmild Church**, a very rare example of an 11C basilica, once forming the north wing of an Augustinian convent. The west part of the nave is part of the original structure. This was a very large church, with aisles on either side of the present nave, both with apses and probably both with square chancels. The low tower in the west is from c 1500. Much of the present richly decorated furniture, including the pulpit and canopy, the organ loft and the pews, is 18C, though the font is Romanesque. In the porch there is a runestone discovered in 1950.

▶Excursion from Viborg to Hald and Finderup

Total distance c 22km.

This is a short trip through beautiful countryside to a site of historic interest. You leave on the A13 south and after 6km turn right on to the A12 to (2km) **Hald**, an estate with a history going back at least to the early 14C. The present house, **Hald Hovedgård**, is the fifth to bear the name. It overlooks a beautiful lake surrounded by wooded slopes, from the top of which there is a view of Viborg in the distance. It is easy to understand why the 19C novelist Meir Aron Goldschmidt called Hald 'one of the most beautiful and most romantic places in the Kingdom of Denmark'.

The first Hald, usually called Brattingborg, is surrounded by still visible earthen mounds and a 20m-wide dry moat. In 1346 Hald was bought by Niels Bugge, one of the mightiest nobles in the land, who built a powerful castle to ensure his influence and safety. He was killed 13 years later, and his castle fell into disrepair. Nevertheless, remains of it (now known as Gammelhald—Old Hald) still stand close to the lake shore southwest of the present building. In 1528 a third castle, surrounded by massive ramparts, was built nearby on a promontory jutting out into the lake east of the present Hald. A good deal of restoration has taken place in this century, in particular the reconstruction of the tower. A fourth, and subsequently a fifth, Hald were built in the 18C. The present mansion is now used as a cultural centre. The converted barn contains an exhibition covering cultural history and natural history (open pm in summer).

If you now continue along the A12 for 2km and turn right, in a further 3km you will come to **Finderup**. This is the scene of the famous murder of King Erik Glipping in 1286. According to tradition he was murdered in a barn here, but there is little to see of this now. A house in which he is reputed to have stayed is undoubtedly not so old. However, a memorial has been placed on the most likely spot for the murder, just west of the church. From Finderup there is a minor road leading straight back to (9km) Viborg. ◀

Returning to the main route, from Viborg the A16 leads east. After 10km you should turn off on the 517 northeast to (6km) **Tjele**, a manor house with long historical associations. Indeed, Tjele claims to be the oldest manor in Denmark. Certainly, part of the present buildings date back to 1380, having survived the ravages of the Count's War, while the remainder was rebuilt in 1585.

Tjele is approached through a gateway near the church. The present offices and cafeteria are in a half-timbered house, formerly the stables dating from 1612, to your right. Here you can buy tickets for the conducted tour of part of the four-winged complex. **Sønderhuset** (The South House) is the oldest wing, perhaps the oldest extant secular building in Denmark, a strongly built two-storeyed house 10m x 17m with walls about a metre thick, a deep cellar, and an upper floor much resembling the hall in Nyborg Castle (p 196), large enough for concerts to be given in it (and the acoustics are good). The present elegant **dwelling house** (not open to the public) adjoins it. It dates from the late 16C, was originally half-timbered, but has now been partly reconstructed in brick. On the west side, facing the dwelling house, are the stables and outbuildings, while the courtyard is entered through a large gatehouse in the north, built slightly later than the dwelling house. Despite the different styles characterising the complex, it is spacious and pleasing, an idyllic and romantic remnant from the past.

The past, however, was not always idyllic. Inevitably, Tjele suffered under Skipper Klement, but it is not on account of this that it has its special place in history. In 1636 the estate was bought by one Erik Grubbe, whose daughter Marie Grubbe (1643–1718) has become famous in literature. In 1660 she was married to King Frederik III's son, Ulrik Frederik Gyldenløve, and went with him to Norway when he was appointed Viceroy. The marriage broke up in 1670, after which Marie Grubbe was married to a less exalted member of the nobility, Palle Dyre, and the couple settled in Tjele. By 1691, however, Marie Grubbe was again divorced, having embarked on an affair with a farm servant, with whom she then settled in Grønsund on the island of Falster (p 159). Here Ludvig Holberg came across her, by now a simple (and coarse) ferrywoman rowing passengers across the straits between the islands of Falster and Møn—while her husband was in prison. Her fate has been the subject of several books—by Steen Steensen Blicher, whose best novel, *The Diary of a Parish Clerk* is inspired by her story, by Hans Christian Andersen ('The Story of Hen Grethe') and by Jens Peter Jacobsen, whose novel *Marie Grubbe* is a bold and penetrating study of the psychological forces which made Marie Grubbe act as she did.

You should not leave Tjele without visiting the adjoining church. Parts of the original Romanesque structure remain, but the church was extended at the same time as additional buildings were put up for the manor in 1572, so the main part, including the tower, is now Gothic. The interior is relatively dark, but it is an impressive small church, with an atmosphere of its own, and containing a massive memorial in alabaster and marble to Geert Diderich Levetzau, who bought Tjele after the Grubbe family. This, like the enormous black Baroque sarcophagus in the porch at the west end, is the work of Fridrich Ehbisch, who was responsible for the stucco ceilings in Rosenborg in Copenhagen. Erik Grubbe is also buried here. The font is from the now vanished church in the nearby village of Foulum.

On leaving Tjele and moving north, on your left you will see the 8km-long **Tjele Langsø** (Tjele Long Lake). In 16km you join the E45, where you turn left and drive a further 4km to **HOBRO** (pop. 14,500), a small, old market town. Its earliest known charter is from 1560, but there were earlier ones going back to c 1300, and the town is certainly older still. It stands at the narrowest part of the Mariager Fjord and was thus a natural place first for a ferry, then for a bridge. In more recent times Hobro's geographical situation was enhanced by the creation of the harbour in 1834 and the advent of the main railway between North and South Jutland, which together helped create an industrial infrastructure. Nevertheless, Hobro's rural character is emphasised by its being the site of one of the biggest cattle markets in Denmark.

■ **Tourist information**: Store Torv; tel. 98 52 56 66.

■ **Hotels**: Alpina, Hostrupvej 83; tel. 98 52 28 00; Motel Hobro, Randersvej 60; tel. 98 52 28 88.

■ **Youth hostel**: Amerikavej 24; tel. 98 52 18 47.

Centred on the fjord, Hobro now spreads up on to the surrounding higher ground. The story goes that at the end of the 19C, a gathering of young people in Zürich was discussing what was the most beautiful place they had seen. Most had been to the most famous places in Europe and spoke in glowing tones. Then a young Dane got up and said, in Jutland dialect: 'Ah, but have you been to Hobro? That is the loveliest place on earth.' You may or may not go all the way with him, but the dictum has stuck, and 'Haa do wot i Hobrow?' has become the motto of the town.

Like so many other Danish towns, Hobro has been severely damaged by fire on several occasions, and thus there are few really old houses left. Nevertheless, there are still a couple in ADELGADE—the old dyer's house (No. 44) and a fine patrician house with an outdoor staircase leading to a gallery overlooking the inner courtyard (No. 73). A long half-timbered house from 1774 in VESTERGADE is now **Hobro Museum**, containing a collection of exhibits from the old Viking fortress of Fyrkat (see below), local silver, porcelain and archaeological finds from the area (open summer).

There are some other interesting buildings down by the river. **Hobro Church**, built 1850–52 by the architect Michael Gottlieb Bindesbøll, who designed the Thorvaldsen Museum in Copenhagen, is quite unusual. It combines the neo-Gothic shape of the traditional Danish village church with the alternate horizontal rows of red and yellow brick usually associated with Byzantine style. The local population must have found it too daring, and in a restoration in 1871 Bindesbøll's bold interior decorations were removed and replaced by something less startling. The present mosaic altarpiece from 1952 is the work of Johan Thomas Skovgaard, based on a 1931 design by his father Joakim Skovgaard.

A visit to **Fyrkat** is a must. To reach it you leave the town via Vestergade and drive c 2km southwest. Here lies the smallest of the four extant Viking fortresses erected towards the end of the 10C, possibly by Harald Bluetooth, all of them built in strict symmetry to the same pattern. The indications are that the original fortress was burned down at some time after it had been abandoned, and consequently only the outlines of the various buildings are now visible. The complex is enclosed inside a circular rampart 120m in diameter, with dry moats to the north and west, and consists of 16 28.4m-long houses with convex walls, arranged in groups of four around a square courtyard. Each house contained three rooms, providing living quarters for some 50 people. (Although Fyrkat was undoubtedly a fortress, it provided living accommodation for both women and children.) A smaller rectangular house stood at the centre of each courtyard.

To the northeast of the complex, which was entered by four gates on the points of the compass, there is the burial ground containing some 30 graves which yielded rich grave finds in the excavations in the 1950s. Of particular interest is a woman's grave in which the corpse was laid in a carriage containing jewels and a chest of personal belongings. A quarter of Fyrkat has not yet been excavated, the decision having been made to leave it for future archaeologists. Just outside the complex itself stands a reconstruction of one of the houses. Remember that the principal treasures found in Fyrkat are on display in the museum in Hobro. In the nearby Fyrkat Møllegård there is a 225-year-old watermill. The fortress area and the watermill are open to the public from Easter to the end of August. There is a cafeteria nearby.

▶Excursion from Hobro to Klejtrup and to Snæbum
Total distance c 29km.

To take this short trip, with something for children and something for those interested in archaeology, you should drive west on the 579 for 11km and then turn left for 3km along a minor road to **Klejtrup**. Here at the south end of the lake there is a large-scale (50m × 100m) **Map of the World**, with land-masses built of boulders and earth in the shape of the continents, and with water from the lake representing the oceans. The main rivers are there, and the major mountain chains, and each country is marked with its own national flag. Close by on a promontory to the southwest lies **Klejtrup Voldsted**, the ramparts of a now vanished castle, by legend said to have belonged to the medieval hero Niels Ebbesen, who slew the Holstein Count Gert and liberated Jutland from foreign rule. However, it is also attributed to other historical or legendary figures. What is certain is that it is early medieval.

Now drive north again, across the 579 to (6km) **Snæbum**, where there are three huge double passage graves dating back to c 3000 BC. One has been badly damaged, but the other two are among Denmark's best preserved passage graves. Nearby you will find 15 burial mounds, of which 13 are aligned on a slope to the southeast of the village. Open all year round.

From Snæbum you return to (9km) Hobro. ◀

20 • Middelfart to Holstebro

Total distance 136km. 421 to (10km) **Fredericia**. *(25km)* **Vejle**. *A18 to (11km)*
Jelling. *(29km) Brande. (26km)* **Herning**. *(35km)* **Holstebro**.

From Middelfart (p 176), you will automatically cross Lillebælt (p 28) via the old
bridge and follow an unclassified road to (10km) **FREDERICIA** (pop. 46,950).

■ **Tourist information**: Danmarksgade 2A; tel. 75 92 13 77.

■ **Hotels**: Kronprinds Frederik, Vestre Ringvej 96; tel 75 91 00 00; Hybylund,
Fælledvej 58; tel. 75 91 15 81.

■ **Youth hostel**: Skovløbervænget 9; tel. 75 93 29 05.

■ **Fredericia Hall**, on Vestre Ringvej, claims to be the largest **sports centre**
under one roof in Denmark, offering a vast range of activities.

History

Fredericia is a city of historical importance, though it was not founded until
1650, when Frederik III created it as a fortress. Seven years later it was
overrun by the Swedes, and all the Danish defenders were killed.

Among pre-19C Danish cities the town planning of Fredericia is unique,
in that all the streets within the original fortifications run in parallel
straight lines, intersecting at right angles. Thanks to its strategic position
and its function from 1679 as a garrison town, Fredericia suffered attack
during the Dano-Prussian wars of 1848 and 1864; it was besieged by
Schleswig-Holstein troops from May to July 1849, and in the 1864 war was
actually taken and occupied by Austrian troops. On 6 July each year the
Battle of Fredericia, which broke the 1849 siege though with heavy Danish
losses, is commemorated in the town. A harbour was opened at Fredericia
in 1808, and has gradually been extended until it now offers some 3000m
of quays. Fredericia's position as a major railway junction began to emerge
in 1866, when the first railway line was opened. This was followed by the
opening of a ferry harbour in 1872 linking Fredericia with Strib on Fyn.
The opening of the first bridge over Lillebælt in 1935 brought increased
railway traffic.

Until 1909 Fredericia remained a fortress, surrounded by the still-
existing ramparts which are the most extensive of their kind in northern
Europe, extending in all for 5.5km and now forming a green belt between
the old town and the modern developments which came post 1909. One of
the old city gateways, **Prinsens Port**, still stands, as do a powder magazine
from 1675 and gun positions from 1849.

A particular feature of Fredericia's history is the right of religious
freedom which it received in 1674 and 1682. The first Jew was granted citi-
zenship in 1679, and by 1719 there was a sufficiently large Jewish
community to warrant the establishment of a synagogue. A Catholic
mission was established in 1674, and by 1686 a small wooden church had

been consecrated. This was replaced by a permanent building in 1767. Around 1720 large numbers of French Protestants (Huguenots) settled in Fredericia, and consequently a Reformed Church was consecrated in 1736.

When permission to expand Fredericia was granted in 1908, one of the first buildings to appear was the **watertower** which stands on the ramparts and dominates the town to this day. Open to the public in the summer, it offers a view of the ramparts and the older part of the town. The ramparts themselves are covered with grass and bushes, but efforts are now being made (especially near the watertower) to restore parts of them to their original state.

In a town with a history such as that of Fredericia, it is clear that there will be national and military memorials to visit. Most famous of these is Herman Wilhelm Bissen's 1858 bronze statue of the Danish Soldier, **Landsoldaten**, standing where DANMARKSGADE and NORGESGADE meet near the ramparts at PRINSENS PORT. The statue was financed through voluntary contributions from the whole country. More bombastic is Bissen's bust of General Bülow standing in a triumphal arch near the town hall. This, too, was paid for by voluntary contributions, as was that to General Olaf Rye standing on RYES PLADS.

Two touching monuments are to be found in the cemetery of **Trinitatis Kirke**. One is to the 500 soldiers killed when the Swedes took the town in 1657, the other, a monument by Bissen showing two soldiers laying a dead comrade in the grave, marks the common grave of those who fell in the 1849 Battle of Fredericia. A memorial of an entirely different kind is that at Oldenborgs Bastion to Danish railway workers killed on duty.

Trinitatis Kirke is the principal church, dating from 1690. It contains eight impressive stained glass windows, an ornate Baroque altar from 1692, and a Romanesque font, presumably moved there from a disused church in the abandoned village of Ullerup. The font is surmounted by a splendid canopy. The neo-classical **Michaelis Kirke**, in VENDERSGADE, was built in 1665–67, but the present building is a modern reconstruction after a fire in 1955. Both the Reformed Church from 1735 and the Catholic Church from 1767 still stand.

Fredericia boasts a great number of parks. One of the best is **Madsbyparken**, close to the railway station, containing a large play park for children—including an Indian encampment and a Stone Age hut for children to play in. There are pens with domestic animals, and a large artificial lake for rowing boats.

Fredericia Museum is in JERNBANEGADE and is centred on six half-timbered houses with relics not only from the military past, but also exhibits relating to the four religious persuasions associated with the town. There is a garden of herbs—including tobacco, which was introduced to Fredericia by the Huguenots.

At RIDDERGADE 15 you will find a plaque in memory of the great 19C novelist Henrik Pontoppidan, born in this house in 1857. The son of a pastor, Pontoppidan broke with family tradition and became one of the leading representatives of the Modern Movement, in the eyes of many Denmark's most important novelist ever.

Leaving Fredericia, you continue north on the 421. At (6km) Egeskov you can turn off right to the beautiful area of **Trelde Næs**, unspoiled natural scenery, studded with half-timbered houses. The village of **Trelde** (2km) consists almost entirely of dwellings of this kind.

From Trelde Næs you proceed to (19km) Vejle, passing on your way near **Brejning** a remarkable twelve-sided church, designed by Mogens Koch and built between 1965 and 1976, and the delightful **Børkop watermill** (the motif of a 1962 postage stamp), now owned by the State and beautifully restored. It is used for cultural events and contains a restaurant.

Approaching **VEJLE** (pop. 52,550) you will see the **Vejle Windmill** (1847) to the left of the road (open summer).

■ **Tourist information**: Den Smidtske Gård, Søndergade 14; tel. 75 82 19 55.

■ **Hotels**: Andersens, Kirketorvet 12; tel. 79 42 79 10; Motel Hedegaarden, Valdemar Poulsenvej 4; tel. 75 82 08 33.

■ **Youth hostel**: Gammel Landevej 80; tel. 75 82 51 88.

Vejle lies in the midst of one of the hilliest and most idyllic parts of Denmark. The name means ford, and Vejle used to be just that. The E45 motorway now by-passes the town, carried across the fjord on yet another of the imposing bridges in this region; but until 1980 all traffic north and south on the east side of Jutland had to go through Vejle's narrow winding streets. Now the town has undergone a period of transformation allowing it to establish new open spaces, carefully regulate traffic, beautify its streets and regain its old charm. This, together with the surrounding tree-covered hills, makes Vejle unique in Denmark. Some would talk of its alpine qualities—though the height of the hills barely qualifies for that—others would say, with some justification, that it is the most beautifully situated town in Denmark. Moreover, it gives easy access to magnificent **beaches**, and offers countless opportunities for outdoor **activities**: bathing, riding, sailing, fishing and, not least, walking in the exquisite surroundings.

History

Vejle is first mentioned at the end of the 13C, receiving a charter in 1327. It did not play a large part in the events of the Middle Ages, but suffered badly during the 17C Swedish wars and, in 1659, from a visitation of the plague. Not until the 19C did Vejle really begin to show signs of life again, and it was only with the completion of the new harbour in 1827 that conditions in the town began to improve. During the Schleswig-Holstein wars Vejle was occupied on several occasions. The great leap came with the arrival of the railway in 1868, bringing in its wake the new and varied industries which still characterise the town.

Once you have crossed the Vejle river, you should make use of the good parking facilities and walk through the winding, hilly streets of the old town. Where the main road crosses KIRKEGADE/HAVNEGADE, you will, on the left, find KIRKETORVET square (parking). The church here, **Sankt Nicolai Church**, can claim to be the oldest building in Vejle, with a north wall from the mid-13C, though most of the rest is 19C. On view inside is a woman from c 450 BC, discovered in a bog in 1835—and fixed in the north wall there are 23 skulls, possibly of criminals executed in the 16C.

From here you could walk down Kirkegade to SØNDERGADE, where you will find **Den Smidtske Gård**. This merchant's house from 1799 was restored in 1985 and now, in addition to housing the tourist information office, forms part of **Vejle Kulturhistoriske Museum** (Vejle Museum of Cultural History). Here you will find an exhibition illustrating the history of Vejle. The section of the museum situated nearby at FLEGBORG 18 is mainly dedicated to local archaeology. Flegborg 16 is the art gallery, **Vejle Kunstmuseum**, with a permanent exhibition of paintings and sculptures from 1850 to the present, with the emphasis on modern works. It also contains a very extensive collection of graphic art.

Also in Flegborg is Vejle's new **Music Theatre** a cultural centre with theatres, workshop facilities, restaurant and hotel. At VEDELSGADE 27 you will find Danmarks Sportsmuseum (Tues–Fri 11.00–16.00) and close by, at GRØNNEGADE 24, there is now a golf museum with four rooms displaying items of both historical and contemporary interest (limited opening).

▶Before continuing your journey, you might make an excursion to **Grejsdal valley** (c 3km), a wooded idyll, a bird sanctuary of great beauty. To reach it, take the A18 and turn right on the outskirts of the town at the top of Gormsgade. ◀

Between Vejle and Brande 40km further on, there are two routes, a fundamental choice between spectacular ancient monuments and the children's paradise of Legoland. The first route goes via Jelling; the alternative route (58km) via Billund.

From Vejle to Brande via Jelling
Total distance 40km.

Leave Vejle by the steep A18 road leading northwest to (11km) **Jelling**, a spot inextricably related to early Danish kingship, and the site of the earliest known residence of a king of all Denmark. (Railway enthusiasts can travel by vintage railway from Vejle on Sun in July.)

Jelling village (**Tourist information**: Gormsgade 4) itself is of modest interest—though the countryside you pass through on the way there is charming. The real attraction is the two enormous ****Jelling Stones**, undoubtedly the most famous of all Scandinavian runestones, and now, together with Jelling church, included on UNESCO's list of the most important cultural monuments in the world. They stand immediately south of the present church, between two huge burial *mounds measuring between 60m and 70m in diameter and standing

The runestones at Jelling

7–8m high—so vast that even the church is dwarfed by them, though it is by no means a small church for its time. The murals inside indicate that it has stood there since the 12C, when it replaced an earlier (probably 10C) wooden structure. Excavations in the 1940s and 1950s revealed traces of a yet earlier heathen temple beneath this wooden church. It appears, therefore, that the present church and churchyard occupy the central positions in what was once a heathen temple complex. A series of standing stones marks the outline of the temple.

The more northerly of the two mounds, known as Gorm's Mound, was excavated in vain as early as 1607, but farmers digging in it in 1820 came across a wooden burial chamber 6.8m × 2.6m × 1.5m. It contained a wooden coffin, but no corpse. The south mound, Thyra's Mound, was excavated in 1861, but no burial chamber was found.

The two *runestones, sometimes referred to as 'Denmark's baptismal certificate' appear to be connected with these mounds. The smaller of them bears the inscription 'King Gorm made these runes in memory of Thyra his wife, the pride of Denmark'. The larger stone stands 2.43m high; on one side it is engraved with the figure of a lion, and on the other a figure of Christ. An inscription runs: 'King Harald had these runes made in memory of Gorm his father and Thyra his mother, Harald who conquered all Denmark and Norway and made the Danes Christian.'

Gorm and Thyra

There is thus a theory that the heathen Gorm built the north mound for his wife Thyra and raised the runestone in her memory, probably himself being buried in the mound beside her. Harald Bluetooth was then responsible for the second, Christian, stone, and it is likely that he had the bodies of his parents removed and buried in the wooden church he had built on the site of the temple which Gorm had erected in his day. The romantic idea was that he did this in order to give his parents a Christian burial, but a modern and more sceptical theory is that he did it in order to ensure his own right of inheritance.

Gorm is generally accepted to be the first Danish king, from whom the present Danish royal family is descended. Thyra may have been an English princess, though this is not certain. Tradition has it that she was responsible for the construction of the Danevirke fortifications which once denoted the border between Denmark and Germany.

There is a small museum providing further information on the site at HYGUMVEJ 36, close to the church.

From Jelling the A18 leads to (8km) **Givskud**, where to the left of the main road there is a large modern zoo and safari park with over 100 different species of animals, including some tame animals for the children (open mid-Apr to mid-Oct).

The Military Road

Just after the safari park you will find a road off right towards Nørre Kollemorten and Øster Nykirke. The road will be marked as an historical monument with the usual sign, and is referred to as **Hærvejen**. In southern and mid Jutland you may already have seen signs indicating Hærvejen, and you are likely to come across more: it means Military Road, but this is a name ascribed to it by a

German cartographer in the 17C, and it gives a wrong impression of its use and its history. Also known at one time as the Ox Road, it is an ancient route following the ridge of high—and hence dry—ground in the centre of Jutland. It was used by travellers, vagabonds, pilgrims and drovers, between the Danevirke fortifications (now in Germany) and Viborg. It was not a single, well defined path, and sometimes divided into different strands. Stretches of it are now a road suitable for traffic, while other parts are still more in the nature of a track. It is a favourite route for cyclists and hikers, well equipped with camping facilities, ancient inns and youth hostels, and although it does pass through a few large villages and smaller towns, it will not take you through the major centres. It thus offers a quiet, idyllic route from north to south often affording panoramic views of the Jutlandic countryside, much of it dotted with burial mounds.

You might like to follow the Hærvej as far as **Øster Nykirke** (9km), where you will find, 130m above sea level, a Romanesque church with a Gothic tower and 19C porch. It stands just west of a medieval place of pilgrimage, a sacred spring, **Sankt Peders Kilde**, traces of which are still to be seen on the opposite side of the road.

From Givskud the A18 continues to (20km) Brande (see below).

Alternative route from Vejle to Brande—via Legoland
Total distance 58km.

Take the A28 west towards Billund. This brings you at 7km to **Skibet**, where there is a Romanesque church with Gothic extensions, largely rebuilt in the 18C, Romanesque tympanum, and a series of frescoes discovered in 1952. Of particular interest is the frieze stretching over five arcades depicting a unique row of knights on horseback. The significance of these riders is uncertain, though one seems to be a Knight Templar, suggesting a possible reference to the legend of the Holy Grail.

A further 8km along the A28 you can turn off to the right to see **Engelsholm** (1.5km), a mansion in the French-Italian Renaissance style, with domed towers which are echoed in the associated Nørup church on the opposite side of the lake, and clearly visible from the park. You can walk in the surrounding woods and even get right up to the house, now a folk high school, but you cannot go inside.

Return now to the A28 and follow it to (13km) Billund where you can visit Legoland (p 27).

From Billund you take the 176 north; this merges with the A30, takes you through Give to (18km) the A18, where you turn left and proceed to (12km) Brande.

Brande (pop. 8535; **Tourist information**: Stationsvej 1; tel 97 18 16 08). The town is associated with Ernesto Dalgas, who was famous for his efforts to cultivate the Jutland heath in the second half of the 19C. There is a memorial stone to him in a park opposite the church. Brande also made itself a name in the 1960s when a group of young artists was allowed to decorate 24 gable ends in very bright colours.

Beyond Brande the A18 leads to 12km **Arnborg**, where the simple, unadorned Romanesque church has a carved altarpiece from 1608. A further 2km ahead a narrow road leads off right to **Søby** (4km). Here you will find a *museum illustrating the development of the nearby lignite mines—to which there is public access. Lignite was mined here in great quantities during World War II, as Denmark could no longer obtain proper coal. Great numbers of unemployed (at one time as many as 5000) flocked here to work the mines, living in primitive conditions; all is graphically presented to the visitor. This strange, desolate area covers some 100 hectares.

Returning to the A18, you continue to (12km) **HERNING** (pop. 57, 570).

■ **Tourist information**: Bredgade 2; tel. 97 12 44 22.

■ **Hotels**: Eyde, Torvet; tel. 97 22 18 00; Corona, Skolegade 1; tel. 97 12 54 44.

■ **Youth hostel**: Holingknuden 2; tel. 97 12 31 44.

From being a tiny, out-of-the-way moorland village, Herning has experienced rapid growth over the past hundred years, and was given a charter in 1913. Conveniently placed for modern transport, it has attracted a large amount of modern industry—clothing, carpets, furniture, printing, computers—and with the space available all has been arranged so as to give a sense of light and air, nothing at all of the traditional industrial atmosphere.

And industry is here closely associated with art. Herning prides itself on its artistic achievements, and they are in turn based on its industries. A far-sighted shirt manufacturer realised that by putting a minute surcharge (less than 1p) on his shirts, he could afford to invest in works by artists some of whom have subsequently achieved international fame—Robert Jacobsen, Sven Dalsgaard and Svend Wiig Hansen. Carl-Henning Pedersen, who is responsible for the murals in Ribe Cathedral (p 205), provided the factory with a 200m-long frieze, and has since established his own gallery nearby. Even the hospital is filled with paintings, to give it an intimate feel far removed from the usual sterile atmosphere.The interest in art is immediately obvious in the town, and a walk through the pedestrian precinct will demonstrate this to the full. The entire area is dotted with **sculptures**, most, but not all, by modern Danish artists. Others are scattered around the town, including a Henry Moore in front of the Congress Centre, **Herning Kongrescenter** in ØSTERGADE.

There are few old buildings in Herning, the oldest being the architecturally outstanding mansion of **Herningsholm**, on the A12 at VIBORGVEJ 72, 2km north of the central area. Said to be the most important piece of secular architecture in central Jutland, this house from 1579 has been tastefully restored and converted into a **museum for Steen Steensen Blicher**. Blicher's stories are so totally identified with the Jutland heath that it is natural for a town which itself has been part of the heath to honour him in this way. In addition to original manuscripts and first editions of Blicher's works, the museum contains illustrations to his work, paintings of the moorland with which he was associated, and the only known painting for which Blicher himself sat. There is also a room illustrating the history of Herningsholm. The carillon plays at 11.00, 13.00 and 15.00 (open May–Oct).

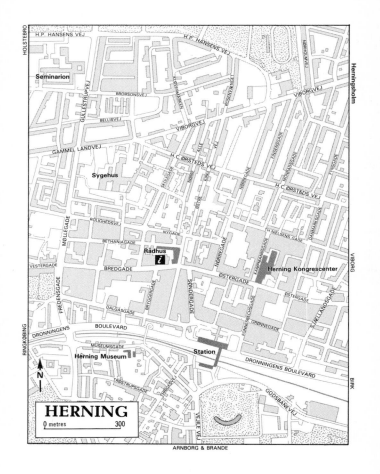

HERNING

0 metres — 300

Just south of the town centre you will find **Herning Museum** in MUSEUMSGADE. This is one of the first public museums to be opened in Denmark, dating from 1892, and is partly an open air museum, with buildings including a traditional moorland knitting room and illustrating the history of Jutland from prehistoric times. In Museumsgade, too, you will find the museum of photography, **Danmarks Fotomuseum**.

Inevitably, some of the places of interest are a little way from the centre. As mentioned above, Herningsholm is about 2km north, on the A12/34. After visiting it, you should go back and take the A15 east in the direction of

Silkeborg. In 3km, in **Birk**, you come to **Herning Kunstmuseum** (Herning Art Gallery). This is the former shirt factory where it all began, and in addition to the impressive frieze by Carl-Henning Pedersen it contains a comprehensive collection of modern Danish and international art. Close by, in a building which is an architectural attraction in itself, is the **Carl-Henning Pedersen og Else Alfelt Gallery**, which, as the name suggests, is dedicated to the work of these two artists. Adjacent is a sculpture park in which modern Danish and international sculptors are represented. And adjoining this again are the **Geometrical Gardens**, a park based on geometrical principles and designed by C.Th. Sørensen, who was also responsible for the layout of both the sculpture park and the Herning Kunstmuseum.

1km further brings you to **Hammerum**, the site of the only Japanese garden in Denmark, 3000 sq m laid out as a typical Zen garden. And from Hammerum it is only 2km along a minor road north from the A15 to **Gjellerup Kirkeby** which boasts the oldest dated church in Denmark. A lintel over a now bricked-up south door bears the date 1140. The nave and chancel are both Romanesque, though there are inevitably Gothic additions. Inside, there is a beamed ceiling, an unusual chancel arch 5m high, and several interesting items of church furniture.

From Herning you continue along the A18 to (6km) **Tjørring**. Here, in what is now a dormitory of Herning, there is an idiosyncratic modern church from 1977 with a roof sweeping up to form a tower, the whole looking rather like a wigwam—though an aerial view shows it to be in the shape of a Maltese cross. Inside, of course, it is circular. It forms a complete contrast to the other, Romanesque, church in Tjørring. Drive on to (14km) **Avlum**, where there is another church, this time one with an unusually richly carved gallery, and then finally to (15km) Holstebro (p 278).

21 • Holstebro to Thisted

*Total distance 84km. A11 to (16km) Struer. (32km) Ydby. (36km) **Thisted**.*

The direct route from Holstebro to Struer on the A11 is quick and easy, but has little of interest to offer. A longer route (33km), east of the direct route, is a little more interesting. So we suggest that you leave Holstebro on the 189 and drive northeast for 8km, turning right here on to a minor road leading to **Borbjerg** (4km), where the Romanesque church has a most unusual antemensale very reminiscent of the golden altar in Sahl (p 260), though the product of a slightly different technique. It dates from 1200, and is made of copper-covered carved oak richly gilded. In the centre is Christ enthroned, surrounded by the Evangelists, and there are 24 more panels representing scenes from the life of Christ. The altarpiece, too, is interesting, the oldest section being English, from c 1425, representing St George slaying the Dragon. On the opposite side of the lake from the church there is an old watermill, now a restaurant.

Driving north on the 189 again you can, at 6km, catch a glimpse of **Rydhave** on your left. The original Rydhave mansion dates back to the 14C and was once in the possession of the Rosenkrantz and Gyldenstjerne families (shades of Hamlet?). The present buildings date from the mid-16C. The adjoining woods, planted in the 19C, constitute the most westerly beech forest in Denmark.

Now follow the 189 to (3km) Vinderup, there turning left on to the 513 to drive along the low-lying coast to (12km) **Struer** (pop. 19,300).

■ **Tourist information**: Rådhuspladsen; tel. 97 85 07 95.

■ **Hotels**: Grand, Østergade 24; tel. 97 85 04 00; Humlum Kro, Vesterbrogade 4, Humlum; tel. 97 86 17 64.

■ **Youth hostel**: Fjordvejen 12, Bremdal; tel. 97 85 53 13.

Struer is one of Denmark's most recent market towns, its charter dating back only to 1917. The home of Bang & Olufsen, Struer has little to offer in the way of old and architecturally interesting buildings, though it is not without the charm of a Danish provincial town. The excellent **Struer Museum**, at SØNDERGADE 23, is housed in the oldest building in the town, and specialises in local cultural history from the last 500 years (open summer; limited opening winter). The old fire engine house in BJERGGADE is now a museum showing the history of a provincial fire brigade.

Take the A11 north now, driving across the bridge, perhaps turning off to the right after 2km to visit the 8km-long island of **Venø** (pop. 147), which is reached by ferry (sailing time 2 minutes). Venø claims to possess the smallest church in Denmark, no more than 9.8m × 4.2m plus a tiny porch.

Back on the A11 you now drive north towards the bridge at (8km) **Oddesund** sound. (West of the road just before you reach the sound there are splendid bathing and camping facilities in the beautiful area of **Toftum Bjerge**.) The 472m-long Oddesund Bridge linking West Jutland with Thy in North Jutland was opened in 1938.

The interest in this immediate neighbourhood is as much in the impressive scenery as in buildings and towns. Almost any road will bring you breathtaking views across the many sounds and fjords, with an archipelago ranging from tiny islets to the largest island in the Limfjord, Mors. These are the waters where many of the great Viking invasions of England were prepared, the place of departure for the invading ships of the Knuds (Canutes).

9km north of the sound you by-pass the village of **Hvidbjerg**, just to the right of the main road. It is one of three villages in the area all called by the same name ('white-hill') because of the limestone in the ground. The large church in Hvidbjerg contains some quite realistic frescoes showing a farmer driving a team of two white horses, with a castle in the background. A figure of Jonas being devoured by the whale hangs in the north chapel. According to legend the Bishop of Børglum was murdered here in 1260, an event depicted in Hans Christian Andersen's *The Bishop of Børglum and his Family*.

13km further north on the A11 you will arrive at **Ydby**.

The area around here has a special character because of the many Bronze Age **burial mounds**—some 200—found in all directions. Some, of course, have been more or less ploughed in, but many are clearly visible and now subject to conservation orders. Some stand singly, but others are grouped together. Thus a group of 35 lies in the immediate neighbourhood of the church, and one of similar size in the Dover Plantation to the east. Slightly further to the south, in **Ydby Hede** heath, you will find a group of over 50. There is also a well-preserved dolmen chamber. On the Boddum peninsula, a couple of kilometres further on, there are the remains of another 80 burial mounds.

There are two possible routes from Ydby to Thisted. The direct route (36km) is listed first; the alternative route is given below.

Direct route from Ydby to Thisted
Total distance 36km.

Continue further along the A11 passing close to (5km) **Hurup**, the birthplace of the painter Jens Søndergaard. Then carry on driving north to (2km) **Heltborg**, where there is a restored old windmill. Yet another kilometre, on the right, there is a farm called **Østergård** where there is a burial mound containing a remarkably well-preserved passage grave, to which there is public access. A stone-lined passage leads to the 6.5m-long burial chamber giving on to a small chamber 2m × 2m.

6km further you reach **Villerslev**, where the outwardly rather modest church contains a wealth of post-Reformation murals discovered in 1973.

Immediately beyond Villerslev we suggest you leave the A11 and turn right on to an equally good coastal road leading through Skyum to (7km) **Skyum Bjerge**, a beautiful stretch of coastline with a magnificent beach suitable for bathing. As you drive north along this road you have the most splendid views across the Vilsund Sound, first of the island of Mors, then (at 6km) of the Vilsund bridge, and beyond that again the fjord with Thisted in the background.

Vilsund Sound is 8km long in all and as much as 1.5km wide. The bridge across it was designed by Anker Engelund, who was also responsible for the old Lillebælt Bridge (p 29) and the Storstrømsbro bridge (p 139), and was opened in 1939. It was widened in 1976.

From Vilsund Bridge it is 10km to Thisted (see below).

Alternative route from Ydby to Thisted—via Vestervig and Vorupør
Total distance c 55km.

From Ydby you drive west on the 527, passing at 4km **Ashøj** hill, the highest point (94m) in Thy.

4km further on, in **Vestervig**, you should visit the **museum** (open school summer holidays) in the old Judge's House as well as the church. Not only does the museum contain a pictorial history of the church but it possesses a collection of materials illustrating the history of schooling in the area.

The famous **Vestervig Church** is the biggest village church in Denmark. Its size is impressive and is explained by the fact that there was a Bishop of Vestervig in the 12C. The present church once formed the north wing of an Augustinian monastery which was destroyed in the 17C. It is 54m long, consisting of a nave and two aisles, and retains something of its original Romanesque character despite much rebuilding in the 15C and subsequently. It was finally thoroughly restored in 1917–21. However, the main attraction for the tourist is undoubtedly the *churchyard, with its unusual number of Romanesque gravestones. One, near the north door, is of particular interest, the traditional grave of Liden Kirsten (Little Kirsten) and her lover Prince Buris, the two placed not side by side, but end to end. The gravestone, 3.4m long and 50cm wide, decorated with two crosses and a now almost entirely illegible inscription, is from c 1200. An examination of the grave in 1875 showed that it does indeed contain two bodies, those of a man and a woman, lying end to end. Tradition has it that they are those of Valdemar I's sister Kirsten, and Burislejf Sverkersøn, the half-brother of Queen Sophie. Attempts to interpret the inscription, however, seem to indicate that the bodies are those of a brother and a sister.

Liden Kirsten

The ballad of *Liden Kirsten* (for which there appears to be no historical foundation) tells the following story: Queen Sophie asks King Valdemar if his sister might marry her brother, Buris. The king scornfully rejects the suit, calling Buris a horse thief, and Sophie vows revenge. While Valdemar is away at the wars, Sophie encourages Buris to seduce Kirsten, and when he at first refuses, she cuts magic runes and thus casts a spell on him. He now does the deed, and Kirsten gives birth to a child on the very day on which King Valdemar returns. When Valdemar discovers what has happened, he whips Kirsten to death and has her buried in Vestervig. He then has Buris' eyes put out, his left foot and right hand chopped off, and his right arm broken, and then chains him outside the church of Vestervig, from where he can just reach the grave of the girl whom he has after all genuinely loved. The supposed burial end to end would be the final act of cruelty representing hatred going beyond the grave, though the ballad says nothing of this. In recent years it has become the custom for local brides to place a bunch of flowers on 'Liden Kirsten's Grave'.

From Vestervig you should drive north up the 527/181 to (19km) **Stenbjerg**, there turning on to the 571 left to visit the lifeboat museum (2km) at STENBJERG KIRKEVEJ 53 right down on the North Sea coast (open summer).

Return now to the 181 and continue a further 4km to the small fishing village of **Nørre Vorupør**, where there is a North Sea Aquarium containing 20 large pools of North Sea fish (open summer).

From Nørre Vorupør you take the 539 east towards Thisted. On the western outskirts of (10km) Hundborg we suggest you take an unclassified road north just to visit **Jannerup Church** (2km). Looking quite modest on the outside, the church here is richly decorated inside and shows signs of considerable wealth, presumably resulting from votive gifts from pilgrims to the holy spring of St Andrew which was once nearby, and, it is thought, from shipwrecked sailors giving thanks for deliverance. It retained its special status after the Reformation, as is indicated by the superb furniture in it. This includes a magnificent carved altar presented to the church in 1648, the work of Peder Jensen Kolding. To the left of the altar there is an equally splendid carved confessional from 1688. The only slightly less elaborate parish clerk's seat to the right of the altar dates from

1693. The pulpit, from 1675, is decorated with ornate carvings, and the ceiling with allegorical paintings.

From Hundborg you continue northeast to (7km) **Sjørring**. Here you will first see on your left **Sjørring Volde**, a 10C mound on which a royal castle once stood, and which is now sometimes used for open air performances. On your right, opposite the mound, is the large Romanesque church from 1160. The north door, still in use, is flanked by a column on either side surmounted by a rounded arch; the south door is still more ornate, with two columns on either side, supporting two concentric arches. The altarpiece is from 1640, and the elaborately carved pulpit from 1639. The tower was built in 1929.

There are two famous Romanesque **bishops' graves** in the churchyard, dating back to the 13C. On one of them there is a carved figure of a bishop, presumably St Nicholas of Myra. According to one legend it is the grave of a bishop from Børglum who was drowned in the North Sea. Another legend has it that it contains an English bishop who fled from the Black Death—but brought it with him.

From Sjørring it is only 7km to **Thisted** (pop. 29,550)

■ **Tourist information**: Det Gamle Rådhus, Store Torv 6; tel. 97 92 19 00.

■ **Hotels**: Limfjorden, Simons Bakke 39; tel. 97 92 40 11; Thisted, Frederiksgade 16; tel. 97 92 52 00.

■ **Youth hostel**: Kongemøllevej 8, Skinnerup; tel. 97 92 50 42.

■ **Thisted has a fine marina**, and this beautiful stretch of the Limfjord affords splendid opportunities for **sailing** and **windsurfing**.

■ There is an open air stage in the Christiansgave park, with regular summer entertainments.

History

Thisted lies in an area which still shows ample traces of prehistoric and Viking settlement. Even its name indicates this, like that of its county, *Thy*, stemming from the name of the god Tyr.

The earliest known allusion to Thisted is from 1367, when it was referred to as a village of the same status as Hovsør. Hovsør, once used as a winter harbour by Thisted, is now a very small village, 10km along the coast to the east. Nevertheless, it was Thisted which grew, and by 1524 it was granted a charter giving its citizens the same rights as those in Viborg. It was the seat of a Lutheran bishop from 1542–48. Yet its situation on the Limfjord, with limited access to the open sea, and with Ålborg in a much more favourable situation, limited its possibilities of expansion. After a series of fires in the 17C, as well the sufferings brought about by the 17C wars, it was steadily reduced in size until the establishment of the harbour in 1840—and the subsequent advent of the railway system—led to steady growth. Before the harbour was built, ships had to be loaded and unloaded away from land, and the cargoes taken to and fro by lighter; and in winter this was not possible. With the establishment of the channel between Agger and Thyborøn in 1825, making the west part of the Limfjord accessible to ocean-going ships, a harbour suitable for year-round sailing had become a near necessity.

Thisted is a charming and lively town with well designed older buildings like the **old town hall** contrasting strongly with its modern replacement from 1978, with its elegant exhibition facilities. Careful restoration work has been undertaken in the area around NYTORV square.

There is a sizeable 16C **church**, replacing an older Romanesque church, and incorporating some of the granite ashlars from it. Some of these are decorated with sculpted heads, animals or designs which are clearly visible. The church was tastefully restored in 1973 to produce an interior of great charm. The large altarpiece, a triptych from c 1520, has the Virgin and Child as its central figures with St Paul and Mary Magdalene on either side; the 12 Apostles are represented in side panels. Beneath is a painting of the Last Supper. The pulpit is from 1594. The slender octagonal spire rises 44m above ground level and is a landmark seen from far around. There is a runestone in the south wall, with the name Thord Amdissøn clearly engraved in runic lettering.

The Thisted Museum, **Museet for Thy og Vester Hanherred**, contains a very large collection of Bronze Age finds from the surrounding area. The museum also has exhibits of local rural life, as well as the Jens Peter Jacobsen room. Art lovers will find several of the Expressionist Jens Søndergaard's paintings exhibited in the **Thisted Library**.

Thisted was the birthplace of Chresten Kold (1816–70), the driving force in the Grundtvigian high school movement. The town was also the site of the first cooperative store in Denmark, founded by Pastor H.C. Sonne in 1866, inspired by the 1844 store in Rochdale, England.

Jens Peter Jacobsen

Thisted is inevitably associated with the great 19C novelist and poet Jens Peter Jacobsen (1847–85). Jacobsen's production was small, consisting of his poetry, two novels and half a dozen novellas or short stories. Yet both as a stylist and as a pioneering naturalist his influence on literature, not only in Denmark and Scandinavia as a whole, but outside Scandinavia (especially in Germany), was enormous in its day. His poem *Gurresange*, telling the story of King Valdemar and his mistress Tove, forms the text for Schönberg's *Gurrelieder*, while the English composer Delius, whose links with Scandinavia were legion, not only set some of his poems to music, but he also used part of the novel *Niels Lyhne* for the action of his opera *Fennimore and Gerda*. Jacobsen's birthplace in Skolestræde is now a scheduled monument. Jacobsen was buried in Thisted, and his grave is marked on the otherwise grassed-over old churchyard opposite the church.

▶Excursion from Thisted to the North Sea
Total distance 45km.

Leave Thisted on the A26 north, turning left into the 557 after 4km. After a further 12km you reach **Klitmøller**, a small fishing village with excellent facilities for bathing, windsurfing and fishing. In the 18C it was a thriving small port, but other towns have long since overtaken it. It is well provided with cafés and restaurants as well as overnight accommodation.

You now have a very fascinating drive north, close to the sea and with the 4000 hectares of the magnificent **Hanstholm Wild Life Reserve** on your right. After 10km you arrive at **Hanstholm**.

■ **Tourist information**: Bytorvet; tel. 97 96 12 19.

■ **Hotel**: Hanstholm, Christian Hansens Vej 2; tel. 97 96 10 44.

Although the presence of a church from c 1200 indicates that Hanstholm has been here for a long time, it is essentially a modern port, mainly built since World War II. The fishing harbour was officially opened in 1967 and has since been extended to take larger ships: you can now sail from here to Norway or to the Faroe Islands. There was a great deal of controversy as to whether a harbour in such an exposed position and so far from the main centres could be justified, but Hanstholm's success has vindicated those who believed in the project. The coastal region here was very heavily fortified during World War II, and there are plentiful signs of this still, including areas still designated as dangerous. One of the biggest gun emplacements, at the end of MOLEVEJ, is now a *museum graphically illustrating the history of Hanstholm during World War II. A second museum at the south end of TÅRNVEJ is centred on the old lighthouse (both museums open in summer).

You now take the A26 south towards Thisted. On your way there, however, it is possible to visit yet another interesting church. At (12km) **Nors**, where the lake is said to contain some of the cleanest bathing water in Denmark, you could turn left to (3km) **Hillerslev**, where there is one of the biggest and most unusual churches in the region, consisting of a Romanesque apse, chancel and nave and late medieval tower. The apse is supported by impressive pillars, and the stone altar also rests on a squat pillar. Like so many of the North and West Jutlandic churches, it reflects toughness together with its elegant lines, and has nothing of the light and gracefulness of the churches in Fyn and Sjælland. West Jutlandic churches are built to withstand the elements, and have the quiet determination which is said to be a characteristic of the people here.

From Hillerslev you can drive direct to (10km) Thisted. ◀

22 • Horsens to Fjerritslev

*Total distance 168km. **Horsens**. A52 to (47km) **Silkeborg**. (34km) **Viborg**. 533 to (71km) **Løgstør**. 533, A29 to (15km) Fjerritslev.*

From Horsens to Silkeborg you have the choice of two routes. The direct route (45km) is given first; see below for the more scenic alternative route.

Direct route from Horsens to Silkeborg

Total distance 45km.

Leave Horsens (p 228) on the A52 in a northwesterly direction, driving to (7km) Lund, where you should not fail to make a short detour straight away, turning left on the 185 to **Tamdrup** (1km). Here, standing so high that it was formerly used as a landmark by shipping in the Horsens Fjord, there is one of the oldest (mid-11C) and most remarkable churches in Denmark. It is too large to have been intended as a village church, and is believed to have been built by a king or some powerful nobleman. Among the interesting features are the murals dating from c 1150 visible over the chancel arch, among the oldest in the country. They have not been radically restored, and are consequently somewhat pale, but an examination in 1973 revealed that the gradual deterioration over the centuries has uncovered the actual drawings made by the artist when planning his work, and they can just be discerned under the paint. Other murals in the chancel are later, from c 1500.

The church, originally a basilica, has been altered and extended in later times, but there are still clear Romanesque sections to be seen. The granite font is late Romanesque, the altarpiece and pulpit early 17C. There is meanwhile another particularly interesting piece in this church, though it is only a copy of the original. This is an elegantly embossed copper antemensale depicting the story of the monk (later Bishop) Poppo who successfully underwent the ordeal by fire and thereby brought about the conversion of King Harald Bluetooth. The original from c 1200, which probably formed a reliquary, was of beaten gold, and is now housed in the National Museum in Copenhagen. This, too, indicates the royal or dynastic connections which the church is thought once to have had.

Close by and clearly visible stands **Tamdrup Bisgård**, a splendid half-timbered house from c 1784.

You now return to the A52 and drive north through beautiful wooded, undulating and increasingly lakeland countryside to (40km) Silkeborg (see p 308), possibly turning left after 18km along the 453 to **Bryrup** (5km), from where a vintage railway runs to the neighbouring village of Vrads (limited opening summer).

Alternative route from Horsens to Silkeborg
Total distance 53km.

Leave Horsens north on the 170 turning left into the 461 after c 6km. 5km further on you will pass the mansion of **Urup** on your right. The history of Urup goes back to the 15C, but the present building is from the late 16C, and was radically redesigned c 1810. A further 3km brings you to **Østbirk**. It is the church here that is of interest. The nave is late 13C Romanesque, with a late Gothic transept and tower, and a 16C chancel. The present south chapel, containing five stone sarcophagi, is all that is left of the transept, the corresponding north wing having been demolished in 1851. Historically, this north chapel is interesting in that it once contained the tomb of the 16C naval hero Peder Skram, who owned the mansion of Urup which you have just passed. He now lies buried in the churchyard, where there is a memorial to him.

The ornate carved altarpiece was brought to the church from a nearby monastery; it is late Gothic, from c 1480; the central panel represents God and Christ standing between the Virgin and a bishop saint. The insides of the side panels each contain eight carved figures representing four Apostles and four Saints, while there are paintings of the Passion on the outsides. The unusually large font is Romanesque and is decorated with carved figures of lions, dragons and human beings. The elegant auricular pulpit is late 16C, possibly the work of the master who carved the pulpit in Århus Cathedral, with which it has some similarity.

▶Excursion from Østbirk to Denmark's highest points
Total distance 18km.

If you want to visit the 5 sq km of moraine plateau from the last Ice Age, which contains the highest points in Denmark, at Østbirk you should follow the 409 to (4km) Yding, turning right there towards (4km) Ejer. On this last stretch you will pass the high **Yding Skovhøj** (Yding Forest Hill) on your left, and in general the area here is where the highest points in Danmark are. At 171m **Møllehøj** (Mill Hill) is just the highest, with **Ejer Bavnehøj** (Ejer Beacon Hill) near Ejer a mere 170.95m. Nevertheless, Ejer Bavnehøj remains the more famous and is picked out from a distance by the tower built at the top. The floor at the top of this tower is 183m, and to those who climb the 60 steps leading to it, it offers a staggering view on a fine day. ◀

A further 6km from Østbirk on the 461 brings you to Voervadsbro, where you should turn left on the 453 to **Sønder Vissing** (4km); there is another interesting church here. Again it has a Romanesque chancel and nave with a Gothic tower (16C), and there are some late 15C fresco decorations on the chancel arch, and a mural depicting St George and the dragon.

More interesting, however is the Romanesque gravestone standing at the gateway, and two runestones, one placed under the organ in the church, the other in the porch. That in the church, which was discovered as part of the stone wall around the churchyard in 1836, is very large and has clear links with the great runestones at Jelling (p 292) in so far as the inscription indicates a family relationship: 'Tove, daughter of Mistive, the wife of Harald the Good, son of Gorm, had these runes carved in memory of her mother.' The other, which was once used as a threshold stone at the entrance to the churchyard, reads: 'Toke made these runes in memory of his father Abe, a wise man.' This same Toke raised a stone with a similar inscription in Gunderup (p 254).

From Voervadsbro the 461 takes you north past **Vissingkloster**, the site of a 13C Benedictine convent, to (6km) the **Gudenå Museum** (open June–Aug). Standing on the actual site of a Stone Age settlement, the museum represents the largest collection in the country of Stone Age hunting and fishing implements (some 30,000 in all) relating to the region, the culture known as the Gudenå Culture. A further 2km brings you to **Gammel Rye**, which lies in outstandingly beautiful and varied hilly countryside, with sudden changes of view and surprising vistas. At one time it must have been an extremely isolated area, and probably for this reason Gammel Rye (or Rye, as it used to be called) became a religious centre and a place of pilgrimage in the Middle Ages. The present church is one indication of this. Originally dedicated to St Severin, it consists of a nave and chancel in one, to which a modern porch has been added. Sizeable as it is, however, it represents only a small part of what was once a huge church on this site, closely associated with the pilgrimages to St Severin's Well in the woods immediately west of Gammel Rye; the site, dry now, can still be seen. After the Reformation, the very large church, with its 52m-long nave and 33m-long transept, fell into disrepair, and it was reduced in size in the 17C. The oldest part of the extant building is from the early 15C. The impressive carved altarpiece is from 1630. Among other old remains in the church are some 15C gravestones from Øm Kloster (see below) and an early 16C crucifix.

A relic of the past of an entirely different kind is the local **Træskomuseum** (Clog Museum). The area has been known for its clog-making, and this museum has preserved both the tools and the styles of a bygone age (limited opening summer).

One site to be visited in this area is the ruined monastery of **Øm Kloster** (open Apr–Oct), standing on an isthmus between the Gudensø and Mossø lakes, 4km southeast of Gammel Rye, and reached on a good minor road.

This Cistercian monastery was founded by French monks with an English abbot in 1172; it was dedicated to the Virgin and originally called *cara insula*. The community had gone to great lengths to find a place where it could be in peace, though according to a 13C history of the monastery that peace scarcely extended to relations between the Øm community and the Bishop of Århus, within whose jurisdiction Øm lay. The later history, in so far as it is known, seems to have been less tempestuous. Øm Kloster together with the school it ran, was even allowed to survive for a time after the Reformation, not being secularised until 1560 when the buildings were converted into a royal residence called Emborg.

The buildings were subsequently used as a source of materials for other purposes, including the building of Skanderborg Castle, but their foundations can still be seen in their entirety, the only Danish Cistercian monastery to be so well preserved. In addition, the canals bringing water to the monks have also survived.

A small museum has been built within the complex to exhibit finds made on the site: keys, chessmen, swords, surgical instruments from the hospital. There is also a valuable collection of medieval skeletons and bones. Just note how perfect the monks' teeth were—though the bones show signs of battle wounds, rheumatism and syphilis. About 1000 graves have been discovered and excavated, and some of them are on show to visitors.

A herb garden such as that used by the monks, and containing some 60 different species, was laid out in 1925. There were in all 14 monasteries and convents in this area, but Øm was by far the biggest of them. At one time it owned no fewer that 380 farms of various sizes.

Just west of Gammel Rye the elevated wooded ridge known as **Rye Nørreskov** (Rye North Forest) sweeps down to the shores of Julsø lake, and here you will find the famous **Himmelbjerget (Sky Mountain). To visit it you turn on to the 461 just north of Gammel Rye and simply drive to the top! You can, of course, reach the top on foot, and this is really the preferable alternative. Although not quite so high as Ejer Bavnehøj, Himmelbjerget stands out considerably more on the terrain; it actually looks like a (small) mountain.

A tower has been built at the top to commemorate King Frederik VII, who granted Denmark its first Constitution in 1849, and it is surrounded by smaller memorials to other historical events. One of these commemorates a meeting of the Danish people led by Steen Steensen Blicher, who was not only a major writer, but also for a time politically active, trying to impart a feeling of political awareness to his a-political fellow countrymen. Another, the women's oak tree, is to mark the granting of votes to women in Denmark in 1915. Over the decades, many political meetings have been held at the top of Himmelbjerget, and indeed, meetings of various kinds are still held here.

The view from the top is splendid, giving a panorama of the lakes and forests all round; to the West Silkeborg can be seen, and to the east Århus. Many is the poetic description of one of the most intriguing and idyllic areas in Denmark. When visiting Silkeborg in 1853 Hans Christian Andersen described it as 'countryside which reminds you of the abundant woodlands of the Black Forest or the grandiose isolation of the Scottish moors'.

The 445 west and the A52 will easily take you from Gammel Rye to (18km) Silkeborg (see below), if you so wish. However, if you do not mind the longer distance (25km) we suggest you take the 445 east instead and reach Silkeborg from the east, having driven anti-clockwise around the lakes.

Your first stop in this case will be at (4km) **Ry**.

■ **Tourist information**: Klostervej 3; tel. 86 82 19 11.

■ **Hotels**: Himmelbjerget, Himmelbjergvej 20; tel. 86 89 80 45; Gammel Ry Kro, Ryesgade 8; tel. 86 89 80 42.

■ **Youth hostel**: Randersvej 88-90; tel 86 89 14 07.

Ry is a modern but quite delightful town which sprang up in the late 19C with the advent of the railway. Its tiny harbour caters for the lake pleasure boats, and there are ample facilities for yachts and the many canoeists who frequent the area. Here, too, there is a freshwater museum, the **Færskvandsmuseum**, with an aquarium containing the fish native to the lakes, and exhibition cases illustrating the flora, fauna and geology of the region (open summer).

From Ry you leave the 445 and take the unclassified road north towards Låsby. In 3km you reach Tulstrup, where you come to a crossroads. If you are interested in church architecture, and if Øm Kloster has whetted your appetite, you ought really to go right here to Nørre Vissing (4km), there turning right again on the 457 to **Veng** (3km).

Veng was the site of the monastery used by the Cistercians before they went to Øm. Previously, Veng monastery had been in the hands of the Benedictines. They had built a magnificent church here, and it still stands. It is the oldest monastery church in Denmark, very big, tall, and unique in design. It is thought to date from between 1100 and 1125. Not only is there an apse at the east end of the chancel, but the transepts are also provided with apses to the east. In style it has many features reminiscent of East English church architecture, and it is assumed that an English builder must have been responsible for it.

Back in Nørre Vissing you follow the 457 n to (4km) Låsby, where you join the A15 west to (8km) **Linå**, where there is yet another large church. The apse, chancel and nave are Romanesque with later extensions. Both the original remarkably elaborate stone entrances, each flanked by three columns on either side, are extant, though the original south door has been moved to form the west door. Inside, there is a brick-built medieval altar, while the altarpiece is dated 1616. The carved font is Romanesque, and the simple pulpit is from c 1630. The church was thoroughly restored in 1966.

Before continuing to Silkeborg, you might like to savour this charming wooded area by driving the 3km south along a minor road to **Svejbæk** on the shore of the Julsø lake and while there you ought to sample the famous Svejbæk eels. Here, too, is the **Hotel og Restaurant Museum Silkeborg**, a splendid collection illustrating the development of the hotel and restaurant trade, housed in the old Hotel Ludvigslyst; one of the attractions is the opportunity to try the food and drink enjoyed at the turn of the century.

There are minor roads from Svejbæk to Silkeborg through Sejs. Alternatively, you can return to Linå, from where it is a mere 8km on the A15 to Silkeborg.

SILKEBORG (pop. 50,000) is not an old town. It was founded in 1844 by one Michael Drewsen, who that year was allowed to establish a paper mill on the lakeside. There is still a paper mill in Silkeborg, which otherwise is known for its teacher training colleges and its schools. It was granted a charter as a market town in 1900. There is no point in looking for very old houses in the straight, intersecting streets, though there are traces of an old castle by the lakeside near the Viborgbro bridge.

- **Tourist information**: Godthåbsvej 4; tel. 86 82 19 11.

- **Hotels**: Dania, Torvet 5; tel. 86 82 01 11; Luisiana, Christian den Ottendesvej 7; tel. 86 82 18 99.

- **Youth hostel**: Åhavevej 55; tel. 86 82 36 42.

- Silkeborg is very much associated with its beautiful lakeland, and a **trip on the lakes** should not be missed. Combine your stay here with a day trip to Himmelbjerget on the old paddle steamer *Hjejlen*, which was launched as long ago as 1861 by Frederik VII and is still going strong—an institution in its own right.

Silkeborg has its own charm, but it is essentially 19C charm, concentrated on the main square, TORVET, and the adjacent area. On the square an outsize chessboard is laid out on the pavement, and at times in the summer tourists can try their skills on it. There are several sculptures by well-known artists adorning the pedestrian area, and many of the buildings can boast artistic ornamentation. Virtually in the centre of the town, too, there is the wooded **Odden** (Headland), jutting out into the Langsø lake, where a large-scale fountain is illuminated at night in the summer.

Two officially designated **bathing areas** are marked out in the Almind Sø, c 1km south of the town centre. Here, as in all the other bathing areas in the district, the water is very clean indeed.

North of Silkeborg lies the Deer Park, **Dyrehaven**, where, in a World War II German bunker, you will find a museum containing exhibits from the Occupation. The fine **Silkeborg Museum**, in HOVEDGÅRDSVEJ, contains one of the most famous of all Danish museum exhibits, the *Tollund Man**. The Tollund Man was discovered in a bog near Silkeborg in 1950; his head, with remarkably clear facial features, was almost entirely preserved; and his body was sufficiently intact for it to have been 'reconstructed', and there he now lies in the position in which he must have been when thrown into the bog some 2200 years ago.

A second, rather less well-preserved body, that of the Elling Woman, is nearby, and the two are surrounded, on the first floor of the museum, by a reconstruction of an Iron Age village, with a comprehensive collection of weapons, tools and clothing, and figures clothed in reconstructions of Iron Age dress. There are drawings and models to illustrate the way of life in the Iron Age and to describe the process of reconstructing the body of the Tollund Man, listing other finds of a similar nature in Danish bogs. Apart from this central feature, the museum contains a collection of local archaeological and historical exhibits.

Silkeborg's other major museum is the art gallery, **Silkeborg Kunstmuseum**, in GUDENÅVEJ. If the Silkeborg Museum is centred on the Tollund Man, this revolves around a more modern, but scarcely less famous figure, the modernist painter Asger Jorn, who was born in Silkeborg in 1914. The gallery contains over 100 of Jorn's paintings in addition to ceramics and tapestries. On top of that, it possesses some 5000 works by 156 other important artists, some going back to the 17C, but mainly from the 20C, all presented to the gallery by Jorn himself. In addition there are many other items acquired independently. All this has established Silkeborg Kunstmuseum, a purpose-built gallery from 1982, as a major Danish art gallery, not to be missed by anyone interested in the visual arts.

The lakes are also responsible for a new attraction, the **Aqua Fresh Water Aquarium** at VEJLSØVEJ 55, just south of the town, claiming to be the largest of its kind in Europe. The bottom floor is submerged under water drawn from the lakes, and you can walk around and watch submarine life as it unfolds. (Open all year; closed Mon.)

From Silkeborg, you take the A52 north for 11km, where you will find a minor road west to **Vinderslev** (1.5km). Here there is a quite elaborate church with a Romanesque chancel and nave, and a late Gothic tower at the west. Built of ashlars, it is richly decorated. In particular it has two ornate (but bricked up)

Romanesque portals in the north and south. The north portal is flanked by three columns on either side, with a figure variously thought to be Christ or St Francis in the tympanum; that in the south has two columns on either side and figures of a lion and an eagle in the tympanum. The tower is of later date, but this, too, contains Romanesque reliefs of lions.

The vaulting and walls are decorated with late 13C frescoes, the most important work of the so-called Vinderslev Master. They portray the Day of Judgement, Heaven, Hell, devils and figures both realistic and fantastic, including Death carrying a scythe, a woman playing cards, a man passing water, and a flock of geese hanging a fox. They were at one time whitewashed over. Some other, 16C, frescoes in the chancel are less drastic and have never been covered. In the churchyard there are two small Romanesque granite crosses.

In Vinderslev, too, there is the 15C Vinderslevgård manor house, probably extensively rebuilt at a later date. According to legend it is the owner of this house, Karen Krabbe, who is seen playing cards in the church mural. The stake was her house. She lost.

5km further north you come to the Kjellerup-Torning crossroads. We are moving now into 'Blicher country', and if you are interested in the author Steen Steensen Blicher, you should turn left here and drive to **Torning** (7km).

Blicher was the pastor in Torning from 1819 to 1825, and it is fitting that the old half-timbered parsonage where he wrote his most famous novel, *The Diary of a Parish Clerk*, should now be a *museum, The **Blicher Museum**, dedicated to a great writer who has been so closely associated with this part of Jutland. This fittingly modest museum gives an impression of life in the region in Blicher's day and earlier, as well as a collection of Blicher memorabilia and an array of stuffed birds and animals from the area (Blicher was a great hunter). The museum also houses the Kjellerup local history archives (open summer; limited opening winter).

There are Blicher relics, too, in the church and the churchyard. The pulpit is that from which he delivered his sermons, and his name figures among the list of Torning pastors. Several of the models for Blicher's characters are buried in the churchyard, and in particular one notices Mads Doss, the lad who looked after the sheep on the moors. One of the exhibits in the museum is thought to be his **snaps bottle**. There is a memorial to Blicher himself just outside the churchyard.

From Torning you can take the A13 straight to (18km) Viborg (p 282). However, there are more places associated with Blicher in the area, and if you want to see them, we suggest you rejoin the A26 just outside Kjellerup.

4km north of the Kjellerup-Torning crossroads there is another crossroads with **Sjørslev** (1.5km) signposted to the right. Here you will find another church with Blicher associations. It used to be owned by one Steen de Steensen, the uncle of Steen Steensen Blicher. The Steensen family's coat of arms is painted on the ceiling, and the family tomb is in a mound to the northwest of the church. The Romanesque font is one of the most elaborately carved fonts in Denmark, and there is an Arab style mausoleum in the churchyard.

Return to the A52, cross it and drive 1km further to the manor house of **Aunsbjerg**, once the home of Steen de Steensen, and a place where the young

Blicher spent much of his childhood. It is also the setting for some of Blicher's best-known stories. The manor goes far back in history, to 1340, but the present building stems from the mid 16C, though it was largely rebuilt in 1872 and 1917.

A further 1km brings you to the large farmstead of **Liselund**, and 1km further on to **Vium**, where Blicher was born in 1782. His father was pastor here, and Blicher was presumably baptised in the Romanesque font which is still in use in the church. The frescoes, restored in 1968, are from the 16C and 17C. The building in which Blicher was born no longer exists, but there is a memorial to him in the wall of the present parsonage.

From Vium you take a minor road northwest, crossing the A13 to (4km) **Lysgård Museum**, once the first stopping place on the Military Road (p 293) on the way south from Viborg. You will now find a sign on a house near the church, saying 'Æ Bindstouw' (The Knitting Room), suggesting that this house is the setting for Blicher's story of that name. In point of fact the house in which he set his story has been pulled down, though the foundations are genuine enough. At all events, the present building still re-creates the wretched surroundings of Blicher's story (open summer).

Return now to the A13, turn left and drive through the delightful and varied **Dollerup Bakker** (Dollerup Hills) to (12km) **Viborg** (p 282)—a town not to be missed.

To leave Viborg you join the 533 north. In 7km, after driving through undulating, partly wooded countryside, you cross the low-lying **Skalsådal** (Skals River Valley). The sheer breadth of the valley here is an indication of the size of Skals Å river in the Ice Age, when it could be compared with the major European rivers. Now little more than a stream, it enters the Hjarbæk Fjord, a branch of the Limfjord, about 1km to your left.

The road by-passes Skals village, keeping to low ground and taking you in a further 4km across the Simested Å river, which also flows into the fjord at this point. Just beyond the river, to your right, lies Låstrup.

Turn left here just to have a look at **Lynderupgård** (3km), a magnificent half-timbered manor house mainly from 1556, standing on a square mound and partly hidden by trees. There is a fountain in the shape of four heads in the courtyard, said to be the oldest fountain in Denmark. Lynderupgård is not open to the public, but the sight of it is well worth the short drive from the main road.

The 533 now continues north to (15km) **Gedsted**. The Romanesque church here dates back to c 1150 and retains many of its original features. Both the north and south portals can be seen, though the south door has been walled up. There are late Gothic frescoes including, in the north chapel, one depicting the martyrdom of St Erasmus. The Romanesque altar contains a reliquary with a relic of the 11,000 virgins. The carillon from 1757 plays every day at noon.

From Gedsted you can drive east along the 561 to **Ålestrup** (10km), where you will find the delightful Jutland Rose Gardens (**Den jydske Rosenpark**) on sloping ground beside the Simested Å river. There is a display of some 15,000 roses of 200 different species as well as an art exhibition in the pavilion (open Jun–Sept).

Also, in Ålestrup you will find the only **Bicycle Museum** in Scandinavia, containing about 100 bicycles ranging from the very oldest to the near-contemporary. This collection is supplemented with an assortment of sewing machines and old radio receivers (open May–Nov).

Ålestrup lies virtually on two rivers and provides excellent **fishing facilities**.

Now follow the 533 north for 4km to the crossing with the 187, where you turn left and follow the 187 southwest to (5km) **Hvalpsund**. Here you will find delightful views across the fjord, though Hvalpsund itself has little to offer.

In Hvalpsund, however, you should turn south on a minor road to **Hessel** (2km), where you will find a most interesting and very special agricultural museum (**Hessel Landbrugsmuseum**) in a large old farm, the last completely thatched major farm in Denmark—some 3000 sq m of thatch altogether (open summer).

The history of Hessel certainly goes back to the 14C, and the present buildings date largely from the 17C and early 18C. Not only is an extensive collection of old implements and machinery housed in the outbuildings, while several rooms demonstrate the conditions under which farmworkers once lived and worked, but the present intention is to run the entire farm as a 'museum project', cultivating the land with reproduction old implements and according to old methods, including the rotation method. It is hoped in this way to keep in being both plants and animals which would otherwise not survive modern methods. Ploughing is done by horses, not tractors. On the first Sunday in July there is what is called a 'horse day', when many of these old implements are demonstrated, and there are other days during the summer when an effort is made to recapture the manner of life of a bygone age.

The main building exhibits rural dress and crafts, and there is plenty of authentic furniture. There is usually a textile exhibition in the summer months (open summer).

From Hvalpsund you drive 6km northwest to **Fovlum Church**, either direct along a minor road or by returning to the 533 and turning left there.

Fovlum church is unique—Romanesque almost entirely as when built. In the view of the mid-20C novelist Martin A. Hansen: 'Surely no nobler church has ever been built in this country.' The porch is 19C, and the south door has been walled up, but the remainder is unspoiled Romanesque demonstrating beautiful workmanship. The granite ashlars are splendidly hewn, and the columns at the two portals are beautifully fashioned. The original Romanesque rounded arches are still in place over the apse and the chancel, and there are original stone sculptures. You will have seen many originally Romanesque Danish churches which have been adapted or extended in the Gothic style. Here is one which has maintained its original character. A must.

From Fovlum you drive north on the 533 to (7km) Strandby. However, those particularly interested in literature might like to take the slightly longer route via Farsø, making the driving distance 14km instead.

To reach **Farsø** (**Tourist information**: Torvet 1; tel. 98 63 16 86) you leave Fovlum, seeking the 187, driving in all c 6km north.

Here Johannes V. Jensen was born, and his home at SØNDERGADE 48 now houses a small museum dedicated to him and his sister. She also has her own small museum at TORVET 1, containing her own furniture and her letters and notes. She is buried in the churchyard here, as is her father.

Johannes V. Jensen felt more akin to pagan Denmark, and it is fitting that a huge memorial stone, inscribed with one of his verses, has been placed close to a prehistoric burial mound just south of the village.

Johannes V. Jensen

Farsø was the birthplace of the authors Johannes V. Jensen (1873–1950) and Thit Jensen (1876–1957). Thit Jensen is known as a novelist, feminist and spiritualist; her more famous brother as a poet, essayist, novelist and short-story writer. He is remembered, too, as one of the great linguistic innovators of 20C Danish literature. He was awarded the Nobel Prize for Literature in 1944, and is particularly associated with stories centred on his native region of Himmerland, which in his childhood was one of the most backward and outlying parts of Denmark—uncultivated moorland with poor communications with the outside world. Here, as the son of the local vet, he came into contact with many of the more colourful figures of the region and has immortalised them in his stories. Thit Jensen used Himmerland as the setting for her large-scale historical novels.

From Farsø you take a minor road left immediately north of the village to (8km) **Strandby**, where there is a large, well-preserved Romanesque church with a Renaissance altarpiece standing on high ground. The main interest though must be centred on the **Strandby Museum**, some 2km north of the village. This contains a large collection of archaeological remains found in the area, and closely associated with the so-called Ertebølle Culture (open summer, on application).

Ertebølle itself can be reached by turning left off the 533 2km north of Strandby. Just south of the village is the site of a Stone Age settlement and its huge kitchen midden dating from 4600–4000 BC. There is relatively little for the layman to see on the actual site, but there is an informative small museum (open summer).

Originally measuring 140m × 20m × 2m, this is thought to contain the remains of 20 million oysters. However, there are the remains of other fish, bones of many different animals, weapons and household implements. The skeleton of a seated human figure has also been found there, and there are sufficient individual human bones here to suggest cannibalism.

When the kitchen midden was established, Ertebølle was on the coast; subsequently the sea rose and flooded it, removing most signs of the actual settlement; then the land rose again and the water receded, so there is now a short distance from Ertebølle to the coast.

As you proceed north from Strandby, you drive through several tree plantations, some of them, like **Trend Skov**, of considerable size. Trend Skov belongs partly to the Queen, who owns a hunting lodge here (not visible from the road).

9km north of Strandby, still on the 533, you reach **Vitskøl Kloster**. This is the ruins of one of the largest of Denmark's medieval religious houses, a Cistercian monastery founded in 1158 by King Valdemar I as a thanks offering for having won the battle of Grathe Hede. Vitskøl was intended to become the biggest monastery in Scandinavia, and at one time it owned no fewer than 400 farms. The 50m × 40m church, of which a considerable portion has survived, is thought by some to have been as splendid as that in the mother foundation of Cîteaux, but it was already in a state of disrepair by the Reformation, and like many other major buildings it was used as a quarry. Vitskøl was allowed to continue after the Reformation, but by 1563 it was secularised, and the school attached to it was closed (the ruins are open to visitors). The original west wing forms the present main building, but is now used as a detention centre and is not open to the public.

The adjoining ***gardens** are particularly interesting. They comprise a copy of the monastery garden in St Gallen with the 16 herbs ordained for each monastery, an apothecary's garden with a systematic arrangement of the herbs according to which part of the body they were intended to heal, a general herb garden, a garden with herbs suitable for making *snaps* and, now, a scented garden for the blind.

From Vitskøl the road continues north to (3km) **Ranum** with a large church built in 1909. The two massive towers were added in 1931. The outstanding feature of this church is the huge fresco on the east wall of the chancel, painted in 1921 by Niels Larsen-Stevns, and depicting the Second Coming, with Christ descending through the clouds over Ranum. Niels Larsen-Stevns, who played a part in the Viborg Cathedral frescoes, is one of the best large-scale artists in 20C Denmark, and this is considered to be one of his finest works.

▶Excursion from Ranum to Livø island

Turn left off the main road in Ranum, drive the 3km to Rønbjerg and there take a ferry to the tiny Limfjord island of **Livø**. The trip takes 20 minutes, and the ferry sails regularly during the summer months. You cannot take your car, and neither can you take a dog with you.

There is a camp site on Livø, and other kinds of overnight accommodation are also available (reservations on 98 67 63 62). A cafeteria and grocer's shop provide for your other needs. The island, which once belonged to Vitskøl Monastery, is rich in wild life (there is a seal sanctuary), and is of particular interest to geologists. A 6.3km route for walking around the island is clearly marked, and maps are available indicating the most interesting areas. ◀

The direct road from Ranum leads you straight to (9km) Løgstør. At 5km you should however make a quick visit to **Lendrup Strand** beach (3km). Much of the coastline here, dotted with summer cottages, is suitable for bathing, but Lendrup Strand is one of the best stretches of beach. Here, too, you will find the southern end of the 4km-long **Frederik VII's Kanal**, which extends all the way to Løgstør and was constructed in the 1850s to avoid the constant difficulties of sailing out from Løgstør, caused by the sandbanks in Løgstør Shallows. Better channels have now been dug, and the canal, no longer needed, was closed off in 1913. It remains, however, as a relic of past initiative, and the old tow-paths provide a much-loved walk along the coast in delightful wooded surroundings.

Løgstør (pop. 10,600) has a history going back to the 11C, when it was connected with the Viking fortress of Aggersborg (see below). By 1514 it was a fishing village engaged in the then lucrative herring fishery. When the herring failed, Løgstør attempted to engage in the corn trade, but was stopped owing to protests from big brother Ålborg. It suffered two major fires in the mid-18C. In the 19C Løgstør benefited from improved conditions for agriculture and from the improvement in communications which led to the establishment of industrial enterprises. The Frederik VII Canal also contributed to its increasing prosperity.

■ **Tourist information**: Sønderport 2A.

■ **Hotels**: Løgstør Parkhotel, Toftebjerg Allé 6; tel. 98 67 40 00; Hotel du Nord, Havnevej 38; tel. 98 67 21 00.

■ There is a **marina**, and excellent facilities for **fishing**.

Løgstør has no imposing architecture, not even an old church (the present church with its lofty spire was consecrated in 1893), but situated at the foot of a gentle slope it is a delightful small town, full of atmosphere, and characterised by narrow streets, fishermen's houses and, inevitably, the harbour area stretching over 2km until it merges with the Frederik VII Canal, which is crossed by the original swing bridge. Here, the former canal manager's house, white-washed and with corbie step gables, now forms the **Limfjord Museum** devoted to the fishing and shipping associated with the area. It contains old implements, models, drawings and photographs illustrating the old way of life, and there is a collection of restored fishing vessels (open summer).

On the hill leading down to the town, Løgstør Bakke, stands the house in which Johan Skjoldborg, the novelist and poet who championed the cause of the Danish smallholders at the end of the 19C, lived from 1917 to his death in 1936. The house was given to Skjoldborg by the smallholders in recognition of his work on their behalf.

5km north of Løgstør the 533 joins the A29 and takes you to the **Aggersund Bridge** spanning the narrows which once provided Løgstør with much of its ferrying income. It is an elegant 210m-long structure dating from 1942; the central part can be raised to allow the passage of ships.

Immediately beyond the bridge you can turn left to drive down to the (1km) **Aggersborg** site. This was the largest of the four Danish Viking fortresses, and probably the biggest in all Scandinavia, three times the size of the far better preserved Trelleborg in Sjælland. Unfortunately for us, however, it was destroyed in the rebellion against Knud II in 1086, and there is little for the layman to see apart from a small section of the ramparts. Excavations have shown that the fortress had a diameter of 285m, containing in all 12 groups of four halls. The whole complex was surrounded by a rampart with four entrances. In addition there was a large Viking village just outside, and many archaeological finds have been made here. The ramparts have been completely rebuilt, and a small **museum** has been established with video facilities. There are **conducted tours** at intervals during the summer, and there is free access to the site and the museum.

The nearby **Aggersborggård** farm itself is scheduled, a beautiful half-timbered building, with a south wing dating back to 1758. It stands on the site of a castle built by Knud II at the end of the 11C. Open June, July and August, it shows an old farming milieu not least illustrating the life of a farmer's wife in the old days. There is also a farm shop.

The novelist Jakob Knudsen, whose father was pastor in the nearby church from 1864, spent part of his childhood in Aggersborg. There is a memorial to him outside the parsonage, where there is also a plan showing what the whole complex is thought once to have looked like.

Return now to the A29 and drive straight to (9km) Fjerritslev (p 264).

23 • Fjerritslev to Copenhagen

Total distance 217km plus ferry. A29 to (65km) **Hobro** *(p 287). E45 to (27km)* **Randers** *(p 239). A16 to (55km)* **Grenå**. *(Ferry Grenå–Hundested 2hr 15min). A16 to (13km)* **Frederiksværk**. *211 to (18km)* **Frederikssund**. *207 to (7km) Slangerup. A6, 211 to (42km)* **Copenhagen** *(p 60 ff).*

From Fjerritslev (p 264) the route goes south along the A29, across (9km) the Aggersund bridge (p 315), and into **Himmerland**, as this area is called. A further 7km brings you to **Skarp Salling**, where there is an unexpectedly large and splendid *church from c 1150.

Why this large-scale basilica should have been built in this place is a mystery. It is far too big for an ordinary village church, and yet there is nothing to indicate that it has had connections with any powerful figure of the realm. One legend has it that it is a thanks offering from three sisters who were saved from drowning. The entire church was restored at the end of the 19C, but it is thought to retain much of its original character, and certainly it has always been this size. The nave and aisles all end in apses, while a notable feature is the massive arcading both between the nave and aisles and at the west end of the nave.

This church is a paradise for students of perspective. The main apse is believed once to have had windows, but is now limited to a single one, while the outside is decorated with blind arcading. The stonework presents several examples of sculptured heads, lions, dragons and geometrical designs. Among the decorations on the Romanesque font there is, unusually, a sculpted child's hand holding a cross. There are two Romanesque gravestones in the churchyard.

Continue further along the A29 to (21km) **Års** (pop. 12,740; **Tourist information**: Himmerlandsgade 113), a lively small town, which lies at the centre of a very beautiful and varied part of Denmark, ideal for walkers, cyclists and anglers, and well equipped to cater for tourists.

Års is proud to recall that the Cimbrians probably originated in this area. They were a prehistoric tribe that, probably because of climatic changes and resultant difficult conditions at home, moved south and ravaged much of southern Europe 2000 years ago. *Cimbrian* and *Himmerland* are thought to be derived from the same word.

Like many other Danish towns, Års has installed works of art in its streets and public buildings. There are sculptures by Per Kirkeby, Knud Nellemose, Jørgen Haugen Sørensen and Yan fra Vendsyssel, and the local grammar school has a large oil painting by Per Kirkeby and a ceramic frieze by Poul Gernes. The **Himmerlands Kunstmuseum**, at SØNDERGADE 44, contains a collection of paintings and watercolours by Jens Nielsen. At the same address you will find the **Vesthimmerlands Museum**, with the Gundestrup Cauldron replica (see below) as its main attraction, but also containing many local archaeological finds as well as items of more recent local history.

There is certainly plenty of evidence of early activity around Års. Several preserved bodies—murdered, sacrificed or executed—have been found in the marshes, while the Roman historian Tacitus has given a graphic description of life here—not always exactly a comfortable experience, if one is to judge by his account. A dozen or so Iron Age settlements are known in the area of Års, and they have yielded large numbers of archaeological finds.

In the marsh near **Gundestrup** c 3km east of Års, known as **Rævemosen** (i.e. Fox Marsh, so called because of the many foxes that used to live here), one of the great archaeological finds was made in 1891. A farmer digging peat came across what has now become known as the Gundestrup Cauldron, a superbly ornamented silver cauldron 72cm in diameter, 43cm high and weighing 8kg, decorated with a figure of the Celtic god Cernunnos, lines of soldiers on foot and on horseback, bullfights and, on the base, the figure of a bull. It is obviously not local work, and must have been brought to the area as war booty. What it was originally intended for is not certain—possibly as a receptacle for sacrificial blood either from bulls or humans. The original, broken in such a way as to suggest that it was itself sunk in the marsh as a sacrifice, is now in the National Museum in Copenhagen, but an exact replica is on view in the Vesthimmerlands Museum in Års. The place where the cauldron was found is marked by a boulder on which there is a deliberately simple, unadorned but subtle inscription by Johannes V. Jensen: 'Her fandtes Gundestrupkarret'—'The Gundestrup Cauldron was (or: was found) here'.

There is also evidence in the area of much later settlements, not least the many burial mounds dotted around the landscape, some of them of considerable size. There are also several runestones, one of the largest being in the churchyard in Års. It stands on its own at the entrance to the church, but it is believed that it was once incorporated into a larger complex consisting of two mounds and a single-stone monument, all of which have now vanished. There are inscriptions on two of its surfaces; that on the front is quite straightforward: 'Asser raised this stone here in memory of his master Valtoke.' For that on the back more than one interpretation has been suggested—either: 'The stone shall long stand here, it shall avenge Valtoke', or 'The stone shall long stand here denoting Valtoke's cairn.'

Approximately 3km south of Års lies **Borremose**, the largest of the Iron Age settlements, possibly once a fortress rather than a village. Discovered in 1929, it is believed to date back to c 200 BC and thus to be the oldest fortified settlement in Denmark. The couple of dozen houses there were clearly surrounded by a double moat and rampart. They have been excavated, and the outlines of some of them, all lying east–west and with a fireplace in the west, are now visible. There is a car park close to the A29, and there you will find a plan of the site.

On your way south from Borremose to (23km) Hobro (p 287), you should perhaps pause in **Stenild** to visit the church, which contains a large and splendidly carved Romanesque font. Even if you decide to by-pass Hobro town itself, the archaeological site of nearby **Fyrkat** (also p 287) should tempt you to spend a little extra time in the region, which is really very attractive.

From Hobro the route continues on the E45 to (27km) Randers. This stretch is described, though in the reverse direction, on pp 239–242, mentioning Handest with its vintage railway, and **Råsted Church** which you must visit to see its outstanding frescoes.

Having passed Råsted you will have to decide whether to visit the old town of Randers (p 239) or to by-pass it. If you opt for a visit, you must leave the E45 3km south of Råsted to join the 180—if not, you stay on the E45 as far as Exit 41, where you take the A16/A21 east. You are actually circling the town, so you have to cross several intersecting radial roads before you really feel out of the built-up area.

16km from Randers centre you come to **Fausing** where those interested in fonts should stop to visit the *church in which there is a most unusual one from c 1300, made of metal and supported by three male figures thought to represent the rivers of Paradise.

From Fausing there is a choice of no fewer than three routes to Grenå and the ferry. The direct route (total distance 39km via the A16), taking you through mid Djursland, is described first; the two alternative routes—one exploring North Djursland, and taking you south of the main route—are detailed below.

Direct route from Fausing to Grenå
Total distance 39km.

3km beyond Fausing you come to ***Gammel Estrup**, one of the finest of Denmark's great houses. Standing in a partly wooded area, the present main building with its 2–3m-thick walls is from the 15C, though the history of Gammel Estrup can be traced back to c 1350. Since 1930 Gammel Estrup has housed the **Jutland Manor House Museum**, and contains a comprehensive collection of furniture and tapestries, much of it comprising the original furnishings in the house, and reflecting changing fashions over the centuries. In addition there is a chapel and, beneath the house, an alchemist's cellar. Each year in June the Randers City Orchestra gives a concert in the Great Hall. The magnificent formal gardens with their lime tree avenues, canals and orangery are open for you to walk in, and there is a cafeteria in the old stable.

The farm buildings have been turned into the ***Danish Agricultural Museum** with a vast collection of 25,000 exhibits relating to the history of agriculture. A blacksmith is there working on his anvil, and children wanting to work off their energy by threshing with a flail in the old-fashioned manner have a unique opportunity.

The author Henrik Pontoppidan, who in 1885 had referred to Gammel Estrup as the 'pearl of Danish manor houses', used it as the setting for the mansion of Favsingholm in his third major novel, *The Realm of the Dead*—which unfortunately has not been translated.

From Gammel Estrup it is only 2km along the A16 to **Auning**, where Jørgen Skeel, one of the owners of Gammel Estrup, was buried in 1695, and where in the church he is commemorated by a huge Baroque marble monument by Thomas Quellinus. The bombastic sarcophagus, surmounted by a reclining figure of Skeel, stands before trumpet-blowing cherubs and heroic figures covering the entire rear wall of the sepulchral chapel. In addition to Jørgen

Skeel's sarcophagus, the chapel contains 14 further sarcophagi. In complete contrast there are some frescoes from 1562.

The A16 continues direct east, first through undulating wooded terrain, which gradually gives way to moorland. At 10km you can turn right and drive 1km south to the large-scale **Djurs Sommerland pleasure gardens**. Much of the area is given over to water, offering rowing and canoeing opportunities, or a sail on a timber raft. There are also facilities for shooting, pony riding, go-carting, trampolining and countless other amusements. And there is a Science Centre in the complex. Once you have paid your admission, all activities are free.

A further 5km brings you to **Ramten**. Here you might make a brief detour and drive south on a minor road to **Tøstrup** (3km), where a wealth of frescoes from 1582 was uncovered in 1984–86 during the restoration of the Romanesque church.

Back on the main road, in **Ørum**, 3km east of Ramten, there is a church in which the centre panel of the altarpiece contains a well-known painting by a major 19C Danish artist, Constantin Hansen, of the Women at the Tomb.

From Ørum it is a further 16km to Grenå (p 322).

Alternative route from Fausing to Grenå—the north Djursland route

Total distance 49km. The route takes you through some interesting villages and intro-duces you to the work of a notable 12C artist.

Turn left off the main road at **Fausing** and drive on the 547 to (4km) Allingåbro, there turning left on to the 531 to **Ørsted** (4km), where the imposing *church glories in some particularly fine stone carvings, including a chancel arch decorated with figures of Christ and the four Evangelists. It is the work of Horder, the outstanding 12C craftsman of Djursland, who is also responsible for the very elaborate decorations around the doorways.

Back in **Allingåbro** you will, in **Vejlby Church**, find more work by this Master. Here again pride of place goes to the stone portals.

4km east of Allingåbro a detour can be made south to **Gjesing** (5km), where the name of the otherwise anonymous Master Horder was established on the basis of a gravestone. Now in the National Museum, this 'Gjesing Stone' bears the inscription 'Horderus', presumably the signature of the artist himself.

East of Gjesing village you will find the manor house of **Løvenholm**, now used as a residential college. The east wing of this forbidding house is the orig-inal main building from 1576, while the south wing, built in the same style, is from 1642–43. The northeast tower is from the original building, but that on the southeast corner is again a later addition, from 1643. After falling into disre-pair, the house was restored in 1783 and given a splendid new interior. A further restoration was undertaken in 1901. Løvenholm, which has retained its original appearance almost unaltered, is approached from the north across an embank-ment and bridge and along an avenue of lime trees planted in the 18C. The park is open to the public.

Return to the 547 and continue to (2km) **Vivild**, from where there is the chance to see two more manor houses—from the outside. You can leave the 547 and drive north to catch a glimpse of **Julianeholm** (1km) and **Hevringholm**

(2.5km further on), continuing perhaps to **Hevringholm Strand** (Hevringholm Beach) (1km), to experience some splendid sandy beaches and a typical Danish weekend cottage area.

Instead of now following the 547 road direct to (9km) Fjellerup, you may like to experience the beautiful countryside around here a little more by leaving Vivild east on the old road, past the church and Vivild Huse towards **Tustrup**. After about 4km you come to a car park and a signpost on your right directing you to an impressive Stone Age burial ground containing a stone circle, three long barrows, a dolmen chamber, a passage grave with a 10m-long chamber, the foundations of a Stone Age house (probably a place of worship) and 16 burial mounds. From Tustrup you then continue to (5km) Fjellerup.

From Fjellerup you follow the 547 to (9km) **Glesborg**, where there is a Romanesque church with 16C frescoes depicting Abraham preparing to sacrifice Isaac. The Renaissance altarpiece and pulpit are from 1618, the gifts of Jørgen Kaas, the owner of the mansion of Mejlgård 5km northwest. **Bønnerup Strand**, 7km north, is another of the splendid beaches in this part of the country.

The route now continues to (3km) **Kastbjerg**, where the rather unusual Romanesque/Gothic church has buttressed walls. It was severely damaged by lightning in 1950 and restored in the 1960s by the architects Johannes and Inger Exner. The untraditional altarpiece, or **altar arrangement**, by Poul Winther, is from 1975.

This area is dotted with several more churches of interest. Leave Kastbjerg on a minor road northeast to (4km) **Rimsø**. Here Master Horder has produced yet another impressive surround to the walled-up north doorway of the ***church**; a column on either side with characteristic cable ornamentation, flanked by four figures with haloes; those on the left are clearly Christ and Mary, both seated. The tympanum represents a carved lion. Inside the porch there is another carved stone, a corbel representing six seated figures in arcading, again with cable ornamentation. There is a runestone close to the church.

Nor is the church the only sight worth seeing here: the ***parsonage**, from 1593, is a beautiful old building, thought to be the oldest parsonage extant in Denmark.

A minor road northeast from Rimsø takes you to (2.5km) **Sostrup**, a large manor house built between 1599 and 1606. In 1960 it was sold to the Cistercian Order, which now uses the main building partly as a convent and retreat centre, and partly as a conference centre and holiday accommodation. There are holiday flats in the old stable buildings, a restaurant in the house and a modern chapel in one of the outbuildings. Note the magnificent main doorway from 1620.

Sostrup lies in the parish of **Gjerrild**, and you should drive the further 500m to see the village, which can boast of numerous half-timbered houses.

In **Sostrup Church** (in Gjerrild) there are some particularly interesting frescoes by the Brarup Master from c 1500, one depicting a horde of devils storming Heaven, and being repulsed by the Divine Hosts. In the vaulting in the nave other frescoes represent the Creation, including a merman and mermaid(!), and the Fall, after which we see Eve spinning and Adam ploughing. From a purely historical point of view this is of special interest, providing a picture of a very early wheel plough.

A road will now take you south through Veggerslev to (5km) Thorsø. Here you should turn left to **Voldby** (1.5km), again to see a church with some fine Gothic frescoes from the end of the 15C, discovered under whitewash in 1891. The most unusual picture here is of a huge man-of-war, filled with soldiers and flying the Danish flag. Others portray grotesque figures, some of which border on the obscene.

From Thorsø it is 7km to Grenå (see below).

Alternative route from Fausing to Grenå—the southern route
Total distance 46km.

Leave Fausing on the A16 east, passing *Gammel Estrup (see above). 7km ahead, just past Auning, you turn right towards (5km) **Pindstrup**. There is a modern church here, from 1969, with a large crucifix over the altar by the important modern sculptor Robert Jacobsen.

Continue through wooded, often steeply undulating terrain to the hamlet of (4km) **Marie Magdalene**, so called after the sizeable church built here between 1425 and 1458.

Made of red brick, with a white washed porch, it is one of Denmark's best-known churches. Frescoes by the Vinderslev Master were uncovered in the apse, chancel and nave in 1904, and these have since been restored: the Day of Judgement on the vaulting of the apse, intertwined plants in the vaulting of the chancel, more plants and geometrical patterns in the vaulting of the nave together with an immodest woman receiving her just deserts. A devil is applying a firebrand to her naked posterior, and the flames are issuing from her mouth. When first discovered earlier this century, this was thought to be unsuitable for a church, and it was covered over again. A later generation thought differently. The ornate pulpit (provided with an hourglass!) and canopy are Baroque, from c 1650, and the altarpiece is splendid rococo work from 1757.

A peculiar feature of the church is the presence of two rowan trees growing out of the mortar of the porch. Legend has it that they have been there since the porch was built; they are scarcely as old as that, though at least one of them is thought to have been there for 250–300 years. There are many local superstitions attached to these trees, as, being without contact with the earth, they are immune from evil. Consequently, wood from them has been used to provide protection from sickness and evil—and the trees still survive.

1km further brings you to the village of Ryomgård, where you will find the **Djursland Railway Museum**, exhibiting uniforms, photographs and equipment from the age of steam trains, together with a large model railway system (open Easter–Oct).

The landscape here begins to show signs of the huge **Kolindsund**, once open to the sea, then, due to land movement, an inland lake, and finally drained at the end of the 19C to provide arable land. The site of the 17C manor house of Gammel Ryomgård on your right was in fact once a headland jutting out into Kolindsund.

5km east of Ryomgård, just before Kolind, you turn left towards Grenå, to (9km) Fannerup, where you turn right to (2km) Fævejle. Here you turn left once more, driving through Allelev to (4km) **Vejlby**, the setting for the most famous miscarriage of justice in Denmark.

Søren Quist

In the 17C there lived in Vejlby a pastor by the name of Søren Quist, who is thought to have been responsible for the renovation of the altarpiece, and whose son's initials are to be found on the back of it. In 1625 Søren Quist was found guilty of murdering his farmhand, and he was executed the following year. His son, also pastor in Vejlby, had the case re-examined, and it emerged that two of the witnesses had committed perjury—for which they were in turn executed in 1634. The case was never fully cleared up, however, and the rumour later arose that it was actually Søren Quist's wife who was the culprit. Søren Quist is the main character in one of Steen Steensen Blicher's best and most moving stories, *The Pastor of Vejlby*.

In Vejlby there is a beautiful 18C farm, the **Ladefoged Farm**. It was used as the setting for the first film on Søren Quist, made in 1920, and has in recent years been completely restored. During the process a well-preserved Iron Age grave was found in the grounds.

The road now leads to (3km) **Ålsø**, where a stone in the church porch is said to be from the grave of Søren Quist, who was buried here in 1626. 3km east of Ålsø, at the end of an idyllic minor road, on a mound in a lake, stands the mansion of **Katholm**, with a principal wing built between 1588 and 1591.

From Ålsø, you now drive to (6km) **GRENÅ** (pop. 18,650), which to most people is just a ferry port with regular sailings to Hundested on Sjælland (but see below!), and to the Swedish ports of Varberg, Hälsingborg and Halmstad. The ferry to the small island of Anholt also leaves from here.

■ **Tourist information**: Torvet 1; tel. 86 32 12 00.

■ **Hotels**: Stena, Kystvej 25; tel. 86 32 25 00; Grenaa Strand, Havneplads; tel. 86 32 68 14.

■ **Youth hostel**: Ydesvej 4; tel. 86 32 66 22.

■ In 1988 Grenå opened its new **yachting harbour**, situated between the commercial harbour and the beach.

■ **Anglers** will find the canals leading to and across Kolindsund ideal for their sport. Licences are obtainable at the tourist information office in Grenå.

History

A market town with a charter probably from c 1300, Grenå has a long history behind it, and excavations have shown that it was built on the site of a Stone Age settlement. In the Middle Ages it occupied an important position as the river provided access to the then 20km-long inland lake of Kolindsund to the southwest.

After a period of stagnation and decay, Grenå experienced growth in the 19C with the establishment of a new harbour. Later in the century, the railway came to Grenå, then better roads, and in 1934 a regular ferry service was established to Hundested. Grenå has since attracted a good deal of industry, particularly the chemical industry and textiles. And as in most

Danish coastal towns there is a thriving fishing industry. The present harbour was opened in 1958.

Grenå suffered a disastrous fire in 1649, which destroyed many of the old buildings, not least the **church** on the main square, TORVET. It was subsequently rebuilt, but there is little left of the original structure. Much of the furniture dates from the period of rebuilding, including the carved pulpit from 1650. There used to be another church in Grenå, to the north west of the town, but this fell into disuse in the 16C and was then demolished. The foundations were rediscovered in 1893 and there is now public access to them from TJØRNEBAKKEN. Close by is the restored 19C **windmill** on Baunhøj, the highest point in the town.

Of older buildings in Grenå, one of the largest and most beautiful, an early 18C galleried merchant's house at SØNDERGADE 1, has been turned into the **Djursland Museum**. It contains extensive collections of local antiquities, coins, weapons, textiles and post-17C pottery. There are exhibits dating back to c 10,000 BC, and a reconstructed grave from the 1C AD. On Wednesdays in the summer there are demonstrations of the various trades represented in the museum. In this same building you will find the **Danish Fisheries Museum**, with exhibits illustrating the history and development of the fishing industry, including models of fishing vessels (both museums open summer; limited opening winter).

In LILLEGADE there are two other delightful preserved half-timbered houses, both from the mid 18C; one of them, known as **Aftenstjernen** (The Evening Star) is now a café. There are other older houses in STOREGADE. At FÆRGEVEJ 4 there is a new aquarium, the **Kattegat Centre**, providing windows for underwater observations of the fish and sea animals (including sharks) in something approaching their natural environment. The main square, Torvet, is now decorated with a huge sculptured vase by Peter Brandes.

From Grenå harbour there is a short and easy 1hr 30min sail by ferry to Hundested on Sjælland. This is one of the longest established ferry routes between Jutland and Sjælland, but **at the time of writing sailings have stopped**. As this *is* such an established route, it is almost unthinkable that a service will not be re-established, but you are advised to make enquiries e.g. from the Grenå tourist office (tel. 86 32 12 00), if planning to travel this way. Your alternative would be to go via Ebeltoft.

Hundested (pop. 9200; **Tourist information**: Nørregade 22; tel. 42 33 77 88) has a history going back to only c 1800, and not until c 1860 was the first attempt made to develop it as a fishing port. By 1886 the harbour was opened, and in 1916 the railway was taken there, enabling the establishment of the Hundested–Grenå ferry route.

There is a memorial in the town to Valdemar Poulsen, the inventor of wireless telegraphy. Art exhibitions are held in the tower of the town hall. The bathing beaches nearby, both to the north towards the high cliffs near **Spodsbjerg** lighthouse, and the south towards **Lynæs** are splendid. Today, Lynæs is a centre for windsurfing, and it is the home of a fine marina.

Spodsbjerg was for many years the home of the polar explorer **Knud**

Rasmussen, and the thatched house in which he lived when not undertaking expeditions is now a *museum commemorating him.

From Hundested there are two good routes to Frederikssund. The main, though longer route (31km) is detailed first; for the alternative route (21km), see below.

Main route from Hundested to Frederikssund
Total distance 31km.

You leave Hundested on the A16 which will take you straight to (13km) **Frederiksværk** (pop. 18,730).

■ **Tourist information**: Nørregade 1; tel. 42 12 30 01.

■ **Hotel**: Frederiksværk, Torvet 6; tel. 42 12 22 88.

■ **Youth hostel**: Strandgade 30; tel. 42 12 07 66.

History
Frederiksværk received its name in 1759, and is Denmark's oldest industrial town, founded in the early 18C by Frederik IV. It became the site of a major ordnance works and the place in which explosives were once manufactured for the armed forces, and, in modern times, a centre for the metal industry. It received a charter in 1907, and grew to its present size as a result of the building of the railway, first to Hillerød (p 114) and then to Hundested (see above). The advent of the railways also opened up the tourist industry which benefited from the unusually beautiful countryside in the north part of Sjælland.

There are few old buildings in Frederiksværk, though Hotel Frederiksværk on the market square dates from c 1800. On the other hand the canal between the Roskilde Fjord and the Arresø lake (the biggest lake in Denmark), around which the town was originally built, is still there, providing stretches of great charm.

A fine bronze statue by Axel Poulsen of a foundry worker stands on the market square, commemorating the principal occupation of the town. On the square, too, close to the canal, is the **Frederiksværk Bymuseum** (Frederiksværk Civic Museum) (open mid-June to mid-Aug; limited opening winter), housed in two half-timbered houses from c 1800. It contains archaeological and other exhibits from the area, especially a collection illustrating the industrial history of the town. The open air **Krudtværksmuseum** (Gunpowder Works Museum) (open Apr–Sep) is also situated by the canal in the middle of the town. The old ordnance foundry, **Gjethuset**, is now an art gallery. Alongside its industrial significance, Frederiksværk has indeed managed to preserve a good deal of charm.

East of Frederiksværk is the **Avderød** peninsula jutting out into the Arresø lake, its idyllic surroundings now a favourite holiday spot. This peninsula was formerly the site of **Dronningholm Kongeborg** (Dronningholm Royal Castle). This, once one of the largest of Danish medieval castles, was said to have been built by Valdemar II for Queen Dagmar. Ruins are all that now remain, but they have been restored as far as possible—and they provide a wonderful view across the Arresø lake. Relics from the castle are now exhibited in Frederiksværk Civic Museum.

Immediately east of Frederiksværk, reached by a path along the canal, stands the neo-classical mansion of **Arresødal**, built in 1782 by Johan Frederik Classen, who was responsible for much of the early development of Frederiksværk; it is now a conference centre. Classen lies in a bombastic sarcophagus by Wiedewelt in the 19C church at **Vinderød**, 1km north of Frederiksværk.

The Frederiksværk area is dotted with summer cottages, of which there are said to be some 6000, and the coast has ample facilities for bathing and sailing. If you take the 205 north from Frederiksværk you come to one of the most varied and beautiful areas of North Sjælland, **Tisvilde Hegn**, an area planted with trees to combat sand drift in the 17C, and now a place of wooded charm. It borders one of the longest stretches of beach in Sjælland, extending 12km from Liseleje in the south to Rågeleje in the north.

Leaving Frederiksværk south on the A16 you arrive at (4km) **Kregme**. Here, standing on high ground, the quite impressive Romanesque church can be seen from afar, and the view from it, across the lake on one side and the Roskilde Fjord on the other, is magnificent.

You now continue your route on the 211 south, until at 5km you come to a minor road leading east to Skævinge (6km). **Skævinge Church** is the outstanding church in this area. It is again frescoes which are the main feature, this time a quite unusual post-Reformation series covering the walls from floor to ceiling. The motifs include David and Goliath, but pride of place goes to a huge painting of Holger Danske, Holger the Dane, the legendary heroic figure said to be sleeping beneath Kronborg Castle (p 107), ready to return to help Denmark in its hour of need. Holger Danske, in 16C dress, is seen confronting his enemy the Sultan Bruher, and both are armed to the teeth. The frescoes are not the only things of interest: there are fine examples of 17C workmanship in the bench ends and pulpit, while the altarpiece portraying Doubting Thomas is by the important 19C artist C.W. Eckersberg.

From Skævinge you return to the 211 through the villages of Lille Havelse and Store Havelse and drive south to (8km) Frederikssund (see below).

Alternative route from Hundested to Frederikssund—via Jægerspris
Total distance 21km.

Leave Hundested on the A16 and at (32km) Amager Ruse turn right to (2km) **Sølager**, where you take the ferry (5 minutes) to Kulhuse. You are now in **Horns Herred**, a beautiful, idyllic peninsula littered with archaeological remains, and now a much favoured holiday area. As you drive south on the 207 on your left is the **Nordskov** forest containing oak trees said to be 1000 years old. From Kulhuse it is a mere 10km to the splendid palace of *Jægerspris, and the 207 goes right past it.

The history of the palace probably goes back to the 11C, though the first direct reference to it is from 1318, when King Erik Menved's four-month-old son was killed here in an accident. Valdemar IV bought it; Queen Margrethe I spent time here, and it has been in the ownership of many Danish queens. It was given to Crown Prince Frederik (later King Frederik V) on his marriage to the English Princess Louise in 1743. However, the most famous of the ladies associated with it is the morganatic wife of Frederik VII, Countess Danner. Countess Danner, a commoner born Louise Rasmussen, was never accepted in royal circles, and the couple spent a great deal of their time here. The Countess is at her own wish buried in an open burial mound in the grounds. Frederik VII left the palace to her, and in 1873 she established it as 'King Frederik VII's Foundation for Helpless and Deserted Young Ladies, More Especially Those of the Humble Classes', much in the style of the English Dr Barnardo's Homes.

The main wing of the palace, the pink Baroque 17C south wing with 18C extensions, is on two floors, with 12 windows in each and towers with onion-shaped steeples midway on each side of the main entrance. The oldest part of the palace, the north wing incorporating the late medieval house known as Abrahamstrup and a substantial heptagonal tower containing a winding stair-case, built by Christian IV, can be seen in the background. While the south wing overlooks the main courtyard, in the centre of which there is a life-sized bronze statue of a stag by Thorvaldsen's pupil Adelgunde Vogt, the north wing looks out on a delightful green. There is an 18C extension to the north wing, while Christian VI had an east wing built in the 1730s in order to join the otherwise separate north and south wings. The royal chambers were then installed in this newly built section.

A considerable part of the palace is now open to the public (Apr–Oct) for conducted tours each hour. In the south wing a number of rooms, including the king's study, are still furnished as they were in the days of Frederik VII and Countess Danner. Other rooms display archaeological treasures found in the area by Frederik VII who was keen to examine the prehistoric sites there. The park is open throughout the year, and is itself of interest, containing not only the open burial mound in which Countess Danner's sarcophagus can be seen, but also 54 statues by Wiedewelt commemorating important Danish figures from early times to the 19C.

Before continuing to Frederikssund, you should drive south on a minor road to **Dråby** (2km) to visit the Romanesque church in which there is a splendid series of frescoes from the 15C Isefjord Master's workshop, including biblical motifs and scenes from the life of St Lawrence.

From Jægerspris it is only 6km to **Frederikssund** (pop. 17,160), which is reached by the Crown Prince Frederik Bridge from 1935. Near the west end of the bridge there is a local museum (**Egnsmuseum**) in an architecturally inter-esting old ferryman's house.

■ **Tourist information**: Jernbanegade 24; tel 42 31 06 85.

■ **Hotel**: Rådhuskroen, Østergade 1; tel. 42 13 44 66.

Frederikssund grew up in the 17C around the ferry connection across the narrow strip of the Roskilde Fjord, linking the east side, North Sjælland, with the west, Horns Herred (County), and was granted a charter in 1809. It is now a centre for food manufacturing, in particular for the soft drinks industry. Its proximity to Copenhagen was underlined in 1989 when the Copenhagen suburban railways, the 'S' trains, were extended as far as Frederikssund.

The town is famous today for two things. It has come to be known as the 'Viking Town', and every summer at the end of June and beginning of July plays with Viking themes are performed on an open air stage on the area called **Kalvø** where the river enters the fjord. This former islet, like the entire area here, does indeed have Viking associations; it is just south of a Viking settlement and was the site of a meeting in 1157 to decide on the succession to the throne.

The other, very different, cultural attraction in Frederikssund is the **J.F. Willumsen Museum**. Willumsen, one of the most important 20C Danish artists, is most famous as a Symbolist painter and sculptor, though he was also a ceramic and graphic artist. Just before his death he presented Frederikssund with all those works of his which were in his possession, on condition that the town built a museum suitable for them. The resultant museum was opened in 1957, but Willumsen, who died in the south of France, where he had lived for many years, never saw it. He is now buried in the park to the east of the museum.

▶ Excursion from Frederikssund to Horns Herred

Total distance 33km. This trip takes you through the middle part of Horns Herred, visiting churches, mansions, a bird sanctuary and a doll museum.

From Frederikssund you cross the strait by the bridge and drive southwest on the A53 to (10km) **Krogstrup**. There is a Romanesque pilgrims' church here. The carved altarpiece is from 1633 and the late Renaissance pulpit from 1625.

Continue 2km west to the small mansion of **Svanholm**, now a collective farm run on ecological principles, and from here a long avenue leads south to (4km) **Skibby**.

Despite an uninteresting exterior, Skibby ***church** is special and rightly famous, not only for its frescoes (which are themselves very splendid), but because it was here that in 1650 a manuscript now known as the Skibby Chronicle was discovered bricked in behind the altar. Written in Latin, it is a history of Denmark from 1046 to 1534, with the main emphasis on the period immediately before the Reformation. Intensely pro-Catholic, this is clearly the work of the great Catholic spokesman of the time, the Carmelite monk from Helsingør, Paul Helgesen. How the manuscript came to be hidden in Skibby church is not known, but the fact that it finishes in the midst of a sentence has given rise to much speculation.

Meanwhile, this is the biggest church in the county, the Romanesque apse, chancel and nave with five mighty pillars dating back to the early 12C. Many of the Romanesque features have survived. A series of outstandingly good frescoes dating back to 1175–1200 was discovered in the apse in 1855. The central feature is a portrait of Christ in Majesty. Restoration work began in 1858, the first (though perhaps rather heavy-handed) restoration of Danish Romanesque frescoes ever. Another series from c 1350 is in the vaulting in the chancel.

You now take a minor road east to (2km) **Selsø** lake. It is thought that—as late as the end of the 17C—this was not a lake but an inlet on the Roskilde Fjord.

Now it forms an important bird sanctuary, the home of large numbers of water birds both native and migratory. The road will take you around the lake, gradually turning north.

You will then come to (2km) **Selsø Church** and, 300m further away, **Selsø House**. Standing in an isolated position, the church was originally Romanesque, with a tall apse filling three quarters of a circle, a very short chancel and a broad and lofty nave. The tower and porch are Gothic. Excavations have shown that there was originally a round church on this site. Selsø House has a history going far back, and the estate was probably established by Bishop Absalon in the 1170s. There was certainly a mansion here in 1288, and the great well in the courtyard, the biggest medieval well in the country, is probably from that time. The present house is over 400 years old, though it was partly redesigned in 1734, when it lost its Renaissance character and received its present Baroque façade.

The interior is largely unchanged from the 18C, and in particular there is a fine great hall, with 4m-high marbled panels and an exquisite stucco ceiling; the enormous mirrors have been compared with those in Versailles. Splendid French tapestries can be seen in some of the other rooms. The rather more modest servants' rooms are also still in existence. Ironically, much of this has been preserved because the house has not been lived in for over a century. Since 1973, however, restoration work has been carried out, and most of the house is now open to the public, including the vaulted cellar from 1565. There are exhibitions of old dresses, weapons and an enormous number of toy soldiers and warship models, while concerts of classical music are regular held in the great hall (open May–mid-June weekends; mid-June–mid-Aug daily; mid-Aug–end Sep weekends).

From the beach of the small Østskov woods, 3km east of Selsø, you will catch sight of the island of **Eskilsø**, where there are the remains of an Augustinian monastery. There is little left of it, and there is no regular connection to the island, but it is nevertheless of historical interest, in that according to an early manuscript the monks of Eskilsø danced the medieval chain dances at an annual festival there in 1165—one of the earliest references to this dance which was widespread throughout Scandinavia in the Middle Ages and beyond, and which is still danced in the Faroe Islands.

Leave Selsø House to the northeast, where a minor road leads to (2km) **Østby**, with an art and handicraft centre housed in a former co-operative dairy. Another 3km north will bring you to **Skuldelev**. It was in the fjord east of Skuldelev that the Viking ships now exhibited in Roskilde (p 54) were found and excavated between 1957 and 1962. Skuldelev is also the site of an important medieval sacred well, known as St Olaf's Well, which still flows. An attraction of a quite different kind is the dolls' museum, **Skuldelev Dukkemuseum**, containing upwards of 250 dolls, many from the 19C; there are also old dolls' prams and a good collection of tin soldiers (open summer).

Now stay on the minor road going north, and you will come to (4km) **Gerlev**, where in the Gerlev Park there is an extensive rose park containing 3000 old-fashioned pre-19C scented roses in addition to 2500 modern varieties. Here, too, there is **Den danske Træsamling**, a plantation containing all the trees native to Denmark. From Gerlev it is only a further 4km back to Frederikssund. ◀

From Frederikssund you take the 207/E53 east to (7km) **Slangerup**, a very old town, once standing on the important road from Helsingør to Roskilde. King Erik Ejegod was born here, and in 1095 he had a church built here. It was the site, too, of the first convent in Denmark, established by Valdemar I and belonging to the Cistercian order.

Like other predominantly ecclesiastical centres, Slangerup found its role diminished after the Reformation. At the same time its importance on the Helsingør–Roskilde route also decreased. Today nothing remains of the convent, and only the tower on the present church is left of the original parish church from 1411. On the other hand, this large and dignified early Renaissance building from 1588, Gothic rather than Renaissance in style, is one of the few large-scale churches of its day, clearly intended for a future which Slangerup never achieved. A memorial to King Erik Ejegod stands outside the church.

Close by there is another memorial, to Bishop Thomas Kingo, who was born here and returned as pastor from 1668 to 1677. Kingo, who later became Bishop of Odense, was one of the greatest of Danish poets, the outstanding Baroque hymn-writer whose best work has surely seldom been surpassed by any writer of hymns in any language. A more modern era is reflected in the new **Aircraft Museum**.

Now go south now on the A6 to (2km) **Jørlunde**, where there is another very old church, early Romanesque, probably built in the 12C by the Hvide family, the most powerful of the great medieval noble families, to which Bishop Absalon himself belonged. The interior has been radically restored. There are fine Romanesque frescoes of scenes from the life of Christ, dating from 1175–1200, in the chancel and nave. The large-scale gilded altar is from 1613.

Continue through (3km) Ølstykke and join the 211 after a further 2km. Turn left here to (3km) **Stenløse**. Here, too, there is a Romanesque church with Gothic transept and porch. The auricular altarpiece from 1663 is the work of Lorentz Jørgensen.

Veksø, 3km further along the 211, has the remains of a Romanesque church, though it suffered from 19C rebuilding which removed the Romanesque nave and replaced the original apse with a new one. There are nevertheless Romanesque features still to be seen together with a magnificent Renaissance pulpit and Renaissance carved bench ends.

Veksø also has a collection of sculptures by well-known sculptors in **Veksølund** in KIRKESTRÆDE. This is the largest gallery for modern sculpture in Denmark, some housed indoors, some on display in the extensive gardens (open June–Sep).

From Veksø the 211 will take you straight to (22km) Copenhagen (p 60 ff).

The area you are moving into now may seem just as uninteresting as any built-up area close to a city, but the ancient villages are also here with their beautiful churches. If you are interested in historical churches, here are three more which ought to be visited.

The first is quite close to the 211, on the left, in (5km) **Måløv**. The Roskilde Fjord once stretched as far as this, and there was a heathen temple here. Sven Estridsen then built his first church in the 11C on the site of the temple. It was dedicated to St James, and the present building consists of Romanesque chancel and nave, with Gothic tower and porch. Many of the original features—rounded windows and doors—are still there, while the round chancel arch has been reconstructed to maintain the aspect of a church of great character. There are numerous frescoes, some from the early 13C on the chancel wall, representing the Virgin, a bishop saint, Christ in Majesty, David and Solomon, and others, all of high artistic quality. Other frescoes on the side walls date from c 1450 and are the work of the Isefjord Master. The pulpit and canopy are from c 1600. St James' Spring is nearby.

Now cross the 211 and drive through Smørumnedre to (3km) **Smørumovre**. Again the church is Romanesque with a Gothic tower and extension to the nave. There are two porches, one late Romanesque, the other Gothic. Of the original Romanesque windows, only one is still discernible. However, there are again some fine frescoes, from c 1500, illustrating the Day of Judgement, the Last Supper and the Passion, but these are offset by a series of humorous, not to say bawdy, scenes, thought possibly to be illustrating light entertainment in the pauses in medieval mystery plays.

Your next stop is at (3km) **Ledøje** which you reach by taking the road from Smørumovre church towards Ballerup, turning right after 1km. The medieval *church in Ledøje is unique in Denmark. Built c 1225 on the orders of an immigrant German knight, Conrad of Reginstein, it follows the pattern he knew from his native Goslar, constructed on two floors and in effect containing two churches, the upper one for the nobility, the lower for the ordinary people. Both the chancel and the nave on both levels are almost square, with columns on the lower floor to support the upper one. There are frescoes in both churches—but they are all from the 19C.

From Ledøje you now return to the 211 via **Ballerup** (where there is yet another church full of frescoes), and Copenhagen (p 60 ff) is then only 15km away.

24 • Bornholm

*Round trip of Bornholm (total distance 98km). 159 from **Rønne** to (10km) Hasle. (13km) **Allinge/Sandvig**. 158 to (16km) **Gudhjem**. (16km) **Svaneke**. Unclassified roads to (13km) Neksø. A38 to (14km) Åkirkeby. (16km) **Rønne**.*

Bornholm, with a total area of only 600 sq km and far from the other Danish islands, 180km out in the Baltic, is the archetypal holiday island. It offers a variety of scenery, woodland, rocky coastlines, idyllic small towns, magnificent beaches (some would say the best in Europe), yachting and swimming opportunities, coastal paths, cycling paths, archaeological remains and a vast ruined fortress. Because of its size and thanks to the services of the bus company BAT (Bornholms Amts Trafikselskab) there are excellent public transport services on the island, making it an ideal place to visit even if you do not come with your own car. There are splendid regular services, and comprehensive tours by bus. Information from **Bornholms Velkomstcenter, Rønne**, tel. 56 95 95 00.

History

The island is known to have been inhabited by 3000 BC, and there are many signs of prehistoric settlement. Seven hundred Bronze Age burial mounds are known, and of these about a third still exist. Those which have been excavated have often yielded valuable material. Other grave finds are from the Iron Age, AD 400–800, which is an age that has not left many traces elsewhere in Denmark. There is also a large number of runestones, mainly—unusually—from the early Middle Ages (1000–1100), and most of the inscriptions reflect early Christianity.

The first historical reference to Bornholm is from c 890 when an Anglo-Saxon skipper, Wulfstan, visited it and referred to it in his account as Burgundaland. According to Wulfstan's account—written for Alfred the Great—Bornholm had its own king at this time, but it subsequently came under Danish rule. Lying close to the North European mainland, it was often the object of attack by the Wends, and for this reason some of the churches were fortified and suitable for defence.

Situated close to the Swedish mainland, Bornholm was also the object of attentions from that direction, and it was for c 200 years in the hands of the Archbishops of Lund, who ran it as their private dominion, giving charters to the market towns and applying their own laws. For a time, Bornholm also tasted the rule of Lübeck. Like the rest of Denmark, it was occupied by Nazi forces in 1940, and was the only part of Denmark to be liberated by Soviet troops in May 1945. The principal town, Rønne, suffered heavily from the preceding bombardment.

Bornholm, with its rugged, impressive scenery, is a rocky island, totally different from any other part of Denmark. Its former isolation from metropolitan Denmark has led to a fierce sense of local pride, many different traditions, and even an accent distinct from what you will hear elsewhere in the country.

Bornholm is a 6–7hr sail from Copenhagen. The trip to **Rønne** is by comfortable modern ferries with excellent facilities. Alternatively, there is an overland route, through Sweden, with a ferry from Ystad to Rønne. There are now also ferry connections between Rønne and two towns on the north German island of Rügen: Sassnitz and Neu Mukran; and for those venturing further afield, between Rønne and Swinoujscie in Poland. By air the flight from Copenhagen takes less than an hour.

RØNNE (pop. 15,180), which received its charter in 1584, is the biggest town on Bornholm and the home of almost a third of the total population. Most of the town consists of single-family houses, many of them half-timbered. There are rows and rows of these charming and well-tended early 19C houses, often in idyllic cobbled streets showing few signs of modern times.

■ **Tourist information**: Bornholms Velkomstcenter, Nordre Kystvej 3; tel 56 95 95 00, providing information on the whole of Bornholm.

■ **Hotels**: Hotel Griffen, Kredsen 1; tel 56 95 51 11; Sverres Small Hotel, Sankt Mortensgade 48; tel. 56 95 03 03.

- **Youth hostel**: Arsenalvej 12; tel. 56 95 13 40.

- The harbour in Rønne is unusually large for a town of this size, reflecting, perhaps, the variety of traffic to this outlying island, not least a new quay to receive cruise ships. There is, naturally, a **marina**, and there are first-rate sheltered **beaches** of white sand, offering good **bathing** facilities, both to the north and south.

A tour of the town would naturally start at the **church** which though pleasing to the eye is not of particular architectural interest, having largely been rebuilt in 1915–18. In ØSTERGADE, immediately east of the church, you will find **Karnapgården**, the only remaining of several former large houses with bay windows. Turning into SØNDERGADE, you cannot miss **Hovedvagten**, from 1743–44, with its overhanging roof supported on columns and its curious rounded gable. Søndergade 11 is another large half-timbered house with an unusual tower-like construction intended to allow the inhabitants to watch the arrival of ships.

Now go north along Søndergade, across LILLE TORV and STORE TORV (the main shopping area) along Store Torvegade, where the splendid **Exsteens Gård** stands, to STOREGADE with the old Sheriff's Residence from c 1800. Nearby is the Commander's Residence (Kommandantboligen) from 1846, a long building with a large dormer. Two streets south is LAKSEGADE, where the fine **Erichsens Gård** (No. 7) is now part of the Bornholm Museum (see below). A building of a completely different kind is the old citadel, **Kastellet**, from c 1650, looking for all the world like one of the round churches—and with walls 3.5m thick. Reached via STRANDPROMENADEN, it stands to the south of the town and is now a *museum illustrating the defence of Bornholm over the centuries (open May–Oct).

Bornholms Museum (open summer; limited opening winter), in SANKT MORTENSGADE, is a regional museum specialising in Bornholm's prehistory and history. Among its prize possessions is part of a large find of Roman gold and silver coins discovered near Vestermarie together with another find of 8C gold pieces all stamped with human figures. Altogether some 2000 of these figures have been found on Bornholm. In addition to these early exhibits there is a splendid collection of paintings by Bornholm artists.

Just as Skagen (see p 271) attracted a group of outstanding artists at the end of the 19C, so, somewhat later, did Bornholm, and their products are well represented here. A new addition to the museum is **Hjorths Fabrik**, a working ceramics museum at KRYSTALGADE 5, where it is possible to follow the whole ceramics process from clay to finished product. **Erichsens Gård** re-creates bygone interiors as well as exhibiting memorabilia connected with the 19C poet Holger Drachmann and his first wife, who was herself an Erichsen. There is also a beautiful period garden with old-fashioned flowers and fruits (open May–Sept).

From Rønne you take the 159 north towards (10km) Hasle, turning right at 5km to look at **Nyker** (2km), where you will find **Nykirke**, one of the four round churches for which Bornholm is famous. It was built of unhewn boulders in 1150, though the steep roof is probably 16C. It is the smallest of the four round churches, and it is on two floors only, the third, fortified floor never having been completed. Some primitive 14C frescoes can be seen on the walls and the central column, and two runestones stand in the porch. There is a free-standing half-timbered belfry in the churchyard, to which access is gained through a gateway of a type commonly found in Bornholm farms.

Return to the 159 and continue to (5km) **Hasle** (pop. 6520), an idyllic little town with winding cobbled streets.

■ **Tourist information**: Havnegade 1; tel. 56 95 44 81.

■ **Hotels**: Hasle Feriepark, H.C. Sierstedvej 2; tel. 56 95 72 95; Pension Svalhøj, Simblegårdsvej 28; tel. 56 96 40 18.

■ **Youth hostel**: Fælledvej 28; tel. 56 96 41 75.

Do not be put off by the simplicity of the 16th-century **church** here: it contains an *altarpiece of rare beauty dating from c. 1450, the oldest in Bornholm. There are various legends as to how this altarpiece came to be here—the favourite being that it was a thanks offering from a sailor saved from ship-wreck—but it is at least certain that it was made in a Lübeck workshop around 1510. The central panel is a crucifixion group, and the side panels portray four scenes from the Passion. The lifelike figures are carved with great skill, and the carved foliage is intricate and beautiful.

Apart from this, Hasle has the charm of its **half-timbered** houses. On STRANDGADE there are the relics of a past age in the herring smokehouses. Bornholm is famous for its smoked herrings, and the island is dotted with such smokehouses, many of which are no longer in use due to changing fishing patterns. One, from 1897, has now been opened as a **smokehouse museum**—and of course, it is possible to buy fresh-smoked herrings (open May-Oct).

The 159 continues north towards **Allinge/Sandvig** but you should turn off left after 5km on a minor road to visit **Jons Kapel** (1km). Despite its name, this is not a chapel, but a group of rocks on the coast, the home of rare rock plants. It is reached by a wooded path and 108 steps. Legend has it that a monk by the name of Jon lived here and preached to the local heathen population. Whatever the truth, this is a remarkable sight.

A further 7km sees you in **Allinge/Sandvig**.

■ **Tourist information**: Kirkegade 4, Allinge. Hotels: Hammersø, Hammershusvej 86; tel. 56 48 03 64; Klintely, Sandkås; tel. 56 48 10 34.

■ **Youth hostel**: Hammershusvej 94; tel. 56 48 03 62.

Allinge and Sandvig are two towns which have now more or less merged into one. The whole area provides a great variety of attractions: sea, beaches, yatchting, countryside walking, archaeological remains. Then there is a group of rock carvings, the **Madsebakke Helleristninger**, the best of such groups on Bornholm, comprising outlines of ships, footmarks, sun symbols and a series of empty circles. And there is the **Moseløkken** quarry. Quarrying has been a major industry on Bornholm, but few quarries now remain. At Moseløkken there is in addition to a working quarry a museum, **Moseløkken Stenbrudsudstilling**, illustrating the traditional methods used for quarrying and treating Bornholm granite (open May–Sept).

However, the outstanding feature is inevitably the castle of ***Hammershus** (open all year), possibly the biggest ruined fortress in Northern Europe, standing on a 74m-high cliff on the west coast. It can be approached either by turning left off the 159, 3km before you reach Allinge, or by a minor road from Sandvig, skirting the northernmost point of Bornholm, Hammeren, and driving past the Hammersø Lake. There are ample parking facilities.

History
Little is known of the origins of Hammershus, but building is believed to have been started c 1255 as a result of the struggles between the Danish King and the Archbishops of Lund. The first direct mention is in connection with the murder of King Erik Glipping in 1286, when the outlawed assassins sought refuge here. Christian II ousted the Archbishop in 1522. Hammershus was leased to the Lübeckers, who extended and strengthened it before leaving Bornholm in 1576. However, strong as the fortress was, it was no longer sufficient to withstand modern artillery, and in 1645 it was taken by the Swedish Admiral Wrangel during the Torstenson War; the admiral only had four cannon at his disposal. It was later used as a state prison, and Christian IV's daughter Leonora Christine was held here for a year. In 1743 Hammershus ceased to be used as a garrison, and from that time it fell into disrepair until it was listed as a national monument in 1822.

The Mantle Tower and courtyard are the oldest parts surviving, standing high above the rest. There were five floors, the top one added by the Lübeckers. It was here that Leonora Christine was imprisoned. The entire complex has been surrounded by a great ring wall probably from the same period. Parts of it still stand, the section to the west being over 9m high. On the east side a length remains near the corner tower, Blommetårnet, which is the best preserved of all the buildings in the castle. The bridge giving access to the castle from the east is the only such bridge to have survived in Denmark, though the drawbridge itself has disappeared.

From Allinge you can take a ferry to the island of Christiansø (see below).

Leave Allinge on the coastal road, 158, southeast to (5km) **Tejn**. This stretch of the coast was the first in north Bornholm to be favoured by tourists for its sandy coves and extensive beaches. At Tejn, the biggest fishing village on Bornholm (containing a post mill from 1859), you turn right and take the steep road leading to (4km) **Olsker** to visit the tallest of the round churches, 112m above sea level, with panoramic views across the north coast of the island.

Originally dedicated to St Olaf (hence the name), it was built on three floors about 1150, and it shows obvious signs of having been constructed for defence, with nine openings clearly intended for dropping boulders on attackers. There are signs, too, of a wooden watchman's gallery having been suspended outside the church at the top. The nave is, of course, round, but there is a small rectangular chancel plus apse, both of them original. The porch is a later addition, but its date is not known. The interior is vaulted, though there are indications of an original flat roof, and there is a half-dome above the apse.

Continue east now on the 158. After 2km you come to **Stammershalle**, where there is a group of Stone Age graves and three standing stones. A further 4km brings you to **Helligdomsklipperne** (Sanctuary Cliffs), a group of rocks on the coast, formerly a place of pilgrimage thanks to the healing qualities of the water from the sacred spring, the **Helligdomskilde**, nearby. There is one tall obelisk-like rock and several deep caves on this spot.

5km further on lies **Gudhjem**, a small and particularly picturesque fishing village on rising ground sloping up from the coast, with steep streets and the usual well-kept half-timbered houses.

■ **Tourist information**: Åbogade 9; tel. 56 48 52 10.

■ **Hotels**: Casa Blanca; tel. 56 48 50 20; Bokulhus, Bokulvej 4; tel. 56 48 52 97.

■ **Youth hostel**: Ejner Mikkelsensvej 14; tel. 56 48 50 35.

A centre for Baltic trade in prehistoric times, Gudhjem is now a busy herring port, and there is usually plenty to see in the harbour. Herring—known simply as Bornholmers—are prepared for smoking in the traditional manner. They are, of course, on sale straight from the smokehouses.

Gudhjem Museum, with a collection of local art, is housed in the old railway station, which is now scheduled (open May–Sept). A recent addition to the attraction of Gudhjem is the brand-new, purpose built art museum, **Bornholms Kunstmuseum**, housing a fine collection of art and applied art that centres on the Bornholm school of painting: Oluf Høst, Edvard Weie, Karl Isakson, Olaf Rude but with a representative collection of other painters of note. The museum claims to have the biggest collection of applied art in Denmark outside Copenhagen. (Open April–Oct 10.00–17.00; Nov–Mar Tue, Thur, Sun, 13.00–17.00.) The church in Gudhjem is 19C, but just behind it you will find the ruins of the 13C St Anna's chapel, with frescoes preserved on the south wall.

The important painter of the Bornholm School, Oluf Høst (1884–1966), is buried in the churchyard here.

▶Ferry-excursion from Gudhjem to Christiansø

Gudhjem is the principal port with regular sailings to the tiny **Ertholme** islands, 17km northeast of Bornholm, two of which, **Christiansø** and **Frederiksø** are inhabited, while the third, **Græsholm**, is a bird sanctuary.

Christiansø was fortified by Christian V, and the stone-lined streets still reflect their military past. The island played a role during the Napoleonic Wars, when it was used as a base for attacks on British ships in the area. The remains of the fortress, including the tower, can still be seen. Frederiksø, on the other hand, was once used as a state prison; here, too, the fortified tower still stands. Apart from their tourist attraction, the islands are a favourite spot for artists. There are no cars on them, and the total population is c 130. A museum, the **Christiansø Museum**, is housed in the small tower, Lille Tårn, in

Christiansø

the Frederiksø fortress, and contains a good collection illustrating the way of life on the islands, with emphasis on its military past on the one hand and its fishing on the other (open May–Sept). ◀

There are two equally interesting routes from Gudhjem to **Svaneke**: the direct coastal route (16km) is described first; for the alternative route (20km) see below.

Coastal route from Gudhjem to Svaneke
Total distance 16km.

1km south of Gudhjem on the 158, in an area much favoured by artists, comes **Melsted**, another tiny fishing village. Here, housed in the 17C half-timbered **Melstedgård** farm, you will find an agricultural museum illustrating the traditional agricultural methods of the island, with implements and interiors from the 19C (open mid-May to Oct).

3km further south comes a rock formation known as **Himmerigsport** (The Gate to Heaven), and a further 3km sees the desolate reef, **Randkløve Skær**, 50m long, with 16m-deep fissures. 4km further on lies the fishing village of **Bølshavn**. Before arriving at (3km) Listed, you will pass a standing stone of granite known as **Helligkvinde** (Holy Woman), just beside a ship burial. According to legend the standing stone represents a woman and the ship burial her nine children, who were all turned to stone when her husband tried to murder them. It used to be the custom to salute the Holy Woman on passing her. You are now 2km from Svaneke (see below).

Alternative route from Gudhjem to Svaneke—via Østerlars and Østermarie
Total distance 20km.

Østerlars Round Church

For this route you take a road south from Gudhjem to (5km) **Østerlars** to visit the biggest and best known of the round churches, like the others built about 1150.

In addition to an oval chancel and apse, the church consists of a round nave, three storeys high. The exterior looks different from that of the other churches thanks to the seven massive buttresses surrounding it, presumably from the 16C and 17C. Once more the walls clearly show that the church has been fortified. There are two porches, that on the north side a uniquely splendid piece of Romanesque work.

The 13m-wide interior is vaulted towards the hollow central pillar which stands on a series of six arcades. The font is beneath these arcades, and the walls of this central pillar are decorated with frescoes depicting the life of Christ, from 1350–1400. There is a free-standing belfry in the churchyard; three runestones at the porch.

A road southeast will take you now to (6km) **Østermarie**. Here there is a very old church ruin standing next to the present neo-Romanesque church from 1891. One unusual feature of this old church is the parallel rows of barrel vaulting clearly seen in the extant east wall. There are four runestones in the church, and two Romanesque stone graves were found beside it in 1932.

From Østermarie the road goes east past **Louisenlund**, the largest group of standing stones on Bornholm, 51 in all, and the very popular and long established **Brændesgårdshaven** pleasure park, and then finally to (9km) **Svaneke**.

■ **Tourist information**: Storegade 24.

■ **Hotels**: Munken, Storegade 12; tel. 56 49 61 12; Østersøen, Havnebryggen 5; tel. 56 49 72 79.

■ **Youth hostel**: Reberbanevej 9; tel. 56 49 62 42.

■ Svaneke is the third port from which you can take a **ferry** to Christiansø.

Svaneke one of the smallest market towns in the country, with a charter going back to the 15C, has been a conservation area since 1967 and was in 1975 awarded a gold medal by the Council of Europe for efforts to preserve its historical character. The harbour, which cannot be used in bad weather, was blasted out of the rocks in the 19C. The town as a whole starts on level ground near the harbour, where the older and larger merchant houses are still situated, and then rises steeply in terraces on the slopes just inland. This has resulted in numerous stone steps leading to the higher parts of the town. The simple church, originally Gothic, was largely rebuilt in 1881. Two listed windmills, an old post mill and a later Dutch model, stand on a hill above the town.

The internationally known philologist and Classical scholar J.N. Madvig (1804–86) was born in Svaneke, and is commemorated in a small park in Storegade.

From Svaneke you follow the coastal road to (3km) Grisby, turning right there to (2km) **Ibskirke**, a church thought to date from the same period as the round churches. It consists of a Romanesque nave, chancel and apse largely as it was when built; particularly notable is the massive tower with warehouse doors opening out on the second and third floors, suggesting that it was used as a butter store in the Middle Ages, its thick walls acting as good insulation. The altarpiece (1846) is by Eckersberg, and there is a statue of the Virgin from c 1500 and a crucifix from c 1300.

Return to the 158 and drive to (7km) **Neksø** (pop. 8620), the second largest town on Bornholm and known to have had a charter in 1451.

■ **Tourist information**: Åsen 4;

■ **Hotels**: Balka Strand, Boulevarden 9A; tel. 56 49 21 50; Bornholm, Pilegårdsvejen 1; tel. 56 48 83 83.

■ **Youth hostel**: Skrokkegårdsvejen 17, Dueodde; tel. 56 48 81 19.

Neksø is cosily situated in a depression near the sea and sheltered by hills to the north and west. It was badly damaged in 1945 when Soviet ships bombarded it prior to the liberation, but careful restoration and rebuilding work has hidden this. As most other towns on Bornholm, Neksø is characterised by houses of modest proportions, many of them surrounded by dry-stone walls. Of larger houses mention must be made of the old sheriff's residence in KØBMAGERGADE. The modest church is late Gothic, but largely rebuilt in the 18C. The foundations of the tower are from the 16C, but the upper part, including the ridge turret, is from 1910.

The author Martin Andersen Nexø (1869–1954) spent six years of his childhood here, from 1877–83, and has described life here in his memoirs as well as, in fictitious form, in Book Two of his novel *Pelle the Conqueror*. There is an Andersen Nexø museum at FERSKESØSTRÆDE 36.

2km northwest of Neksø lies **Paradisbakkerne** (The Paradise Hills). Much of this wooded and hilly area is now protected as an area of outstanding natural beauty. One feature of the hills is the large number of erratic boulders, one of which, **Rokkestenen**, still can actually be rocked, despite its 30 tonnes. In these hills, too, you can find the remains of an old castle, Gamleborg. Clearly, this is an area for walking, and suitable paths are marked for one, two or three hour walks.

South of Neksø you will find wide flat **beaches**, a total contrast to the rocky shores of the north. This is a favourite holiday area with countless holiday cottages. **Dueodde** (9km) is the southernmost point of Bornholm, characterised by sand drift, and with huge expanses of white sand and extensive dunes. The area is now protected, though there are both hotels and a camping ground there.

Your round trip of Bornholm now continues west along the A38. After 4km you reach **Bodilskirke**, called after the English St Bottolph. As in Ibskirke church, the tower, broader than the nave, has been used as a store. Close by the church there is the large group of standing stones called **Gryet**.

10km further on you will be in Åkirkeby, passing at 5km a road leading south to **Pedersker** (5km), where there is a Romanesque church with the nave, chancel and apse largely as when built, except for window and door openings. The stubby tower is 16C and the porch a 19C addition.

Åkirkeby (pop. 6762), received its charter in 1346 from the Archbishop of Lund and in the Middle Ages was the most important town on the island. The regional council met there until 1776. Since then it has been overtaken by the coastal towns and is now little more than a large village.

■ **Tourist information**: Torvet 2; tel. 56 97 45 20.

■ **Hotels**: Strandhotel Boderne, Boderne 1; tel. 56 97 49 33; Dams på Bakken, Haregade 14; tel. 56 97 46 66.

Åkirkeby was also once the centre of Bornholm's ecclesiastical administration, and so it is not surprising that there should be a particularly impressive *church here. The oldest parts stem presumably from c 1150, and the tower, with a saddle roof, must have been completed c 1200. The thickness of its walls suggests that it was fortified. The fine late Romanesque porch is from the same time and is the oldest extant Romanesque porch on Bornholm. Note in particular the corbels with carved lions' heads at the top.

The altarpiece is from c 1600, and there is a late Gothic crucifix from c 1500. The Renaissance pulpit is from c 1610. Pride of place, however, goes to the magnificent late 12C Romanesque font of Gotland sandstone, decorated with eleven reliefs of scenes from the New Testament, each of which is explained by runic inscription. The foot of the font is decorated with intertwined plants and the heads of lions and rams. Two runestones stand in the porch.

▶Excursion from Åkirkeby to Almindingen

North of Åkirkeby lies **Almindingen** (The Common), a wooded area covering c 24 sq km and the third largest forest in Denmark, harking back to the days when all Bornholm was covered by trees. There are roads through this area, but to be savoured to the full it really requires that you walk. There are plenty of marked paths and recommended walks, and a map can be obtained from the tourist information offices.

Ekkodalen (Echo Valley) on the south edge contains rocks up to 20m above ground level, and other groups of rocks are also to be found in the forest. Near Ekkodalen there are the ruins of another castle called **Gammelborg** and close by, standing by the lovely Borresø lake are the ruins of **Lilleborg** which despite its name is the second largest fortress on Bornholm. It dates from the 12C and was destroyed by fire. Just south of Lilleborg is the highest point in Bornholm, **Rytterknægten**, topped with a granite observation tower standing 184m above sea level, known as **Kongemindet**.◀

The A38 will now take you direct to (16km) Rønne, passing through **Nylars**, where you will find the fourth of the Bornholm round churches, dedicated to St Nicholas. Three storeys high, it is the best preserved of them all, with the original defence installations still in place. Built before 1200, this church consists of a nave, oval chancel and apse, with a porch added in 1879. The vaulted nave is supported by a relatively slender column. The small northwest window high in the barrel vaulting is the only Romanesque window in Bornholm preserved intact. There are frescoes from c 1250 depicting scenes from Genesis. Two runestones stand in the porch.

There is much more to be seen on Bornholm, smaller things too numerous to list. We suggest that you make good use of the Tourist Information Offices, especially Bornholms Velkomstcenter in Rønne, if you are going to spend a holiday here.

History of Denmark

History

The story of Denmark is that of a territorially small country which, once it was organised as a unity, came to play a dominant role in northern European history. Placed at the crossroads of trade north and south and east and west, and long in control of the entrance to the Baltic, it is a country which has had an importance far in excess of its size. It led the Kalmar Union comprising mainland Scandinavia plus Finland, Iceland, the Faroe Islands and Greenland. Even when the Union was dissolved, Denmark retained the whole of Norway, the southern Swedish provinces and the islands in the north Atlantic. To the south Denmark was long in at least partial control of what is now northern Germany, and the North German coast has also known Danish rule. Yet in the course of time, Denmark had to relinquish her Baltic domains to Sweden and subsequently her southern duchies to Germany, becoming for a period at the end of the 19C even smaller than she is today.

The expansionist dream came with the Vikings. By 878 the Danelaw (those parts of Anglo-Saxon England subject to Danish rule) was established, and by 1033 all England was under the Vikings. The year 911 saw the Viking Rollo in possession of Normandy as the first Duke after his warriors had laid waste to the land around the Seine. Just how many of these Vikings came from Denmark, it is difficult to say, as the English tended to call them all Danes, whether they came from Denmark or Norway, while the French tended to call them all Norsemen. There was little to distinguish them from each other.

While the Vikings were ravaging far and wide, the population at home was gradually fashioning Denmark in the shape she was to have for centuries. The southern frontier with Germany stretched roughly to the Ejder—a fact that was to have repercussions in the 19C Schleswig-Holstein problem—while the sea formed a natural boundary between Denmark and the other Nordic lands. The people were farmers, and by about 1250 they had settled the entire country and founded the villages which to this day are the basis of Danish rural society.

Denmark was an elective monarchy, and although it was customary to choose the new king from among the sons of the previous one, it was by no means an unbreakable rule, something the early medieval nobility learned to exploit.

The first attempt at converting Denmark to Christianity was made by the Anglo-Saxon bishop Willibrordus around the year 700, but it was not until the baptism of Harald Bluetooth in 960 that the Church can really be said to have thoroughly established itself on Danish territory. The conquest of England in the following century further strengthened the influence of the Church in Denmark, for it must be remembered that England had long been Christian, and although politically dominated by Denmark was able to exert a significant cultural influence.

Even so, the Church was by no means an established Church. It fell to King Knud (Canute) II (St Knud) and his next successor but one, King Erik Ejegod (Erik the Kind-Hearted), finally to establish it in all its power and independence.

Knud did much to liberate the Church from the legal authority of the state, and he also sought to introduce tithes and enforce celibacy, but he succeeded in neither of these objectives. His piety stood in some contrast to his treatment of his subjects, and finally, after an attempt by him to launch a new Viking expedition to England in 1086, the Jutland peasantry rebelled. Knud fled, but was caught and murdered in Odense. Nine years later Erik was elected king, and he succeeded in separating the Church in the North from the archbishopric of Hamburg. A new archbishopric was created in Lund in Skåne, and in 1104 Asser was made Archbishop of Lund and thereby Primate of the North. With his appointment the temporal authorities saw the possibility of greater political independence from the German states. The king now managed to introduce a system of tithes which made the Church financially independent and enabled it to increase its influence. One result of this was that it was now possible to build churches in stone instead of wood as hitherto, and so permanent buildings, many of them still at least partially extant, were erected, not least among which were the great cathedrals.

The Age of the Valdemars and Danish Expansion

For a generation after the death of the powerful King Erik, Denmark suffered a series of civil wars, and it was not until 1157 that true stability was brought to the country with the acceptance as king of Valdemar I. The period of growth and power, known as the Age of the Valdemars, had begun. It lasted until the death of Valdemar II in 1241, and alongside the kings the central figures in this age of glory were the three great archbishops of Lund—Eskil, Absalon (the founder of Copenhagen) and Anders Sunesøn.

When Valdemar I came to the throne, Denmark was weak. Like his predecessors, Valdemar had to acknowledge the Holy Roman Emperor as his overlord, but he began to turn this dependence to his own advantage. During the period of weakness, the Wends, the Slavic peoples of the Baltic, had taken the opportunity of ravaging the Danish coasts. Valdemar set about putting an end to this. To do so he needed the help of the Saxons, who were also enemies of the Wends. His armies supported theirs and took a small share of the booty, until they were powerful enough to conquer the Wendic stronghold of Rügen on their own.

Denmark was gradually fortified and began to assert herself as a power to be reckoned with both in Scandinavia and in the Baltic as a whole. Yet Valdemar had other plans which were equally ambitious and equally important to the country's internal affairs. So far the monarch had been elective, and the main voice in choosing the new king had been that of the people expressing themselves in *things*—, gatherings of the people where laws were formulated and recited and lawsuits heard. Valdemar wanted to strengthen the monarchy and make it independent, and between 1165 and 1170, with the support of Archbishop Eskil, he succeeded in his aim. No longer was kingship to be the gift of the people; it was to be bestowed by the Church. Although in theory the *things* continued to influence the choice of king, in practice hereditary monarchy was introduced. It was still not absolute monarchy, and until the 17C it became the practice for each elected king to sign a charter limiting his powers. But in effect the system was in full flower, the monarchy strong internally as well as externally.

When, as an old man, Eskil was forced to resign his archbishopric, the obvious choice as his successor was Absalon, who had so far been Bishop of Roskilde and Valdemar's right-hand man. Absalon was not merely a zealous churchman, but a first-class organiser and military mind, and he was bent on centralising power in Denmark and diminishing the influence of the various regions. When Valdemar died in 1182 and was succeeded by his son Knud, Absalon was able to continue the policies of Valdemar for the next two decades. It was Absalon who fused the reigns of the two Valdemars into one glorious age.

While Valdemar I had been forced to acknowledge the Emperor, Knud refused to do so. This led to war, but Denmark was now strong, and gradually took possession of Mecklenburg and Pomerania as well as the territory as far south as the Elbe, including Lübeck. The most important trade centres in the north of Europe were thus under Danish rule. Only one year after Absalon's death, Knud was succeeded in 1202 by Valdemar II, and the expansionist policy continued. By 1219 Denmark possessed the whole Baltic coast as far as the eastern boundary of Estonia. But Valdemar had gone too far. In 1223 he was taken prisoner by Count Henrik of Schwerin, and before he was released Denmark had to give up most of her Baltic possessions, while the southern boundary was drawn at the Ejder. The seeds of future trouble were sown, for the population in the area was no longer purely Danish. It contained many Saxons who had moved in from Holstein, and their presence was to be felt again in the 19C with the Schleswig-Holstein problem.

Instead of external expansion, Valdemar II now worked for internal growth, and his reign saw profound internal changes in the country's administration. The legislative power passed more and more into the king's hands, as was made plain by his giving the people the Jutland Law of 1241. It was a law of good government, and it codified what in fact had been traditional law before this time. The country was now unified both administratively and legally, and a change was taking place from a primitive society to one which was sophisticated for the Middle Ages. A community based on the three estates was emerging, and as a whole it was a community which could equal those of other European countries, with a literature and a culture of its own, a country with the ability to build and to fashion an architectural style distinct from that of other countries.

The following period, until c 1300, was one of economic growth. Skåne became a great trade centre, and a wealthy merchant class emerged. Towns were established, and with the development of new skills the craft and trade guilds were established. In the country districts life was less good, and the number of independent farmers fell from about 50 per cent of the total about 1250 to between 10 per cent and 12 per cent around 1400. the remainder having sacrificed their freedom for the protection of the wealthier nobility. By 1350 the system which was to last until the 18C was beginning to take shape.

Politically these were troubled times. Valdemar II made his sons dukes in various parts of the country, and they quarrelled over the succession and their rights under the new king, Erik Plovpenning (Erik Ploughpenny). Under these conditions Schleswig acquired a degree of independence not enjoyed by any other part of the country. Duke Abel of Schleswig, one of Erik Plovpenning's brothers, fought for the independence of his duchy, and finally, with the support of the counts of Holstein—still completely independent of Denmark—murdered his brother and was made King of Denmark. Two years later he fell in battle, and although he left two sons, the Danes chose another of Valdemar II's sons as Christoffer I. Abel's sons could do little in face of this, but they did manage to secure the semi-independence of Schleswig. Schleswig drifted closer to Holstein, and when in 1460 King Christian I of Denmark was elected Duke of both Schleswig and Holstein against a promise never to divide the duchies, the seeds of the 19C conflict were planted deep.

Meanwhile, after the death of Valdemar II, a struggle developed between the nobility and the Crown. The nobles won, but they brought untold trouble to the country as a whole. In order to maintain power, and in an attempt to put down a rebellion in Jutland and Fyn, Christoffer II had to pawn large areas of the country. Holstein was in virtual control of Jutland, having taken it as a pledge for a sum of money which Christoffer had no hope of raising. Another Holstein count, Johan, was in control of Sjælland and Skåne. For a time it even seemed possible that Denmark might cease to be a unified state, and for eight years after the death of Christoffer II it was without a king.

In 1340 the Holstein Count Gert was murdered in Jutland. The Danish nobility, disunited as they were, saw their only hope in the re-establishment of a strong monarchy, and negotiations led to the election of Christoffer II's son Valdemar, whose task it was to free the country from foreign domination.

Valdemar IV was strong and determined, combining these qualities with shrewdness and ruthlessness. Within 20 years he had reunited the country and restored its total independence. As had happened before, however, a king went too far. In 1361 Valdemar attacked the Swedish island of Gotland and won it, but this move was to lead to his downfall. Sweden, Holstein, Schleswig and, most important, the Hanseatic League joined forces against him. The ensuing Peace of Stralsund (1370) gave the Hansa a number of outposts in Skåne and the right to trade there for 15 years.

The Kalmar Union

Valdemar died in 1375 and was succeeded by his five-year-old grandson Oluf, the son of his daughter Margrethe. Oluf's father, King Haakon VI of Norway, died five years later, and Oluf automatically succeeded to the Norwegian throne, thus uniting the two kingdoms.

During Oluf's infancy, his mother ruled in his place, and when Oluf died in 1387, she was chosen as queen in her own right. Thanks to internal strife in Sweden, Margrethe was invited to become Queen of Sweden as well, and so by 1389 the whole of Scandinavia was united under her rule. To ensure the continuance of the union, Margrethe had her nephew, Erik of Pomerania, crowned King of the North in 1397, and she also executed a formal document of union, known as the Kalmar Union. Despite complaints that Margrethe, herself a Dane, showed too many favours to the Danes, she managed to maintain the union, but Erik of Pomerania was less successful, finally losing his throne in 1439. This was not, however, before he had carried out important economic reforms within Denmark. In order to increase the wealth of the towns, he insisted that much foreign trade should go through Danish merchants instead of direct from Hanseatic merchants to his subjects. He also introduced a toll on ships passing Helsingør (Elsinore), so 1429 saw the start of the Sound Dues which were to be a bone of contention in later centuries.

The Union outlasted King Erik, but it fell apart under Christian II, who sought to crush opposition to his rule in Sweden. In 1520 he had himself crowned in Stockholm, celebrating the occasion by summoning the flower of the Swedish nobility to Stockholm Castle. He arrested them on charges of heresy and had 82 of them executed, after which he carried out a series of bloody reprisals against opponents in the Swedish provinces. The result was a full-scale rebellion leading to the end of the Union.

Christian's policies made him enemies not only in Sweden, but also in Lübeck, while the Danish nobility felt itself threatened. In August 1522 a Lübeck fleet sailed against Denmark, to be joined by ships from Danzig and other Hanseatic cities. This action coincided with unrest in Jutland, where one of the king's sheriffs had been murdered. The king repaid in kind, burning the city of Ålborg where the murder had taken place. By the end of the year a group of Jutlandic noblemen joined in a conspiracy aimed at bringing down Christian, and in January 1523 they renounced their oath of allegiance to him. By April Christian had fled to Holland, and in his place Duke Frederik of Gottorp, who had supported the rebellion, was proclaimed King Frederik I.

There was more, however, to the discontent in the country than mere political oppression. Already in the final years of Christian II's reign, the first signs of the Reformation had appeared in Denmark, and Christian had shown some sympathy for the Lutheran cause. He aimed, however, at reforming the Church from within, without breaking with Rome. When Frederik I came to the throne, he sought to avoid taking sides; a Catholic himself, he sought to be neutral and to allow the Lutherans a certain freedom, even providing protection for the leading Reformer, Hans Tavsen. He thus avoided giving offence to the Emperor while gaining the favour of the Danes, many of whom supported the Lutheran cause.

And popular support was just what he needed, for Christian II was making an attempt to return. He landed an army in Norway, and was invited to Denmark under safe conduct. He accepted the invitation, but was arrested and kept prisoner until his death in 1532.

Frederik I died in 1533, and his likely successor was the zealous Protestant Duke Christian, to whom there was considerable opposition from the still Catholic nobility. An attempt was now made to reinstate Christian II, with the help of a Lübeck army led by Count Christoffer of Oldenborg, from whom the resultant civil war has received the name of The Count's War. This army occupied Sjælland and Fyn, but was then opposed by the Jutlandic nobility who supported Duke Christian. At the same time, in opposition to him, a peasant revolt was organised in North Jutland under the leadership of Skipper Klement. This was put down with great brutality in 1534 by the Holstein Johan Rantzau, who then proceeded to defeat the Lübeck army at Øksnebjerg in Fyn in 1535. Christian III was finally proclaimed king. He then imprisoned all the Catholic bishops and in 1536 declared Lutheranism the Danish national religion.

Rivalry between Denmark and Sweden

During the following century Denmark became preoccupied with more worldly matters, and under Christian IV there was a period of veritable mercantilism with the establishment of an East Indies Company based on the small Danish colony of Tranquebar.

Meanwhile, Denmark was still in control of the entrance to the Baltic, deriving considerable profits from the tolls exacted from all ships entering and leaving. Sweden decided to try to put an end to this. The result was a series of wars covering the greater part of a century. First, there was the Nordic Seven Years War (1563–70), which led to enormous devastation and brought about little change. Then, Sweden turned on Russia and gradually acquired the entire eastern Baltic, as far as Estonia, gradually extending her dominions until she bordered on Denmark to the south as well as to the north. Christian IV tried to counter this by entering the Thirty Years War and securing the north coast of Germany. The episode, which lasted from 1625 to 1629, led to a resounding defeat and the occupation of Jutland by Wallenstein's forces, until the Danes agreed not to take any further part in the war.

It was then Sweden's turn, and Swedish soldiers under Gustav II Adolf joined the Protestant North Germans and helped decide the outcome of the war in the North. From the Swedish point of view, however, mastery of the Baltic was of paramount importance. Having established themselves there, the Swedes, infuriated by continued Danish opposition, followed Wallenstein's example and occupied Jutland. By the resultant Treaty of Brömsebro in 1645, Sweden acquired some of the Danish provinces in the north of the Sound, and also ensured freedom from Sound Dues both for the Swedish mainland and for all Swedish possessions in the Baltic.

The next stage in the struggle between Denmark and Sweden came in 1657 when Sweden faced a nationalist uprising in Poland. Denmark, now under Frederik III, saw the chance of revenge and declared war on Sweden. Again the Swedes immediately occupied Jutland, while the Danes withdrew to Fyn, where they appeared to be safe. Then the unforeseeable happened. In the extremely harsh winter of that year the water between Jutland and Fyn and between Fyn and Sjælland, froze over and enabled the Swedish army to march across the ice and make for Copenhagen. By the terms of the Treaty of Roskilde, Denmark had to give up her possessions north of the Sound, and Sweden acquired the entire coastline south of the Norwegian border. Peace seemed to be restored, and Denmark humiliated, but Sweden did not trust her southern neighbour to keep out of the war still being waged in North Germany, and consequently broke the treaty within months by invading Sjælland without warning, with the object of taking over the whole of the country.

This was too much for the Dutch. Little as they had liked the Danish mastery of the Sound, they did not relish the prospect of Swedish domination either, and they sent a fleet to relieve Copenhagen, which had withstood a lengthy siege. Sweden was forced to sue for peace. The 1660 Treaty of Copenhagen acknowledged that Sweden had been defeated, but did not give back to Denmark all the provinces that Sweden had taken after the Treaty of Roskilde. In particular, Sweden was allowed to keep the Sound provinces, whereby that country took on something like its present shape.

The Establishment of the Absolute Monarchy

Despite the cost of the many wars, the end of the 17C was one of economic growth, symbolised especially by the architectural glories of the age of Christian IV. Not everyone benefited from the economic changes, and the less affluent rural population became yet less affluent and subject to exploitation by the increasingly rich and demanding landowners. On the other hand, the towns did benefit, not only directly from improved trade patterns, but also because it became the policy of Christian IV to give state support to trade both at home and abroad. An increasingly influential middle class appeared, and the period saw the emergence of a Copenhagen bourgeoisie which was to play an important part in establishing the absolute monarchy when the final struggle between the Crown and the nobility got under way.

Since the rise of the nobility as a political power, with the privilege of forcing a charter upon each king before allowing him to take the throne, there had been an obvious source of strain between them and the king. In practice the nobles had not been as strong as the theory might suggest, but no king was happy at having his power limited by them. Nevertheless, each king had been to a great extent militarily dependent on the nobility. In times of war he looked to the nobles to provide his armed forces, and in return they were given widespread privileges. Things changed in the 17C. The wider use of firearms made the king less dependent on the foot-soldiers whom the nobles could provide, and at the same time the nobles found themselves less wealthy than they had been. The king's power, on the other hand, was obviously in the ascendant.

His chance to break the power of the nobility once and for all came immediately after the siege of Copenhagen. In order to encourage the citizens to hold out, he had promised them special privileges, including that of deciding how much tax they should pay. A meeting of all the estates in 1660 decided that all, including the nobility, should pay taxes. Sensing their new influence, the Copenhagen citizens then went on to suggest a hereditary monarchy, which would, of course, put an end to the power of the nobility. After a show of reluctance, the king went along with this. When the new constitution was drawn up in 1661, it was not quite what the citizens had foreseen, as the king was proclaimed not only a hereditary monarch, but also an *absolute* hereditary monarch. Whether Frederik III actually intended it is not certain, but absolute power in the style of Louis XIV of France was certainly introduced, lasting in differing forms until the middle of the 19C.

The rather exaggerated love of grandeur which has often accompanied absolutism also appeared in late 17C Denmark. It resulted in magnificent palaces and squares of which Kongens Nytorv in Copenhagen is one example, and it gave rise to the Baroque style in architecture and poetry. But the one field in which glory could be won by the absolute kings would be in the recovery of the Swedish provinces. Denmark was allied to Holland, and Sweden to France, and it was obviously impossible for Denmark to wage war on Sweden while Sweden had such an ally. However, in 1675 the pretext and the opportunity came. France, herself at war with Holland, persuaded Sweden to attack Brandenburg, where the Swedes suffered a defeat. Denmark could not resist the opportunity, and after occupying Sweden's small ally to the south, Gottorp, the Danes landed an army in Skåne, where it was well received by the local population. Denmark won the war, but once more, the wishes of a major power, France, prevented the return of the old Danish territories.

However, Denmark was still not prepared to give up the attempt, and a rapprochement with France took place just at the same time as Sweden made a move to improve relations with England and Holland, who had previously supported Denmark. This new constellation was in existence at the beginning of the Great Nordic War, which lasted from 1700 to 1720. The final outcome was that Sweden once and for all lost most of her Baltic possessions, while Russia for the first time came to play a dominant role in the Baltic. Denmark failed to regain the Swedish provinces, however, and merely achieved an end to the Swedish freedom from Sound Dues and the cessation of Swedish support for Gottorp. Consequently, Frederik IV was able to strengthen his own position in Schleswig, while allowing the Duke of Gottorp to keep Holstein. It was hoped thereby to remove the frontier problem both to the north and the south. Peace between Denmark and Sweden now seemed possible.

18C Pietism and Enlightenment

The Lutheranism which came to Denmark with the Reformation in 1536 had quickly led to a new orthodoxy and intolerance. However, the close connection existing between the Lutheran Church and the Crown meant that little could be done to overcome this or to allow new ideas to be established. It was not until the beginning of the 18C that new developments occurred with the arrival from Germany of the pietist movement. There was no obvious desire to stray from the strictly Lutheran teaching, but merely to intensify the spiritual life, and so it was difficult for the Church to prevent the spread of pietism. By 1720 Frederik IV himself was sympathetic towards the new movement, and his successor Christian VI was himself a convinced pietist. Under his rule there was a period of intensification of Danish religious life, accompanied by increasing intolerance. Not only were all forms of entertainment forbidden on Sundays, but pietist influence also brought about the closing of Copenhagen's Royal Theatre for a period, just when Ludvig Holberg, the greatest dramatist in the North, was at the height of his creative powers. On the other hand, the pietists laid great store by charitable acts and help for those in need. Into this category fell children in want of education, and under the pietists an attempt was made to provide a minimum of schooling for all.

The pietist interest in education can be seen not only as a special aspect of their creed, but as the forerunner of the 18C Enlightenment, which replaced pietism later in the century and led to increased interest in education generally. At the end of the century schools such as the School for Civic Virtue were founded, a private, liberal experimental school aiming at as broad an education as possible. A school commission was set up in 1789, and its report formed the basis of the 1814 Education Act, providing for free schooling for all.

Alongside educational reform went peasant reform, one of the major achievements of the late 18C. Stemming from a happy combination of philanthropy, a period of increasing prosperity, an enlightened monarch and perhaps a touch of Rousseauist idealism, the peasant reforms saw a reversal of the trend towards the oppression of the farming community. Landowners lost their grip on their tenant farmers, and it became common for a farmer to buy back his farm instead of leasing it. By 1814 some 60 per cent of Danish farmers were once more independent. They were not thereby made wealthy, and many had a hard time because of falling prices, but they acquired a self-esteem which they had not had for centuries.

Prosperity, War and Poverty

The agricultural reforms had coincided with a period of increased agricultural and national prosperity. Thanks to the Industrial Revolution, England's population had risen rapidly, and from being a corn-exporting country, England had started importing corn. Denmark had been among those countries which bene-fited from this turn of events, which, combined with the introduction of a corn monopoly in Norway (then still part of Denmark), was good news for farmers.

Denmark's economy benefited also at first from the wars between Britain and France at the end of the 18C and from the American War of Independence, in all of which the country declared itself neutral and set about trading with both sides. Copenhagen achieved its old objective of becoming the centre of Baltic trade. By 1784 trade restrictions were abolished, and Denmark was able to enter the 19C in a period of affluence and free trade.

However, none of the belligerent powers was happy to see Denmark trading with its enemies, and in particular Britain sought to stop and search Danish ships and confiscate cargoes whenever there was the slightest excuse. In 1780, therefore, Denmark joined with Russia, Prussia and Sweden in an armed neutrality aimed at safeguarding trading rights in America, and was largely successful in doing so until the end of the War of Independence in 1783. However, when Britain was again embroiled in war with revolutionary France, Denmark was less successful, and the decision to organise a convoy system met with immediate British opposition. Denmark gave in, but went on to join the second Armed Neutrality with Sweden and Russia. After this apparent disrespect for an agreement just made, Britain in 1801 sent a fleet to Copenhagen and succeeded in forcing Denmark to withdraw from the Armed Neutrality.

The difficulties in which Denmark found herself, caught between two major warring powers, were a sign of things to come. In particular the situation became difficult when Napoleon announced the Continental Blockade in 1806, and even more so when Britain set in motion a counter-blockade. Denmark, dependent as always on the sea for communication, both between the islands and between Denmark and Norway, was at the mercy of the British fleet. It was not surprising that the British Government, after the events of 1801, was scarcely sure of the Danish attitude, though in fact Denmark was mainly inter-ested in keeping out of trouble.

However, after pressure from Britain culminating in a three-day bombard-ment of Copenhagen in 1807, Denmark did finally enter the war—on the French side, though it soon became obvious that this was a mistake. However, attempts to break with France and join the alliance against Napoleon were thwarted by Sweden, where the new king had been promised Norway once the war was over, provided Denmark was on the losing side. Thus, in 1814, a year after a state bankruptcy had been declared, Denmark had to sign away Norway in the Treaty of Kiel and found herself reduced from a medium-sized but affluent state to a minor and poverty-stricken one.

The period up to 1828 was marked by the struggle to recoup the national finances on the one hand and on the other by the start of the Schleswig-Holstein troubles which were to persist until 1864. Should Denmark plus the duchies become a unified state, or should Holstein be allowed to join the German Confederation, formed in 1815? In this case, what was to become of Schleswig, which was tied to both? The end of the Napoleonic Wars brought about an upsurge of nationalism in all the elements forming the Danish state, and it also brought about a demand for democratic reforms to bring about the end of the absolute monarchy, for although the king was accessible and delighted in being a father to his people, he *was* still an absolute monarch.

In 1831 the king gave in to some of the demands and ordered legislation to establish four consultative assemblies to allow a voice to public opinion throughout the country—though he made sure that none of them met in Copenhagen. When they met, they consisted of individual delegates only, as no political parties as such existed. However, these delegates soon divided into two broad camps of conservatives and liberals, with the liberals predominating. The movement towards democratic government had begun, but it was not to be completed until 1901.

Nevertheless, this was a period of reform and reconstruction. Agricultural reforms, begun in the 18C, were taken a step further, and efforts were made to improve the lot of the poorer members of the rural community, in particular by means of loans to enable them to buy their own land. Trade within the country, which had hitherto been subject to ancient restrictions, was liberalised, and the Sound Dues were abolished, allowing Copenhagen to compete on equal terms with its great rival Hamburg as a trading centre. By 1844, the first railway line was established and by 1870 the railway system of today had in essence been laid out.

Meanwhile, the pressure for constitutional reform gathered impetus, and by the 1840s the king, Christian VIII, decided to give in to it and renounce his absolute authority. He ran into trouble, however, when the new written constitution had to take account of Schleswig and Holstein, where different conditions obtained. Christian died before the constitution was signed, but despite hesitations, his successor, Frederik VII, was persuaded to put the proposals into effect in January 1848. It was a notably liberal constitution, but it led to a reaction in the duchies, which sought a common constitution for themselves and demanded permission for Schleswig to join the German Confederation. Danish national feeling was also running high, and the government proved intransigent. Consequently, Danish troops were sent to Flensburg in Schleswig, where they encountered a force of 30,000, including Prussian soldiers. Ultimately, Denmark appeared to win this war, though this was largely due to pressure on Prussia from abroad, a fact that was lost on many Danish politicians. Consequently, when further trouble ensued in 1863, Denmark thought it could repeat the performance. This time, however, Denmark was thoroughly beaten, and the border was drawn just south of Kolding in 1864.

The king, who still had the prerogative of appointing his government, now brought in new men to lead the country. They were, however, still predominantly wealthy landowners, and there was a period of political stagnation—though a number of much-needed social reforms were carried out. It was at the same time a period of internal conflict, as improved educational standards and a changing social pattern made people unwilling to accept a form of aristocratic, semi-authoritarian government. The last years of the 19C thus became a battleground for parliamentary government, with the king maintaining his conservative cabinet in the face of an increasingly liberal parliament. By 1901 the principle of parliamentary government was accepted.

Meanwhile, alongside the parliamentary struggles, Denmark had been making progress in other spheres. The final liberalisation of internal trade in 1862 led to a period of eager industrial activity, and something like 1000 new firms were established within two years. A free harbour was established in Copenhagen, bringing a marked increase in international trade. Easier transport meant that industry could develop in the provinces as well as in Copenhagen, and the period saw an increase in the populations of the provincial towns as well as in the capital.

In the country districts changes were also taking place, not least in the form of intensified farming. Here, too, there was a reaction against the power of the wealthy farmers and their conservative supporters. Perhaps the most striking feature of rural developments was the establishment of the co-operative movement, which is still a potent force in Danish life. Inspired by the English movement, the first co-operative store was opened in Thisted. Then the smaller farmers joined forces to open co-operative dairies and slaughterhouses, thus providing the foundations for the efficient organisation of the modern Danish meat and dairy industries. This movement went hand in hand with the Folk High Schools, inspired by the principles of N.F.S. Grundtvig, and aimed at providing a Christian education for the rural population which had been deprived of an academic schooling. These schools, which quickly spread throughout the country, provided relatively short courses to give the rural population an appreciation of Danish culture and history, to inspire a sense of nationhood with Christian virtues and, not least, to teach them an appreciation of traditional crafts. These schools, which are still an important feature of Danish life even if they have changed somewhat in character, are doubtless a product of the National Romantic movement, but they have played a huge role in educating and enlightening the broad population, and are to be thanked for the widespread appreciation of art, design and culture which is such a striking characteristic of modern Denmark.

The advent of democratic government in 1901 brought calls for a liberal reform of the constitution, and a great deal of time and energy was spent on this. Before this process could be completed, however, World War I broke out, and new preoccupations replaced the subject of constitutional change. As had happened before, Denmark had good relations with both sides in a war (though 1864 had not been forgotten) and decided to remain neutral. Initially the country's balance of payments went into surplus as a result of an increase in demand for Danish goods abroad. The new conditions brought the different parties in Denmark together, and agreement was reached on a new constitution, which was signed on the by now traditional constitution day of 5 June in 1915.

The war nevertheless brought shortages and economic problems after the initial buoyant months. The national debt grew, and taxes were increased, while profiteering was rife. The workers did not benefit from the new conditions, and became a prey to syndicalists and bolsheviks. These influences continued after the war, and in 1920 there was a confrontation between the king and the workers which, in the eyes of some, was a potentially revolutionary situation. However, the trouble blew over, and once more Denmark sought to stabilise its situation. The most immediate effect of the post-war period was the holding of a referendum in the lost territories of Schleswig and Holstein. This was done on a parish-by-parish basis, and resulted in the present border being drawn, very largely reflecting the cultural boundary between the Danish and German-speaking populations. Minorities there were, and bitterness there was for many years, but of late the problems have disappeared, and the two populations now mix easily and peacefully.

In the 1930s, Denmark's economic problems were compounded by the world-wide slump. It was, however, also a time of reform, first of the penal system and then of the social system. K.K. Steincke's Social Reform was introduced in 1933, producing one of the most advanced social security systems of its day, and forming the basis for Danish social legislation for the next 50 years. Other practical measures were effected, and the same egalitarian principles also prompted the government to introduce a new Education Act, with the aim of improving the quality of schools and to ensuring equal opportunities for all.

When war broke out again in 1939, there was no doubt where Danish sympathies lay, but Denmark hoped once more to remain neutral. By April 1940, however, Hitler's troops had invaded. By general standards, Denmark had a 'good' occupation, and its elected politicians were, within limits, allowed to run the country until 1943. Then, under the pressure of increasing opposition, the occupation forces introduced a state of emergency and took over full administrative powers, which they retained until the end of the war.

Since 1945, Denmark has undergone a period of increasing prosperity, despite balance of payments problems caused by huge loans to finance a new infrastructure. Denmark joined NATO, then EFTA, and after a referendum in 1972, became a full member of the EEC on 1 January 1973. In 1992 a referendum went against accepting the Maastricht Treaty, but this was reversed the following year when various opt-outs were agreed for Denmark at the Edinburgh Conference.

Today, Denmark stands as a country with a very high standard of living, a country notable for efficiency and humanity, and for the respect in which it holds all its citizens. Equality was one of the claims made by the Vikings in their day, and it seems that that instinct has either survived the ages or been revived in the twentieth century.

Brief Chronology

Danish monarchs and the most important events in their reigns

Gorm den Gamle (Gorm the Old) died c 940

Harald Blåtand (Harald Bluetooth) c 940–86
Introduction of Christianity

Svend Tveskæg (Svend Forkbeard) 986–1014 (died in Gainsborough; buried in Roskilde)
Conquest of England 1013

Harald II 1014–18

Knud I den Store (Canute the Great) 1018–35 (died in Shaftesbury; buried in Winchester)
The Ejder defined as South border of Denmark
Denmark frequently at war with the Wends from 1022

Hardeknud (Hardicanute) 1035–42 (died in London; buried in Winchester)
The last Danish King of England 1040–42

Magnus den Gode (Magnus the Good) 1042–47
Svend II Estridsøn 1047–74
  Nephew of Svend Forkbeard, born in England
  Responsible for ecclesiastical organisation of Denmark; many churches built
  during his reign
Harald III Hen 1074–80
  Established unified monetary system in Denmark
Knud II den Hellige (St. Canute) 1080–86
  Murdered and buried in Sankt Albani Kirke in Odense
  Canonised
Oluf I Hunger 1086–95
Erik I Ejegod (Erik the Kind-Hearted) 1095–1103
  The first Danish king to undertake a pilgrimage to the Holy Land
Niels I104–34
Erik II Emune 1134–37
Erik III Lam 1137–46
Oluf II c 1140–43
Svend III Grathe 1146–57
  Killed in the Battle of Grathe Heath by Valdemar I
Knud III 1146–57
  Co-regent with Svend Grathe, by whom he was murdered at a
  banquet in Roskilde
Valdemar I den Store (Valdemar I, The Great) 1157–82
Knud IV 1182–1202
  The first Danish king to be anointed and crowned by the Church
  Assumed the title of 'King of the Wends'
Valdemar II Sejr (Valdemar II, The Victorious) 1202–41
  Made an unsuccessful attempt to establish a Kingdom of the Baltic
Erik IV Plovpenning (Erik IV, Ploughpenny) 1241–50
Abel 1250–52
Christoffer I 1252–59
Erik V Glipping (or Klipping) 1259–86
  Murdered by Rane Jonsen in Finderup Barn near Viborg
Erik VI Menved 1286–1319
Christoffer II 1320–26; 1330–32
Valdemar III 1326–30
Valdemar IV Atterdag (Valdemar IV, Another Day) 1340–75
  Concluded peace with the Wends 1365
Oluf III 1375–87
Margrethe 1375–97 (died 1412)
  Kalmar Union 1397
Erik VII af Pommern (Erik VII of Pomerania) 1397–1439
  Øresund Dues introduced 1429
Christoffer III af Bayern (Christoffer III of Bavaria) 1440–48
  Copenhagen created the capital of Denmark
Christian I 1448–81
  Copenhagen University founded
Hans 1481–1513
  Defeated in the Ditmarshes 1500

Christian II 1513–23
  Stockholm Bloodbath 1520
  Driven into exile by the nobility 1523
  Union with Sweden breaks down 1523
  Prisoner in Sønderborg Castle 1532–49
  Prisoner in Kalundborg Castle 1549–59
Frederik I 1523–33
  Governs from Gottorp Castle
Christian III 1534–59
  The Count's War 1534–36
  Last battle against the Wends 1536
  The Reformation proclaimed 1536
  The Government returns to Copenhagen 1539
Frederik II 1559–88
  The Nordic Seven Years War 1563–70
Christian IV 1588–1648
  The architect king, founder of many of Denmark's finest buildings
Frederik III 1648–70
  The Karl-Gustav Wars 1657–60
  Svend Poulsen (Gøngehøvdingen) leads guerilla warfare 1658–1660
  The storming of Copenhagen
  Establishment of Absolute Rule 1660
Christian V 1670–99
  The Scanian War 1675–79
  The Battle of Køge Bay 1677
Frederik IV 1699–1730
  Serfdom abolished 1702
  Great Northern War 1709–20
  240 cavalry schools established
Christian VI 1730–46
Frederik V 1746–66
Christian VII 1766–1808
  Coup d'état by Struensee 1771
  The abolition of adscription (the liberation of the peasantry) 1788
  Napoleonic Wars
  The Battle of the Copenhagen Roads 1801
  Bombardment of Copenhagen 1807
Frederik VI 1808–39
  State bankruptcy 1813
  Loss of Norway 1814
  Advisory Provincial Assemblies 1834
Christian VIII 1839–48
  Was King of Norway May–October 1814
  First public State accounts 1841
Frederik VII 1848–63
  End of absolute monarchy 1848
  First Schleswig War 1848–50
  First Constitution June 1849
  End of Sound Dues 1857.

The death of Frederik VII marked the end of the Oldenburg dynasty, which had ruled through 16 reigns for 415 years

Christian IX 1863–1906

Glücksborg dynasty founded. Christian IX elected as a descendant of Christian III

Second Schleswig War 1864

Schleswig and Holstein surrendered to Germany 1864. Introduction of parliamentary democracy 1901

Frederik VIII 1906–12

Christian X 1912–47

World War I 1914–18

Revision of Constitution 1915, providing for universal suffrage—also for women

Return of South Jutland 1920

World War II 1939–45

Occupation of Denmark 1940–45

Frederik IX 1947–72

Denmark joins NATO 1949

Revision of Constitution 1953, resulted in: abolition of the Landsting (the Upper House); the possibility of female succession to the Throne; Greenland becoming an integral and equal part of the Kingdom of Denmark

Danish membership of EFTA 1959

Margrethe II 1972–

Danish membership of EEC after referendum 1973

Denmark signs the Maastricht Treaty 1993 after a second referendum

On Danish Churches

A Benedictine monk, Ansgar (801–865), subsequently canonised as St. Ansgar, is usually given credit for converting Denmark. He certainly had a church built in Ribe during his lifetime. Conversion was a slow process, however, and it was c 1000 before it could reasonably be claimed that Denmark was a Christian kingdom. Adam of Bremen wrote in 1070 that there were 150 churches in Sjælland and 100 in Fyn, and there is a view that there were altogether some 500–600 churches in Denmark as a whole. The main period of church building, however, was between 1100 and 1200, when some 1500 churches were built. These have provided the foundations for Danish churches to this day, even when, as has happened in most cases, the original Romanesque buildings were extended in the Gothic period. They are a unique source of insight into both architecture and custom, while the frescoes decorating them provide a lively, sometimes amusing, commentary on beliefs and ways of life. Some are almost like strip cartoons in the way in which they present tiny scenes, often revealing an unspoken criticism of authority both ecclesiastical and temporal. The names of some of the fresco artists are known, such as the Elmelunde Master; he is probably the greatest of them all and was a gifted artist by any standards. Others are more homespun, some quite primitive.

Village churches are often small, occasionally intimate, and with their corbie-stepped gables and, often, their whitewashed walls, they are very much a part of the Danish countryside. They are usually open during daylight hours, and when they are not, the key can normally be obtained from an address shown on the noticeboard outside. Visit them: they grow on you—they are an inexhaustible source of historical knowledge, and in their furniture they are often a storehouse of artistic inspiration.

Glossary

Antemensale. The decorative panelling in front of an altar
Antependium. Cloth hanging over the front of an altar
Auricular. An ornate Baroque style, also known as Ohrmuschel style.
Baroque. Ornamented, decorative style of art and architecture stretching from the late 16C to early 18C.
Epitaphium. Memorial Tablet
Gothic. Style of architecture usual between the 12C and 16C, characterised by pointed arches
Rococo. Style of architecture and decoration common in the 18C, ornate and intricate, but more graceful than Baroque
Romanesque. The earliest style of Danish church architecture, lasting until the 12C, when it was replaced by Gothic. It is characterised by massive, relatively undecorated walls, and rounded arches and windows.

Early Church Artists

One of the delights of the early Danish churches is the wealth of frescoes found in them. Many are by unknown artists, but some of the painters are either known from their signatures or identifiable by their styles, and several of these are referred to in the text. Among other early artists there are some outstanding sculptors, ranging in time from the early Middle Ages to the Reformation period. The following provides brief information on some of the most interesting of them.

Berg, Claus: born c 1470, died after 1532. Sculptor and painter centred on Odense. Main works: altarpiece and memorial in the Greyfriars' Church in Odense, now in St Knud's Cathedral; altarpieces in Nørre Broby, Sanderum, Holmekloster (Fyn), Tirstrup near Randers, Bregninge on Ærø; crucifixes in Vejlby, Skamby, Asperup, Vindinge (Fyn) and Sorø; Ivar Munk's tombstone in Ribe Cathedral.
Brarup Master: active around 1500. Fresco painter. His late Gothic frescoes are characterised by rather primitive figures. Main works: Tågerup, Sædinge (Lolland), Kongsted (South Sjælland), Gjerrild, Hyllested (Djursland).
Elmelunde Master: active c 1480–1500. Fresco painter. Based his work on a book of biblical illustrations with short rhymed texts. Characterised by expressionless faces amidst wealth of decorative invention. Main works: Elmelunde, Fanefjord, Keldby (all on Møn), Nørre Alslev, Tingsted, Åstrup (all on Falster), Bogø.
Goti: early medieval sculptor, probably Swedish, active in Jutland and in Sweden. In the church in Gjøl he not only left his mark, but included a portrait

of himself in the Paradise motif which he sculpted. Also responsible for the reliefs in Voldsted.

Helligtrekonger (The Three Kings) Master: active late 15C. Fresco painter called after exquisite late Gothic frescoes in the Helligtrekonger Chapel in Roskilde Cathedral. Apparently influenced by German and Dutch art. Other work: Tyrstrup (Christiansfeld); Vordingborg.

Horder: worked c 1200 in the Djursland area of East Jutland, responsible for Romanesque portals in many churches, of which those in Rimsø, Vejlby and Ørsted are the most important. He takes his name from a signature on the Gjesingholm Stone, found near Randers and now in the National Museum.

Isefjord Master: worked c 1450. Fresco painter. Lively biblical scenes, of which the best preserved are in Mørkøv. Characterised by figures with rounded cheeks and big eyes, tapestries and rugs with diamond patterning. Main works: Bregninge, Herlev, Kirke Hyllinge, Lynge, Mørkøv, Måløv, Over Dråby, Skamstrup.

Jørgensen, Lorentz: worked c 1644–81. Sculptor. His early work is on Langeland, but he later moved to the area around Holbæk and is responsible for work in many Sjælland churches. His main works are the auricular altars in Kalundborg, Køge and Helsingør, and the pulpit in Sankt Peders Kirke, Næstved.

Kolding, Peter Jensen: died c 1670. Sculptor. Main work is the auricular Clausholm Bed. Also altarpieces in Odder, Jannerup, Glud, Saksild, Vor Frue Kirke in Horsens, Ølsted.

Kongsted Master: worked c 1430–50. Fresco painter, possibly pupil of Martinus. His faces often have characteristic small chins, and he fills his space with foliage and other decoration. Main works: Kongsted near Fakse, Ballerup and the Slagelse region.

Lily Master: worked c 1500 in South Jutland and West Fyn. Fresco painter responsible for some 15 churches, recognisable by the stylised lilies of which he made frequent use. Main works: Janderup, Nørre Løgum.

Martinus Maler: worked in early 15C. Fresco painter, responsible for Gothic paintings in Sjælland, some bearing his signature. Characterised by ornamentation based on branches, leaves and shells. Main works: Gimlinge (dated 1409), Kirke Såby, Mogenstrup, Gerlev (his most important), Flakkebjerg, Hjembæk, Nordrup, Sankt Peders Kirke in Næstved, tower chapels in Roskilde Cathedral.

Quellinus, Thomas: (1661–1709). Sculptor. Dutch, but mostly worked in Denmark. Monuments in Copenhagen Cathedral; Tølløse; Hørning; St Knud's Cathedral, Odense; Sankt Petri Kirke, Copenhagen; Auning; Herlufsholm; Fraugde; Århus Cathedral.

Sødring Master: worked end 15C. Fresco painter. Feminine faces are characteristic of his work. Main works: Sødring, Udbyneder and Randers area.

Torum Master: worked c 1530. Fresco painter. Late Gothic frescoes in North Jutland. Often filled his pictures with inscriptions and painted several scenes in a single panel. Main works: Grinderslev, Torum, Vester Hornum.

Træskomaleren (The Clog Master): worked in East Fyn in 1480s. Named after clog in Ørbæk Church, but also recognisable by his suns and dedication crosses with flames. Main works: Hesselager, Skrøbelev, Vindinge.

Union Master: also known as the Undløse Master. Worked 1440–60 in Denmark and Sweden. One of the most important late Gothic artists.

Characterised by men's faces with long noses and graceful femalefigures. Main works in Denmark: Undløse, Nødebo.

Vinderslev Master: worked c 1500. Fresco painter. Recognisable by the face he always painted on the Virgin. Main works: Vinderslev, Maria Magdalene, Marved and Ottestrup.

Index

Æ, ø and å are positioned at the end of the alphabet. Note that å is sometimes writtem as aa, an old-fashioned form.

H

372   INDEX

Å

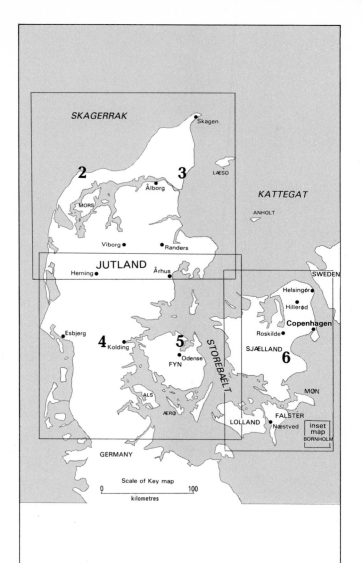

SKAGERRAK

2

Skagen

3

LÆSO

Ålborg

KATTEGAT

MORS

ANHOLT

Viborg ●   ● Randers

JUTLAND

Herning ●   Århus ●

SWEDEN

Helsingør ●

Hillerød ●

Esbjerg ●

Copenhagen

Roskilde ●

4 ● Kolding

5

STOREBÆLT

● Odense

FYN

SJÆLLAND

6

ALS

MØN

ÆRØ

GERMANY

LOLLAND

FALSTER

Næstved ●

inset
map

BORNHOLM

Scale of Key map

0   100

kilometres

KEY TO ROUTE MAPS

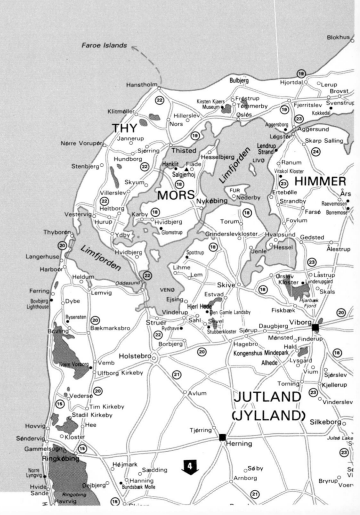

2

SKAGERRAK

Faroe Islands

Blokhus

Bulbjerg
Hjortdal ○Lerup
Hanstholm (19) Brovst
Kirsten Kjaers ●Frøstrup Svenstrup
Museum ○Tømmerby Fjerritslev
Klitmøller (22) ○Oslos (19)
Hillerslev (23) Kokkedal
THY ○Nors Aggersborg ○Aggersund
Jannerup (19) Skarp Salling
Nørre Vorupør Løgstør
○Sjørring Thisted (24)
Stenbjerg○ Hundborg Hesselbjerg Lendrup
Hanklit ▲Flade LIVØ Strand●
Skyum○ (18) ●Salgjerhoj Ranum HIMMER
Villerslev○ MORS Vitskol Kloster
(22) Nykøbing (23) ○Ars
Heltborg FUR ○Ertebølle Raevemosen●
Vestervig○ (22) Karby (18) ○Nederby ○Strandby Farsø ○Borremose●
Hurup Hvidbjerg Torum○ ○Fovlum
Thyborøn ○Glomstrup Gedsted
(20) Grinderslevkloster○ ○Hvalpsund
Langerhuse Limfjorden Hvidbjerg Spottrup (18) ○Hessel Ålestrup
Harboør ○Jenle ○Hessel
Heldum ○Lihme (23)
Ferring○ Oddesund Lem Skive ○Orslev ○Låstrup
Bovbjerg ○Dybe Lemvig VENØ Estvad (18) Kloster ●Lynderupgard
Lighthouse● Ejsing○ Hjerl Hede ○Fiskbæk ○Skals
Rysensten○ Viderup Den Gamle Landsby Hjarbæk
(20) Struer Sahl● Sjørup Daugbjerg Fjord
Bovling Bækmarksbro (22) Rydhave● ●Sevel ●Stubberkloster ○Sjørup ○Daugbjerg Viborg (20)
Borbjerg Mønsted○ ○Finderup
Norre Vosborg○ Vemb○ Holstebro (20) Hagebro○ Hald
Vederso ○Ulfborg Kirkeby (21) Kongenshus Mindepark Lysgard (18)
(20) ○Alhede ○Vium
Hovvig ○Tim Kirkeby Avlum○ ○Torning Sjørslev○
(15) Stadil Kirkeby Kjellerup
○Hee JUTLAND (23) ○Vinderslev
Søndervig○ ○Kloster (JYLLAND) Silkeborg○
Gammelsogn○ Tjørring○ Julsø Lake
Ringkøbing (15) Herning ■ (23)
Norre ○Højmar Sæding ○Søby
Lyngvig ○Hanning Se
Hvide○ ●Bundsbæk Molle Arnborg○ Vi
Sande Ringobing ○Dejbjerg Bryrup○ Voen
(15) Havrvig (21)

4

3

Skagen
Den Tilsandede Kirke
Kandestederne
Råbjerg
Mile
Hulsig

Norway

Hirtshals
Tversted
Ålbæk

Norway

Horne
Tornby
Bindslev
Strandby

Lønstrup
Mårup
Rubjerg
Knude
Vennebjerg
Hjørring
Frederikshavn

Løkken
Flade
Bangsbo
Cloostarnet

Borglumkloster

VENDSYSSEL
Sæby

Saltum
Brønderslev
Voergård
Præstbro

Jetsmark
Tylstrup
Kås
Gammel Vrå
Slot
Hjallerup
Åbybro
Birkelse
Sulsted
Dronninglund
Gjøl
Oksholm
Lindholm
Høje
Nørresundby
Ålborg

LÆSØ

0 kilometres   30

② Route numbers in text
■ Towns with plans in text

Troldkirken
Frejlev
Klarup
Sejlflod
Sønderholm
Gunderup
Egense
Nibe
Lille
Vildmose
Støvring
Volsted
Komdrup
Muldbjerge
Lindenborg
Dokkedal
Sønder
Kongerslev
Kongestedlund

LAND
Gravlev
Øster Hurup

Årestrup
Rold Forest
Norlund
Rold
Als
Villestrup
Astrup
Visborg

Stenild
Hadsund
Overgård

KATTEGAT

Snæbum
Hobro
Havndal
Udbyneder
Klejtrup
Frykat
Mariager
Sødring
Tjele
Langså
Gjerlev
Råby
Tjele
Handest
Spentrup
Øster Tørslev
Tvede
Mellerup
Ørsted Vivild
Fjellerup
Bønnerup
Strand
Anholt

Råsted
Harridslev
Stovringgård
Hevringholm
Strand
Sostrup

Albæk
Lovenholm
Glesborg
Rimsø
Voldby
Kastbjerg

Gammel
Estrup
Ørum
Sweden

Randers
Fausing
Gjesing
DJURSLAND
Auning
Ramten
Grenå

Hørning
Marie
Magdalene
Tøstrup
Fannerup
Vejlby
Ålsø
 Årslev
Clausholm
Voldum
Mørke
Thorsager
Katholm

Tange
Rosenholm
⑧
Tange Sø
Kongensbro
Hornslet
Rønde
Bjødstrup
Hyllested
Rugård
Farvang
Frijsenborg
Løgten
Kalø
Mollerup
Stubbe Sø
Tvilum
Gjern
Voldby
Todbjerg
Kalø
Bay
Agri
Dråby
Fuglsø
Ebeltoft

Linå
Låsby
Nørre
Vissing
Tved
Knebel
Øer Maritime
Ferieby
Himmelbjerget
Ry
Veng
Vistoft
HJELM
Gammel Rye
Hørning
Moesgård
Helgenæs
Peninsula

Århus
Marselisborg
⑦

Skanderborg
Malling
⑤

Øm Kloster
Yding
Ejer Bavnehoj
Odder
TUNØ
⑦

Urup
Ørting
Overby

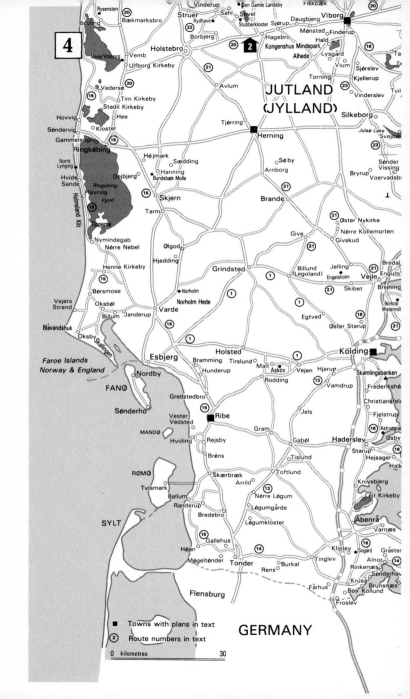

4

Rysensten
Bøvling
Bækmarksbro
Struer
Rydhave
Borbjerg
Holstebro
Vemb
Nørre Vosborg
Ulfborg Kirkeby
Avlum
Vedersø
Tim Kirkeby
Stadil Kirkeby
Hovvig
Hee
Søndervig
Kloster
Gammelsogn
Ringkøbing
Nørre Lyngvig
Højmark
Sædding
Hvide Sande
Dejbjerg
Hanning
Bundsbæk Mølle
Ringøbing Fjord
Skjern
Havrvig
Tarm
Tipperne
Nymindegab
Nørre Nebel
Ølgod
Hjedding
Henne Kirkeby
Grindsted
Vejers Strand
Børsmose
Norholm
Oksbøl
Norholm Hede
Billum
Janderup
Varde
Blåvandshuk
Oksby Skallingen
Esbjerg
Bramming
Tirslund
Malt
Askov
Vejen
Hjarup
Hunderup
Rødding
Nordby
FANØ
Gredstedbro
Sønderho
Vester Vedsted
Ribe
MANDØ
Hviding
Rejsby
Gram
Gabøl
Brøns
Tislund
Skærbæk
Toftlund
RØMØ
Arrild
Tvismark
Nørre Løgum
Ballum
Løgumgårde
Randerup
Bredebro
Løgumkloster
SYLT
Gallehus
Højer
Tønder
Burkal
Møgeltønder
Rens
Flensburg
Fårhus
Bov Kollund
Frøslev

Vinderup
Sahl
Den Gamle Landsby
Sevel
Sjørup
Stubberkloster
Hagebro
Kongenshus Mindepark
Alhede
Tjørring
Herning
Søby
Arnborg
Brande
Give
Givskud
Billund (Legoland)
Jelling
Engelsholm
Vejle
Skibet
Brejning
Egtved
Øster Starup
Kolding
Holsted
Rodding
Jels
Vamdrup
Frederikshåb
Christiansfeld
Fjelstrup
Astrupgård
Haderslev
Øsby
Starup
Hejsager
Halk
Knivsbjerg
Løjt Kirkeby
Åbenrå
Varnæs
Kliplev
Sogård
Græsten
Tinglev
Alnor
Rinkenæs
Sønderhav
Krusaa
Brunsnæs

FISKBÆK
Viborg
Daugbjerg
Mønsted
Finderup
Hald
Lysgård
Vium
Sjørslev
Torning
Kjellerup
Vinderslev
Silkeborg
Julsø Lake
Svejbæk
Sønder Vissing
Bryrup
Voervadsbro
Øster Nykirke
Nørre Kollemorten
Bredal
Engum

JUTLAND (JYLLAND)

Faroe Islands Norway & England

Route numbers and town circles: 20, 22, 21, 18, 23, 15, 1, 13, 14, 16, 2

■ Towns with plans in text

② Route numbers in text

0   kilometres   30

GERMANY

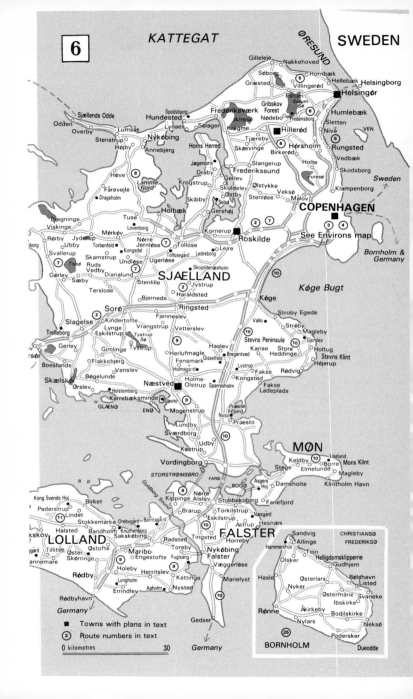